Applying Life Skills

Eighth Edition

Joan Kelly-Plate, Ed.D. • Eddye Eubanks, Ph.D.

McGraw Hill **Glencoe**

New York, New York   Columbus, Ohio   Chicago, Illinois   Peoria, Illinois   Woodland Hills, California

Safety Notice

The reader is expressly advised to consider and use all safety precautions described in this textbook or that might also be indicated by undertaking the activities described herein. In addition, common sense should be exercised to help avoid all potential hazards and, in particular, to take relevant safety precautions concerning any known or likely hazards involved in using the procedures described in *Applying Life Skills*.

Publisher and Authors assume no responsibility for the activities of the reader or for the subject matter experts who prepared this book. Publisher and Authors make no representation or warranties of any kind, including but not limited to the warranties of fitness for particular purpose or merchantability, nor for any implied warranties related thereto, or otherwise. Publisher and Authors will not be liable for damages of any type, including any consequential, special or exemplary damages resulting, in whole or in part, from reader's use or reliance upon the information, instructions, warnings or other matter contained in this textbook.

Brand Name Disclaimer

Publisher does not necessarily recommend or endorse any particular company or brand name product that may be discussed or pictured in this text. Brand name products are used because they are readily available, they are likely to be known to the reader, and their use may aid in the understanding of the text. Publisher recognizes that other brand name or generic products may be substituted and work as well as or better than those featured in the text.

The McGraw·Hill Companies

Send all inquiries to:
Glencoe/McGraw-Hill
3008 W. Willow Knolls Drive
Peoria, IL 61614-1083

13-digit ISBN 978-0-07-874435-8 (Student Edition)
10-digit ISBN 0-07-874435-0 (Student Edition)

Printed in the United States of America
2 3 4 5 6 7 8 9 10   027   10 09 08 07 06

Contents in Brief

Unit 1: You & Your World

Chapter 1   Growing & Changing 18
Chapter 2   Building Character 36
Chapter 3   Taking Responsible Action 50

Unit 2: Exploring Careers

Chapter 4   Pathways to Careers 64
Chapter 5   Workplace Skills 84
Chapter 6   Entering the World of Work... 102

Unit 3: Building Relationship Skills

Chapter 7   Communicating with Others 122
Chapter 8   Conflict Resolution 140
Chapter 9   Dealing with Peer Pressure 154
Chapter 10   Enjoying Friendships............... 166

Unit 4: Relating to Family & Children

Chapter 11   Building Strong Families 182
Chapter 12   Family Challenges 198
Chapter 13   How Children Grow 218
Chapter 14   Caring for Children................. 232
Chapter 15   Understanding Parenting 248

Unit 5: Managing Your Life

Chapter 16   The Balancing Act.................. 262
Chapter 17   Making Consumer Choices... 276
Chapter 18   Living with Technology 294

Unit 6: Your Health & Wellness

Chapter 19   Staying Healthy & Fit 306
Chapter 20   Health Risks 326
Chapter 21   Personal Safety 340

Unit 7: Food & Nutrition

Chapter 22   How Nutrients Work 354
Chapter 23   Guidelines for Healthy Eating.. 370
Chapter 24   Buying & Storing Food 390
Chapter 25   Eating Together 404

Unit 8: Working in the Kitchen

Chapter 26   Kitchen Equipment 418
Chapter 27   Safety & Sanitation................. 434
Chapter 28   Recipes & Measuring........... 448
Chapter 29   Quick Meals & Snacks 464
Chapter 30   Basic Cooking Techniques....480
Chapter 31   Preparing Grains, Fruits & Vegetables 492
Chapter 32   Preparing Protein & Dairy Foods.. 506

Unit 9: Clothing

Chapter 33   Clothing That Suits You 518
Chapter 34   Fibers and Fabrics.................. 534
Chapter 35   Caring for Clothing 546
Chapter 36   Preparing to Sew.................... 560
Chapter 37   Basic Sewing Techniques 580

Unit 10: Housing & the Environment

Chapter 38   Where You Live 594
Chapter 39   Decorating Living Space........ 610
Chapter 40   Clean & Safe Environments 628

Technical Reviewer

Marsha Markle, M.A., M.A., Ed.S.
Professor
National University
San Diego, California

Teacher Reviewers

Cindy L. Bowman
Family & Consumer Sciences Teacher
McFarland Unified School District
McFarland, California

Ann L. Branch, M.Ed.
Family & Consumer Sciences Instructor
Jefferson High School, School District 206
Alexandria, Minnesota

Annette Bunce, M.Ed.
Family & Consumer Sciences Instructor
West Jefferson School District
Terreton, Idaho

Jennifer Burch
Family & Consumer Sciences Teacher
Choctaw Junior High School
Choctaw, Oklahoma

Kathryn P. Crawford, Ed.S., NBCT
Family & Consumer Sciences Teacher
Huffman Middle School
Birmingham, Alabama

Doreen Lee
Family & Consumer Sciences Teacher
Harper Junior High School
Davis, California

Elizabeth Stokes Lewis
Family & Consumer Sciences Teacher
Powhatan County School System
Powhatan, Virginia

Judy Obrecht
Family & Consumer Sciences Teacher
Irwin-Kirkman-Manilla Community Schools
Manilla, Iowa

Kathy Sue O'Dell
Family & Consumer Sciences Teacher
Calhoun R-8 Schools
Calhoun, Missouri

Lynn Savelle
Family & Consumer Sciences Teacher
Northview High School
Dothan, Alabama

Jereta Davis, M.Ed.
Family & Consumer Sciences Instructor
Altus Public School
Altus, Oklahoma

Contents

Unit 1: You & Your World

Chapter 1   Growing & Changing........................**18**

- Understanding Changes in Your Life
- Developing a Positive Self-Concept
- Reaching for Your Dreams
- Resources Affect Potential
- The Importance of Goals
- Moving Toward Maturity

Chapter 2   Building Character **36**

- Recognizing Character
- Letting Character Be Your Guide
- Personal Responsibility
- Becoming a Responsible Citizen
- Making a Difference

Chapter 3   Taking Responsible Action **50**

- Making Responsible Decisions
- Putting Problem-Solving Skills to Work
- Responsible Leadership

Unit 2: Exploring Careers

Chapter 4   Pathways to Careers...................64

- Considering a Career Path
- Investigating Careers
- Thinking About the World of Work
- Looking Toward the Future

CAREERS

Consumer & Design Services 82

Chapter 5   Workplace Skills 84

- How to Succeed at Work
- Employee Characteristics
- Workplace Issues
- Skills for a Changing World

CAREERS

Nutrition & Wellness Services 100

Chapter 6   Entering the World of Work........102

- The Job Application Process
- Starting a New Job
- Balancing Work and Family
- Aiming for Success

CAREERS

Child & Family Services 120

Unit 3: Building Relationship Skills

Chapter 7   Communicating with Others 122

- What Is Communication?
- Avoiding Communication Roadblocks
- Delivering Your Message
- Starting a Conversation
- Developing Listening Skills
- Communicating Respect

Chapter 8   Conflict Resolution 140

- Understanding Conflict
- Responding to Conflict
- Resolving Conflict
- Working Through Conflicts

Chapter 9   Dealing with Peer Pressure 154

- Recognizing Peer Pressure
- Developing Refusal Skills
- Developing Confidence

Chapter 10   Enjoying Friendships 166

- Focus on Friendships
- Diverse Friendships
- Hanging Out with Friends
- Love and Infatuation
- When Friendships End

Unit 4: Relating to Family & Children

Chapter 11   Building Strong Families 182

- The Anatomy of a Family
- Building Family Strengths
- Pulling Together

Chapter 12   Family Challenges 198

- Changes and Challenges in the Family
- Violence in the Home
- Getting Help

Chapter 13   How Children Grow 218

- A Look at Child Development
- Developmental Stages
- Considering Special Needs

Chapter 14   Caring for Children 232

- Providing Care
- Put Safety First
- Accidents and Emergencies
- Caring for Children

Chapter 15   Understanding Parenting 248

- Considering Parenting
- Parenting Responsibilities
- Sources of Help

Unit 5: Managing Your Life

Chapter 16   The Balancing Act 262

- The Importance of Balance
- Balancing Your Life
- The Stress Factor

Chapter 17   Making Consumer Choices 276

- You, the Consumer
- Becoming a Smart Shopper
- Your Consumer Rights and Responsibilities
- Resolving Consumer Problems
- Managing Your Money
- Using Financial Services
- Understanding Credit

Chapter 18   Living with Technology 294

- A Look at Technology
- Managing Technology

Unit 6: Your Health & Wellness

Chapter 19   Staying Healthy & Fit 306

- Health and Wellness
- Your Physical Health
- Managing Your Weight
- Your Emotional and Social Health
- Health and Wellness Resources

Chapter 20 Health Risks 326

- Keeping Your Best Interests in Mind
- Frequently Abused Drugs
- Sexually Transmitted Diseases
- Negative Effects of Early Pregnancy
- Preventing Suicide
- Avoiding Health Risks

Chapter 21 Personal Safety 340

- Why Think About Safety?
- Taking Emergency Action

Unit 7: Food & Nutrition

Chapter 22 How Nutrients Work 354

- Nutrients at Work
- Deficiencies in Nutrition
- Digestion
- Energy and Calories

Chapter 23 Guidelines for Healthy Eating 370

- Eating, Exercising, and Good Health
- MyPyramid
- Individual Food Choices
- Getting the Facts
- Individual Nutritional Needs

Chapter 24   Buying & Storing Food 390

- Getting Ready to Shop
- Shopping for Food
- Food Quality
- Finishing Your Shopping
- Storing Food

Chapter 25   Eating Together 404

- Enjoying Meals Together
- Setting the Table
- Basic Table Manners
- Clearing the Table
- Eating Out

Unit 8: Working in the Kitchen

Chapter 26   Kitchen Equipment 418

- Selecting Kitchen Equipment
- Utensils
- Small Kitchen Appliances
- Large Kitchen Appliances
- Cookware

Chapter 27   Safety & Sanitation 434

- Working Safely in the Kitchen
- Sanitation in the Kitchen
- Preventing Accidents in the Kitchen
- Children in the Kitchen

Chapter 28   Recipes & Measuring.............. 448

- Selecting a Recipe
- Measuring Ingredients
- Understanding Recipe Terms
- Altering Recipes

Chapter 29   Quick Meals & Snacks............ 464

- It's Time to Eat!
- Budgeting for Food
- Working in the Foods Lab
- Working in Your Home Kitchen

Chapter 30   Basic Cooking Techniques 480

- Choosing Cooking Techniques
- Conserving Nutrients

Chapter 31   Preparing Grains, Fruits & Vegetables 492

- Grains in Your Diet
- Fruits and Vegetables in Your Diet

Chapter 32   Preparing Protein & Dairy Foods 506

- Nutrients in Protein and Dairy Foods
- Buying Protein Foods
- Preparing Protein Foods
- Storing Protein Foods
- Dairy Foods
- Preparing Dairy Foods
- Storing Dairy Foods

Unit 9: Clothing

Chapter 33   Clothing That Suits You 518

- The Importance of Clothing
- Individualizing Your Clothing
- Wardrobe Assessment
- Shopping for Clothes

Chapter 34   Fibers and Fabrics 534

- Selecting Fabric
- Fibers
- Fabric Construction
- Fabric Finishes

Chapter 35   Caring for Clothing 546

- Routine Clothing Care
- Clothing Storage
- Washing Clothes
- Drying Clothes
- Pressing and Ironing
- Dry Cleaning
- Repairing Clothing

Chapter 36   Preparing to Sew 560

- Learning About Sewing Equipment
- Small Sewing Equipment
- Sewing Machines
- Serger Sewing
- Selecting a Pattern
- Selecting Fabric and Notions
- Using the Pattern
- Fitting the Pattern
- Preparing Fabric
- Pattern Layout

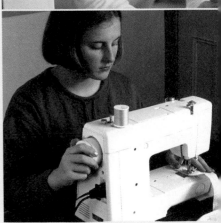

Chapter 37   Basic Sewing Techniques 580

- Developing Your Sewing Skills
- Basting
- Machine Stitching
- Sewing Techniques
- Simple Alterations

Unit 10: Housing & the Environment

Chapter 38   Where You Live..........................594

- Housing to Fulfill Human Needs
- Influences on Housing Decisions
- Types of Housing
- Ways to Obtain Housing
- Choosing a Place to Live

Chapter 39   Decorating Living Space 610

- Using Design
- Sharing Space

Chapter 40   Clean & Safe Environments ...628

- The Earth—Your Home
- Conserving Earth's Resources
- Creating a Clean and Safe Home Environment
- Maintaining a Healthy Home Environment
- Keeping Your Home Safe
- Making Repairs

FCCLA 646
(Family, Career and Community Leaders of America)

Glossary 647

Credits 656

Index 658

HOW TO . . .

Unit 1
Set Goals 30
Be a Good Listener 46
Make Decisions 56

Unit 2
Direct Your Career 68
Be an Effective Team Member.......... 91
Get the Word Out 108

Unit 3
Be Cell Phone Savvy 130
Deal with Bullies 148
Stand Up for Yourself 160
Make New Friends 170

Unit 4
Make Time for One Another 190
Recognize Sibling Abuse 210
Handle Tantrums 224
Entertain Children 240
Be a Positive Example 258

Unit 5
Take Good Notes 266
Protect Personal Identity 282
Stay Safe on the Internet 300

Unit 6
Protect Your Skin 312
Say "No" to Drugs 330
Prevent Falls 348

Unit 7
Maintain a Healthy Weight 364
Lower the Fat 374
Store Groceries 401
Plan a Celebration 414

Unit 8
Grill Healthy Food........................... 430
Store Food Safely............................ 444
Make Salsa...................................... 460
Put It All Together........................... 476
Check for Doneness 488
Buy Great Grains 498
Explore a Variety of Dairy
     Products 514

Unit 9
Select Quality Clothing 528
Choose the Right Fabric.................. 543
Pack a Bag....................................... 556
Select Notions 572
Serge Seams.................................... 591

Unit 10
Meet Special Family Needs 598
Hang Borders................................... 624
Keep Up with Cleanup 638

Reading with Purpose

Practice your reading skills with the ideas provided at the beginning of each chapter.

TIPS

Try these techniques that link to chapter content.

Character Check ✓

Read what it means to have strong character—and to show it.

Safety ✓ Check

Stay alert to safety issues with these features.

Highlighted Topics

Volunteer Opportunities for Teens 45
Career Clusters 72
Using a Résumé 105
Importance of Play 226
Understanding Your Paycheck 286
Reconciling Bank Statements.............. 291
The Heimlich Maneuver....................... 350
Fat-Soluble Vitamins........................... 360
Water-Soluble Vitamins 361
Important Minerals 362
MyPyramid 377
Nutrition Facts Panel 394
Set the Table....................................... 408
Measuring Utensils 422
Mixing Utensils................................... 423
Other Kitchen Utensils 425
Small Kitchen Appliances 426
Cookware & Bakeware......................... 429
Sanitation in the Kitchen 437
Units of Measure................................. 452
Estimates of Common Ingredients 453

Mixing Terms 454
Cutting Terms 455
Cooking Terms 456
Substitutions That Work...................... 459
Cooking with Dry Heat........................ 482
Cooking with Moist Heat..................... 485
Recipe: Banana Muffins...................... 496
Recipe: Green Bean Salad................... 502
Recipe: Minted Beans and Tomatoes ... 515
Recipe: Foolproof Cheese Soufflé 521
Using the Elements of Design 522
Using the Principles of Design 526
Fabric Care Symbols............................ 551
Small Sewing Equipment 562
Sewing Aids... 563
Sewing Machine 564
Serger 569
Sewing Pattern 570
Taking Measurements 571
Simple Alterations............................... 590
Using Color 614

CAREERS

Consumer & Design Services 82
Nutrition & Wellness Services 100
Child & Family Services 120

STEPS TO SUCCESS

I Can . . .

Appreciate My Heritage 22
Try Out Careers.................................. 73
Be a Better Listener............................ 132
Break the Silence of Abuse 212
Manage My Time................................ 268

Handle Stress 322
Eat Healthfully 384
Help with Family Meals 468
Sort My Laundry 552
Take Action Against Trash.................... 634

Teens Speak

About Gaining Understanding.............. 53
About Learning Skills........................... 87
About Community Pride...................... 163
About What Children Need................ 243
About Products Generating Ideas 280

About Exercise and Nutrition.............. 315
About Enjoying Mealtime 407
About Cooking Techniques................. 486
About Fabric and Function 539
About Housing Options...................... 603

Growing & Changing

Objectives

- Describe the physical, social, emotional, intellectual, and moral development that occurs during adolescence.
- Compare self-concept and self-esteem.
- Relate heredity and environment to personality development.
- Plan strategies to reach your potential and make the most of your resources.
- Explain why goals are important.

Vocabulary

- **adolescence**
- **puberty**
- **hormones**
- **personality**
- **heredity**
- **environment**
- **potential**
- **priorities**
- **resource**
- **goal**

Reading with Purpose

1. **Read** the title of this chapter and describe in writing what you expect to learn from it.

2. **Write** each vocabulary term in your notebook, leaving space for definitions.

3. **As you read** Chapter 1, write the definition beside each term in your notebook.

4. **After** reading the chapter, write a paragraph describing what you learned.

Understanding Changes in Your Life

At the beginning of this school year, did you notice that some of your classmates had grown much taller over the summer, while others looked the same? You may be aware of some changes in yourself as well. **Adolescence**, the stage of growth between childhood and adulthood, is a time of amazing changes. During adolescence, you'll change more in a shorter time frame than you ever will again.

Physical Changes

Your body's rapid changes during adolescence affect the way you think and feel about yourself and your relationships with others. Learning about adolescence helps you understand and deal with these changes.

Adolescence begins with **puberty**, the time when teens start to develop the physical characteristics of men and women. For girls, the start of menstruation—a monthly discharge of blood from the uterus—is an early sign that puberty has begun. For boys, the reproductive system begins producing sperm. Both girls and boys usually experience a growth spurt, or rapid increase in height. Girls may notice that their body shape changes. Boys notice growth of facial hair and their deepening voices. Both boys and girls feel strong surges of physical energy.

During puberty, your **hormones**, or chemical substances in the body, reach a very high level. Hormones help stimulate body changes and the development of the reproductive system. Puberty, which lasts an average of three years, starts at different ages for teens. Changes for both boys and girls usually start between the ages of 10 and 15. The changes end between the ages of 16 and 20.

Many teens worry that they change too slowly or too quickly during puberty. Girls often undergo physical changes earlier than boys. Some look older than their peers; others look younger. It's normal for teens to develop at different rates. See **Fig. 1-1**.

Fig 1-1 ▶ As you move through adolescence, it's important to remember that everyone—not only you—is experiencing many physical changes.

Social and Emotional Changes

Changing hormones in the body can make you feel like you're on an emotional roller coaster. One moment you may feel restless and irritable, and the next you may be happy and full of life. If you feel down about something, remember that this emotion will likely change after a short time.

You can take positive actions to deal with your changing emotions and energy during adolescence. Play a sport, exercise, or volunteer in your community. You'll feel better and worry less about yourself. Take advantage of opportunities to make new friends. Positive friendships will help you feel better about yourself and help you develop important social skills.

Intellectual Changes

During adolescence you also change intellectually. With increased experience and knowledge, you learn to solve more complex problems and to make more mature decisions. Your education—along with your school, family, and community activities—provides new insights and experiences that contribute to your intellectual development.

Moral Development

Zach is afraid of failing a class and asks José if he can copy José's homework. In the past, José has always come through for Zach. How should José handle the situation? As a teen, you start to make more decisions that deal with issues of right and wrong behavior. Although you want to do what's right, sometimes it's not clear how to act. Your choices may also be more difficult if you feel pressure from your friends. See **Fig. 1-2**.

The challenge, as in José's case, is to base moral decisions on a set of generally accepted guidelines for right and wrong behavior. From the time you were born until now, your parents and other adults in your life have set the standards for right and wrong behavior. As you move through adolescence, it's up to you to apply these standards in the choices you make. For example, telling the truth and treating people fairly are commonly accepted standards of moral behavior. Lying and cheating are not. Having a strong sense of right and wrong can guide you through tough times. Parents, teachers, religious leaders, and counselors can help you deal with difficult situations.

Fig 1-2 Adults can help guide you in making good choices. Which adults can you turn to for advice?

Developing a Positive Self-Concept

The mental picture you have of who you are, and the way you think others see you, is your self-concept, or self-image. Your self-concept is shaped and influenced by positive and negative comments about you from family, friends, and other people in your life—including yourself. Since infancy, you have heard these messages, and they have affected your view of yourself. Positive messages are more likely to lead to a positive self-concept. Hearing—and believing—negative messages, both from yourself and from others, can lead to a negative self-concept.

Building Confidence

A positive self-concept is related to high self-esteem, or the confidence and worth you feel about yourself. Your self-esteem affects many aspects of your life. For example, when you have high self-esteem, you feel good about yourself, believe you can be successful, and have the confidence to try new things. This might mean you join the swim team instead of spending another summer at home watching TV.

STEPS TO SUCCESS

I Can Appreciate My Heritage

It's perfectly natural to wonder about who you are. Along with understanding your thoughts, feelings, and interests, part of discovering yourself is learning about your family heritage.

It's often easy to see how your immediate family and your environment shape who you are. You may have red hair like your mother and a love of baseball like your father. However, your unique combination of characteristics that you inherited from your ancestors also plays a major role in who you are. Therefore, getting to know your ancestors is an effective way to get to know yourself.

Discovering—and appreciating—your heritage can be fun and interesting detective work. Families leave clues to their heritage in different ways. Some pass on stories that are retold by their children and their grandchildren, and some pass on photographs or keepsakes from one generation to the next. Others don't leave much information behind, so uncovering their clues may be more of a challenge.

Here are some ways to explore—and better appreciate—your family heritage.

- Interview family members. **Contact family members in person, by telephone, or by e-mail. Find out what they know about your family heritage. Keep a journal of what you learn.**

Your self-esteem can be higher at some times than at others. Your successes, your thoughts, and the way people treat you can cause you to feel down about yourself. To strengthen your self-esteem, you can do the following:

- **Analyze the messages you send to yourself.** Don't put yourself down. Instead, send yourself positive messages such as "I can do this" and "I'm doing better today than yesterday."

- Create a family-heritage scrapbook. Fill your scrapbook with photographs, stories, and keepsakes. Ask family members to help you document as many items as possible, with names, dates, and places.

- Research your ethnic background and culture. Everyone in the United States has roots in another country. Find out your family's country of origin and study its culture. Choose a tradition from the culture and make it part of your own family's traditions.

- Surf the Internet. Many online sources are now available for researching genealogy (gee-nee-AH-luh-gee), or family history. Simply type in your family surname and see what comes up.

- Establish long-distance relationships. Because of the Internet, distant relatives are closer than they used to be. Share family stories and photographs with relatives by e-mail. Try to reunite occasionally with distant relatives so that you can strengthen your family ties.

- **Concentrate on what you do well.** Keep a record of past and present successes. Review your achievements often, and remind yourself that you are capable of even more success in the future. See **Fig. 1-3**.

- **Spend time with positive, supportive people.** It's important to be around family and friends who believe in you. Their positive messages will build your confidence.

- **Improve your strengths.** Constant improvement will help you meet challenges, which in turn will help you feel better about yourself.

Appreciating Who You Are

Kim is an outgoing teen who enjoys people. She makes friends feel comfortable with her kindness and sense of humor. Life hasn't been easy for Kim since her father died and her mother took a full-time job. However, Kim appreciates who she is, which shows in her behavior. Kim's self-concept and self-esteem are reflected in her friendly, outgoing personality.

Your **personality** is the combination of feelings, traits, attitudes, and habits that you show others. This combination of characteristics makes you unique, or one of a kind. The stage was set for your personality before you were born. You received genes from each of your parents. These genes determined physical traits, such as your height, eye color, and hair color. **Heredity**—characteristics passed from parents to children—also influences your personality.

Your personality may have begun with your heredity, but it's shaped even further by your environment. Your **environment** is everything around you, including people, places, things, and events. Your family is usually your most important environmental influence. Children raised in an environment filled with love and emotional support are more likely to appreciate their worth—and develop healthy personalities.

Unfortunately, it's not always easy to appreciate who you are. When Matt's parents divorced, his grades went down. He was upset about the divorce and felt powerless to deal with the situation. His self-confidence took a nosedive. He struggled to stay in school. Fortunately, Matt's school counselor helped him deal with his emotions about his parents' breakup. Gradually Matt recovered his positive self-esteem.

Reaching for Your Dreams

What does it take to achieve a dream? How do you know where to start? A good place to begin is in your mind. Think about something you want to do and picture it as clearly as you can. Maybe you want to learn to play the guitar, get a summer job, or run for office in a school club. Each day can bring you closer to achieving your dream. See **Fig. 1-4**.

Success and self-confidence go together. Self-confidence means being confident in your abilities. Self-confident people feel good about themselves and their accomplishments. When success comes, they feel there are other things they can achieve—if they work at them. When they're not successful the first time, they try again. They learn how to deal with obstacles and learn from them.

Think of things you weren't able to accomplish when you were younger. Maybe you hadn't learned to read yet, make a sandwich, or throw a basketball. How did you learn to do these tasks? In the process, did you tell yourself, "I'll never be able to do this," or did you look at yourself more positively? Maybe you said to yourself, "I want to learn to do this. I know I can do it!"

Fig 1-4 You may have heard the saying, "Anything worth having doesn't come easily." What does this mean?

Growing Toward Independence

Hopefully, many of the experiences you've had since you were a young child were positive as you learned to walk, talk, and understand more of your world. Although what you want to achieve today is different, every past success helps you build self-confidence and become more independent.

Jason has won several science awards and hopes to be a doctor someday. He has a friend who enjoys building things and wants to build homes someday. Like everyone, Jason and his friend have **potential**, or the possibility of becoming more than they are right now. Reaching your potential means becoming all you can be. See **Fig. 1-5**.

What's your potential? How can you reach it? Try these suggestions:

- **Keep your efforts focused.** It's important to set priorities. **Priorities** are things that are important to you, ranked in order of importance. Once you decide what you want to accomplish, stay focused and avoid distractions.

- **Consider your interests and activities.** Make a list of each one. Next, compare your interests and activities to your priorities. Tom enjoys working on cars. Because he wants to own his own auto repair shop someday, he chooses to spend more time fixing cars at his uncle's shop than playing soccer.

- **Choose friends who support you.** To be your best, surround yourself with friends who have positive attitudes and who encourage you to reach your goals.

Fig 1-5

Many people spend years overcoming obstacles and striving to meet their potential.

- **Use your potential in positive ways.** Laura probably has more computer skills than anyone at school. She wants to become a software designer and create computer programs that can help doctors find cures for diseases.

- **Be health-smart.** You're much more likely to reach your potential if you're healthy and full of energy. Eat a variety of healthful food. Get enough sleep, and take time to exercise. Avoid substances that can harm your health, such as tobacco, drugs, and alcohol. These substances can keep you from reaching your goals. See **Fig. 1-6.**

Resources Affect Potential

Anything you use to help accomplish something is a **resource**. There are many types of resources, often categorized into four groups. Material resources include money, supplies, and property. Community resources include libraries, schools, places of worship, hospitals, and parks. Natural resources include everything in the natural environment, such as air, water, and trees. Human resources include people, time, energy, knowledge, and skills.

Family members, teachers, and other school personnel are human resources who can help you grow toward independence and reach your potential. Friends, neighbors, and employers offer other possibilities to help you achieve a goal. Community members, such as medical workers, police officers, teachers, and counselors, are also valuable resources. In addition to these resources, you have your own set of human resources. They include your health, interests, skills, knowledge, abilities, and attitudes. See **Fig. 1-7.**

Fig 1-6 Healthy practices, such as eating healthful food and exercising regularly, can help you reach your potential. How are you striving to meet your potential?

Fig 1-7 These teens are enjoying nearby natural resources. Why do you think community members value natural resources?

Make the Most of Your Resources

Identify the resources available to you and put them to work. Whether they're plentiful or limited, you can make the most of the resources you have by following these suggestions:

- **Expand your resources.** Get to know a variety of people. Individuals you meet may be able to help you learn a skill or find a job. Read newspapers, bulletin boards, and pamphlets available in your community to get a sense of the opportunities available to you. Develop your own knowledge and abilities. When you train and sharpen your skills in a subject that interests you, you start down a path that can lead to a successful adult career.

- **Conserve your resources.** Spending all your money on video games may be fun at the moment, but it wastes a valuable resource. Putting some of your cash in a savings account rewards you with more money in the long run. You can also save money, time, and energy by taking care of your possessions. They'll last longer, and you won't have to replace them.

Fig 1-8 Besides sharing CDs, people share their time and friendship. What other resources can friends share?

- **Substitute resources.** What if you're short on cash, and your best friend's birthday is approaching? Substitute time and energy for money and make a birthday gift. If you enjoy books and tapes, save money by borrowing them from the library instead of buying them. You also can save money by renting a video and having friends over, rather than going to the movies.

- **Share resources.** You can share resources and increase your brainpower at the same time by working with a study group on a difficult class assignment. You also share resources when you trade books, CDs, or sports equipment with friends. Often, sharing can be beneficial for everyone involved. See **Fig. 1-8.**

Resources are everywhere. Look for them, and learn how to use them effectively. By doing so, you'll be resourceful and develop the ability to solve problems.

The Importance of Goals

Everyone has goals in life, but not everyone is able to achieve them. A **goal** is something you plan to do, be, or obtain. It's ultimately what you're willing to work for. A goal should be positive and something you really desire. Your goals should also be realistic, or possible to reach. Chris set a goal to start a pet-sitting business. After thinking about her goal, she realized it wasn't realistic because she's allergic to animal hair!

Like road signs, goals give you direction, keeping you focused on where you want to go. Goals can also help you see what you achieved—and did not achieve. People who set goals and work to achieve them are much more likely to gain success and satisfaction in life. Without goals, it's easy just to drift along, letting circumstances control your future.

Personal Goals

Some goals, like trying out for the school play or applying for a part-time job, are short-term goals—goals that can be accomplished in the near future. Finishing high school, going to college, starting your own business, and getting married are examples of long-term goals. Long-term goals are more far-reaching and take longer to achieve.

Both short- and long-term goals are important. Short-term goals, such as reading a book, cleaning your room, or writing a letter, are easier to complete than long-term goals. By setting and reaching short-term goals, you gain a sense of accomplishment. Short-term goals can also serve as stepping stones to long-term goals. As a Chinese proverb says, "The journey of a thousand miles begins with a single step." See **Fig. 1-9**.

HOW TO SET GOALS

Children set remarkable goals for themselves. As a young teen, you see those goals were only fantasies. With a better sense of reality, you set more realistic goals. Yet these goals can be just as exciting if you know how to set goals you can achieve. These tips can help:

STEP 1 | **Be specific.** Giving yourself a clear target has several advantages. First, it's easier to chart your course and mark your progress when you know exactly what you're aiming for. Also, achieving precisely what you set out to do gives a greater sense of satisfaction and confidence.

STEP 2 | **Look at the big picture.** Consider how a proposed goal could affect other commitments, other people, and even other goals. Deciding in advance what is most important can help if conflicts arise later.

STEP 3 | **Be realistic.** In deciding which goals to set, you need to draw the line between dreams and reality. Some dreams may be out of reach. If you have no athletic talent, are you likely to become a professional athlete? Millions of teens share this dream, but for most of them, it is highly unrealistic.

There are also flexible and fixed goals. Both flexible and fixed goals can be either short or long-term. A flexible goal is one that has an outcome, but no time limit. A savings account would be an example of a flexible goal. A fixed goal means the outcome has a specific date or time, such as saving for your best friend's birthday gift. Deciding ahead if something is a flexible or fixed goal helps you manage your time and meet your goal.

Fig 1-9 ►
Daily practice helps people reach long-term goals.

STEP 4 | **Compare needed and available resources.** First, make a list of the things you would need to reach your goal. Then think of how you would obtain them. The easier it is to acquire needed resources, the more likely you are to achieve your goal.

STEP 5 | **Expect potential problems.** Try to imagine potential problems and plan positive, creative ways to deal with them. This helps you predict your chances of success. Working toward your goal is also a good way to add a variety of skills to your personal resources.

STEP 6 | **Stay active with your goal.** Action, not wishful thinking, is the key to success. Do something every day to work toward your goal.

TAKE **ACTION**

Choose a goal for yourself that you think is possible but challenging. Analyze this goal using the steps listed here. On reflection, does the goal seem more realistic or unrealistic? What conditions, if any, would have to change to make the goal more attainable? Could you change them? If so, would the effort be worthwhile? Why or why not?

Group Goals

People often work with members of a group to achieve common goals. Families may have common goals, such as planning a holiday dinner or planting a garden. As a group, the family maps out steps to take and works together to meet its goals. Working together to reach a goal can be fun. It can be as rewarding as the end result.

Groups outside the family often share organizational goals. A community or religious youth group may decide to help less fortunate families. They meet their goal by holding a car wash, cookout, or sports event to raise money. When people pull together for common goals, they can accomplish great things.

Moving Toward Maturity

"I can't wait to grow up!" How many times have you said that? The desire to become an adult is normal and necessary. That's what gives you the incentive to learn about your own life and the world as you move toward adulthood.

Becoming an adult is not the real goal, however. Becoming mature is. Maturity means reaching full development—physically, emotionally, socially, intellectually, and morally.

Signs of Maturity

Some people seem to be older than their actual age, possessing attributes that can come from a variety of factors. These factors can include personality, environment, heredity, past experiences and parental modeling.

One of the most common signs of maturity is age. Some laws require you to be a certain age before you can obtain a driver's license or vote. However, just because you are no longer a young child doesn't mean you're mature in all areas.

As you age, you change along the way. You may look older, your verbal responses may be more adult-like, but you may feel awkward in social situations. Someone else may look young but seems to have it all together when it comes to making good decisions.

Character Check ✔

Put Your Best Foot Forward!

- **Make a commitment.** People who do their best often do so because they know why they are doing something and have made a commitment. Before you begin a project, be clear on why you are doing it. As you continue, remind yourself of your commitment.

- **Start where you are.** Break a large goal down into smaller, reachable goals. Do your best by taking one step at a time toward each goal.

- **Prepare to do your best.** Take charge of your performance even before it begins by making sure you eat well, sleep enough, and get enough practice and training.

- **Be proud of your best efforts.** Your best may not be the same from day to day. Be proud of yourself no matter how well you do, as long as you do your best.

People don't mature at the same rate. Some people mature faster than others, and some people mature rapidly in one area but lag behind in others. For most people, personal development continues throughout life. Some signs of maturity include the following:

- **Independence.** Think about what you need to know before being on your own. You need to understand how to make good decisions, how to manage money, and how to take care of housing and health needs, for example.

- **Emotional control.** Mature people are in charge of their emotions and don't allow their emotions to overwhelm them.

- **Dependability.** Being dependable means you can be counted on. You go to school or work every day, keep a promise, and show up on time for appointments.

- **Willingness to work hard.** Little is accomplished without hard work. Good grades come with effort. Winning teams develop with practice. Successful employees are rewarded for working hard.

Fig 1-10 ▶ Teens can make a difference in the world by helping others succeed.

Helping Others Succeed

Think about times when someone encouraged you to succeed. Did encouragement make you feel more capable and worthwhile? Give the same encouragement to people in your life. Positive comments such as "I know you can do it," "I'm proud of you," and "I'm glad you're my friend" go a long way toward motivating others to do their best. See **Fig. 1-10**.

It's easy to get caught up in your life and forget about others. But your life is closely intertwined with many people. The positive way you treat others comes back to you when others treat you positively. You truly can make a difference in the world by helping others succeed.

Review & Activities

Chapter Summary

- Adolescence is a time of many changes that affect the way you think and feel about yourself.
- Your experiences in life shape your self-concept and self-esteem.
- Your heredity and environment help create your personality.
- Your potential and resources can help you achieve your dreams.
- Goals help you think about what you want and the steps needed to reach your dream.
- People mature at different rates over a lifetime.

Reviewing Key Terms & Ideas

1. When does **adolescence** occur?
2. What physical changes take place during **puberty** in boys and girls?
3. What is the function of **hormones**?
4. What four characteristics make up a person's **personality**?
5. What is **heredity**?
6. Which **environment** is usually most influential?
7. How can friends help you reach your **potential**?
8. Define **priorities**.
9. List one type of **resource**.
10. How can short-term **goals** help you accomplish your dreams?

Thinking Critically

1. **Analyze challenges.** Think about your own personal development. What roadblocks or challenges do you face on your path to adulthood? How can you conquer those challenges?
2. **Compare and contrast.** Think of the community resources you have available to you. How do they compare with the community resources your parents or guardians had when they were your age?
3. **Make generalizations.** Which distractions do you think challenge teens the most as they work to reach their potential? Explain your answer.

Review & Activities

Applying Your Learning

1. **Family history.** Interview adult family members about changes they went through during adolescence and how they dealt with them. Which changes were the most difficult? Which were the easiest? Write a brief report of your findings.

2. **Development timeline.** Use photographs of yourself to create a timeline of your development. Write brief descriptions of your development to accompany each photo. Afterward, write a brief reflection on your accomplishments.

3. **Success skills.** Read newspaper and magazine articles about three people you think are reaching their potential. List the individuals and write the reasons you believe each person is successful in achieving goals.

4. **Goal achievement.** Choose one of your long-term goals. Explain how you will use priorities now to help you move closer to that goal.

5. **Life simulation.** Enact a scene in which several family members work together to achieve a group goal. Show how they make plans and identify resources they can use.

6. **Personal development.** Evaluate your maturity level using the characteristics of maturity listed in the chapter. Which characteristic do you need to improve? Create a personal development plan to improve that characteristic.

Making Connections

1. **Reading** Read a biography of a successful person, such as a politician, an activist, or a celebrity. What obstacles did the person overcome to be successful? How did self-esteem help the person attain success?

2. **Math** Calculate the costs of buying movies and books. How can you and your friends share these resources to save money?

3. **Reading** With a partner, review local newspapers and community newsletters to determine some of your community's goals. Then develop activities you can do to help improve your community. If possible, carry out one of your ideas and report the outcome to your class.

CAREER Link

Setting Goals.
You are more likely to be happy with your career choices if you consider your interests and abilities when setting goals. List three goals at the top of a sheet of paper. Divide the bottom of the paper into two columns. Write "Interests" in the left column and "Abilities" in the right column. How closely do your goals match your interests and abilities?

Building Character

Objectives

- Explain why character is important.
- Describe how values influence actions.
- Distinguish learned values from shared values.
- Demonstrate personal responsibility.
- Summarize what it means to be a responsible citizen.

Vocabulary

- **character**
- **ethical principles**
- **role models**
- **values**
- **universal values**
- **responsibility**
- **familial**
- **citizen**
- **citizenship**

Reading with Purpose

1. **Write down** the colored headings from Chapter 2 in your notebook.

2. **As you read** the text under each heading, visualize what you are reading.

3. **Reflect** on what you read by writing a few sentences under each heading to describe it.

4. **Continue** this process until you have finished the chapter. Reread your notes.

Recognizing Character

Think of people in your community whom you admire. Perhaps they are friends, family members, teachers, or religious leaders. What makes them stand out? Chances are they are people of character.

Calling someone a person of character may be the biggest compliment you can pay that individual. **Character** is a combination of traits that show strong ethical principles and

Fig 2-1 Role models are chosen for their character and integrity. How are you a role model for others?

maturity. **Ethical principles** are standards for right and wrong behavior. People's character shows in both their public and their private behavior. Character gives them the strength and courage to do the right thing every day. By doing so, they often become **role models**, or people who set a positive example for others.

You may be a role model for younger children. Perhaps they see you as someone they want to be like when they're older. They watch you closely and follow your example—in behavior, language, and even the way you dress. Picture yourself as a role model for young children. Does your behavior show your true character? See **Fig. 2-1**.

Values and Character

Values and character go hand in hand. **Values** are beliefs and ideas about what is important. Your character is based on a set of values you've learned since childhood. You use your values to guide the choices you make every day. For example, bringing an extra sandwich to give to a classmate who cannot afford to buy lunch shows your value of compassion. You show the value of honesty when you refuse to shoplift, even though your peers may be pressuring you to steal.

Values also show in what you say—and how you say it. For example, you display the value of courtesy when you speak kindly and respectfully to others. Your values also can be seen in how you spend money. Buying a gift for someone who's been ill shows the value of caring.

Finally, your values show in what you're willing to stand up for. A person who risks criticism from others to stand up for a principle sends a clear message about moral strength, or integrity. How have your values influenced your behavior in a positive way?

Learned Values

You learn values from your family and others in your life directly through what they teach you and indirectly through the examples they set. For instance, Kevin's mom donates time on weekends to a neighborhood cleanup project. She shows Kevin that concern and a sense of responsibility for the community are important values.

Throughout life you may also learn values from other sources. Schools and places of worship teach values, as do friends, books, and community youth organizations. Some of these sources reinforce the values you learned earlier, but others may not. The Internet and television may show people who display unacceptable values. What values might a person learn from each of these sources? Which are most likely to keep your best interests and the best interests of others in mind? See **Fig. 2-2**.

Fig 2-2
You set an example for others when you exhibit caring and respect.

Shared Values

Think about your family's values and the values of other families you know. Are they the same? Which values do all families share? Look around and you'll see that people's values often vary. However, people of all cultures share some common values.

Values that are generally accepted and shared worldwide are sometimes called **universal values**. They are the "glue" that makes positive and peaceful interaction among people possible. The following values are examples of universal values:

- Caring and compassion
- Fairness
- Honesty
- Integrity
- Respect
- Responsibility
- Self-discipline
- Trustworthiness

Although these values are held around the world, people place different levels of importance on them. Even among your own friends, you may share similar values but express them differently. For example, Tanya believes respect is important. Her friends often confide in her because they know she'll listen and show respect without making judgments. Her best friend thinks honesty is most important—even when sharing her opinions leads to debates and disagreements with others. What are your most important values? See **Fig. 2-3**.

Fig 2-3 The universal value of respect is shown in various ways in different countries around the world. How is respect shown in your community?

Letting Character Be Your Guide

When Stacy was younger, she was quick to become angry when things didn't go her way. After becoming angry with friends, Stacy would speak to them in a nasty tone of voice. With her parents' help, Stacy learned how to behave more maturely when angry. Stacy's choice affected her character and her friendships in a positive way.

Personal character develops over time. It comes from thinking about and consciously living by your values. In time, putting your values into action becomes automatic—good habits are hard to break. Which of the following values have become habits in your life?

- **Caring** and compassion is how you show concern about a living being—whether it's a person or an animal—or the environment.

- **Fairness** is being open-minded and willing to look at all sides of an issue. People who show fairness are accepting and tolerant toward other people.

- **Honesty** means you're truthful and act real, not fake. Honest people don't try to be something they're not. They don't cheat or take things that don't belong to them.

- **Integrity** is when you always act according to your values. Integrity gives you the strength to make wise choices when you're pressured to go against your values.

- **Respect** is how you treat others as you would like to be treated. People who show respect aren't hateful or cruel.

- **Responsibility** means you are accountable for choices you make and things you do. **Responsibility** involves making a decision and accepting the consequences of your choice and behavior.

- **Self-discipline** is when you have control over your behavior. You can control your temper, your actions, and your tendency to put off tasks at work, school, or home.

- **Trustworthiness** means people can trust what you say and do. When people are trustworthy, you can take them at their word.

TIPS
Control Your Emotions

Most people respond in a positive, healthy way to emotions such as love and hopefulness. However, learning to control emotions such as anger in a positive way is easier for some teens than for others. Here are several tips to help you control difficult feelings:

▶ **Wait before reacting.** If you feel angry, count to ten, take deep breaths, or walk away from a stressful situation. Calm down and then rethink your response before reacting.

▶ **Let go of the little things.** Try not to let small irritations upset you. You'll see yourself improve if you give up stressing out over little things.

▶ **Talk it out.** Find a friend or trusted adult and tell him or her how you feel. Name your emotions as you talk. Sharing your feelings can help you get a fresh perspective on the situation.

Personal Responsibility

Most teens look forward to being more independent and to having the freedom to make their own choices. Remember that with this freedom comes responsibility. Personal responsibility is character in action. See **Fig. 2-4**.

Responsibility in Action

It's easy to identify people who accept responsibility. It shows in their words and in their actions. Responsible people say things like, "Let me help," "I'll do it," or "I made a mistake, and I'll correct it if I can." Responsible people don't need to be reminded or pressured to do a job. They simply work to accomplish things that need to be done. They keep their own and others' best interests in mind.

Think about ways those in your family show responsibility. Maria's grandmother asked her to help make tamales for their community center's fundraiser. Maria enjoys helping her grandmother and listening to stories of her early years. In her family's culture, older people are held in esteem and respected. How does your **familial**—or family—responsibility influence personal and family decisions?

Every day you have dozens of ways to show whether you are responsible. Do you keep promises and avoid gossip? How do you refuse to be pressured into negative behavior and activities? Do you try to get the most out of school? How do you choose friends and activities that reflect your personal values?

Fig 2-4 You show responsibility when you pitch in and help. How might this type of responsibility help you later as an adult?

Becoming a Responsible Citizen

Each year Kelsey wins an award for "good citizenship" in school. What do you think the award stands for? A **citizen** is a member of a community, such as a school, city or town, or country. Unfortunately, just being a citizen doesn't automatically mean you are a good one. The way that you handle your responsibilities as a citizen is known as **citizenship**.

As community members, citizens are entitled to certain rights and privileges. For example, community members have the right to vote for city officials and the privilege of fire protection. In return, citizens owe certain responsibilities to the community, such as following its laws. This allows the community to run smoothly and serve the needs of its citizens. A thriving community requires responsible citizens. Kelsey follows the rules of her school, respects her fellow school citizens, and behaves responsibly. Her good citizenship not only earns her an award each year but also earns her the respect of her peers and teachers.

Citizenship in Action

You first learn and practice good citizenship in your home and school, where you have a chance to exercise your personal values. The two most important qualities of citizenship are caring for the greater good of individuals or the community and acting on your concerns. See **Fig. 2-5**.

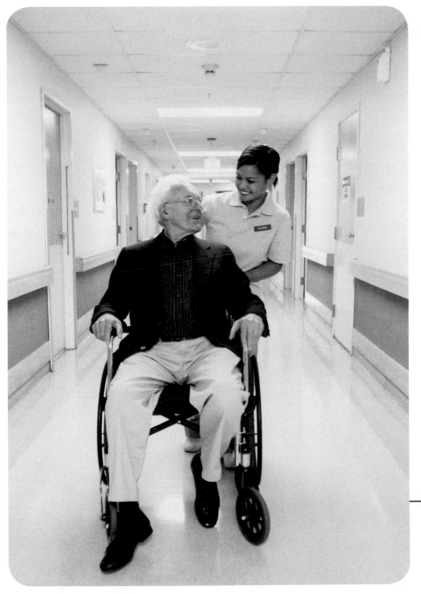

Fig 2-5
Small actions can make a big difference to others. What small act of caring and compassion can you do today to make a difference in your community?

Character Check ✓

Be Worthy of Your Word

- **Keep promises.** If you give your word that you will do something—no matter how small it is—do it. People will learn over time that you are reliable and that they can count on you.

- **Know your limits.** Take on only as much as you can handle. It does no good to say you can do something when the honest answer should have been "no."

- **Take responsibility.** If something goes wrong and the mistake is all or partially your fault, take responsibility by apologizing and accepting your mistake—then correct it. You'll learn a valuable lesson, and others will know you make an effort to do the right thing.

When searching for a volunteer opportunity, consider your skills and interests. Often you can find opportunities that match your talents.

Dan shows concern for and commitment to his community by coaching a Little League baseball team. Beth is elected to a class office because she treats classmates equally, with honesty and respect. Beth's brother volunteers at the local animal shelter. Some teens incorrectly think they have to reach adulthood before they can make a contribution to their community. The good news is you can become a valuable member of your community now.

When you know what's going on—and get involved—you're more likely to make a positive difference in your community and the world. Eventually, as a voter, you'll help choose public officials. The more information you have about your community, the more educated decisions you'll be able to make. By reading newspapers and listening to radio and TV news, you can keep up with what's happening in your local community and throughout the world. See **Fig. 2-6**.

Finding Volunteer Opportunities

Many teens would like to volunteer for a "good cause" or an organization they've heard about, but they don't know where to find volunteer opportunities. Opportunities exist in most communities for volunteer service.

Before jumping in to help local groups or organizations, spend a moment thinking about your own skills and interests. What causes are you interested in? Perhaps you'd like to help older people. You might find volunteer work at an adult care facility, visiting and reading to the residents. What skills can you lend to an organization? Perhaps, like Beth's brother, you like and are good with animals. Your local animal shelter might be able to put you to work feeding and walking dogs. **Fig. 2-7** lists some volunteer opportunities for teens. You can use ideas from the list or contact local service organizations to find out about other opportunities in your community.

Making a Difference

Learning to develop and display positive qualities of character and values takes time and effort, but the rewards are great. People in your community come to respect you for who you are. They observe your commitment and willingness to be a part of your community.

As you grow older and become more involved in your community, people may begin to see you as a leader. Whether you choose to be a leader or not, being a responsible citizen makes it possible for you to make a difference in your life and in the lives of others.

Fig 2-7

Volunteer Opportunities for Teens

Most communities have nonprofit service organizations that offer volunteer opportunities. Contact a local organization you're interested in to begin volunteering in your community. Many teens find volunteer work like the following:

▶ Tutoring young children.

▶ Working as a hospital volunteer.

▶ Delivering meals to people confined to their homes.

▶ Collecting recyclable materials.

▶ Participating in food, clothing, and toy drives for people in need.

▶ Working in a community garden.

▶ Making audio recordings of books for people with visual impairments.

HOW TO BE A GOOD LISTENER

Being a good listener doesn't get as much notice as some other personal qualities, maybe because it looks easy. Yet listening well shows respect for others, their opinions, and their knowledge. In that sense, it's a sign of character.

Listening well is also work. A job description for listening might look like this:

STEP 1 | **Eliminate both interior and exterior distractions.** Obstacles to focusing on the speaker may be physical or mental. You may need to turn off a television, for example, to both physically hear the words and mentally concentrate on their meaning.

STEP 2 | **Keep a positive attitude.** Believe the speaker has something meaningful to say. Look for ways to make the message useful.

STEP 3 | **Maintain objectivity.** Keep an open mind, even if you and the speaker disagree. If you judge ideas before they're spoken, you may miss important points and misunderstand the message. You may miss areas of agreement that could foster better understanding and communication.

STEP 4 | **Give nonverbal feedback.** Use body language to show you are listening. Make good eye contact. Nod or smile when you understand, and frown if you are confused. Personal responses like these tell the speaker whether the message is getting through. They also can inspire and encourage the speaker, which often makes for a more interesting talk.

Let the speaker finish speaking.
This sounds basic, yet it can be easy to interrupt when a speaker's opinion or story triggers one of your own. Such interruptions may even seem like positive feedback, but they can derail the speaker's train of thought. Constant interrupting can also create the habit of planning your response rather than focusing on what is being said.

**STEP
5** **Repeat the message to yourself in your own words.** This technique lets you know whether you understand the message. Also, you probably process information more quickly than the speaker talks. Silently repeating the message fills the time gap between your comprehension and the speaker's rate of delivery and helps avoid mental distractions.

TAKE **ACTION**

Tell a friend or family member about an interesting experience you had, a book you read, someone you met, or any other topic. Notice the person's reactions. Does he or she help or hinder you in delivering your message? How can you use the person's responses to help you become a better listener?

Review & Activities

Chapter Summary

- Character, shown through behavior, gives people courage to do the right thing.
- Values you learn from people you respect, your family, your school, places of worship, friends, books, the community, and youth organizations are learned values.
- Values you share with others worldwide are universal values.
- Character comes from putting your values into practice in a positive way.
- With freedom comes personal responsibility.
- Citizens have certain rights and privileges and have certain responsibilities to their community.

Reviewing Key Terms & Ideas

1. What is **character**?
2. Define **ethical principles**.
3. What makes people **role models**?
4. Give three examples of **values** in action.
5. What are **universal values** and why are they important?
6. How can you show integrity?
7. Explain the difference between honesty and trustworthiness.
8. How can you show **responsibility**?
9. What is **familial** responsibility?
10. What is a **citizen**?
11. Name the two most important qualities of **citizenship**.
12. How can you make educated decisions about your community?

Thinking Critically

1. **Making generalizations.** Describe someone whom you consider a person of character. How has the person's character influenced your values and actions?
2. **Making comparisons.** Compare your values with those reflected in the actions of your friends. How are they different and how are they alike?
3. **Drawing conclusions.** Imagine a trusted friend copied your assignment. When questioned by the teacher, your friend lied and said you were the one who copied. What value is this friend lacking? How would your view of this person's character change?

Review & Activities

Applying Your Learning

1. **Personal integrity.** Imagine a woman unknowingly drops a $20 bill on the floor of a large department store. You're the only person who sees the money. You feel torn between returning the money and keeping it. What will you do? Why?

2. **Media evaluation.** With a partner, discuss criteria a TV program should meet to be considered a "program of values." Consider how characters on the program exhibit values and whether they are good role models for young children. Create an evaluation sheet for parents and guardians to use based on your criteria.

3. **Perseverance promotion.** Many people give up in the face of challenges and do not achieve their goals. Create bookmarks that encourage teens to persevere.

4. **Active listening.** Observe teens speaking with each other. Note how they show respect through listening. What respectful listening behaviors do most teens display? Which behaviors do they lack? Discuss your findings.

5. **Volunteer call.** Visit several places where volunteers are at work. Take photographs or videotapes of volunteers in action. Create a public service announcement that motivates people to volunteer using the visuals and your descriptions of the benefits of volunteering.

Making Connections

1. **Language Arts** Research various facial expressions used during communication and what messages they send. Create a book illustrating facial expressions that communicate respect and courtesy.

2. **Reading** Choose a short story or novel about a teen growing up in another country or culture. Present a report sharing what you learned about the teen's values and responsibilities.

3. **Writing** Think about a citizen in your community who has served as a role model to you or others. Write a letter, expressing thanks for the effort he or she has made, and send it to the individual.

CAREER Link

Commitment.
Success, in the classroom, on the playing field, or at work, doesn't just happen. It results from commitment. When you make a commitment at work, you are promising that you can be relied on to be on time, do your part, and be honest in all your actions. Interview adult family members or friends about the level of commitment required of them on the job. Write a paragraph comparing their level of commitment at work with your level of commitment to school and related activities.

Taking Responsible Action

Objectives

- Identify the factors that influence decisions.
- Explain the decision-making process.
- Predict the consequences of decisions.
- Propose solutions to complex problems.
- Describe the qualities of responsible leaders.

Vocabulary

- **decision making**
- **needs**
- **wants**
- **leader**
- **leadership**

Reading with Purpose

1. **As you read** Chapter 3, create an outline in your notebook using the colored headings.

2. **Write** a question under each heading that you can use to guide your reading.

3. **Answer** the question under each heading as you read the chapter. Record your answers.

4. **Ask** your teacher to help with answers you could not find in this chapter.

Making Responsible Decisions

"Should I put up banners for the Martin Luther King, Jr. Day parade or study for tomorrow's math test?" You make decisions every day. Many decisions you make are almost automatic. You choose to brush your teeth, comb your hair, or pick out a jacket to wear to school.

Other decisions are more complicated. Should you continue a friendship that seems troubled? Should you become involved in a school activity? These decisions take time and consideration. They affect not only you but also your family and friends, and some of your decisions even affect the society you live in and future generations.

Decision making is the act of making a choice. Making responsible decisions helps you achieve personal goals. Each year you'll make a number of major decisions about school, health, work, and how you can contribute to society. Your decisions determine your behavior. At times, you may choose to do nothing about a situation, or you may let someone else decide for you. That's a decision, too.

What Influences Your Decisions?

Think about a recent decision you made. Did you make the decision yourself? Did you get help from a family member or teacher? A variety of influences shape your decisions. Some influences are external, like family, friends, and society. Others are internal and come from your own knowledge and attitudes. Which of the following influences have played a major part in your decisions?

- **Family.** Family members can strongly influence your decisions. Sometimes parents or guardians make a decision for you—especially if they feel you aren't ready or able to make the decision on your own. They know that you learn from mistakes, but they choose to make the decision because it's their responsibility to protect and teach you. See **Fig. 3-1**.

Fig 3-1
Caring family members influence you to make good decisions.

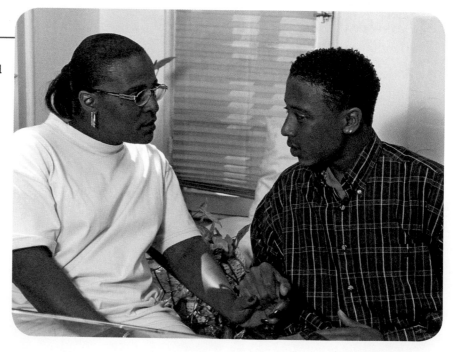

Michelle spotted her friend Ken at the florist shop, carrying a single red rose in a small vase. "What special lady are you buying flowers for?" she teased.

"My sister. She just found out she didn't get a job she wanted. Flowers always cheer her up."

"Is this the same sister you used to call 'my sister from another planet'? You squirted food dye in her hair that time—"

"I was a kid," Ken defended himself. "Besides, since I missed out on making captain of the hockey team, I know how she feels."

Michelle nodded. "It's like my Aunt Norene and me. I always hated to hear her complain about her arthritis. Then I broke my ankle and got a taste of what it feels like not to be able to do things you like." She brightened. "Aunt Norene loves flowers. Does that florist sell marigolds?"

Teen Connection

Think of a situation in your past in which you reacted immaturely. Describe how you would react now and how your emotional growth contributes to your more mature reaction.

- **Culture.** Your family's beliefs and customs directly affect your decisions. For example, Maria had to choose between attending her sister's Quinceañera (kin-see-ah-NYAIR-uh) and going on a class trip. A Quinceañera is a celebration in Hispanic families of a girl's move to adulthood at age 15. It emphasizes family values and social responsibility.

- **Friends.** As you grow older, you may turn to friends for help with decisions, which is natural. Some friends will have a positive influence on your decisions. Others, however, will have a negative influence. Your friends often have no more experience or knowledge than you do and might give you poor advice. Some may want to influence you to do things that aren't in your best interest. You can always listen and learn from others, but in the end you must make your own decisions.

Know Your Community Resources

Your time and knowledge are just two resources you have. Other helpful community resources exist for almost any decision you need to make:

▶ **Health care professionals,** such as your family doctor, can provide information related to your physical health.

▶ **Police departments** can provide safety resources, such as neighborhood watch programs and personal safety pointers.

▶ **Counselors** from a community counseling agency or a school can help you make decisions related to your emotional health and well-being.

▶ **Bank employees** can help you with money-related decisions.

• **Values.** Many decisions you make are based on your values. As a result, your decisions express your values loud and clear. Choosing to complete your homework instead of going to the movies shows that you know the value of responsibility.

• **Resources.** Your decisions are also affected by your resources, such as people, time, money, energy, knowledge, skills, and technology. If you're low on money, do you go to the game or go cycling in the park? If you just got paid from an after-school job, do you use your earnings to buy a new bike or use your skills to repair the bike you already have?

• **Demographics.** Changes in the characteristics of the population, or demographics, affect everyone. Our society has more older adults than ever before. How might that affect your career choice? What other demographic changes can you name? What effects do they have on your behavior?

• **Needs.** People's needs exert a strong influence on their decisions. **Needs** are those things essential to your survival and well-being. Food, clothing, and shelter are physical needs, and affection, security and safety, belonging, and achievement are emotional needs. Your desire to learn is an intellectual need, and maintaining positive relationships with other people is a social need.

• **Wants.** Those things you desire, even though they aren't essential, are **wants**. A new DVD, makeup, or a video game are wants, not needs, because those items are not essential to your survival or well-being. Wants can have a powerful influence on your decisions. See **Fig. 3-2**.

• **Society.** Society refers to a group you belong to, such as your school, community, or country. Your decisions and behavior are influenced by the society in which you live. For example, Jamail's neighborhood takes pride in keeping the area safe. Jamail and his friends decided to attend next weekend's neighborhood watch meeting to find out how they can contribute to neighborhood safety. What are some ways society can influence your decisions?

Fig 3-2
Many items, and their advertisements, are designed to have a powerful influence on your decisions.

Learn from Your Decisions

Good decisions are choices you can be proud of. Think through your decisions carefully. Are they realistic, responsible, and respectful for everyone involved? Making choices you feel good about can result in the following:

- Improved self-esteem

- Increased respect from family and friends

- More independence as you become responsible for yourself and your actions

Every decision can't work out the way you might expect it to. When you make a mistake, don't blame others. Take responsibility for it, and learn as much as you can about the experience. Sometimes you have to live with the consequences of a wrong decision and say, "I'll make a better choice next time."

Consider the Consequences

The consequences of some decisions you make affect only you. Some consequences may be minor, and some may be very serious. Many decisions affect other people, too. That's why it's important to think about the impact of your decisions on your family, your friends, and ultimately your community. When you care about other people and want their respect, you'll make decisions carefully. Even minor decisions, such as deciding not to wear a safety belt when riding in a car, can have far-reaching consequences. See **Fig. 3-3.**

HOW TO MAKE DECISIONS

Until now, the major decisions in your life have been made by adults. Many decisions still are. As you mature, however, more decisions—and more important decisions—are in your own hands. Now is the time to learn how to make them wisely.

The following steps show one way to make sound decisions. The process is not like a math formula, which always gives the correct answer if followed exactly. Rather, it's an outline that allows some flexibility. Using it successfully takes judgment and honesty, qualities that also come with maturity.

STEP 1 Identify the decision to be made. State or write the decision as specifically as possible. Having a clear image from the start will help reveal the best course of action.

What Do I Do?

Choose elective classes.

STEP 2 List options and resources. Available resources strongly influence your options. Suppose you're trying to choose among several after-school activities. You need to know whether you have— or can acquire—the skills and time each option demands.

Kent Academy

Course Catalog

Art 101
Learn basics of art. Students will experiment with different media as they learn the principles of design.
Semester: Fall

Painting 201
Learn to paint with oils and acrylics. Students will paint one still life and nature scenes.
Semester: Spring

Remember that the personal decisions you make may alter the direction of your life. Think about what and who has influenced those decisions. For example, what do you think would happen if you decided to drop out of school? What effect would such a decision have on your life? What effect would it have on your family? Choosing to stay in school and graduate is a responsible decision that will set you on a winning course in life.

Fig 3-3
The consequences of a seemingly minor decision—failing to wear a safety belt or to stop at a red light—can affect you and your family and friends in big ways.

STEP 3 | **Analyze your options.** Once you've settled on some promising options, reflect on possible outcomes of each one. Be realistic and include both pros and cons.

STEP 4 | **Choose the best option.** For some people, this step is the hardest. If no option seems right, you may need to go back a step or two. Perhaps you can't decide because you need more facts. Maybe you sense that you are ignoring a possible, unpleasant outcome. On the other hand, it could be that several options look equally good. Let your goals and values guide you.

STEP 5 | **Act on your decision.** Give your best effort, backed by the confidence that you have made the best decision possible.

STEP 6 | **Evaluate the results.** Are you happy with your decision? If so, congratulations! If not, try to pinpoint the cause of the problem. Maybe you overlooked a resource that would have led to a different choice. Then again, even working through each step carefully does not guarantee success. The unexpected can happen. Facts that you could not have known before may come to light. Either way, remember the experience—and refer to it when it's time to make the next important decision.

Kent Academy

Elective Course Registration

Name: Josephine Mills

Address: 123 Shumard Oak

Grade: 9

Elective: Art 101

Semester: Fall

TAKE **ACTION**

Give an example of how a streamlined version of this process can be useful for making simpler decisions, such as whether to subscribe to a magazine or buy a CD or whether to pack a lunch or buy one at school.

Effective leaders can promote an understanding and appreciation of cultural diversity by using some of the following techniques:

▶ Provide resources that reflect various cultures and backgrounds.

▶ Include people of varying ages and cultural backgrounds in groups or on teams.

▶ Provide an inclusive environment that is free of discrimination or harassment. Inclusive environments let people share their unique talents and experiences.

▶ Use an interpreter to communicate with others when language barriers exist.

▶ Avoid imposing personal values that may be different from the values of others.

▶ Set an example by treating all team members equally.

Putting Problem-Solving Skills to Work

Michelle has to make a decision. Her best friend is using drugs, and she needs to decide whether to continue the friendship or back away. Making decisions is part of solving complex, or practical, problems. Practical problems are problems that involve morals and values. Problem solving helps break problems into pieces you can handle better and keeps you from becoming overwhelmed. This in turn helps you make better decisions.

When solving a problem, consider the available resources and possible options. What are the short- and long-term consequences of each option? What results do you want to achieve? Keep in mind that few solutions are perfect. Michelle might choose to keep her friend and risk her parents' disapproval, or she might choose to end the friendship, which means losing her best friend.

Problem solving is a continuous process—and an opportunity to grow. Apply what you learn to new situations. Using what you've learned in previous situations can help keep problems from becoming bigger issues. Michelle's decision to continue or end her friendship will take some time and careful thought, but the experience will help her use the decision-making process.

Responsible Leadership

Do you see yourself as someone who leads or someone who prefers to follow? A **leader** is a person who has influence over and guides a group. It takes a leader to motivate others to action, and it takes followers—as well as leaders—to get things done.

Leadership is the ability to lead, not just hold an office, such as student body president. When Danielle organizes her friends to go bowling, she acts as a leader. Leaders have two main functions: to get a job done and to keep the group members together. The "job" is whatever the team is organized to do. The job might be to play a game, win a contest, or make a committee decision. See **Fig. 3-4**.

Fig 3-4 Not all leaders are born leaders. Many people learn the skills to be an effective leader. What leadership skills do you have?

Leadership Skills

To lead others, you must learn certain skills. Sometimes being a follower first can teach you how to be a good leader later. As a follower, you can observe leadership skills in action and practice them at home, at school, and with your friends. The following are some of the skills you'll need as a leader:

- **Management skills.** Effective leaders can manage time, money, and other team resources. They know what must be done and what resources their team needs to meet its goals. They manage human resources by using the skills and talents of everyone in the group.

- **Motivational skills.** Effective leaders are skilled at motivating others to take action. As leader of the school's debate team, Mike uses praise and encouragement to motivate his team to work hard. Mike's motivational skills helped his team earn first place at the state competition.

- **Do more than is asked of you.** Think about the kind of people whom everyone likes. They are the ones who put in a little extra time and effort to make things go well.

- **Think of others.** Consider what you can do to make a friend's or neighbor's life a little easier—such as hold a door, help carry a heavy load, or return a stray pet.

- **Make things happen.** Investigate issues important to students in your school. Take a stand on the issues and run for office, or work with a group of students to change your school for the better.

- **Communication skills.** Leaders are able to explain the goals of the team and each team member's specific job. Leaders not only talk to but also listen to team members and respond to their suggestions, problems, concerns, and feelings.

- **Problem-solving skills.** The problem-solving skills of leaders help them solve the varied problems they encounter. They use decision-making skills and are willing to look for new ways to achieve goals. For example, a good leader can solve problems among team members that might divide the group. The leader's solutions help the team move forward toward its goals.

The leadership skills that you develop now will help you prepare for your future roles at home and in the workplace.

Leadership Opportunities

Where can you find opportunities to lead? Opportunities for leadership are all around you. In a group of friends, someone leads and directs others in deciding where to go and what to do. In class, student leaders spark discussions and influence others by what they say.

You can also find leadership opportunities in student organizations, such as Family, Career and Community Leaders of America (FCCLA). FCCLA is a dynamic and effective national student organization. Students in middle and high schools who are currently or previously enrolled in a family and consumer sciences class can join FCCLA. FCCLA teaches students personal growth and leadership development. It helps teens focus on their multiple roles as family member, wage earner, and community leader through fun and challenging activities and competitions.

Opportunities for leadership in FCCLA are limitless. In your local FCCLA chapter, or group, you can lead a committee or become a chapter officer. In these roles, you coordinate projects and manage people. For example, you might create a program that teaches young children how to deal with bullies, or you might coordinate a canned food drive for a local food bank.

FCCLA also offers leadership positions at the district, regional, state, and national levels. Teens nominated and elected to these positions work in groups to raise awareness of teen issues and create positive changes. As a state or national officer, you might meet with legislators to address problems such as teen substance abuse, teen pregnancy, or workplace safety for teens.

If you're interested in leading but unsure of your leadership skills, FCCLA can help. Among other programs, FCCLA offers the Dynamic Leadership program, which helps teens model good character, solve problems, foster relationships, manage conflict, and build teams.

In families, older brothers or sisters show leadership when they model positive behavior for younger family members. Just as you may look to someone for guidance and behavior worth imitating, young people may do the same with you as their role model.

In sports, a junior on the track team can show a freshman what it means to win or lose with a positive attitude. At work, a long-time employee at a fast-food restaurant can show someone new on the job how to work well as a team member. Making the effort to practice leadership today can prepare you for bigger opportunities in the future. See **Fig. 3-5**.

Fig 3-5 A job provides many opportunities for leadership. What opportunities for leadership do you have in your daily life?

Review & Activities

Chapter Summary

- Your decisions influence your behavior.
- Decisions are influenced by a variety of factors.
- The decision-making process can help you make effective decisions.
- Decisions have positive and negative consequences.
- Complex problems often involve in-depth decision making.
- Leadership skills you develop now will help you as an adult.
- Leaders have certain qualities and skills that can be learned and practiced.

Reviewing Key Terms & Ideas

1. What can making responsible decisions help you achieve?
2. List five influences that affect people's decisions.
3. What is the difference between **needs** and **wants**?
4. Name four resources that affect your decisions.
5. What are the six steps of **decision making**?
6. What are the results of good decisions?
7. What are the benefits of problem solving?
8. What are the two main functions of a **leader**?
9. How do teens display **leadership** in their family?
10. List three qualities of responsible leaders.

Thinking Critically

1. **Analyzing results.** What results of good decisions have you experienced? What might have been the results if you had made a different choice? Explain.
2. **Make generalizations.** Describe a practical problem faced by some of your friends or classmates. What are some of the decisions related to the problem?
3. **Making comparisons.** Think of two leaders in your community. Compare the leadership skills of each. Which person do you think is more effective? Why?

Review & Activities

Applying Your Learning

1. **Ad analysis.** Select five newspaper advertisements that you believe are effective in influencing teens' consumer decisions. Share your examples with the class. Ask students to discuss and rank the ads according to their effectiveness.

2. **Personal choices.** In a small group, develop and present several short skits, each depicting a teen confronted with a different decision to be made and weighing possible consequences of his or her choice. Afterward, ask the classroom audience to evaluate each decision and suggest other consequences that may not have been identified.

3. **Decision inventory.** Make a list of decisions teens your age are likely to face before finishing high school. Put a check mark beside the decisions you feel will be most difficult for you. What can you do now to make those decisions easier?

4. **Personal assessment.** Think of at least two times you have assumed the role of leader at home, at school, or in extracurricular activities in the last month. List and describe the situations. Note the leadership skills you used and ways you might improve them.

5. **Community search.** Write a help wanted ad seeking a teen leader for an after-school community service club. Describe the kind of person who could fill the job and the skills needed to do it well.

Making Connections

1. **Writing** Think about one of the hardest decisions you have made. Write a short essay identifying the decision you made, describing the way you worked through it, and evaluating the result of your decision.

2. **Math** Imagine you're going to purchase a new software program. Follow the steps of the decision-making process. Compare prices and product advantages. Choose the software you would purchase. What role did price play in your final decision? Explain.

3. **Reading** Select a book on leadership to read. Give a short presentation, sharing what you learned about leadership by reading the book.

CAREER Link

Attendance.
Once you've been hired to do a job, it's vital that you show up—on time and ready to work—when required. Just as in school, your attendance is important on the job. Your boss and your coworkers depend on you. Imagine being the supervisor of a small group of employees. Write a memo to the employees explaining the importance of good attendance.

Pathways to Careers

Objectives

- Describe the connection between school and work.
- Identify interests, skills, and aptitudes.
- Explain different strategies for exploring career options.
- Compare ways that people and resources can help you learn about careers.
- Classify different types of businesses.

Vocabulary

- **career**
- **lifelong learning**
- **aptitudes**
- **mentors**
- **job shadowing**
- **career cluster**
- **networking**
- **fringe benefits**
- **entrepreneur**

Reading with Purpose

1. **Read** the title of this chapter and describe in writing what you expect to learn from it.

2. **Write** each vocabulary term in your notebook, leaving space for definitions.

3. **As you read** Chapter 4, write the definition beside each term in your notebook.

4. **After reading** the chapter, write a paragraph describing what you learned.

Considering a Career Path

Imagine your life after high school. Will you go to a trade school or college? Will you find a job? What kind of work will you do? You may not know the exact answers to these questions, but it's important to start thinking about them now. Many decisions you make as a student will affect your future.

As you consider a career path, think about the kind of adult life you want to have. The type of work you choose will affect many aspects of your life, including the place where you live, the way you spend your work and leisure hours, and the money you make.

Work is a natural part of everyday life. Work is doing something productive with your time, and you may or may not be paid for it. Paid work is called a job. Similar jobs are grouped to form occupations. A **career** is a series of related jobs in a particular field over a lifetime. To choose a career, you need to identify your skills and interests, as well as available opportunities. There are tens of thousands of occupational titles in the United States. That's a lot of jobs!

Why People Work

All over the world, people spend their days learning, making things, providing services, solving problems, and traveling. They perform a variety of jobs that provide goods and services. It's not possible for one person to make all of the goods and provide all of the services needed in life. See **Fig. 4-1**.

Work fulfills human needs in several ways. One way is directly from things that are made and services that are performed. Another way is from the income that people earn. Paid work provides money to buy things you need and want, gives

Fig 4-1
Many people learn new skills on the job. What are some other benefits of work?

you a sense of pride, and contributes to your success. Most people work to make money that can be used to purchase these goods and services. Can you imagine what life would be like if you had to make all of your own clothes, shoes, electronics, and sports equipment?

Money isn't the only reason people work. Many people enjoy what they do and wouldn't trade their work for another job, even if it paid more money. Work gives people a sense of doing something worthwhile. Many people develop strong friendships at work and feel a sense of belonging. When people work, they help themselves, their families, and their communities.

The School-Work Connection

School and paid work have several things in common. Learning in school can be hard work. Like work, school requires practice and commitment, even when you'd rather be somewhere else. Most skills learned in school are necessary to succeed at work. Employers want to hire people who are committed to learning, work hard, and have good attendance records. See **Fig. 4-2**.

Fig 4-2 Hobbies you have now can lead to a career later in life.

There are also differences between school and paid work. In school, students spread their efforts across a variety of subject areas. In the workplace, people try to choose jobs that allow them to work in areas that they like and in which they do well.

Another difference between school and work is that employers pay wages and require people to do a good job in return for those wages. Because of this, employers often have less patience than teachers have. When a worker fails to show up at work, somebody else has to do his or her job. In the workplace, people who don't meet expectations often lose their jobs. Those who have not performed well in past jobs may not be considered for future ones.

Many jobs require **lifelong learning**—keeping skills and knowledge up-to-date throughout your life. Some companies provide or help pay for employee training and education. Wherever you work, it will be important to keep your skills and knowledge current. In other words, you will need to become a lifelong learner.

Investigating Careers

Current research shows most people change careers several times in their lifetime. Now is a good time to do some detective work and learn as much as possible about careers you

HOW TO DIRECT YOUR CAREER

Some teens know their exact career path before they enter high school. For most teens, however, career plans are much less clear-cut. In fact, career planning may seem of little use before your senior year of high school. Technology and social trends change the job scene rapidly, and jobs that look appealing now may be drastically different when you enter the workforce.

Yet it's this unpredictability that makes some preparation essential. You want to be ready for whatever the future brings. These strategies can help:

Gain a variety of experiences. You may be surprised at the different learning experiences that are open to young teens. From attending a science camp to volunteering in a soup kitchen—the more you learn about the world, the more you learn about yourself. For example, one teen discovered a real empathy for older adults when she went on rounds with her mother, a home health aide.

Focus on goals and priorities. What do you want to accomplish with your life? What matters to you? For many people, the answers to these questions develop over time. Each career path brings its own

might enjoy. You can use career information as a road map, choosing your destinations and determining the best route to reach your workplace goals.

To understand your possibilities in the working world, start by looking at yourself. The more you know about your interests and skills, the easier it will be to pick your career path.

What Are Your Interests and Skills?

Interests are the things you like to do, and skills are things that come easy to you. Skills are easy because you have a natural talent or have practiced them enough. Over time, people tend to like most the activities they can do well. Remember,

rewards. Staying aware of your values and expectations can help you decide which path to take and when, or whether, to change course.

Develop transferable skills. These are "seed" abilities that can be grown and used in numerous job situations. For example, time management skills help a head cook create a work schedule for the kitchen staff. A teacher might use time management skills to decide how two students can share a computer so that both finish an assignment on time.

Look at general trends. You cannot always predict what a job will be like in the future, but you can make assumptions based on trends in society. You know that global events have a growing effect on the local job market, for instance. This can help you decide whether to consider jobs in a certain field.

TAKE **ACTION**

Ask an expert on careers, such as a school counselor or job recruiter, what skills are always in demand. Use this information to analyze the classes you're taking. How are your classes helping you learn these skills? Make a list of future classes that would help you gain necessary workplace skills.

Fig 4-3 Discovering your talents will help you choose a career path. What talents do you have?

however, that skills and interests are two very different things. A person may be interested in an occupation but may not be willing to invest the time and effort to develop the skills needed to succeed at it. Another person may have natural talent but may not be interested in using these skills for paid work. See **Fig. 4-3**.

To help identify your interests and skills, ask yourself which activities you enjoy most and which you think you would enjoy doing more than 2,000 hours each year. This is the average number of hours people spend at work in a year.

If your answers to the questions are different, don't be surprised. Some activities seem interesting but lose their attraction when you have to do them constantly. Pat, for example, likes camping and working outdoors at her uncle's ranch, yet she has no desire to work outside in the snow, rain, or heat. She decided that, for her, outdoor activities were hobbies to enjoy rather than occupations.

People also have **aptitudes**, which are natural tendencies that make it easy for them to learn certain skills. Students may possess different aptitude levels in school subjects, athletics, mechanical ability, public speaking, leadership, and the ability to understand the feelings of others. You can become aware of your aptitudes through school activities and career aptitude tests. Pat chose accounting as a career goal for several reasons, including her aptitude for mathematics and her excellent memory for details.

Exploring Career Pathways

There are many ways to explore career paths. The best way to learn about jobs is to try them out. Firsthand experiences, such as field trips, internships, and employment, are some ways to discover what you like. Field trips are visits to job locations that let students see a sample of what a certain job involves. Internships provide opportunities to actually do work, generally without pay. See **Fig. 4-4**.

You can also gain firsthand experience through part- or full-time paid employment. Although interns may have a broader range of experiences, student employees are being paid and therefore feel they are doing purposeful work.

Students can also benefit from developing special relationships with experienced workers. **Mentors**, or informal teachers or guides, demonstrate correct work behavior, share knowledge, and help new employees adjust to the workplace. You can learn a lot by working closely with a mentor.

Job Shadowing

Did you ever wonder how much you could learn if you could see what a person actually does at work? Following a worker for a few days on the job is called **job shadowing**. The individual you're observing follows a regular workday while providing a sample of the real work done on the job. You stay nearby and quiet—like a shadow. The person being shadowed may take time to answer questions and listen to your comments. Job shadowing can provide valuable information about the education and training needed for various jobs.

Because job shadowing is an individual experience, you'll need permission from a parent or guardian and from the person you are shadowing. You may also need permission from your school. Some schools permit students to do job shadowing as a school-related activity. If so, you may receive credit for shadowing and for reports you write about your experiences. Teachers and counselors can often help you find a person to shadow. Ask them about shadowing opportunities.

Many businesses allow parents to bring their children to work on a special day each year so that young people can explore careers. If this applies to your family, ask your parents if you can participate.

Career Clusters

As you explore career options, you may feel overwhelmed by the number of available opportunities. One way to narrow your career search is to use a career cluster system.

A **career cluster** is a large grouping of occupations that have certain characteristics in common. Many states have

Fig 4-4 In addition to school field trips, some student organizations provide opportunities to explore different types of work.

identified career clusters to encourage career decision making and to help you choose appropriate academic study areas.

A career cluster system is an efficient method of exploring occupations. Each career cluster often requires the same types of skills. If you have the skills necessary for success in one occupation, there probably will be other occupations in the same cluster that appeal to you. The career cluster system helps you focus on an occupation yet remain flexible to pursue a variety of job opportunities.

Career clusters also identify areas of academic emphasis for different occupations. You may now be studying a variety of subjects in school, but eventually you'll need to narrow your studies to gain the necessary skills to succeed in certain occupations. Career clusters can help you focus your education. **Figure 4-5** shows some common career clusters and the academic areas of study for each.

You can receive information about career clusters and career opportunities from private companies, associations, and government agencies. Your teachers, guidance counselors, and media specialists can help you gain access to these valuable resources.

Fig 4-5 Career Clusters

Cluster Name	Product or Service	Sample Study Areas	Sample Occupation
Arts & Communications	Art, Music & Literature	Communications	Editor
Business & Management	Accounting & Management	Business Administration	Office Manager
Health & Medical Services	Medicine & Nutrition	Nursing	Nurse
Human Services	People & Education	Sociology	Social Worker
Engineering & Industrial Systems	Manufactured Goods	Manufacturing or Engineering	Engineer
Natural Resources	Food and Agriculture	Agricultural Services	Farmer

Name a career cluster in which your "dream job" might fall.

STEPS TO SUCCESS

I Can Try Out Careers

Imagine this scenario: You've done everything you can to figure out which career is right for you. You have completed an inventory of your skills and interests, and you have interviewed and shadowed people in the workforce.

But what happens if you begin a job on your career path and realize it's not what you thought it would be? What if you aren't enjoying yourself or the work is more stressful than you can handle? What if your priorities change—for example, you realize having time off is more important to you than having a high-paying job?

Coping with Change

If you change your mind about your career—for whatever reason—there is no reason to feel as though you've failed or that you are trapped in one career. People change and so do their careers. People in all stages of life change careers for a variety of reasons.

As your life changes, your plans may need to change. What's important is to keep your options open. If you find that you are not happy with the career you've chosen, you don't have to stick with it. Instead, think about your interests and figure out what you want to do next.

Changing Jobs

If you decide to leave a job, think carefully about how and when to do so. If you need the money, you may want to stick with it until you find something new.

Whether or not you need the job, it is always a good idea to leave on good terms with your employer. After all, if you make a good impression and leave the job responsibly, you can use your employer as a reference for future jobs.

Discovering a New Career

Once you've made the decision to try a new career, retrace the career exploration steps outlined in this chapter. Now that you have some experience under your belt, you might think differently about your skills and interests. Maybe you've discovered a new talent, or maybe you think you need more training or education. Do your research, be open to opportunities, and stay flexible.

Personal Connections

Networking, or making use of personal connections to achieve your goals, is one of the best ways to get a job. Many people credit someone else with helping them find work. Some help by serving as references. Others help by encouraging people to explore career opportunities in a given area. They may be able to answer your questions or put you in contact with someone who can.

Personal connections are helpful for several reasons. Word-of-mouth contacts are the best source of information about job openings in most communities. Personal connections also allow employers to verify a job applicant's skills, experience, and positive attitude before offering a job to the individual. See **Fig. 4-6**.

Researching Careers

Your school's and local library's resources can help you explore careers and plan for the future. As you look for up-to-date information about jobs, workers, employers, and educational opportunities, consider these categories of information to make the best career choice:

Fig 4-6 Networking can be done almost anywhere. Social events provide an opportunity for you to share your career goals with others.

- **Required education or training.** Educational requirements range from short-term, on-the-job training to as much as ten years of college and a doctorate degree. Most employers require post-high-school education or training for job applicants.

- **Compensation.** Earnings vary greatly among occupations and employers. Some jobs include regular pay increases based on the length of time a worker is employed. Employees can earn wages on an hourly rate of pay, or they may earn a fixed annual salary.

- **Employer benefits.** It's important to consider the fringe benefits offered with a job when comparing the income of two jobs. **Fringe benefits** are services and products you receive for little or at no cost to you. They can include vacation time, sick leave, child care, health insurance, and retirement programs.

Fig 4-7 Working conditions vary from job to job. Some occupations require working nighttime hours or overnight.

- **Nature of work.** This refers to the actual activities you do on a job, including the equipment used and the supervision received. It also includes whether you work alone or as part of a team.

- **Working conditions.** Working conditions refer to the environment in which you work. Will you work inside or outside? Other conditions include work schedules, chances of job-related injury, and perhaps travel requirements. Are you willing to work nights, weekends, or holidays? See **Fig. 4-7**.

- **Future job opportunities.** Job outlook refers to the future opportunities in an occupation. Job opportunities are often created because of new jobs, the replacement of existing workers, or a shortage of skilled applicants for job openings.

Attend a Job Fair

The Internet is not the only place to find career information. If you would rather learn about a career in person, try attending a local job fair. Job fairs feature companies who are looking to hire employees. When talking to company representatives at a job fair, keep these points in mind:

▶ **Prepare.** Find out which companies will be at the job fair and create a list of questions for their employees.

▶ **Wear appropriate attire.** Company representatives are more likely to take time to talk with you if you look professional.

▶ **Ask FAQs (frequently asked questions).** Approach a company's booth, be polite and friendly, smile, and introduce yourself. Ask if the representatives have time to answer your questions.

Three excellent sources of career information from the federal government are available in most libraries. The *Career Guide to Industries* provides general information about whole industries. The *Occupational Outlook Handbook* (OOH) provides information about occupations within whole industries. The *Occupational Outlook Quarterly* (OOQ) provides updated information about changes in the workforce. It also has interesting articles about training opportunities and new occupations.

Researching Careers Online

The Internet offers an almost unlimited amount of career information. Web sites set up by companies, schools and colleges, and youth and trade organizations can be helpful in your career exploration. Company profile directories can also be found online, so you can read in-depth, current information about companies in all industries.

The U.S. government also offers valuable career information online, including information from the *Occupational Outlook Handbook,* the *Occupational Outlook Quarterly,* and the *Career Guide to Industries.* The Occupational Information Network (O*NET) is another helpful resource. It provides information you can use to research career clusters and occupations and to determine which occupations match your skills and interests.

More companies are using the Internet to post job openings and look for help. Job seekers may also find career information on Web sites of online employment agencies. Be sure to choose online job boards carefully because some do not update their job postings regularly. Applicants using these sources might apply for jobs that are no longer available.

Thinking About the World of Work

The more you know about the world of work, the better your chances are of finding a career that's right for you. The world of work consists of two major categories: the public sector and the private sector. The public sector is funded by taxes and made up of local, state, and federal government agencies. Teachers, police officers, and firefighters are some of the people who work in this group. The private sector consists of businesses that sell goods and services to make a profit. Examples are grocery stores, insurance companies, and restaurants. Depending on your occupation, you may have the choice of working in either the public or the private sector.

Types of Businesses

Businesses in the private sector range from very small businesses with one employee to large companies with thousands of employees. There are three main types of businesses in the United States:

- **Sole or individual proprietorships.** These businesses are owned and controlled by one person—the proprietor—who receives the profits if the business succeeds but loses money if it fails. See **Fig. 4-8**.

- **Partnerships.** These businesses are owned and controlled by two or more people who share profits and risks.

- **Corporations.** Corporations are owned by many people, called shareholders, who share in the profits and lose money if the business doesn't do well.

Fig 4-8 Most private sector businesses are small businesses. What might be the benefits and drawbacks of working in a very small business?

Entrepreneurship

There are millions of businesses in the United States, each started by an **entrepreneur**, someone who sets up and operates a business. Perhaps you know some entrepreneurs in your community. With their new ideas and their willingness to take risks, entrepreneurs create the businesses that give millions of people a place to work.

Entrepreneurship provides the satisfaction of being one's own boss and the possibility of earning substantial sums of money. However, entrepreneurs risk losing the money they invest in the business if it fails. The failure rate of a new business is high, especially during its first years. Most entrepreneurs work long, hard hours to keep their businesses profitable. See **Fig. 4-9**.

Employment Options

Both the public and the private sectors offer full-time, part-time, and temporary employment options. Most full-time jobs require seven or eight hours of work each day, five days a week, although some full-time jobs require more hours per week. Part-time positions, such as after-school jobs, vary and can range from 1 to 40 hours a week. Temporary jobs can be either full-time or part-time, but they only last a certain number of days.

Fig 4-9 Entrepreneurs can be any age. This teen entrepreneur has her own babysitting business. After college, she might open her own child care facility.

Looking Toward the Future

The job market is constantly changing with increasing speed. Some occupations will be eliminated because of changes in technology, and other jobs will be added because of new inventions and new ways of doing things.

Many of today's jobs and products didn't exist when your grandparents were young. You can expect to work in occupations that don't even exist today. With huge growth in the global economy, you may consider working in another country and experiencing a different culture. Career opportunities will be unlimited for people who are willing to continue learning and can adjust to change. See **Fig. 4-10**.

Fig 4-10 If you're good with languages and enjoy new experiences, you may find job opportunities in another country.

Review & Activities

Chapter Summary

- School and work have some common features, but they are very different in some ways.
- People tend to make better career decisions when they understand their interests, skills, and aptitudes.
- You can learn about careers through firsthand experiences, a career cluster system, and job shadowing.
- Many print and online resources are available to help you make informed career decisions.
- Most businesses are classified as a sole proprietorship, a partnership, or a corporation.

Reviewing Key Terms & Ideas

1. Name two reasons why people work.
2. Explain the difference between a job and a **career**.
3. If a job requires **lifelong learning**, what must you expect to do?
4. Explain the difference between interests and **aptitudes**.
5. What are **mentors**? List three ways mentors can assist new employees.
6. Explain **job shadowing** and its purpose.
7. Describe two ways a **career cluster** can help you choose a career.
8. Why is **networking** one of the best ways to find a job?
9. Why might it be important to consider **fringe benefits** when comparing jobs?
10. What are two advantages and disadvantages of being an **entrepreneur**?

Thinking Critically

1. **Drawing conclusions.** How can paid and unpaid work experiences help someone prepare for a career? How can they prepare someone to be successful in a future job?
2. **Summarizing sources.** Think about job or career discussions you have had with adults you know. Who did you talk to? What did you learn? Who was the most helpful?
3. **Comparing strategies.** How are networking and online job searching alike? How are they different? Which do you think is more valuable to people entering the workforce? Why?

Review & Activities

Applying Your Learning

1. **School reflection.** Think about how your school experiences are helping prepare you for your adult role as an employee. Write a short reflection on the value of your school experiences.

2. **Shadowing opportunities.** Brainstorm employers in your community who might provide opportunities for job shadowing. Which might be of interest to you? Which might not? Why?

3. **Career skills.** Choose a job of interest to you and research the required academic skills for the job. Use the *Dictionary of Occupational Titles* available from the U.S. Department of Labor or another source to gather information. Which skills do you already possess? Which do you need to learn?

4. **International discoveries.** Use print or Internet resources to identify several international career possibilities of interest to you. Report your findings to the class.

5. **Personal interview.** Conduct an interview with a community member who is an entrepreneur. Find out how this person adapts to change to be successful.

CAREER Link

Adapting to Change. Change is part of life, and being able to deal with change is a trait that employers appreciate in a worker. Interview family members or friends about changes they've encountered at work and how the changes affected them. What did they do to adapt to the changes? Write a short report based on your interviews.

Making Connections

1. **Writing** Imagine you're nominating someone you know for "Outstanding Mentor of the Year." Write a letter explaining the reasons for your nomination and the traits that make the person a good mentor.

2. **Reading** Select print or Internet resources to read about current job opportunities in an industry that interests you. Share your findings in a report to the class.

3. **Math** Determine how much money you spend in one week, including food, entertainment, and clothing. Then calculate the number of hours you need to work if your job pays $6 per hour.

4. **Reading** Use the Internet to gather information about a professional or student organization in a career field of interest to you. Write an essay describing the organization and the roles and responsibilities of its members.

CAREERS

Consumer & Design Services

LOAN OFFICER
Regional bank seeks consumer loan officer with excellent computer skills. Must work well with people and be good with details. Training provided. Bachelor's degree required. Good benefits.

LANDSCAPE ARCHITECT
Park district seeks certified landscape architect to assist with the design and development of city park and recreation areas. Must be able to manage new and renovation projects in a team effort. BLA or MLA from an accredited program is required.

KITCHEN PLANNER
Seeking kitchen planner to organize spaces and select appropriate fixtures and appliances that suit customer demands. Ability to work within budgets and building codes are essential. An understanding of ventilation systems and solar options is a plus.

FASHION BUYER
Mature, dependable, creative person needed to choose suppliers, negotiate prices, and monitor quality. Must be able to anticipate customer demands and work well under pressure. Frequent travel required.

LIBRARIAN Large metropolitan library has immediate opening for librarian with supervisory experience. Responsibilities include public relations, fund raising, and purchasing. Master's degree in library science required.

FASHION DESIGNER Apparel manufacturer has opening for fashion designer of men's clothing line. Degree and at least two years of work experience required. Working knowledge of textiles and construction is a must. On-the-job customized training is provided. Nice benefit package.

CONSUMER JOURNALIST City newspaper has entry-level opening for journalist to research and write articles related to family health and education issues. Meeting deadlines is critical. Degree in journalism preferred.

INTERIOR DESIGNER Established design firm adding a new position in our commercial division. Seeking an experienced designer who has made a mark in the region. This position requires a degree, working knowledge of ADA and EPA regulations, and an excellent eye for detail.

URBAN PLANNER Regional planner needed to oversee the development of water-front properties within an urban renewal project. Master's degree preferred and knowledge of EPA regulations an asset. Excellent communication and negotiation skills are required.

Career Connection

Research Careers. A good way to learn about a career is to talk to people who already work in that field. Interview three people with jobs in Consumer & Design Services. Find out about the demands and rewards of their jobs. Write a short report based on one of your interviews.

MORE CAREER OPTIONS

Entry Level	Technical Level	Professional Level
• Mortgage Loan Processor • Bank Teller	• Assistant Apparel Designer • CAD Technician	• Hospitality Interior Designer • Actuary

Workplace Skills

Objectives

- Identify employability skills necessary in the workplace.
- Explain characteristics of workplace leaders.
- Demonstrate effective teamwork skills.
- Classify assertive, passive, and aggressive communication.
- Propose solutions to workplace issues.

Vocabulary

- **academic skills**
- **thinking skills**
- **work ethic**
- **teamwork**
- **discrimination**
- **harassment**
- **downsizing**

Reading with Purpose

1. **Write down** the colored headings from Chapter 5 in your notebook.

2. **As you read** the text under each heading, visualize what you are reading.

3. **Reflect** on what you read by writing a few sentences under each heading to describe it.

4. **Continue** this process until you have finished the chapter. Reread your notes.

How to Succeed at Work

"Should I try to get a job this summer, and if so, doing what? Sometimes I feel like I don't know how to do anything!" Thinking about your future and what will be required at work can be scary. It's normal to question whether you have the skills to be a successful employee.

Success in the workplace begins with the skills you learn at home and in school. These skills form the foundation needed

Fig 5-1 Many skills you learn in school are skills you'll use on the job. What skills is this teen using?

to succeed at work. Today's jobs require a combination of skills that help you function in life and at work. Using these skills every day is the most effective way to develop them.

Core Academic Skills

What skills do employers really want? The answer may vary from job to job, but you can build skills now and apply them at home and at school. You can't be a success in the workplace unless you understand—and develop—the required skills. See **Fig. 5-1**.

Competencies in reading, writing, mathematics, and science are known as core **academic skills**. Speaking and listening are basic communication skills. These skills are tools, or building blocks, for learning and include the following skills:

- **Reading skills.** Workers need to be able to understand what they read, summarize the information, and apply it to their jobs. You use reading skills to read and interpret written text, including newspapers, magazines, instruction manuals, encyclopedias, dictionaries, and maps. Most jobs require a variety of reading skills. Higher-level jobs may also call for the ability to read financial reports, technical journals, architectural plans, or legal documents. See **Fig. 5-2**.

Fig 5-2
Expressing your creativity and using problem-solving skills help prepare you for challenging careers.

Teens Speak About Learning Skills

Darcy dropped her books on the lunch table and pulled out the letter she had saved from the morning mail. Seeing Eric's curious face, she explained, "It's from my cousin Alicia."

"Does she like being in the Marines?" he asked.

Darcy nodded. "Now that she survived boot camp. She's studying engineering."

"I wish we could learn something useful. Not like algebra. When are we ever going to use that?"

Darcy laughed. "That's just what Alicia said. She wanted to be a civil engineer because she wanted to build things. What's the first thing she has to study? Math!"

Eric bit into his sandwich, eyeing his literature book. "We're reading poetry from the Middle Ages. You think that will be useful someday?"

"Are you kidding? If you can understand that stuff, you can understand anything!"

Teen Connection

List the courses you are currently taking. Explain how each of these courses might strengthen the following skills: problem-solving, creative thinking, logical thinking, and interpersonal skills.

- **Writing skills.** At work, writing skills are used to communicate information, ideas, thoughts, and messages in written form. All occupations require the completion of job applications, business forms, and correspondence, such as written letters and e-mail. Higher-level jobs may also require the ability to take notes and write reports, speeches, and journal articles. The widespread use of computer-based communication has resulted in an increased need for writing skills and good grammar.

- **Speaking skills.** These are needed to organize ideas and communicate messages to individuals and small and large groups. Much verbal communication in the workplace takes place in person, over the phone, and in meetings. Verbal communication is most effective when you present information in an organized way using effective communication skills. In any organization, you'll need to talk to coworkers and to your supervisors. If you're promoted, you may have people who work under your direction. Speaking skills are important in all three types of work relationships.

- **Listening skills.** Effective listening skills let you hear another person's message, read body language, and understand the speaker's tone of voice. When listening to others, it's important to show them that you hear what they're saying, whether you agree with them or not. When people are focused only on getting their ideas across, they often fail to hear what someone else is saying. See **Fig. 5-3**.

- **Science skills.** Science skills, along with reading and math skills, help you understand basic chemical and physical reactions that occur in everyday life at home and at work. For example, Sandy used her knowledge of chemistry and her reading and math skills to develop a set of safety procedures for handling chemicals at work. All three skills helped her research the situation and calculate the costs of implementing the procedures.

- **Math skills.** As an employee, you will likely be expected to know how to add, subtract, multiply, and divide. You also might have to work with decimals, fractions, and percentages and know how to use a calculator. A combination of math and reading skills is needed to figure out such things as wages, credit card expenses, bank statements, and budgets.

Fig 5-3
Speaking and listening skills help you work effectively in groups. When have you needed good speaking and listening skills?

Employability Skills

Besides core academic skills and communication skills, there are other employability skills that almost all employers will expect of you:

- **Technology skills.** Being able to use a computer and other current technology is essential for almost every employee. These skills will also prepare you for workplaces that must constantly adapt to changing technology. Whatever future jobs you hold, you will use technology in various forms and will need to keep up with changes in technology throughout your career. Take advantage of opportunities now—and in the future—to learn and update these skills for success. See **Fig. 5-4**.

Fig 5-4 Learning new technology is important in getting and keeping a job.

- **Information skills.** The ability to obtain information when you need it is important in most workplaces. Analyzing and processing information—and communicating it to your employer, coworkers, and customers—are other components of information skills you will need.

- **Interpersonal skills.** "People skills" will continue to be important in an increasingly diverse workplace. Interpersonal skills include being able to work effectively with people from different backgrounds, cultures, and experiences. Employees also must be able to work in teams, teach others, and serve customers.

- **Thinking skills.** The mental skills you use to learn, make decisions, analyze, and solve problems are commonly referred to as **thinking skills**. Workers need to be able to think creatively and make the best decisions possible based on sound reasoning and facts. Both everyday and long-term decisions call for thinking skills.

- **Leadership skills.** Leadership skills are essential in the workplace. Leaders often motivate others with their positive attitude, enthusiasm, and work ethic. **Work ethic** means working hard, being honest, and staying committed to work. To set group goals and delegate tasks, leaders must be skilled at listening and working with others. Brad is a leader at school. He organized a group of students to create the school's float in the city parade. Because of his leadership, the students finished the job and won first prize.

There are many kinds of leaders. Some lead quietly, preferring to lead by example. Others are more vocal, frequently giving encouragement. Some leaders become involved in every part of a job, and others prefer to stay in the background until they are needed. Regardless of their leadership style, good leaders encourage tolerance and understanding. They help others in the group accept and appreciate all who contribute.

- **Teamwork skills.** How does playing on a soccer team, organizing a recycling drive, and working with your family to prepare a meal relate to your future work and adult roles? Teamwork skills are central to all these things. **Teamwork** occurs when team members work together to reach a common goal. Members cooperate rather than compete. Working cooperatively allows you to work as part of a team, to achieve team goals, and to share the credit for the work.

Whether as an employee or as a family member, you need teamwork skills. For example, teamwork skills help you work cooperatively with family members to plan a family trip or paint the kitchen. Teamwork skills are also used when employees work together to accomplish a task, such as serve customers quickly or clean up a store after closing.

People with good teamwork skills can work through conflicts that might arise among team members. Conflict resolution techniques allow the team to discuss and solve problems, strengthen relationships, and make better team decisions. Left unresolved, conflict can be a major obstacle to a successful team.

What do a promising athlete and a preschooler have in common? Both need to learn how to play well with others. The same is true of workers. Employers realize that in this competitive, global economy, valuable employees are people who add to a company's success.

To be an effective team member, take the following actions:

Be results-oriented. Focus on making progress, not taking credit or placing blame. With this perspective, put aside personality disputes and individual pride.

Appreciate diversity. Respect each team member's cultural background and personal qualities. View these traits as assets. Each person's background and personality

influence how he or she meets needs, solves problems, and deals with the world. Encourage others to bring these skills to the job and find ways to use them.

Understand human nature. Recognize when someone needs praise, support, and even gentle criticism. Deliver this message in a way that inspires others to give their best.

Keep an eye on "the big picture." Ask, "How does my contribution affect your contribution? How does my team's work affect the work of other teams?" Seeing these relationships helps you decide how to direct personal and group efforts to best achieve goals. On a practical level, this might mean knowing whose job must be done first and pitching in to help do it. On a larger scale, it might mean seeing how the project could affect a company's ability to stay competitive in the future.

TAKE **ACTION**

Choose a situation in which you can act as a team member—helping prepare a younger sibling for school or working on a small-group assignment, for instance. Use the strategies described here at the next opportunity. Note the effect of the strategies. What are the costs and rewards of teamwork?

Fig 5-5 Customers and employers appreciate workers who communicate clearly and respectfully.

• **Communication skills.** Whether you're speaking to one person or a crowd, you want listeners to understand your message. To get your point across to listeners, you need to be clear about your message and how you say it. See **Fig. 5-5**.

Making sure your body language and your words say the same thing is important to effective communication. Body language—messages you send with your face and body—can communicate something different than your verbal message. When this happens, you risk sending a mixed message. A mixed message, such as smiling while speaking angrily, is confusing to listeners and hinders good communication. Successful employees avoid sending mixed messages.

Effective communicators in the workplace use assertive communication, which lets them say what they mean in a firm but positive way. People are more likely to listen to assertive speakers and take them seriously. On the other hand, aggressive communication is overly forceful and negative and tends to push others away. A third style of communication, passive communication, is the opposite of aggressive communication. Passive communicators are too timid to say what they mean or tend to follow the crowd rather than state their own ideas. Often, passive communicators fail to gain the respect of others.

Employee Characteristics

"Most people I fire are let go because they can't get along with others," said Mr. Ruiz. "Everybody has to cooperate with each other or the work doesn't get done, and I lose a lot of money."

Employers not only expect employees to have appropriate skills but also expect certain traits or characteristics in the people they hire. Most of these traits are the same ones that help you at school or in social situations. At work, these traits produce successful employees and successful employer–employee relationships:

• **A positive attitude.** Your attitude is your way of looking at the world and the people in it. People with a positive attitude usually get along well with others and tend to be cheerful and enthusiastic most of the time. See **Fig. 5-6**.

Fig 5-6
Employees who keep a positive attitude are more likely to be recognized by their employers. What strategies can you use to stay positive in tough situations?

- **Initiative.** Most employers expect their employees to take initiative. Taking initiative means doing what needs to be done without being asked. Your willingness to find tasks that need to be done will help you achieve success at work.

- **Honesty.** Be honest with your employer and coworkers. Being honest includes not stealing property and being truthful about the time you spend on the job. Misusing time on the job by arriving late, taking long breaks, conducting personal business on company time, and stopping work early can be costly for employers.

- **Flexibility.** Flexible employees are willing to help with different tasks or learn new skills and technology. Flexibility allows workers to adapt to new situations, deadlines, or unexpected problems.

- **Work ethic.** Employees with a good work ethic are willing to do tasks that need to be done, and they are likely to be recognized by their employers for having the company's interests in mind.

Fig 5-7
Following your employer's dress code and maintaining your work wardrobe help show others you're a professional.

TiPS

Use Manners in the Workplace

Manners in the workplace help ease conflict and promote positive relationships. The following strategies will help you put manners first:

▶ Treat customers, coworkers, and employees with the same respect that you have for your supervisor.

▶ Always say thank you for any service received from others. It's nice to feel appreciated.

▶ Apologize when you make a mistake. Everyone makes mistakes sometimes, but good employees accept responsibility and act to prevent mistakes.

▶ Listen intently when others speak to you. Make eye contact and lean slightly toward the speaker.

▶ Don't cut off others when they speak. In an effective conversation, people take turns speaking and listening.

- **Responsibility.** Responsible employees show up for work on time, ready to work. Employers can depend on them to finish their work correctly and efficiently and to not waste time or money.

- **Professionalism.** Employees show professionalism in several ways. It is reflected in their appearance when they dress appropriately and in their behavior when they interact well with others. Successful employees choose to look and act their best so that they represent the company well. See **Fig. 5-7**.

Workplace Issues

Workplaces are not perfect. At times, various problems need to be addressed. If handled positively, things go well, and work gets done. Your employability skills and characteristics can help you deal with workplace issues that might occur.

Criticism

Constructive criticism is an employer's means of evaluating what you're doing and letting you know what you can do to improve your tasks. To improve your work performance, it's important to learn to deal with criticism in a professional way.

By doing so, you can learn and grow as a valued employee. Here are some suggestions to help you deal with criticism.

- **Listen to the criticism.** While you listen, think honestly about your performance. Don't become defensive or sulk. Doing so will keep you from being honest with yourself. See **Fig. 5-8**.

- **Understand the criticism.** Ask your employer to clarify the problem with your performance, if necessary.

- **Make a plan.** What exactly do you need to do better or in a different way to improve your work? List the steps needed to meet your improvement goal.

- **Take action.** Depending on the problem, you may need to break the solution into steps and take one step at a time.

Workplace Conflicts

Conflicts occur among people who have differing ideas or goals. Many conflicts are small and are quickly resolved. Others are serious and take time and effort to resolve.

One type of conflict at work occurs when an employee feels a need to be in control of certain situations, creating a power struggle. Power struggles, or conflicts over roles and responsibilities, may take place and disrupt the work environment

Fig 5-8 By listening to criticism, you learn how to be a better employee. What are these teens doing to listen actively?

for everyone. Other common causes of conflict are personality differences, poor communication, and jealousy.

Working to resolve a conflict can be a valuable experience. You strengthen many of the skills you need in the workplace, and you help strengthen relationships at work.

Employer Discrimination

Every employee has a legal right to fair treatment. Even so, some employees suffer **discrimination**—unequal treatment based on factors such as race, religion, nationality, gender (male or female), age, or physical appearance. See **Fig. 5-9**.

Various state and federal laws make it illegal for employers to engage in discrimination. One law, the Americans with Disabilities Act, protects the rights of individuals with disabilities, such as visual or hearing impairment, mental illness, or paralysis. The Equal Employment Opportunity Act prohibits discrimination by employers on the basis of race, hue, age, religion, gender, or national origin. These laws protect employees on the job and people who are applying for jobs.

Fig 5-9 Diverse employees contribute different viewpoints in the workplace.

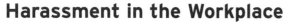
Fig 5-10

Fig 5-10
Keeping your skills up-to-date will help you in a changing job market.

Harassment in the Workplace

Behavior that is unwelcome and disturbing to others is called **harassment**. Persistent teasing, insulting, bullying, and stalking are all forms of harassment. Sexual harassment consists of disturbing comments or conduct with sexual overtones. It includes inappropriate touching, gestures, and jokes. Spreading sexual rumors and pressuring someone for dates are other examples of sexual harassment.

Any kind of harassment is unacceptable. When another person's behavior makes you uncomfortable, you may choose to ignore it at first and stay away from that individual. If that isn't possible, or if the actions continue, speak up. First, let the harasser know that the behavior is offensive and unwanted. A confident and assertive response may be all that's needed. If not, tell your employer. When harassment happens at work, your employer has the responsibility to make it stop.

Skills for a Changing World

In past generations, many people took jobs when they were young and stayed with the same business until they retired. Today the workplace is different. You can expect to change jobs numerous times before you retire. See **Fig. 5-10**.

Some of these career changes will be your choice. At other times, job changes may be forced on you, especially if a company moves work overseas or downsizes. **Downsizing** occurs when a company eliminates jobs to save money. Downsizing affects everyone in the workplace—some employees lose their jobs, and others are often given additional responsibilities. Mastering and updating your employability skills will help you stay employed in a changing job market.

Character Check ✓

Be Trustworthy

- **Be honest.** Trusting relationships aren't built on lies. Telling the truth, in a nice manner, shows others they can rely on your opinion.

- **Keep your word.** People decide who they can count on based on others' actions. By doing what you say you will do, people learn that they can trust you.

- **Trust yourself.** As you gain more experience in life, you learn more about yourself—your strengths and limitations, your talents and struggles. Be honest with yourself about who you are and what you can reasonably accomplish.

5

Review & Activities

Chapter Summary

- Today's jobs require a variety of employability skills.
- Leadership styles vary, but good leaders motivate others and encourage tolerance and understanding.
- Teamwork skills help employees work through conflicts and accomplish goals.
- Employers look for specific characteristics in potential employees.
- Employability skills and characteristics can help workers deal with workplace issues.

Reviewing Key Terms & Ideas

1. Name the core **academic skills** needed in the workplace.
2. What are **thinking skills**?
3. How do leaders motivate others?
4. Define **work ethic**.
5. What is **teamwork**?
6. What causes mixed messages?
7. List three styles of communication.
8. Name three characteristics employers look for in employees.
9. How should employees deal with criticism?
10. What laws help prevent **discrimination** in the workplace?
11. Define **harassment**.
12. Why does **downsizing** occur? How does downsizing affect employees?

Thinking Critically

1. **Defending opinions.** Think of students in your school who display good leadership skills. Would these students be effective leaders in the workplace? Why or why not?
2. **Drawing conclusions.** Think of school activities that encourage young people to develop teamwork skills. Do you think these activities do a better job of teaching cooperation or competition? Why?
3. **Predicting outcomes.** What might happen to employees who are unable to deal with criticism in the workplace?

Review & Activities

Applying Your Learning

1. **Skill identification.** Interview a local employer about employability skills he or she considers most important when evaluating job applicants. Share your findings with your class.

2. **Personal growth.** Reflect on your academic, employability, leadership, teamwork, and communication skills. Create a list of skills you need to improve to be ready for a job. Then list the steps you can take to practice and improve your skills.

3. **Interpersonal skills.** Imagine that you are part of a school news team. With five or six of your classmates, prepare a newscast about recent events at school, including school issues, student council, sports, and even the weather. Practice your presentation before presenting your newscast to the class.

4. **Life simulation.** Create workplace scenes in which one of several employees tends to find teamwork difficult. Demonstrate how communication skills can be used to promote teamwork.

5. **Conversation guidelines.** As a class, develop a video demonstrating conversations appropriate in workplace settings. Be sure to include guidelines for dealing with harassment. Present your video to a local employer for feedback.

Making Connections

1. **Writing** Assume the role of a school newspaper reporter. Write a short article about teamwork skills in action. Share your article with the class.

2. **Math** Imagine an employee who costs an employer $150 each day the employee does not show up for work. How much would this employee cost the company if he or she did not show up for work two days each month for one year?

3. **Reading** Read a story in which a character is teased or harassed. How does the character overcome the problem? Do you think the character's solution would work in real life on the job?

CAREER Link

Solving Problems. Workplace problems that you don't know how to solve can be frustrating and might cause you to act quickly without thinking the problem through. Talk to your school counselor, teachers, or other adults about problems they encounter at work and how they solve them. What advice would they give a young employee trying to develop problem-solving skills? Write a short report summarizing your findings.

CAREERS

Nutrition & Wellness Services

FOOD TECHNOLOGIST
Create new products and solve technical problems as you team with food science professionals. Involved in product formulation and designing plant start-ups. Must communicate well with a variety of audiences. MS in Food Science or Agricultural Engineering required.

REHABILITATION SPECIALIST
Full-time position available in a live-in rehab facility. Work involves developmentally disabled adults requiring direct care. Must have work experience and be able to teach daily living skills.

CHEF
Contract foodservice provider has opening for self-directed individual in the Central region. Good supervisory, leadership, management, financial, and coaching skills are necessary. Proficient computer skills required. Degree and three years of catering experience a must.

HOME HEALTH AIDE
Caring individuals needed to provide personal care to patients in their homes. Must be able to check vital signs and assist patients in bathing, exercising, and dressing. High school diploma, valid driver's license, and reliable transportation required. Training provided.

FOOD EDITOR Generate stories for quarterly publication based on trends in food, restaurants, and grocery shopping. Assign and edit articles and recipes from freelancers. Guide the publishing process. BA/BS in journalism or English and three years of experience are required.

DIRECTOR OF YOUTH PROGRAMS Community center needs organized director to plan and manage recreation programs. Will supervise staff, athletic programs, and community events. Excellent people skills necessary. Degree in recreational programming with knowledge of first aid preferred.

PERSONAL TRAINER Health club looking for an energetic trainer to supervise fitness plans for clients on an individual basis. Must be physically fit, personable, and have at least five years of experience.

FOOD MARKETER Individual will lead the development of our new marketing strategy in regional stores. Create effective brand messages in a visual format. Requires 10+ years experience in retail design and food merchandising and project management.

CLINICAL DIETITIAN Local hospital has immediate opening for a licensed dietitian. Responsible for providing basic nutrition assessments, planning special diets, and developing nutrition education programs. Bachelor's degree and extensive experience as a registered dietitian required.

Career Connection

Career Pathways.
Read the want ads on this page and list at least five job requirements for careers in the field of Nutrition & Wellness Services. Describe what you would need to do in order to meet these requirements. Explain why this career area does or does not interest you.

MORE CAREER OPTIONS

Entry Level	Technical Level	Professional Level
• Caterer • Food Stylist	• Physical Therapy Assistant • Food Services Manager	• Weight Reduction Specialist • Exercise Physiologist

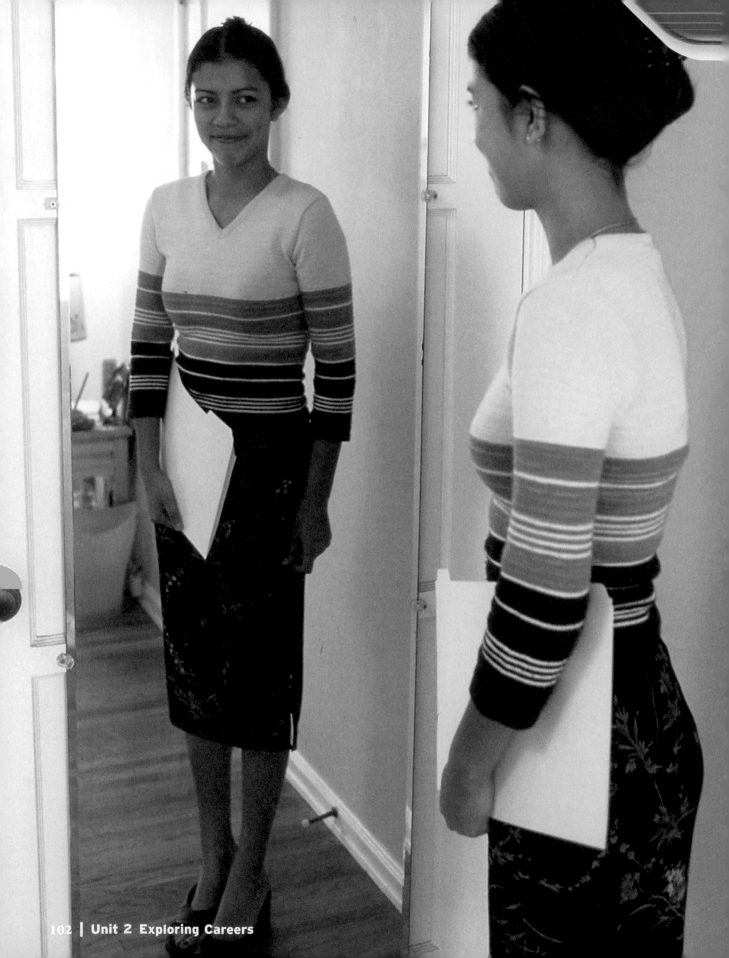

Entering the World of Work

Objectives

- Explain how to apply for a job.
- Practice writing a résumé.
- Create a career portfolio.
- Prepare for a job interview.
- Discuss strategies for balancing work and family.

Vocabulary

- **résumé**
- **cover letter**
- **portfolio**
- **interview**
- **stress**
- **flextime**
- **telecommute**
- **job sharing**
- **benefits**

Reading with Purpose

1. **As you read** Chapter 6, create an outline in your notebook using the colored headings.

2. **Write** a question under each heading that you can use to guide your reading.

3. **Answer** the question under each heading as you read the chapter. Record your answers.

4. **Ask** your teacher to help with answers you could not find in this chapter.

The Job Application Process

Ryan thought he could get a job anytime he wanted. After all, he was on the football team and had just been elected class president. However, after applying at several places for a summer job, he hadn't had any success—no job offers came his way.

Getting a job can be challenging. The employer wants the best person for the job, and you want a job you can do well

Fig 6-1 Find out what performance tests an employer requires, and brush up on your skills before applying.

and that pays an acceptable wage. A job offer is a two-way agreement that benefits both the employer and you, the employee.

Applying for a Job

Once you have one or more job leads, or information about specific job openings, you can begin applying for a job. The process of applying for a job is important in getting the job you want and shouldn't be taken lightly.

Employers have several ways of obtaining the information they need to choose the best person for the job. Most employers start by asking you to fill out an application form—either on paper or on the computer—and to submit a résumé and cover letter. For some jobs, you may have to take a blood or urine test to check for illegal drug use. Other tests may include a performance test to evaluate how well you can do a particular task, such as typing. Some employers also conduct background checks, which inform them of any criminal convictions you might have, and credit checks, which let them know whether you pay your bills on time. For most jobs, you will also need to interview with the employer. How you go about providing employers with the information they want often determines whether you get the job. See **Fig. 6-1**.

Preparing a Résumé

Many employers ask for a résumé in addition to a job application, and they want to review your résumé before they grant you an interview. A **résumé** provides a brief history of your work experience and education. It also highlights your interests and skills and includes some personal information. There are many kinds of résumés. A chronological résumé is shown in **Fig. 6-2**.

A résumé may be delivered in person, sent by postal mail, or sent by e-mail. Some employers prefer to receive résumés a certain way, so be sure to check before sending yours. Because a résumé can get you an interview—or ruin your chance for a job—it's important that your résumé looks its best and is factual before a potential employer sees it.

Using a Résumé

Fig 6-2

A résumé identifies work experience, accomplishments, and your educational background.

James Smith
123 Main Street, Springfield, IN 55555
(555) 555-555

CAREER OBJECTIVE A paid position as a preschool teacher assistant.

WORK EXPERIENCE AND ACCOMPLISHMENTS
- Three years of experience babysitting for five families
- Two years as an assistant coach for Little League baseball and helping care for my two younger brothers
- Class president of Family, Career and Community Leaders of America (FCCLA)
- Completed Red Cross CPR and first aid training courses
- Sophomore student at Hayes High School, currently on the honor roll

EDUCATION AND TRAINING
Present   Hayes High School, 23 Oak Street, Springfield, Indiana
2006   Red Cross CPR Training Program Certificate of Completion

SCHOOL ACTIVITIES
- Active member of FCCLA for two years, current class president
- Manager of junior varsity football team
- Member of National Honor Society

COMMUNITY ACTIVITIES
- Assistant coach for Little League baseball, Springfield Recreation Department

REFERENCES
References available upon request

When employers receive a large number of résumés for a position, they often narrow the field by selecting those candidates with the best-prepared résumés. Poorly written résumés, or those with misspelled words and poor grammar, are often eliminated regardless of an applicant's skills. If an employer is looking for someone with a specific skill, the reviewer will eliminate résumés that fail to identify the requested skill.

Writing a Cover Letter

Generally, a résumé is sent with a cover letter, although some employers don't require a cover letter. A **cover letter** tells the employer that you are applying for a position in the company. A successful cover letter has four major parts:

- A salutation and a reference to the specific job for which you are applying.

- Information regarding your knowledge of the company.

- A positive statement about the contribution you can make to the company.

- Your request for an interview, plus follow-up information.

Creating a Portfolio

Some employers want to see a career **portfolio**, a collection of work samples demonstrating your skills. See **Fig. 6-3**. The work samples—or photographs and copies of the samples—are placed in a folder to protect them and may include writing samples, artwork, or photographs of visual displays or models.

Instead of putting your samples in a folder, you can place your collection on a CD or DVD. A computer-generated, or electronic, portfolio is another way to show your skills. An electronic portfolio helps you demonstrate a variety of skills you have mastered. For example, you might include an audio file documenting your fluency in another language or your debating skills, or you might create a digital video spotlighting your theatrical talents. As with a traditional portfolio, keep your electronic portfolio files up-to-date.

Fig 6-3 Your portfolio is a reflection of you. Make sure it contains your best work organized in an attractive manner.

Fig 6-4
Learning as much as you can about a company will help make an interview go smoothly and demonstrate your interest in the business.

Interviewing for a Job

An **interview** is a meeting between a job applicant and an employer. It is the employer's chance to meet you and learn more about you and your specific job skills. The time you spend with an interviewer may play a major role in the course of your life. Unfortunately, many people fail to prepare for an interview and have no idea what they will say or how they will act.

The way you present yourself when applying and interviewing for a job usually determines whether you get the job. You can expect to be judged by the first impression you make. Employers tend to rate highly those candidates who are prepared, who appear genuine and enthusiastic, and who share the same values as the company.

Steps to a Successful Interview

Before an interview, study your résumé and be prepared to answer any questions you might be asked about it. Also, learn about the company, the products or services it offers, and how many people it employs. Studying a company's Web site, ads, and brochures can show the interviewer that you are interested in the business. In addition, ask your family or teachers about the business. Perhaps they know someone who works there who can give you more information. See **Fig. 6-4**.

The following tips can also help prepare you for a successful interview:

- **Plan your wardrobe.** It's always better to overdress than underdress for an interview. If you can, visit the workplace beforehand to see what the employees are wearing.

- **Know the time and place.** If necessary, check out the location of the business the day before the interview so that you're sure to arrive on time. Also, find out the interviewer's name and how to pronounce it.

HOW TO GET THE WORD OUT

Many people dream of being their own boss, of being self-employed. For younger teens, that option is not only possible but is also often easier than working for someone else. You may be too young to work in a car wash, but you can start your own car-washing service.

One thing every business needs is publicity. Of course, a teen pet-sitter doesn't need to rent a billboard or hire a marketing consultant. Simpler techniques such as the ones described here will do:

STEP 1 | **Choose a catchy name.** You have to call your business something—why not something memorable? Be careful that it's not offensive or questionable, and make sure it won't be confused with another business that offers a similar service.

STEP 2 | **Use community bulletin boards.** Ask permission from librarians, store managers, and postal office workers about placing homemade flyers in their business or facility. Cut one end of the flyer into strips with your name or business name and phone number for potential customers to tear off and take home.

STEP 3 | **Advertise on site.** If your business is visible to the public, make a large sign to place at the location while you work—for example, "This lawn lovingly mowed by . . ." You can also barter with a skilled seamstress to have your logo stitched onto your shirt or jacket.

SUDSY PUP DOG WASHING

Call Mike: 555-0347

- **Take resources.** Take a pen, a notepad, and a copy or two of your résumé and letters of recommendation to the interview. Only present letters of recommendation if asked and be sure to have the telephone numbers and addresses of each of your references, just in case you need them. Also, make sure you have your Social Security number.

- **Listen.** Let the interviewer take the lead in the conversation. Focus on hearing questions and answering them directly.

STEP 4 **Write a press release.** Local publications, such as neighborhood newsletters and small newspapers, often print press releases as a public service. A press release should be short and to the point. It should include information customers need to decide whether to try your service and how to contact you. Use humor or personal elements to make it stand out. Stress specialized skills that set you apart from others in the field.

STEP 5 **Take to the airwaves.** Many television and radio stations feature local personalities in "meet your neighbor" segments. If you're confident before a camera or microphone, contact the station about doing an interview.

STEP 6 **Generate word of mouth.** Recommendations from satisfied customers are most effective but often overlooked. They are also free. If someone compliments your work, reply, "Thank you. If you know people who could use me, please give them my name."

TAKE **ACTION**

In small groups, design or demonstrate one low-cost method of publicizing a real or fictitious teen business. Use an idea listed here or generate one of your own.

Dress for Success

An employer's first impression of you often relates to your clothes and grooming. The following tips will help you succeed in an interview and on the job:

▶ Wear business-like clothes for interviews and clothes that fit the job after you're hired.

▶ Be sure your clothes fit well and are comfortable.

▶ Wear clothes that are clean, pressed, and in good condition.

▶ Be well-groomed, with clean hair, clean fingernails, and polished shoes.

▶ Avoid excessive jewelry and makeup.

▶ If you use nail polish, choose a light, neutral color.

▶ Avoid multiple piercings, tattoos, and hairstyles that reflect an unprofessional image.

- **Ask questions.** Bring a list of questions to ask about the job and its requirements. Wait until after the interviewer asks for your questions, and save questions regarding wages and benefits until you know that you're a finalist for the job.

- **Be confident.** Sit up straight and speak clearly. Your job is to sell yourself.

- **Leave professionally.** Don't overstay your visit. When the interviewer has no more questions, or has risen from his or her chair, the interview is over. If you are not offered the job during the interview, thank the interviewer for talking to you and ask when a decision may be made. You might say, "May I call next week to find out your decision?" Then shake hands with the interviewer and leave. If you pass a receptionist or assistant on your way out, thank that person, too.

Following Up

Following up after a job interview is as important as the preparation you did beforehand. Start by promptly writing a brief, handwritten thank-you letter to the interviewer. The letter helps remind the employer of your interview and restates your wish to work for the company. Remember to include your telephone number and e-mail address. If you decide you aren't interested in the job, send a letter to thank the interviewer for the time he or she spent with you. See **Fig. 6-5**.

If you told the interviewer you would follow up with a phone call, make the call when you said you would. When the interviewer answers the phone, state your name and when your interview took place. Then ask if a decision has been made about the job. If the employer has not made a decision, ask when a decision might be made. If the employer has already hired someone for the job, kindly thank him or her again for taking time to consider you for the position.

If you don't get the job, keep looking—and learning. Going through the process of applying and interviewing for a job is educational in itself. Make a list of what you think you did well and what you could have done differently, and use your notes to prepare for future interviews.

Fig 6-5 Employers appreciate a thank-you note within one week of an interview.

Starting a New Job

The interview went well, you got the job, and you start work next week. What can you do to prepare? What will your employer expect of you? What can you expect from your employer?

Looking the Part

How you appear to your employer and to any customers and coworkers is important. The clothing and accessories you wear must be appropriate for the workplace. One way to find out what to wear is to ask about a dress code. Some jobs require a uniform, and others allow more casual wear. If your job involves meeting the public, it is especially important to choose clothing that is clean and neat.

When creating a work wardrobe, select easy-care items that can be coordinated with each other. This is more easily done when basic—rather than bright or flashy—colors are chosen. If you wear jewelry, keep it simple and not too large. Avoid trendy or faddish clothing.

Fig 6-6 Employees who use dangerous equipment and materials should have access to safety equipment and guidelines. What safety precautions is this employee taking?

Staying Safe on the Job

Many people are injured on the job every year. Part of your job is to make sure you're not one of them. The government, employers, and employees all have a part to play in preventing accidents. See **Fig. 6-6**.

The federal Occupational Safety and Health Administration (OSHA), a branch of the U.S. Department of Labor, sets job safety standards and inspects job sites. Its goal is to make sure employers provide a place of employment free from recognized safety and health hazards, such as exposure to toxic chemicals, excessive noise levels, mechanical dangers, heat or cold stress, or unsanitary conditions.

The employer's role is to provide a safe workplace, furnish equipment and materials needed to do the job safely, teach employees how to use the equipment and materials, inform employees when conditions are hazardous, and keep records of job-related illnesses and injuries. The employer is also expected to follow policies for conservation and environmental protection. The U.S. Environmental Protection Agency (EPA) sets standards for workplace environments, including the safe disposal of hazardous wastes.

Fig 6-7

This employee uses critical-thinking and decision-making skills to perform office tasks.

Your role as an employee is to learn and follow the safety regulations of your employer and OSHA. These include learning to perform your job safely, knowing how to operate and maintain tools and equipment safely, and reporting unsafe conditions or practices immediately to your supervisor. Failure to follow these guidelines can result in human errors that may affect both you and others.

Making Good Decisions

You'll make many decisions during your career. The chances of making good ones will be increased if you follow the decision-making process (see Chapter 3). The process, a series of steps involved in making a choice, can be used in a variety of workplace situations. Decisions ranging from choosing what to wear to selecting the kind of tool needed to do a certain job safely require critical-thinking skills. These skills will help you analyze problems and deal with them effectively. See **Fig. 6-7**.

Balancing Work and Family

Sandra starts her new job next week. She knows that being successful will take hard work, and she knows that, like most jobs, her job will include a certain degree of stress.

Stress is the pressure people feel as the result of their ability or inability to meet the expectations of others and themselves. Stress can result in a variety of physical reactions or symptoms, such as sweaty palms, the feeling of butterflies in the stomach, sleep difficulties, loss of appetite or overeating, and headaches.

Stress can be either positive or negative. Positive stress helps you meet challenges by giving you the extra push you need; negative stress causes discomfort and decreases performance. See **Fig. 6-8**.

The cause and the intensity of stress determine whether stress is a positive or negative force in your life. Tragedies and crises, such as the death of a loved one, a serious illness, or the loss of a job, cause feelings of negative stress. Uplifting events, such as a wedding, graduation, or job promotion, result in positive stress. Positive stress is usually connected with a sense of accomplishment and, if kept at a low level, can improve your performance. However, too much stress decreases performance levels.

Because employees are expected to work hard, meet deadlines, and interact with coworkers and supervisors, they often have difficulty balancing their commitments to their jobs, family, and friends. Some individuals feel they have no time for their own interests and hobbies. You can use several strategies to decrease the stress of balancing work and family commitments.

Fig 6-8 Even though celebrations can be fun, they can also be stressful because they require a lot of planning and work for the event to turn out successfully.

- **Set and prioritize activities.** Identify the activities that are most important to you. Which activities are enjoyable and help promote your health and well-being?

- **Budget time.** Set aside time for your hobbies, school events, and activities with your family and friends. Also make time for household chores, study time, and after-school jobs.

- **Avoid overload.** Don't fill your schedule with work-related activities. Before getting a part-time job, Julie used to babysit for a neighbor. Now that she's working, she can't babysit as much as she used to. If she did, she wouldn't have any time to enjoy family activities.

Work and Family Challenges

Most people are aware of the close connection between work and home life and try to develop strategies to keep them in balance. When they do, workers and employers both benefit.

Some companies help employees deal with the challenges of work and family by allowing flexible work schedules, or flextime. **Flextime** lets workers adjust their work schedules to meet family needs as long as the workers put in the required number of hours on the job. See **Fig. 6-9**.

Fig 6-9 Flextime allows parents or guardians to adjust their schedules so that they can drop off and pick up their children from day care.

An increasing number of employees **telecommute**, or work at home and communicate with customers and coworkers by phone, fax, and computer. In some work situations, **job sharing** is allowed, in which two part-time workers share one full-time job, splitting the hours and the pay. See **Fig. 6-10**.

Some companies provide reimbursement for child care or provide onsite child care facilities. Other **benefits**, or rewards for employment besides salary, may include health insurance, personal financial savings plans or retirement plans, and paid vacations. Vacations offer employees opportunities to release stress and time to be with their family and friends. Paid vacations are usually available to new employees once they have completed six months or a year of work. Some employers also increase employees' vacation time as they accumulate years on the job. For example, after five years, an employee might earn another week of vacation.

Fig 6-10 Many people who telecommute work from home. Others work from satellite offices. What might be some benefits of telecommuting?

Another benefit, an employee assistance program, provides confidential counseling services to help workers deal with personal or work-related problems. Some of the services include marital and family counseling, drug and alcohol abuse programs, and financial and legal assistance.

Benefits vary from employer to employer. They are one way an employer can attract and keep quality employees.

Aiming for Success

Successful workers are usually in jobs that they like and find satisfying. See **Fig. 6-11**. You will be most successful in a job under the following conditions:

- You feel comfortable and safe in the work environment.
- You have the tools and equipment you need to do the job.
- You earn wages and benefits that are appropriate for your skills.
- Your job gives you the opportunity for personal development and learning.

Fig 6-11 Personal interests often direct people toward a career path. Which of your personal interests would you like to pursue as a career?

TIPS
Achieve Workplace Harmony

Getting along with coworkers can be a challenge sometimes. Here are some suggestions for building and maintaining positive relationships at work:

▶ **Respect others.** No two people are exactly alike. It helps to understand and appreciate people's differences. Someday, you may be the one in need of some extra understanding, tolerance, and respect.

▶ **Communicate effectively.** It's important to send and receive messages accurately. Make your messages positive and supportive.

▶ **Focus on the job rather than the person.** You may dislike some people at work. If so, you must separate your personal feelings from the job requirements and learn to work together.

▶ **Stay neutral in disputes.** Mind your own business and don't take sides. By taking sides, you may strengthen your friendship with one person for the moment, but you may damage your working relationships with others.

▶ **Keep a sense of humor.** Try to laugh when the joke is on you. People tend to like and respect people who can laugh at themselves.

Review & Activities

Chapter Summary

- The application process is an important part of getting a job.
- A résumé summarizes your qualifications, work experience, education, interests, and skills.
- Career portfolios can be used to demonstrate certain skills to prospective employers.
- A successful interview requires planning and preparation.
- You can use several strategies to decrease the stress of balancing work and family commitments.

Reviewing Key Terms & Ideas

1. Name two tests you may have to take when applying for a new job.
2. What are three ways a **résumé** may be submitted to an employer?
3. List four parts of a successful **cover letter**.
4. What is the difference between a traditional **portfolio** and an electronic one?
5. What should you consider when planning your attire for a job **interview**?
6. Explain the difference between positive and negative **stress**.
7. How does **flextime** help workers reduce stress?
8. What does it mean to **telecommute**?
9. What is **job sharing**?
10. What are job **benefits**? Give four examples of benefits.

Thinking Critically

1. **Analyzing careers.** Some occupations offer more flextime than others. Which of the following occupations have a better chance of having flextime: farmer, writer, school teacher, house painter, mechanic, or hairdresser? Explain your choices.
2. **Making generalizations.** Think about interesting careers. Write down the expected rewards, the potential demands, and future expectations.
3. **Predicting loss.** Imagine what it would be like to lose a job. What challenges might the job loss present? What coping strategies can a person use to deal with stress caused by the job loss?

Review & Activities

Applying Your Learning

1. **Application readiness.** Develop a personal information sheet to use when filling out a job application. Fill it out and keep the information current.
2. **Résumé writing.** Imagine you are applying for a summer job. Create a résumé and cover letter using information in this chapter.
3. **Personal analysis.** Determine opportunities you will have in the near future to make a positive first impression. List those opportunities and suggestions for making a good first impression at each of them.
4. **Life simulation.** Pretend you have applied for a job and have been asked to interview for the position. Practice your interview skills with a partner.
5. **Job evaluation.** Make a list of questions you would like answered before accepting a job offer, such as pay, hours of work, and education assistance. Ask an adult or employer to review your list and give you feedback.
6. **Benefits research.** Interview a local employer about his or her employee benefits, such as health insurance and paid vacations. Determine the various plans available to the employees and the costs. Share what you learn with your class.

Making Connections

1. **Language Arts** Imagine you're a famous scientist in history. Create a résumé and cover letter for your job. For example, pretend to be Albert Einstein applying for the job of an astronaut or Madame Curie applying for a job as a physicist.
2. **Writing** You have just completed a job interview. Write a thank-you note to the employer to express your thanks for the interview and to restate your interest in the job.
3. **Reading** Read information about OSHA and the EPA. Compare their roles in protecting American workers and the workplace. Write a paragraph summarizing your findings.

CAREER Link

Appropriate Attire. Appearances count, especially at job interviews and at work. Body piercings, obvious tattoos, excessively long nails, and nontraditional hairstyles and hair colors can influence whether you get—and keep—the job you want. Although your job will determine the clothes you wear, a clean and neat appearance is important to most employers. Research local dress codes by interviewing several employers about their requirements. Share your findings with the class.

Child & Family Services

CHILD WELFARE WORKER
Qualified candidate performs professional investigation, casework, and casework services for the Department of Human Services under the Family & Children Services program. Work may include nights and weekends. A Master's in social work or counseling is preferred. Supervised fieldwork must be completed prior to applying for this position.

SPEECH PATHOLOGIST
Join a growing practice in evaluating and treating speech disorders for regional school districts. Good rapport with preschoolers and elementary children is a must. Master's degree, clinical experience, and state license required.

EXTENSION AGENT
Caring individuals needed to plan, organize, teach, and implement adult Family & Consumer Sciences and 4-H youth programs in the tri-county area. Day travel is common. Must recruit, train, and supervise volunteer leaders. Master's degree and dependable transportation required.

FACS TEACHER
Growing school district has immediate opening for a creative Family & Consumer Sciences teacher at the junior high school. Bachelor's degree and current teaching certificate required. Experience preferred. Ten-month position with excellent benefits.

EMPLOYMENT COUNSELOR
Search firm specializing in placement of computer analysts/programmers needs employment counselor to interview potential candidates. Bachelor's degree and good communication skills needed. Salary plus commission.

CHILD PSYCHOLOGIST
School district seeks psychologist to observe, interact with, and help children who have behavior and learning problems. Good observation skills and the ability to communicate with children, teachers, and parents are critical. Doctoral degree required.

PRESCHOOL TEACHER
Early learning center has opening for enthusiastic teacher to lead afternoon class for three-year-olds. Positive work environment. Associate's degree and certification required.

CHILD CARE PROVIDER
Mature, dependable, creative people needed to join our teaching team! Must enjoy working with children from 6 months to 6 years of age. Self-directed people with excellent communication skills should apply. High school diploma required. Course work in child development preferred.

SOCIAL WORKER
Licensed social worker needed to assist with patient recovery and rehabilitation plans. Must maintain accurate case records and help clients locate necessary services. Master's degree preferred. Must be available to work evenings and weekends.

Career Connection

Entrepreneurship. Research how a person might go about starting a Family Services business, such as at-home child care services or older adult care services. What education and training would be needed? How could you pursue these options?

MORE CAREER OPTIONS

Entry Level	Technical Level	Professional Level
• Teacher Aide • Nanny	• Preschool Director • Dental Hygienist	• Guidance Counselor • Family Therapist

Communication with Others

Objectives

- Distinguish between verbal and nonverbal communication.
- Explain how body language affects communication.
- Produce effective written communication.
- Describe communication roadblocks and how to avoid them.
- Demonstrate effective listening techniques.
- Show respect for yourself, for others, and for your community.

Vocabulary

- **communication**
- **verbal communication**
- **nonverbal communication**
- **body language**
- **rapport**
- **assertive**
- **tact**
- **empathy**
- **stereotype**
- **prejudice**

Reading with Purpose

1. **Read** the title of this chapter and describe in writing what you expect to learn from it.

2. **Write** each vocabulary term in your notebook, leaving space for definitions.

3. **As you read** Chapter 7, write the definition beside each term in your notebook.

4. **After reading** the chapter, write a paragraph describing what you learned.

What Is Communication?

Every second of every day people all over the world send messages to each other. In the time it takes you to read this sentence, millions of messages will have been sent in person, over the phone, through the mail, or by e-mail. Each of these messages is a form of communication.

Communication is the process of sending messages to—and receiving messages from—others. Messages include facts, opinions, and feelings. You send messages in what you say and how you say it. You receive messages when you listen to what others say to you.

Verbal communication includes spoken messages. A message sent without speaking is called **nonverbal communication**. Most communication is a mixture of both verbal and nonverbal messages.

Verbal Messages

Has someone ever told you something and you later thought, "What did that person mean?" Just talking to another person doesn't guarantee good communication. Although verbal communication isn't the only component of good communication, you need to use words effectively to communicate accurate messages. Whether you're speaking to a friend or in front of your entire school, you can improve your verbal messages if you do the following:

- **Be specific.** Organize your thoughts before you talk—in your mind or on paper.

- **Think before you speak.** Consider what you want to say before the words come out of your mouth. Once they're out, you can't take them back. Don't embarrass yourself or hurt others by saying things you'll later regret. See **Fig. 7-1**.

- **Express a positive attitude.** Try to express yourself positively and enthusiastically whenever you can. No one likes to hear others whine, complain, or criticize all the time.

Fig 7-1

Just talking to another person doesn't guarantee good communication. Good communication is a skill that needs to be learned and practiced.

- **Consider the person receiving your message.** The way you talk to a close friend differs from the way you communicate during a class discussion or how you express yourself to a young child.

- **Speak clearly and at the appropriate volume.** Speak up so that others can hear you. Pronounce words correctly and distinctly, and don't talk too slow or too fast.

- **Make sure your listener understands you.** Check to see that the person or group you're speaking to understands what you're saying. If you're not getting your points across effectively, try expressing your ideas in a different way.

- **Be aware of give-and-take in conversation.** Find a balance between talking and listening. If you do all of the talking, your listener might become bored and stop listening. This should be a two-way street. See **Fig. 7-2**.

Nonverbal Messages

You don't always need to talk to communicate. You send many nonverbal messages without ever speaking a word. Your smile or frown instantly expresses delight or disapproval.

Body Language

Body language, or the use of gestures and body movements to communicate, can often say more than spoken words. All forms of body language—facial expressions, posture, gestures, eye contact, physical distance, and even your appearance—communicate your inner feelings and attitudes.

- **Facial expressions.** A smile expresses happiness, attracts others to you, and encourages communication. Frowns, yawns, and snarls definitely discourage communication.

- **Posture.** Standing or sitting comfortably upright as you talk shows interest and confidence. So does walking with your shoulders back and head up. On the other hand, if you stand or walk with stooped shoulders and your head down, you send a message—true or not—that you lack confidence or feel sad. When people's body language sends a different message than their words, they risk sending a mixed message. For example, when Sharon crosses her arms and pouts after giving another girl a compliment, others don't know if Sharon is being sincere. To avoid sending mixed messages, make your body language match your words.

Fig 7-2 Eye contact is an essential part of verbal communication. It connects the speaker with the listener to be sure that the correct message is conveyed.

- **Hand and head gestures.** Hand gestures are often used to emphasize a key point or excitement. A clenched fist might show others that you are determined, angry, or hostile. Nodding or shaking your head shows that you are in agreement or not with what's being said or done. See **Fig. 7-3**.

- **Eye contact.** Looking into another person's eyes shows that you are friendly, confident, and interested in the speaker. However, be aware that in some cultures looking directly into the listener's eyes is a sign of disrespect.

- **Physical distance.** The space between you and another person often sends a message without words. Usually, the closer the relationship, the less distance people put between each other when they speak. However, people in conflict often stand close when sending messages of aggression.

- **Appearance.** A neat, clean, and healthy appearance sends a message that you respect and care about yourself. It also shows respect for others. What does your personal appearance say about you?

Fig 7-3 Nonverbal messages can be used to communicate feelings of respect and joy. What nonverbal messages do you see in this photo?

Written Messages

When you want to write to a faraway relative or friend, do you write a handwritten note and drop it in the mailbox or do you send your message by e-mail? In the past, most written messages took the form of letters, notes, and cards. Today, billions of messages are sent daily over the Internet, by e-mail, by text message, on electronic bulletin boards, or in chat rooms.

No matter how you send your message, you will need solid communication skills to write it. Before sending written messages, read them carefully to make sure your words are clear. Be sensitive to other people's feelings and use humor with care. Your message may be received differently than you intended. When sending messages online, make certain not to put anything in writing that you wouldn't say to someone in person. Also, remember that written communication in the workplace is often more formal than written messages to friends and family. Be sure your workplace messages are punctuated correctly and use correct grammar.

Avoiding Communication Roadblocks

Roadblocks stop traffic at the site of a major accident. Vehicles are backed up for miles, and travel is impossible. Just like bad traffic, certain obstacles can block communication:

- **Gossip, lies, insults, threats, and accusations.** Hurtful talk closes the lines of communication, shows no concern for others, and destroys relationships. See **Fig. 7-4**.

- **Nagging and preaching.** Comments like "You better exercise more" or "I tell you all the time to clean your room" turn listeners off.

- **A "know-it-all" attitude.** No one is all-knowing. Not being open to alternate views hinders communication.

Fig 7-4
Gossip often consists of lies about another person. What harmful consequences of gossip have you witnessed?

Learn to Listen, Listen to Learn

- **Listen anyway.** You never know what you might learn. Even if you think you know what another person is going to say or you feel you don't need to hear more about a topic, you will likely learn something.

- **Be a friend.** Telling people your thoughts and feelings is part of building strong relationships with others. Learning about other people is the other part. Listen to what your friends think and feel. You will become closer to each other as a result.

- **Show you're listening.** People send signals with their eyes, hands, faces, and bodies that tell when they are listening—and when they're not. Look at friends when they're talking, face them, and nod occasionally to show that you're paying attention.

- **Sarcasm.** Sometimes people use a tone of voice that expresses the opposite of what they're saying. By doing so, they are using sarcasm. For example, someone may say, "You're so smart," but if his or her tone of voice is sarcastic, the message sent is "you're not smart."

- **Interruptions.** How should you respond to people who interrupt you before you finish speaking? It will have to be brought to their attention by saying, "Pardon me. I didn't get to finish what I was saying."

Delivering Your Message

The way you speak is just as important as the words you use. Your emotions—whether you're happy or sad, relieved or upset—can come through in your tone of voice. Strive to use a tone and inflection (pitch and loudness) that accurately conveys your message. Controlling your emotions makes it easier for you to achieve the right tone and for people to understand what you are saying.

Choosing the right time to communicate is also important for good communication. Pick a time when listeners are interested in communicating with you. Bringing up your curfew to your dad when he's trying to nap won't result in a meaningful conversation!

For good communication, establish rapport with your listener. **Rapport** (rah-POHR) is harmony or understanding among people. It's the feeling of being listened to and accepted. One way to establish rapport is to put other people at ease. Show interest in them by involving them in the conversation. Call them by name and make them feel comfortable. Ask questions or ask for their opinions on a topic and give them time to respond. If you act relaxed and comfortable, others will react in the same way, too.

Assertive Communication

Have you ever been afraid to express your feelings? Many people feel uncomfortable saying what they think or asking for what they want. When people are passive, they don't stand up for themselves. They're afraid to say something that might make others angry. Some passive people end up following the crowd—whether or not the crowd is making good decisions.

Some people are aggressive and have the need to be in control. They are often viewed as pushy and rude, concerned mostly with their own needs and wants. Failing to respect the rights of others, they may try to get their way by bullying people who do not stand up to them. Most people are turned off by aggressive people.

Individuals who communicate assertively are neither passive nor aggressive. **Assertive** people stand up for themselves and for their beliefs in firm, but positive, ways. They don't bully others, but they don't give in either. They state their opinions and respectfully listen to other people's opinions. When opinions differ, they try to reach an agreement that's acceptable to all involved.

Starting a Conversation

James doesn't like being a loner at parties, but he just can't bring himself to talk to people he doesn't know very well. He's unsure of what to say and afraid of embarrassing himself. As a result, he either sits by himself at parties or doesn't go. What advice would you give to James?

The key to good conversation, especially among acquaintances, is to show interest in them. Here are some ways to start a conversation:

- **Encourage listeners to talk.** Ask open-ended questions that require a response in addition to yes or no answers, such as, "What do you think of . . .?" This will encourage the other person to keep a conversation going.

- **Show interest.** Pay attention to what is being said and respond to it—nod your head, maintain eye contact, and make occasional positive comments.

- **Be friendly.** Smile and be enthusiastic in what you say.

Developing Listening Skills

Listening is as important to communication as speaking. Unfortunately, it's often the most overlooked communication skill. If you've ever tried to make a point when others weren't paying attention, then you know how important it is to listen when someone is speaking.

TIPS
Speak with Confidence

Some people fear public speaking more than flying or heights. Even thinking about public speaking causes them to panic. Whether you're about to give a speech to your class or to your city council, the following tips will help you overcome your fears and speak confidently:

▶ **Make eye contact.** If you're afraid of making eye contact, look at the eyebrows of audience members. People will think you are making eye contact.

▶ **Breathe.** Breathe regularly during the speech. It helps you stay relaxed.

▶ **Move.** Casually move around, without hurrying. This keeps you from appearing stiff and nervous.

▶ **Focus.** Focus on the message, without rambling.

▶ **Wear comfortable clothes.** Wear shoes and clothing that are comfortable so that you won't be distracted by ill-fitting clothes. Also, avoid wearing too much jewelry.

▶ **Prepare your body.** No speech will be successful if you're not feeling your best. Get plenty of rest the night before. Eat lightly and avoid drinking beverages containing caffeine, which can increase your anxiety.

Active Listening

Active listening means listening and responding with full attention to what's being said. When you listen actively, you concentrate on what the speaker is saying, rather than on what you want to say. It also means you stay focused on the whole conversation, not just a part of it. Distractions are easier to avoid when active listening is taking place.

HOW TO BE CELL PHONE SAVVY

A cell phone can open doors to communication, but cell phone communication is not always welcome—ask anyone who has tried to enjoy a movie or a meal while someone in the seat behind chats on the phone. Even worse, imagine a driver running a red light while absorbed in a phone conversation. How can you use cell phones to advance communication and relationships, rather than strain them? Try these tips:

STEP 1 **Respect silent spaces.** Quiet is expected in certain settings. Cell phone conversations are as inappropriate as any other type of conversation at a museum, in a library, or during a worship service.

STEP 2 **Delay conversations when possible.** Not every issue is urgent. If a phone call interrupts a meal or disturbs others, explain the situation to the caller. Arrange for another, more convenient time to talk. A better option is to turn off your phone in a restaurant or any environment that is not conducive to conversation.

STEP 3 **Switch from a ring to a vibration.** Cell phones have a vibration option. The phone vibrates, rather than rings, to signal an incoming call, which is less disruptive.

Active listening involves giving both verbal and nonverbal feedback to the speaker. Verbal feedback might be a simple "Yes" or "Okay," or it might be a question or statement. Nonverbal responses include maintaining eye contact, nodding your head to show you understand, or shaking your head when you don't understand. This type of communication is responsive and interactive. Active listening promotes real understanding.

STEP 4 | **Ask companions' permission.** It's always polite to let others know if you need to make a call or expect to receive one.

STEP 5 | **Give yourself room.** If you choose to make or take a phone call, find a place where you won't bother others—the lobby of a movie theater, for instance.

STEP 6 | **Consider the ringtone.** Choosing or creating a special ringtone or melody is a fun way to express your personality. Before you program your phone, however, think of the people who are likely to hear the ringtone. Songs and sounds that you like may be unappealing or even offensive to others.

STEP 7 | **Practice safety first.** Making or taking a call while doing another activity can be a recipe for an accident. Going for a long walk might be compatible with talking on the phone. Riding a bicycle down a busy street while chatting on the phone is not.

STEP 8 | **Tell others about your cell phone rules.** Make sure friends and family members know general and specific times when you may and may not be called.

TAKE **ACTION**

Review your school's policy on students using cell phones. How does it relate to the tips given here? Do you find the rules reasonable? If not, how would you change them, and why?

I Can Be a Better Listener

Listening is a skill, but most people think it comes naturally, like breathing. The truth is, you have to learn how to listen effectively and then practice what you learn. The following tips can help you become a better listener:

- **Maintain eye contact with the speaker.** Eye contact helps keep you alert and focused on what is being said.

- **Avoid internal and external distractions.** Some days you simply have a lot on your mind, and it's hard to concentrate. However, to listen effectively you have to ignore internal distractions, such as thoughts and worries. You need to ignore external distractions as well, such as background activity or noise.

- **Evaluate the message.** Avoid communication barriers by evaluating the words, not the person speaking. Avoid letting preformed ideas or feelings influence your evaluation.

- **Be responsive to the speaker.** Your response shows the speaker whether or not you understand the message. Nod your head as you listen or comment on the speaker's message to show you understand.

- **Ask questions.** If you don't understand what is being said, ask for another explanation or an example. Try rephrasing in your own words what you think the speaker said. This can be especially helpful when you are given step-by-step instructions.

- **Avoid interrupting.** When you interrupt, you don't receive all the information the speaker meant to give you, and you discourage the speaker from continuing your conversation. Wait for your turn to speak, and if you have to interrupt, do so politely by saying "excuse me" first.

Communicating Respect

Good communication occurs when you respect others. You consider others before speaking and listen with an open mind to what others have to say. Respect means you are willing to appreciate another person's point of view—even though you may not understand or agree with what is said. When you show regard for the worth of someone or something—including yourself—you're showing respect. You gain respect with your positive words and actions. When you refuse to be pressured into going against your values, for instance, you send a message that you demand respect.

Respect also means showing regard for all forms of property and the environment. Respect for other people's property means you understand that their property belongs to them. Respect for the environment includes keeping your community clean and safe.

Respect is important in all areas of life—from friendships to international cooperation. When people send verbal and nonverbal messages of respect and common courtesy to each other, they help make life easier and more positive.

Respecting Yourself

Self-respect means the value you have for yourself. You show self-respect when you treat your own life and body as worthy. Caring enough about yourself to be your best also shows self-respect. Avoiding what could hurt you—physically, emotionally, and morally—also shows self-respect. You show respect for yourself when you refuse to take part in self-destructive behavior, such as drug or alcohol abuse. See **Fig. 7-5**.

People with self-respect have healthy self-esteem. Taking care of your health, developing your skills and abilities, and choosing friends who have similar values to your own are clear signs of self-respect.

Fig 7-5
There are many positive ways to say "no." Say it like you mean it. In the end, you'll feel good about yourself because you stood your ground and did what was right.

Be a Good Sport

When you play a sport, many opportunities exist for you to treat others with respect. Even if you don't play a sport, the "rules of good sportsmanship" can help you communicate respect in other aspects of life. The following tips can help:

▶ **Encourage others.** Give teammates or others in your group the same encouragement you would like to have from them.

▶ **Communicate positive messages.** Speak positively not only about members of your own group but also about the opposing groups.

▶ **Share your expertise.** Help your teammates or other group members to learn new skills.

▶ **Solve conflicts responsibly.** Discuss problems with coaches, instructors, and teammates to find a solution that works for everyone involved.

Respecting Your Community

What evidence of respect do you see for your own community? Are sidewalks and streets, playgrounds, parks, libraries, and recreational centers clean and well maintained? Or, are they in disrepair and littered with trash?

Respecting your community and the environment involves doing your part to take care of them. This includes disposing of trash in appropriate places and refusing to vandalize, or destroy public or private property by breaking things or painting them with graffiti (unwanted drawings and writing on walls and other property). When you respect your community, you take care of public property—whether library books or playgrounds—as if it were your own.

Respect at Home

Your family was the first community you were ever a part of. At home, you learned to respect yourself and those in your immediate family. As a teen, you show respect at home when you do the following:

• Act with consideration for the feelings of family members, including differences of opinion.

• Take initiative and help willingly around the house.

• Clean up after yourself.

• Follow rules, including curfews, and tell the truth about the people you're with and what you're doing.

• Treat siblings as equals.

• Treat the possessions of others with care.

• Take responsibility for your actions instead of blaming others.

Respect at School

How many ways can you show respect at school? Making time for friends, listening considerately to teachers, completing assignments on time, and following school rules are just a few ways to show respect at school.

Respect also shows in your communication at school. When you take an interest in your classmates' activities and opinions, you show them respect. You don't have to agree with them—only listen—to show respect. You also show respect when you're tactful with others. **Tact** is communicating something difficult without hurting another person's feelings. To be tactful, you need **empathy**, the ability to understand what someone else is experiencing. You empathize by putting yourself in another person's place and trying to see things from his or her point of view. In most cases, the more respect you show, the more you'll gain in return—from teachers, other school staff, classmates, and friends. See **Fig. 7-6**.

Fig 7-6 Empathy begins with listening. How have your friends shown empathy toward you?

TIPS

Overcome Stereotypes and Prejudice

The best way to overcome stereotypes and prejudice is to learn more about the people in your community. Here are some steps you can take:

▶ **Learn about other cultures.** Knowledge and understanding can help get rid of stereotypes and prejudice.

▶ **Identify and solve problems.** Find out the types of problems caused by stereotypes and prejudice in your school and neighborhood. Work on solutions to the problems with others.

▶ **See people, not their disability.** People with disabilities are people first. See them for the people they are—their interests, values, and goals.

Respect in the Neighborhood

Neighbors show respect by watching out for each other's safety and well-being. They stay informed about community issues and consider the needs of others by keeping their music at lower volumes. Other respectful actions are keeping front lawns mowed, properly disposing of trash, and participating regularly in recycling efforts. Courtney shows respect for the children in the neighborhood when she drives at safe speeds down neighborhood streets.

When Respect Is Missing

It's easy to see when people fail to respect themselves or other people. Teens who lie, cheat, or steal show little respect for themselves. Negative pressure from others, physical violence, and vandalism of property are just a few ways lack of respect is shown in the community.

Stereotypes and Prejudice

Each evening after dark, Nathan plays his electric guitar in his family's garage, even though his neighbors have several young children who have already gone to bed. His neighbors have asked Nathan to play at other times of the day or to turn down the volume, but Nathan refuses. He figures he should be allowed to play when and as loud as he wants. What opinion do you think Nathan's neighbors have about him?

A lack of respect can have many negative consequences and can lead to stereotypes and prejudice. A **stereotype** is the belief that an entire group of people fit a fixed, common pattern—that they're all alike in certain ways. People who hold stereotypes fail to see others as individuals, only as a group sharing the same characteristics. People with disabilities, the homeless, and those of different ethnic cultures are often stereotyped. Older adults and teens are sometimes stereotyped as well. In Nathan's case, his neighbors have begun to think that all teens are selfish and loud. See **Fig. 7-7.**

Stereotypes can lead to prejudice. When people dislike or hurt others because of their differences, they show **prejudice**—an unfair or biased opinion made without knowledge of the correct facts. Unfortunately, prejudice often is directed against people because of their race, religion, gender (male or female), age, economic status, or disabilities.

136 | **Unit 3 Building Relationship Skills**

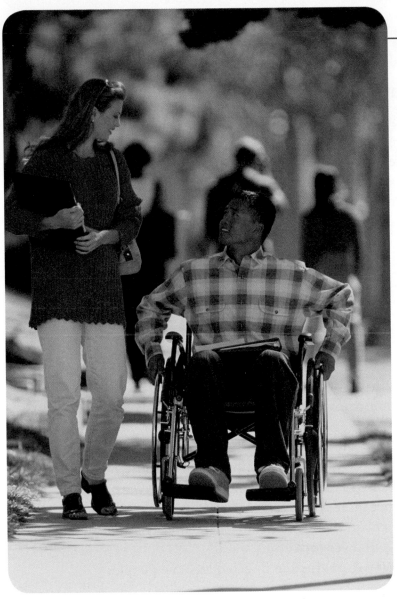

Fig 7-7

When you ignore stereotypes and view people as individuals, you create the opportunity to make new friends. What are some other benefits of knowing people who are different from you?

Prejudice causes distrust and hate without just cause. People on the receiving end of prejudice often respond with anger, frustration, and sometimes despair. Rather than smoothing the path to understanding, prejudice creates a widening gap between people.

How do you want to be treated? No doubt, you want people to get to know—and respect—you as a person. You in turn must practice the same principles.

Review & Activities

Chapter Summary

- You communicate with others when you send and receive messages.
- Messages are sent using verbal and nonverbal communication.
- Body language communicates your feelings and attitudes.
- Written communication can take many forms.
- Communication roadblocks prevent effective communication.
- Active listeners concentrate on the speaker, not on what they want to say.
- Respect means you show regard for people, the community, the environment, and yourself.

Reviewing Key Terms & Ideas

1. What is **communication**?
2. What is the difference between **verbal** and **nonverbal communication**?
3. List three forms of **body language**.
4. How can you establish **rapport** with others?
5. How do **assertive** people communicate?
6. Why is respect important?
7. List three ways teens can show respect at home.
8. Explain the relationship between **tact** and **empathy**.
9. Define **stereotype**.
10. Why is **prejudice** directed at some people?

Thinking Critically

1. **Analyzing situations.** Think about a time you failed to give or receive a clear message. What happened? What could you have done to make the message clear?
2. **Making predictions.** Imagine you sent an e-mail to a teacher, asking about an assignment, and the e-mail was full of punctuation and grammatical errors. Would the teacher's impression of you be affected by the e-mail? Why?
3. **Drawing conclusions.** What advice would you give younger friends or siblings who fail to use tact with people they want as friends?

Review & Activities

Applying Your Learning

1. **Communication game.** Sit across from a partner and take turns using one- or two-sentence communication roadblocks. Have the listener share how he or she felt when experiencing the roadblock. Discuss with your partner appropriate strategies for dealing with each obstacle.

2. **Presentation skills.** Write a short speech on a subject that interests you. List three main points and their supporting facts. Practice your speech in front of a mirror, using effective body language. Then present your speech to the class.

3. **Assertiveness skits.** With a partner, think of three difficult situations teens might encounter in which assertive communication would be helpful. Develop a skit, based on these situations, that includes passive, aggressive, and assertive communication. Present your skit to the class.

4. **Leadership skills.** Describe some volunteer activities you could do as a class to clean up a local park, recreation center, or other community property. Share your ideas with the class. If possible, select one idea and carry it out.

Making Connections

1. **Reading** Read print or Internet resources that discuss body language in various cultures. Share your findings with the class.

2. **Writing** Using the information in this chapter, write an article for your school newspaper that fits one of the following titles: "Unmixing Your Mixed Messages," "Watching Out for Written Messages," or "Listen Up!" Submit your article for publication.

3. **Math** Contact city officials to determine how much your city spends repairing property that has been vandalized. Then find out how much the city spends helping homeless people. How many more people could the city help if it didn't have to repair property?

CAREER Link

Speaking Skills.
Some people practice and improve their workplace speaking skills through organizations such as Toastmasters International. With practice, members lose their fear of public speaking and learn skills that help them be more successful in their career. Invite a local politician or public figure to talk to your class about public speaking. Ask about the public-speaking challenges the person faced and how he or she overcame them.

CHAPTER

8

Conflict Resolution

Objectives

- Identify the causes of conflict.
- Demonstrate ways to respond to conflict.
- List the steps in the conflict resolution process.
- Explain how tolerance and anger management contribute to conflict resolution.
- Explain how mediation is used to resolve conflicts.

Vocabulary

- **conflict**
- **escalate**
- **conflict resolution**
- **compromise**
- **tolerance**
- **negotiation**
- **mediation**
- **peer mediator**

Reading with Purpose

1. **Write down** the colored headings from Chapter 8 in your notebook.

2. **As you read** the text under each heading, visualize what you are reading.

3. **Reflect** on what you read by writing a few sentences under each heading to describe it.

4. **Continue** this process until you have finished the chapter. Reread your notes.

Understanding Conflict

Rachel loved her younger sister Brenda, but sharing a room with her wasn't fun. The sisters fought over everything, and no matter how small the disagreement, it always blew up into a big fight. "I wish we could find a way to get along," thought Brenda.

People are different, with different thoughts and emotions. Sometimes these differences can create conflicts. A **conflict** is a disagreement, dispute, or fight between people with opposing points of view. It can involve individuals or groups, such as friends, family members, community organizations, or even nations. Sometimes conflicts are easily resolved, but other times they become continuous struggles or turn into fights. When violence occurs, it's usually because the people involved don't know constructive ways to settle their differences. Fortunately, a conflict does not have to end in violence. See **Fig. 8-1**.

Types of Conflict

People experience two types of conflict: external conflict and internal conflict. Whenever one person's wants, needs, or values clash with those of another person, an external conflict can occur. Disagreements between family members, friends, and community members are external conflicts.

Conflicts may also be internal—inside your heart or your head. For example, Joseph found out his friend Christine had been plagiarizing, or copying, reports for school. Joseph strongly disapproves of Christine's behavior but doesn't know what to do about his feelings. Should he keep quiet or speak to Christine?

If people in conflict use destructive tactics to try to resolve a problem, the outcome is likely to be negative, but not all conflicts need to end poorly. Positive outcomes are possible if each person involved approaches the conflict with mutual respect, an honest effort to listen, and a commitment to finding a solution.

Successful conflict resolution can actually bring people closer together. In Joseph's case, he decided to speak to Christine. He found out that she plagiarized the reports because she was unsure of her writing skills. Joseph worked with Christine on her next report. He helped her improve her writing skills, and his caring actions reinforced their friendship. See **Fig. 8-2**.

Causes of Conflict

Have you ever argued with someone and later couldn't remember what caused the conflict? No matter how small, every conflict has a cause. Some big conflicts, such as inter-

Don't let conflict ruin a special friendship. Think about what you respect and admire about each other, and work together to resolve your problem. Why do you think friends let conflicts spoil their friendship?

national problems, have many causes. In general, conflicts are caused by the following:

- **Instant flare-ups.** Many kinds of situations can trigger sudden disputes or arguments. Anytime people interact—whether they live, work, or play together—conflicts can occur. Some people just overreact and have a flare-up based on their emotions alone. Fortunately, such instant conflicts typically don't last long. Most people deal with a quarrel and go on with their relationships.

- **Personality differences.** Differences help make life exciting and fun, but they can also create conflict. Perhaps you like being around large groups of people, but your friend feels uncomfortable in groups. As a result, conflict over what to do when you get together may be an occasional part of your friendship.

- **Power issues.** Power struggles often take place when different people try to control a situation. Many arguments in families with teens involve power issues. For example, sometimes a teen's choice of friends leads to a power struggle with a parent.

▶ Listen for verbal signs that a problem exists:

  Name-calling
  Insults
  Arguments
  Yelling
  Threats

▶ Leave the scene if a conflict has the potential to become physical:

  Shoving, pushing, or
    grabbing
  Slapping
  Kicking
  Showing or using weapons

Other causes of conflict include prejudice, jealousy, and revenge. In addition, poor communication, stress, and drugs and alcohol frequently trigger conflict. Understanding the cause of a conflict can help you respond to it.

Responding to Conflict

When a conflict develops, you can either face it or ignore it. Before deciding which action to take, consider these points:

- **Think safety.** Your personal well-being and safety should be your first concern.

- **Weigh your options.** If the other person is someone you don't know well, you might decide it's best to ignore the situation. If it's someone you care about, try to communicate your feelings in a calm and reasonable way.

- **Leave the conflict behind.** Avoid physical violence by walking away. Leaving a potentially dangerous situation is a positive choice—not a sign of cowardice. See **Fig. 8-3**.

In some cases, people let conflicts **escalate**, or grow into disagreements that are destructive or unsafe to everyone concerned. Some teens think that becoming involved in a conflict may prove they're tough and fearless. Unfortunately, getting out of a difficult conflict isn't as easy as getting into one. You can suffer legal consequences, lose friends, and lose your family's trust if you engage in violent conflicts.

Fig 8-3
Sometimes walking away is the best choice. Otherwise, conflict may get out of hand and a fight may result. What situations can you imagine walking away from?

Resolving Conflict

Whether a conflict seems unavoidable or tests your pride or values, you can resolve it peacefully. **Conflict resolution**, the process of settling a conflict by cooperation and problem solving, is a proven approach. Conflict resolution lets people involved in a dispute work out a solution to their problem. Resolving conflicts takes work, but anyone can learn problem-solving and communication skills.

The Conflict Resolution Process

How can you resolve conflicts? One way is to brainstorm with the other people involved to bring the conflict to an end by following these steps:

1. **Define the problem.** Each person takes a turn describing the problem from his or her point of view. Everyone speaks and listens with respect.

2. **Suggest a solution.** Each person suggests a solution to the problem.

3. **Evaluate a solution.** Each person identifies the parts of a solution that he or she agrees with or can't accept.

4. **Compromise.** If the parties are close to an agreement, they may compromise. When people **compromise**, they settle a conflict by each agreeing to give up something that he or she wanted.

5. **Brainstorm.** If individuals can't compromise, they brainstorm different ways to approach the problem and try again to reach a compromise. See **Fig. 8-4**.

6. **Seek help.** If no solution is reached, the people ask a mediator, a neutral third party, to listen to their problem and make suggestions to resolve it.

Character Check ✓

Forgive Others

- **Put yourself in another's place.** Have you ever been forgiven for your mistakes? Remember what a relief that was? Share that feeling with others by forgiving people who have made mistakes.

- **Accept apologies.** It takes a lot for people to admit that they were wrong and to apologize. When people apologize to you, show respect for their courage by accepting their apology graciously.

- **Let go of the past.** Avoid holding grudges against people. After forgiving them, move on.

Fig 8-4
It helps when everyone works together to try to resolve a conflict. This way, each person feels a part of the solution, and the result is likely to be successful.

Practice Peace

You can help prevent the spread of violence by keeping these factors in mind:

▶ **Friends.** Choose friends who value peaceful behavior. Don't become a member of a gang.

▶ **Skills.** Learn and practice the skills of communication and conflict resolution.

▶ **Distance.** Walk away from physical conflict and other acts of violent behavior.

▶ **Self-esteem.** Work at building your self-esteem. When you feel good about yourself, you're more likely to deal with difficult situations in positive, nonviolent ways.

Respect and Tolerance

You use respect in the conflict resolution process, but did you know that you can avoid and resolve many conflicts simply by showing others respect? When you show respect, you value another person as an individual. You also make it more likely the person will respect you. People who respect each other tend to listen with an open mind, consider the other person's views and feelings, and honor each other's basic values.

Tolerance is also vital to prevent and resolve conflict. **Tolerance** means accepting and respecting other people's customs and beliefs. People who are willing to accept others as they are tend to have fewer conflicts than people who are unaccepting of others. Tolerance helps you understand that different people have a right to behave and express themselves in ways different from your own, as long as they don't hurt others in the process.

Tolerance also involves getting along with people of all ages and generations. Teens sometimes find it hard to get along with older adults because they have different ways of talking, dressing, and acting. You need to be willing to accept all people and learn to understand their points of view. You are deserving of respect and so are others. Be fair in respecting others, even older adults. (After all, you will be an older adult someday, too!)

Anger Management

Everyone feels angry at times. When people are angry, they may feel annoyed and walk away or use a harsh tone of voice. Other times, they may yell, argue, or fight. If you learn to manage—or control—your anger, you can redirect these surges of energy to reach your goal.

When anger isn't controlled, conflict becomes worse. Dwelling on how angry you are doesn't help defuse your anger. Instead, your anger can build and lead to rage. At this stage, you may no longer be able to think clearly. The ancient martial art of jujitsu teaches those who practice the art to remain calm, to empty themselves of anger, and to gain the advantage in a conflict by using their opponent's tendency to strike out in blind rage. This type of self-control isn't just for martial artists. You can develop these techniques to control your anger and resolve conflicts in positive ways. See **Fig. 8-5**.

Fig 8-5
Strenuous exercise is a great way to put "anger energy" to work. You'll feel better when you're finished and more in control of your emotions.

Anger can take two forms. The first form can be called pent-up anger. It builds over time, and if not released in a healthy way, pent-up anger can explode when you least expect it. When you feel angry, here are positive ways to release pent-up feelings:

- Exercise: walk, jog, swim, or shoot some baskets.

- Talk out your feelings with a good friend.

- Listen to soothing music.

- Find a private place where you can feel emotional and cry or yell if you need to.

- Sit quietly for a while.

The second form of anger can be called hot anger and occurs suddenly when conflict flares between you and another person. To control hot anger, try these suggestions:

- Tell yourself, "I choose to be focused; I choose to be relaxed."

- Think of your anger as energy. View this energy as a way to get things done and positively resolve conflicts.

- Breathe deeply by pulling air in through your nose and letting it flow evenly and slowly out through your mouth.

- Think of either a peaceful place in nature or of someone you love who loves you, too.

If you need help in dealing with your anger, talk to an adult family member, a teacher, a counselor, or another caring adult. Don't let anger take control and ruin your present—and your future.

Negotiation

Ashley worked all summer to save enough money to buy a new stereo. When they heard of her plans, Ashley's parents told her to put all of her earnings into the bank to save for a car. Instead of fighting with her parents, Ashley asked them to set a time when they could negotiate an agreement about how to spend the money. **Negotiation** is a process of discussing problems face-to-face to reach a solution. Negotiation involves talking, listening, considering the other person's point of view, and compromising.

Safety Check

Anger can be particularly dangerous for drivers. These tips can help drivers keep their anger in check:

- **Avoid making driving a battle.** Competition can be deadly—to you and others.

- **Share the road.** It belongs to everybody.

- **Calm down.** Take deep breaths or listen to your favorite music.

- **Drive friendly.** Remember that hostility is contagious, but so is courtesy.

- **Avoid blocking drivers.** Let hurried drivers go on their way. They probably believe they have a good reason to hurry, and it has nothing to do with you.

- **Give up trying to punish wrongdoers.** You're not going to change their behavior. Model good driving behavior and leave punishment to the authorities.

HOW TO DEAL WITH BULLIES

The word "bully" comes from the German word for brother, yet bullies are far from brotherly. Through continual taunts, threats, and physical violence, they can make life miserable for others. Most bullying occurs at school, which can make it hard to concentrate or care about learning. Some bullying occurs at home, when one sibling bullies another.

Bullies themselves are usually unhappy and insecure. Humiliating those who are weaker gives bullies a sense of importance. They may believe they are earning respect, but they are only instilling fear. For some, the abuse confirms the low opinion they hold of themselves.

Bullies are not open to conflict resolution because their conflict is really within themselves. They need help dealing with their anger. Meanwhile, this is what you can do to keep bullies at bay:

- **Show confidence.** Bullies choose easy targets. If you show that you aren't likely to be bothered by their aggression, they look elsewhere. Show positive self-esteem by carrying yourself with pride, looking people in the eye, and being friendly to others.

- **Stand up for yourself.** Tell—do not ask—the bully to stop the hurtful behavior. Avoid criticizing, name-calling, or other emotional responses, which only encourage and provoke further attacks. Then leave calmly.

- **Ignore verbal abuse.** Show no reaction to insults or cruel jokes aimed at you. Bullying is like a game that takes two or more to play. If you don't go along, the game ends.

- **Stand up for others.** There is strength in numbers. Come forward to defend someone who is being abused, and encourage others to do the same. Bullies often back down when faced with a show of real power—the power of people with courage. They see that their actions make them unpopular.

- **Talk to an adult.** Tell a parent, teacher, or other trusted adult if you are bothered by a bully. Take a friend if you need support. Adults' intervention may not be needed at that point. If the bullying continues or escalates, however, they will be ready to act. If you're being bullied by e-mail, ask your service provider to help you block the bully's messages. Bullying can also be a form of sibling abuse. Parents need to be made aware of any intimidation or inappropriate physical contact by one sibling to another.

- **Put safety before possessions.** If a bully demands money, shoes, or any other thing you own, hand it over. Your physical well-being is more important than any material items. Report the incident to an adult.

TAKE **ACTION**

Suppose a friend tells you that a schoolmate is sending threatening e-mails. Your friend says it's not really bullying because the schoolmate doesn't make threats in person. How do you respond?

Fig 8-6 There is a right time and place to resolve conflict. It is best to find a quiet place to discuss the problem alone or with a third party.

Keep the following guidelines in mind when you're negotiating to resolve a problem:

- **Select an appropriate time and place to work out your problem.** Choose a quiet place and a time that are agreeable to everyone. Avoid meeting if you feel rushed or impatient.

- **Keep an open mind.** Listen carefully to each other and consider all points of view.

- **Be flexible.** Be willing to meet others halfway.

- **Accept responsibility for your role in the conflict.** Be willing to apologize if you see you've unfairly hurt the other person. Accepting and correcting your mistake is a sign of maturity.

- **Work together to find a positive solution.** Brainstorming possible solutions together can be productive.

- **Don't give up.** If negotiating isn't going well, it's okay to work at it another time. Suggest a future time and place to continue the process.

- **Find help.** Consider asking another person to help you reach a solution.

Learning to negotiate can help you resolve problems before they turn into big conflicts. In Ashley's case, negotiation kept Ashley and her parents from fighting about the money. They all agreed some of the money would be put aside for a new car, and the rest could be spent on the stereo. See **Fig. 8-6**.

Mediation

Sometimes people can't resolve a conflict on their own using either negotiation or conflict resolution. Deadlocks, in which no one will budge, occur when two or more people can't agree on a solution to a conflict. To resolve a deadlock, they may need mediation. During **mediation**, a neutral third party is used to help reach a solution that's agreeable to everyone. With a mediator, people can often agree on a solution.

Many schools have instituted peer mediation programs. A **peer mediator** is a young person who listens to both parties in conflict and helps them find a solution. Mediators are

trained to withhold judgment and to be careful listeners. They ask questions of both parties and respond fairly and calmly. Although mediators try to resolve conflicts by using problem solving, they don't solve problems. Instead, they help both parties seek a solution, usually through compromise. See **Fig. 8-7**.

Schools with peer mediation programs tend to have more cooperation, fewer fights, and less overall violence. Many families and communities now use mediation to resolve disagreements and prevent violence. When people resolve differences peacefully, everyone benefits.

Fig 8-7 Sometimes teachers, parents, guardians, counselors, or even your own peers are needed to help you resolve conflicts. Don't be too embarrassed or afraid to ask for help.

Working Through Conflicts

Although some conflicts are never resolved, both sides can learn to accept and respect each other's differences. Jacob and his parents may never agree on which music is best, but they can agree to respect each other's choices.

Fortunately, most conflicts can be resolved when people are willing to cooperate and work toward positive solutions. By learning as much as you can about conflict resolution, you can do your part to bring about and keep peace at home, at school, and in your community.

Review & Activities

Chapter Summary

- Conflict is a part of everyday life. Some conflicts are settled easily; others may last indefinitely.
- Conflicts are caused by a variety of factors. What creates conflict for one person may not matter to someone else.
- When responding to conflict, think safety first.
- The conflict resolution process is a proven method for successfully resolving conflicts.
- People who are tolerant and can control their anger are better able to resolve conflicts peacefully.
- When disagreeing parties are deadlocked, they may need mediation.

Reviewing Key Terms & Ideas

1. What is a **conflict**?
2. List the two types of conflict.
3. Why do some people let conflicts **escalate**?
4. What are the steps in the **conflict resolution** process?
5. What should people do if they cannot **compromise**?
6. What is **tolerance**? How does it help prevent and resolve conflict?
7. List five positive ways to release pent-up anger.
8. Define **negotiation**.
9. When should people go to **mediation**?
10. Name three benefits of using a **peer mediator**.

Thinking Critically

1. **Making comparisons.** Compare ways you dealt with conflict when you were younger and how you deal with conflict now. How are they different? How are they similar? How would you rate your current conflict resolution skills? Why?
2. **Making generalizations.** Why is it important to control emotions both at school and in the workplace? What suggestions would you give teens for managing their emotions so that they can work with others effectively?
3. **Drawing conclusions.** Imagine you're selecting peer mediators for your school. What qualities would you look for in a peer mediator? Why?

Review & Activities

Applying Your Learning

1. **School conflicts.** Take an anonymous survey asking students which types of conflicts they observe at school. Review the results and create a poster campaign that promotes a more peaceful school.

2. **Life simulation.** With a partner, enact a scene in which you use the conflict resolution process to resolve a problem. Present your scene to your classmates and ask them to evaluate how well you used the steps in the process.

3. **Cultural diversity.** Use print or Internet resources to locate news articles about conflicts caused by a lack of respect and tolerance in our country and around the world. As a class, discuss the consequences of these conflicts.

4. **Negotiation skills.** With a partner, create a comic book depicting two or more teens who resolve a problem by negotiating. Share your comic book with the class and donate it to the school library for other students to check out and read.

5. **Peace promotion.** Work in small groups to develop a list of volunteer activities you could do individually and as a class to resolve disagreements, prevent violence, and promote peace at home, at school, and in the community. Share your list with the class. If possible, implement one of the ideas on your list and evaluate the results.

Making Connections

1. **Reading** Read a short story or novel and identify the conflict. Write a description of the conflict, the characters involved, and the resolution.

2. **Writing** Using print and online sources, research road rage. Write your results in an informational essay, explaining the consequences and proper responses to road rage.

3. **Reading** Find articles in newspapers and news magazines about conflicts or disagreements between athletes and team owners. Describe how negotiation was used to settle these disputes. If negotiation failed to resolve the situation, identify the reasons for failure.

CAREER Link

Harassment.
Inappropriate, unwanted behavior that disturbs others is known as harassment. Harassment can happen at school, at work, online, on the phone, or on the road. In all cases it's harmful, and in some cases it's illegal. Interview a school counselor and other adults about workplace harassment and suggestions for dealing with it. Outline the steps you would take if you were harassed at school, at a school-related event, or in the workplace.

Dealing with Peer Pressure

Objectives

- Give examples of manipulative behavior.
- Identify alternatives to joining a gang.
- Classify responses to negative peer pressure.
- Demonstrate refusal skills.

Vocabulary

- **peers**
- **peer pressure**
- **manipulation**
- **refusal skills**

Reading with Purpose

1. **As you read** Chapter 9, create an outline in your notebook using the colored headings.

2. **Write** a question under each heading that you can use to guide your reading.

3. **Answer** the question under each heading as you read the chapter. Record your answers.

4. **Ask** your teacher to help with answers you could not find in this chapter.

Recognizing Peer Pressure

Julia, one of the most popular girls in school, stopped Lea in the hall. "There's a party tonight at Jim's house. His parents are away for the weekend, and everyone's going!" Lea knew her parents would never let her attend a party if parents weren't present. "I don't think I can make it," Lea said meekly. "Tell them you're going to a friend's house to study for finals," Julia said with a secretive smile. "They'll never know. What do you say?"

It's normal for **peers**, or people the same age, to try to influence each other. The pressure you feel to do what others your age are doing is called **peer pressure**. Because most teens are sensitive to their peers' opinions, peer pressure can be hard to resist.

Positive Peer Pressure

Have you ever been influenced by friends to do something positive for yourself, others, or your community? Positive peer pressure is what you feel when people your age encourage you to do something worthwhile. When a good friend influences and encourages you to study for a big test, you are experiencing positive peer pressure. The same is true when you pressure a friend to eat healthy and get in shape.

True friends don't ask each other to do things that either friend feels is wrong or hurtful—to themselves or anyone else. Positive peer pressure supports your values and beliefs, and it almost always results in positive consequences for everyone involved.

Role Models

Good role models—peers or others whom young people look up to—exert a positive influence. They inspire you to work harder, to think about your future, and to choose correct behaviors. You may be a positive role model to someone who looks up to you and follows your actions. See **Fig. 9-1**.

Fig 9-1 ▶

It's an honor when someone sees you as a role model. By being a positive role model, you can inspire others around you.

Role models can also serve as good examples of what not to do. A teen whose role models don't use tobacco, alcohol, or other drugs may be positively influenced to follow their example. Unfortunately, not all role models are positive ones. Some people—including celebrities and others on television or on the radio—may encourage you to act against your own values and beliefs.

Negative Peer Pressure

When you hear the words "everybody's doing it," how do you feel? Do you think true friends use these phrases with each other? These are just a few words people say when they're using negative peer pressure. Negative peer pressure is what you feel when your peers try to persuade you to do something you don't want to do or something that has negative consequences. Some peers may try to persuade you to do something to hurt others or to do something unhealthy, dangerous, or illegal, such as use tobacco, alcohol, or other drugs. They may urge you to try something you feel you aren't ready for or that goes against your better judgment.

People who use negative peer pressure often know that what they're pressuring others to do is wrong. Convincing friends to join them fills their own needs—not the needs of their friends—and makes them feel important and in control.

Manipulation

People sometimes pressure others through **manipulation**—a dishonest way to control or influence someone. People who manipulate others aim to get what they want, regardless of the consequences. Manipulators try to do the following:

- **Appeal to your courage.** They may use put-downs, such as "What are you, chicken?" to shame you.

- **Appeal to your desire to belong.** Besides the familiar statement "Come on, everybody's doing it," other appeals include, "We only ask people we think are cool to join us" or "Only losers say 'no.'" See **Fig. 9-2**.

- **Appeal to your guilt.** "Man, I thought I could count on you!" is an example of manipulation with guilt.

Understand Negative Peer Pressure

If you're pressured by others to act against your beliefs or take part in behavior that has negative consequences, stop and think carefully. Ask yourself these questions:

▶ Will this hurt anyone or any property?

▶ Will it be harmful to me?

▶ Are there risks involved?

▶ Would my actions negatively affect the way my family, teachers, friends, and people in the community view me?

If one or more answers are "yes," then respond with a firm "no." If you think you need to, give a simple reason for not going along with what your peers want you to do. Then change the subject or walk away. You don't need friends who don't care about your well-being. Look around to find friends who do.

Watch out for manipulative behavior by friends and acquaintances who do the following:

- Make threats to use violence or other negative actions to get their way.

- Make you feel guilty to get what they want.

- Flatter or praise you insincerely to influence you.

- Promise you money or favors if you do what they ask.

- Tease you in nasty or destructive ways.

Fig 9-2 Manipulation comes in many forms and can result in serious school and legal troubles. This teen was pressured to shoplift. What other choice did he have?

How do you feel when people try to manipulate you into doing things that are wrong? True friends won't push you to do something you don't want to do. In the same way, your peers should be able to count on you to respect their values and beliefs and to not manipulate them.

Bullying

Bullies pick on others as a way to gain power, to get their way, or to feel important. Bullying can take many forms, including gossiping, teasing, and physical violence. When bullies use these tactics to pressure others, they're using negative peer pressure.

You don't have to let bullying get the best of you. Sometimes appearing confident and telling the bully to stop is enough to make a bully back down. Other times, ignoring the bully makes the pressure go away. Whenever bullying gets out of hand, tell an adult. Don't bully back. Fighting back just satisfies a bully and makes the bullying worse.

Fig 9-3

You show courage when you ask for advice from someone in authority. Often, this will stop the problem you're experiencing.

Gangs

A gang is a group of people who associate with one another because they have something in common and are looking for acceptance. Not all teen groups are bad. However, many gangs are involved in illegal activities, and they use negative peer pressure to convince others in their group to go along.

There are many alternatives to joining a gang. If you're lonely or bored, search out a youth group, sports team, volunteer opportunities, or other activities in your neighborhood or community. If peers are negatively pressuring you, think about starting a group that works for positive change, such as a group that tutors young children or collects items for a homeless shelter. Talk to adults and local businesses to sponsor sports, music, or art events for teens who don't participate in gangs. See **Fig. 9-3**.

If you're harassed by gang members, seek help. A family member, community group, school counselor, or police officer can help protect you and give you support.

Responding to Negative Peer Pressure

Standing up to negative peer pressure is one of the most important skills you can learn. It's never easy to say "no" to friends when you want to be part of a group. You may be afraid of hurting someone's feelings or losing a friendship. You may fear being laughed at or excluded.

How you respond to negative peer pressure is up to you. You can give up your self-control, or you can decide to be the one who is in charge of your life.

- **Passive response.** Giving in to peer pressure is a passive response. So is backing down instead of standing up for your needs and wants. You may know someone who is passive and thinks he or she wins friends by going along with peers. Instead, this person is viewed as a pushover and not worthy of respect.

- **Aggressive response.** Hostile responses that violate the rights of others are aggressive responses. Even though aggressive people think they'll get their way and be seen

HOW TO STAND UP FOR YOURSELF

Suppose a classmate frequently asks to borrow money. You always end up loaning it, although you've yet to see a dime in repayment. You decide today is going to be different. You're going to insist on being paid back before making another loan. How can you turn this image of the assertive new you into reality?

These pointers can help you stand up for yourself—and help ensure that you don't resort to manipulative tactics:

- **Know what you want.** If what you want is abstract, like respect, identify actions or behaviors that demonstrate it. You might decide that you don't appreciate being teased about the way you dress or waiting for people who are always late.

- **Prepare yourself.** Rehearse the scene with a friend. Have the friend give responses designed to sway you from your stance. Counter with arguments of your own.

I understand your situation, but I've made up my mind.

- **Speak with conviction.** Politely state exactly what you want, and don't apologize or weaken your message with appeasing phrases such as, "It would be nice if . . ." Avoid asking "Could you . . .?" or "Is it possible to . . .?"

- **Keep your body "on message."** Reinforce your words with body language. Stand straight and keep eye contact to show determination.

as powerful and popular, their approach often backfires. People either tend to avoid those who are aggressive or jump in and fight back.

- **Assertive response.** When you respond assertively to peer pressure, you stand up for your rights in firm but positive ways. You directly and honestly state your thoughts and feelings. You show that you mean what you say. Most people respect others who show the courage to be true to themselves.

Refuse to be interrupted. Finish your thought, even if you have to talk over someone who tries to interrupt. Raise your voice only enough to be heard.

- **Allow an acceptable compromise.** Decide in advance what compromises would be satisfactory. Would you be willing to change some of your habits if other people agree to change theirs?

TAKE **ACTION**

Think of a situation in which teen peers make decisions together, such as picking a place to eat lunch. Use the techniques here to demonstrate an assertive response from a teen who feels taken advantage of. In class, discuss how this response prevents manipulation.

Show You're Responsible

- **Follow through.** When you agree to do something, you become responsible for it. Others have trust that you will come through as you said you would.

- **Back it up.** You choose which words to say; you decide which actions you will take. Take responsibility for yourself by standing behind all that you say and do.

- **Step up to the challenge.** Leaders are responsible for their groups, but group members can help out. Let your parents or guardians, teachers, and coaches know that you would like to help them with their responsibilities.

Developing Refusal Skills

What if a friend tries to convince you to do something you don't want to do or that goes against your values? If you say "yes" to something that doesn't feel right, you'll end up feeling disappointed in yourself. Saying "yes" to something risky may harm you physically and emotionally. It also may hurt the people you care about most.

Refusal skills can help. **Refusal skills** are basic communication skills you can use to say "no" effectively. Use these skills to say "no" without feeling guilty or uncomfortable. People will respect you for your honesty and firmness. See **Fig. 9-4**.

When it's time to take a stand against negative peer pressure, use the following refusal skills:

- **Say "no" and mean it.** If you're pressured to do something you don't believe is right, say "no" and mean it. Practice saying "no" out loud until you sound like you really mean it. If you seem to waver, the other person may try to change your mind. Use eye contact to show you mean what you say. If the other person won't take "no" for an answer, repeat your refusal and your reason for it.

- **Offer alternatives.** If a friend presses you to do something that makes you uncomfortable, suggest another activity that's acceptable to you.

Fig 9-4 ▶
Direct eye contact, facial expression, hand gestures, a firm tone of voice, and an erect posture send the message that you really mean "no" when being pressured to do something you know is wrong for you.

- **Take action.** Back up your words with actions. If you're pressured to act against your better judgment, make it clear that you won't do it. If that doesn't work, just leave an uncomfortable situation. It's okay to say, "I'm going home."

Developing Confidence

Doing what you believe is right can be especially hard when peers pressure you to make certain decisions. Decisions about the friends you choose, the clothes you wear, and how you treat your body can be particularly difficult.

When you're struggling with peer pressure, remember that it's your life—not someone else's. Rather than letting others pressure you into behavior you may regret, start now to follow your own values and dreams. Most people will respect you more as you become more confident and show that you respect yourself. Individuals who stand up for what is right for themselves and others are the ones who are most admired in the long run.

Teens Speak About Community Pride

Kayla rested her basketball on her hip and stared at the trash collecting in the park. "Did a garbage truck lose a few bags passing through?"

Nicki shrugged. "It's always like this. I guess people around here don't care."

"It's not people around here; it's everyone who uses the park." Kayla tossed her friend a plastic soda cup. "See those trash cans over there? Let's use them."

Working together, the teens cleared the courts of assorted boxes, bags, and fast-food wrappers. They saved one plastic bag for aluminum cans.

"Look over there." Nicki nodded toward the play area, where children were helping adults do the same thing.

Kayla smiled. "See? People do care. Sometimes they just need a push in the right direction. Now, let's wash our hands and practice our game-winning, buzzer-beating, three-point shot."

Teen Connection

Identify ways that teens can show pride in various communities, including the home, school, and workplace. Carry out one idea and report on the effect.

Review & Activities

Chapter Summary

- Peer pressure may be positive or negative.
- Positive role models encourage you to be your best.
- People who use manipulation aim to influence others to get what they want, regardless of the consequences.
- If you're tempted to join a gang, search out a youth group, sports team, or other activities in your community instead.
- When you respond assertively to peer pressure, you stand up for your rights firmly and positively.
- Refusal skills help you say "no" without feeling guilty or uncomfortable.

Reviewing Key Terms & Ideas

1. Who are a person's **peers**?
2. Describe positive **peer pressure**.
3. What is a role model? Explain how a role model can be a good example of avoiding a risky activity.
4. What is negative peer pressure?
5. What is **manipulation**?
6. What are three ways people might try to manipulate you?
7. Why do bullies pick on others?
8. What should you do if you're harassed by gang members?
9. List the three types of responses to negative peer pressure.
10. What are **refusal skills**? How can they help you deal with peer pressure?

Thinking Critically

1. **Making comparisons.** Define the words "friend" and "peer." In what ways are peers and friends similar? In what ways are they different?
2. **Drawing conclusions.** Think about a family member or friend who has served as a role model for you. Make a list describing this person's qualities.
3. **Analyzing behavior.** Compare several responses to peer pressure that you have observed in friends and acquaintances. Which responses were the most effective? Which were the least effective? Explain.

Review & Activities

Applying Your Learning

1. **Classification skills.** For one week, observe and list instances of peer pressure. Classify the instances as positive or negative peer pressure, and explain your reasoning.

2. **Children's activity.** In small groups, create an activity for young children that teaches them how to respond effectively to bullying. Analyze your activity.

3. **Community research.** Research community resources that provide alternatives to joining a gang, such as community recreation centers or school-related clubs. Share your list with your class.

4. **Short story.** Write a short story, with two different endings, that depicts a teen responding to peer pressure. In the first ending, describe the consequences of giving in to negative peer pressure. In the second ending, describe what happens when the teen successfully resists the pressure.

5. **Refusal skills.** Think ahead about a situation in which your peers might try to pressure you into doing something you don't want to do. Plan how you will use refusal skills.

Making Connections

1. **Reading** Read information about an organization such as Alcoholics Anonymous. Give a short presentation, sharing what you learned about the organization's purpose and history of positive peer pressure.

2. **Writing** Think of a role model you admire. Write a short essay about the individual, including how his or her behavior has influenced you.

3. **Language Arts** Research the work of drug and alcohol rehabilitation centers in your community or state. In what ways does addiction hinder people's ability to refuse drugs and alcohol? How are rehabilitation centers addressing this issue?

4. **Math** Imagine you want to show a friend who is pressuring you to smoke cigarettes that it's not financially worth it. Using current prices, calculate the cost of smoking one package of cigarettes a day for 10 years.

CAREER Link

Making Decisions.
Peer pressure sometimes leads teens into making decisions that negatively affect their future careers, such as getting facial piercings or tattoos. Interview several employers about their opinions and policies regarding obvious tattoos, body piercings, and unconventional hairstyles. How can these traits affect a job interview and an employer's opinion of a worker? Share your findings with your class.

Enjoying Friendships

Objectives

- Describe qualities of a true friend.
- Demonstrate ways to make and keep friends.
- Give guidelines for responsible relationships.
- Suggest ways to end a friendship when necessary.
- Practice positive ways to handle rejection.

Vocabulary

- **acquaintances**
- **dependable**
- **cliques**
- **infatuation**

Reading with Purpose

1. **Read** the title of this chapter and describe in writing what you expect to learn from it.

2. **Write** each vocabulary term in your notebook, leaving space for definitions.

3. **As you read** Chapter 10, write the definition beside each term in your notebook.

4. **After reading** the chapter, write a paragraph describing what you learned.

Focus on Friendships

Lorna's best friend, Dana, recently moved to another part of the country. Lorna misses her friend and sometimes feels lonely. She and Dana have known each other since preschool, spending most of their free time together. They hope to remain friends for the rest of their lives, regardless of the distance between them.

Some people form childhood friendships that last a lifetime. Others make new friends as they move to high school and beyond. Good friends enjoy their time together. They go to each other for advice and view their friends as people who are always there for them. Friends listen to one another and offer support. They help each other through problems. True friends are there for each other in good times and bad.

Qualities of True Friends

Qualities you may want in friends vary depending on the degree of friendship. People you may know—but who are not personal friends—are called **acquaintances**. For example, a neighbor down the street or someone you say hello to at school may be an acquaintance. In time, the person may become a friend, someone you know well and like to spend time with. A friendship generally goes through stages on the way to becoming a close relationship.

You may have known some of your friends for as long as you can remember. Other friendships may have recently grown. Regardless of how you met, or how long you've known each other, the following qualities are generally true of all good friends:

- **Caring.** Friends care for and about each other. They accept each other's weaknesses and focus on their strengths. Also, caring friends value and respect each other's feelings.

- **Dependability.** Friends are **dependable**, or able to be counted on. They keep their word.

- **Loyalty.** Real friends stick by you. They like you for who you are—not for what you have or what you can do for them. They will take your side as necessary. A friend believes in you. Loyal friends are there when you need them. See **Fig. 10-1**.

- **Respect.** Your true friends respect your values and never ask you to go against what you value as important. They respect your position on sensitive issues and respect your opinion. They may not always agree with you, but they always hear you out.

- **Empathy.** Good friends show you empathy, or the ability to understand what others are experiencing. They put themselves in your place and try to see things from your point of view.

Fig 10-1 If you expect loyalty from friends, you must be loyal to your friends. When have you shown loyalty in the past?

Fig 10-2
Some popular teens seem to choose friends based on looks. Remember, true friendships are not based on appearances.

- **Forgiveness.** True friends understand that they each can make mistakes. Friends apologize when they've made a mistake, forgive each other, and remain friends without holding grudges.

- **Common interests.** Good friends often share similar interests. Whether it's baseball or sewing, common interests give friends something to talk about and do together. However, it's not necessary for friends to share interests. People sometimes are interested in each other because of their unique differences.

Strengthening Friendships

To have a friend is to be a friend. Friendships take effort. People with lifelong friendships know how to give as well as take. This involves spending time with your friends, listening to what they have to say, and offering them help when they need it.

Diverse Friendships

Think about the friends you have. How are they different from you? Perhaps they're much older or from another country. Although many of your friends will be similar to you, not all friends have to be. A variety of friends makes life interesting. Friends come in different ages, shapes, sizes, and colors. When you have friends who are different and have different qualities, it brings a different aspect to your personality—it makes you a more interesting person. Some friends can be very different from you. You may not have common interests, just a sort of chemistry between you. Embrace the differences and enjoy your friendship. See **Fig. 10-2**.

HOW TO MAKE NEW FRIENDS

Making friends seems to come naturally to young children. Strangers sharing a sandbox can be "best friends" within days. For many teens, especially those who are going to a new school, making friends can be awkward and stressful. Yet reaching out in friendship has great rewards. Whether you're "the new kid" or part of the "ranking class," these pointers can help:

- **Strive for friendship, not popularity.** The desire for friendship leads some teens to take on what they think are the keys to popularity—wearing certain clothes, for instance, or using certain language. Actually, popular teens attract people through their personalities. You can do the same.

- **Prepare.** Making friends is a skill. Even people with a natural talent don't master it without effort. Make a list of activities, sports, and other local events that you'd like to share with a friend. Before attending an event, practice conversation starters or dialog with a family member.

- **Be positive.** Do you enjoy the company of people who always complain or feel sorry for themselves? Avoid behaviors and attitudes like these that drive away potential friends—and remember to smile. People are more willing to begin a friendship with someone who appears positive.

- **Extend an invitation.** Instead of waiting to be asked, take the first step. You may be surprised to learn that the other person was hoping you'd reach out. If someone turns you down, don't worry about it. This happens to everyone. Just try later with another person.

- **Lend a hand.** What could make a better impression than offering help? Ask first before helping, and be sure that you know what you're doing. Whether the problem is understanding algebra or fitting a wheelchair through a doorway, give help in a spirit of service, not superiority.

- **Keep expectations realistic.** Even best friends don't share every quality or interest. In fact, the contrast can help keep relationships fresh. Don't let differences in things like musical tastes or favorite foods discourage you from developing a friendship. Likewise, give people space. Don't overwhelm potential friends with constant demands on their time or energy. Give your friendships room and time to grow.

- **Make a fresh start.** If you have trouble keeping friendships, ask yourself the question, "Why did it end?" Did you do something to cause the friendship to dissolve? Identify the causes of past problems so that you can avoid them in future friendships. For example, some teens with low self-esteem try to be friends with anyone, at any cost. They need to work at developing a positive self-image.

TAKE **ACTION**

Choose one of the suggestions outlined here. Using creative thinking skills, list practical ways to help teens apply it. Compile your ideas with those of your classmates in an "action plan" for making friends.

People who share what they have are often rewarded with greater self-respect, the respect of their family and friends, and an overall positive attitude. You can share many things, not simply your possessions. Consider the following ways to share:

- **Share your knowledge.** Teach a friend or family member a skill or tutor someone who's struggling in school.

- **Share your company.** People often appreciate the company of others. Read to an older neighbor, visit a friend who's feeling down, or mentor a young child.

- **Share the work.** Help out by doing chores for other family members when you notice they're busy.

Peer Friendships

Your peers—people your own age—are likely the people you associate with the most. During teen years, peer friendships are often the most common.

There is no rule about the number of peer friendships you should have. Some people are happy with one or two close friends. Others appear to have many friends. Some teens struggle to be popular—even to the point of doing things they shouldn't. Their popularity can sometimes cause them to miss out on having special close friends.

Cliques

In any setting where people gather, they tend to move into groups in which they feel comfortable. There is nothing wrong with that. Many teens, as well as adults, form groups to feel a sense of belonging.

Unfortunately, some groups form **cliques**, or groups that exclude others from their circle of friendship. The members of a clique reject people they think don't fit in. Only by the group's approval can someone be a part of the group. The basis for acceptance is often superficial, based on external qualities such as their appearance, their clothing, where they live, or the amount of money they have to spend. When this kind of rejection occurs, people get hurt.

Perhaps you've been in a clique and have seen someone rejected by the group. Or maybe you've been the one excluded. To belong to a group without rejecting others, avoid groups that treat others unfairly. This may mean forming your own circle of friends who don't judge others. If the "clique mentality" comes up in your group, challenge it.

Younger Friends

Although most of your friends are probably other teens, children can be good friends, too. Because you're older, your attention is special to them. They may look up to you and see you as both a role model and a friend. You might teach them a skill you have or just talk with them. In today's world, children can use your friendship.

Having some younger friends may broaden your understanding of people—including yourself. These kinds of friendships can help you gain insight into your own thoughts, feelings, and actions. You may find you like being a guiding force, which could lead you to a career choice later on, perhaps as a teacher, a child care worker, a counselor, or a therapist. See **Fig. 10-3**.

Older Friends

Sometimes it's hard to think of adults as friends, but older people, such as grandparents, can be very good friends. Many adults have authority over teens and set rules to be followed. When teens are aiming for independence, it isn't easy for them to be friends with adults in authority.

Being the adult in charge isn't always easy, either. Mr. Rodriguez, the school's algebra teacher, cares about his students. He knows he must enforce behavioral rules so that his students can have a successful class experience and become proficient in math skills. For Mr. Rodriguez and many other adults, setting and enforcing rules is part of their responsibility to teens, and it's not always fun. Rules are made to provide guidance for appropriate behavior—a necessary part of functioning in an orderly world.

Most adults, even when they have authority over you, enjoy friendships with teens. They're people, too, with personal problems and concerns. Like you, adults can make mistakes sometimes. When you fail to understand why an adult acts in a certain way or sets a rule you don't agree with, try talking about it with that person. Put yourself in the person's place and be respectful and considerate. After all, you'll be an adult someday, too.

Fig 10-3 Teaching a young friend a new skill can be fun and rewarding. Both of you will learn more about the other and about yourselves.

Hanging Out with Friends

Hanging out with friends tends to become all-important to teens. Generally, teens like to be in mixed-gender groups, both guys and girls. Also, by being in a group, people tend to have less pressure than they do in one-to-one dating (going together) situations. Without the nervousness of a date, you can relax and have a good time. You can get to know everyone better at your own pace—without being rushed into pairing off with one particular person. See **Fig. 10-4**.

Places to Go, Things to Do

Some communities offer plenty of fun places to go and things to do. Other communities have fewer choices. Activity costs and transportation also can restrict what many teens are able to do. In such cases, creative thinking helps. Create carpools, use public transportation, or ask a willing parent to drive. An afternoon or evening spent watching DVDs at a friend's house, listening to music, skateboarding, making jewelry, scrapbooking, popping popcorn, making smoothies, or preparing an actual meal can be as much fun as going out. Where do you like to go with your friends? What activities could you plan for a day with your friends?

Your Responsibilities

When you spend time with others in a group, don't forget that you have some important responsibilities. Remember that most places teens go are used by other people as well. When you and your friends gather in community places, think about how your actions affect others. For example, what might happen to a restaurant if a large group of people routinely took

Fig 10-4 Even the simplest activities can be fun when you're with friends. How do you spend time with your friends?

up table space and ordered only soft drinks? Without a chance to make enough money to pay its expenses, the restaurant would go out of business. Also, hanging out in front of shops does not create an inviting or welcoming situation for adult customers.

Personal Responsibilities

Going out with people of the opposite sex involves other responsibilities and decisions. You must make decisions about your personal conduct ahead of time. Set standards of behavior and keep them in mind while you're out with your friends.

Any time you hang out with your friends, difficult situations might arise. Your friends might pressure you to do something that goes against your standards of behavior. In these cases, use your refusal skills—the communication skills you use to say "no." Tell your friends "no" and offer an alternative activity. If you can't convince your friends to change their minds about the behavior, then leave. Walking away from a bad situation does not have to end your friendship, but it will keep you safe—and your friends will respect you for sticking to your values. See **Fig. 10-5**.

Fig 10-5 True friends consider each other's safety when they hang out together. How do your friends look out for each other?

Consider Your Family

Following the family rules shows you care about your family. When planning to go out with friends, remember the following:

▶ **Where, who, and when.** Adult family members should always know where you're going, whom you're going with, and when you'll return home.

▶ **Respect.** Keep in mind the responsibilities you have and show respect to yourself, to others, and to the community.

▶ **Safety.** If the activities of an individual or group get out of hand or don't follow your values or standards of behavior, leave! Call your parents or guardians, other relatives, a taxi, or the police to ask for a ride home.

Responsibility to your friends is a different issue. Your friends deserve your respect. By meeting them on time and treating them as you would like to be treated, you show them respect. When you are out, stay with your friends. Never leave your group or let another friend leave alone. Instead, leave together so that everyone returns home safely—and by curfew. If you're out with a mixed-gender group, shoot for equal numbers of girls and guys. Teens who are outnumbered—for example, one guy with four girls—can experience problems.

Responsibilities to Your Family

Over the last year, Melinda has become friends with a group of guys and girls. They have most classes together, and they eat lunch together almost every day. Melinda would like to go out with them as a group, but her parents won't let her. They feel that Melinda's friends are too young to go out unsupervised in mixed-gender groups. For now, Melinda invites her friends to her house where there is supervision.

Another responsibility you have to your family is to follow family rules. Common family rules involve curfews, transportation, and where teens may and may not go. Once rules are set, follow them. Parents and guardians make rules because they're responsible for your safety and well-being. Breaking rules can cause family members to worry and lose trust. If you disagree with a rule, talk it over with your parents or guardians. You might find there's room for compromise.

Deciding to Go Together

Adolescence is when most people develop an interest in the other gender. Because teens mature at different rates, not all of them develop an interest in the opposite sex at the same time. For example, Shelly likes guys as friends, but she's not interested in going out with them yet. To her, spending time with her girlfriends is more fun. If she's like her older sister, she might not start going out with a boyfriend until after high school. See **Fig. 10-6**.

Keith, one of Shelly's classmates, is just the opposite. He is going out with a girl and rarely spends time with his old group of friends. You probably know teens like Shelly and Keith. Some are interested in going together, and others aren't. Holding off on a one-to-one relationship until you are ready is entirely normal. If you're not ready for that step, don't take it!

Fig 10-6
Healthy relationships with the opposite sex are based on respect. How can teen friends of the opposite sex show respect for each other?

Love and Infatuation

Last year, you thought your sister's friend was a pest. Nowadays, you find yourself checking out your appearance whenever you know she's coming to your house. You're attracted to her and would like her to spend time with you, rather than with your sister.

What you're experiencing is **infatuation**, or a crush, a type of love experience based on an intense attraction to another person that may or may not be one-sided. You may have had similar feelings about a movie star, one of your teachers, or a classmate.

When people are infatuated, they're in love with what they imagine the other person is like. Infatuation can be pleasant or painful, depending on the attitude and actions of the other person involved. Although it's not mature love, infatuation can help you learn about loving, mature relationships.

Crushes are common feelings, especially for teens, and the emotions that go with them are real and powerful. Crushes seldom last long, especially when the other person shows interest in someone else. Once a crush is over, you may even wonder why you felt the way you did.

When Friendships End

Not all friendships last forever. Some friendships end because one person moves away and there are fewer opportunities to keep in touch. In these cases, remaining emotionally close takes work. Long-distance friendship can survive with a great deal of effort. Some friendships that seem to have faded may rekindle at another time, sometimes many years later. See **Fig. 10-7**.

Some friendships end because of conflict or misunderstandings. Feelings of jealousy and possessiveness can threaten—or end—a friendship. In other cases, people mature, change, and no longer want the same things from their friendship. Changing interests, goals, and experiences can end friendships that aren't strong enough to deal with the changes.

Fig 10-7
It takes time to get over the sadness you feel when a friendship ends.

Other times, friendships no longer work or may simply fade because you don't give enough time to each other. In other situations, friendships may be unhealthy or destructive and you need to walk away from the relationship. If a friend is abusive, causes you serious problems, or is unpleasant to be around, you need to end the friendship. Unhealthy friendships are not the kind you want to collect.

If you must deliberately end a friendship, do it with sensitivity. One way to end a friendship is to ease out of the relationship. Find other activities that gradually take more of your time. Accepting a part-time job, volunteering in the community, and making other friends can be effective ways of stepping back from the relationship.

In the case of a friendship that's unhealthy or destructive, you may need to be direct, but kind, in your actions. Explain why you need to end the friendship. Focus on how you feel, not on the other person, by using "I" messages, or statements that begin with the word "I." For example, you might say, "I don't feel comfortable being around people who smoke," or "I don't like putting down other people." Giving reasons rather than blaming the other person takes courage. However, doing so can help you end a friendship in as positive a way as possible.

If a relationship ends against your wishes, understand that this simply happens sometimes. You may feel sad or angry for a while, and you may even blame yourself. In time these negative feelings will go away. As you move on to other friendships, you can take what you've learned with you.

Handling Rejection

Sometimes two people seem out of sync with one another or just don't hit it off. Some relationships that are pure friendships just dissolve over time. In either case, one party experiences rejection. Almost everyone experiences rejection at some point. Remember these are not lifetime commitments. If feelings of rejection are difficult to deal with, here are some ideas to consider:

- **Share your feelings.** Talk with a friend or family member, and be open to advice and suggestions.

- **Be kind to yourself.** Just because your friendship was rejected doesn't mean you are a bad person or not good enough. The friendship may have simply outgrown itself, and your friend responded first.

- **Appreciate yourself.** On bad days, make a list of your positive points and refer to your list when you need a boost. See **Fig. 10-8**.

- **Evaluate your actions.** Think about your behavior toward the other person. Did you do something that was hurtful? If so, learn to behave differently.

- **Don't spread rumors or gossip.** Avoid making negative comments to peers about the person who rejected you. That kind of behavior gets you nowhere. You may be the rejecter, not the rejectee, next time.

- **Move on.** Become involved with other friends and activities. In time, it will all be just a distant memory.

Fig 10-8 Not everyone you want to be friends with will share your feelings. Appreciating yourself will help you move on and make new friends.

10

Review & Activities

Chapter Summary

- True friendships share common qualities.
- You can follow specific steps to make new friends.
- When spending time with others in a group, you have important responsibilities to yourself, to your friends, and to your family.
- Many people experience crushes or feelings of infatuation.
- Friendships can end for a variety of reasons. If you end a friendship, do so with sensitivity.
- Almost everyone experiences rejection at some point. You can take steps to overcome rejection.

Reviewing Key Terms & Ideas

1. What is the difference between **acquaintances** and friends?
2. Name four qualities that are generally true of all good friends.
3. How can you identify friends who are **dependable**?
4. What is the most common form of friendship?
5. What are **cliques**?
6. How can younger friends help you?
7. Name four activities friends might enjoy when cost and transportation are limited.
8. What do common family rules involve?
9. What is **infatuation**? What positive experience might come from it?
10. List three tips for handling rejection.

Thinking Critically

1. **Analyzing relationships.** What qualities would you look for in an ideal friend? Does anyone you know have all those qualities?
2. **Making generalizations.** Think about friends from your past. What did you learn from them that you can carry over to other friendships?
3. **Making comparisons.** How is rejection from a friend similar to rejection from someone you have a crush on? How is it different?

Review & Activities

Applying Your Learning

1. **Art project.** Using magazines or photos, create a collage that reflects the qualities of true friendship. Display your collage in the classroom.

2. **Life simulation.** Imagine you've just moved to a new community. With a partner, role-play how you would make new friends. Ask the audience for feedback.

3. **Community service.** With a small group, select a service project to conduct in your community that involves older adults. If possible, dedicate several weeks or months to the service project so that you can get to know some of the older adults you meet. Afterward, reflect on your new friendships.

4. **Entertainment plans.** Create a plan to entertain friends at your home. What activities will you make available? Share your plan with your family and make adjustments based on their feedback. If possible, implement your plan.

5. **Friendship benefits.** Using print or Internet sources, research the benefits of friendship on a person's health. You might include information about reduced stress and positive attitude. Report your findings to the class.

6. **Safety announcement.** In a small group, create a public service announcement about safety when hanging out with friends. Record your announcement and share it with the class.

CAREER Link

Listening Skills.
In the workplace, success often depends on hearing directions and interpreting them correctly. Interview adult friends and family members about the importance of listening skills in their workplace. Ask about any misunderstandings that occurred because someone failed to listen well. Share the information with your class.

Making Connections

1. **Reading** Read print and online sources about teen friendships in other cultures around the world. Compare the friendships of teen friends in other cultures to your own friendships.

2. **Writing** Choose one of the following topics for a newspaper article: "What Works in Friendship" or "When a Friendship Must End." Write the article and read it to your class.

3. **Math** Determine how much money you would spend to have dinner in a restaurant and go to a movie. Be sure to include the cost of transportation. Then calculate the cost of cooking a meal at home and watching a DVD. How much, if any, money do you save by staying home?

Building Strong Families

Objectives
- Identify the functions of families.
- Contrast the various types of families.
- Explain the family life cycle.
- Describe the characteristics of strong families.
- Give guidelines for building strong families.

Vocabulary
- **traditions**
- **family life cycle**
- **empty nest**
- **siblings**
- **age span**
- **sibling rivalry**

Reading with Purpose

1. **Write down** the colored headings from Chapter 11 in your notebook.

2. **As you read** the text under each heading, visualize what you are reading.

3. **Reflect** on what you read by writing a few sentences under each heading to describe it.

4. **Continue** this process until you have finished the chapter. Reread your notes.

The Anatomy of a Family

Picture your family as a human body, a structure of connected bones from the skull to the toes. Although every bone is important, each bone must depend on the other bones to function in harmony. Like your bones, when all members of a family function together, the family is happier and more effective. Family members laugh and learn together. They enjoy one another, and they help one another through tough times.

Make a conscious effort of thinking of yourself as part of the whole family—as "us" instead of just "me." This will help you remember that your actions affect other members of your family. If you wipe up a spill, then no one will slip on it and fall. If you phone your grandfather or your grandmother, his or her day—and yours—will be brighter. It's easier to make good choices when you remember to keep others in mind. Your family "body" stays together only when all family members work together.

The Importance of Families

Without families there wouldn't be neighborhoods, cities, or countries. That's because families provide the structure, or the building blocks, for society. You will find this is true in every culture. Children are born into families. In families they grow and learn to become independent adults, and many go on to have children of their own.

This process of growing and learning doesn't just magically happen. Families encourage the growth process through the following:

- **Meeting basic needs.** Families provide food, shelter, clothing, and education.

- **Providing a safe trial-and-error environment.** Being a part of a family allows you to try new things and make mistakes. This is a safe environment in which to learn and experience new things.

- **Giving emotional support.** Family members believe in one another and themselves, and they help one another through difficult times. See **Fig. 11-1**.

- **Teaching moral values and social skills.** By example and through direct instruction, parents teach children right from wrong and what's most important in life. Parents also help their children learn social skills—ways of relating to other people. Children use these skills in their childhood relationships, as well as adult relationships.

Fig 11-1 What you do affects others in your family. How do the actions of your family members positively affect you?

- **Passing on traditions.** Within the family, children learn about their family's cultural heritage and **traditions**—customs passed from one generation to another.

Types of Families

Families come in all sizes, shapes, and personalities. They also differ in who the family members are and how these individuals are related. These characteristics make each type of family special. Which family type describes your family?

- **Nuclear family.** This family consists of a mother, a father, and one or more children.

- **Single-parent family.** In this family, one parent raises the children. The parent may be divorced, widowed, or never married.

- **Blended family.** This family is formed when two people marry and at least one already has children. A parent, a stepparent, and the children of one or both parents are expected to "blend" into the new family.

- **Extended family.** This family includes relatives besides the parents and children, such as grandparents, aunts, uncles, and cousins. Sometimes extended families live in the same household; other times they live in different homes.

- **Adoptive family.** In adoptive families, the parents adopt a child who is not born to them. The adopted child has the same legal rights as a birth child. See **Fig. 11-2**.

- **Foster family.** A foster family includes one or more children who are not related to the foster parents but are cared for as family members.

Fig 11-2

Adoptive families need to be patient and understanding as they make their new family member feel safe and secure.

Family Changes

Over the centuries, family life has changed. In the 1800s, many people lived and worked on farms. In the early 1900s, many of today's conveniences hadn't yet been invented, and many daily tasks were time-consuming. Having large families meant more help with household and family tasks. Sharing the load saved time and helped family members bond.

Today, life is changing faster than ever, and so are families. No family remains exactly the same over the years. Children grow up, and parents grow older. Some changes, however, aren't simply the result of passing years. They are a result of social trends, such as separation, divorce, and remarriage. When a parent divorces and marries into another family, members of both families must adjust to new relationships. If a parent divorces and doesn't remarry, the result is a single-parent family. Many single-parent families are headed by women, who often struggle with time, energy, and money as they raise their children.

The Family Life Cycle

Although social trends and changes have affected today's families, most families still go through certain predictable stages—from their beginning as a couple until their final years. The process families go through as they grow and change is called the **family life cycle**. Some researchers label the stages of the family life cycle differently. However, the basic pattern remains the same. Knowing about the family life cycle will help you better understand your current—and your future—family.

- **Beginning stage.** The first stage begins with a couple. The couple's major tasks include setting up a home, setting goals for the future, and learning to live comfortably with each other.

- **Parenting stage.** During this period, new members— children—are added to the family. When children are young, most parents are involved with home and family life. They have less time for themselves as a couple. Great amounts of time, attention, and money are required to care for the children's needs. See **Fig. 11-3**.

- **Launching stage.** In this stage, teens and young adults begin to leave the family home and assume work and household responsibilities of their own.

Fig 11-3

Special activities can help family members develop strong bonds with one another. What special activities does your family do together?

- **Middle years stage.** This stage allows parents to focus on being a couple once more. Having an **empty nest**, or a home children have left to be on their own, allows couples more time to enjoy hobbies, community activities, and volunteer work. There can be an adjustment period once grown children leave the home.

- **Retirement stage.** For many people, the final stage of the family cycle involves retirement from a job. During this stage of life, people have time to reflect on the past and share with others what they have learned over their lifetime. Many older adults remain active, spending time with children, grandchildren, and friends; enjoying hobbies; and traveling. Age-related health issues and declining ability to live independently may be major concerns during this stage.

There are variations of these stages. For example, some couples don't have children, some marry at an older age and have children later in life, and some couples separate and divorce. Other couples find themselves parenting one or more grandchildren as they enter the middle years stage or the retirement stage. Some couples have their adult children move back in with them, with or without their own children. Further, by choice or because of financial need, an increasing number of retirement-age people are continuing to hold either full-time or part-time jobs.

The Cultural Background of Families

Do you know a family that is similar to your own? You may think this family is just like yours, but if you were to spend a day with that family, you would be able to make a list of dozens of differences.

Cultural background helps create interesting differences among families. For example, some cultures emphasize large families, and others prefer smaller ones. Families in some cultures have several generations of the family living in one home. Some cultures place emphasis on having a close-knit family that participates in many activities together. In other cultures, independence is important, and children are encouraged to develop their own interests and activities and to live on their own as adults.

Families who value their cultural history usually make a point of carrying on its traditions and beliefs. They encourage their children to learn traditional ways and to stay in touch with their cultural heritage. At the same time, they teach their children to respect and appreciate other cultures.

Family Roles and Responsibilities

All family members have specific roles. Some roles—like mother, father, child, or older sister—come with the person's position in the family. Others, such as income earner, at-home parent, or student, refer to the way the person spends his or her time. Generally, everyone has more than one role. You might be a son, a younger brother, and a grandson all in one. You also might be a friend, a soccer team member, and a paper carrier outside the family.

For the family to function effectively, all members must be responsible and do their part. Major responsibilities, such as providing basic needs, fall primarily on the parents and other adult family members. Parents are also responsible for setting limits and maintaining rules regarding behavior, health, and safety.

Children have responsibilities as well. Maybe you help with cleaning, cooking, and grocery shopping. Perhaps you take care of your younger **siblings**—brothers and sisters. It's easy to complain, "I have to do everything around here!" Is the complaint really true? Take another look at your family and evaluate how responsibilities are divided. What are each person's roles inside and outside the home? What responsibilities go with each role? In your family, who pays the bills,

Fig 11-4
Being willing to help out with a variety of responsibilities helps you learn more about what is involved in making a family function well.

keeps the car running, cooks the meals, cares for sick family members, and does laundry? Every person can and should do some things to help. When you share these tasks, you not only help the family run more efficiently but also develop life skills you will need as an adult.

Building Family Strengths

What does it take to have a strong family? Researchers have identified some characteristics of strong, successful, loving families. No family will have all the characteristics—and certainly not at all times. However, strong families don't just happen. It takes time and effort from everyone to make and keep a family strong. You can positively affect your family relationships through the actions you take. You can help make your family strong by doing the following:

- **Having a positive attitude about life and family.** Family members who look for the best in one another have great potential for getting along. They believe that if they work together, they can achieve family goals. See **Fig. 11-4**.

- **Arranging to spend time together.** This includes quality time spent either in a group or one on one.

- **Showing appreciation and love for one another.** A hug, a compliment, a card or note of thanks, a task done without asking—these are all actions of loving family members.

- **Sharing beliefs, values, and goals.** The family's daily actions reflect what it considers important. A family teaches a sense of right and wrong. Members share their hopes and dreams.

- **Staying committed to one another.** Family members care about one another's well-being and happiness for a lifetime. They are willing to work out difficulties among themselves.

HOW TO MAKE TIME FOR ONE ANOTHER

Have you ever watched sitcoms from the 1950s or 1960s, in which a family ate meals together every day and siblings walked home together after school? That togetherness was an ideal, but it was also more likely for families at that time than for today's families.

Parents and children are busier than ever. Families cannot assume they'll naturally spend time together. Instead, they must deliberately make time. These ideas can help them find ways:

- **Have fun with family chores.** Making meals and cleaning are some tasks that families do together. Add an enjoyable element that helps you appreciate one another's company. For example, you can take turns picking a CD to play and telling why you like certain songs.

- **Start new traditions.** Traditions don't have to be elaborate, just fun. A weekend dinner made from scratch or a Saturday morning at a farmers' market can be a treat if it's something you look forward to every week.

- **Take advantage of passing moments.** You can fit in some meaningful exchanges while riding to school or waiting in line at a store. Listen carefully when someone shares an opinion or a funny story. You might gain insight into a family member's interests and concerns. Those moments will someday become fond memories.

- **Showing consideration and respect for one another.** This includes respecting one another's privacy and space and accepting differences of opinion.

- **Being tolerant and forgiving.** No one's perfect. Strong families may have their differences. They may even quarrel, but they are successful in working out solutions.

- **Volunteer as a family.** Look for volunteer activities that lend themselves to a family effort. Collecting for a food drive, helping at a walkathon, and visiting a nursing home are a few examples of how families can make a contribution together. Being charitable comes from the examples you have been given at home—sometimes you need to ask or remind your parent.

- **Spend time with individual family members.** Trying to include every family member in family time is not always practical. Special bonds can still form when siblings spend time together without parents or when you share time with only one parent.

- **Make togetherness a priority.** The bottom line is this: spending time together must be seen as important. Intentionally carve family time out of busy schedules, even if it means giving up other activities.

TAKE **ACTION**

In small groups, list specific ways that families can make more time to be together, based on the suggestions offered here. Choose and carry out two ideas that fit your family situation.

- **Sharing traditions and family history.** Old family stories, daily and seasonal rituals, photo albums, and special mementos link the family to its past. Creating new traditions is valuable, too. The children will someday base their traditions on their own experiences.

- **Taking time for laughter and play.** The ability to laugh together, even in rough times, can mean a lot. Strong families know that their time together is valuable. Activities such as a picnic or a soccer game in the yard or at a nearby park can bring family members closer.

Getting Along in Your Family

Getting along presents challenges in every family. Think about all the ways family members are different—age, gender, personality, and life experiences. Add differing interests, abilities, and responsibilities, and you have quite a mix of people.

What can you do to improve family relationships? More than you may realize. You can start by controlling your own attitudes and actions. It's easy to just react to what happens by saying or doing things without thinking. Often that hurts others and pulls your family apart. If you think about the situation first, you will make better choices. Talk through problems without an "I win, you lose" attitude. See **Fig. 11-5**.

Fig 11-5
Strong families share good times and stick together through times of trouble. How does your family show its strengths?

You and Your Parents

As teens move toward more independence, their relationships with their parents may change or feel like a roller coaster. Some have difficulty finding ways to get along and stay close. Think about your own family. How do you maintain strong relationships with your parents or guardians? Do your relationships periodically change?

Increase Your Understanding

How well do you really know your parents or guardians? What have their lives been like? What responsibilities and problems do they have? Understanding means learning about the reasons behind your parents' beliefs and actions. Maybe they are trying to protect you from problems they had at your age.

Understanding also depends on how well your parents know you. Unless you share your thoughts and feelings with them, how can they understand you? Find time when you can talk to your parents or guardians. Jared and his mom talk as they walk the dog in the evening. Carmen has become closer to her dad and stepmother by talking with them during mealtime each night.

Show Respect

Unfortunately, it's easy for disrespect to creep into a family. Disrespectful words and actions often result in anger and hurt feelings. When that happens, everyone's happiness suffers. Try making mental movies of how you interact with your parents or guardians. What message do your words give? What does your tone of voice or body language say about you and your feelings? How can you change your words and actions so that they show respect?

Act Responsibly

Teens who are responsible are often given more privileges. Here are some examples of responsibility:

- Be honest with your parents and admit mistakes when you make them.

- Complete your chores at home without constant reminders.

- Tell your parents where you are when you're away from home.

TIPS

Plan a Family Meeting

Meeting regularly to discuss problems, assign chores, and celebrate good news can help family members get along and strengthen their bonds. The following tips can help you plan a successful family meeting:

▶ **Set a date.** Make sure everyone knows the time and place for the meeting. Every family member should be included in the meetings. If someone cannot attend the meeting, find another time to meet.

▶ **Appoint a meeting leader.** A meeting leader helps guide the discussion and keep everyone on track. Rotate the responsibility so that everyone has a chance to lead.

▶ **Give everyone a chance to speak.** Any family member, even the youngest child, should be allowed to voice their concerns or suggestions.

▶ **Avoid the blame game.** Attacking or blaming other family members for their actions creates a negative environment. Instead of bringing up what a family member did wrong, list what the person did right and then build on it.

▶ **Make meetings fun.** Serve a favorite snack or dessert. Have some soft, relaxing music during the meeting. Perhaps family members could rotate turns choosing their favorite music.

- Call your parents as soon as you know you're going to be late—don't wait until you have exceeded your curfew.

- Do your best in school.

- Watch out for your younger brothers or sisters—whether your parents ask you to or not.

Fig 11-6 Sometimes you can show appreciation simply by listening to one another.

Show Appreciation

How often do you give a friend a compliment or say "thank you"? Appreciation is just as important in families, but it's often overlooked. A willing smile, an offer of help, or even a request for advice can show that you realize how much your parents and guardians help you. See **Fig. 11-6**.

You and Your Siblings

Understanding, respect, responsibility, and appreciation are traits of all healthy relationships, including your relationships with your siblings. How well you get along with your siblings depends on many factors. Sharing common interests can help you get along. The **age span**—the number of years between siblings—also plays a part. Siblings who are close in age often have more in common than those who are many years apart. Being close in age is not a guarantee that siblings will be or will remain close to one another. Some older siblings are overly protective of the younger ones. Others feel frustrated when a younger brother or sister hangs around and asks questions all the time. Try to figure out what your sibling thinks and feels. Then you can find better ways to get along.

Are You Rivals?

Sibling rivalry, or competition for the love and attention of parents, is common. Have you ever felt that unfairness was a problem in your family? Do you keep track of gifts, awards, privileges, and compliments that each sibling receives? Try not to fall into this trap. Every situation is different. If you were a parent, how would you keep track of everything said to, bought for, or rewarded to each child? It's impossible!

Fig 11-7
Older siblings often are special people in the eyes of their younger brothers and sisters.

When you feel competitive, remember that you have your own special qualities and abilities. They may not be the same as those of your siblings, but that doesn't matter. Discover what you do well, and develop those skills. Remember, too, your parents have the ability to love more than one child. See **Fig. 11-7.**

Pulling Together

When you think about all of the things that combine to make families strong, there's one last point to remember. People need the support, love, and friendship of their family. Friends can drift apart, but parents and siblings share a bond like no other. This goes for grandparents as well. If you want your family members to be there when you need them someday, then it's well worth your effort to work toward building strong family ties now. You get out of family relationships what you put into them. These relationships last a lifetime.

11

Review & Activities

Chapter Summary

- There are different types of families, but they all have the same functions.
- Families go through a cycle, or stages, of change.
- Every member fulfills several roles in a family and has many responsibilities.
- Strong families have common characteristics that foster family bonds.
- Showing understanding, respect, responsibility, and appreciation can help you improve relationships with your family members.

Reviewing Key Terms & Ideas

1. Name four functions of families.
2. What are **traditions**?
3. Briefly describe four types of families.
4. How does divorce affect families?
5. Summarize the five stages of the traditional **family life cycle**.
6. What is an **empty nest**? How do you think your parents will feel when they have an empty nest?
7. Define **siblings**.
8. Identify at least four characteristics of strong families.
9. List six ways you can show others that you're responsible and dependable.
10. How can **age span** affect a sibling relationship?
11. What is **sibling rivalry**? Give examples in your own family.

Thinking Critically

1. **Analyzing relationships.** Which types of families have you observed among your friends and acquaintances? What characteristics of strong families do they share?
2. **Making generalizations.** Which stage in the family life cycle do you think is the most important? Which do you think is the most difficult for adults? Explain.
3. **Comparing roles.** Compare the roles you currently fill in your family and the roles of your other family members. What similarities and differences do you see?

Review & Activities

Applying Your Learning

1. **Communication skills.** Use a state map, a U.S. map, or a world map—whichever is appropriate—and place stickers or pins on the places where your family's ancestors came from and where various family members live today. Write letters or cards to extended family members you've located on the map, filling them in on news about yourself and your family or, in some cases, introducing yourself.

2. **Life stages.** Develop a list of interview questions to ask a grandparent or older friend about his or her experiences in each stage of the family life cycle. Conduct the interview. What answers surprised you?

3. **Family additions.** Use print or Internet resources to research current information about adopting a child or becoming a foster parent. Report your findings to the class.

4. **Life simulation.** Working in a small group, enact a scene in which two or more siblings are engaged in sibling rivalry. Ask classmates for suggestions on how to solve the problem.

5. **Family plan.** Create a plan on paper to strengthen your family unit using information from this chapter. Keep a journal of positive actions you took each day to build a strong family. After one week, analyze your results. How have your actions affected your family?

Making Connections

1. **Reading** Read about a family whose culture is different from yours. Give a short presentation sharing what you learned about some of the customs and traditions that are part of that culture.

2. **Math** Research the number of single-parent families in the United States today, 50 years ago, and 100 years ago. Graph the results. What can you conclude from the information?

3. **Writing** Imagine that you are the parent of a teen your age. Write a letter to the teen explaining your reasons for making a decision or taking an action that the teen thinks is unfair.

4. **Reading** Read a book about communicating effectively with family members. Choose several tips and try them with your own family members. What response did you receive?

CAREER Link

Building Consensus. One of the best ways to ensure that family members share household responsibilities is to build consensus, or come to a decision agreeable to everyone. Like family members, employees often have to build consensus to work effectively. How do you think consensus building helps both employees and employers? What skills do you think are required for successful consensus building?

Family Challenges

Objectives

- Identify specific changes that affect families.
- Describe the effects of different crises on families.
- Summarize coping strategies for specific crises.
- Name sources of help for families facing challenges.

Vocabulary

- **financial**
- **creditors**
- **credit rating**
- **crisis**
- **closure**
- **addiction**
- **alcoholism**
- **alcoholics**
- **spouse**
- **neglect**

Reading with Purpose

1. **As you read** Chapter 12, create an outline in your notebook using the colored headings.

2. **Write** a question under each heading that you can use to guide your reading.

3. **Answer** the question under each heading as you read the chapter. Record your answers.

4. **Ask** your teacher to help with answers you could not find in this chapter.

Changes and Challenges in the Family

Whenever people live in the same household, they are sure to experience changes and challenges. Some changes are exciting. For example, your older sister graduates from college and moves into her first apartment, so the room you shared is all yours now. Or perhaps your dad just got a new job that gives him weekends off with the family.

On the other hand, some changes can be more difficult and stressful. For example, your older brother volunteers to work in a developing country for a year, and your family misses him and worries about his safety. Or, the company your mom works for makes some changes that require your mom to work nights and weekends.

Changes and challenges are part of the normal ups and downs in life, and often families adjust fairly easily. However, when families experience major problems, they may have difficulty coping. Knowing what to expect and how to react can help family members deal effectively with the challenges. See **Fig. 12-1**.

New Family Members

Many families experience change because of a new addition. The new family member may be a new brother or sister or may be a cousin who has come to live with you while attending a local college. Anytime a family adds another member, everyone needs to make adjustments. A new brother or sister can shake

Fig 12-1 When you need advice about a problem you are experiencing, you may not need to go far to find help. Sometimes an understanding family member can keep your problem confidential and help you work things out.

up everyone's daily routine, and a college-age cousin might need to sleep in your room. It's only natural to feel a little stress, insecurity, and resentment. That's the downside—if you choose to see it that way.

However, you have the option to view the change as a way to learn more about yourself and your family. Loving and entertaining a new baby can be more fun than you ever imagined. Having a college student around means obtaining feedback and advice from someone closer to your age, not just your parents or guardians. Thinking of ways to value a new addition to your family makes it easier to see the change as a positive experience.

Teenage Pregnancy

Having a child is a life-changing event. This is especially true when the pregnancy is unplanned and the parents are still teenagers. Parenthood involves many responsibilities, and they are best handled when the parents are independent adults who have prepared for them. Unfortunately, this is not always the case. See **Fig. 12-2**.

Teen parents and their families face many challenges. Teen parents usually experience financial difficulties, and they often find child care to be overwhelming. Many teen parents give up their dreams, such as a college education, to meet the responsibilities of parenthood. The families of teen parents

Fig 12-2 Becoming a parent is a lifelong commitment with many responsibilities. Balancing school, a child, and daily routines is hard and leaves little or no time for a social life.

TIPS

Make New Friends in Five Easy Steps

1. **Look friendly.** Don't be afraid to smile at other people.

2. **Take the first step.** Don't wait for others to make friends with you. Instead, make the first move to let others know you want to get to know them.

3. **Make a call or write an e-mail.** Contact someone you talked with in class or during lunch. Keep the conversation balanced so that both of you can participate.

4. **Sign up for activities.** Try out for a part in a play or volunteer in a lakeside cleanup. Chances are there will be other teens involved who are looking to make friends, too.

5. **Help new students feel at home.** Ask new students about themselves, and offer to show them around the school or your community.

are also affected. Many teen parents continue to live with their families because they cannot afford housing costs. Despite the difficulties, however, some teens make parenthood work with great effort, sacrifice, and the support of their families.

Moving

Karen placed the last box into the moving truck and looked at her childhood home. Her mother had accepted a job in another town 200 miles away, which meant that the family had to move. "I just made the basketball team this year, and now we're moving," thought Karen. "This is so unfair!"

How does moving affect the whole family? How might Karen's mom be affected by her new job? What issues might her siblings be having related to the move? Moving to a new community can be both challenging and exciting. Most moves involve adjusting to a new school, finding your way in unfamiliar surroundings, and getting to know new people. Feeling strange about a new community is perfectly normal, but usually the feeling disappears after awhile. Soon it can feel as though you've lived there your entire life.

You can fit in faster at a new school by signing up for a sport or other activity you enjoy. That can make it easier to meet other teens with similar interests. Be friendly and show interest in others. Discovering classmates who share your interests is a first step to cementing new friendships.

Unemployment

Sometimes you have to deal with a parent or guardian who loses a job. Layoffs and other situations make temporary unemployment difficult for many families. When people suffer a job loss, they can experience feelings of low self-esteem, anger, and frustration. These feelings may result in depression or a sense of despair. Financial problems that usually occur with a job loss cause families stress. Fortunately, these feelings are usually temporary and go away after the family member finds another job and the family regains its financial stability. See **Fig. 12-3**.

Financial Problems

Financial, or money-related, problems are often triggered by the loss of a job, a natural disaster, a serious illness, or even a death. Many families routinely struggle with financial problems because their income simply doesn't stretch far

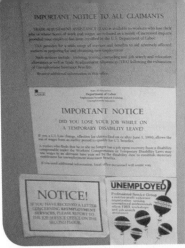

Fig 12-3
Many people find it's not easy to land another job after they have been laid off. In some communities, jobs may be scarce.

enough. Here are some strategies that can help families deal with financial problems:

- **Create a bill-paying plan.** When bills are overdue, most **creditors**—people or companies you owe money to—are willing to schedule new arrangements for payment. This can protect your **credit rating**—a record that shows your ability and willingness to pay your debts.

- **Find help.** Many communities offer consumer credit counseling services to help individuals and families with financial problems. They help people create plans to control their spending and get out of debt. In some situations, they work with creditors to arrange realistic payment schedules. See **Fig. 12-4**.

- **Tighten your spending.** Understanding goes a long way when finances are tight. Money for clothes and entertainment may be scarce. Mending the clothes you have or buying "gently used" items at thrift and consignment stores can help. So can preparing most of your meals at home, instead of eating at restaurants or buying prepared foods. Another way to help out is to take advantage of free and low-cost entertainment. (Make up some games or activities, go to the park, or make a craft project with items you have at home.)

- **Be understanding.** Putting other family members' needs ahead of your own wants helps everyone get through tough situations more easily. Although it may be stressful at the time, learning to carefully handle financial resources makes people far better money managers throughout their adult lives.

Fig 12-4 Consumer credit counseling is one way of many ways that families can learn to cope with financial problems.

Fig 12-5 Homelessness is often the result of natural disasters. For some families, their homes, possessions, and finances are destroyed. How are these people helping one another cope with a disaster?

Natural Disasters

Families all over the world have been victims of natural disasters. Earthquakes, hurricanes, tornadoes, floods, and fires are just some of the disasters that can occur—with or without warning. Perhaps you have experienced a natural disaster in your community. See **Fig. 12-5**.

Homes—or entire communities, including workplaces and schools—may be damaged or destroyed. The loss of a home, and perhaps a job, can seriously affect family finances. Government agencies, private organizations, and religious groups often provide some money, clothing, food, and temporary shelter. However, family members may need substantial time and emotional support to overcome the effects of a disaster and return to normal.

Homelessness

Homelessness—having no permanent place to live—is a problem all over the world. This problem has become more common in recent years. When people lose their homes, it is often because of financial troubles or job loss. Other times people lose their homes through natural disasters. Even temporary homelessness puts a major strain on a family. Many communities have agencies, such as the Salvation Army and the Red Cross, that can provide temporary shelter for people who lose their homes.

Health Problems

When a parent, guardian, child, or close relative becomes seriously ill or disabled, the whole family experiences worry and stress. Family members may need to make adjustments so that the person with the illness or disability can receive proper care. Parents or guardians may need to decrease their working hours to help provide care. Children may need to pitch in and pick up extra household chores.

Learning about a family member's illness or disability can help you better understand his or her daily and long-term needs. Doctors, clinics, libraries, and Web sites offer valuable information. People who have had similar difficulties can provide advice and support. Becoming well informed and showing an attitude of understanding, direction, and compassion can help the family stay strong.

Death

Lauren's father was killed in a work-related accident. The suddenness of the loss created a **crisis**—an immediate difficulty that can be life altering. Whenever death strikes, it's natural to experience grief. The closer you were to the person, the greater your loss. The person's age and the circumstances of the death can also affect how you feel.

People handle the grieving process in different ways. For each individual, it is different. Some people need to express intense emotions. Others need to talk quietly to a trusted relative or friend. Family members need to respect one another's grief process and allow others to mourn in their own way for as long as necessary. Participating in or attending a gathering such as a funeral or memorial service can help people better accept the reality of death. For some, the funeral provides the **closure** (finality) that helps them deal with the reality of the loss. See **Fig. 12-6**.

Fig 12-6 The grieving process lasts different lengths of time for different people. It's important to be patient with family members who grieve longer than you do.

Think of Others

- **Show empathy.** Learn to empathize, or see things from another person's point of view. For example, your parents or guardians may be tired after a long day's work. Look for low-key ways to interact in the evenings. Save activities that make larger demands on their time and energy until the weekends.

- **Offer support.** When you see a friend having a hard time handling things, try not to react in a negative way. Instead, think of specific ways that you like to be supported when things are tough and offer that support to your friend.

- **Welcome others.** It's hard being the new kid. You may belong to a group of friends who hang out regularly. Be open to and welcome new people who may want to join you.

Conflict among family members is common because of increased emotional stress during this period. However, families can grow closer and stronger as a result of loss. Sharing emotions and memories with one another—and with good friends—can be valuable and can ease the pain of coping with loss. Talking to a counselor who specializes in this type of therapy can also help with the grieving process.

Suicide

When a death is caused by suicide—the taking of one's own life—the family may be faced with unanswered questions and guilt. Family members may feel they are to blame in some way or that they could have taken steps to prevent the tragedy. There seems to be little or no closure with all of the questions remaining.

Sometimes there are warning signs that a person is thinking about suicide. Warning signs for suicide include severe depression and frequent mood swings. The person considering suicide may also give away personal items, act irrationally, and talk about death. If you suspect that someone is suicidal, don't be afraid to show that you care and to seek help from a responsible adult. However, your best efforts might not prevent a suicide. It may just be like a runaway train—there's no way to stop it. If a friend or family member does commit suicide, remember that it is the person's own decision and you are not responsible. There was nothing you could do, and you should not feel guilty.

Separation and Divorce

When parents separate or divorce, usually one parent moves out of the family home. Some couples separate for a period of time but then resolve their differences and get back together. In other cases, they decide to end the relationship and divorce, leaving the family to go through major changes.

The children of parents who separate or divorce often go through a difficult period of emotional adjustment. They may think their behavior caused the breakup and blame themselves. For this reason, they need to receive loving support from both parents and reassurance that this is not the case. It's about the parents and their issues.

Teens whose parents divorce often feel isolated and lonely. They may feel that they are the only young people who have experienced the effects of divorce. At such times it's important

Fig 12-7 It's normal for children to feel grief, anger, fear, and frustration when they learn their parents are divorcing. Children should remember that the divorce is not their fault.

to realize that many marriages end in divorce, and many teens experience similar feelings. See **Fig. 12-7**.

Parents often make mistakes when a separation or divorce process involves bitter feelings. They may make negative comments about each other to their children and want the children to take sides. One parent may even try to take custody of the children illegally. It's easy to feel torn between parents who are going through a separation or divorce. For this reason, you need to spend time with both parents and share your feelings. You have the right to express how your parents' actions make you feel. If you are unsure about how to tell your parents what you feel, talk to a trusted adult. Talking things out with a teacher, school counselor, or religious leader can help.

Adjusting after a divorce takes a lot of time, emotional healing, and special effort. Teens may have increased responsibilities in the home and spend less time with both parents—not just the absent one. Although many effects of divorce are unpleasant, most people adapt, and they grow to accept the way things are.

Help Someone Who Abuses Alcohol

If you're concerned about someone close to you who is abusing alcohol, the following guidelines can help:

▶ **Express concern.** Let the person know you're concerned and willing to help. In your discussion, speak calmly and call the problem by its name: alcoholism.

▶ **Don't be an enabler.** Don't cover up or make excuses for the drinker. Avoid doing things that the person should be doing for himself or herself. Set boundaries. Not setting boundaries just enables the person to continue drinking without facing the consequences.

▶ **Suggest help.** Let the person know that help is available. Provide information about community resources and their locations. Realize, however, that the alcoholic must be ready to seek assistance.

▶ **Remain safe.** Never argue with someone who's been drinking. The person isn't able to think clearly and may react violently. Also, refuse if the person offers to drive you somewhere. You don't want to be a victim in a drunk-driving accident.

Substance Abuse and Addiction

Substance abuse often puts a family on the fast track to a crisis. In some cases, substance abuse occurs when medications for illness are misused. It also occurs when people use alcohol and illegal drugs. Serious health problems, and even death, can result from substance abuse. People who use drugs can develop an **addiction**—a physical or psychological dependence on something. People addicted to drugs will do almost anything, even commit crimes, to obtain the drug they crave.

Alcohol is the most commonly abused substance. The result of alcohol use is often a disease known as **alcoholism**—physical and mental dependence on alcohol. People who are addicted to alcohol, in the form of beer, wine, or other liquor, are called **alcoholics**.

Effects on the Family and Society

Whether young or old, people with a substance abuse problem can make life difficult for their families. They may neglect their responsibilities and act irrationally or violently. Their behavior often causes other family members to live in tension and fear, never knowing how the addicted person will act. Abusers may deny they have a problem, which makes it discouraging for family members who try to help them. The abuser's denial can cause anger, frustration, stress, and pain for a family. See **Fig. 12-8**.

Substance abuse affects society as well. Drug abusers may be violent and physically harm others. They may drive a car under the influence and seriously injure or kill another person or themselves. Many crimes are committed by addicts who steal money and objects to pay for drugs.

When teens use alcohol and other drugs, they face serious consequences that can affect them for life. Long-lasting physical, psychological, and emotional problems can interfere with how well teens perform in school or at work. They may frequently fight with parents or guardians and show a "don't care" attitude. Because their use of alcohol and other drugs is against the law, they may face serious legal troubles.

Solutions

Prevention is the best solution to the problem of drug abuse. If you don't start using alcohol or any other drug, you won't have a problem! That means resisting pressure from

Fig 12-8 Facing a drug problem requires courage—from the person abusing drugs and other family members.

peers to try drugs and avoiding places where drugs will be available. Refusing drugs might be hard at times, but doing so can prevent a lifetime of problems and heartaches. When your family's well-being is threatened by drug use, all of the members need help. Seeking help from a counselor or support group, such as Al-Anon or Alcoholics Anonymous, is a way of caring for your family.

Violence in the Home

Sometimes a family member harms or threatens to harm another's physical or mental health. This abuse can be directed toward any member of a family, including children, older family members, or a **spouse**—one's husband or wife. **Neglect**, another form of abuse, occurs when people fail to meet the needs of their children or older adults in their care.

Abuse may take various forms. Jackie grew up feeling she was worthless. Emotional abuse in the form of constant put-downs from her mother fueled this feeling. Trevor's cousin physically abused his wife by hitting her when he was angry.

Jake's friend suffered sibling abuse when his brother routinely hit and taunted him. Neglect was cited when a two-year-old child was found alone in an apartment without food or adult supervision. Sexual abuse occurred when a young girl was forced into sexual activity by an adult.

There is no excuse for any kind of abuse or neglect. Every type of abuse is wrong and severely damaging to the victim. Anyone who is abused would benefit from professional help. An abused person must find someone who will listen and provide shelter if needed. Some teens run away from abusive situations. Running away can turn out to be just as dangerous—

HOW TO RECOGNIZE SIBLING ABUSE

It's true that squabbles among siblings are part of growing up. Many people look back on them with laughter. Yet parents, guardians, and health experts are realizing that some cases of teasing, arguing, and other types of conflict go beyond typical and are harmful. These conflicts become abusive. Children can be physically, emotionally, and sexually abused by a sibling. The following conditions can contribute to sibling abuse:

- The parents or guardians are not involved in their children's lives.

- Adults in the family use physical or emotional violence against one another.

- Parents or guardians "play favorites" among children, which fosters rivalry that can turn into abuse.

- Older children are rushed into adult roles and responsibilities. They may be resentful and even feel entitled to hurt younger siblings if that attitude is modeled by adults.

- Children are exposed to TV shows, video games, and other types of entertainment that promote violence as a way to solve problems.

or even worse—than staying in the home. Strangers may take advantage of runaways and abuse them.

Many communities provide safe shelter for victims of abuse. You can locate them by calling 911 (or the emergency number in your area). You can also ask for a referral at a hospital emergency room or from various community organizations.

Cycles of Abuse

Any kind of abuse is destructive to families. In many cases, abuse is almost certain to be repeated. This cycle continues within the family until someone seeks help. Causes of abuse

How can you recognize when a sibling is being abusive? Here are some signs:

- An abused child may avoid the abusive brother or sister.
- The child may refuse to stay alone with the sibling.
- The child may choose to stay in his or her room, not in common areas of the home.
- The child may have bruises or unexplained cuts and marks.
- Play activities may include violence or sexual acting out that is advanced for the child's age.
- The child's behavior may change, especially eating (loss of appetite) and sleeping habits. Nightmares are common among abused children.

Not every incident that looks like abuse really is. Rough-and-tumble play is not physical abuse. Name-calling that causes both children to laugh is not emotional abuse. However, once one child wants the activity to stop and the other refuses, the situation has crossed the line. Even

that sign is not always reliable, however, because abused children often learn not to stand up to the abuser.

If you care for children or count them among your friends and you notice signs of sibling abuse, take your concerns to a trusted adult at once.

TAKE **ACTION**

Imagine that a neighbor's child is sometimes violent toward a younger sibling, yet the younger child acts lovingly toward the older one. Would you suspect sibling abuse? Why or why not?

usually have little, if anything, to do with a victim's actions. Even if an action triggers the abuse, the action is not the cause of abuse. Many abusive adults were abused as children, and they often lack skills to cope with anger, fear, or stress. They had abuse as a model, and the cycle continues. Many child abusers lack basic parenting skills and cannot make responsible child guidance decisions. Low self-esteem, marital conflict,

I Can Break the Silence of Abuse

If you or someone you know is being abused, it is time to seek help. Silence will not make the abuse go away. It will only allow the abuse to continue. By seeking help now, you may prevent the abuse from happening to someone else.

- **Acknowledge the problem.** The first step in breaking the silence of abuse is to acknowledge the abuse, or accept that the abuse happened. This may be especially difficult for people being abused by a trusted adult, such as a parent. It's never easy to accept that someone who is supposed to love, protect, and care for you is hurting you.

- **Don't accept the blame.** People who are abused often think they did something wrong to deserve the abuse. Abusers often encourage their victims to believe they deserve it. Abusers usually also urge their victims to be silent about the abuse, threatening trouble or physical attack if anyone finds out about it. It's important to remember that abuse is never the victim's fault and that the best course of action is to seek help.

- **Get help from a trusted adult.** Talk to someone you can trust—a family member, a school counselor or teacher, a doctor, or someone who works in a place of worship. Counselors are trained to work with people

and employment problems can also lead to an adult's abusive behavior. The same is true for drug or alcohol abuse, none of which are an excuse for the behavior—abuse is abuse.

Prevention of abuse and neglect starts with respect for each family member. Learning about child development and parenting skills, and reducing stress can also help prevent abuse. Community outreach programs link family members with people who will listen and help guide them.

who have been abused. They know how to help. If you feel you cannot report the abuse face to face, try calling or even sending an e-mail.

- **Call a help line.** If you can't discuss the problem with an adult you know, call a crisis hotline. Sometimes it's easier to talk with someone you don't know. Telephone books list local child abuse and family violence telephone help lines.

- **Call the police.** Safety of the victim is the primary concern. In cases of physical or sexual abuse, the police should be contacted immediately. You can contact them yourself or ask an adult you trust to make the call for you. The police can remove the abuser from the situation and provide the victim with sources for support and counseling.

Help Prevent Youth Violence

Many teens are concerned about youth violence in their schools. Luckily, there are actions you can take to help make your school a safer place:

▶ **Be a constructive problem solver.** Solving problems through communication takes practice. Make a point to use words instead of violence to solve problems and encourage your friends to do the same.

▶ **Speak out before violence occurs.** If you learn that someone intends to commit a violent act or is carrying a gun or other weapon, tell a trusted adult. You can do so anonymously, if you're worried about your own safety.

▶ **Get involved.** When you participate in your school community, you help create a positive atmosphere for other students. Join an after-school program, a sports team, or a club. You can also join or create a nonviolence club in your school to help prevent teen violence.

Crime

Have you, or someone you know, been a victim of crime? It can happen to anyone. Children, teens, older adults, and people with disabilities are often at high risk. Victims of crime can become emotionally scarred. Family and friends need to rally around the victim to give support. If you become aware of a crime, talk to an adult you trust and report the crime to the police.

When a family member commits a crime, the rest of the family suffers. The best approach is to obtain legal help and work to shift the person's life back on track.

Getting Help

Most families have to deal with unexpected changes and challenges. Through love, care, and support for one another, family members are better able to cope with stress and crisis. At times, however, family members may need to seek help from the following groups or people:

• **Extended family.** Often another family member who understands the problem can help. The person's support and fresh perspective may help you find a solution.

• **Trusted adults outside the family.** Sometimes it's wise to talk with someone outside the family who is not involved in the situation, such as a teacher, counselor, religious leader, family physician, or trusted neighbor.

• **Friends.** Close friends may be able to offer emotional support and help you clarify your problem. They may suggest that you seek counseling.

• **Support groups.** Members of support groups share similar experiences. They meet to discuss specific problems, solutions, and sources of help.

• **Community organizations and agencies.** Look for a guide to human services on the Internet, in the telephone directory, or at the library. Many of these services are provided for free or for little cost.

• **Law enforcement agencies.** When a person is abused or neglected, immediate action must be taken to stop the abuse. A police officer can stop the abuser and help the victim seek support. You must report the abuse before you can obtain police help. See **Fig. 12-9**.

Fig 12-9 When you observe instances of abuse or neglect, contact the police.

Review & Activities

Chapter Summary

- Every family faces changes and challenges.
- Some unexpected changes in the family can create a crisis that may affect family members in different ways.
- Abuse can harm any member of a family, including a spouse, children, and others in the household.
- There are positive strategies you can use to handle changes and challenges.
- Although most families can deal with changes and issues, outside help is sometimes necessary and is usually helpful.

Reviewing Key Terms & Ideas

1. Explain the challenges of unplanned pregnancy.
2. How is a family affected by a move? What are three steps you can take to adjust to a new school more easily?
3. What are **financial** problems?
4. List four things families can do when faced with a financial challenge.
5. Why is it helpful to learn about a family member's illness or disability?
6. What is a **crisis**?
7. List the warning signs of suicide.
8. What is an **addiction**?
9. What causes **alcoholism**?
10. How does **neglect** occur?

Thinking Critically

1. **Identifying facts.** Some people think homelessness is always caused by substance abuse, unwillingness to work, or other faults of the homeless person. How would you respond to this position? Explain.
2. **Drawing conclusions.** Why do children of separated or divorced parents often suffer guilt?
3. **Making generalizations.** Which two sources of help do you think would be most beneficial for families trying to cope with the challenges of the cycle of abuse? Why?

Review & Activities

Applying Your Learning

1. **Generational diversity.** Interview older adults to find out how their families dealt with changes and challenges when they were your age. If they were faced with similar problems today, would they handle them the same way? Share your findings with the class.

2. **Positive interactions.** Working in a small group, create and implement a welcome program for teens who have just moved into the community. Include information about local entertainment, school activities, and community resources.

3. **Life simulation.** With a partner, enact a scene in which a teen tells a friend that his or her parents are getting a divorce. The teen feels responsible for the divorce. Model positive responses and ask for classmate feedback.

4. **Teamwork skills.** Imagine that an older disabled family member is coming to live with your family. Describe specific ways you and your other family members can make the transition simple while providing care and comfort to your older relative.

5. **Community resources.** List community resources that are available for individuals experiencing physical or sexual abuse, substance abuse, or homelessness. Share the list with your classmates.

Making Connections

1. **Math** List all unnecessary purchases you made in the past two weeks. Include all frills—even phone calls. Total the purchases. How could this information help you during a family financial crisis?

2. **Reading** Read newspaper articles about recent natural disasters. What types of economic costs are expected? What were the emotional factors for survivors?

3. **Reading** What other kinds of addiction exist? Gambling and food can be addictive. Read about other addictions and research their causes and effects.

CAREER Link

Respect for Authority.
At almost any worksite, someone has the authority, or the right, to make decisions, give orders, and enforce rules. Working well with others includes learning to accept and get along with people in authority. Interview your parents and other adults about positive qualities they have observed and come to respect in authority figures at work. How do you think their attitude toward authority figures has affected their job performance?

How Children Grow

Objectives

- Describe the five areas of development.
- Relate heredity and environment to development.
- Summarize the stages of development.
- Explain the types of play and their importance to healthy development.
- Describe the special needs of children with disabilities.

Vocabulary

- **large motor skills**
- **small motor skills**
- **eye–hand coordination**
- **genes**
- **developmental milestones**
- **parallel play**
- **conscience**
- **cooperative play**
- **puberty**
- **acne**

Reading with Purpose

1. **Read** the title of this chapter and describe in writing what you expect to learn from it.

2. **Write** each vocabulary term in your notebook, leaving space for definitions.

3. **As you read** Chapter 13, write the definition beside each term in your notebook.

4. **After reading** the chapter, write a paragraph describing what you learned.

A Look at Child Development

Think back to some of your first school experiences. What skills did you have? How have you developed over the years? The process of growth and change during a person's lifetime is called development. Although changes in adults may proceed slowly, children develop rapidly. If you were to watch a child develop, you would see that many changes occur very quickly—from month to month or even from week to week. Over time, children grow and learn many skills, including walking, talking, and solving problems. These developmental changes, as well as certain influential factors, create unique individuals.

Developmental Areas

Do you remember learning how to ride a bike? You had to learn how to balance, how to control your speed, and how to stop. All of these tasks required specific physical skills. You also had to understand bike safety, which requires intelligence. If you rode with friends, you needed social skills. Almost everything you do requires many skills, all of which fall into five developmental areas:

- **Physical development** involves the growth of the body and the strength and coordination of muscles. Walking, running, and throwing a ball involve **large motor skills**, or the movement and control of the back, legs, shoulders, and arms. Writing requires **small motor skills**, or the movement and control of smaller body parts, such as the hands and fingers. Physical development also includes the development of **eye–hand coordination**—the ability of the eyes and the hand and arm muscles to work together to make complex movements. When you hit a tennis ball with a racket, you're using eye–hand coordination. See **Fig. 13-1**.

- **Intellectual development** involves the ability to think, understand, reason, and communicate. Infants use their senses to understand the world. As children's language skills develop, they use words to express and understand concepts.

Fig 13-1
Photo albums keep a record of how you've changed over the years. What traits do you have now that you had as an infant?

- **Emotional development** relates to emotions and their expression. Infants show emotions through body movements, facial expressions, and sounds, such as cooing or crying. As children grow older, they experience more emotions and they learn to express them in socially acceptable ways.

- **Social development** refers to children's interactions with others. Sharing, getting along, and making friends all require social skills.

- **Moral development** involves an understanding of right and wrong. Very young children do not understand the difference between right and wrong. Over time and with guidance, they learn how to behave appropriately and how to monitor their own behavior. Parental guidance continues through the teen years and into young adulthood.

Fig 13-2 Heredity and culture contribute to a child's development. What "other relatives" do you inherit from?

Developmental Influences

Have you ever met someone who looks exactly like you, wears the same clothes, likes the same movies, and has the same abilities? You probably haven't because no one is just like you. Even if you have an identical twin, each of you is different is some ways. Two factors work together to shape you into a one-of-a-kind individual:

- **Heredity** refers to all of the traits you inherited from your parents, grandparents, and other relatives. These traits are passed on through **genes**, the basic units of heredity. Genes determine your body type and the color of your hair, skin, and eyes. You also may inherit certain talents, such as musical or athletic talent, and personality traits, such as shyness. See **Fig. 13-2**.

- **Environment** is what surrounds you and affects your development and behavior. Your environment includes your family, friends, home, school, and community. It even includes technology, such as computers, television, and video games.

Although heredity is permanent, environmental influences are strong. For example, praise, encouragement, and support from family members are crucial to developing healthy self-esteem. Children who feel good about themselves are better able to complete challenging tasks and be successful in future relationships and in the workplace. On the other hand, children who are not encouraged often feel insecure and are afraid to try new things.

A family's level of education, income, access to health care and technology, culture, and traditions also influence a child's development. Culture influences parents' and caregivers' roles and what and how children are taught. What differences do you see between your family and that of a friend from a different culture? What similarities do you see?

Developmental Stages

Your development began before you were born, in the prenatal stage of life. During this period, you developed from a single cell into a baby capable of surviving in the outside world. Since birth, you have continued through several developmental stages to become who you are today. The developmental stages correspond to a person's age, beginning in infancy and continuing through young adulthood.

For most people, development in all areas follows a general and progressive sequence. As people develop, they accomplish certain **developmental milestones**—skills achieved at a particular stage of life. For example, before you could walk, you had to learn to stand. Walking and standing are developmental milestones. Everyone proceeds through developmental stages in the same sequence, but the rate of progress differs from person to person. For example, you may have learned to stand two months earlier than your best friend did.

Young Infants

Imagine an infant in the early part of infancy, no older than six months of age. You probably notice the infant has little hair, wears a diaper, and cries for food or comfort. If you observe the infant carefully, however, you will notice much more. Infants younger than six months of age can do many things. Newborn infants look at faces and can recognize primary caregivers' voices. A few months after birth, their neck muscles strengthen, allowing them to hold up their head. Soon they learn to kick their legs and roll from their stomach to their back. Young infants communicate by cooing, laughing, and crying. See **Fig. 13-3**.

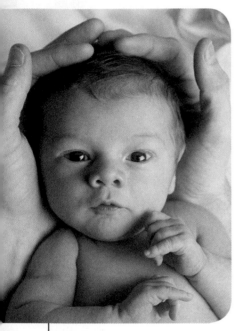

Fig 13-3 Infants younger than six months are more than what they seem. They can learn and communicate, and they develop at a rapid pace.

Older Infants

The period between 6 and 12 months of age is an exciting time because infants make many changes. Older infants can eat solid foods and drink from a cup. They learn to sit alone, crawl, and stand. Some may even begin to walk. See **Fig. 13-4**.

At this stage, infants interact more with their caregivers. They raise their arms to be picked up and can recognize close family members. They also imitate others' actions and facial expressions and listen to others speak. Infants this age spend much of their time looking and reaching for objects. They explore many objects by putting them in their mouths, so they must be supervised closely. They like music, picture books, and simple games, such as peek-a-boo. Their language has developed from cooing to babbling, and they usually speak their first word by their first birthday.

Young Toddlers

After infancy, children become toddlers. Young toddlers, those between 12 and 24 months of age, master quite a few skills before their second birthday. Not only are they eating table foods, but they also can hold their own spoon to eat and may use a straw to drink. They can walk, climb steps without help, and run, although they may do so clumsily. Increased coordination in their arms and hands allows them to roll a ball, turn pages of a book, and scribble with crayons or markers.

Safety Check

Toys can be hazards. Follow these tips when choosing toys for children:

- Toys should be age appropriate—for example, clay is an appropriate choice for preschoolers, not for infants.

- Be sure toys are nontoxic and nonflammable.

- Don't allow children to play with toys that are broken or have sharp edges.

- Check eyes, buttons, and other sewn-on parts of stuffed animals to be sure they are secure.

- Do not allow children to play with small objects that can be swallowed. Any toy small enough to fit through a toilet paper tube is small enough for a child to swallow.

Fig 13-4 This toddler's natural curiosity has him reaching for objects. What safety hazard is this toddler facing?

Young toddlers are very curious people. They enjoy exploring their surroundings, which means they have to be monitored constantly. They want independence and will try hard to do many tasks for themselves. For this reason, they may tell adults "no" when adults try to do something for them. Although toddlers want independence, they also need love, care, direction, and comfort from their parents and caregivers.

HOW TO HANDLE TANTRUMS

Imagine you've been craving a double-dip ice cream cone all day. When you reach the ice cream shop, you find the shop is out of your two favorite flavors. Young children may know this frustration daily. For every skill they learn, it seems another one is denied them. They can slip on shoes but cannot tie laces. They're urged to eat with a fork, but knives are off limits. Life seems unfair, and they react in the only way they know: screaming, thrashing, and throwing things—in other words, by having a tantrum. A tantrum is an early attempt at problem solving. Parents and caregivers need to address tantrums in an appropriate manner, or this will become a pattern for children to get what they want.

As a teen, you've learned better ways to deal with problems, and you can help children deal with theirs. Try a few of these constructive techniques the next time a child throws a tantrum:

- **Ignore the tantrum.** Ignoring a tantrum shows the child you're not giving in. Make sure children cannot hurt themselves, others, or anyone's possessions.

They need to be held and comforted when they're upset or afraid. They also need to be taught how to behave in public, share, and deal with frustrations in a nonphysical manner. Biting is not uncommon, but it is inappropriate. During this stage, children use more words to communicate their feelings, wants, and needs and can even use short sentences. See **Fig. 13-5**.

- **Maintain the rules.** Giving in only teaches children that poor behavior gets results. Likewise, don't reward children for stopping the tantrum by giving them what was wanted.

- **Distract the child.** Becoming involved with a game or other activity has two effects: it shows that you aren't bothered and encourages the child to join you in something more enjoyable.

- **Remove the audience.** If you're in a public place, find a quiet spot away from "center stage." Attention from others can encourage the child and put pressure on you to end the tantrum. You might resort to actions that only make the situation worse.

- **Hold the child.** Sometimes a firm but gentle embrace gives the comfort that an angry or frightened child needs.

- **Stay calm.** This teaches children that you are in control. It shows control of the situation and gives them a sense of security. They learn trust when they see that you keep your word, even when they don't like it. They see that you care about them even after they behave poorly.

TAKE **ACTION**

Think of three situations in which a child might have a tantrum and a constructive response to each. Then describe each situation and response to a partner. Give reasons for your choices.

Older Toddlers

Children round out their toddler years with physical energy—they run, jump, walk on tiptoes, climb, pedal a tricycle, and throw and catch balls. At times, they seem as if they'll never stop moving! Between 24 and 36 months, many

Fig 13-5 ▶ Importance of Play

Experts agree that play is a child's work. Play nurtures all areas of children's development and allows children to explore their world. Jean Piaget, a noted child expert, described three stages of play:

▶ **Sensorimotor Play—Infancy to 24 Months** Infants and young toddlers experiment with motor movements. Once they master coordination, they enjoy playing with objects that respond to them. For example, they shake rattles to hear a sound or push a ball to watch it roll.

▶ **Games with Rules—School-Age Children** Because older school-age children understand cooperation and teamwork, they are able to play more complicated games with rules. These games can be formal games, such as sports, or games the children create on their own.

How can parents and caregivers support children's play? They can provide safe play environments and age-appropriate toys and arrange for play dates with other children. Parents should also join in on the fun!

▶ **Symbolic or Pretend Play—24 Months to 6 Years** In this type of play, children pretend by taking on roles. They may play "house," pretending to be parents, siblings, or even pets. As their experiences grow, so do their imaginations. Soon they take on roles of construction workers, princesses, or doctors. This fantasy play helps them understand reality.

children become toilet trained. They can also wash their own hands and dress themselves. Although many older toddlers have trouble sharing, they are interested in other children and may play with them. Older toddlers will often engage in **parallel play**, in which they play alongside other children but not with them. Their increased vocabulary helps them interact with parents and caregivers. Older toddlers can ask questions and use longer sentences to express their thoughts and feelings. Gradually, with help from parents and caregivers, they develop a **conscience**, an inner sense of right or wrong. A developing conscience helps children monitor their own behavior.

Preschoolers

By preschool age—three to five years—children's large motor skills are well developed. Their fine motor skills are becoming more refined, allowing preschoolers to cut paper with scissors, draw shapes, print their own name, and shape clay into recognizable forms. During the preschool years, children develop the skills they need for school. They learn the alphabet and how to count. Their vocabulary continues to grow, and they learn that printed symbols have meaning.

Their increased vocabulary helps preschoolers express their feelings. Preschoolers can experience many emotions, such as jealously, curiosity, fear, joy, and affection. They have a sense of right and wrong and are beginning to understand that adults set rules that they need to follow. During the preschool years, children move from parallel play to **cooperative play**, in which they play with other children and learn to share, take turns, solve problems, and control their emotions. These early play experiences build important social skills that are needed throughout life.

School-Age Children

When children reach five years of age, they enter the school-age stage of life. During this time, they begin to spend more time away from home—at school and in structured activities outside of school, such as swim lessons and art classes. These activities foster their independence, help them develop their sense of self, and teach them skills they will use later in life.

School-age children can ride a bicycle and participate in activities that require skilled movements, such as team-related sports. Their fine motor skills have become more refined, which allows them to write and draw more precisely.

TIPS

Cut Back on TV Time

Carefully chosen TV programs can be an effective and interesting way for children to learn. However, too much television can negatively affect children's health. The following tips will help you cut back on the time children spend watching television:

▶ Limit TV viewing to no more than ten hours each week.

▶ Create a weekly viewing schedule that includes age-appropriate programs—and stick to it.

▶ Choose physical and social activities, such as reading and active play, over TV viewing.

▶ When TV time is over, turn the television off. If the house is too quiet, play some age-appropriate music or talk to one another.

During this stage, children can read and do arithmetic, reason, and problem solve. Because they face increased academic pressure, they can also experience stress. They may worry about school or family life, and they can be sensitive and easily suffer embarrassment. Their range of feelings increases, and friendships become more complex. School-age children learn teamwork and compromise and can consider others' feelings. They understand right and wrong and generally want to do what is right.

Adolescents

The period of adolescence is a time when teens experience many changes in preparation for adulthood. Adolescence begins with **puberty**, the bodily changes that indicate sexual maturity in the physical sense. These changes are most noticeable in teens' physical appearance—their bodies begin to look like those of adults. Some awkward changes may also be taking place, including **acne**, a skin problem that develops when glands below the pores (tiny openings) in the skin become blocked. These physical changes can also affect emotions. Many teens experience mood swings, or sudden changes in behavior that feel like an emotional roller coaster.

Teens have the ability to reason and think of alternatives to problems or actions, which helps them deal with social situations and academic work. During adolescence, friendships become more solid, and some may even develop into more one-on-one relationships. Although friends are important at this stage of development, the family remains a stable base for teens.

Considering Special Needs

Not all children follow the typical pattern of development that most people follow. Some children who do not progress in a typical sequence have physical, emotional, social, or intellectual needs. See **Fig. 13-6**.

Some children with special needs have health-related conditions that can affect their ability to function in some way. For example, children with cystic fibrosis (SIS-tik fie-BRO-sis)—a lung and digestive system disorder—may need special treatment to keep their lungs clear. Some children with special needs have problems with movement, vision, or hearing.

Fig 13-6 Children with special needs might need extra help with schoolwork to succeed. How can parents and caregivers help promote self-esteem in children with special needs?

Children with learning disabilities struggle with language concepts and reading. Some children experience an emotional disability that affects their behavior in a negative way. Children with certain disabilities can also be highly intelligent. Gifted children, who achieve higher intellectual levels, should be given challenging academic tasks.

Children with special needs require special guidance from parents, caregivers, teachers, and sometimes health professionals to reach their full potential. These children want to be treated just like other children. They have the same basic needs for praise, support, and encouragement as anyone else.

Knowing how children grow can help you better understand yourself and those around you. You will be more prepared to care for children, whether they're your siblings, younger relatives, neighbors, or ultimately your own children when you become a parent later in your life.

Review & Activities

Chapter Summary

- The skills you use in your daily activities involve five developmental areas.
- Both heredity and environment influence children's growth and development.
- As people develop, they accomplish certain developmental skills.
- Play nurtures all areas of children's development and allows children to explore their world.
- Children with special needs require assistance to meet their full potential, but they have the same basic needs as other children.

Reviewing Key Terms & Ideas

1. What are the five developmental areas?
2. What activities involve **large motor skills**?
3. What are **small motor skills**?
4. Describe an activity that uses **eye–hand coordination**.
5. What does intellectual development involve?
6. What are **genes**?
7. What does environment include?
8. Define **developmental milestones**.
9. Describe **parallel play**.
10. What is a **conscience**?
11. What do children learn in **cooperative play**?
12. Define **puberty**.

Thinking Critically

1. **Defending positions.** Some people think that heredity is the most important influence on a child. How would you respond to this position?
2. **Predicting outcomes.** Imagine that a child's physical development slowed after infancy and the child was unable to walk as a preschooler. How might this delay affect the child's intellectual, social, and emotional development?
3. **Drawing conclusions.** How might parents and caregivers encourage a child's moral development?

Review & Activities

Applying Your Learning

1. **Developmental support.** With a partner, imagine one of you is a parent and the other is a teacher. Conduct a dialog about how the two of you might work together to promote a child's overall development.

2. **Intelligence assessments.** Use print or Internet resources to research intelligence tests used in schools. What kinds of things are measured? Based on your findings, what are the pros and cons of intelligence testing in schools?

3. **Observation skills.** Observe a parent or caregiver interacting with a child. Note the adult's statements and actions that encourage social and moral development.

4. **Service project.** With a small group, list items, such as books and home learning tools, that make your home a positive learning environment. Organize a donation station in your school to collect these items and deliver them to a local shelter for disadvantaged children.

5. **Activity plans.** Plan an activity for preschool children with language disabilities. Demonstrate your activity to the class.

Making Connections

1. **(Writing)** Write a persuasive essay encouraging people to learn more about how children grow. In your essay, cite some of the ideas you learned from this chapter.

2. **(Reading)** Read parenting magazines that describe activities for young children. Based on what you know about development and play, how would you rate the activities?

3. **(Writing)** Choose one of the following topics to research and write about: juvenile diabetes, visual impairment, or cystic fibrosis. Include if the disorder affects development. Share your findings with the class.

4. **(Reading)** Read one or two books about individuals with disabilities and how they managed to achieve their potential.

CAREER Link

Reading Skills.
Whether your future career involves working with children, teens, or adults, you will need good reading skills. You might need to skim reading material for general information. Other times you will need to read carefully for specific facts. Find out what reading is required in a job of interest to you. How can you improve your reading skills to meet the demands of the job?

Caring for Children

Objectives

- Give guidelines for keeping children safe.
- Explain how to respond to emergencies.
- Compare behavior management techniques of infants, toddlers, and older children.
- Prepare nutritious meals and snacks for children.
- Discuss strategies for managing children's bedtime.

Vocabulary

- **childproofing**
- **poison control centers**
- **concussion**
- **shock**
- **cardiopulmonary resuscitation (CPR)**
- **nightmare**
- **night terror**
- **sleepwalking**

Reading with Purpose

1. **Write down** the colored headings from Chapter 14 in your notebook.

2. **As you read** the text under each heading, visualize what you are reading.

3. **Reflect** on what you read by writing a few sentences under each heading to describe it.

4. **Continue** this process until you have finished the chapter. Reread your notes.

Providing Care

Imagine that you just received a call from your new next-door neighbor. She asks you to care for her toddler one afternoon next week. What would your answer be? Do you have any past child care experience that might be helpful?

Many parents need the help of others to care for their children on a temporary basis. Trusted teens who take child care responsibilities seriously can be valued caregivers. Many teens your age take jobs caring for infants, toddlers, or children. Some have had practice caring for younger siblings. For others, caring for a child is a new experience. Whether you're an old pro or just starting out, caring for children is a fun way to spend some time with children while making extra money. See **Fig. 14-1**.

Fig 14-1▶ You can be a positive influence on young children you care for.

Put Safety First

Whether you're caring for a younger sibling or your neighbor's toddler, you are in charge of the child's safety and welfare. Being in charge of children is an enormous responsibility. Chances are it's the biggest responsibility you've ever had.

Safety in the Home

When caring for small children, think about how they see things. Anticipating children's natural curiosity can prevent accidents. Taking steps to identify possible hazards and removing them, or **childproofing** the home, helps ensure children's safety. The following guidelines can help you keep children safe inside the home:

- **Remove objects that create hazards.** Check for debris, objects, furniture, or equipment that could hurt a crawling baby. Remove from tables any heavy items that infants or toddlers might pull off and put away small items they might choke on. Also, it's good to pad any sharp corners of tables or other furniture to avoid accidents.

- **Monitor use of stairs.** Infants and young toddlers often attempt to climb stairs. Keep them away from stairs, lock any gates at stairways, and provide temporary gating when necessary. Remind older toddlers and preschoolers to hold on to a handrail to prevent falls on stairs.

- **Keep doors and windows locked at all times.** This is especially important in any home with more than one story. Doors should never be opened to strangers, even if they appear to be friendly. Children should never indicate to strangers that they are home without their parents or guardians.

- **Supervise children constantly.** Accidents can happen in the blink of an eye. Never leave children alone in any room, especially a bathroom. They may lock themselves inside, open medicine cabinets, or fall into toilets or tubs containing water. Also, when bathing children, never leave them alone. Most drownings of small children occur in bathtubs. In the kitchen, be sure to keep children away from ranges, heaters, hot-water faucets, knives and other sharp utensils, heavy pot covers, and hot drinks. See **Fig. 14-2**.

Fig 14-2 ▶
Remember that many children like to climb, so keeping harmful materials on a high shelf might not be enough. If possible, childproof drawers and cabinets should be used to store potentially dangerous items.

Bathe a Baby Safely

Follow these tips for safety and comfort when bathing an infant:

1. **Prepare the bath.** Use a basin of water, infant tub, or the family tub. Check the water temperature before putting an infant into a tub. The water should be warm, not hot or cold. Put a towel or rubber mat in the tub to make the infant comfortable and to prevent slipping.

2. **Put the infant in the tub.** Place the infant in the tub with a secure grip. Hold the infant securely under the arm with your hand supporting the back of the head. Keep the infant seated in the tub.

3. **Wash the infant.** Start by washing the infant's face with clear water and then patting it dry. Continue to wash and rinse the rest of the infant's body. While in the bath, the infant shouldn't be allowed to drink bathwater or suck on a washcloth. Instead, offer a drink of fresh water or a teething toy to suck on.

4. **Dry the infant.** Lift the infant from the water with a secure grip. Place the infant on a clean towel and immediately wrap the towel around the infant to prevent chilling. Then gently pat the infant dry.

- **Place harmful chemicals and matches out of reach of children.** Most ordinary household products are poisonous and can cause death. Common poisons include insecticides, cleaning supplies, and medicines. Chemicals and medications should be in locked cabinets, out of reach of children. Swallowing chemicals is obviously dangerous, but damage can also be caused when chemicals are inhaled into the lungs or if they come into contact with skin or eyes.

Be alert to signs of poisoning, such as coughing, stomach pain, dizziness, rashes or burns, vomiting, unconsciousness, and swelling in the mouth or esophagus, which causes choking and breathing difficulty. If you think a child has been poisoned, immediately call 911 and a poison control center in your area. **Poison control centers** give advice on treatment for poisoning. Their staff will tell you what emergency action to take.

Toy Safety

Children enjoy toys of all types. Although they can be fun to play with, toys can also have safety hazards. Before giving a toy to a child, make sure it's clean, unbreakable, free of sharp edges, and too large to swallow. Any object that can pass through a tube of toilet tissue is too small to give to children younger than three years of age.

Some loud toys can scare small children and even permanently damage hearing. Toys with long strings or cords may cause choking and should not be placed in cribs or playpens where children might become tangled in them. Toy safety is important for older children, too. Check to see that their toys are in good working condition with no broken pieces or sharp edges. Broken toys can cause serious injuries. Also, provide children with safety equipment for activities such as biking—as a rider or a passenger—and rollerblading.

Outdoor Safety

Most children enjoy playing outdoors, but they must be supervised at all times when they're outside. In some cases, you can remain inside and watch children who are playing in an enclosed backyard. Other outdoor areas, such as playgrounds, require extra caution. When choosing a playground, select one that has a soft surface, such as shredded tires beneath the equipment. Make sure to keep children off playground equipment that has peeling paint, is developmentally inappropriate, or is broken. Playground outings should always be supervised by an adult caregiver. See **Fig. 14-3**.

Streets are dangerous areas for children. Never let children play in streets or roads. If older children need to cross the street, explain to them how to cross safely and monitor them as they do. Bicycle safety rules need to be established before children ride.

Wading or swimming pools are another type of outdoor danger. Although they are lots of fun, pools can also be deadly. If you're taking children to a pool, don't take your eyes off them. Children who get cramps while swimming, or those who are inexperienced swimmers, can easily drown within minutes. Swim activities, as well as other outdoor activities, also can cause sun-related problems, such as sunburns. Be sure to apply sunscreen to children before they swim or play outdoors.

Fig 14-3 Taking a child to a nearby playground can be a lot of fun for both of you. What safe playgrounds are available in your community?

Accidents and Emergencies

Would you know what to do if a child fell from a swing or into a swimming pool? The action you take can be the difference between a minor injury and a more serious injury. To prepare yourself for dealing with an emergency while caring for children, commit these suggestions to memory:

- **Remain calm.** Breathe deeply and focus your thoughts on actions you need to take. Also, try to keep the child calm by speaking in a soothing, controlled manner. The child will pattern his or her behavior after yours.

- **Assess the situation.** Is this a minor or major injury? Is the child burned, bleeding, or unconscious? If eye pupils are different sizes, if the child vomits, or if the child just wants to sleep after an injury, he or she may have a **concussion**, or a type of head injury. Can you handle the situation by yourself, or do you need to call for help? See **Fig. 14-4**.

Fig 14-4
Emergencies can happen without warning. It's best to learn basic first aid before caring for young children.

- **Call for assistance.** If the child is seriously injured, call 911 or your local emergency number for help. If the child appears abnormally cold, he or she could be going into shock. **Shock** is a physical condition characterized by inadequate blood flow and can be very serious. In this case, use a blanket, jacket, or large towel to cover the child. If the child is overheated, he or she may be experiencing sunstroke. Make sure the child has adequate fluids and has a chance to cool down naturally. Providing shade can help.

- **Give the minimum necessary first aid treatment.** Knowing what you should not do in an emergency is as important as knowing what you should do. Some injuries, such as broken bones, can be made worse by moving an injured person. Only treat injuries if you know how!

Classes that provide instruction in basic emergency care, or first aid classes, can teach you how to treat minor injuries and how to respond to serious ones. You can also take a class to learn **cardiopulmonary resuscitation (CPR)**, a rescue technique used to keep a person's heart and lungs functioning until medical care arrives. These classes are offered in schools and through the American Red Cross and other community agencies.

Caring for Children

Responding to emergencies and providing a safe environment are vitally important. Caring for children also includes playing with them, dressing them, feeding them, putting them to bed, encouraging them, guiding their behavior, and promoting their self-concept.

Managing Behavior

Children of different ages have different needs, and they behave differently to have their needs met. For example, infants have many physical needs. When infants cry, you need to find out what's troubling them. Are they too cold or too warm? They may be hungry or sick or need a clean diaper. Changing diapers is a necessary part of infant care. To change a diaper, make sure all necessary supplies are nearby before you begin. Never leave an infant alone on a changing table. It is too easy for the child to fall off. If an infant is crying to be held, try holding the baby while walking or rock the baby in a chair. Always support the head and neck when holding infants.

The needs and behavior of toddlers and preschoolers are different from those of infants. For example, toddlers tend to get into things that can be hazardous, and many like to climb, which can lead to falls. You'll need to watch them every moment and provide safe play activities and toys. Preschoolers also need your attention, but they can do more for themselves. They enjoy it when you read to, play with, and talk to them.

Safety Check

The following tips will help you and the children in your care remain safe in case of fire:

- If a fire starts in the oven, turn off the oven and close it. If a fire starts in a frying pan, put a frying pan cover on it. If the fire is out of control, leave the house and call for help.

- If there is smoke in the home, cover your nose and mouth with a wet cloth and do the same for the children. Tell the children to crawl under the smoke as they escape the home.

- Before leaving a room, touch the door. If it is hot, do not open it. Find another exit. If you are unable to escape, stand by a window and signal for help.

- Never stop to take personal belongings or to call 911 while escaping. Wait to call until you are safely outside.

- If you are in an apartment building, locate the nearest stairway marked "fire exit," or a fire escape if a stairway is not accessible. Never use an elevator in a fire.

- If clothing is on fire, stop, drop, and roll until the flames are out.

HOW TO ENTERTAIN CHILDREN

Children like to be involved in activities. Yet if you ask, "What do you want to do?" a child may respond, "I don't know." These ideas for simple, low-cost fun can help you keep a child's hands—and mind—active:

- **Fascinate infants with simple, sensory experiences.** Take time and help them safely explore things that draw their interest. Let them feel the cool smoothness of a metal wind chime, hear its music, and watch it sway in the breeze.

- **Play peek-a-boo with infants.** Slowly lower a stuffed toy down one side of the sofa and pop it up (making appropriate popping noises) on the other. Repeat and cheer when the child turns to await the reappearance. See if the child tries to find a toy that you hide under a pillow.

- **Make mealtime fun.** Generations of parents have made train noises as a spoonful of strained peas "pulls in" to a child's mouth. You can make the train a honking car or a rumbling truck.

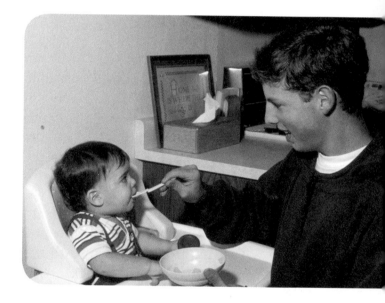

- **Play pretend with toddlers.** Pretend to be cats, dogs, or jungle or farm animals. Toddlers are also great imitators. Teach them dance steps (but don't expect coordination).

- **Make play out of work.** Encourage toddlers' can-do spirit and channel their energy by giving them "jobs." They can wash socks in tubs of water or dust chair legs.

- **Explore nature.** Most toddlers and preschoolers enjoy nature activities. Gather and crack acorns. Compare colors of autumn leaves. Watch ants at work. Feel different types of grasses and leaves.

- **Encourage preschoolers' imagination.** Play dress-up or make-believe. Help with props but leave the "storyline" to them. You might help set up a diner and write the menu as they dictate it. Take turns playing the grouchy customer, the clumsy waiter, or the master chef.

- **Make edible sculptures.** Find a recipe for edible paint in a craft book or on the Internet. Decorate graham crackers for snacking and sharing. Peanut butter, celery, and raisins make wonderful sculpting tools. (Watch for allergies.)

- **Create prints.** Use textured fabric pieces, rubber stamps, cut vegetables, sponge pieces, and leaves to make impressions in clay. You can also dip the materials in paint to make prints.

TAKE **ACTION**

In small groups, discuss ways to include a young child of a certain age in daily activities. Choose one activity and develop a simple "lesson plan."

Caring for older children requires different skills. Some children may feel they're old enough to take care of themselves. Be friendly to them and show a sincere interest in their ideas and activities. Sometimes older children are jealous of the attention you give to their younger siblings. They may misbehave to get your attention. If a child deliberately misbehaves, remain calm and discipline the child. The most effective discipline has a clear connection to the misbehavior. For example, if a child bumps into others with a bicycle after being told not to, you might take the bicycle away. Be fair, but firm. You can be friendly and still be in charge.

Clothing

Although dressing yourself is easy now, as a young child, this was a challenging task. Most young children and all infants need help getting dressed. When dressing infants, keep in mind that they lose body heat more easily than adults do, but they are also sensitive to overheating. As a general rule, dress infants in one layer more than you would wear. Unless the weather is cold, socks and booties are not necessary, and shoes are not required until a child starts to walk outside.

Fig 14-5 Preschoolers can do many tasks independently, but they still need guidance from parents and caregivers.

Toddlers and young preschoolers are very mobile, and their clothing often becomes dirty quickly. Choose clothing that stretches and can be cleaned easily. Guide them in their clothing choices. Children this age have no concept of weather. Offer clothing appropriate to the time of year, the daily weather, and the activity. Because many children at this age are learning to use the toilet independently, they need clothes that can be removed easily and quickly. Pants with elastic in the waist are a better choice than those with buttons.

Older preschoolers and school-age children are usually able to dress themselves, but they may need help tying their shoes. Because children this age have definite likes and dislikes, allow them to choose from several clothing options. See **Fig. 14-5.**

Mealtime and Snacks

When you care for children, you may be responsible for feeding them. Find out what food should be served, when to serve it, and how much to serve. Also, ask parents or guardians about any food allergies or special diets. Here are tips for feeding children:

- **Infants.** When caring for an infant, you may need to feed him or her with a bottle. Before feeding, put a bib on the infant to protect clothing. You can feed an infant formula at room temperature, or you can warm it by placing the bottle in warm water for several minutes. Check the formula's temperature by shaking a drop out on the inside of your wrist. It should feel warm, not hot. Never warm a bottle in a microwave oven. The liquid might become dangerously hot. When you feed an infant, hold the infant upright and hold the bottle while the infant eats. You will need to burp the

Teens Speak About What Children Need

Corey slid the toy catalog across the lunchroom table to his classmate Paul. "You have a little brother, don't you? I have to get my nephew a birthday present. What do you think a twelve-year-old would like?"

Paul scanned the pages, shaking his head. "I don't think my brother would like this stuff. I got him a kid's recipe book. He gets a kick out of 'cooking' for us. His granola bars are really good."

"Joe might like that. But doesn't that need some kind of supervision? My sister works nights."

"What about you?" Paul asked. "Weren't you complaining last Saturday that you didn't have anything to do?"

"I guess I could spend more time with him. That's it. I'll make him coupons for things we can do together, like a trip to the pet shop."

Teen Connection

Think of a skill you have that a child would like to learn. With a classmate, demonstrate how you would teach this skill. Remember that the lesson should suit a child's understanding and physical abilities.

baby during and after eating. Older infants may be eating baby cereal or baby food. Be prepared for messiness. Protect the baby's clothes and your own. The child is likely to play with the food, as well as eat it. That's normal. Have a sense of humor and make mealtimes fun and enjoyable.

- **Toddlers.** Toddlers can eat some regular food. They like simple finger foods—small, bite-sized pieces they can pick up with their fingers. If you use a high chair, keep it clean and in a handy spot. Never give young children hard candy, hot dog pieces, nuts, or any other food that might cause choking.

Fig 14-6
Foods you feed to children should be nutritious and safe. Be sure to ask parents or guardians about any food allergies before giving children food.

- **Preschoolers.** Simple foods, such as milk, cheese, crackers, peanut butter, fresh and dried fruit, and vegetable sticks are popular and healthful foods for preschoolers. (Peanut butter can be dangerous for children allergic to nuts.) Avoid foods that are high in fat and sugar. Preschoolers may lack good manners, but they're somewhat skilled at eating. See **Fig. 14-6**.

Bedtime

Bedtime is often a challenge. Toddlers, preschoolers, and young school-age children may not want to go to bed. They will protest bedtime by crying, climbing out of bed, making excuses to get up for water or restroom visits, and refusing to return to bed. Ask parents or guardians what the bedtime routine is and follow it. Putting on pajamas, brushing teeth, and listening to a quiet story can help prepare children physically and emotionally for bed.

A sleeping child is still in your care. Be sure to stay close by in case the child needs your attention. Many children experience bedwetting during the night and need a change of pajamas and bedding. Some children may experience a **nightmare**, or bad dream, and need your help and comfort. Occasionally children experience a **night terror**, a type of sleep disorder that is more intense than a nightmare. These often occur when a child has a high fever or illness. Children experiencing a night terror might scream, cry, and act confused while still asleep. For nightmares and night terrors, stay with the child and provide comfort until he or she falls back asleep. If the child is asleep, don't wake him or her. Simply provide comfort until the child quiets down.

Sleepwalking, walking while still asleep, occurs in some children, usually between 5 and 12 years of age. Most children who sleepwalk return to their beds on their own, and there is no need to wake the child. Be sure the doors are locked, so the child does not leave the home, and the stairs are gated. Taking extra care at bedtime can keep children safe and calm while they are in your care.

TIPS

Follow Your Child Care Checklist

Follow these tips when you agree to accept a child care job:

1. **Learn about the job.** Before you go, find out the time and date, names and ages of children, how long you will be needed, and transportation details. Also, agree on your fee.

2. **Inform your family.** Write down the name of the people you're working for and their address and phone number. Give this information to your family. Have a phone handy for emergencies. Your family can be a good resource in emergencies.

3. **Arrive early.** Give yourself about 15 minutes to get to know the children and talk to the parents or guardians before they leave. Ask for special instructions about medication, bathing, and mealtime and bedtime routines.

4. **Ask for emergency phone numbers.** Write down the numbers of the family's doctor, the poison control center, and the fire and police stations. Also, ask for the number where the parents or guardians can be reached.

5. **Keep your attention on the children.** You are here to watch the children. That is all you should be doing. Personal calls and TV favorites are activities to do at home.

Review & Activities

Chapter Summary

- Childproofing the home helps keep children safe.
- Caregivers must know what not to do, as well as what to do, in case of an emergency or accident.
- Children of different ages require different behavior management techniques.
- A successful caregiver knows how to prepare and serve children healthful meals and snacks.
- Following regular routines can help when preparing children for bedtime.

Reviewing Key Terms & Ideas

1. Define **childproofing**.
2. Name three signs of poisoning.
3. What do **poison control centers** do?
4. What kind of toy safety procedures should be followed for older children?
5. What actions should you take in an emergency?
6. What is first aid? Name three places where you might learn about first-aid procedures.
7. List four possible causes of an infant's cries.
8. What general rule should you follow when dressing infants?
9. List six simple and nutritious foods that are popular with preschoolers.
10. What is a **night terror**? What is the difference between a **nightmare** and night terror?
11. What should you do if a child is **sleepwalking**?

Thinking Critically

1. **Evaluating skills.** What criteria would you suggest parents and guardians use when selecting a teen to care for their toddler several times a week?
2. **Solving problems.** Think of a difficult situation you might encounter during your first child care job. How would you handle the situation?
3. **Making generalizations.** Which emergency response step do you think is most important? Why?

Review & Activities

Applying Your Learning

1. **Evacuation plan.** Draw a floor plan of your home or a home where you care for children. Show the location of doors, windows, stairways, and outside fire escapes, if applicable. Work with family members to diagram a plan for escape in the event of a fire or other emergency.

2. **Personal preparation.** Read a book on babysitting basics and a first-aid manual. Then create a babysitting kit that includes basic first-aid supplies, emergency phone numbers, and materials to entertain children, such as craft supplies and books. Include any additional items recommended in your reading.

3. **Dressing practice.** Using a life-sized doll, diapers, and infant clothing, practice changing a diaper and dressing an infant. Remember the safety guidelines described in the chapter. After you've practiced, demonstrate a diaper and clothing change for the class.

4. **Snack plan.** Imagine that you have been hired to care for two preschoolers each afternoon for the next two weeks. Think of ten creative and healthful combinations of snacks you might serve each day, not repeating any of them. Share your completed menu with the class.

5. **Bedtime basics.** Invite a child psychiatrist to speak to the class about bedtime rituals and childhood sleep disorders. Prepare questions in advance.

Making Connections

1. **Math** Make a list of first-aid supplies that should be kept at home. Price out the products. Compare that cost with the cost of a first-aid kit.

2. **Writing** Using a catalog, choose three toys you think would be safe for an infant, a toddler, or a preschooler. Write a short description of each toy and explain what makes the toy safe.

3. **Reading** Read a book about first aid for children. Choose three first-aid tips you think would be most useful when caring for children, and share them with your class.

CAREER Link

Benefits.
When you're considering a job offer, you need to consider more than the salary. Fringe benefits, or extra benefits an employer provides for little or no cost, include vacation time, paid sick leave, and health insurance. Some employers also provide on-site child care as a benefit. Read about common benefits offered by employers. Which benefits do you think would be most important to working teens? Which do you think are most important to parents and guardians? Explain.

Understanding Parenting

Objectives

- Explain lifestyle, financial, and career changes related to parenthood.
- Give guidelines for responsible parenting.
- Identify the needs of children and how parents meet them.
- Summarize strategies for positive parenting.
- Demonstrate discipline techniques.

Vocabulary

- **parenting**
- **vaccines**
- **nurturing**
- **discipline**

Reading with Purpose

1. **As you read** Chapter 15, create an outline in your notebook using the colored headings.

2. **Write** a question under each heading that you can use to guide your reading.

3. **Answer** the question under each heading as you read the chapter. Record your answers.

4. **Ask** your teacher to help with answers you could not find in this chapter.

Considering Parenthood

How old were your grandparents when they had children? Chances are, they began their families at a young age. In the past, it was common for couples to marry and have children right after high school. Today, couples often wait until they are older, with established careers, before having children.

Fig 15-1

One of the best things you can do for your future children is to complete your education. Couples who finish school before starting a family have a head start on a successful life for themselves and their children.

These couples know that having a baby is the beginning of a lifelong commitment. They know that a child needs much physical care, financial support, love, and guidance until adulthood. Wise couples also know that once they become parents, they must put the needs and wants of their children first. See **Fig. 15-1**.

People have children for various reasons—and not all of them are good ones. For example, some people may feel pressure from family or friends to have children. Others have children because they want to feel loved and important. However, any potential parent needs to consider seriously whether the decision to have children is the right one.

The Parent Test

What if everyone had to pass a test before becoming a parent? Unfortunately, unlike driving a car, there is no test, license, or training required for parenting. Instead, for some people, parenthood happens with little or no preparation. Before deciding to have children, couples need to ask themselves the following questions and reflect carefully on their answers:

- Do we really want children? Are our reasons sound?

- Are we old enough and mature enough to be parents?

- Have we completed our education?

- Is our relationship as a couple mature and stable? Will it be able to withstand the challenges of parenthood?

- Do we have a good understanding of the principles of child growth and development?

- Are we ready to meet all of the needs of a child?

- Do we have enough money to support a family?

- Are we willing—and able—to make the long-term personal sacrifices needed to care for another person?

Lifestyle Changes

When a child is born or adopted into a family, parents have the unique experience of getting to know and love a new family member and the added responsibility of taking care of a child. A child brings many changes and adjustments to daily life. For example, a newborn infant must be fed every few hours—every day, around the clock. In addition, an infant needs diapering, bathing, positive interactions with others, love, and comfort. When you add a job and household tasks, it is easy to see why new parents have little time for themselves or each other. Movies, dinners out, and other entertaining activities the couple used to enjoy are often put on hold to care for the baby. See **Fig. 15-2**.

Fig 15-2 The responsibilities of parenting are different from responsibilities you have as a student. As a parent, you must take care of your child's needs in addition to your own.

Financial and Career Changes

Have you ever thought about how much it is costing your parents to raise you? Since you were an infant, your parents have provided you with clothing, food, health care, and shelter. If you attended a day care or preschool, they paid the bill. They probably purchased toys, books, and school supplies for you. If you ever played a sport, participated in an after-school activity, or went to camp, they likely paid the fees for you. Add all of these costs, and it is easy to see why parents must make financial sacrifices to meet their child's needs. Parents generally want to give their child every advantage possible.

Parenthood also affects parents' careers. People who worked overtime and weekends, or who traveled as part of their job, often find that their job interferes with their role as a parent. To keep up with their parenting tasks, they need to cut back on working hours or find another job, which might pay less than their current job does. One parent may need to stop working to care for the children, or alternatives may need to be developed. Plans may have to wait or be adjusted to accommodate the situation.

Challenges of Teen Parenthood

Think about your plans for yourself and your future. Where do you want to be five and ten years from now? Would having a child fit into your plans? Adolescence is a full-time job. Add pregnancy and the birth and care of an infant, and life becomes complicated. Under the best of circumstances, parenthood is full of challenges. When the parents are teens, they usually lack the money, education, emotional maturity, and skills to raise children. The time, energy, and money needed to raise a child are far greater than most teens can even imagine. See **Fig. 15-3**.

The majority of teen pregnancies are unplanned. As a result, many children are raised by teen parents who aren't ready for the responsibility or the emotional demands of parenting. Often the primary care of the child falls on the mother. Although some teen fathers take an active role in parenting, many don't live up to

Fig 15-3 Many times, teen parents are unable to assume full responsibility for the care of their children. Grandparents, or other extended family members, often return to the parenting role when they least expect it. What effects might this have on the children?

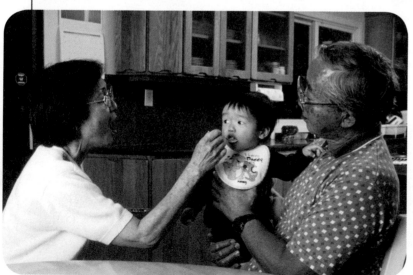

their fatherly responsibilities. Even when teen parents marry, it's unlikely the couple will remain married. If either parent drops out of school, the lack of a high school diploma can be a lifelong barrier to better-paying jobs. Many teen parents spend their lifetime working in low-paying or minimum wage jobs. All of these hardships can negatively affect children.

The happiest and healthiest children are those born to parents who honestly want and are ready for them. The decision to become a parent is a permanent one. A child's birth changes the lives of the parents—and their families—forever.

Parenting Responsibilities

It's hard not to smile when you see a baby. Babies are adorable, especially when they're clean, newly diapered, and wearing cute clothes. It's easy to see them as cuddly little dolls to hold and love. Many people only see the charming side of babies and have little or no understanding of what parenting involves. **Parenting**, the process of caring for children and guiding their growth and development, is incredibly demanding work.

Parenting Education

Parenting requires knowledge of child growth and development. It also requires teaching, counseling, and even nursing skills. Large amounts of patience, understanding, and a sense of humor are needed, too. Unfortunately, many parents learn these difficult skills by trial and error. Taking time to learn them ahead of time can help. See **Fig. 15-4**.

Many school, hospitals, and community groups offer classes in parenting and child development. People can also gain parenting skills by working with or caring for children and by observing the interactions of responsible parents and their children. After they have children, people can continue their education by reading books, magazine articles, and online information about parenting. Your own parents may be a wealth of information.

Fig 15-4
Even simple parenting tasks can be challenging. Resources can help couples prepare for parenting before their children arrive.

TIPS

Read Aloud to a Child

Reading aloud helps build comprehension, memory, and critical thinking skills. It also shows the child that you value reading. Here are some ways to make the experience special:

▶ **Get close.** Let the child sit on your lap or cuddle next to you as you read aloud. Children who are comfortable and feel safe are more receptive to learning. Plus, the child will associate reading with the warm, positive feeling of being close to you.

▶ **Use voices and sounds.** Make stories more interesting by using silly voices for different characters, adding sound effects from the story, and varying the volume of your voice.

▶ **Make a point.** As you read, point to the words. This helps the child see that reading moves left to right and shows that speech is made up of individual sounds and words. Point out pictures, shapes, colors, and numbers on the page.

▶ **Do it one more time.** Although you may tire of reading the same story, repetitive reading helps a child recognize and remember words.

Meeting Children's Needs

Think about an infant or young child you know. What needs does the child have? Who meets his or her needs? All children have basic needs, and their parents or guardians must meet them. Food, clothing, and shelter are a few of the physical needs of children. Children also need plenty of rest, play, exercise, and medical care. Protection against common childhood diseases with vaccines is usually also provided. **Vaccines** are small amounts of disease-carrying germs introduced to the body so that the body can build resistance to a disease. Children receive vaccines for measles, mumps, chicken pox, and other diseases.

Children also need **nurturing**—the giving of love, affection, attention, and encouragement. When caregivers nurture children, they are fulfilling children's emotional and social needs. Nurturing makes children feel secure and accepted and gives them a sense of worth and confidence. It also helps them relate well to others. Children who learn to be comfortable with themselves can reach out to others more easily.

Because children begin learning as soon as they're born, caregivers must provide tools and learning opportunities to meet the developmental needs of children. How can parents and caregivers create a nurturing environment for children? How can they help children learn? Talk, read, and listen to children from the time they are born. Provide opportunities for children to play and learn. Take advantage of community resources, such as library story hours, children's museums, community-owned zoos, and petting farms, that help meet children's intellectual needs.

Positive Parenting

When people compliment you for doing what's right, how do you feel? You probably feel good and want to continue doing the right thing. This same idea is behind positive parenting, which helps children learn to behave in acceptable ways. Many people think of guidance or discipline only in terms of punishment. However, effective **discipline** helps children learn to get along with others and control their own feelings. Gradually, children begin to see why certain actions are right or wrong. They learn to manage their behavior and take responsibility for it. Here are some ways to practice positive parenting:

- **Give praise.** Children feel good about themselves when they receive genuine praise for appropriate behavior. They're also more likely to continue the behavior.

- **Set good examples.** Young children model, or imitate, what adults say and do. Modeling appropriate behavior often works better than long explanations about how a child should act. See **Fig. 15-5**.

- **Set clear limits.** By setting clear limits for behavior, children learn what is acceptable, appropriate, and safe for them to do.

- **Give simple explanations.** As children grow, they need simple explanations about expected behavior. When they have done something wrong, children need to know why it's wrong and what should be done instead. Messages must match a child's age and level of understanding. For example, with a younger child you might say, "Pet the dog," along with a simple demonstration. With an older child you could say, "It hurts the dog when you pull his ears. You have to be gentle to play with him."

Fig 15-5 Children are great imitators. They learn best by being shown what to do, rather than by simply being told. How would this characteristic affect your behavior around children?

Dealing with Misbehavior

Even the best children misbehave from time to time, and wise parents and caregivers are prepared to respond in an appropriate way. Caregivers should agree on discipline methods beforehand so that they respond in similar ways each time a child misbehaves. By not brushing off a child's misbehavior one day and punishing the child for the same action the next day, caregivers are consistent in their discipline. They show that they mean what they say.

Discipline should be immediate and fit the misbehavior. The goal is to help children learn suitable behavior. Knowing when to punish misbehavior can be tricky. A mistake is not misbehavior. Don't become angry with a child who drops a glass of juice because she lacks coordination. Instead, teach her how to carry a glass, and help her clean up the spill. A young child who draws on a wall may be experimenting with a new tool or trying out a big drawing board. In this case, you need to explain, not punish. If a child leaves something undone, ask him or her to return to the task to finish it. See **Fig. 15-6**.

Fig 15-6 Parenting children can often be overwhelming. Babysitting for parents can give them some much needed time away from their children.

Deliberate misbehavior calls for a reaction that fits a child's level of understanding and the misbehavior. Taking away a privilege, such as not allowing a child to go outdoors to play, is one way to deal with misbehavior. Having the child sit quietly without playing for a few minutes is another way. Caregivers can also ignore misbehavior. For example, if a child cries because he or she wants a toy at the store, caregivers can simply say, "No, we aren't buying toys today." The child learns that crying for something doesn't get the toy or the caregivers' attention.

It is important that parents continue to show the child that he or she is cared for but that the actions aren't acceptable. Be prepared to repeat your instructions and explanations many times. Young children don't realize that what applies to one situation also applies to another, similar situation. Above all, discipline should never be an outlet for an adult's anger or abuse. Physical and verbal responses to anger often occur because parents become frustrated with the responsibilities of parenthood—or with each other. See **Fig. 15-7**.

Fig 15-7 ▶ Parents can become frustrated. It is important that they refrain from disciplining their children when they are experiencing frustration.

Safety ✓ Check

If your emotions threaten to put a child at risk of physical or emotional harm, stop and do the following:

- If you're holding an infant, put the infant down in a safe place. Never shake an infant!

- Take several deep breaths. Then count slowly to ten.

- Have someone look after the child while you take a walk.

- Call a parent, a friend, relative, or religious leader. Ask how he or she deals with parenting a child while frustrated, fatigued, or angry.

- Check the Internet or phone book for social service and mental health agencies and crisis hotlines. Call and ask for help.

Sources of Help

Caring for children is demanding both physically and emotionally. Anyone who cares for children needs some time away on a regular basis. Many couples share child care so that the responsibility doesn't fall on one adult. Couples need time to themselves, too. If a paid babysitter isn't possible, family members and friends may be willing to help out with child care. Also, consider taking turns with other parents to care for each other's children.

Sometimes parents need help communicating with each other over parenting issues. Sometimes parents disagree about how to handle a situation or behavior. Learning conflict resolution skills helps many caregivers deal with problems brought on by the challenges of parenting. Most communities have state and local agencies that can help caregivers deal with child-rearing problems. Doctors, schools, places of worship, and support groups are also sources of help.

HOW TO BE A POSITIVE EXAMPLE

Don't look now, but you may be someone's role model. Even without becoming a parent, you can influence a child's growth and development. Children naturally imitate the speech, actions, and attitudes of other older family members. Encouraging children to follow your good example not only benefits them but also helps you. Setting a positive example now is good practice for when you start your own family as an adult. These guidelines can help:

- **Give reasons for your actions.** Examples are most effective when a child connects your behavior to your values. Enforcing a bedtime may seem unfair until you explain that you are respecting a parent's rule and how that rule is good for the child. Knowing your motives also helps you make sure they are good ones.

- **Admit your mistakes.** Would you trust someone who claims to never make mistakes? Children don't either. In contrast, letting children know that you sometimes fall short, just like they do, shows them that they don't have to be perfect to do well.

- **Be consistent.** As often as possible, make your words match your actions and your actions match your values. Children can tell when someone says one thing and does another. They become confused and lose confidence in the person.

grows socially and emotionally, so will the ability to give. These are behaviors instilled in children by example or by loving direction. You started with those same small steps.

- **Point to other role models.** Tell children why you admire your role models. Perhaps a parent taught you the importance of honesty, or you learned a solid work ethic from a favorite athlete.

- **Respect their limitations.** Expect no more than children are capable of. To you, generosity may mean giving half your lunch to a classmate. To a five-year-old, it means parting with one cracker from a whole box. As the child

TAKE **ACTION**

For the next three weeks, make a deliberate effort to set a good example in situations where children are present. Describe the effect on your actions and on your feelings about yourself.

Review & Activities

Chapter Summary

- Parenthood often results in lifestyle, financial, and career changes.
- Parenting is incredibly demanding and comes with many responsibilities.
- Parents encourage good behavior by praising children for good behavior, setting good examples, setting clear limits, and giving simple explanations.
- Effective discipline is immediate and fits the misbehavior.
- Many communities have resources that can help parents deal with the responsibilities of parenting.

Reviewing Key Terms & Ideas

1. List six questions couples need to ask themselves before deciding to have children.
2. Explain how parenthood often affects parents' careers.
3. What is **parenting**?
4. How can people learn parenting skills?
5. What are **vaccines**?
6. What physical needs do children have?
7. What is **nurturing**? Why is it important to children?
8. What can caregivers do to help children learn?
9. What is the goal of **discipline**?
10. List four strategies for positive parenting.

Thinking Critically

1. **Making a generalization.** When do you think is the ideal time for a married couple to have children? Why?
2. **Analyzing reasons.** How would you respond to a teen who says, "Babies are so cute. I want one of my own to play with"?
3. **Making predictions.** Think of some personal sacrifices that parents often make. Which of the sacrifices would be most difficult for you at this stage of your life?

Review & Activities

Applying Your Learning

1. **Career choices.** Use print or Internet resources to research careers related to child care. Make a list of the rewards of each career. Report your findings to the class.

2. **Family discussion.** Interview family members about which parenting experiences were the most rewarding to them. Which were the most challenging?

3. **Health analysis.** Research recommended and required vaccines in your community and state. Look for the most current information about vaccines. Discuss your findings with the class.

4. **Discipline skills.** Create three scenarios involving a preschooler who misbehaves. With a partner, demonstrate appropriate discipline techniques that address the behavior. Ask classmates for feedback.

5. **Anger management.** Interview a peer mediator, school counselor, religious leader, or mental health worker about ways that communication and conflict resolution skills can be used in parenting situations. Share your findings with the class.

Making Connections

1. **Math** Assume an infant consumes 3 ounces of formula every 2 hours, 24 hours a day. Find an ad or visit a store that sells baby formula. Determine the cost of baby formula for the infant for one week.

2. **Reading** Read recent articles on brain development in young children. Discuss with classmates how parents and caregivers can stimulate brain growth. Ask how brain growth can affect development and learning.

3. **Reading** Ask a librarian to recommend a book about positive parenting. Read the book and discuss what you learned with your classmates.

4. **Writing** Write a dialog between a parent or caregiver and a preschooler who has intentionally misbehaved. Be sure the adult uses appropriate discipline techniques.

CAREER Link

Setting Priorities. Most people have to prioritize, or rank tasks according to importance, every day. This can be a difficult task. People must set priorities at home and at work, especially if they have young children. Ask your parents, teachers, and other adults to share instances in which they set priorities. What are some ways they deal with work and family priorities that conflict with each other? Write a short report based on your interviews.

The Balancing Act

Objectives

- Discuss the importance of a balanced life.
- Create a plan to manage time.
- Apply work simplification techniques to save time and energy.
- Design a storage system to manage belongings.
- Describe strategies for managing stress.

Vocabulary

- **goal**
- **priorities**
- **obligations**
- **work simplification**
- **stress**

Reading with Purpose

1. **Read** the title of this chapter and describe in writing what you expect to learn from it.

2. **Write** each vocabulary term in your notebook, leaving space for definitions.

3. **As you read** Chapter 16, write the definition beside each term in your notebook.

4. **After** reading the chapter, write a paragraph describing what you learned.

The Importance of Balance

"Everything was going along just fine," said Rob. "I was passing all my courses, and I had just been selected for the soccer team. Then, all of a sudden, everything crashed in on me. Mom got real sick, and now she needs me to do more around the house and help with my little brother. I'm sleeping less, and I can't concentrate in school. I need to keep my grades up, but I can't seem to find time to study." Have you ever been in a situation like this?

A balanced life is important and difficult to achieve. Balance involves making wise use of your time and energy. When you achieve balance, your values and actions work in harmony. Balance gives you strength and confidence to meet life's demands.

When life shifts out of balance, as in Rob's situation, you may feel like your life is spinning out of control, with too many problems to solve, too many things to do, or too many decisions to make. A hectic schedule, too many commitments, and unrealistic expectations are just a few factors that can tip a life out of balance. Besides negative feelings, a loss of balance can cause fatigue, loss of appetite or overeating, disturbed sleep patterns, and difficulty concentrating.

Balancing Your Life

Regaining balance in your life isn't easy, but it is possible. A management plan can help you reach your goals. A **goal** is something you plan to do, be, or obtain. People who manage their resources, such as time and energy, accomplish more. See **Fig. 16-1**.

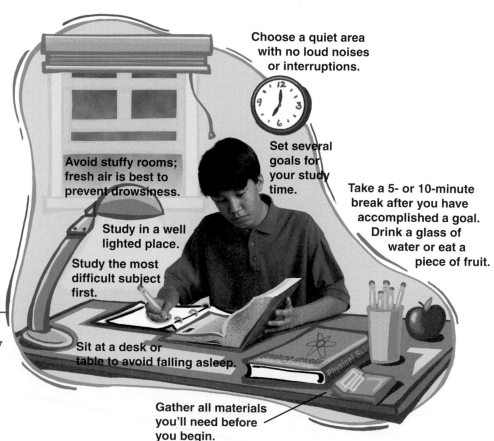

Choose a quiet area with no loud noises or interruptions.

Set several goals for your study time.

Take a 5- or 10-minute break after you have accomplished a goal. Drink a glass of water or eat a piece of fruit.

Avoid stuffy rooms; fresh air is best to prevent drowsiness.

Study in a well lighted place.

Study the most difficult subject first.

Sit at a desk or table to avoid falling asleep.

Gather all materials you'll need before you begin.

Fig 16-1
A management plan can help you organize your study time to finish schoolwork on time. In what other areas of life can a management plan be helpful?

The following steps will help you manage your life:

1. **Identify what's important.** Write down what you need to accomplish. Perhaps you need to do laundry, write an essay for school, and call one of your friends.

2. **Prioritize your tasks.** Look at your list. Which are your top priorities? **Priorities** are the things that are most important. Number the tasks, starting with "1" for the most important. For example, if writing the essay is most important, label it "1." Your last priority should have the highest number.

3. **Make a plan.** Decide how you're going to accomplish your tasks. Use tools, such as a day planner or calendar, to help you organize your plan. Also, list any resources you need, such as books for researching your essay.

4. **Put the plan into action.** Begin working on your tasks, starting with your highest priority.

5. **Evaluate the results.** Did you accomplish everything on your list? If not, what would you do differently next time?

Once you see positive results, the negative feelings will lessen, and your confidence will return. To maintain balance, keep your priorities. Staying focused will help you manage your resources.

Manage Your Time

Everything you do takes time. Do you ever say "yes" to activities, then wonder how you will find the time to do them? Having enough time for all you need and want to do isn't easy. You most likely have **obligations**, or things you must do, such as homework assignments, household chores, and after-school activities. Obligations often require most of your time. After you finish these obligations, you can spend what time you have left on other activities of your choice, such as your hobbies or favorite sports. By making the most of your time, you can accomplish most tasks yet maintain a balanced life. See **Fig. 16-2**.

Fig 16-2 ▶ Effective time management is key to meeting your goals. What time management skills do you currently use?

Time for Learning

You spend at least half of your waking hours at school or doing homework. Education is vital at this point in your life and for your future. To get the most out of your school-related hours, follow these suggestions:

• **Focus on learning.** This means paying attention and listening closely to your teacher and to class discussions. You have a better chance of understanding what is going on if you stay focused, especially if the subject matter is difficult.

HOW TO TAKE GOOD NOTES

The planning and organization that help you balance different aspects of your life are just as useful for taking notes for school. Taking good notes, in turn, streamlines studying. Taking good notes is more than repeating a teacher's words or lines in a book. It means writing the most important ideas in ways that help you remember and make connections among them. Try these tips for taking notes in class:

STEP 1 | **Get organized.** Use a divided, three-ring binder. This lets you neatly add or rearrange notes as needed. Date and label all notes. Preview or review the material to be covered. Jot down anything you don't understand and ask for clarification in class. Double or triple space your notes. Use the blank lines to answer questions or add new information.

STEP 2 | **Listen.** Use the listening skills described in Chapter 2. Listen and watch for the teacher's cues that signal important points. If a teacher repeats something or writes it on the board, it's probably worth remembering.

- **Take notes.** Good notes help refresh your memory when you study. Write down important points that are presented and discussed in class. Also write down assignments, instructions for doing them, and the dates they're due. If you are unclear about any information, ask questions.

- **Stay on top of homework.** You will get more out of class time if you do your homework as soon as you can each day. Also, start projects soon after they are assigned. A little work on a report every week until it is due will give you time to complete it and add quality to your work.

STEP 3 **Rewrite the main ideas.** Use your own words and add just enough details or examples to make them clear. Emphasize important ideas with stars, arrows, underlining, or a highlighter marker. Develop a system of shorthand. Just make sure you can understand your abbreviations when you review your notes.

STEP 4 **Create graphics.** Diagrams, pictures, tables, and charts can create "snapshots" that help fix the information in your mind.

STEP 5 **Read your notes.** Find a quiet place and review your notes later that day. Rewrite them only if needed to make them more understandable.

STEP 6 **You can adapt these steps to take notes from a text.** First read the material for understanding. Then review, looking for clues to main ideas, like section titles and boldface print. Rewrite them in your own words. Double-check your notes against the text.

TAKE ACTION

With a partner, practice the skills described here while watching a news program or reading a magazine article. Compare notes. Did your partner include points that you left out? Why did he or she decide they were important?

Time for Family, Friends, and Activities

"I wish I could join the jazz band, but I work in the library after school. That doesn't leave me time to practice." Like many people, Jerry cannot find the time to do all of the activities he would like, so he has to make a choice. For Jerry, being a library assistant is more valuable than being in jazz band. This experience gives him the additional skills necessary to fulfill his ultimate goal—a real job.

STEPS TO SUCCESS

I Can Manage My Time

You have the same amount of time each day—24 hours. In these hours, you need to squeeze in time to eat, sleep, go to school, do homework and household chores, work on hobbies, and spend time with your family and friends. These tips can help you manage your time and accomplish everything you need:

- **Start with a to-do list.** A to-do list helps you keep track of your responsibilities and goals. Write a list of tasks you need to accomplish each day, such as school assignments and chores. If a project on your list seems too big to handle, break it down into smaller tasks.

- **Determine your priorities.** Prioritize your to-do list. Put a "1" next to tasks that must be done, such as homework. Put a "2" next to tasks that should be done, such as making your bed. Put a "3" next to tasks you hope to do, such as playing disc golf with a friend.

- **Plan your schedule.** Record tasks that must be accomplished at a certain time, such as school assignments or doctor's appointments, on a calendar, on a personal digital assistant (PDA), or in a day planner. Be sure to give yourself enough time to accomplish each task. Check for any scheduling conflicts and resolve them immediately. Also, think of ways to overlap activities. For example, perhaps you can do your assigned reading on the bus or car ride home.

Almost everything you want and need to do requires time. It takes time to be a good family member or friend. Personal interests, such as hobbies, sports, exercise, and even relaxation require time. A little planning can help you do more of the things you need and want to do, without overscheduling your time.

Planning your time means you have to make choices based on what you value. If you value time with your brother, plan

plans. For instance, if your computer network goes down for several hours, finish your reading assignment while you wait for the computer to come back online.

- **Get things done.** As you finish a task, check the item off on your to-do list. Avoid procrastinating, or putting off what you need to do. Procrastination can cause stress, which in turn keeps you from accomplishing things. Instead of waiting until the zero hour to finish a project, do a little at a time. Also, be flexible. Anticipate problems and have backup

- **Keep the right attitude.** Be fair to yourself. Set realistic goals about what you can accomplish. If you set unrealistic goals, you set yourself up for failure. A good attitude begins with good health. Eat a nutritious diet and get plenty of sleep. When you're tired, even the easiest tasks can cause frustration. Good health will give you the energy to accomplish all of your goals and obligations.

an activity you both enjoy or just sit and talk. If you and a friend share an interest in sports, make plans to go to a game. Remember to make time for yourself, too. Creating time for yourself each day to read, listen to music, write in a journal, or exercise is important to help regain your sense of balance. Making time for yourself also helps you learn more about who you are and what is important to you.

Manage Your Energy

Jenna is an early riser. She is at her best in the morning and early afternoon. Maybe you're just the opposite. You may start slowly but pick up steam later at night. Like everyone else, you have a regular energy cycle. Try to schedule tasks that require alertness and energy when you are at your peak. You can increase your energy level in general by improving your health habits. Eat healthful foods, exercise regularly, and get enough rest. Check out Chapters 19 and 23 for more information about health, nutrition, and fitness.

Another important aspect of energy management is **work simplification**, or the easiest and quickest way to do a job well. By simplifying tasks, you save energy. Follow these guidelines to help conserve your energy as you work at home, at school, or in the workplace:

- **Analyze each job.** What are the steps you need to take to do a project? Can any steps in the process be omitted or combined?

- **Use the most appropriate tools for the job.** The right tools can save you time and frustration. A toothbrush might clean a floor, but it won't finish the job quickly. This same principle applies to almost any job.

- **Organize your workspace.** Place items you use frequently where you can easily reach them. Use free or inexpensive containers to separate items in drawers and on shelves.

Manage Your Possessions

Jared looked around his room. The closets and drawers were bulging with clothes, and the shelves were stuffed with papers and books. The computer equipment he bought last week was stacked in boxes on the floor, with CDs scattered around them. Jared let out a defeated sigh. "It will take me a year to find my brother's MP3 player in this mess."

Many people have experienced Jared's problem. They spend much time searching for items in cluttered and disorganized spaces. Locating items in sloppy spaces can also cause frustration. Taking charge and organizing what you own can ultimately help you save time, leaving you more time and energy for other activities.

To begin, take a mental tour of your room, noting places where you might eliminate some unused items. Assess clutter realistically. What items do you need? Set any needed items aside. If an item isn't necessary, decide whether or not you need to keep it. If you think you will want the item a year from now, keep it. Sentimental items, such as photos, and collectable items are usually worth keeping. Put all remaining items in a pile to be recycled, donated, sold, or discarded. See **Fig. 16-3**.

After reducing clutter, create or purchase an efficient storage system. Proper storage will help you feel more organized and will save you time. It can also reduce frustration and **stress**, or the pressure people feel as the result of their ability or inability to meet the expectations of others or themselves. Check out how some teens used storage to manage their belongings:

Fig 16-3 When you donate used items, you help others and yourself at the same time.

- **Frequently used items.** Put items you use often in the same place after each use. Have a spot designated for items. Make sure items are in view and easy to reach. This way you won't waste time looking and reaching for wanted items. Greg keeps his workout gear in a duffle bag in the mudroom. This way he can grab it on his way out the door. If he knows it is always in this spot, he can direct someone else to bring it to him if he is elsewhere.

- **Seldom-used items.** Store items you use less frequently in out-of-the-way places. Shannon's family camps out only once a year. Instead of storing camping gear in a closet, they keep the camping gear in the attic where it is out of the way.

- **Similar items.** Keep similar belongings, such as school supplies, craft items, hair care products, or sports equipment, in one place. Marla stores her gift-wrapping supplies in a labeled container under her bed. When she needs to wrap a friend's birthday gift, she's all set.

- **Papers and photos.** Develop a simple filing system for important papers and treasured photos. Emma uses an alphabetical system to file her papers, and Karen has begun making scrapbooks to keep her photos organized.

Fig 16-4
Balancing your life will help you manage stress. What can you do to gain more balance in your life?

The Stress Factor

Disorganization and unmanaged time and energy can lead to stress. The level of pressure varies with each situation. Participating in a hockey match might cause enough stress to motivate you to perform your best. Some situations, however, can cause overwhelming, negative stress. A family illness and intense academic pressure are just two causes of negative stress. This negative stress can cause you to feel pressured, frustrated, hopeless, jittery, or out of control. When negative stress begins to affect your health, schoolwork, and relationships, your life can quickly slip out of balance. If this happens to you, it's important to remember that you can manage your stress and regain balance. See **Fig. 16-4**.

To successfully manage stress, first identify the cause. Some sources of stress are easy to identify, such as a major exam or a piano recital. Others may be less obvious. For example, you may feel uncomfortable talking to classmates who frequently pressure you to give them answers on unfinished homework. That uncomfortable feeling causes you constant stress.

The next step in a stress management strategy is to take action. If the stress is caused by an event, such as an exam, prepare yourself. Not only will the preparation help you do your best, but it will keep your mind busy, so that you don't become occupied with worry and anxiety. After the event ends, the stress will probably go away.

If the stress is caused by something other than a specific event, such as pressure from a friend or a difficult class, the stress might not go away completely. However, you can keep it to a low level. If you can avoid the situation or person, do so as much as possible. Removing yourself from the situation will help decrease stress.

You can also try to change the way you perceive or react to the stress. Rethinking, or gaining a new perspective on, a stressful situation can help you make it a learning opportunity rather than a threat. For example, instead of thinking of math as too difficult to learn, think of it as an interesting puzzle to figure out. Other effective ways to manage stress include exercising, getting plenty of rest, and spending time with family and friends.

Get Support

Sometimes when life gets out of balance, people become overwhelmed and feel unable to cope. If this happens to you, reach out to people who care about you. Talk to a family member, close friend, favorite teacher, counselor, coach, or religious leader. Share your concerns and ask for help when you need it. See **Fig. 16-5**.

Keeping a sense of balance in your life will require effort. Remembering your values and priorities, managing your time and stress, and getting support from others who care about you can help you maintain a balanced life.

Fig 16-5
Don't be afraid to ask for support when you need it. Many adults, including your parents or guardians, have experienced a loss of balance and can relate to your feelings.

TIPS
Control Test Anxiety

Have you ever studied thoroughly for an exam only to panic and freeze up after the first question? If so, test anxiety is to blame. These tips can help you get through an exam without all of the test-related stress:

▶ **Study properly.** Studying over time helps you retain information. Facts that have been crammed in your brain right before a test usually don't stay long enough to get you through exam time.

▶ **Test yourself.** Use the same method your test will use. If the test is multiple choice, ask a family member or friend to ask you multiple-choice questions.

▶ **Think positively.** Don't let negative thoughts put you in a panic. You might not know all of the answers on a test, but with preparation, you can know most of them.

▶ **Prepare physically.** Get plenty of rest the day before a test, and eat a healthy breakfast before school. Also, take short breaks during the test if possible.

16

Review & Activities

Chapter Summary

- Balance involves making wise use of your time and energy.
- By making the most of your time, you can accomplish most tasks yet maintain a balanced life.
- Work simplification is a very important part of energy management.
- People who manage their belongings effectively have more time and energy to concentrate on other activities.
- Stress varies with each situation.
- Some stress goes away after an event ends. Other stress is continuous and must be managed.

Reviewing Key Terms & Ideas

1. What does balance involve?
2. What are **priorities**? Why are they important in maintaining balance?
3. Define **obligations**.
4. What does it mean to be focused on learning?
5. Why is time alone important?
6. How can you increase your energy level?
7. Define **work simplification**.
8. List some negative effects of clutter and disorganization.
9. What is **stress**?
10. Who can teens turn to if they are unable to cope with an out-of-balance life?

Thinking Critically

1. **Analyzing behavior.** What would you do if you were granted 1,000 hours to spend exactly as you chose? What values are reflected in your answers?
2. **Drawing conclusions.** Think about the following saying: "You don't own your possessions. Your possessions own you." What do you think this means?
3. **Defending positions.** Which do you think is more important, managing time or managing stress? Explain your position.

Review & Activities

Applying Your Learning

1. **Life skills.** List the tasks you want or need to accomplish for one day. Do not prioritize them. At the end of the day, check your list, noting which tasks you accomplished, which you put off, and which you forgot. At the beginning of the next day, repeat the exercise but prioritize your tasks. At the end of the day, compare your lists. Which system worked best?

2. **Homework schedule.** Create a homework schedule for one month, using a calendar or spreadsheet. Try to do homework as soon as possible after school. Was your homework finished on time? How did the schedule affect the quality of your work?

3. **Scheduling technology.** Investigate PDAs, cell phone calendars, or scheduling software. Use the technology for a week, if possible. In your opinion, are technical scheduling methods better or worse than paper calendars?

4. **Organization plan.** Use the information in this chapter to organize your belongings and clear clutter from your living space. Stick to your management plan for one week. How does an organized space help keep your life in balance?

5. **Stress management.** Interview three people about how they handle stress. Include a teacher or other adult, a classmate, and a family member. Ask them to suggest tips for coping with stress. Share the tips with the class.

Making Connections

1. **Reading** Read a book on time management and study strategies. Try three strategies from your reading that you think would help you improve your learning. How were your time management and study skills affected?

2. **Math** Record the amount of time you spend in each activity of your day, including school, time with friends and family, meals, and hobbies. Graph the results. What conclusions can you draw?

3. **Writing** Stress is a contributor to health problems. Research the effect of prolonged stress on the body. Write a short report of your findings.

CAREER Link

Work Ethic.
Employees who are committed and honest and who value their work are said to have a good work ethic. They choose to arrive promptly, work hard, and perform their best. Teens can also have a good work ethic by working hard in school and other activities and staying committed to their education. Reflect on your own work ethic. How often do you arrive on time to school and other events? How much effort do you put into your assignments?

Making Consumer Choices

Objectives

- Identify factors that influence consumer choices.
- Summarize the rights and responsibilities of consumers.
- Create a budget to meet financial goals.
- Practice procedures for using savings and checking accounts.
- Analyze the types and uses of credit.

Vocabulary

- **consumer**
- **income**
- **impulse purchases**
- **comparison shopping**
- **redress**
- **warranty**
- **budget**
- **expenses**
- **interest**
- **endorse**

Reading with Purpose

1. **Write down** the colored headings from Chapter 17 in your notebook.

2. **As you read** the text under each heading, visualize what you are reading.

3. **Reflect** on what you read by writing a few sentences under each heading to describe it.

4. **Continue** this process until you have finished the chapter. Reread your notes.

You, the Consumer

What was the last thing you bought? Maybe it was the haircut you received yesterday or the video game you picked up last weekend. Any time you pay for something, you're a consumer. A **consumer** is someone who buys and uses goods and services produced by others. As a teen, you are among a group of active consumers, whose total annual spending is in the billions of dollars! No matter how much money you spend, you will be more satisfied with your purchases if you make wise shopping decisions. See **Fig. 17-1**.

Becoming a Smart Shopper

How can you determine the right products and services to buy? How can you get the best price? Like any consumer, teens want the most value for their money. To become a smart shopper, you need to realize that each purchase involves a choice—a choice affected by many factors, including the following:

- **Your income.** Whether it's from a paycheck or an allowance, your **income**, or the amount of money that you receive, is the single most important factor that affects what you buy.

- **Your environment.** Your environment may affect your purchases. If you live in a cold climate, you need different kinds of clothing than people who live in a hot climate.

- **Your personal interests and values.** You choose to spend money on goods and services that you value and that interest you. Often clothing falls into this category.

Fig 17-1 You're a consumer not only when you buy goods but also when you purchase services, such as a haircut.

- **Your family and culture.** Each family and family culture has customs and traditions that influence how people shop and what people purchase.

- **Advertising.** Most advertising is designed to tempt you to buy something. Clever ads can make it easy to lose control of your purchasing decisions.

- **Peer pressure.** Keep in mind that you—not your friends—know what you need, want, and can afford.

Planning to Shop

Have you ever bought something and later decided it wasn't what you wanted? This is a common problem for many shoppers. One way to gain control of what you buy, and to be pleased with the results, is to develop a shopping plan.

What Do You Want and Need?

The most important part of a shopping plan is to figure out what to buy. Make your decisions based on your needs and wants—with your values and resources in mind. For example, Thomas needs a baseball glove. He knows if he buys the glove, he won't have enough money to pay for a movie Friday night. Because Thomas values his performance on his baseball team, he's buying the glove and skipping the movie.

A shopping plan can help you resist **impulse purchases**, or items you buy without thinking them through. Felicia saw some earrings she liked and immediately bought them. When she got home, she realized the earrings didn't match any of her outfits. The money Felicia impulsively spent on earrings was money she could have saved for something else. See **Fig. 17-2**.

Where Can You Find Product Information?

Smart consumers research products they plan to buy. What sources of product information are available? One of the best sources is other consumers. Ask friends and relatives about their experiences with certain goods or services. Written material from manufacturers, available either online or in print, can be another source of valuable information.

Consumer magazines, such as *Consumer Reports*, test and rate different brands for quality, safety, and price. Check for them at local libraries or at newsstands. You can use consumer information for **comparison shopping**, or comparing products, prices, and services to get the most value for the money.

TIPS
Look Before You Buy

You're more likely to be happy with your purchases if you follow these steps:

▶ **Inspect a product's quality.** Check to see how well the item is made. For example, look inside or on the bottom of products you're considering. Don't let the outside be the only part you examine.

▶ **Look at the price tag.** Is the product worth its cost? Can you find a better buy? Remember, a high price tag doesn't always mean good quality.

▶ **Check to see whether it is a name brand or a store brand.** Name brands usually cost more than store brands. The quality of store brands is often equal to that of name brands, but the price is usually much lower.

▶ **Read product labels.** Labels can give information that may affect your buying decisions. Does the garment require dry cleaning? Does it have to be hand-washed?

▶ **Find out if the product has a warranty.** If so, read it carefully and fully understand all of its conditions.

Fig 17-2 Many of the choices consumers make reflect their interests. How do your interests affect the way you spend your money?

Government and consumer organizations also provide consumer information. The Consumer Product Safety Commission is a government agency that provides information about the safety of various products. The Better Business Bureau (BBB) is an organization supported by businesses that follow ethical practices. You can use the BBB Web site to locate a reputable business near you.

Product advertisements—in print, online, or on the radio—can alert you to sales, which help save you money. Read and listen to all ads carefully. Some ads can be misleading. Don't rely on them as your only information source.

When Will You Buy?

Knowing when to shop can be as important as deciding what to buy. Smart shoppers plan their purchases to coincide with sales. For instance, end-of-season summer clothing sales are often held in July or August. Sales also occur around major national holidays. See **Fig. 17-3**.

Teens Speak About Products Generating Ideas

Annie slipped into the seat next to her friend in the cafeteria. "Another catalog?" she asked.

Gabrielle looked up from the pictures of clothing. "It's full of retro styles, from the 1930s. They are so cool. Look at the bangles on this dress."

Annie peered at the photo. "Look at the price on that dress. Where's the catalog from?"

Gabrielle showed her the catalog cover. "I've never heard of this business. But then, I had never heard of most of the places I ordered from—until I got their catalogs. I always try to check them out before I buy."

"That's smart," Annie said. "But can you pay that much?"

Gabrielle stuffed the catalog in her backpack. "No way. But it's fun to look. And sometimes I get ideas for sewing projects."

Annie raised her brows. "I can see Ms. Meyerhoff's face if you showed her that dress. And where would you buy 20 feet of bangles?"

Gabrielle grinned. "I get a catalog . . ."

Teen Connection

As a class, list some favorite local places for teens to shop. Discuss why these stores are popular. How do you think store managers have made the shops appealing to teens? How does understanding these techniques help you as a consumer?

Fig 17-3
Smart shoppers search for the lowest price before they purchase an item. What techniques do you use to compare prices?

Where Will You Buy?

Consumers have more shopping options than ever before. Deciding where to shop depends on what you want to buy and the price you are willing to pay. Depending on where you live, you might have some or all of the following shopping options:

- **Department stores** sell a variety of products and may offer a number of customer services, such as gift wrapping and delivery.

- **Mail-order companies** sell items you can order from a catalog and have sent to you. Remember to add shipping and handling fees, and in some cases sales tax, to mail-order items. You may also have to pay shipping fees if you return items.

- **Specialty stores** usually sell one type of merchandise, such as sporting goods or shoes. They offer a wide selection of these products but sometimes charge more than other stores.

- **Discount stores** buy in large quantities and limit the number of customer services. One benefit of discount stores is lower prices.

- **Factory outlets** are manufacturers' stores that sell products directly to shoppers. Prices may be lower than those at department stores. Some items may be seconds, with slight imperfections, or they may be discontinued.

Safety ✓ Check

When shopping, take the following safety precautions.

- Keep your bag or wallet closed and close to your body.

- Stay alert while shopping. Tell a security guard or call your parents or guardians if you notice someone following you or acting suspiciously.

- Shop during daylight hours. If you need to shop at night, don't go alone. Go with family members or friends.

- Check the car before climbing in. Look under the car and in the back seat to make sure no one is hiding there.

- Lock your car doors and put packages in the trunk or out of sight.

- **Warehouse clubs** charge lower prices than most supermarkets or department stores because they buy in bulk and offer little or no services. They also charge a membership fee.

- **Electronic shopping** options are available through television shopping channels or on the Internet. Generally, you need a credit card for electronic shopping. Some Web sites will accept personal checks.

HOW TO PROTECT PERSONAL IDENTITY

With today's technology, a thief can take your money and ruin your reputation without your knowing it. Identity thieves illegally obtain and use someone else's personal information, such as name, date of birth, and Social Security or bank account numbers. With this information, thieves can raid savings and run up debts in the victim's name. Fortunately, a few simple steps can help families protect personal identity:

- **Secure your mail.** Drop mail in a public collection box, rather than leaving it in your house or apartment mailbox. If you go on vacation, ask a trusted friend to pick up your mail while you're gone or ask the post office to hold it.

- **Keep personal information private.** Give personal information only when initiating contact with reputable companies—to sign up for cable service, for instance. Never give this information to someone who calls or e-mails and asks for it.

- **Properly dispose of documents.** Tear or shred papers such as bills and bank statements.

- **Other shopping alternatives**, such as thrift stores, garage and yard sales, flea markets, auctions, and swap meets, often sell merchandise for low prices. These shopping options usually have no customer service, and items are sold "as is," which means you are purchasing them with flaws. "As is" items are generally nonreturnable.

- **Watch the mail for regular bills.** Contact utility or credit card companies if bills are late, and always look them over right after receiving them to check for any unusual charges.

- **Choose creative passwords.** Letter and number combinations make the best passwords. Don't choose obvious words and numbers—birth dates and names of family members aren't the best choices.

- **Protect computers from viruses.** Install a virus protection program from a reputable software vendor. Avoid buying "spyware" protection software from pop-up ads. These may actually install the spyware, which tracks your Internet use. Update protection software regularly.

- **Secure wireless computer connections.** If your wireless home computer is not secure, strangers can read your files and steal your information. Most wireless equipment comes with built-in security features that you need to turn on.

TAKE **ACTION**

Read the privacy policy on a Web site you visit regularly. (Look for a link at the top or bottom of the Web page.) What information about users does the company gather? How does it use this information? How does it protect against identity theft? Do you think these measures are adequate?

Your Consumer Rights and Responsibilities

Have you ever returned an item to a store because it didn't work or was broken? If so, you practiced one of your consumer rights. As a consumer, you have the following rights, which are protected by state and federal law:

- **The right to safety.** Consumers are protected against sales of products that endanger life or safety.

- **The right to be informed.** Consumers should be protected against dishonest advertising, labeling, or sales practices. Businesses must give consumers honest and relevant facts about goods and services.

- **The right to choose.** There should be a choice of goods and services available at fair and competitive prices. Businesses are forbidden to take actions that limit competition.

- **The right to be heard.** Consumers have a right to speak out about consumer laws.

- **The right to redress. Redress** is the right to have a wrong corrected quickly and fairly. See **Fig. 17-4**.

- **The right to consumer education.** All consumers are entitled to information about consumer issues.

- **The right to service.** Consumers have the right to expect courtesy, convenience, and responsiveness from a business.

With every right, there is a responsibility. For example, with your right to information about products and their safety is your responsibility to learn about products and to use them safely—according to the manufacturers' directions. Some other responsibilities include the following:

- **Being fair and honest with stores.** As a consumer, you are expected to take care of merchandise you handle or try on. You are also required to pay for your purchases. If you don't pay, you are stealing, which is punishable by the law, and you can be sent to jail.

Fig 17-4 Be calm and polite when returning an unsatisfactory item to a store. Most problems between consumers and businesses can be resolved fairly easily.

Fig 17-5
Always review your product information after you purchase an item and file it for future use.

- **Paying attention while a sales transaction is taking place.** When you check out, you should watch the register to make sure the price is correct. If you paid with cash, count the change you get back. If you receive too much change, you are responsible for returning it.

- **Saving sales receipts, instructions, and guarantees.** It's your responsibility to furnish these materials as proof of purchase if you return an item. See **Fig. 17-5**.

Resolving Consumer Problems

Have you ever paid for a service that wasn't performed correctly? Or paid for a product and later found out the store overcharged you? Most consumer problems involve refunding a customer's money or replacing a purchased product. Whenever you need to resolve a consumer problem, the following steps may prove helpful:

1. **Check your warranty.** A **warranty** is a guarantee that a product will work properly for a specific length of time unless misused or mishandled by the consumer. If your problem is covered by a warranty, follow the warranty instructions for service. If the product has no warranty, or if the problem isn't covered in the warranty, take the product and your records to the store's customer service department. If your problem isn't resolved, politely ask to speak to the manager.

2. **Write the manufacturer.** If your trip to the store doesn't resolve the problem, put your complaint in writing. Briefly state the problem and the solution you think is fair. Include your name, address, and telephone number, as well as copies of your receipt and warranty.

3. **Take further action.** If your letter doesn't bring results, you may contact the BBB to help you resolve the problem. As a last resort, you may choose to go to small claims court. In this type of court, you present your complaint before a judge, and the business involved must respond within a certain period.

Character Check ✓

Practice Honesty

- **Do the right thing.** Sometimes being honest is not the easiest thing to do, but it is the right thing to do. If you've done something wrong, own up to it. It will be out in the open, and you will be able to move on.

- **Small lies add up.** Small lies might seem harmless, but they can hurt others. Your lies might cost you your friend's trust. Instead of lying, don't say anything.

- **You are enough.** When getting to know new people, you do not need to exaggerate or make up stories about yourself. Tell people about the real you. When you make a point to interact honestly with someone else, you experience a real connection.

Managing Your Money

Money is an important resource that must be managed. Some people manage money with ease. They make smart purchases and save money with seemingly little effort. For others, money management requires discipline. Saving money for a future goal means cutting back on spending, which can be difficult. A budget can help. See **Fig. 17-6**.

Fig 17-6 ▶ Understanding Your Paycheck

When budgeting, it's important to understand your paycheck. When you are paid, look at the pay stub carefully and make sure it's correct.

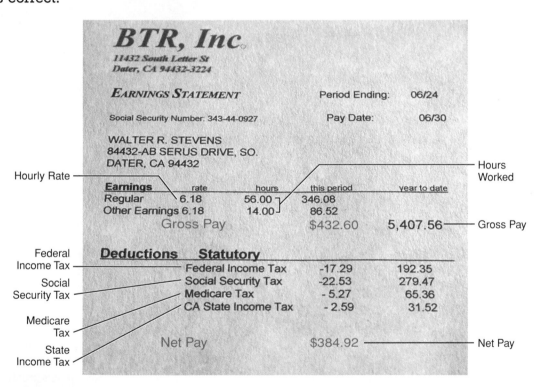

- ▶ **Hours worked.** This is the number of hours you worked during a pay period.

- ▶ **Gross earnings.** This is the total amount of money you earned during the pay period.

- ▶ **Deductions.** These are monies subtracted from your gross pay. Tax deductions for federal, state, and local income taxes may be included. Other government deductions known as Social Security and Medicare use the abbreviation FICA.

- ▶ **Net pay.** This is the amount of your check.

Create a Budget

A **budget** is a plan for spending and saving the money you have available. When you make a budget, you make a plan for saving and spending your money in ways that will fulfill your needs and wants and help you meet a goal. See **Fig. 17-7**.

To make the best use of your budget, first identify your most important expenses. **Expenses** are the goods and services you purchase. Using paper and pencil or a computer spreadsheet program, list your expenses in order of importance, deciding which are needs and which are wants. Then take steps to make your budget a reality:

1. Record your expected income during the period of your budget. For example, if your budget is for one month, write down all of the money you will receive in that time.

2. Write down your planned expenses. This information should reflect your most important goals.

3. Subtract your expenses from your income. Do you have enough money to pay for all of your planned purchases? If not, you will need to cut back on your spending.

4. Review your budget periodically to see how it's working. If you allowed too much or too little for some budgeted items, readjust your plan. If you forgot one or more expenses, include these as you update your budget.

Fig 17-7
Managing money is easier when you keep a simple financial record and update it frequently.

Using Financial Services

Financial institutions, such as banks, credit unions, and savings and loan associations, offer checking and savings accounts. These accounts help you manage your money in a safe place. Financial institutions offer a variety of services. Some services are free, and some cost money. Before opening an account, compare the fees and services of different institutions. Is "free checking" really free?

Savings Accounts

Saving money is important. Many people open a savings account to save for a major goal, such as a college education, a vacation, or a car. People also save for emergencies, such as home repairs.

You can earn money simply by putting your money in a savings account. Savings accounts earn **interest**, or money a financial institution pays customers at regular intervals. The interest is a certain percentage of the amount in your savings. For example, if you have $500 in a savings account that earns 1 percent interest, you would earn $5 during one interest period.

You may deposit cash or checks into your savings account using a deposit slip. Before depositing a check, you must **endorse** it, or sign your name on the back. This transfers your right to the check over to the bank, which deposits it in your account. You can withdraw money from your savings account when you need it. However, you must maintain a certain amount in the account to keep it open. To take out money, complete a withdrawal slip. See **Fig. 17-8**.

Checking Accounts

Another type of financial account is a checking account. Checking accounts allow you to pay with checks, instead of cash. A check is a written order to a financial institution to pay a specific amount of money. To write checks, you must deposit money in your account. Checking accounts are convenient. Carrying cash can be unsafe, and cash sent through the mail can be stolen. Bills are often paid using checks.

Fig 17-8 Some banks require a deposit slip each time you deposit money.

Commercial National Bank

Member Midwest Financial Group, Inc.
ANYTOWN, USA

DATE _____ Oct. 22 _____ 20 07

DEPOSITS MAY NOT BE AVAILABLE FOR IMMEDIATE WITHDRAWAL

SIGN HERE FOR LESS CASH IN TELLER'S PRESENCE

JANE SMITH
12235 LAKE FOREST DR.
ANYTOWN, USA

099:5600 250000: 223 0007 289394

DEPOSIT TICKET
70-4
711

CASH	CURRENCY	15	00
	COIN		
CHECKS LIST CHECKS SINGLY	70-8/711	27	63
TOTAL CHECKS FROM OTHER SIDE			
TOTAL		42	63
LESS CASH RECEIVED			
NET DEPOSIT		42	63

CHECKS AND OTHER ITEMS ARE RECEIVED FOR DEPOSIT SUBJECT TO THE PROVISIONS OF THE UNIFORM COMMERCIAL CODE OR ANY APPLICABLE COLLECTION AGREEMENT.

**Fig 17-9**

If you lose your checks or they are stolen, contact the bank immediately to cancel the checks and protect your account.

When you open a checking account, you agree to certain terms, or rules. One term is to pay any charges applied to your account. You also agree to not write checks for more money than you have available. If you write checks for more money than you have in your account, the account will be overdrawn. Institutions charge a fee for over-drawn, or "bounced," checks. They may also send a check back to the business that presented it for payment, causing you embarrassment and additional charges. For these reasons, it pays to keep careful track of your account.

Using a Checkbook

You receive a checkbook when you open a checking account. A checkbook contains two important features:

- **Checks.** Always fill these out in ink, as needed. Write the date and name of the person or business you are paying. Then write the amount, first in figures and then in words. Make sure the amount in figures is the same as the amount written in words. Sign the check. See **Fig. 17-9**.

- **Check register.** This small booklet is used to keep a record of your account. Each time you make a deposit or withdrawal of any type, you record the date, the amount, and the check number if the withdrawal was by check. Then adjust your balance, or the total amount in your account. To adjust the balance for deposits, add the deposit to the balance in your register. To adjust for withdrawals, subtract the withdrawal from the balance showing. The result is your new balance. Addition and subtraction are the only math skills needed to use a checkbook. Be sure to double-check all calculations!

Using Debit and ATM Cards

Many people with bank accounts use debit cards and auto-matic teller machine (ATM) cards. A debit card can be used to withdraw cash from an ATM machine or to make a purchase in a store. An ATM card can only be used for ATM withdraw-als. When you use a debit or ATM card to withdraw cash or

Safety ✓ Check

When using an ATM:

- Only use ATMs located in well-lit public places, and be aware of the surroundings, especially at night.

- Fill out deposit slips and have your card ready before approaching the ATM.

- Protect your privacy by positioning yourself in front of the ATM keyboard. This will help prevent someone from observing your personal identification number (PIN).

- If you make a withdrawal, put your money away immediately and take your receipt with you.

- Cancel your transaction at the first sign of suspicious activity. Take your card and leave.

- If someone follows you after you leave the ATM, go to a heavily populated, well-lit area immediately and call the police.

Control Credit Card Use

Credit cards can cause serious money problems. Whether the credit card belongs to you or your parents or guardians, the following tips can help you keep the credit card bill low:

▶ **Set limits.** Use your budget or talk to your parents or guardians to determine how much you can spend. Then stick to your limit.

▶ **Save your receipts.** Total your receipts after shopping to make sure you haven't overspent. Verify the credit card statement's accuracy using the receipts.

▶ **Keep your card to yourself.** Never let friends use your card, even if they say they will pay you back. Also, keep passwords private.

▶ **Get help.** If you overcharge, be honest with your parents or guardians. Tackling credit card debt is not easy, but if you let it go your bill will only increase with interest and late fees.

to make purchases, you are using your own money at your financial institution. When you use a debit card to make a purchase, the amount of your purchase is transferred electronically from your checking account to the store's account.

Many people use debit cards in place of cash or checks. Always make sure to keep your receipts from purchases or withdrawals and record them in your checkbook register. Compare the receipts with the information on your monthly statement. This will help you check the accuracy of your statement, as well as identify any unauthorized purchases. If your card is lost or stolen, you may be responsible for charges made on the card. Report a lost or stolen debit card to your bank immediately!

Reading Financial Statements

Your financial institution will keep records of your account and send them to you. These records, called statements, list checks that have been paid, deposits that have been made, and fees that have been charged. Some banks allow you to view your statements online. Keep all statements and any check copies sent to you. They serve as proof of purchases you have made.

When you receive your statement you need to reconcile your account, or make sure your own records and the bank statement are in agreement. This process is similar to balancing your check register. See **Fig. 17-10**.

Understanding Credit

Credit allows people to buy things now and pay for them later. Sometimes using credit is a good decision. For example, it would take most people years to save enough cash to pay the entire cost of a college education. Using credit makes large purchases possible. Consumers have several credit options:

- **Cash loans** are usually used to pay for large items, such as cars or homes. With loans, you borrow money from financial institutions or loan companies and pay the loan back in specific amounts.

- **Sales credit** allows you to charge a purchase and pay the store for it over time.

- **Credit cards** are the most widely used type of credit. Credit cards can be used to pay for goods and services in person, over the phone, or online. Financial institutions that issue credit cards require minimum monthly payments.

Fig 17-10

Reconciling Bank Statements

To reconcile your checkbook register with your account statement, do the following:

1. Write down the last balance shown on your checking account statement.

2. Total the deposits you've made that don't appear on the statement. Add this total to the amount that appears on your statement.

3. Make a list of checks that you've written that don't appear on the statement. These are called outstanding checks. Total all of these checks.

4. Subtract the total of your outstanding checks from the total you reached in Step 2. This amount should agree with the balance in your checkbook register.

The Costs of Credit

Using credit costs money. In addition to the money you owe, you pay the lender interest. Unless you pay the total of your credit card bill on time each month, you must pay interest. The interest is usually high. That's how credit card companies make money. Fees are charged if payments aren't made on time. Credit is easy to use and misuse. Credit card bills can quickly increase, and people can sink into serious credit trouble. For this reason, use credit only when necessary.

17

Review & Activities

Chapter Summary

- Every purchase involves a choice that is affected by certain factors.
- Consumers have certain rights and responsibilities that are protected by law.
- Good money management means not spending more than you can afford. It also means planning for future spending goals.
- A budget helps you make the most of your money.
- Before opening a savings or checking account, compare fees and services of different institutions.
- Credit allows you to buy now and pay later. However, there are certain costs when you use credit.

Reviewing Key Terms & Ideas

1. What factors influence the choices a **consumer** might make?
2. What is **income**?
3. What are **impulse purchases**?
4. Define **comparison shopping**.
5. List four shopping options available to consumers.
6. What is **redress**?
7. What is a **warranty**?
8. List three steps to resolve a consumer problem.
9. What is a **budget**?
10. Define **expenses**.
11. From what type of bank account might you receive **interest**?
12. What does it mean to **endorse** a check?

Thinking Critically

1. **Analyzing behavior.** Excluding your income, what factors do you think influence your consumer choices the most? Explain.
2. **Making comparisons.** Think of two similar purchases you made in the past year, such as two clothing items. Which would you consider the better buy? Why?
3. **Drawing conclusions.** Many people have trouble sticking to a budget. Why do you think this is so?

Review & Activities

Applying Your Learning

1. **Ad analysis.** Bring advertisements from newspapers, magazines, and other print sources to class. Do any of the ads target teens? How can you tell? How do you think the ads persuade consumers?
2. **Consumer research.** Read an article of your choice in a consumer magazine, such as *Consumer Reports*. What value does the article have for consumers?
3. **Life simulation.** With a partner, enact a scenario in which a consumer is unhappy with a purchase and is trying to resolve the problem with a store manager. Ask the audience for feedback.
4. **Budget creation.** List the expenses you currently have. Imagine you receive $25 each week in allowance money. Create a budget that allows you to save $20 each month, leaving the rest for expenses.
5. **Budget software.** Compare several budget software programs. Consider their ease of use and cost. Give reasons why you would choose one program over the others.
6. **Account comparisons.** Find ads for checking accounts offered by a local financial institution. Compare the costs and features of each type of checking account offered. Select the account that you think fits your needs. Share your reasons for your selection.

CAREER Link

Managing Your Money.
One of the most important steps you can take to prepare for your future is to learn to manage your money well. Arrange to talk to a banking professional or a financial adviser. Ask about methods of saving and the best use of credit. Summarize what you learned in a short report.

Making Connections

1. **Reading** Read product brochures and consumer magazine articles about two items you would like to purchase. Based on your reading, which product seems the better value?
2. **Writing** Imagine you purchased a computer that stopped working after only one week. The warranty does not cover the problem, and the store manager will not refund your money. Write a letter of complaint to the manufacturer to resolve the problem.
3. **Math** Research interest rates for savings accounts at several local financial institutions. Calculate the amount of interest you would earn in one interest period if you deposited $200. Use the following formula:

$200 × (percentage of interest) = interest earned

Living with Technology

Objectives

- Discuss the benefits of technology.
- Identify the drawbacks of technology.
- Plan strategies for technology management.

Reading with Purpose

1. **As you read** Chapter 18, create an outline in your notebook using the colored headings.

2. **Write** a question under each heading that you can use to guide your reading.

3. **Answer** the question under each heading as you read the chapter. Record your answers.

4. **Ask** your teacher to help with answers you could not find in this chapter.

Vocabulary

- **technology**
- **video teleconferencing**
- **cost-effective**
- **hybrids**
- **obsolete**
- **identity theft**
- **repetitive stress injuries**

A Look at Technology

Imagine a world in which phones, televisions, and computers don't exist. There are no cameras, no stereos, no DVD players, no MP3 players, and no movies. It's not unlike the world a little more than a century ago. Today, it's hard to imagine a life without technology. **Technology**, the application of science to help people meet needs and wants, is everywhere. It includes time-saving, energy-saving, and life-saving devices.

TIPS

Put Your Technology Skills to Work

Are you computer savvy? If so, you may be able to earn extra money by using some of your computer skills. Consider the following options:

▶ **Install software programs.** People new to computers often need help setting them up and installing new software.

▶ **Create Web sites.** If possible, use a digital camera to enhance the Web sites with photos.

▶ **Publish newsletters.** Many community groups need help designing and publishing newsletters.

▶ **Tutor other students.** Share your computer knowledge with others.

Although new advances continually occur, technology itself isn't new. Technology has been advancing for thousands of years, from simple stone tools to complex spacecraft. Throughout history technology has affected the lifestyle of many people in positive ways, and it will continue to do so. The effect of technology can be complicated. Your role as a technology user is to understand the benefits and drawbacks of this important resource. See **Fig. 18-1**.

Benefits of Technology

Sharla used to spend hours writing assigned essays. Each assignment meant piles of wadded up drafts in her trash can. This year has been different. Sharla learned to use her computer's word processing software. She can now delete and rewrite words with no wasted paper, and the printed assignments are much neater than her handwritten versions. By using technology, Sharla is saving energy, time, and money—and her grades reflect the change.

Like Sharla, many people experience the benefits of technology every day. Technology positively affects almost all aspects of life, including the following:

• **Communication.** Cell phones, telephones, instant messaging, e-mail, fax machines—communication technology seems almost endless. People today have more methods of talking to each other than ever before. They can also learn

Fig 18-1
Thinking about future technology can be exciting. The creativity of scientists, engineers, designers, and others results in many new products.

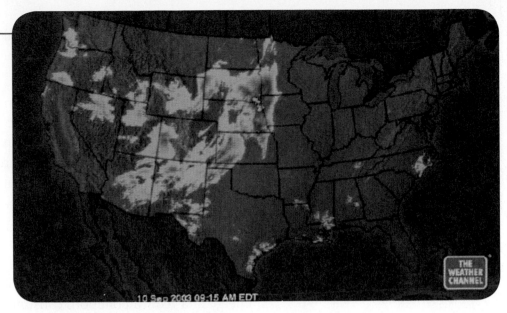

Fig 18-2
Advanced tracking systems monitor storms, tornadoes, flash floods, and hurricanes. Up-to-the-minute reporting can help keep you safe in dangerous weather conditions.

about events as they unfold around the world through television, radio, and Internet news. Businesspeople have also benefited from communication technology. In the past, people had to travel to do business with distant companies. Today they can use **video teleconferencing**, which enables people in different locations to see and hear each other at the same time. Compared with face-to-face meetings, this method of meeting is often faster and more **cost-effective** (less expensive for the benefits produced).

• **Home and community safety.** Technology helps protect people, their property, and their community. Many homes have alarms to detect unauthorized entry, smoke, and carbon monoxide. Business owners use video cameras to record shoplifters, and police officers can use their vehicle's computer to access information about suspects. Weather technology helps communities around the world remain safe in the event of natural disasters, such as flash floods, hurricanes, tornadoes, and earthquakes. See **Fig. 18-2.**

• **Health care.** Technology is helping people live healthier and longer lives. Health care professionals use computerized tomography (CT) and magnetic resonance imaging (MRI) scans to detect diseases. With telemedicine—the use of streaming audio and video and robotics to perform medical procedures—doctors can treat patients without ever seeing them in person. At home, people can use the Internet to gather information about healthy lifestyle practices and specific medical conditions. Surgical procedures are performed with technology-filled equipment, such as scopes with microscopic cameras attached.

- **Transportation.** Technology has changed how we travel. Early automobiles did not have air conditioning, radios, DVD players, power windows, or turn signals. Today, radios are common features of vehicles, as are MP3, CD, and DVD players. Safety is another important automobile feature. Most vehicles today are equipped with air bags that inflate in a car crash to protect the driver and passengers. Global positioning systems in vehicles inform emergency personnel of a car's location in case of emergency or give drivers directions and shopping and restaurant options in any state. To conserve energy and reduce pollution, consumers can drive **hybrids**, vehicles that use a combination of electricity and fuel.

- **Home management.** Do you use a washing machine to wash clothes, or do you wash your clothes by hand? If you use a washing machine, you're benefiting from technology. Washing machines today are sophisticated. Some front loaders have a multitude of features and are extremely energy and water efficient. Other devices in the home save people time and energy. Smart refrigerators track their contents and print grocery lists. Some products cool and cook. Newer microwaves can read package information to program themselves. With home monitoring systems, people can control their home's appliances and lighting from anywhere in the world.

- **Entertainment.** Satellite television and radio, gaming stations, and home theaters provide endless hours of entertainment at home with just the touch of a button. Outside the home, global positioning systems are used for geocaching, a real-life treasure-seeking game. With wireless technology, it is possible to surf the Internet while hanging out in cybercafes. Amusement parks are also using virtual reality technology to create thrilling rides for park goers. See **Fig. 18-3**.

Fig 18-3 Technology has changed how people spend their leisure time. In what ways has technology affected how you and your family spend your free time?

- **Banking and shopping.** With online shopping and banking, people save the time they used to spend traveling to businesses. Debit and credit cards can be used to make purchases quickly in person, over the phone, or online. Self-scan registers allow customers to pay for store items without ever talking to a cashier. How has technology affected your shopping experiences?

- **Education.** Technology has made education more accessible. People can take courses online without ever sitting in class. With audio and video technology, students can view live, long-distance demonstrations from experts, such as engineers, teachers, and doctors.

The Drawbacks of Technology

"I can't believe it," Matt complained to his friend. "I just bought the latest graphics software to finish my class project, and it won't run. I'll have to upgrade my computer or use someone else's program. So much for modern technology!"

Almost everyone has complained about technology at some point. Although it helps people in many ways, technology has some serious disadvantages. Have you ever bought a device and had trouble figuring out how to use it? Perhaps you have experienced being out of range with your cell phone or have lost information on your computer when your hard drive crashed. If so, you're familiar with the frustration technology can cause.

Many people experience frustration because of the rapid changes in technology. Quickly learning new technology to keep up with the changes can be difficult. Broken devices, computer viruses, and power outages can also cause frustration.

The cost of technology is a drawback for many people. The newest devices are often expensive. Rapid changes in technology also affect people's budgets. Quickly changing technology often means devices are quickly **obsolete**, or out of date and no longer useful. A software program you buy today can be obsolete in just a couple of years, which might mean you have to buy a new program.

Technology has also raised privacy concerns. Some phone calls can be illegally tapped, which means you should be careful about what you say on a cell phone. Computers and the Internet have made identity theft easier. **Identity theft**, or stealing and illegally using personal information, is a concern for anyone who uses a computer.

Manners Matter

- **Make a good impression.** Good manners show off your personality. When you use polite words and actions, others think better of you.

- **Be a role model.** You are a role model to young friends and family members. By using good manners, you teach them how to speak and act courteously.

- **Take action.** Good manners don't just happen. You have to put good manners in action. Write a thank-you note or say "thank you" after you receive a gift. Say, "excuse me" when you bump into someone in the hallway. Hold a door open for someone whose arms are full.

HOW TO STAY SAFE ON THE INTERNET

Like the physical world, the World Wide Web has both people you want to know and those you want to avoid. The two groups can be harder to distinguish on the Internet, however. How can teens stay safe from sexual predators and others who try to exploit their trust? These precautions can help:

- **Get permission first.** These general words of wisdom apply to almost anything you do on the Internet, from logging on to sending pictures of yourself or your home. Parents and guardians may not have grown up with the Internet, but they have experience and can often spot potential dangers that teens might not see.

- **Monitor discussion groups before joining.** Get a feel for the topics and personalities. If they make you uncomfortable, find another group.

- **Choose usernames thoughtfully.** Consider the impression your name might make on people who don't know you. What might people assume about "Wacky Wanda" compared with "Egghead"?

- **Treat Internet communications like any other.** Respect the rules, or "netiquette," of different chat rooms and mail lists. Use emoticons (punctuation that shows facial expressions) and abbreviations to indicate when you are serious or joking. If a conversation gets out of control or sexually suggestive, log off. Do not subject yourself to this kind of behavior!

- **Be alert to signs of imposters.** Someone may claim to like the same music as you do, but avoid discussing favorite groups. Another person may use teen slang heavily. Try stating something you know is false. Does the other person go along? Maybe he or she is just a polite teen—or maybe the "teen" is not a teen. Tell a trusted adult if you have suspicions.

- **Word messages carefully.** Replies to chats and discussion groups can be read by all members. Carefully word your responses to avoid revealing information that you wouldn't want a stranger to know about you or your family. The same goes for e-mail and blogs.

- **Resist "cyberpeer" pressure.** Peers can exert the same pressure online as they do in person. Politely but firmly tell fellow chatters if their talk offends you. If you receive a hostile response, leave the chat room.

TAKE **ACTION**

On a piece of paper, write a short, questionable message that might be sent to a teen or to a chat room frequented by teens. Exchange papers and discuss the message you received. What "red flags," or warning signs, do you see? How would you handle this situation?

To prevent the theft of handheld electronic devices and protect your personal safety, follow these tips:

- Never leave devices in your desk at school, in view inside a vehicle, or in an unlocked locker.

- Be cautious about where and how you use devices. Don't use expensive headphones or equipment in public. Keep MP3 players, PDAs, and cell phones inside your jacket, in your pocket, or in your backpack.

- Remember that your safety is more important than an electronic device. If a thief demands your device, hand it over. Then report the theft to the police.

Technology can also negatively affect people's health. Too much time spent working on a computer or playing video games can result in back pain, eyestrain, and hand and wrist injuries. Even very young children who spend many hours clicking a mouse or pushing video game buttons can suffer from **repetitive stress injuries**, or joint injuries caused by repeated motions. General health also suffers when people choose television, video games, or the computer over physical activities.

Besides health risks, the increased use of technology can cause isolation. Hours spent watching television, surfing the Internet, and playing video games means hours away from family and friends. This isolation can negatively affect people's social and emotional health. How can you lessen your technology use and increase face-to-face time with the people you care about?

Managing Technology

Technology is a resource, and despite its drawbacks, it is here to stay. Like any other resource, technology needs to be managed. People who manage technology well enjoy its benefits and experience fewer of its disadvantages. The following strategies can help you stay in control of the technology in your life:

Fig 18-4
It's easy to become wrapped up in computer work and forget to take breaks. If this often happens to you, use a kitchen timer to signal that you should take a break.

- **Practice healthy habits.** Avoid working at the computer or playing video games for hours at a time. Take breaks often to walk around or stretch. When sitting at the computer, sit up straight, with your feet flat on the floor. When you are not using electronics, be active—swim, ride a bike, jog, or take a walk. See **Fig. 18-4**.

- **Take time to learn.** Take available classes. By keeping up your technology skills, you are more likely to use technology successfully, without feeling frustrated or overwhelmed. Read current magazine articles and books, and talk to tech-savvy friends and family members.

- **Be a smart shopper.** Before buying a high-tech product, ask yourself the following questions: How will it improve my life? How often will I use it? Can I justify the expense? Do I want it just because my friends have it? You might find that the device you thought you needed isn't that important. If you decide you do need it, research the product to find the best buy. Read consumer magazines and product reviews. If possible, wait a few months to buy the product. Many consumers who buy the latest device to hit the shelves end up frustrated with the product's bugs, or defects. Waiting gives the manufacturer time to fix the bugs.

- **Protect your privacy.** Losing control of your personal information can cost you and your family money. Always keep your personal information private. The tips on pages 282–283 in Chapter 17 can help protect you from identity theft and other crimes.

- **Make time for others.** The latest technical devices may be cool, but they can't replace people. Family and friends bring joys that technology cannot. Make time for the people you care about. Doing so will prevent isolation and help strengthen your relationships.

- **Remember your values.** Will your use of technology hurt you or anyone else? Disrespectful chat room or e-mail messages can hurt friendships and turn arguments into fights. How does the technology you use affect the environment? The growing problem of e-waste is a concern to everyone. Investigate ways to reuse or recycle old equipment. It's up to you to make the best possible use of present and future technology.

Mind Your E-Manners

Whether you are e-mailing family members or instant messaging friends, here are a few pointers to help you communicate respectfully and effectively:

▶ **Bite back angry words.** When you are upset or angry, wait to send your message. Review it after you calm down. If it's hurtful, delete it. Words said, or sent, in anger can never be taken back.

▶ **Avoid embarrassment.** Don't write anything you wouldn't say to someone face to face. You have no control over where your messages might be sent.

▶ **Think of others.** Don't interrupt people with instant messages when they are working. Also, avoid using all capital letters in messages. A message in all capitals comes across as shouting to the reader.

▶ **Delete suspicious messages.** If a message tells you to forward it to other people, delete it. The message may contain a virus. Even if it doesn't, forwarded jokes and chain e-mails are annoying to many people.

Review & Activities

Chapter Summary

- Technology includes time-saving, energy-saving, and life-saving devices.
- Technology positively affects almost all aspects of life.
- Although it helps people in many ways, technology has some serious disadvantages.
- Technology is a resource that needs to be managed. People who manage technology well enjoy its benefits and experience fewer of its disadvantages.

Reviewing Key Terms & Ideas

1. Define **technology**.
2. What is the benefit of **video teleconferencing**?
3. How does technology help protect people, their property, and their community?
4. What are **hybrids**?
5. How has technology affected education?
6. How does rapidly changing technology negatively affect people?
7. What is **obsolete** technology?
8. Define **identity theft**.
9. What are **repetitive stress injuries**?
10. What should you ask before buying a high-tech product?
11. How can you prevent technology-related isolation?

Thinking Critically

1. **Making generalizations.** Imagine you had to spend a week in a remote area with no electricity, and you could only take your clothing. Which technology device would you miss the most? Which would you miss the least? Explain.
2. **Drawing conclusions.** Does technology always make life more convenient and safe? Explain.
3. **Defending positions.** Some experts blame technology for people's weight problems. Take a stand either with or against these experts. Defend your position.

Review & Activities

Applying Your Learning

1. **Electronic etiquette.** Cell phone and Internet communications require their own etiquette. Create a poster campaign that promotes cell phone, instant messaging, and e-mail manners. Display your posters in the school.

2. **Expert demonstration.** Invite a police officer to demonstrate the technology devices used in law enforcement. How do these devices help the officer perform on the job? How do they keep you safe?

3. **Health promotion.** Research recommendations to reduce the risk of repetitive stress injuries while using technology. Choose several recommendations to implement at home. Ask your family to also follow the recommendations. After one week, evaluate the results.

4. **Community service.** Charity organizations often accept donated technology devices, such as old cell phones and computers. Find a local charity organization that could use these donations. As a class, plan an e-donation drive for the charity.

5. **Shopping savvy.** Think of a technology device you would like to buy. Research the device using consumer magazines and the manufacturer's Web site. What are the drawbacks of owning the product? What are the benefits? How can you get the most value for your money?

6. **Technology design.** Design a technology product for people with a specific disability, such as a hearing impairment. Identify the disability and explain how the device would help assist individuals at home, at work, or in school.

Making Connections

1. **Math** Find out the average miles per gallon of a hybrid car and a sport-utility vehicle (SUV). How many miles could you drive in each vehicle on ten gallons of gas?

2. **Writing** Research two different calling plans for cell phones. Compare the plans' features to their costs. Which plan is the better value? Write down your results.

3. **Writing** Imagine you are transported in time 200 years into the future. Write a letter to your family describing the types of technology available to you.

CAREER Link

Using Technology. Almost every career field uses a form of technology. Workers who are flexible and willing to learn new technology will be more successful in their chosen career. Use classified ads and company Web sites to find out the technology skills required in a career that interests you. Which of these skills do you have now? How can you learn skills you don't have?

Staying Healthy & Fit

Objectives

- Describe overall health and wellness.
- Discuss factors that affect physical health.
- Relate exercise and nutrition to overall well-being.
- Plan an exercise program.
- Identify factors that influence a person's weight.
- Explain the dangers of eating disorders.

Vocabulary

- **wellness**
- **grooming**
- **acne**
- **dermatologist**
- **dandruff**
- **plaque**
- **basal metabolic rate (BMR)**
- **anorexia**
- **bulimia**
- **binge eating disorder**

Reading with Purpose

1. **Read** the title of this chapter and describe in writing what you expect to learn from it.

2. **Write** each vocabulary term in your notebook, leaving space for definitions.

3. **As you read** Chapter 19, write the definition beside each term in your notebook.

4. **After** reading the chapter, write a paragraph describing what you learned.

Health and Wellness

What does good health mean to you? Some of your friends might reply, "not being sick" or "feeling good." Another person may say, "being happy." They would all be partly right. Health is the condition of your body and your mind and includes three components:

- **Physical health**—The condition of your body

- **Mental and emotional health**—As reflected in your thinking, attitudes, and feelings

- **Social health**—As reflected in your relationships with others

Physical, mental, emotional, and social health are interrelated. All are affected by your day-to-day actions and decisions. For instance, one night you might not get much sleep. The next day you may be irritable, do poorly on a math test, and have an argument with your best friend. How would you rate your overall health that day?

Wellness is an approach to life based on healthy attitudes and actions. When you are feeling good, you may not think about what you do to make that attitude happen. If you take care of your body and keep a positive attitude, you are more likely to enjoy good health.

Your Physical Health

Your everyday activities—such as sleeping, grooming, eating, and exercising—all contribute to your physical health. When you enjoy physical health, you have energy to engage in the activities you need and want to do every day. You also look and feel your best.

To maintain your physical health, it makes good sense to seek regular medical checkups. Checkups give you the chance to talk to a doctor about any health problems or questions

Fig 19-1

Doctors can usually identify and handle small problems before they turn into major ones.

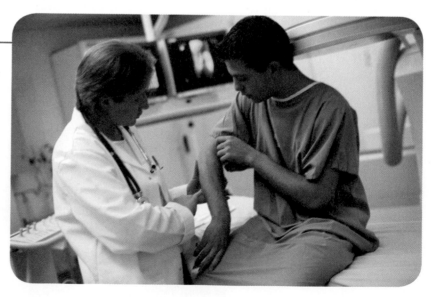

you may have. As part of a medical exam, your doctor may ask questions about your general health. Unusual fatigue, unexplained weight loss, ongoing pain, and sores that do not heal would be definite red flags. These physical conditions might be the result of lack of sleep or overactivity, or they may be signs of a serious illness. Cancer would be an example of a serious illness. See **Fig. 19-1**.

Your doctor is experienced at diagnosing different types of cancer and can teach you how to perform self-examinations so that you can find signs of cancer early. For example, a self-examination of your skin might reveal recent changes in the size or coloration of the skin around a mole or birthmark. Your doctor should examine the change to eliminate the possibility of skin cancer.

All teens should perform regular self-examinations. Girls should examine their breasts and guys their testicles for any thickening or lumps. Testicular examinations are particularly important because testicular cancer is the most common form of cancer in teen males age 15 years and older. Screening for cancer is important because early detection increases the chance for successful treatment.

Sleep and Rest

Have you ever wondered what your body does during the night? While you sleep, your body repairs itself, removes waste products from cells, and builds a supply of energy for action the next day. See **Fig. 19-2**.

TIPS

Promote Family Health

The health and wellness of family members is just as important as your own. Here are some tips to improve your family's wellness:

▶ Help plan and prepare regular, healthful meals for your family.

▶ Encourage family members to get enough rest.

▶ Plan active family events that promote good health.

▶ Reduce others' stress level by helping out.

▶ Hold family meetings to discuss weekly and monthly schedules to avoid schedule conflicts.

Fig 19-2
Relaxing activities, such as reading, help calm you and prepare you for sleep. How can you improve your sleep?

You may think that you can accomplish more if you sleep less. But when you don't sleep enough, everything feels like an effort. It is hard to concentrate, and you are more likely to make mistakes. Your need for sleep actually increases as you move into adolescence. Teens should aim for about nine hours of sleep a night. You will feel a lot better the next day—and will be more likely to accomplish everything you want to do!

Good Grooming

Grooming means the personal care routine you follow to keep yourself clean and well-groomed. Everyone is not born with natural good looks, but anyone can be attractive by making the most of what he or she has.

Cleanliness is vital for your health and appearance. As you read about grooming and cleanliness, think about how your own routine measures up.

Your Skin

Your skin is like fabric that covers and protects your body. It warns you about hot, cold, and pain. It produces oils to keep itself soft and moisture (perspiration) to help regulate your body temperature.

One step in taking care of your skin is to take a bath or shower as part of your daily routine. Soap and water remove dirt, dried skin, extra oil, and surface bacteria that can cause

Fig 19-3
Take the time to wash your face thoroughly, especially before bedtime.

body odors and infections. If you can't bathe or shower, fill a basin with water and use a towel or sponge to wash yourself from head to toe. This is often called a sponge bath.

Everyone perspires. Perspiration is a natural body process that regulates body temperature. Your body contains glands called sweat glands. These glands are located under your arms. When you perspire, skin bacteria react with the perspiration and produce an odor. How can you control body odor? By using deodorant or antiperspirant every day, you can prevent body odor.

Acne

Another skin concern is acne. **Acne** is a skin problem that develops when glands below the pores (tiny openings) in the skin become blocked. The oils that normally move through your pores to soften the skin are trapped beneath it. As more oil becomes trapped, blackheads and whiteheads develop. Often these areas become irritated or infected and develop into pimples, or acne. Despite what you might think, no medical evidence links your diet—chocolate, cola drinks, or potato chips—to the cause of acne. See **Fig. 19-3**.

Most teens develop acne. Acne is most common on the face, upper chest, and back. The best treatment for mild cases of acne is to wash your face twice daily. You can also blot your face with a tissue between washings to remove the oil. Over-the-counter acne medicine that you buy without a doctor's prescription may help. Avoid picking and squeezing the pimples. This injures the skin, spreads bacteria, and can leave lifelong scars. Serious cases of acne need to be treated by a **dermatologist**, a doctor specializing in skin problems.

Your Hair

Did you know that hair reflects your general health? Attractive hair begins on the inside. A poor diet, emotional stress, or even a bad cold can alter the appearance and texture of your hair.

How often do you need to shampoo your hair? Many teens have so much natural oil in their hair that they need to shampoo it every day, while others need to shampoo it less often. Wash your hair often enough to keep it looking clean.

Dandruff, or scales and flakes on the scalp, is a problem for many teens. To help control dandruff, keep your hair clean. Special dandruff shampoos available over the counter can often be effective. Keep combs, brushes, and other hair-care

Wash Your Face

Washing your face isn't difficult, but there are things you can do to help make it as clean as possible:

▶ Wet your face completely by splashing it with warm water.

▶ Lather cleanser or facial soap between your clean hands. Use your fingertips or face brush to gently massage your face, using a circular motion.

▶ Start at the forehead, move down the nose, lather the cheeks, and then move down to your neck.

▶ Rinse the cleanser or soap off by repeatedly splashing cool water over your face. Spend more time rinsing than cleansing.

▶ Use a clean soft towel to blot, not vigorously rub, your face.

HOW TO PROTECT YOUR SKIN

Bright, sunny weather and exercise seem to go together. In fact, exposure to sunlight is a proven promoter of good mental health. A bit of sunlight throughout the week helps your skin manufacture vitamin D.

However, the sun can damage skin as well. The culprits are ultraviolet (UV) rays, a type of solar energy that affects the cells. UV rays are responsible for a so-called healthy tan, which is actually a sign of skin cells under stress. At best, these rays can lead to burns and wrinkles. At worst, they change cells' genetic makeup, leading to skin cancer.

How can you enjoy the healthful effects of exercise but minimize the unhealthful effects of the sun? These tips can help:

- **Duck the sun.** Enjoy the sun for only short periods of time. Limit your exposure especially between 10 a.m. and 4 p.m., when the sun is most intense.

- **Check the UV index.** The UV index is a zip code–specific prediction of the strength of the UV rays for the following day. It's often mentioned in local television and newspaper forecasts. An index of 5 or greater indicates a high intensity. Avoiding the sun altogether on these days may be a good idea.

- **Choose the best sunscreen.** Choose a sunscreen lotion based on its sun protection factor (SPF). This number indicates the amount of time the sunscreen protects you from UV rays. Health experts recommend formulas with an SPF of 15 or more, which protects your skin about 15 times longer than if you did not use it. Apply it liberally, and reapply it often. Know, however, that reapplying sunscreen is not like adding coins in a parking meter. It does not give you more time but only ensures that the protection doesn't wear off earlier. A more effective option is sunblock. As the name suggests, these creams reflect the sun completely. Be warned, however: they may go on chalky white depending on the company that produces the product.

- **Make skin care a year-round regimen.** The sun can be a concern in the winter if you spend a lot of time outdoors, especially if sunlight is reflected onto your skin by snow. That's added reason to wear those gloves and scarves, even if it doesn't feel that cold. Colder, drier winter air can also dry skin. Include a skin lotion in your daily hygiene routine.

- **Dress the part.** Clothing is a physical sunblock. A wide-brimmed hat and long-sleeved, tightly woven garments are basic cover-ups. Clothing labeled "sun protective" has an ultraviolet protection factor (UPF) of 15 or more, meaning it allows one fifteenth of UV rays to penetrate. Some specially treated fabrics have a UPF of 50 or higher.

- **Eat right.** As with all health matters, a nourishing diet is a good, basic defense. Nutrients help your skin resist and rebound after exposure to the sun.

- **Know the skin you're in.** Some people tan—and burn—more easily than others. You may know from experience if you fall into this group. Respect your body's limits. Also, obtain medical advice on any changes in moles or freckles.

TAKE **ACTION**

Find ads that show people enjoying an outdoor activity. Do these models follow the skin care precautions described here? If not, why do you think the advertiser chose to show them this way?

Clean Your Teeth

Taking good care of your teeth and gums improves your appearance, smile, and long-term dental health. Try these suggestions:

▶ Use short back and forth strokes when brushing.

▶ Angle the brush gently but with enough pressure to feel the bristles on your gums.

▶ Use a toothbrush with soft bristles and rounded ends.

▶ Replace your toothbrush every three months.

▶ Use dental floss daily to clean between your teeth where a toothbrush can't reach.

equipment clean, and change your pillowcases often. Avoid scratching your scalp with sharp combs or fingernails. If your dandruff is severe and doesn't improve, you may find a dermatologist helpful.

Your Teeth

"Look, no cavities." Now there's a phrase to make you smile. Good dental hygiene is important for healthy teeth, clean breath, and an attractive smile.

Brushing your teeth after eating and before going to bed helps remove decay-causing plaque. **Plaque**, a sticky film that clings to your teeth, is formed by the food, bacteria, and air in your mouth. Together, plaque and sugar combine to form acid, which eats away your tooth enamel and forms a cavity. Sugary and starchy foods feed the bacteria in plaque. See **Fig. 19-4**.

How do you fight plaque? Following some simple tips can help you prevent tooth decay:

- **Floss regularly.** Dental floss removes food particles between your teeth that a toothbrush can't reach. Floss between your teeth every day.

- **Monitor snacks.** Eat starchy and sugary foods at mealtime rather than snack time. The liquids you drink at meals, along with your saliva, help rinse sugar from your mouth.

- **See a dentist regularly.** A dentist can check out minor problem areas before they become major ones.

Fig 19-4
Dentists and dental hygienists can remove plaque from your teeth and help you learn proper dental hygiene.

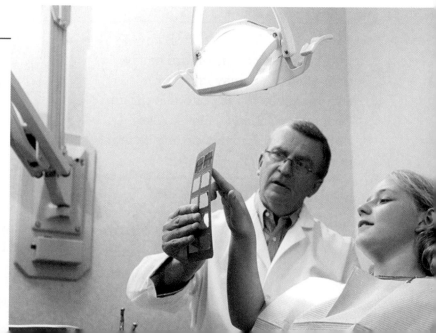

Exercise and Nutrition

Exercise and good nutrition are a powerful combination. People who are more physically active and maintain a healthy weight over their life span have fewer health problems, more energy, and a better mental outlook.

In some ways, your body is similar to a machine. Machines need oil to run smoothly, and your body needs nutritious food to function efficiently. Eating a variety of foods keeps you well nourished and gives you the energy you need to keep on top of your schedule. Exercise helps your body's organs function more efficiently.

When growing up and going through the normal life cycle—childhood, adolescence, adulthood, and finally old age—dietary needs change. Establishing good food habits now can minimize illness later. Infancy and adolescence are the most rapid growth periods; therefore, teens have an increased need for most nutrients. Although older adults continue to need the same nutrients, they need them in smaller amounts.

Teens Speak About Exercise and Nutrition

Jody and Mia sank onto the park bench after their morning run. "That hill didn't look so big from the bottom," Mia said, panting. "Next time we stick with our regular route."

Jody wiped her brow. "Good idea. On the other hand, think of all the good we did our heart and bones and muscles."

"I'm thinking of those big cinnamon buns they sell at the bakery we jog by on our way here," Mia replied. "I'm thinking I'll stop for one on the way home."

Jody laughed. "That's not the idea!"

"But it's the only thing that kept me going up that hill!"

"Tell you what," Jody offered, "we'll cool down by walking to the bakery, and we'll split a cinnamon roll. After all, everyone needs a reward now and then."

Teen Connection

Describe ways in which society sends contradictory messages about exercise and nutrition. Suggest ways to balance these views to maintain a healthful lifestyle.

Your Exercise Program

In addition to nutritious foods, your body needs daily exercise. To benefit the most from exercise, make it a regular habit. Your program should include the following four elements of fitness:

- **Heart and lungs.** Your heart, lungs, and blood vessels deliver oxygen to every part of your body. You can train them to work more efficiently with regular aerobic exercise. Aerobic exercise is any vigorous activity that causes your heart to beat faster for a sustained amount of time. Jumping rope, dancing, cycling, swimming, and walking at a fast pace are healthful aerobic exercises. See **Fig. 19-5**.

- **Muscular endurance.** The ability of your muscles to work continuously over a long time is called muscular endurance. Most aerobic activity improves your muscular endurance.

- **Muscular strength.** Strength enables your muscles to push or pull with force. Having strong muscles can also improve your posture and help prevent injury. Weight lifting, leg lifts, and push-ups are examples of weight-bearing exercises. They increase the strength of your muscles, bones, and joints.

- **Flexibility.** You should be able to move your muscles and joints easily, without pain or stiffness. Slow, gentle stretching exercises help improve flexibility.

Fig 19-5
Aerobic activity not only helps strengthen the heart but also helps relieve stress and burns calories. What types of aerobic activity do you engage in?

You don't need to work on all four elements every day. Follow the tips that some experts suggest to plan a personal exercise program:

- **Strength building.** Include a strength-building session two times a week. Work all the major muscle groups: chest, stomach, back, legs, and arms. Allow at least 48 hours between strength workouts to rest your muscles and build new tissue.

- **Stretching.** Perform stretching exercises several times a week. You might do them before and after your workouts or before going to bed.

- **Aerobic exercise.** Most health experts recommend performing aerobic exercise every day for 30 minutes.

It is easier to stick with an exercise program if you are active and have fun at the same time. Make a date with a friend to play tennis, hike, run track, shoot baskets, or go line dancing. Plan to meet at least twice a week to exercise together. Make sure to try different types of physical activities to avoid boredom. Exercising with friends combines two important parts of your life—physical fitness and socialization.

Workout Safety

Just as important as exercising is doing it safely. If you overdo your workouts or develop an injury, you'll set yourself back and miss out on the fun and benefits of your exercise program.

Pick a safe place and time to exercise. Surfaces with some cushioning, such as a track, are better for running than hard surfaces, like concrete. On hot days when you may become dehydrated, try to exercise in the early morning or early evening when it is cooler and take a water bottle on your runs. See **Fig. 19-6**.

Start each exercise session with a warm-up period, which prepares your body for more vigorous activity and helps prevent injury. Begin by stretching for 5 to 10 minutes. Then start a "light and easy" version of the activity you are planning to do before beginning more intense exercise.

Fig 19-6 A balanced exercise program won't be effective if it is not safe. How can these teens keep their workouts safe?

- **Keep at it.** Often the only difference between those who reach their goals and those who do not is that the successful kept going when things got difficult.

- **Stay focused.** If you want something badly enough, keep it in mind and imagine achievement.

- **Check in.** Evaluate your progress regularly as you move toward your goal. Are there any skills, information, or training that you need to reach the next stage? Obtain them yourself and keep going.

- **Stop and celebrate.** Acknowledge what you accomplish along the way. Celebrate your hard work before you move on to the next step.

After you have exercised, end each session with a cooldown period to allow your heart rate to slow and return to normal. A cooldown lets you gradually slow your body down rather than bring it to a sudden halt. Walking at a slower pace is a good way to cool down. After your cooldown, stretch again to help prevent soreness. Also, remember to drink plenty of water before, during, and after any vigorous exercise.

Managing Your Weight

Your weight is not the result of any single factor. One person can eat an unbelievable amount of food every day and never seem to gain a pound, and another person may have to struggle just to stay at the same weight. Although weight management is hard work, it's important to your health. Hundreds of thousands of people die each year due to poor diet and lack of physical activity. Now that's a reason to eat right and exercise!

Factors Affecting Weight

Your weight is affected by your metabolic rate, your genetic makeup, your body composition, your physical activity, and the food you eat. Each of these factors influences the number of pounds that registers when you step on a scale:

- **Your basic energy needs.** Your **basal metabolic rate (BMR)** is the rate at which your body uses energy when you are inactive. Your body is always working for you. It needs energy to make your heart beat, to breathe, and to keep your body warm. It also cools your body down, sends messages to your brain, and produces thousands of body chemicals. Your basal metabolism consumes about 60 percent of your body's energy needs.

- **Genetic makeup.** Your genetic makeup is what you inherit from your family. It helps determine your skin and hair color, your height, your size, and your body shape. Genetics also affect your basal metabolism. See **Fig. 19-7**.

- **Body composition.** Your body is made up of lean tissue (muscle and bone) and body fat. Exercise develops muscles. Muscles burn more calories than fat tissue but take less space. So if you develop muscles through exercise, you can improve your body and appearance.

- **Physical activity.** When you move your body, you use energy. Active people use more energy than sedentary (inactive) people. Physical activity generally accounts for 30 to 40 percent of your energy needs. When you are physically active, you increase your basal metabolic rate for at least 24 hours after exercise. So while sleeping, your exercise routine is still working for you!

- **Food.** Nutrients in food supply energy, so it's important to eat healthful foods—and to eat at regular times throughout the day. When you go too long without food, your body lacks the fuel it needs. People who skip meals make up for it by overeating later.

Weight Management Plan

You may keep a record of how you spend your money or how many hours you babysit in a month, so why not keep a record of your eating and exercise habits? People who keep fitness records are often more successful in staying fit than those who do not. You are not always aware of the habits you develop, some of which may be poor. A fitness record can help you identify and correct poor habits.

Try keeping a fitness record for at least a week. List the foods and beverages, along with the amounts, that you consume. Note the place and time you eat and drink. Comment on how you feel and your mood at the time. List your physical activities and the length of time you do them.

After a week, take a look at your record. You will probably see some patterns emerging. Are you pleased with what you see? Are you exercising enough? What would you continue to do the same? What changes would you make?

Fig 19-7 Body shape and size are genetic traits. What genetic traits have you inherited?

Safety Check

Be sure to evaluate a weight-loss plan and consult your doctor before you try it. A safe weight-loss plan:

- Is based on real foods, not pills, powders, or special liquids.

- Has enough calories to maintain energy.

- Includes a variety of foods from all the food groups.

- Doesn't promise weight loss without exercise.

- Doesn't promise weight loss of more than one-half to one pound a week.

Eating Disorders

It is normal for teens to be concerned about their weight, but sometimes those concerns get out of control. Obsession about food, combined with mental and emotional problems, may indicate an eating disorder. Eating disorders are extreme, and serious eating behaviors can lead to sickness; deterioration of the body, hair, and teeth; and even death. See **Fig. 19-8**.

There are three main types of eating disorders:

- **Anorexia** is an eating disorder characterized by self-starvation. People with this disorder have a strong fear of being overweight. They eat little and become extremely thin, yet they still think they weigh too much.

- **Bulimia** is a condition in which people eat large quantities of food in a short period of time and then purge. They induce vomiting, abuse laxatives, or overexercise to keep from gaining weight.

- **Binge eating disorder** is characterized by compulsive overeating. People with this disorder may be overeating due to low self-esteem, stress, or mental or physical abuse.

Eating disorders carry a number of severe health risks, including severe dehydration, sleep problems, a lack of mental acuity or sharpness, heart-related problems, and muscle-tone loss. People suffering from eating disorders need medical help and qualified counseling immediately. Although recovery takes time, early diagnosis greatly improves the chances of recovery. To identify an eating disorder, look for the following signs:

- Obsessing over weight, weight loss, calories, and food
- Chewing gum excessively
- Going to the bathroom immediately after eating
- Eating excessive amounts of food and not gaining weight
- Pretending to eat by moving food around on a plate
- Overexercising
- Vomiting or using laxatives
- Stealing, hiding, or hoarding food

People who develop eating disorders usually cannot get well on their own. They need medical help and qualified counseling for a healthy recovery.

Fig 19-8 People with eating disorders often think they're overweight, even when they are not.

Fig 19-9
Hobbies are important to maintaining balance in your life. How do you keep your life balanced?

Your Emotional and Social Health

In your everyday activities, you want to strike a balance among your emotional, social, and physical health. If one of these areas is seriously out of balance, the other areas often suffer, too. When you balance all aspects of your health, you're able to get along with others and manage problems and stress. See **Fig. 19-9**.

Stress

Stress is the physical or emotional strain or tension that is the body's natural response to conflict. Everyone has to deal with stress. Anyone who moves to a new city or school experiences stress. Family problems can trigger stress. Trying to meet a deadline for school can cause stress. You may never be completely free of stress, but you can definitely learn how to manage it.

Stress is not entirely negative. When you prepare for a major sports event or test in class, it is natural to feel a certain amount of stress. The stress you feel compels you to work harder to succeed. When the event or test is over, the stress you felt usually vanishes. On the other hand, too much stress can cause emotional strain and even lead to long-term health problems.

How do you know when you are suffering from an overload of stress? Your body gives you physical and emotional signals. For example, physical clues include a racing heart if you're scared and sweating hands if you're nervous. Other physical signs of stress can include headaches, tightness in your shoulders or neck, tiredness, overeating, and irritability. Signs of emotional stress can include edginess, feelings of frustration, and crying.

Signs of stress are like warning signals. They could be warning you of serious problems. When you see signs of stress in yourself, try to find healthy ways to reduce it.

Health and Wellness Resources

Everyone has health-related concerns or questions from time to time. Government and community resources can provide you with health and wellness information to help guide your decisions. You can obtain reliable health maintenance information by checking with your doctor or searching Web sites and publications from government agencies, such as the

STEPS TO SUCCESS

I Can Handle Stress

There's no doubt about it: just being a teenager is stressful. You have to balance many things in your life—homework and tests, a changing body, parents, friends, and sports and other after-school activities. And for many teens, there are additional stressors, such as parental divorce, pressure to try drugs or alcohol, or pressure to fit in with the "in crowd." Too much stress can take a toll on your emotional and physical health. Fortunately, you can take positive action to get a handle on stress.

U.S. Food and Drug Administration and the U.S. Department of Health and Human Services.

Professional health organizations, such as the American Medical Association, the American Heart Association, and the American Cancer Society, also help people understand different health issues. Community-level organizations, such as health clinics and your own doctor, are local resources you can use to keep your life on a healthy track.

- **Exercise regularly.** It's a good idea to be physically active at least 60 minutes each day. Take a walk, swim some laps, or ride your bike.

- **Eat for your health.** While stress may cause you to eat on the run or indulge in junk and "comfort" foods, such as cookies and chips, these foods do your body more harm than good. Instead, eat regular meals. When you're in a hurry, reach for fruit, yogurt, and other healthy foods.

- **Get plenty of sleep.** When you're well rested, you are better able to tackle what life throws at you. In addition, sleep gives your body a chance to recover from stress. Everyone needs recovery time.

Health experts recommend that teens sleep about nine hours each night.

- **Avoid caffeine.** Caffeine, which is found in chocolate and many sodas, teas, and coffee, can increase feelings of anxiety. This, in turn, can make you feel more stressed.

- **Prioritize your activities.** You can reduce the number of activities you choose to do. Figure out which activities you truly enjoy and stick to only those. Make sure that the things you choose to do are those that have the highest priority.

- **Talk it out.** Talk about your problems with an adult or trusted friend. Sometimes just letting out your fears or frustrations can do wonders for your stress level.

- **Be realistic.** Don't put pressure on yourself to be perfect. After all, no one is perfect. Do your best and make a promise to yourself to accept yourself at your best, not at a level of perfection.

CHAPTER 19

Review & Activities

Chapter Summary

- Physical, mental, emotional, and social health make up your overall health.
- Your everyday activities affect your physical health.
- A good personal care routine is important to your health.
- Forming good nutrition and exercise habits now can benefit you throughout your lifetime.
- Understanding the factors that determine weight help you manage your weight more effectively.
- Eating disorders can result in severe health problems.

Reviewing Key Terms & Ideas

1. Define **wellness**.
2. What four daily activities contribute to your physical health?
3. Why is **grooming** important?
4. How can **acne** be handled?
5. What is **dandruff**?
6. What role does **plaque** play in tooth decay?
7. How do exercise and nutrition contribute to your health and well-being?
8. List the four elements of fitness.
9. What is a **basal metabolic rate**?
10. List four factors that influence body weight.
11. What are some consequences of eating disorders?

Thinking Critically

1. **Predicting actions.** Imagine addressing a group of teens about the importance of developing a plan for lifelong health practices. What would you say to influence their behavior now and in the future?
2. **Making comparisons.** Imagine two people, one with good grooming practices and the other with poor grooming habits. Contrast their daily grooming routines. How might their appearances differ?
3. **Showing relationships.** In addition to fear of being overweight, suggest other reasons people might develop eating disorders. How can our society help prevent eating disorders?

Review & Activities

Applying Your Learning

1. **Sleep observations.** Keep a record of the number of hours you sleep each night and how you feel each day. Reflect on your daytime performance and how sleep might have affected it.

2. **Skin care.** Create a how-to pamphlet explaining proper skin care techniques for teens. Include information about available skin care products and their use.

3. **Dental awareness.** Research common dental problems of teens and how to prevent them. Then create a public service announcement to help teens be more proactive with dental hygiene.

4. **Food choices.** Using magazine clippings or computer graphics software, create a picture book of nutritious food choices for teens. Present your book to a local parent group.

5. **Exercise evaluation.** Evaluate your present exercise routine using the suggestions in this chapter. Follow your exercise plan for two weeks and then report on the effects of any changes you made.

Making Connections

1. **Writing** Some schools require uniforms, and others do not. Take a position either for or against school uniforms and defend your position in a brief essay.

2. **Math** Find out the cost of a tube of toothpaste and a spool of dental floss. Estimate how long each item would last if you used it every day. Calculate the cost of these items for one month.

3. **Writing** Develop and write a one-minute commercial designed to encourage the general public to become more fitness conscious. Videotape the commercial and present it to your class for feedback.

4. **Reading** Read articles on health routines in several health or sports fitness magazines. Compare the information from each article and make three generalizations that apply to your own health.

CAREER Link

Leaving a Job.
When you quit a job, it's important to tell your employer you will be leaving. It's reasonable to let your employer know you're leaving two weeks in advance. Some employers may also require a letter of resignation, which explains why you are leaving. Practice writing a letter of resignation for a summer job you plan to quit.

Health Risks

Objectives

- Describe the effects of frequently abused illegal and legal drugs.
- Explain safety precautions for prescription and over-the-counter drugs.
- Discuss the dangers of sexually transmitted diseases.
- Explain the risks associated with teen pregnancy.
- Demonstrate strategies for refusing drugs.

Reading with Purpose

1. **Write down** the colored headings from Chapter 20 in your notebook.
2. **As you read** the text under each heading, visualize what you are reading.
3. **Reflect** on what you read by writing a few sentences under each heading to describe it.
4. **Continue** this process until you have finished the chapter. Reread your notes.

Vocabulary

- **inhalants**
- **addiction**
- **stimulants**
- **depressants**
- **marijuana**
- **hallucinogens**
- **anabolic steroids**
- **sexually transmitted diseases (STDs)**
- **abstinence**
- **acquired immunodeficiency syndrome (AIDS)**

Keeping Your Best Interests in Mind

Who is ultimately responsible for your health? Your family? Your doctor? The answer is you. To do the best job possible, you need to become informed about good health practices and some of the dangers you will confront. One danger you may encounter as a teen is drugs.

Drugs pose a risk to anyone who uses them. Drugs that are prescribed by doctors often help people fight disease or control pain. Physicians are aware that the positive effects of prescribed medication outweigh negative risks to the body. They carefully regulate the dosage of drugs they prescribe to patients. But what about drugs that aren't prescribed by doctors or that are illegal?

Making wise decisions is a critical part of becoming an adult. It's hard enough to make certain choices when you are alert and in control. It becomes much harder if you use illegal drugs that can alter your judgment. When teens are under the influence of drugs, they are more likely to do things they would not normally consider doing and even chance deadly risks. See **Fig. 20-1**.

Drugs have negative effects on others, too. The people who care most about the person using drugs find it difficult to help when help is most needed. Communication and relationships with friends and family members change. The effects of drug use don't stop with friends and family. The local community is also affected. Substance abuse is a contributing factor in many crimes committed in communities.

Fig 20-1 You are more influential than you may think. How might your behavior affect your friends?

Frequently Abused Drugs

What drugs are frequently abused? Tobacco, alcohol, inhalants, stimulants, marijuana, and steroids are among the most commonly abused drugs. Although different, they all have one thing in common: These drugs affect the user's feelings, behavior, and outlook on life. They also can cause serious injury to your physical health. See **Fig. 20-2**.

Tobacco

Think about the following statements: "No one's going to tell me not to smoke. No one's going to tell me what's good for me." What's the difference between someone who tells you not to smoke and media sources that may glamorize smoking? Both seek to influence your behavior.

You can choose to ignore what someone says about the dangers of smoking. On the other hand, you can choose not to

be influenced by what others do and by subtle, manipulative messages about smoking. Consider the following risks related to tobacco:

- **Nicotine cravings.** Cigarettes, cigars, pipes, and chewing tobacco (smokeless tobacco) all contain nicotine, an addictive drug. Most tobacco users crave greater amounts of nicotine and use more tobacco products.

- **Health problems.** Studies prove that tobacco causes cancer and is related to various other health problems, such as emphysema, heart disease, and high blood pressure.

- **Stress.** Some people claim that smoking calms their nerves. In reality, smoking releases a substance that creates physical stress rather than relaxation.

- **Secondhand smoke.** The smoke given off by a burning cigar, cigarette, or pipe is secondhand smoke, and it's a danger to your health. To promote personal health, some states have passed laws that ban smoking in public places.

Alcohol

Why is it against the law for anyone under the age of 21 to drink? As a teen, you risk serious harm to your health if you drink. You can become addicted to alcohol more rapidly than adults do because your body is still developing. Alcohol consumption interferes with your natural growth and development. Excessive use of alcohol can cause serious damage to nearly every part of your body.

Alcohol is a depressant that reaches the brain in a matter of minutes. Over time, drinking destroys brain cells, which cannot be repaired or replaced like other cells in the body. As

HOW TO SAY "NO" TO DRUGS

"Just say 'no' to drugs!" Teens have heard the message for years, but hearing those words may not be enough. Good advice is useless without realistic strategies to carry it out. Here are some practical ways to avoid drugs:

- **Choose friends wisely.** Find people who don't use drugs and look for underlying qualities that show why they don't use them. Teens who are confident, secure with themselves, and hopeful about the future are living antidrug messages. They are also more fun to be around.

- **Choose activities with care.** Negative peer pressure can undermine the most positive intentions. Avoid places or events where you think drugs will be available.

- **Use your parents or guardians.** This is one time when parents or guardians don't mind taking the blame for your decisions. "My parents would make my life miserable" is a reason most teens can accept for refusing an invitation to use drugs.

- **Know the facts.** Knowledge alone won't ensure positive behavior. Knowing the dangers of drug use can, however, reinforce your commitment to staying drug free.

a result, the brain can't function properly. Body movements, speech, vision, and good judgment are dramatically altered.

People have many ways of persuading you to drink. They may tell you that everyone's doing it, that you'll appear more grown up while drinking, or that you'll relax and forget your problems if you drink. Some teens might say they will not socialize with you unless you drink.

The truth is that drinking doesn't make underage drinkers look or act more like adults, but it can make them look foolish. Drinking doesn't help anyone forget problems; the problems remain after the alcohol has worn off.

- **Find ways to solve problems.** Many people use drugs to escape problems in life. Instead, drugs themselves become a problem, sometimes worse than those the user was trying to avoid. Face problems rather than running from them. Friends, family members, teachers, and counselors are all there to help.

- **Remind yourself of what you could lose.** Money, friends, a starting position on the team—these are just a few of the costs of using drugs. Put reminders of the things you might forfeit in strategic places: your locker, mirror, refrigerator, or any place you look often.

TAKE **ACTION**

Collect antidrug pamphlets from your school counselor or local health department. Analyze the design, arguments, and overall tone. Do you think these elements are used effectively to appeal to teens? Why or why not?

Inhalants

Inhalants are substances with dangerous fumes that are sniffed to produce a mind-altering high. More than a thousand household and commercial products can be abused by sniffing or "huffing"—inhaling through the mouth. Glue, hair spray, nail polish, and spray paints are a few examples of inhalants.

What's wrong with inhaling these products? Inhalants contain volatile solvents that starve your body of oxygen, which causes your heart to beat more rapidly. Sniffing highly concentrated inhalants can cause dizziness, headaches, vomiting, loss of coordination, memory loss, and even heart failure. They can cause death!

Illegal Drugs

Illegal drugs are simply that—illegal. It is illegal to buy, sell, or possess them. If a person is found guilty of an illegal drug charge, he or she can be suspended from school, placed under court supervision, or sent to jail. See **Fig. 20-3**.

Illegal drugs are not generally prescribed for medical purposes, and they are dangerous to use. They can have adverse psychological effects (confusion, depression, or anxiety) and adverse physical effects (blurred vision, tremors, sweating, or chills). Taking illegal drugs gives an intense sensation or "rush," which lasts only a short time. However, the long-term effects are serious. To maintain that rush, you need more drugs more often. You have to ask yourself, is it worth the physical damage, the psychological problems, and the legal consequences?

Stimulants, depressants, marijuana, and hallucinogens can all lead to dependence, or **addiction**.

- **Stimulants** increase a person's heart rate, speed up the central nervous system, increase breathing rates, and raise blood pressure. Illegal stimulants include cocaine, crack cocaine, methamphetamine, and ecstasy. They give a short-term rush followed by a "crash," or sense of coming down.

Fig 20-3

When friends choose to sell and use drugs, you may have to choose new friends. How might this teen's life be affected if he stays friends with teens who use drugs?

- **Depressants** reduce blood pressure and slow heart and breathing rates. They result in a loss of coordination, poor attention span, mood changes, and extreme anxiety. Examples of depressants include barbiturates (sleeping pills) and tranquilizers (anxiety-reducing drugs). See **Fig. 20-4**.

- **Marijuana** is a drug made from the hemp plant. It is the most commonly used illicit drug in the United States. There are numerous street names for marijuana, including pot, weed, grass, ganja, and reed. Marijuana is rapidly absorbed by the body and has dangerous effects. The short-term effects of marijuana use include loss of motivation, memory loss, and learning difficulties. Long-term use can lead to serious health problems, such as cancer.

- **Hallucinogens** are street drugs that distort the user's thoughts, moods, and senses. PCP and LSD are hallucinogens. Hallucinogens change the way your brain functions and affect your self-control. People under the influence of hallucinogens may think they are hearing voices, seeing images, or feeling sensations that don't exist. Hallucinogens can cause heart and lung failure and induce a coma.

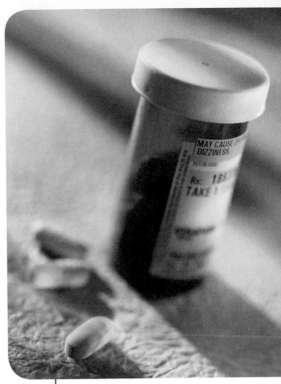

Fig 20-4 Prescribed depressants can be addictive and dangerous. If prescribed one of these drugs; strictly follow your doctor's orders.

- **Anabolic steroids** are manufactured substances that alter body characteristics. Anabolic refers to muscle building, and steroids are simply a class of drugs. Athletes and others have abused anabolic steroids to enhance performance and to improve their physical appearance. The major side effects of abusing anabolic steroids include cancer, increased aggressiveness, and severe mood swings.

Reaching Out for Help

Alcohol and drug abuse can and should be treated. There are many kinds of addictions, and many communities offer counseling services, support groups, treatment services, and interventionists to help people beat their addictions and change their lives. Organizations such as Alcoholics Anonymous, Alateen, and Al-Anon help alcohol users and their family and friends. Narcotics Anonymous is helpful to people dealing with drug abuse, and Gamblers Anonymous can help those with a gambling addiction. People struggling with food addictions can contact Overeaters Anonymous.

- **Stand up for others.** Don't walk the other way when someone's being teased. Imagine the strength and good feeling you can give others by sticking beside them.

- **Say a kind word.** An unexpected compliment can brighten someone's day. Think of something kind to say to a friend. This small gesture can go a long way.

- **Care for yourself.** Sometimes teens care about others and forget to care for themselves. Be your own best friend and praise yourself for your accomplishments, no matter how small.

Prescription and Over-the-Counter Drugs

Prescription and over-the-counter (OTC) drugs (those sold without a prescription) are beneficial in treating many health conditions. Doctors will tell you that everyone responds to these drugs differently. That's why it is important to follow your doctor's and pharmacist's directions for prescription and OTC drugs. What can you do to avoid misusing medicine?

- **Stay away from others' medications.** Do not use a drug prescribed for someone else. You don't know how your body will react to it.

- **Follow directions.** Take the amount prescribed by your doctor or the dosage listed on the OTC drug label, not more or less. If you are taking a prescription, use all of the medicine. See **Fig. 20-5**.

- **Don't mix drugs and alcohol.** Drugs, even OTC drugs, should never be mixed with alcohol. Alcohol can severely change the beneficial effects of any drug and cause serious physical harm.

- **Obtain doctor's approval for supplements.** OTC products such as diet pills and herbal supplements can also be dangerous to your health. Do not use these products unless advised by your doctor.

Sexually Transmitted Diseases

Sexually transmitted diseases (STDs) are diseases passed from one person to another through sexual contact. There are numerous STDs, including chlamydia, gonorrhea, syphilis, and herpes. STDs are dangerous and can even be fatal. Symptoms and complications range from feelings of discomfort to permanent physical and mental damage. Symptoms are not always obvious, however, and if symptoms do appear, they may be confused with symptoms of other diseases.

Fig 20-5
Read all information on boxes and bottles of OTC products and note any side effects.

No vaccines or treatments exist to prevent STDs. Your body cannot build up immunity (resistance) to STDs. The way to avoid contracting an STD is by practicing sexual **abstinence**—not engaging in a sexual activity. An important benefit of abstinence is that you maintain a healthy sense of self-respect. Abstinence puts you in charge of your body and your future.

AIDS and HIV

Acquired immunodeficiency syndrome (AIDS) is a life-threatening disease that interferes with the body's natural ability to fight infection. The virus that causes AIDS is called the human immunodeficiency virus (HIV).

HIV is spread from one person to another by the exchange of body fluids during sexual activity. It is also transmitted by unclean needles used to inject illegal drugs. HIV carriers might not display symptoms, so you cannot identify who is or is not carrying the disease. For your own protection, it is important to guard against HIV and AIDS by not using illegal drugs and by practicing sexual abstinence. See **Fig. 20-6**.

Fig 20-6 True friends will understand your choice to abstain from sexual activity. How might your choice affect your friends' choices?

People who have AIDS can contract many life-threatening diseases. AIDS weakens the body's immune system and makes it difficult to fight off infections that could normally be controlled. There is no cure for AIDS, so it's in your best interest to become knowledgeable about it. You can obtain information about HIV, AIDS, and other STDs from the U.S. Centers for Disease Control, state health departments, and community health organizations.

Negative Effects of Early Pregnancy

Teen pregnancy can create harmful health risks for both young mothers and their children. A teen girl's body is still developing and may not be able to support and nourish an unborn child. Many pregnant teens receive inadequate prenatal care, or care received during pregnancy. Their children are often born with low birth weights, which lead to health problems later on, as well as other physical and mental disabilities. The majority of teenage mothers are unmarried, which can create emotional and financial problems for young children and their mothers.

Many teen mothers choose to keep their babies, despite a lack of money, education, and emotional maturity. Raising children is a major challenge for mature adults. For teens, the demands of parenting are overwhelming and can negatively affect the rest of their lives. Many teen mothers and fathers are unable to pursue their education, which can open doors to higher-paying jobs. While their friends are enjoying the freedom and fun of being teenagers, teen parents often feel trapped by having become parents too soon.

Fig 20-7 People who suffer from depression feel alone and overwhelmed. Counselors, teachers, and caring adults—as well as friends—can help teens feel better about themselves and their life.

Preventing Suicide

Every teen experiences a certain amount of stress, disappointment, and confusion. Sometimes these feelings can be overwhelming, causing some people to view suicide, or taking their own life, as a solution. See **Fig. 20-7**.

People who are considering suicide need help, and it's important for others to know the warning signs of suicide. Be concerned if a friend or family member who has been under stress or has been depressed says, "You won't have to worry about me anymore." This person may also display dramatic changes in personality and appearance and may give away prized personal belongings.

What can you do if you suspect someone is contemplating suicide? Be attentive to what this person says by listening carefully and asking questions for clarification. Suggest that many problems have solutions that are not obvious at the moment. Encourage the person to obtain help by speaking with a counselor, a trusted adult friend, a parent, or a well-liked teacher. If the person refuses help, seek a trusted adult yourself and request help for your friend. Above all, do not dismiss the person's remarks and actions as unimportant. See **Fig. 20-8**.

Fig 20-8 Listening to and respecting your friend's feelings shows your friend you care. What else can you do to express a caring attitude?

Avoiding Health Risks

What can you do to avoid sexual activity and illegal drugs? Try to develop friendships with people who share your interests and values and who won't pressure you to have sex or do drugs. Consider joining a school service organization or pursue your interests in sports or the arts. Keep in mind that when you are busy doing positive things, risky activities seem less appealing.

Saying "no" to illegal drugs or sexual activity is one of the most important decisions you will ever make. By taking a stand, you show that you value your health and that you are in charge of your own life.

By refusing to use drugs or have sex, you will not suffer any negative consequences, you won't be any less popular, you won't be any less loved, and you won't be any less attractive. You will be making an important choice. If you abuse drugs or become involved in sexual activity, you often hurt other family members and friends who care about you. Even more important, you hurt yourself, and the effects can last a lifetime.

Review & Activities

Chapter Summary

- Frequently abused drugs have a variety of negative physical and psychological effects.
- Always follow doctor's orders and instructions on OTC and prescription medicines.
- STDs can cause serious physical and mental damage.
- Children of teen mothers are often born with low birth weights and are at risk for physical and mental problems.
- Refusing risky activities helps keep you safe and shows others that you value your health and life.

Reviewing Key Terms & Ideas

1. Name three drugs that are commonly abused.
2. What are the effects of **inhalants**?
3. What is **addiction**?
4. Explain the difference between a **stimulant** and a **depressant**.
5. What are the dangers associated with **marijuana** and drugs that are **hallucinogens**?
6. Why do some people use **anabolic steroids**?
7. Identify at least two precautions to follow when using prescription and OTC drugs.
8. Define **sexually transmitted diseases (STD)**.
9. What effect does **acquired immunodeficiency syndrome (AIDS)** have on the body?
10. How does pregnancy affect a teen mother's life?

Thinking Critically

1. **Understanding effects.** What effects do you think drug abuse has on a family? What problems does teen drug use cause for parents or guardians and siblings? How do you think parents or guardians should react to teen drug use?
2. **Analyzing behavior.** What motivates someone to use tobacco, despite the health risks? How do the media influence a person's decision to smoke or chew tobacco?
3. **Drawing conclusions.** How does involvement in school and community activities help teens refuse drugs?

Review & Activities

Applying Your Learning

1. **Media analysis.** Find advertisements for cigarettes in newspapers and magazines. Who do you think the ads target? Do you think they accurately reflect the image of real-life smokers?

2. **Personal safety.** With a partner, enact a scene in which a friend who has been drinking offers to drive you home from a party. Practice refusing the ride and preventing your friend from driving.

3. **Drug education.** Working with a small group, develop a drug awareness program for your school. What are your objectives? What approaches will you use? Present your program to your teacher, counselor, or principal for feedback.

4. **Safety warnings.** Using art supplies or computer graphics software, create a poster that warns young children about the dangers of household chemicals.

5. **Student interviews.** Interview school athletes to find out their knowledge and attitudes about steroids. Write a short article based on your findings.

6. **OTC research.** Choose an herbal supplement you think might benefit teen health. Interview a doctor or pharmacist about the benefits and dangers of the supplement.

Making Connections

1. **Writing** Imagine a friend has written you telling you he has been taking steroids. You became concerned because of what you have heard about steroids. Write a letter to him explaining your concerns.

2. **Reading** Read newspaper and magazine articles about the problem of AIDS in Africa. How is the international community addressing the problem? Summarize your findings.

3. **Writing** Imagine you are an advice columnist for a local newspaper. A teen has written you asking how to keep friends while refusing to participate with them in risky activities. Write a response to the teen.

CAREER Link

Health and Safety. The U.S. government sets safety standards, or guidelines, to help protect workers. A special branch of the U.S. Department of Labor, the Occupational Safety and Health Administration (OSHA) is in charge of setting safety standards and inspecting workplaces to make sure that the standards are being followed. Interview a local employer about OSHA standards. How does the employer meet the federal guidelines?

Personal Safety

Objectives

- Explain crimes of opportunity.
- Recognize ways to make your home safer.
- Identify safety measures to practice away from home.
- Practice safety precautions in sports.
- Summarize steps for handling emergencies.

Vocabulary

- **crime**
- **exploitation**
- **telemarketing**
- **fraud**

Reading with Purpose

1. **As you read** Chapter 21, create an outline in your notebook using the colored headings.

2. **Write** a question under each heading that you can use to guide your reading.

3. **Answer** the question under each heading as you read the chapter. Record your answers.

4. **Ask** your teacher to help with answers you could not find in this chapter.

Why Think About Safety?

Safety is everybody's concern. You are responsible for your own safety and sometimes the safety of others at home, at school, and even at work if you have a part-time job. Most people around you are citizens who care about the safety of their family and others in the community. They're ready to help someone in trouble. Are you prepared to help?

Fig 21-1 By carrying her purse over her shoulder, this girl makes it more difficult for a thief to steal her valuables. What other safety precautions can she take?

Safety ✓ Check

You can help prevent crime and make your community safer by taking the following actions:

• Observe the rules and laws of your school and community.

• Report any suspicious activity to the proper authorities.

• Make it a point to know your neighbors and where they live.

• Work with others to set up a neighborhood crime watch program that encourages people to look out for one another.

A small minority of people commit criminal acts. A **crime** is an illegal act committed against someone or something. Many crimes are crimes of opportunity—a criminal sees the opportunity to commit a crime and does. For example, a criminal might spot an open window and decide to enter a home unlawfully. One way to prevent crime is to avoid creating opportunities for criminals. See **Fig. 21-1**.

Many factors contribute to crime. Some experts believe that the violence seen on TV and heard on CDs encourages crime. They think the media make crime seem glamorous and acceptable. Still others believe that traditional family life has weakened and that moral values are no longer stressed. What do you think?

Safety at Home

You and your family want to feel safe at home. Some neighborhoods are safer than others, but even in the safest areas, law enforcement authorities suggest that you and your family follow some basic safety precautions:

• **Keep contact information private.** Never give your phone number or address to anyone you do not know, and don't share information about your family or their schedules. This includes giving personal information over the Internet or the phone.

• **Keep doors and windows locked.** Deadbolt locks are the most secure locks for doors. When you turn the key from inside or outside the door, a strong metal bar slides into the door frame. Use ventilation locks on windows. These locks, which you can find at hardware stores, are inexpensive metal stops you can adjust to any level for air to enter.

• **Secure sliding glass doors.** Prevent sliding glass doors from being opened from the outside by placing a piece of thick wood, such as a dowel, in the door track or purchasing and placing a rod made for that purpose.

• **Light entryways.** Make sure that the areas around outside doors are well lit. This is especially important in an area with large bushes among which someone could hide.

- **Keep alert.** Form a neighborhood volunteer patrol system. Many neighbors make it a point to look out for each other and report any suspicious activity.

- **Be prepared.** Have your house key ready when you enter or leave your home. If you witness suspicious activity near your home, do not go into the house. Go to a neighbor's home and contact the police. Be prepared to explain why you are concerned. Accurate descriptions of people, cars, and license plates are helpful.

- **Enter your home safely.** If someone drops you off at home, ask the driver to wait until you are safely inside. Flash a light when you are inside to show you entered safely.

- **Don't allow strangers in.** If a stranger asks to come inside your home, have an adult come to the door. If you're alone, do not open the door. Tell the person to come back at another time. Always check the identification of repair workers and community employees. See **Fig. 21-2**.

Internet Safety

Millions of people are now going online to exchange e-mail, surf the Internet, post and read messages on bulletin boards, and join chat rooms. The Internet community is like any other community—there are plenty of good people online and a few people who will harm others. Some people online are rude and insulting, and others commit **exploitation**—they use others for selfish purposes. The Internet has many benefits, but if you are not cautious online you can become a target of crime and exploitation. Follow these guidelines to be "cybersmart":

- **Do not give out personal information.** Keep private information such as your address, telephone number, parents' or guardians' workplace addresses and phone numbers, and the name and location of your school.

> **TIPS**
> ## Stock a First Aid Kit
>
> A well-equipped first aid kit includes these basic items:
>
> ▶ Adhesive strip bandages in a variety of shapes and sizes
>
> ▶ Sterile gauze pads
>
> ▶ Gauze rolls
>
> ▶ Hydrogen peroxide
>
> ▶ Adhesive tape
>
> ▶ Medicated soap
>
> ▶ Antibiotic ointment
>
> ▶ First aid manual
>
> ▶ List of emergency telephone numbers

Fig 21-2

Talk about home safety with your family and establish rules to keep everyone safe. What rules does your family have in place for answering doors?

- **Get help.** Tell your parents or guardians if you come across any information that makes you feel uncomfortable.

- **Say "No" to face-to-face meetings.** Never agree to meet in person anyone you "meet" online. If someone suggests that you meet, tell your parents or guardians.

- **Keep your image private.** Do not send photos to people you "meet" online, and don't post them to Web sites without your parents' or guardians' approval.

- **Ignore bullies.** Do not respond to any messages that are insulting or mean. These messages are a form of harassment, and responding to the sender usually increases the conflict. If you feel bullied on the Internet, tell your parents or adults in charge so that they can contact your Internet service provider. The service provider can help you block the bully's messages.

- **Don't give passwords away.** Keep your passwords private from everyone except your parents or guardians. No one—not even your best friend—should be able to access your passwords.

- **Follow family rules.** Rules for going online may involve the time of day that you can be online, the length of time you can be there, and the sites you can visit. Some families install filters to protect teens from unsafe online experiences. See **Fig. 21-3**.

Fig 21-3
Meeting friends online can be a positive and safe experience if you follow safety precautions. What precaution is this teen taking?

Fig 21-4

To be safe, going places with a friend or a group of friends is a good idea. How can having friends nearby be a protection when you're in public places?

Telephone Scams

Telemarketing, or selling over the telephone, is a million-dollar business. Although most telemarketers are honest, some dishonest callers are scam artists. They tell lies to steal money or valuables, which is **fraud**.

People who commit telephone fraud are skilled at sounding believable. They might use phrases such as "specially selected," "free bonus," "valuable prizes," and "only if you act right away" to motivate you to give them money. You may believe you're buying a product or giving money to a charity, when in reality the scammer is stealing your money.

When you receive a telephone solicitation, be cautious about the information you share. Personal information can be used for illegal means. When in doubt, the best way to handle the call is to say, "No, thank you," and hang up the phone.

Safety Away from Home

Whether you are alone or with friends in a crowd, keep safety in mind. Act confident—always look as if you know where you are going, even if you don't. Carry personal identification and the phone numbers of people to contact in case of an emergency, and make sure someone at home knows where you are and when you will be home. Also, learn where the police and fire stations are located.

Here are some other "street smarts" to keep in mind:

- **Use the "buddy system."** There is safety in numbers. Go places with friends whenever you can. See **Fig. 21-4**.

- **Use well-traveled routes.** Don't take risky shortcuts or travel through isolated areas. Be aware of your surroundings, and stay in well-lit areas. Try to walk in the middle of the sidewalk and not next to buildings.

- **Make a plan in case you become lost.** If you're in a public area and are separated from your friends or family, do not wander around looking for them. In advance, designate a specific place to meet them in case you become lost.

- **Ignore strangers.** If anyone attempts to verbally harass you, keep walking. Responding can make the situation worse.

- **Don't get into strangers' cars.** If someone tries to force you into a car, scream to get attention and fight to escape. Some experts suggest that you yell, "Fire!" People are more likely to pay attention if they think there is a fire.

- **Watch your belongings.** Keep your personal items with you to prevent others from taking your identification or money. Identity theft is a serious crime. It occurs when someone uses your personal information, such as your name, Social Security number, or credit card number without your permission. If you think your identity has been stolen, contact the police immediately.

- **Trust your instincts.** If a situation doesn't feel right to you, leave quickly.

Sports Safety

When you are exercising or playing a sport, remember that safety comes first. Unfortunately, many teens ignore simple safety precautions that can keep them from being sidelined. The following guidelines can help prevent sports-related injuries:

- **Follow the rules of the sport.** When bicycling, ride on the right side of the road with traffic, not against it. When skating, avoid parking lots, streets, and other areas with traffic. See **Fig. 21-5.**

Fig 21-5 Learning about the proper safety gear is part of playing sports. Why do you think some teens choose not to wear safety gear?

Fig 21-6
Keeping a cool head in any emergency is the first step in handling it effectively. What emergency procedures are these teens following?

- **Always wear a helmet.** This is especially important for sports such as football, hockey, baseball, biking, skateboarding, and inline skating.

- **Use eye protection.** The eye gear offering the most protection is made from a plastic called polycarbonate, which has been tested especially for sports use. Goggles are often worn for soccer, basketball, racquet sports, snowboarding, street hockey, and baseball and softball.

- **Wear a mouth guard.** Mouth guards can protect your mouth, teeth, and tongue if you play a contact sport or other sport for which head injury is a risk.

- **Protect your bones and joints.** Wrist, knee, and elbow guards are important gear for inline skating and skateboarding.

- **Stay off the phone.** Anytime you are involved in an active sport, such as skateboarding or biking, do not use a cell phone. The sport requires your complete attention. Losing your focus can result in a serious accident.

Taking Emergency Action

Emergencies happen, usually unexpectedly. How can you and your family be better prepared to handle emergency situations? See **Fig. 21-6**.

Calling for Help

Post the following emergency phone numbers near the telephone so that everyone can see them:

- Police, fire, and ambulance (911 or dial 0).

- A poison control center.

- A doctor or clinic.

- Parents' or guardians' work numbers.

- Nearest relative.

- Friend or neighbor.

HOW TO PREVENT FALLS

Compared with other accidents, falls may not seem serious. Yet they send about two million people to the emergency room every year. Older adults are particularly at risk because age often slows reactions, making falls more likely. Also, adults' bones grow thin as they age, making the injuries more serious. Young children are also at risk, with their unsteady balance and natural curiosity.

To help keep all people in your home on their feet, take these simple precautions:

- **Use stairway railings.** As you may have guessed, stairways are the most common site of household falls.

- **Light the home adequately, especially stairways.** Besides overhead lights, place nightlights throughout the home as needed. Keep a table lamp or flashlight next to your bed. Make sure to have extra lightbulbs and batteries on hand.

- **Create clear traffic areas.** Arrange furniture for easy passage. Avoid running electrical cords across widely traveled areas. Remove clutter.

- **Secure area rugs.** Use tacks, foam backing, or double-sided tape.

Stay calm if you need to make an emergency telephone call. Wait for the dial tone, then dial 911 or 0 for an operator. Speak clearly and state the emergency. Give the dispatcher your name, address, and phone number. If you are not at home, describe your exact location. Do not hang up the phone until someone tells you to do so. It may be important to stay on the line to receive additional instructions. Follow any directions the dispatcher gives you. You may want to repeat the instructions to be sure that you understand them.

- **Place nonskid mats or strips in bathtubs and showers.** Be sure a bathroom rug that grips the floor awaits wet feet as people step out of the tub.

- **Keep paved surfaces outside the home in good condition.** Home improvement stores sell concrete fillers and patches to smooth uneven spots and fill cracks and holes in sidewalks and driveways. Contact the local public works department to repair damage on public property. Clear walkways of snow and ice.

- **Use a sturdy stepladder or stepstool to reach high places.** These items are designed to support a person's weight securely—chairs are not. Be sure to keep both feet on the stepladder at all times, and steady yourself by placing one hand on the ladder or a counter or wall.

- **Choose the right footwear for working around the home.** Low-heeled, rubber-soled shoes give the best traction and balance.

TAKE **ACTION**

Use this information to create a "Fall Prevention Checklist" to share with your family.

Giving First Aid

Every emergency situation is different, and it is critical to know when and how to act. Become familiar with the basic principles of first aid. The American Red Cross offers classes and information on first aid, as do other community service organizations.

Timing and action are important in the case of choking. Food lodged in the throat, or airway, can cause a person to choke. When you see someone choking, perform the Heimlich maneuver, as shown below. See **Fig. 21-7**.

Fig 21-7 ▶ The Heimlich Maneuver

The Heimlich maneuver can be performed on a person who is standing or sitting.

1. If the person can speak, cough, or breathe, do not interfere. Often, the person can cough out the food or blockage.

2. If the person cannot speak, cough, or breathe, ask someone to call for help or call 911 immediately for medical assistance.

3. Stand behind the person and wrap your arms around his or her waist. Make a fist with one hand and wrap your other hand around the fist. Make a sharp inward and upward thrust just above the person's waist. Repeat six to ten times until the blockage is expelled. If the blockage does not come out, repeat the procedure.

Performing CPR

Giving first aid to an injured or ill person may include performing CPR—cardiopulmonary resuscitation. This technique is used to keep a person's heart and lungs functioning until medical care arrives. The rescuer breathes into the person's mouth and applies pressure to the chest to force the heart to pump. You should be trained in CPR before performing it. The American Heart Association and the American Red Cross have information about this technique and about classes you can take to learn it.

Responding to Fire

Fires usually take everyone by surprise. Do you know how to respond in case of fire? If the fire is inside your home, leave as fast as possible and call for help from the nearest phone. Do not go inside a burning building. If someone is on fire, remember to immediately have him or her "stop, drop, and roll" to put out the flames. It's important that all family members have an emergency plan in place so that everyone knows how to act if a fire occurs.

Every minute counts in an emergency. Do not leave an emergency situation unless you are in danger. Look for ways to help; others may be depending on your actions.

Community Resources

All communities have emergency services you can contact for help. Your local telephone book has a section listing important emergency numbers. Call the local police department to help you or refer you to services you may need. Before a situation becomes a crisis, try to find help. Don't be afraid to speak to people at the police department or an emergency hot line. People who work at these locations are trained to help you. They will ask questions to obtain necessary information from you and will provide you with the assistance you and others may need. See **Fig. 21-8**.

Fig 21-8 You don't need to wait for an emergency to happen before talking to police officers. Feel free to get to know the police officers in your neighborhood.

Review & Activities

Chapter Summary

- One way to prevent crime is to avoid creating opportunities for criminals.
- Law enforcement authorities recommend simple guidelines to keep you safe at home.
- Observe safety practices away from home to prevent dangerous incidents from occurring.
- Use proper sports equipment and follow the rules of the game to enjoy sports events and remain safe.
- It is important to handle emergencies quickly yet calmly.

Reviewing Key Terms & Ideas

1. Define **crime**.
2. List three safety precautions to take at home.
3. What should you do if a stranger comes to your door?
4. Explain **exploitation**.
5. How should teens respond to bullying on the Internet?
6. What is **fraud**?
7. List two safety precautions you can take when away from home.
8. What are three examples of sports gear people can wear to help prevent injury?
9. Name three emergency telephone numbers to have near your phone.
10. Explain the procedure for making an emergency phone call.

Thinking Critically

1. **Making evaluations.** Some experts believe violence on TV, in movies, and in video games can cause crime. Imagine you're speaking to a parent group about how to evaluate TV programming for teens. What criteria would you suggest that they use to evaluate programs for their family?
2. **Analyzing viewpoints.** What Internet rules would you make to keep children safe? How do you think those rules would differ from the rules adults would set for themselves?
3. **Drawing conclusions.** Why do people sometimes panic when emergencies occur? What are some signs of panic? What advice would you offer others to help them stay calm when an emergency occurs?

Review & Activities

Applying Your Learning

1. **Crime prevention.** Develop a public safety announcement emphasizing procedures people can take to prevent crime at home. Arrange to show your public service announcement to students in your school or a local crime prevention organization.

2. **Internet safety.** Plan an instructional program for young children regarding Internet safety. Present your safety program to a class.

3. **Fraud prevention.** Create a brochure for teens that provides tips for preventing telemarketing fraud and identity theft.

4. **Sports safety.** Interview physical education teachers or coaches to identify ways to participate more safely in sports programs. Share your findings with your class.

5. **CPR demonstration.** Invite an American Heart Association representative or an emergency medical technician to demonstrate the CPR emergency response techniques. Be prepared to ask questions of the speaker.

Making Connections

1. **Writing** Develop a story about a teen superhero who works to prevent crime. Illustrate your story and arrange to share it with a class of young children.

2. **Reading** Read community safety pamphlets from the police and fire departments or read a book about community safety. Summarize the information for your class.

3. **Math** Find out the cost of protective sports gear for a sport of your choice. What is the range of prices for the gear? How much does the price of the gear relate to the quality of the item?

4. **Writing** Take a position either for or against blocking software that prevents teens from browsing certain Web sites. Write a persuasive paragraph convincing readers of your position.

CAREER Link

Community Involvement.
Many businesses are actively involved in their community to help promote the well-being of its citizens. As an employee, you might be involved in your employer's community service activities. Identify a local nonprofit organization in your community. Make a list of ways a business can work with the organization to benefit the community and the business.

How Nutrients Work

Objectives

- Summarize the role nutrients play in your diet.
- Explain how nutritional deficiencies can affect health.
- Describe how food is digested in your body.
- Relate calorie intake to energy.
- Propose strategies for meeting energy and nutrient needs.

Vocabulary

- **nutrients**
- **carbohydrates**
- **fiber**
- **proteins**
- **amino acids**
- **complete proteins**
- **incomplete proteins**
- **cholesterol**
- **phytochemicals**
- **deficiency**
- **calories**
- **nutrient density**

Reading with Purpose

1. **Read** the title of this chapter and describe in writing what you expect to learn from it.

2. **Write** each vocabulary term in your notebook, leaving space for definitions.

3. **As you read** Chapter 22, write the definition beside each term in your notebook.

4. **After** reading the chapter, write a paragraph describing what you learned.

Nutrients at Work

Think about how you feel today. Do you feel energized? Are you alert and able to concentrate in class? If so, you can thank the food you ate this morning or at lunch. You can also credit your diet with the condition of your hair and skin. Your body relies on the nutrients found in food for good health and proper functioning.

The substances found in food that keep your body in good working order are called **nutrients**. Your body needs nutrients for energy and growth and to repair your body. Nutrients also help your body maintain basic functions, such as circulating your blood and breathing. Six categories of nutrients work together to keep you in good health: carbohydrates, proteins, fats, vitamins, minerals, and water. See **Fig. 22-1**.

Carbohydrates

Carbohydrates are the nutrients that provide your body with most of its energy. The two main types of carbohydrates are sugars and starches. Sugars, which are simple carbohydrates, can be either natural or refined. Refined sugar is sugar that has been removed from its natural source. Candy and soft drinks contain refined sugar, but most do not provide you with other nutrients. Fruits, vegetables, and milk contain natural sugars and other important nutrients.

Starches, which are complex carbohydrates, are broken down into sugar when digested. Breads, cereals, pasta, rice, dry beans, and some vegetables, such as potatoes and corn, contain starch and other nutrients.

Many complex carbohydrates also contain **fiber**, or plant material that does not break down during digestion. Although fiber is not a nutrient, it's an important part of healthful eating. Insoluble fiber comes from grains. It helps move food through the body and helps eliminate waste. Soluble fiber, which is found in fruit and other foods containing pectin, helps reduce the risk of heart disease.

Where can you find fiber? The cereal you ate this morning probably contains some fiber, as do the fruits and vegetables you ate with lunch or as a snack. Other sources of fiber include whole-grain bread, oatmeal, whole-wheat crackers, and popcorn.

Fig 22-1 ▶ Colorful vegetables and fruits contain important nutrients. Be sure to eat a variety of foods to maintain a well-balanced diet.

Proteins

Think about your hair, skin, and nails. What do they have in common? And what feature do they share with your vital organs? The answer: they're all made of protein. Nutrients used to build, maintain, and repair body tissues are called **proteins**. Protein is especially important during your teen years to help you grow and develop.

Fig 22-2 Combining incomplete proteins supplies your body with the protein it needs. Which of these foods do you eat each day?

Protein foods are made up of chemical compounds called **amino acids**, which are known as the body's building blocks. Every type of protein food contains a different combination of amino acids that helps your body function. Your body makes all but nine of the amino acids that you need. Those nine are called essential amino acids. Because your body cannot manufacture these amino acids, the food you eat has to supply them.

Meat, fish, poultry, milk products, eggs, and other foods from animal sources are called **complete proteins** because they have all of the nine essential amino acids your body needs. Plant foods such as grains, dry beans and peas, nuts, seeds, and vegetables also contain proteins. These proteins are called **incomplete proteins** because they lack one or more of the nine essential amino acids. See **Fig. 22-2**.

Incomplete proteins can work together to form complete proteins. For example, when eaten together, beans and rice form a complete protein. You can also make complete proteins by combining a complete and an incomplete protein. For example, when you eat milk with your cereal, the complete proteins in the milk fill in for the missing amino acids in the cereal. To make sure that your body gets enough complete proteins, you should eat a wide variety of foods each day.

Fats

Darren decided to lose a few pounds before the Saturday wrestling match. "I'll cut all fat from my diet, and the pounds should drop right off," he thought. Although Darren might have a good reason to lose weight, cutting out all fat isn't the best way to do it.

A small amount of fat is vital to good health. Fats help regulate body temperature, cushion vital organs, and provide substances your body needs for normal growth and healthy skin. Fats are the most concentrated form of food energy you eat, and they act as your body's energy storage trunk, saving energy for you to use later. Fat works as a partner with other nutrients in your food. Some vitamins need to dissolve in fat before they can be carried to other parts of the body that need them.

Foods such as butter, margarine, sour cream, and salad oil are fats you can easily see. Fats you may not see as easily are called hidden fats and are found in meat, fish, egg yolks, whole milk, cheese, donuts, and nuts. There are three main types of fat:

- **Saturated fats.** Saturated fat is solid at room temperature and should be used moderately. You can find saturated fat in animal foods, such as meat, poultry, egg yolks, and whole-milk dairy products. Saturated fats are also found in tropical oils, such as coconut and palm oil.

- **Unsaturated fats.** Unsaturated fat, which is liquid at room temperature, can be found mainly in vegetable, olive, and nut oils. Try to use these fats instead of saturated fats in your cooking. See **Fig. 22-3**.

Fig 22-3
Try to limit the amount of saturated, or solid, fats you eat. What substitutions can you make for the saturated fats shown here?

- **Trans fats.** Also known as trans fatty acids, trans fats are made when food manufacturers turn liquid oils into solid ones through a process called hydrogenation. Trans fats can be found in vegetable shortenings, French fries, doughnuts, fried foods, and salad dressings. If you see the words "partially hydrogenated" on a food label, this is a clue that the product contains trans fat.

Cholesterol

Cholesterol is a soft, fatlike, waxy substance found in the bloodstream and in all of your body's cells. Despite its bad reputation, it's needed for several important bodily functions, such as digestion.

Your body manufactures all the cholesterol it needs, so you don't need the additional cholesterol contained in certain foods. Eating too many cholesterol-rich foods, such as meat, eggs, butter, and cheese, can be harmful to your health. Many experts also advise people to avoid eating too many foods containing saturated and trans fats because they help your body produce cholesterol.

How can cholesterol affect your health? Cholesterol can build up on the walls of your arteries, which carry blood and oxygen to the heart. If enough cholesterol builds up, the blood and oxygen cannot reach the heart. When this happens, you can suffer a heart attack. High cholesterol, which is a leading cause of heart disease, can also cause high blood pressure.

Vitamins

Vitamins trigger many of your body processes. They function like spark plugs in an engine by setting off chemical reactions in your body's cells. Each vitamin regulates a different process. Their roles are very specific, and one cannot substitute for another. Your body requires a variety of vitamins each day, and generally you get all the vitamins you need when you eat a variety of healthful foods. See **Fig. 22-4**.

Vitamins fit into two categories:

- **Fat-soluble vitamins.** Vitamins A, D, E, and K are absorbed with the help of fats. Your body can store fat-soluble vitamins. However, too much of these vitamins can be harmful to your health. For example, too much vitamin D can cause nausea, confusion, weight loss, and muscle weakness. See **Fig. 22-5**.

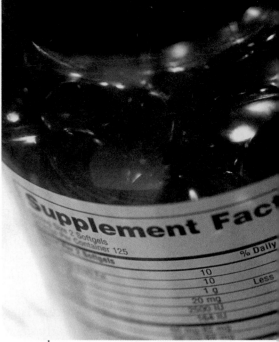

Fig 22-4 Vitamin supplements are not a substitute for good nutrition.

Fat-Soluble Vitamins

Vitamin	Where It's Found	What It Does
Vitamin A	Dark green, leafy vegetables (spinach, kale); deep yellow and orange fruits and vegetables (cantaloupe, carrots, sweet potatoes, apricots); liver; milk, cheese, and eggs	Helps keep skin and hair healthy; aids night vision; builds strong bones and teeth
Vitamin D	Milk with vitamin D, egg yolk, salmon, liver	Helps build strong bones and teeth; helps the body use calcium and phosphorus
Vitamin E	Whole-grain breads and cereals; dark green, leafy vegetables; dry beans and peas; nuts and seeds; vegetable oils, margarine; liver	Helps form red blood cells, muscles, and other tissues
Vitamin K	Dark green, leafy vegetables; cabbage	Helps blood to clot

Fig 22-5 The key to good nutrition is to eat a variety of foods. Too much of a vitamin can be just as harmful as too little.

- **Water-soluble vitamins.** Vitamin C and the B vitamins dissolve in water and easily pass out of the body as waste. You need a frequent supply of these vitamins, but again too many may be harmful. Water-soluble vitamins are also shown in **Fig. 22-5**.

Phytochemicals

Phytochemicals are substances that plants produce naturally to protect themselves from harm. They do the same for you by improving your body's immunity, which helps you fight diseases, such as heart disease and cancer. As an added bonus, they give many foods their attractive color. You can find phytochemicals in fruits, vegetables, dry beans, nuts, and whole grains.

Water-Soluble Vitamins

Vitamin	Where It's Found	What It Does
B-complex vitamins (riboflavin, niacin, B_6, B_{12}, thiamine)	Whole-grain and enriched breads and cereals; dry beans and peas; peanut butter; nuts; meat, poultry, and fish; eggs and milk	Helps the body use carbohydrates, fats, and proteins; helps produce energy in cells; helps maintain healthy nervous system, muscles, and tissues
Folate	Fruits; enriched and whole-wheat breads; dark green, leafy vegetables; liver; dry beans and peas	Helps build red blood cells and genes
Vitamin C	Citrus fruits (oranges, grapefruit, etc.), strawberries, broccoli, tomatoes, potatoes	Helps maintain bones, teeth, and blood vessels; helps heal wounds

Fig 22-5 continued

Minerals

Like vitamins, minerals also have certain jobs to perform. Minerals are an essential part of your bones, teeth, and internal organs, and they help regulate body functions. To work efficiently, your body needs at least 16 minerals each day. Your body needs small, or trace, amounts of some minerals and larger amounts of others. When you eat a variety of foods every day, you usually get the minerals you need.

Calcium is an especially important mineral for teens because it helps teens develop strong bones and teeth. Most of the body's calcium is stored in your bones. Bone mass accumulates rapidly when you're a teen, creating a strong bone structure. Many people who don't get enough calcium when they're young risk developing osteoporosis—or brittle bones—later in life. It's important that you get enough calcium now so that your bones remain strong for a lifetime. Drinking and eating dairy products is a good way to get the right amount of calcium. See **Fig. 22-6**.

Important Minerals

Mineral	Where It's Found	What It Does
Calcium	Milk and milk products; dark green, leafy vegetables; dry beans and peas; sardines and salmon (eaten with bones)	Builds and maintains strong bones and teeth; helps heart, muscles, and nerves work properly; helps blood to clot
Magnesium	Whole-grain products; green vegetables; dry beans and peas; nuts and seeds	Helps build bones; helps nerves and muscles work normally; contributes to proper heart function
Phosphorus	Meat, poultry, fish, and eggs; dry beans and peas; nuts; milk and milk products	Builds and maintains strong bones and teeth; helps body use carbohydrates, fats, and proteins
Iodine	Saltwater fish, iodized salt	Helps produce substances needed for growth; helps regulate rate at which body uses energy
Iron	Red meats, liver, and egg yolk; dark green, leafy vegetables; dry beans and peas; nuts; whole-grain and enriched breads and cereals; dried fruits (raisins)	Helps red blood cells carry oxygen to all parts of the body; helps cells use oxygen
Sodium	Salt, many foods	Helps maintain fluid balance in body; helps muscle and nerve action
Zinc	Meat, liver, poultry, and fish; dairy products; dry beans and peas; whole-grain breads and cereals	Promotes normal growth; helps wounds heal; helps body use carbohydrates, proteins, and fats
Potassium	Oranges and orange juice; bananas; dried fruits; dry beans and peas; peanut butter; meats	Works with sodium to help maintain fluid balance in body; helps heart and muscles work properly; helps regulate blood pressure

Fig 22-6 Your body may need only trace amounts of certain minerals, but that small amount is vital to good health.

Water

Do you know what water does after it leaves your glass and enters your body? Water is an essential nutrient. It makes up most of your body weight, and you couldn't survive long without it. Water helps regulate body functions and carry other nutrients to your cells. It also helps carry waste from your body. Think about the last time you exercised outside or in physical education class. Did you sweat? Perspiring is how your body regulates its temperature, and water helps it to do so. Water even keeps your nasal passages from drying out. Moist nasal passages help trap germs and keep them from entering your body. See **Fig. 22-7**.

Getting the right amount of water is important. You should drink at least eight glasses of water each day. Foods with high water content, such as fruits and vegetables, provide some of the water you need. Liquids you drink, such as milk, juice, and sports drinks, provide more water. Even if you eat and drink these foods and beverages, you still need to drink the minimum amount of water.

Fig 22-7
Water feeds and cleanses your body and is an important element for all life forms. How do you supply your body with sufficient water each day?

Deficiencies in Nutrition

When your body does not receive enough nutrients, a **deficiency**, or shortage, occurs. The symptoms, or effects, of the deficiency depend on its seriousness.

At first, the symptoms of a nutrition deficiency may not seem serious. People may feel a little tired, have difficulty sleeping or concentrating, have frequent colds, gain weight,

HOW TO MAINTAIN A HEALTHY WEIGHT

At one time, few people worried about maintaining a healthy weight. Life was physically demanding and diets were limited, so weight gain was not a problem. Today the situation is reversed. Modern technology makes life easier and expands the food supply.

At the same time, modern nutrition science is learning more about what constitutes a healthy weight. Certainly, having a clearer idea of what is the right weight for you can help you take charge of your health. However, finding your healthy weight can be a challenge, as new findings shape scientific opinion.

How can you solve the healthy weight riddle? The best advice is to talk to your family health care provider. He or she can give you information to help with each of these steps:

STEP 1 | **Learn your healthy weight range.** Health experts are developing increasingly exact methods to determine a healthy weight for any one person. Besides looking at traditional height and weight charts, learn your body mass index (BMI). BMI uses a formula that compares weight to height to find what percentage of weight is fat, which many experts believe is a more important factor than weight alone.

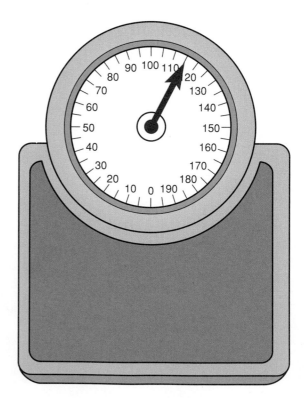

or lose weight. However, more serious symptoms of a nutrition deficiency can occur, such as hair loss, brittle nails, skin problems, nervousness, and extreme fatigue.

Nutritional deficiencies are more common than you might expect, even among people who think they eat well. Even though many people eat plenty of food, their diets frequently lack many important vitamins and minerals. To keep your body in top shape and avoid deficiencies, it's important to eat a variety of foods.

STEP 2 | **Calculate calories.** Once you identify your healthy weight range, you need to know how many calories you need to maintain it. Compare your calorie needs with your current calorie intake, which you can learn by reading food labels and keeping track of the foods you eat in a food diary.

Food Diary

Breakfast
Oat cereal
Milk
1/2 banana

Snack
Carrots and dip
Glass of water

STEP 3 | **Choose your course of action.** This is where you need to make some decisions—namely, whether your eating and activity habits are helping you reach and maintain a healthy weight. If not, will you change them? If you choose to gain or lose weight, will you pay as much attention to nutrition as to the numbers on a scale? What role will exercise play?

City Recreation Center

Weight Training Class: 1:00 p.m.

Kickboxing Class: 3:15 p.m.

Yoga Class: 5 p.m.

Sign Up Now!

STEP 4 | **Give yourself room to grow.** Remember that young teens are in the early stages of a great and somewhat unpredictable period of physical growth. What now looks like excess weight may look just right after a growth spurt in a few months. Likewise, an underdeveloped body may be on the verge of filling out.

TAKE ACTION

Bring to class an article on recent findings on the relationship between weight and health. How do the findings compare with established beliefs? How might they apply to maintaining a healthy weight?

Digestion

To get nutrients from food, your body must first digest it. Eating begins with what your eyes see. The smell and taste of food start the flow of saliva. When food enters your mouth, your teeth break it into small pieces, which releases the food's flavor. Your tongue pushes the food around in your mouth, and your saliva combines with the food. The chemicals in saliva, along with chewing, begin to break down the food. The path food takes through the digestive system can be seen in **Fig. 22-8**. Any undigested food is eliminated as body waste.

Energy and Calories

Your body gets its energy from the food you eat. You need some energy for normal body processes, such as breathing and pumping blood. You also need energy for schoolwork and other activities, such as playing sports and doing homework.

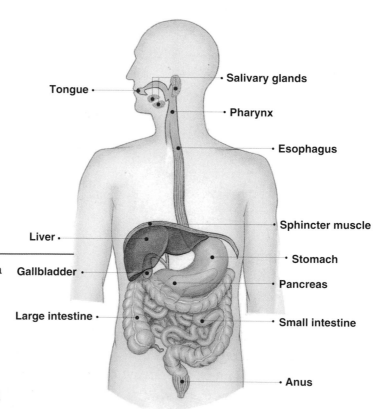

Fig 22-8
Food moves from the mouth through the esophagus to the stomach, where digestive juices break it down further. Food remains in the stomach about three to five hours. From the stomach, food moves to the small intestine, where nutrients are absorbed into the bloodstream. Unneeded nutrients and undigested food become body waste.

Tongue ·
· Salivary glands
· Pharynx
· Esophagus
· Sphincter muscle
Liver ·
· Stomach
Gallbladder ·
· Pancreas
Large intestine ·
· Small intestine
· Anus

Calories are units for measuring energy. Calories are used to measure both the energy you obtain from food and the energy you use when you are active.

How many calories do you need each day? The answer to that question depends on several things, such as your age and your level of activity. The number of calories you take in should balance with the amount you burn. If you take in more calories than you need, you'll gain weight. If you take in fewer calories than you need, you'll lose weight.

Sources of Calories

Do you eat mainly grains, fruits, and vegetables, or do you eat mostly meat and dairy foods? Where your calories come from is important. The energy in foods comes from fats, carbohydrates, and proteins. Vitamins, minerals, water, and fiber, although good for your health, do not provide energy. Fat is the most concentrated source of energy, with 9 calories per gram. (A gram is a metric unit of weight.) However, you do not want to eat large amounts of fat for your energy needs. Most of your energy needs will be met by carbohydrates and proteins.

Nutrient Density

Choosing food is more complicated than simply grabbing the first snack you spot in the store. When making healthful food choices, use nutrient density to guide your decisions. **Nutrient density** is the amount of nutrients in a food item in relation to the number of calories.

Candy, potato chips, and sugary soft drinks have low nutrient density. They increase your calorie count but contribute few nutrients. Which foods do you think have high nutrient density? If you answered fruits, vegetables, whole grains, lean meats, fish, poultry, and low-fat milk, you would be correct. These foods supply energy and important nutrients, such as proteins, minerals, and fiber.

You can eat some foods that have low nutrient density because they taste good, but these foods should not make up a large portion of your diet. If you eat mainly low-nutrient foods, you not only miss out on good nutrition but also may experience weight problems and nutritional deficiency.

You have probably heard the expression "you are what you eat." It may sound funny, but there is a lot of truth in this statement. After all, food fuels your body, and you want to give it the best fuel possible.

Tame Your Sweet Tooth

Most people enjoy sweets, but cookies, cakes, and other high-calorie, high-fat desserts contribute to weight gain. When you crave a sweet treat, try one of the following low-calorie options:

▶ Fresh fruit and fresh fruit parfaits

▶ Sugar-free pudding

▶ Low-fat or fat-free yogurt, plain or topped with fruit

▶ Low-fat fig cookies

▶ Fruit smoothies

▶ Sugar-free frozen juice bars

Review & Activities

Chapter Summary

- Six categories of nutrients work together to help your body function effectively.
- Nutritional deficiencies can cause health problems. Some may be mild, others can be serious.
- Digestion begins when you chew food and continues as food is transported through the body.
- You get energy from the food you eat, and energy is measured in calories.
- To meet nutritional needs, eat a variety of nutrient-dense foods each day.

Reviewing Key Terms & Ideas

1. Define **nutrients**.
2. What are the two types of **carbohydrates**?
3. What is **fiber**?
4. Explain the difference between **complete** and **incomplete proteins**.
5. Where are **amino acids** found?
6. List three foods that contain **cholesterol**.
7. What are **phytochemicals**?
8. What are the effects of a nutritional **deficiency**?
9. What is the relationship between energy and **calories**?
10. List four foods with high **nutrient density**.

Thinking Critically

1. **Analyzing situations.** How would you respond to a friend who thinks sugar is harmful and refuses to eat fruit because it contains sugar?
2. **Making comparisons.** Think of two people, one who maintains a healthy weight and another who does not. How do their food choices compare? What can they do to improve their eating habits?
3. **Drawing conclusions.** Many professional athletes follow strict diets. How do you think food affects their athletic performance? How might their diets change if they were to stop competing?

Review & Activities

Applying Your Learning

1. **Fiber assessment.** Research foods that are rich in fiber. Using this information, assess the fiber content of foods in your school's lunch program. How could the menu be changed to serve more high-fiber foods?

2. **Vitamin mural.** As a class, create a mural depicting different foods classified according to vitamin content. For example, carrots would be grouped with other foods labeled as vitamin A. Display the mural in your school's cafeteria.

3. **Calcium promotion.** Teen girls do not get enough calcium in their diets. Create a public-service advertisement that encourages teens to eat calcium-rich foods.

4. **Culture comparisons.** Research diets from other cultures. How do the diets compare with yours? What are the nutritional differences? Would it benefit you to incorporate foods from other cultures into your diet?

5. **Designing products.** Create a new food product that is tasty and nutrient dense. Design a label for your food product that lists the nutrients it contains and a description of its taste.

Making Connections

1. **Writing** Write a children's story incorporating a healthful food, such as broccoli. Emphasize the role the food plays in the body's functioning. Share your story with younger children.

2. **Reading** Read print and Internet sources to find out more about phytochemicals. Summarize the health benefits of phytochemicals and share your summary with your class.

3. **Math** Assume you need 2,000 calories a day to maintain your weight. Find out the number of calories burned in one hour of your favorite physical activity. How many calories a day do you need to eat to participate in your favorite activity and maintain your weight?

CAREER Link

Terminology.
Every career field has jargon, or terms that are unique to a field. Knowing the unique words used in your career of interest will help you communicate with your supervisors and coworkers on the job. Interview employees in a career field you're interested in. Ask them about the jargon used in the field. How did they learn the terminology? How does knowing the jargon help them at work?

Guidelines for Healthy Eating

Objectives

- Summarize the recommendations of the Dietary Guidelines for Americans.
- Demonstrate how to use MyPyramid to plan daily meals.
- Explain factors that influence individual food choices.
- Distinguish between accurate and misleading nutritional information.
- Compare food needs to food choices.

Vocabulary

- **Dietary Guidelines for Americans**
- **sedentary**
- **obesity**
- **MyPyramid**
- **dietary supplements**
- **additives**
- **functional foods**
- **irradiated foods**
- **allergies**
- **vegetarian**

Reading with Purpose

1. **Write down** the colored headings from Chapter 23 in your notebook.

2. **As you read** the text under each heading, visualize what you are reading.

3. **Reflect** on what you read by writing a few sentences under each heading to describe it.

4. **Continue** this process until you have finished the chapter. Reread your notes.

Eating, Exercising, and Good Health

How do food and exercise fit into your life? Do you eat junk food with low nutrient density for dinner and exercise by pressing the buttons on the television remote? Or do you eat a variety of foods and exercise at least 60 minutes every day? Your eating and exercise habits play a big role in your overall health now and throughout life.

Good habits can help you avoid serious diseases, such as heart disease, diabetes, and some forms of cancer. The choices you make today will affect your health for the rest of your life. Fortunately, information on this topic is plentiful and will assist you in making wise food choices.

Dietary Guidelines for Americans

The federal government provides information to guide you as you make food and exercise decisions. The **Dietary Guidelines for Americans** includes scientifically based advice for making smart food choices, balancing food choices and physical activity, and getting the most nutrition out of your calories. These guidelines are updated and published every five years. The Dietary Guidelines are suggestions for healthy people age two and older. They are not for infants and toddlers because their nutrition needs are age-specific to early growth. See **Fig. 23-1**.

Making Calories Count

Every person's calorie needs are different. Your calorie needs depend on your age, activity level, and whether you're trying to gain, maintain, or lose weight. To meet your individual calorie needs and get the required nutrients, choose a variety of nutrient-dense foods and beverages from the basic food groups.

Fig 23-1
Playing sports is a good way to get exercise, maintain your health, and be with your friends at the same time.

Managing Your Weight and Physical Activity

Balancing calories from foods and beverages with the calories used in physical activity is key to maintaining a healthy weight. Many teens lead a **sedentary**, or inactive, lifestyle and take in too many calories. This way of life, combined with extra calories, can lead to **obesity**, or being seriously overweight because of an excess of body fat.

Regular physical activity promotes health, well-being, and a healthy body weight. Most teens should be physically active for at least 60 minutes every day or almost every day. Weight concerns should be discussed with your doctor.

Choosing from Key Food Groups

When creating a healthy eating plan, choose foods from the following key food groups:

- **Grains group.** Make half of the grains you eat whole grains. Check the label to make sure grains such as wheat are referred to as "whole."

- **Vegetable group.** Eat a variety of dark green vegetables, such as broccoli and spinach; orange vegetables, such as sweet potatoes and carrots; and dry beans and peas.

- **Fruit group.** Eat a variety of fruits—fresh, frozen, canned, or dried—rather than fruit juice for most of your fruit choices. Juice contains more calories per serving than whole fruit.

- **Milk group.** Children age nine and older, including teens, need 3 cups of fat-free or low-fat milk per day. If you cannot consume regular milk or milk products, choose lactose-free options or calcium-fortified foods and beverages.

- **Meat & Beans group.** Select lean proteins over fatty options. Vary your protein choices by including beans, peas, nuts, and seeds, along with meat, poultry, and fish.

Limiting Fats

Although it has a bad reputation, fat is an important component of a healthy diet. Fat helps supply energy and is important to body functions. Eating a limited amount of healthy fat, such as olive oil, is a good idea. Look for foods low in fat, saturated fat, and cholesterol.

Make half your grains whole.

Vary your veggies.

Focus on fruits.

Eat calcium-rich foods.

Go lean on protein.

HOW TO LOWER THE FAT

Many people have trouble following the Dietary Guidelines when it comes to limiting fats. Yet avoiding fat is as easy as adding it. Here's how:

- **Cut the fat in meats and poultry.** Choose lean ground meat and poultry and reduced-fat versions of luncheon meat and sausage. Trim visible fat and remove skin from poultry and fish before or after cooking. Eat fish often, especially those that contain fish oil, such as salmon.

- **Choose lower-fat dairy foods in meals and recipes.** High-fat dairy foods often have low-fat versions. A reduced-fat variety of sour cream has about 10 fewer grams of fat than regular sour cream. Also look for low-fat substitutes. Buttermilk, which tastes similar to sour cream, contains only 1 gram of fat.

- **Choose snacks wisely.** To satisfy a sweet tooth, you can choose a brownie, with 10 grams of fat, or fresh fruit, which has none. When you crave a crunchy snack, chose a small bag of low-fat pretzels instead of potato chips.

- **Use low-fat condiments.** Dress up a sandwich with salsa, relish, horseradish, or wasabi (the Japanese version of horseradish). Make potato salad with more vinegar and less mayonnaise. Explore ethnic condiments, such as chutneys (spicy fruit relishes) and hoisin, a spicy Asian ketchup. Beware, however: some condiments are high in sodium and sugar.

- **Spice up your foods.** Experiment with the incredible variety of herbs, spices, and other seasonings. Try salads with fruit vinegars instead of oily dressings. Toss pasta with an herb blend.

- **Learn cooking and menu terms.** How a food is described can be a clue to how it's prepared. Learn terms that denote high- and low-fat methods. Roasted vegetables are a lower-fat choice than scalloped vegetables, which are served in a cream sauce and topped with breadcrumbs.

- **Reduce fat in baking.** Learn tips for cutting the fat in baked recipes, such as using applesauce to replace oil. You might start by following specially developed low-fat recipes, applying principles of low-fat cooking as you gain experience.

TAKE **ACTION**

Bring in Nutrition Facts panels from three foods your family eats regularly. Add these to panels brought in by classmates. From this collection, draw three panels at random. In small groups, discuss the fat content of your selections. How would you suggest including the food in a healthful diet?

Recognize Fad Diets

Fad diets often promise dramatic results, but they can be dangerous to your health. Talk to your doctor before beginning any diet and be especially cautious when considering diets that do the following:

▶ Exclude certain food groups in MyPyramid or overemphasize one particular food or food group.

▶ Make misleading claims, such as rapid weight loss or weight loss while sleeping.

▶ Omit physical activity or exercise.

▶ Use actors who are paid to promote the diet.

Reducing Sodium, Increasing Potassium

Sodium, or salt, helps the body keep a balance of fluid, and it helps regulate blood pressure. Too much sodium, however, can have unhealthy effects, such as high blood pressure. Chances are most of the sodium you consume comes from processed foods. To keep your sodium intake at a healthy level, choose and prepare foods with little salt and eat plenty of potassium-rich foods, such as fruits and vegetables.

Limiting Added Sugar

Do you have a sweet tooth? Many popular foods, such as cookies and sweetened cereals, contain high amounts of added sugar. Too much sugar can lead to weight gain.

Limit your sugar intake by choosing foods and beverages that are low in added sugars. Read food labels carefully to make sure that added sugars are not one of the first few ingredients on the list. Examples of added sugars include sucrose, glucose, high-fructose corn syrup, corn syrup, and fructose.

Handling Food Safely

Keeping food safe from harmful bacteria and other hazards is vital to healthful eating. The following guidelines can help you prepare, handle, and store food safely:

• Wash your hands with soap and warm water before preparing, handling, and eating food.

• Clean food-contact surfaces to avoid spreading bacteria.

• Use different, clean cutting boards for preparing different types of food.

• Wash fruits and vegetables thoroughly before eating.

• Separate raw, cooked, and ready-to-eat foods while shopping, preparing, and storing food.

• Chill perishable foods promptly and thaw foods properly. Make sure food is not left on the counter!

MyPyramid

MyPyramid is a personalized way to approach healthful eating and physical activity every day. The pyramid, shown in **Fig. 23-2**, sends the message that food and exercise go hand in hand. The figure shows a staircase on one side of the pyramid with a person climbing the stairs. This is your cue to be active and exercise each day.

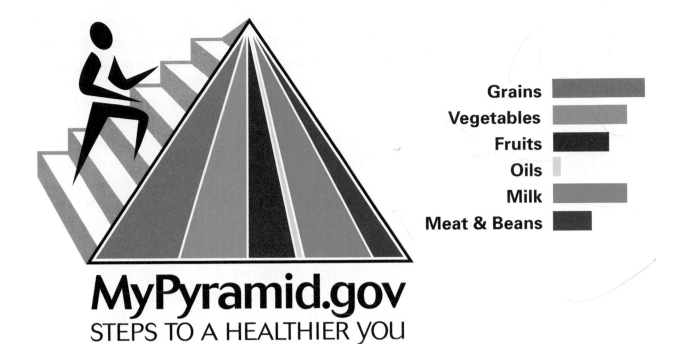

Fig 23-2 Serving amount examples are as follows:

MyPyramid Food Equivalents

Grain Group
What equals 1 ounce?
- 1 slice bread
- 1 cup dry cereal
- ½ cup cooked rice, pasta, or cereal
- 1 ounce dry pasta or rice

Vegetable Group
What equals 1 cup?
- 2 cups raw, leafy vegetable
- 1 cup cooked or chopped raw vegetable
- 1 cup vegetable juice

Fruit Group
What equals 1 cup?
- 1 large fruit (depends on fruit)
- 1 cup fresh, frozen, or canned fruit
- ½ cup dried fruit
- 1 cup fruit juice

Milk Group
What equals 1 cup?
- 1 cup milk or yogurt
- 1½ ounces natural cheese
- 2 ounces processed cheese

Meat & Beans Group
What equals 1 ounce?
- 1 ounce lean meat, poultry, or fish
- ¼ cup cooked dry beans or peas
- 1 egg
- 1 tablespoon peanut butter
- ½ ounce nuts or seeds

The bands of color on the pyramid represent the five food groups, plus oils. Here is how you can identify them: Orange—Grain group; Green—Vegetable group; Red—Fruit group; Blue—Milk group; Purple—Meat & Beans group; and Yellow—Oils. You should choose foods from every food group on a daily basis in order to get the balance you need.

Notice that the color bands on the pyramid are different widths. You should eat more of the foods with wider bands, such as grains and vegetables. The bands also narrow as they near the top of the pyramid. Foods at the top have more added sugar and solid fat. Very active people may be able to eat more of these foods.

Eat the Right Amount

How much food does a teen need each day? The list below gives recommended daily amounts for teens. These numbers apply if you get less than 30 minutes of daily physical activity beyond normal activities:

- **Grains.** Females need 6 ounces and males, 7 ounces, or the equivalent. At least half of daily grains should be whole.

- **Vegetables.** Females need 2½ cups and males, 3 cups.

- **Fruit.** Females need 1½ cups and males, 2 cups.

- **Milk.** Females and males need 3 cups or the equivalent.

- **Meat and beans.** Females need 5 ounces and males, 6 ounces, or the equivalent.

The numbers above don't fit every teen. For example, if you're very active, you may need larger amounts. The MyPyramid.gov Web site allows you to personalize your eating plan. If you enter your age, gender, and activity level, the results will tell you how much food to eat each day. Fig. 23-2 on page 377 shows how to compare what you eat with recommended daily amounts.

Individual Food Choices

Why do people make the food choices they do? Why might they select pasta rather than salad, or fish over beef? The following factors influence people's food choices and the way they feel about food:

- **Geographic area.** Different regions of the country often feature their own food availability and traditions. Meals in New England may emphasize fish and baked beans, whereas Southern menus might include barbecue and coleslaw. Also, the local resources of an area can factor into food choices. For example, fish and seafood are usually more available and affordable in coastal areas than in other areas of the country. See **Fig. 23-3**.

- **Religious beliefs.** Many of the world's religions have guidelines concerning food and eating. For example, some religions restrict certain foods, some require some foods to be prepared in certain ways, and some promote certain foods or promote fasting on religious holidays.

- **Family and culture.** People tend to follow their family's food customs. Perhaps your grandparents always celebrated summer holidays by serving grilled food in the backyard. Now your parents carry on this tradition, and someday you may as well.

- **The media.** Have you ever bought food after seeing a clever advertisement for it? Radio, television, and print advertisements can easily influence the foods you buy and eat. Some cooking programs also offer recipes and cooking methods that can influence your eating habits.

- **Technology.** Advances in technology allow people the convenience of microwavable and convection-oven foods and online ordering for restaurant takeout. Many people choose convenience foods over foods they need to prepare themselves.

Fig 23-3 Where you live affects your food choices. How can you incorporate healthy eating habits with the foods in your region?

Getting the Facts

You've probably heard this statement about food: "An apple a day keeps the doctor away." Because food is so important to people's health and way of life, they have a lot to say about it. How can you tell whether statements you hear are accurate?

Food Myths

Some information you read and hear turns out to be myth. A myth is an untrue statement that people believe. Look at the following myths and the facts that disprove them:

- **Frozen foods are not as nutritious as fresh foods.** Many frozen foods are just as nutritious as fresh foods. Frozen foods are processed right after being harvested, at the peak of their nutritive value. See **Fig. 23-4**. On the other hand, fresh produce that is transported long distances can lose nutritional value.

- **Carbohydrates make you fat.** Carbohydrates are an important part of a healthy diet. Eating too many carbohydrates and not being active enough can be a bad combination. Carbohydrates turn to sugar after they are consumed, which can lead to weight gain. When choosing carbohydrate-rich foods choose unrefined foods, such as whole grains and vegetables, over refined processed foods, such as soft drinks and sugar.

- **Certain foods burn body fat.** No one food can decrease fat in your body. The best way to lose weight is to eat in moderation from all of the food groups and exercise daily.

Fig 23-4
When you can, choose frozen foods over canned foods. They typically contain more nutrients and less sodium, or salt.

- **Exercise makes you eat more.** Although some people who exercise eat more to maintain their weight, exercise doesn't cause them to eat.

Questioning Information

Health information is readily available to you. Before deciding whether food information is reliable and accurate, ask the following questions:

- **Where did the information come from?** Rely on the experts in the field—registered dietitians, health care professionals, researchers in the nutrition field, family and consumer science teachers, extension agents, and professional organizations, such as the American Dietetic Association.

- **Could the statements be false?** Many businesses make false claims to persuade you to purchase their products. On the other hand, statements by health organizations, such as the American Heart Association or the American Cancer Society, are meant to educate the public about health issues of interest. They usually base their information on scientific research. See **Fig. 23-5**.

Fig 23-5 When you read food claims, try to understand what is being said and what is not being said. Many claims can be made, but not all are reliable.

Natural and Organic Foods

Perhaps you've noticed "health" foods in the stores or foods labeled "organic." Some people prefer to eat natural or organic foods. Natural foods contain no artificial ingredients. Whereas many regular foods can contain preservatives to keep them fresh longer, natural foods do not. Organic foods are foods grown without the use of pesticides or artificial fertilizers. People choose natural and organic foods because they want to avoid consuming substances they feel are unhealthy.

Many grocers offer natural and organic foods, usually at a higher price than regular foods. As with any food, read the nutrition label and compare it with the labels of other foods to be sure you're getting the most nutrients for your money.

Beware of outrageous claims involving dietary supplements. Many companies who sell these products are really selling false hope.

Dietary Supplements

Karen's older sister thinks Karen should take vitamins every day. "You don't get enough vitamins from the food you eat," she told Karen, "and, besides, they're vitamins—they have to be good for you, right?" What do you think?

Most health care professionals agree that you don't need to take dietary supplements if you eat a variety of healthful foods. **Dietary supplements** include pills, capsules, and powders that are taken in addition to, or to supplement, a person's diet. Dietary supplements include not only vitamins and minerals but also herbs and other botanical products. Only take supplements prescribed by a doctor!

Health care professionals may recommend dietary supplements for certain people. For example, people recovering from an illness or pregnant women may need to take dietary supplements to increase nutrients or specific vitamins. If you can't eat dairy products, your doctor might recommend an additional calcium supplement.

If your doctor recommends a supplement for you, read the label carefully to make sure you're getting the proper dosage. Check the expiration date and throw away expired supplements. Also, avoid taking megadoses, or large amounts, of dietary supplements. Often, it will simply pass through your system with no health benefit. Taking a large dose can also lead to severe illness or death! See **Fig. 23-6**.

Food Additives

Have you ever wondered why ice cream is so smooth and creamy? Or why oil separates from some peanut butters and not others? The answer is food **additives**, or substances added to food for a specific purpose.

Additives keep peanut butter from separating and make ice cream smooth. In these cases, the additives make the texture of the product more pleasing. Additives can also improve the flavor of products and increase the shelf life of food, or the length of time the food can be stored. All additives must pass rigid governmental tests for safety. Even so, some people choose not to eat foods that contain additives.

Functional Foods

Perhaps you've noticed the words "calcium-fortified" on some cartons of orange juice. These juices are **functional foods**, or foods that provide benefits beyond basic nutrition. They have added calcium to help ensure you get enough calcium in your diet.

People have been consuming functional foods for many years. Almost a century ago, many people suffered from diseases caused by nutrition deficiencies. Adding nutrients to foods helped eliminate these diseases. Today, functional foods include not only staples but also beverages and snacks. Why is there so much interest in functional foods? The food technology needed to create functional foods is advancing rapidly. People are also becoming more interested in the connection between the foods they eat and their health.

When choosing functional foods, always read the nutrition label to make sure you're getting the nutrients you expect. Also, remember that nature produces its own functional foods. Fruits and vegetables, whole grains, beans, and low-fat dairy products are packed with nutrients and phytonutrients that can help minimize the risk of many diseases.

Irradiated Foods

Some stores advertise irradiated foods. **Irradiated foods** are foods that have gone through a process that destroys bacteria, mold, and insects by passing them through a field of radiant energy similar to X rays. Irradiation extends the shelf life of foods and helps maintain their quality.

The irradiation process is controversial. Some people think that irradiated food is radioactive, but this is not true. Most of the radiant energy used in food passes through the food in much the same way as microwaves pass through foods. According to law, a food's label must state whether the food has been irradiated.

Individual Nutritional Needs

Nutritional needs vary from one individual to the next. Your size, activity level, age, and other factors, such as any medical conditions you might have, determine what you need to eat to maintain good health.

TIPS
Sideline the Supplements

For some thin teens, especially some athletes, being "skinny" feels like a curse. To gain weight, teens sometimes turn to supplements, such as protein powders, to fill out. Unfortunately, supplements don't create the body teens would like to have. If you're trying to put on a few pounds, follow these tips:

▶ **Think safety first.** Always consult your doctor before you begin an eating or exercise regime.

▶ **Grow strong, not big.** Focus on your health, not your size. When you are healthy, you will feel better about yourself—and you'll probably look better, too!

▶ **Eat a healthful diet.** The foods people eat to lose weight are the same foods you should eat to gain weight. Eat a variety of foods, including vegetables, fruit, and grains, and avoid high-calorie, high-fat foods.

▶ **Follow an exercise routine.** For overall health, exercise every day. To increase your strength and gain muscle, try strength-training exercises. Because some weight-lifting exercises can injure teens' growing bodies, be sure to consult a doctor before you begin a strength-training routine.

▶ **Get plenty of rest.** Your body grows at night, so be sure you get the recommended eight to ten hours of sleep every night.

I Can Eat Healthfully

You know you should eat healthfully, but it isn't always easy. You often have to eat quickly between school and after-school activities. You usually don't have time to stop at home, so you eat on the go, grabbing prepackaged snacks from the nearest vending machine or eating at a fast-food restaurant. Unfortunately, these choices are often high in fat, calories, and sugar, and low in nutrients.

Packing a Snack

Bringing along healthy snacks is a good way to eat on the go, meet your calorie needs, and squeeze in some good nutrition. When you choose snacks, keep MyPyramid in mind. The following snack choices can be packed ahead of time in your backpack or in an insulated cooler:

- Whole fruits
- Celery with peanut butter or low-fat cheese
- Baby carrots
- A whole-grain bagel with low-fat or nonfat cream cheese or peanut butter
- Peanut butter on low-fat crackers
- Yogurt with low-fat granola or fruit
- Low-fat cheese and crackers
- Dried fruit
- Low-fat cheese slices

Choosing from Vending Machines

Sometimes hunger takes over, and you have to buy a snack from a vending machine. If you find yourself in this situation, look for the following healthy options:

- Low-fat or "light" popcorn
- Pretzels
- Nuts
- Dried fruit
- Trail mix
- Whole-grain cereal bars
- Baked chips
- Cheese and crackers
- Peanut butter crackers
- Water
- 100 percent juices

Eating Fast Food

Fast food doesn't have to ruin your healthy meal plan. When ordering at fast-food restaurants, use the following tips:

- Order smaller portions.
- Choose grilled or baked chicken or fish instead of fried.
- Hold the cheese, mayonnaise, and other high-fat condiments.
- Choose salads with low-fat dressings.
- Skip the soda and choose low-fat milk or water.

People with Medical Conditions

Some medical problems, including high blood pressure, high cholesterol, diabetes, and obesity, require people to follow special or modified diets. For example, doctors may suggest to people with high blood pressure that they consume less salt. Added salt should be avoided. People who are obese or diabetic may need to regulate the portions and types of foods they eat. People with medical conditions that might be affected by food should consult health care professionals, such as physicians and dietitians, to obtain expert nutritional and medical advice.

People with Food Sensitivities

Scott likes peanut butter sandwiches and would eat them every day if he weren't allergic to nuts. Food **allergies** are reactions of the body's immune system to ingested food. People allergic to food might break out in a rash, suffer stomach cramps, experience nausea, or have difficulty breathing after eating certain foods. In Scott's case, even the tiniest peanut makes breathing difficult for him and can cause death. Other foods besides nuts that commonly cause problems include eggs, milk, wheat, fish, and shellfish.

Some people have what is called a food intolerance. This condition can cause severe digestive problems. You may know someone who is lactose intolerant. This means that the person is unable to digest lactose, or the sugar contained in cow's milk. People with lactose intolerance often substitute lactose-free or soy products for milk and other dairy products.

Vegetarians

What is a vegetarian? A **vegetarian** is someone who does not eat meat, poultry, or fish. Meals typically consist of grains, beans, fruits, vegetables, and sometimes eggs and dairy products. People who don't eat any animal products, including dairy products and eggs, are known as vegans. See **Fig. 23-7**.

Vegetarian meals are rich in fiber and complex carbohydrates. Because vegetarians do not eat meat, chicken, and fish, their protein comes mainly from plant sources, such as dry beans and peas, nuts, and soy products. Vegetarians should strive to eat a variety of foods to maintain a well-balanced diet. It's important to get nutritional counseling before following a strict vegetarian or vegan diet.

Fig 23-7 ▶ If you are going to follow a vegetarian diet, you should obtain nutritional counseling from a dietitian to make sure your diet has a balance of nutrients.

Athletes

Are the nutritional needs of competitive athletes different from those of people who exercise for health and enjoyment? The answer is no. Athletes need carbohydrates, protein, fat, vitamins, minerals, and water. However, athletes may need more of these nutrients.

Athletes must be extra careful to drink plenty of fluids. Everyone sweats when they are physically active. The perspiration evaporates from your skin to cool your body. Drinking fluids before, during, and after activities, even when you are not thirsty, replaces the fluids you lose to perspiration. Waiting until you are thirsty to drink is risky because thirst is a sign of dehydration. As a general rule, drink water if your workouts are fewer than 60 minutes and are not very strenuous. For longer, strenuous activities, drink sports beverages or fruit juices diluted to half-strength. These drinks provide important nutrients lost during exercise.

Along with water, athletes need plenty of energy, and the best source for energy is complex carbohydrates. You can increase your fitness and endurance by eating foods rich in complex carbohydrates, such as whole-grain breads and cereals.

Review & Activities

Chapter Summary

- The Dietary Guidelines for Americans provide suggestions for a healthy lifestyle.
- MyPyramid is a personalized way to approach healthful eating and physical activity.
- People's food choices depend on a number of factors.
- Distinguishing between accurate and misleading nutritional information is important for a healthy lifestyle.
- Food needs vary from one person to another.

Reviewing Key Terms & Ideas

1. Name three recommendations of the **Dietary Guidelines for Americans**.
2. What is a **sedentary** lifestyle?
3. What leads to **obesity**?
4. What are the five key food groups?
5. What do the stairs indicate on **MyPyramid**?
6. Identify three factors that influence people's food choices.
7. What questions should you ask yourself when analyzing information?
8. Compare and contrast natural and organic foods.
9. What are **dietary supplements**?
10. Define food **additives**.
11. What are **functional foods**?
12. What concern do people have regarding **irradiated foods**?
13. List the common symptoms of food **allergies**.

Thinking Critically

1. **Analyzing behavior.** Which of the recommendations in the Dietary Guidelines for Americans is the easiest for most teens to follow? Which is the hardest to follow? Explain your answers.
2. **Defending statements.** Do you believe that teens today are more sedentary than a generation ago? Defend your response.
3. **Making predictions.** Functional foods have captured people's interest. Predict some functional foods you expect to see in the future.

Review & Activities

Applying Your Learning

1. **Information hotline.** Imagine you work for a nutrition hotline that helps inform callers about the Dietary Guidelines for Americans. "Take calls" from classmates and answer their questions using the information from the chapter.

2. **Nutrition planning.** Go online to MyPyramid.gov and use the interactive features to personalize your daily food plan. Follow the plan for one week. How difficult was it to follow? Do you feel differently after following the plan? Write a brief reflection of your experience.

3. **Regional study.** Research the regional foods in your area. Choose a regional favorite and prepare it for your class.

4. **Panel discussion.** In two small groups, research the benefits and drawbacks of natural and organic foods. Present the information in a panel discussion for remaining classmates.

5. **Menu planning.** Develop a one-day vegetarian food plan that follows the nutrition recommendations in this chapter. If possible, ask a dietitian or health care professional to evaluate your plan.

6. **Dehydration awareness.** Create a public-service announcement for television that addresses the issue of dehydration. Be sure to include guidelines for staying hydrated while exercising. Videotape your announcement and show it to athletes in your school.

Making Connections

1. **Writing** Write a letter to parents outlining the recommendations of the Dietary Guidelines for Americans and requesting that they provide their own students snack options that follow the recommendations.

2. **Math** Keep an activity log for two weeks. Record the number of minutes you exercise each day. Afterward, analyze your log.

3. **Reading** Read and analyze print advertisements for various food products. How might the ads influence people? Which ads seem to target teens specifically? Share your advertisements and analysis with your class.

CAREER Link

Constructive Feedback.
Test scores, conferences, and report cards tell you how you're doing in school. Employers also have methods of letting you know how well you do your job and what you need to improve. Many employers use constructive feedback—they tell you what you need to improve so that you can perform better. Talk to an adult about constructive feedback they receive on the job. How do they use the feedback to improve?

Buying & Storing Food

Objectives

- Organize a food-shopping trip.
- Propose strategies for cutting food costs.
- Explain comparison shopping techniques.
- Identify quality food products.
- Demonstrate food storage techniques.

Vocabulary

- **staples**
- **unit price**
- **food product dating**
- **pasteurized**
- **homogenized**
- **legumes**

Reading with Purpose

1. **As you read** Chapter 24, create an outline in your notebook using the colored headings.

2. **Write** a question under each heading that you can use to guide your reading.

3. **Answer** the question under each heading as you read the chapter. Record your answers.

4. **Ask** your teacher to help with answers you could not find in this chapter.

Getting Ready to Shop

"Should I buy organic cereal or the regular cereal that's cheaper?" "How many pounds of chicken do I need for dinner?" Food shopping requires many decisions. Think about the times you've been food shopping. What decisions did you make?

To get the most out of your shopping experience and make good decisions, you'll need to do a little planning beforehand. If you take time to plan, you'll be happier with your decisions—and your purchases.

Making a Shopping List

Have you ever gone to the supermarket without a shopping list and come back with items you didn't intend to buy? Or perhaps you got home from the store only to realize you didn't have an important item for dinner. A shopping list can help you plan your shopping trip so that you come home with what you need. Besides reminding you of what you need, shopping lists help you stick to a budget by keeping you from buying impulse items. Impulse purchases are purchases you make quickly without thinking. Use the following tips to create your shopping list:

- **Keep a running list.** Find a handy spot in your kitchen for your shopping list. Everyone in the family can add to the list as they notice items are running low.

- **Plan weekly meals.** Look over recipes for upcoming meals and add needed ingredients to your list.

- **Take stock.** Check the food you have on hand, paying particular attention to **staples**, or to foods you are likely to use often, such as milk, eggs, pasta, rice, and bread.

- **Buy items on sale.** Read grocery store flyers and news-papers to find items on sale and add them to your list.

- **Organize your list.** Group items according to the store's layout, and then shop in the order of your list. This will help you save time. See **Fig. 24-1**.

Fig 24-1
All family members—even the very young ones—can add to a shopping list if it's posted in a central location. What else can younger family members do to help with food shopping?

The Family Food Dollar

Most families have a food budget they need to follow. Being organized helps you stay within your budget. What can you do to stretch your food dollars?

- **Scan newspapers for supermarket specials.** Planning meals around specials can help you to save money. You can also compare advertised prices of several stores to find the lowest prices. Keep in mind that stores often advertise items at everyday prices, not sale prices. Be sure you're choosing items that are discounted, not simply advertised.

- **Clip coupons.** Although coupons can help you save, coupon items may not always be the best buys. Use a coupon for a needed item you normally buy and if it's less expensive than similar brands.

- **Buy in bulk.** When you buy in bulk, you buy larger quantities of an item to get a lower price. Before buying in bulk, be sure you can either eat the food before it spoils or store it for future meals.

- **Shop on a full stomach.** If you're hungry when you shop, you're more likely to buy extra food that you may not need. See **Fig. 24-2**.

- **Take advantage of seasonal specials.** Generally, fresh fruits and vegetables are less expensive when they are in season.

Fig 24-2 Using a shopping list will also help you stick to your budget.

Shopping for Food

If helping to shop is one of your jobs, how are you going to organize your shopping? First, keep your grocery list handy. As you select items, cross them off the list. Some people use a calculator as they shop to track their spending and make sure they stay within their budget.

Store Layout and Displays

Food stores use a number of techniques to encourage you to buy their goods. Bright, colorful packaging and eye-catching displays are designed to attract your attention. Products are arranged in special end of aisle displays, which are called end caps. Featured items are sometimes on sale, but not always.

Higher-priced and impulse items are typically placed at eye level or at the checkout stand so that you'll be more likely to notice them and make a purchase. Some stores offer food samples. Store managers hope the samples, along with pleasant background music, will encourage the customers to stay in the store longer and buy more products. By sticking to your shopping list and being aware of these techniques, you'll be less likely to make unnecessary purchases.

Reading Labels

Would you buy any product without knowing what was inside? Food labels tell you more about what's in a package, including the name of the product, the weight of the package contents, the ingredients listed from most to least, and often the name of the manufacturer. Take a look at the Nutrition Facts panel. It can help you make healthful food choices. See **Fig. 24-3**.

Fig 24-3 ▶ Nutrition information is located on the Nutrition Facts panel.

NUTRITION FACTS

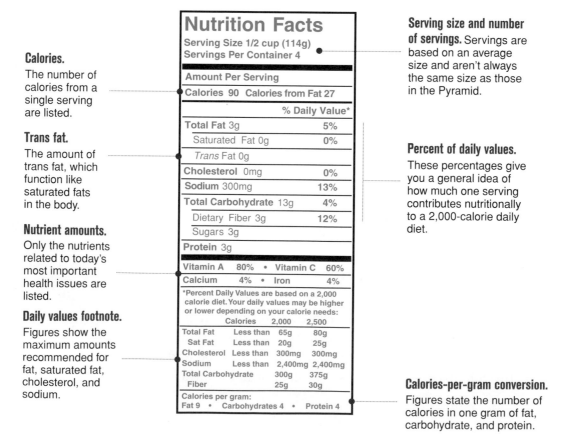

Calories. The number of calories from a single serving are listed.

Trans fat. The amount of trans fat, which function like saturated fats in the body.

Nutrient amounts. Only the nutrients related to today's most important health issues are listed.

Daily values footnote. Figures show the maximum amounts recommended for fat, saturated fat, cholesterol, and sodium.

Serving size and number of servings. Servings are based on an average size and aren't always the same size as those in the Pyramid.

Percent of daily values. These percentages give you a general idea of how much one serving contributes nutritionally to a 2,000-calorie daily diet.

Calories-per-gram conversion. Figures state the number of calories in one gram of fat, carbohydrate, and protein.

Comparison Shopping

Instead of picking up the first package you see, take time to do some comparison shopping. When you compare different items, you can be sure you're buying what you want at a fair price. Knowing about labels, pricing, freshness, and quality can help you put comparison shopping into practice.

Comparing Brands

As you scan the shelves of breakfast cereals, you notice the various brands. "Is one brand really better than another?" you ask yourself. You can only answer that by comparing national brands, store brands, and generic products. See **Fig. 24-4**.

- **National brands.** Major food companies produce many of the products you see on store shelves. National brands are sold in stores throughout the country and are advertised nationally on radio and television and in magazines.

- **Store brands.** These products are produced and packaged for a particular chain of stores and carry the store's brand name. Store brands and generic brands usually have prices that are lower than the prices of national brands. There can be differences in quality among products, but generally they're comparable.

- **Generic products.** Identified by their plain packaging, generic products are usually less expensive than both national brands and store brands.

Fig 24-4 Comparing products enables you to get the most for your money and ensure quality.

Unit Pricing

Taking time to compare unit prices will also help you get the most for your money. The **unit price** is the price per ounce, pound, or other unit of measure. Look for the unit price on the shelf near the item. The total price for the package is also given.

If a store does not list unit prices, calculate them yourself. Divide the total cost of the package by the number of units (ounces or pounds) to find the cost per unit.

Fig 24-5 Always check the "sell by" date before purchasing milk products.

Food Quality

The idea of shopping used to almost scare Emily. She never knew how to select food at its freshest point and often came home with overripe fruit and vegetables. Lately, though, Emily's mother has been showing her how to evaluate food for quality, and she's been much happier with the results of her shopping trips. As Emily's experience shows, choosing the freshest and best-quality items can pose the biggest challenge as you shop.

Food Product Dating

One way to make sure you buy the freshest food possible is to check the date on the items. **Food product dating** is the process of dating food to indicate product freshness. You'll see four types of dates stamped on product packages:

- **"Sell by" date** or "pull date" is the last day a product should be sold if the food is to remain fresh for home storage. This date is usually found on meat, milk, eggs, and other items that spoil quickly. See **Fig. 24-5**.

- **"Packed on" date** is the day the food was packaged.

- **"Use by" date** tells when you should use the food for best quality. A food item may still be safe to eat after this date, but the quality and nutritional content may not be at their best.

- **Expiration date** indicates the last day a product should be eaten. After this date, the product may not be safe to eat.

How can you use these dates? If the "sell by" date has passed, do not buy the product. Buy the item with the latest "sell by" date. Always choose the latest "packed on" date for items that spoil quickly, such as meat, deli items, and baked foods. Refer to the "use by" date when planning meals to make sure food is at its freshest.

Buying Produce

Knowing some signs of quality will help you buy the freshest fruits and vegetables, or produce. See **Fig. 24-6**.

Fig 24-6 A little time spent checking for signs of quality in produce can save you money. Why might this be true?

- **Avoid bruised and wilted produce.** It's a sign that produce has passed its peak of freshness or was not handled properly. It's also a sign that nutrients have been lost.

- **Inspect produce to determine quality.** Produce has certain qualities that indicate freshness. For example, head lettuce and cabbage should feel solid. Softness may be a sign that the produce is overripe. Celery, asparagus, and green beans should be crisp, not limp. Citrus fruit, squash, cucumbers, and tomatoes should feel heavy for their size.

- **Avoid buying root vegetables with sprouts.** When root vegetables, such as potatoes and onions, begin to show sprouts, it is a sure sign of age.

- **Look for items in season.** Although items can be shipped to stores at any time of the year, try to buy items when they are in season. For example, acorn and butternut squash are in season in fall, and strawberries are in season during early summer.

Buying Protein Foods

Many foods are highly perishable, meaning they spoil quickly, so you'll want to choose them carefully. The following suggestions can help you:

- **Look at color.** Freshness of meat and poultry is indicated by color. Look for bright red beef and pinkish pork. Poultry should be pinkish, without bruises or torn skin. Some chicken will appear more yellow. The yellow color is caused by the food the chicken was fed. See **Fig. 24-7**.

- **Check the odor.** Fish should have a mild smell and be firm to the touch. Raw meat should have little odor. Your nose will immediately know the smell of bad fish or meat. Fresh fish should be iced and refrigerated in the store. If buying frozen fish, the package should feel solid and cold.

- **Examine shells on shellfish.** The shells of clams, oysters, and mussels should be tightly closed. On whole fish, the gills should be bright red and the eyes should be clear, not cloudy.

Fig 24-7 In addition to color, check the "sell by" date and do not buy meat that is expired.

In addition to checking for freshness, you should check the fat content of meat you purchase. The percentage of lean meat on ground beef packages is a clue to the fat content. Ground round is usually the leanest.

Eggs are another type of protein food you might buy. When purchasing eggs, you'll have the choice of grade (usually AA or A) and size (usually medium, large, extra large, or jumbo). Open egg cartons to check the eggs, making sure no eggs are cracked, broken, or discolored.

Buying Dairy Products

There are many varieties of milk. Fresh milk is sold as whole milk (at least 3.25% milk fat) and milk with lower fat content (skim, 0.5%, 1%, 1.5%, and 2% milk fat). Except for the fat, the nutrient content of all milk, including chocolate milk, is about the same.

Fresh milk is generally labeled as "pasteurized" and "homogenized." **Pasteurized** (PAS-chur-ized) means that the milk has been heated to destroy harmful bacteria. **Homogenized** (HO-ma-ju-nized) means that the fat particles in the milk have been broken up and distributed throughout the milk. See **Fig. 24-8**.

Before purchasing any dairy products, such as sour cream, yogurt, or cheese, check the package. If the package is broken, the seals are disengaged, or the product is leaking, inform a store employee and do not buy the product. Also, check cheese labels carefully and choose low-fat varieties whenever possible.

Fig 24-8 ▶ Soy milk is an option for many people who cannot digest regular milk. Scientists believe soy products can help reduce cholesterol and bone loss.

Buy Canned Food

Some canned food contains a "use by" date, but many only display a code that allows manufacturers to track them. How do you know whether a canned food is safe to eat? Follow these tips:

▶ **Consider shelf life.** The shelf life, or length of time food remains fresh, varies by food product. As a general rule, highly acidic canned food, such as fruit juices and tomatoes, remain fresh for 12 to 18 months. Canned meat and most vegetables can be stored for two to five years, and canned milk lasts one year if stored properly.

▶ **Inspect lids.** Do not purchase jars of food if the jars' lids are rusted or damaged. For home-canned foods, be sure the lid is properly sealed and not bulging or swollen.

▶ **Look for bulges, leaks, and dents.** Cans that are damaged, leaking, or bulging may contain harmful bacteria.

Buying Grain Products

Grains are the seeds or fruits of cereal grasses. Grain products include bread, cereal, rice, and pasta. These products are made from a variety of grains, including wheat, oats, corn, barley, and rye. The following tips can help you shop for grains:

- **Buy nutrient-dense grains.** Try to select grain products that contain whole grain or bran for more nutrients. Also, look for grains that are enriched.

- **Think whole grain.** Whole-grain products should make up half of your grain servings per day. Examples of whole grains include whole wheat bread, brown rice, and old-fashioned oatmeal (not the instant version).

- **Avoid sugar, sodium, and fat.** Don't assume that a cereal that seems good for you really is. Many cereals contain an abundance of added sugar, and some "healthy" cereals, such as granola, can be high in fat.

- **Experiment with different varieties of products.** Pasta comes in a variety of shapes, sizes, and colors. Rice is available in brown, black, red, and white forms. It can be instant or regular and short, medium, or long grain. Wild rice is a type of grass, not a grain like rice. Most pasta is dried and sold in boxes or bags. Fresh pasta is often available in the refrigerated foods section of the store.

- **Examine legumes.** **Legumes** are plants in which seeds grow in pods, such as beans, peas, and lentils. Legumes are available dry or canned and ready to use. If you're buying dry legumes, make sure they are firm and uniform in size and color. Legumes need to be washed thoroughly before cooking.

Finishing Your Shopping

After you've selected all your items, you will need to check out at the register. Watch the register as the cashier totals your items to be sure the prices scan correctly.

Some stores offer self-service checkout lanes that allow customers to scan and bag their items and pay for them without the help of a traditional cashier.

HOW TO STORE GROCERIES

Purchasing food is only one part of your shopping trip. After you return home with your groceries, you'll need to store them. To retain foods' freshness and prevent it from spoiling, follow these steps:

STEP 1 | **Keep food cold.** If you live far from the store, pack perishable groceries in coolers for the drive home. This is also a good idea for summer shopping.

STEP 2 | **Store frozen first.** At home, put away frozen foods first, then refrigerated foods. As you put away the cold foods, check the refrigerator and freezer temperatures. Refrigerators should be set between 32° and 40°F (0°F to 5°C). Freezers should be 0°F (–18°C) or below.

STEP 3 | **Store dry and bulk foods.** Put cans and boxes in cabinets. If you bought bulk foods in containers too large to store in cabinets, separate the contents into airtight containers. Then label the containers with the date and put them away.

TAKE **ACTION**

Investigate different types of food storage containers, such as plastic bowls with covers, plastic wrap, and aluminum foil. Which container would be best for storing dry foods? For cold foods? For liquid foods? Explain your reasoning.

24

Review & Activities

Chapter Summary

- Organizing your food shopping will help you make good purchasing decisions.
- Making a shopping list can help you avoid impulse purchases and cut food costs.
- Knowledge of brands, labels, and unit pricing can help you comparison shop.
- Look for indicators of quality when buying produce, protein foods, dairy items, grains, and milk products.
- Storing food properly is as important as shopping carefully.

Reviewing Key Terms & Ideas

1. What are **staples**?
2. How should you organize your shopping list? Why?
3. When should you use a coupon?
4. How do stores encourage you to buy items?
5. What is the difference between national brands, store brands, and generic products?
6. What information is found on food labels?
7. What is a **unit price**?
8. List the four types of **food product dating**.
9. What does bruised or wilted produce indicate?
10. How do you determine whether meat and poultry are fresh?
11. Explain the terms **pasteurized** and **homogenized**.
12. Define **legumes**.

Thinking Critically

1. **Analyzing situations.** What advice would you give to teens who are about to shop for the first time?
2. **Making assumptions.** What assumptions do you think people make about different brands of products? Do people favor national brands over generic brands? Why or why not?
3. **Drawing conclusions.** Why do you think storing food properly impacts its freshness?

Review & Activities

Applying Your Learning

1. **Shopping preparation.** Create a brochure that will help teens prepare to shop. Talk to local grocers about distributing your brochure in their stores.

2. **Ad analysis.** Gather several weekly newspaper ads showing grocery store specials. Compare the ads and then choose the store you think offers the best quality for the lowest price. Be prepared to defend your choice.

3. **Community options.** Using a phone book and newspapers, determine the types of stores available in your community. How do you think the availability of stores affects people's decision about living in your community?

4. **Online shopping.** Browse Web sites of food stores, noting the products available, the cost, and the delivery options. Based on your findings, write a brief essay describing the benefits and drawbacks of online shopping.

5. **Sales strategies.** Imagine you've been promoted to food store manager at a local supermarket. Your main job is to increase sales. Write a proposal describing the specific sales strategies you would use and why.

6. **Produce assessment.** Speak with the manager of a store's produce department to find out how the store ensures freshness of its produce. Ask for buying tips. Share the information you learn with your class.

Making Connections

1. **Math** Keep a running grocery list for one week. Estimate the total cost of the groceries on your shopping list. Compare your actual total with your estimate.

2. **Writing** Imagine you write a weekly newspaper column titled "The Savvy Shopper." Write an article for your column that provides strategies for avoiding impulse purchases.

3. **Reading** Read and compare two nutrition labels for a national brand, a store brand, and a generic brand. What differences, if any, are there in nutritional content?

CAREER Link

Presentation Skills. Working with others means presenting information—whether you're presenting to one person or a hundred. To give an effective presentation, prepare first. Focus on the information you need to give, and speak clearly and confidently. Maintain eye contact with your listeners and ask if they need clarification. Think about your presentation skills as they are now. How would you rate them? What can you do to improve your skills for the workplace?

Eating Together

Objectives

- Explain the importance of family mealtime.
- Arrange place settings for meals.
- Identify basic table manners.
- Describe common sections of a menu.
- Demonstrate appropriate restaurant behavior.

Vocabulary

- **etiquette**
- **place setting**
- **tableware**
- **flatware**
- **courses**
- **appetizer**
- **entrée**
- **à la carte**

Reading with Purpose

1. **Read** the title of this chapter and describe in writing what you expect to learn from it.

2. **Write** each vocabulary term in your notebook, leaving space for definitions.

3. **As you read** Chapter 25, write the definition beside each term in your notebook.

4. **After** reading the chapter, write a paragraph describing what you learned.

Enjoying Meals Together

Mealtime can come with what looks like a set of rules. How should a table be set? Where does a napkin go during meals? And when should all the different utensils be used? Although **etiquette**—the accepted rules of behavior at mealtime—might seem overwhelming at first, mealtime can bring you and your family much enjoyment. It can also socially prepare you for adult life.

Every family works out its own approach to handling meals. Sometimes meals have to be hurried because of conflicts in family schedules. Other times, people can spend more time and enjoy the food and each other's company. Some families welcome friends who drop by and don't mind a loud dinner table. Others prefer a quiet meal. Many families follow the same routine at mealtime because it works best for them. However, when company comes or on special occasions, their routine may change.

Mealtime should provide families with a chance to relax and spend time together. During meals, families can share news about their day, listen to each other's news, and enjoy each other's company. Because mealtime communication is so important, many families turn off the television and do not answer the phone during meals. This focus on mealtime helps strengthen family relationships. See **Fig. 25-1**.

Fig 25-1 Meals are one time when families with hectic schedules can meet to reconnect with each other. How can teens help make mealtimes enjoyable?

Luisa saw Blake at his locker the day after he had dinner with her family. She approached hesitantly. "Sorry about last night," she said. "My uncle shouldn't have made you try his pickled eggs. Just because he loves them. . . ."

"He was just being polite," Blake said. "They were . . . interesting."

"And you weren't supposed to end up at the kids' end of the table."

"I didn't mind. Your sister showed me how to tie green beans in knots."

Luisa sighed. "She is always embarrassing me!"

Blake laughed. "It's okay, really. Dinner is always quiet at our house. I like that, too, but—you have fun!"

Luisa smiled gratefully. "That's not what my mom calls it. But I'm glad you had a good time."

"I had a great time. In fact, tonight I think I'll show my mom a new way to fix green beans."

Teen Connection

Show manners in an informal eating situation. Compliment cafeteria workers on the foods' look and smell. Use table manners at a fast-food restaurant and use your napkin and utensils correctly. How do others react? How does taking the added time and effort affect your enjoyment of the meal?

Setting the Table

Have you ever been confused about the arrangement of plates, glasses, and utensils on a restaurant table? You're not alone in your feelings, but table settings aren't as complicated as they first seem.

Except at picnics and buffets, most tables are set with individual place settings. A **place setting** is the arrangement of tableware and flatware for each person. **Tableware** includes dishes, glasses, and **flatware**, or eating utensils. The tableware at each person's place has a logical organization. Each place setting usually has at least one plate, glass, fork, knife, spoon, and napkin. Depending on what food is being served, other tableware may be used, such as a salad plate, a cup and saucer, a salad fork, or a soupspoon. Flatware is positioned by use, from the outside in. An appetizer fork is placed farther from the plate than a dinner fork. Sometimes the dessert fork and spoon are placed above the plate.

Fig 25-2 ▶

Set the Table

These steps will help you set an attractive table.

1. Place the fork to be used first farthest from the plate.

2. Place the dinner knife so that the blade faces the plate.

3. Place spoons to the right of the knife. If soup is the first course, the soupspoon should be placed at the far right.

4. Line up the bottom of the flatware with the lower edge of the plate.

5. Only put out the tableware you need to eat a meal.

6. Be sure your placemats and tablecloths are clean and free of wrinkles.

Table Coverings

Think about attractive tables you've seen in restaurants, store displays, or events you may have attended, such as weddings. Besides the place setting, what makes them attractive? One way to make an ordinary table more eye-catching is to use a table covering. When setting a table, you can choose to use a tablecloth or placemats—or both. You may also choose a table runner, which goes down the center of the table. Tablecloths come in sizes to fit different table dimensions and shapes, such as oval, rectangular, and round. See **Fig. 25-2**.

An Added Touch

At times you may want to use your creativity and add something special to the table to make it look more attractive. If your family has a flower garden, you could cut a few flowers or make an arrangement and place it in a vase at the center of the table as a centerpiece. Fruits and vegetables also make nice centerpieces. An edible centerpiece can also include a variety of breads and breadsticks.

Candles add elegance to a dinner table. You can use large candlesticks or put small floating candles in a shallow bowl of water. Remember to blow out the candles when you leave the table and remove any candle wax that has dripped onto the table.

Fig 25-3 Using the correct flatware will help prevent unnecessary spills.

Basic Table Manners

Kari and Jamie had been best friends for three years, but Kari couldn't bring herself to eat dinner at Jamie's house. Although Kari liked Jamie's family, she was insecure about table etiquette and thought she would surely embarrass herself at their table.

Knowing basic etiquette, or table manners, will give you confidence in different social situations and will make a positive impression on others. Although it seems like a lot to remember, once you start to follow these tips they'll become automatic:

- **Use the correct flatware.** If you're not sure which piece of flatware to use, observe what the person at the head of the table uses. See **Fig. 25-3**.

- **Wait before eating.** If you have been invited to eat at someone's house, don't begin eating until everyone has been served or a host encourages you to start. At a buffet, everyone does not have to be seated for you to begin eating, but wait until a few people are seated.

- **Ask for food to be passed to you.** If an item is not placed in front of you, ask for the item to be passed to you. Don't reach across the table.

Good table manners allow everyone at the table to have a good time. How do your table manners affect people's perception of you?

- **Put your napkin in the correct place.** Your napkin should be on your lap when you're eating. At the end of the meal, place it to the left of the plate. Don't blow or wipe your nose with a napkin. If you need to do this, excuse yourself from the table and use tissues in the restroom.

- **Use fingers for finger foods only.** Eat with a fork unless you're eating actual finger foods, such as corn on the cob, sandwiches, or raw carrot and celery sticks. Never use your fingers to push food onto your fork. Instead, use your knife to place food on your fork or spoon.

- **Eat slowly.** Eating quickly is not only bad table manners but also bad for digestion. Also, avoid stuffing your mouth with food. It looks terrible and can cause you to choke.

- **Eat quietly.** Always chew with your mouth closed, and refrain from making noises while you eat. Finish eating your food before talking.

- **Keep your flatware in the right place.** During a meal, do not rest the fork or knife gangplank style from the plate to the table. Instead, place them across the edge of your plate. After eating, put your knife and fork across the center of your plate. See **Fig. 25-4**.

- **Cut food correctly.** Cut one bite of food at a time and eat it. When eating a dinner roll, break off and butter one piece at a time.

- **Don't clean your teeth at the table.** Don't pick anything out of your teeth while seated at the dining table. If something seems caught in your teeth, excuse yourself and go to the restroom to deal with the problem. This also applies to combing your hair!

- **Calmly correct mistakes.** Don't let a mistake ruin your dinner. If you do something incorrectly, calmly correct the behavior. More than likely, no one noticed.

- **Always offer to help.** As a guest it is appropriate to ask if you can help. The hostess or host will let you know what to do. See **Fig. 25-5**.

- **Say "thank you."** If invited to someone's home for a meal, it's thoughtful to bring a small gift. When eating at someone's home or as a guest in a restaurant, always thank the host or hostess. If you don't like what's being served, take a small portion.

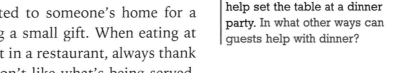

Fig 25-5 This teen offered to help set the table at a dinner party. In what other ways can guests help with dinner?

Clearing the Table

Think about how family meals end at your home. In many families, everyone is responsible for clearing his or her own place setting from the table. However, if you're serving guests in your home, here are some suggestions:

1. Clear one or two plates at a time, placing the flatware across each plate.

2. Scrape the plates when you reach the kitchen.

3. Stack the scraped plates quietly.

4. Clear all plates before serving dessert.

Eating Out

When you think about eating out, what pictures flash through your mind? Do you see a fast-food restaurant or a restaurant in which food is served to you? At fast-food restaurants, you order your food at the counter or drive-through window. At many casual restaurants, you wait for a table to become available. Someone may seat you or you may seat yourself, and a server takes your order after you're seated at the table. See **Fig. 25-6**.

Fig 25-6 ▶ When greeted by a restaurant employee, you can request a preference for a table location.

At more formal restaurants, you may need to reserve a table. In this case, phone ahead and make a reservation. You will be asked what time you plan to dine and how many people are in your group, or party. Many fine-dining restaurants have dress requirements. If you're not sure what the restaurant requires, ask when you make the reservation.

Once you make a reservation, the restaurant depends on you to arrive on time. If you can't get there on time, call. You can either cancel the reservation or reserve a table for another time.

Ordering from the Menu

Casual and formal restaurants have menus categorized by type of food, or **courses**, which are parts of a meal. For example, the menu might include appetizers, soups, salads, entrées, desserts, and beverages. An **appetizer** is an optional first course, and generally a small portion. The **entrée** is the main course, and a larger portion than the appetizer.

Some menus list and price food separately, or **à la carte**, which means each item has an individual, or separate, price. Other menus list a complete meal for a certain price.

Restaurant Behavior

Have you ever been seated next to a loud, disruptive group of people at a restaurant? You probably know how annoying that kind of behavior can be to others. Most people go out to eat to enjoy their meal and each other's company, not be around rude people.

To keep from being a diner no one wants to sit next to, avoid talking loudly with others at your table. If you need something during the meal, go to the counter where you ordered your food or ask your server when he or she comes to your table. If you want to get a server's attention, raise your hand to catch the server's eye or say, "Excuse me" in an ordinary voice as the server passes your table. See **Fig. 25-7**.

Paying the Bill

Unlike counter-service restaurants, which require you to pay before you eat, sit-down restaurants bill you after you eat. Before paying, check the bill to be sure it's accurate. You may notice a sales tax, which some states require restaurants to add to customer bills. If a server brought food to your table, you should leave the server a tip. Tips are generally 15 to 20 percent of the bill before tax. No matter what you thought of the food, if the service was good, leave a tip. If something is wrong, and an item is deducted from your bill, it is still appropriate to tip on the original amount.

If your check reads "Pay the cashier," leave a tip on the table and pay the cashier on the way out. Sometimes the server takes your money and pays the cashier for you. If you're paying by credit card, write the tip and the total on the charge receipt.

When eating out with friends, agree on who will pay before you go to the restaurant. If you're invited out and aren't sure about who's paying, bring enough money to cover your own bill—just in case.

Fig 25-7 Servers work hard to make your restaurant experience pleasurable. In addition to using good etiquette, treat your server with respect.

HOW TO PLAN A CELEBRATION

From the everyday to the once-in-a-lifetime, some events call for celebrating. Any celebration, even an informal gathering, can benefit from some preplanning. Follow these guidelines to make your next event a memorable one:

STEP 1 **Extend invitations.** Send written invitations for casual events at least two weeks in advance. Allow for four weeks for a major event. Include the date, time, address, and reason for the occasion. Add "RSVP," meaning "response if you please." Guests should tell you whether they can come by replying using a phone number or e-mail address you have included on the invitation.

STEP 2 **Set the menu.** Foods should fit the occasion. An elaborate meal might be right for a holiday. New neighbors may feel more comfortable sharing favorite family recipes. A selection of snacks or pizza would probably be better at a teen party. Learn beforehand whether any guests have a food allergy or follow a restricted diet.

STEP 3 **Consider space needs.** Space can be a limitation but also an asset if it's creatively used. If you have little space but a big crowd, think in terms of "cozy," rather than "cramped." Serve simple finger foods on unbreakable plates and encourage guests to mingle on the porch or patio, in the backyard, or on the balcony.

STEP 5 **Choose decorations.** These aren't essential, but they do add a festive touch. Look for things you can borrow or buy at little cost. Decorations are fun for creating a theme. For example, for a sports theme, decorate with new or borrowed sports equipment and serve dips in bowls set in well-lined football helmets or baseball caps.

STEP 4 **Plan your time.** As with space, you may need to be creative to fit tasks into your schedule. If you're going to prepare foods, look to convenience foods for help. Buy refrigerated biscuits and canned sauce for pizza cups, for example. If your friends enjoy making their own pizzas, the food can double as entertainment, saving you time and effort.

TAKE **ACTION**

In groups of four or five, plan a simple celebration for a small group, such as a lunch for adult volunteers who help your class. Discuss and assign each of the tasks described here. Carry out your plans if possible.

Review & Activities

Chapter Summary

- Families use mealtime to strengthen their relationships.
- Place settings at a meal are arranged in a logical order.
- People observe generally accepted rules of behavior when eating to show consideration to others.
- Knowledge of restaurant etiquette can give you confidence and increase your enjoyment while eating out.

Reviewing Key Terms & Ideas

1. What is **etiquette**?
2. Define **place setting**.
3. What items make up **tableware**?
4. What **flatware** does a typical place setting contain?
5. List four basic table manners to keep in mind when eating a meal.
6. List the steps in clearing a table after dinner with guests.
7. What are the typical **courses** you would find on a restaurant menu? Are courses served at home?
8. What is the difference between an **appetizer** and an **entrée**?
9. What does it mean if items are listed **à la carte**?
10. How much should you tip the waitperson in a restaurant?

Thinking Critically

1. **Making comparisons.** What would you consider a formal dining experience? How can you transform a casual meal to a more formal meal?
2. **Drawing conclusions.** Why do you think a concentration on table etiquette makes some people nervous?
3. **Making predictions.** Imagine you have friends with poor table manners. How might their lack of manners affect their future lives?

Review & Activities

Applying Your Learning

1. **Family time.** With a small group, brainstorm ways to make family meals more enjoyable. Select three ideas and create a plan to incorporate them at home. Try it out!

2. **Table settings.** Using tableware and flatware, create two place settings—one correct and one incorrect. Ask a classmate to identify the correct place setting and identify the errors in the incorrect place setting.

3. **Table designs.** Look through home decorating magazines for photos of table settings. Then, using art supplies or graphic software, design a table setting that includes tableware, flatware, table coverings, and a centerpiece.

4. **Life simulation.** With a small group, enact a mealtime scene that includes good and poor table manners. Have the audience critique your table manners and offer suggestions for improvement.

5. **Restaurant etiquette.** Using props, videotapes, Power-Point, or other visual aids, create a presentation for teens who may not have knowledge of restaurant etiquette. Practice your presentation and ask a classmate for feedback before you present the information to others.

Making Connections

1. **Reading** Not all etiquette is about food. Read a book about etiquette. Choose three points of etiquette not covered in this chapter and write a short description of each.

2. **Writing** Imagine you're the owner of a new restaurant, and you're creating your menu. List the different courses you'll offer and the items available in each. Write short, appealing descriptions of each food item.

3. **Reading** Research the customary table manners of people in a different country. How do their table manners differ from yours?

CAREER Link

Teamwork.
Many employers require their employees to work in teams. Generally, people on teams accomplish more than they could individually. Team members also feel good when they collaborate with others to get a job done. Describe your experiences working as a team member. What benefits did teamwork provide? What challenges did you encounter?

Kitchen Equipment

Objectives

- Explain factors to consider when selecting kitchen equipment.
- Classify different kitchen utensils.
- Name small kitchen appliances and explain their use.
- Describe features of large kitchen appliances.
- Identify different types of cookware and explain their use.

Vocabulary

- **utensils**
- **immersible**
- **microwaves**
- **cookware**

Reading with Purpose

1. **Write down** the colored headings from Chapter 26 in your notebook.

2. **As you read** the text under each heading, visualize what you are reading.

3. **Reflect** on what you read by writing a few sentences under each heading to describe it.

4. **Continue** this process until you have finished the chapter. Reread your notes.

Selecting Kitchen Equipment

Setting up a new kitchen is a lot of fun, but it takes careful planning. Imagine you're moving into a new house with no kitchen equipment. What items would you select? Your home kitchen doesn't need dozens of supplies for you to be a successful cook, but you do need to consider the kinds of foods you make or the kinds of foods you like. Most kitchens are stocked with basic equipment that lets you perform an amazing number of food preparation tasks. The role of kitchen equipment is to simplify the task at hand.

Selecting kitchen equipment requires decision making. You need to determine how much money to spend. Large equipment, such as stoves, refrigerators, and dishwashers, can be costly, so you have to consider these purchases carefully. Although small equipment is less expensive, you should avoid spending money on clever gadgets you may not need or will use only once or twice. Another important consideration is quality. Get the best quality for your money. Make sure to do some research before you shop! See **Fig. 26-1**.

The following questions can help guide you as you furnish your kitchen:

- **How large is my kitchen?** If your kitchen is small, it probably has little cabinet and counter space. You'll need to think carefully about storage before you buy kitchen items.

- **What kinds of food do I like?** If you like Chinese food, you might want to purchase a wok and an electric rice cooker or steamer. If hamburgers are your favorite, you might need an indoor or outdoor grill.

- **Does quality count?** High-quality equipment may cost more, but it usually lasts longer with proper care.

- **Do I need it?** If you can make a dish just as easily with equipment you have on hand, then the new item probably isn't worth the money. Also, think about how often you will use the new equipment. If you'll use it often, then you might want to buy it. If not, pass it by.

Fig 26-1 ▶ Select kitchen equipment wisely. Look for good construction for a fair price.

Utensils

Kacy and her grandmother bake cakes every year for a charity bake sale that benefits Kacy's dance team. Kacy remembers the first time she watched her grandmother bake cakes. Kacy was amazed by all of the **utensils**, or small kitchen tools, her grandmother used. Kacy had never seen so many different sizes of spoons, turners, and measuring cups in one kitchen before!

If you have already done some cooking, you know how helpful utensils can be. Without them, it would be hard to measure, mix, or prepare food. Sturdy, well-made utensils last a long time. If you have a dishwasher or microwave oven, it is helpful to have utensils that are dishwasher and microwave safe. See **Fig. 26-2**.

Cutting and Chopping Utensils

Cutting and chopping tools are used to cut food into pieces of different sizes. A good set of sharp knives is essential. If you can only afford two knives, purchase a good-quality slicing knife or chef's knife and a knife that has a serrated (sawtooth) blade for cutting things like bread. Knife choices have a lot to do with personal preference. What fits well and comfortably in your hand? A good choice would be a paring knife. Make sure the knife handle is attached to the blade with two or three rivets. See **Fig. 26-3**.

Fig 26-2 You can find these utensils and more at a gourmet cooking store. How necessary do you think these utensils are?

- **Paring knives** are helpful for peeling fruits and vegetables.

- **Utility knives** are all-purpose knives for cutting and slicing foods.

- **Chef's knives** are used for cutting, mincing, and dicing.

- **Bread knives** are serrated and designed for slicing bread or baked goods.

- **Cleavers** are used to cut through thick meats and bone.

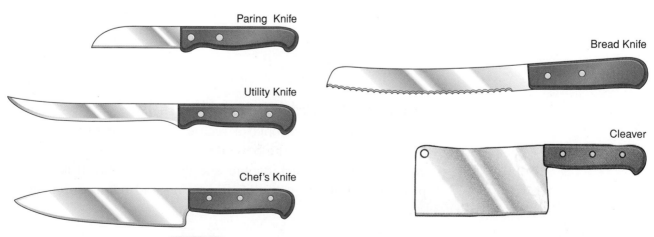

Paring Knife

Utility Knife

Chef's Knife

Bread Knife

Cleaver

Fig 26-3 These are common knives for kitchen use.

Fig 26-4 ▶

Measuring Utensils

▶ **Dry measuring cups** are used to measure dry ingredients, such as flour and sugar. They usually come in sets: ¼ cup, ⅓ cup, ½ cup, and 1 cup. Sizes in a set of metric measures include 50 mL (milliliters), 125 mL, and 250 mL.

▶ **Liquid measuring cups** are often clear plastic or glass. They have a spout for pouring and measurements marked on the side in cups, ounces, and milliliters. Common sizes are 1 cup, 2 cups, and 4 cups (250 mL, 500 mL, and 1,000 mL in metric).

▶ **Measuring spoons** are used for measuring smaller amounts of liquid and dry ingredients. The most common sizes are ¼ teaspoon, ½ teaspoon, 1 teaspoon, and 1 tablespoon. A set of small metric measures includes 1 mL, 2 mL, 5 mL, 15 mL, and 25 mL.

Measuring and Mixing Utensils

Have you ever seasoned a recipe by pouring salt directly from the shaker into the bowl without measuring it? Or have you tried to mix thick cookie dough with a fork? If so, you probably know the value of measuring and mixing utensils.

Fig 26-5

Mixing Utensils

▶ **Mixing bowls** hold the ingredients that you mix and come in graduated sizes. They can also be used in a casual setting to serve food.

▶ **Mixing spoons** have long handles and are used to combine ingredients.

▶ **Plastic or rubber scrapers** are used to scrape bowls and mix ingredients together. They have a wide, flexible rubber blade.

▶ **Sifters** sift and mix dry ingredients together as they pass through a mesh screen. They come in various sizes.

▶ **Pastry blenders** cut shortening into flour for pie crusts and biscuits.

▶ **Wire whisks** are used for beating and blending. Whisks are especially efficient to combine liquid ingredients and to beat eggs.

▶ **Rotary beaters** are also known as hand beaters. You use a rotary beater to beat eggs and mix thin batters, such as pancake or cake batter.

Measuring utensils help you accurately measure ingredients for recipes. Mixing utensils easily combine ingredients. Some mixing utensils can be helpful for a variety of tasks; others can be used only for a specific task. See **Fig. 26-4** and **Fig. 26-5**.

To operate electrical appliances safely, apply the following guidelines:

- Be sure to read all instructions before using appliances.

- Use an appliance only for its intended purpose.

- Be sure to dry your hands before using any electrical appliance.

- Do not touch any moving parts of an appliance when it is operating.

- Be careful that power cords are not hanging over the edge of counters.

- Keep power cords away from heat.

- Do not use appliances with frayed power cords.

- Unplug power cords from outlets when not in use and before cleaning or attaching any parts.

- Keep your instruction manual.

Other Kitchen Utensils

A variety of other tools can make work in the kitchen easier. See **Fig. 26-6**. In addition to these, what other utensils does your family find helpful?

Small Kitchen Appliances

When you make toast, do you bake slices of bread in the oven, or do you pop bread into a toaster? If you use a toaster, you're using a small kitchen appliance. There are hundreds of small appliances available today. Along with toasters, you can find mixers, coffeemakers, blenders, food processors, and indoor grills, just to name a few. Small appliances perform specific cooking tasks for you, such as toasting your bread, which can speed up your cooking time. Small appliances, which are generally powered by electricity, are portable, so you can move them from place to place. Portability not only allows you to use the appliances in different areas of your kitchen but also provides you with different options for storage.

Some appliances are **immersible**, which means that the entire appliance can be put safely into water to be washed. On these appliances, the electrical unit has been sealed so that no water can enter it. Immersible appliances have the term "immersible" written on them. If you don't see the term, do not put the appliance in water. See **Fig. 26-7**.

Large Kitchen Appliances

Most kitchens are equipped with basic large appliances, such as a gas or electric range and a refrigerator. Additional large kitchen appliances include microwave ovens, convection ovens, dishwashers, upright or chest-type freezers, trash compactors, and garbage disposals.

Large appliances are considered major purchases. The costs vary depending on the style, size, and features you choose and whether you buy new or used appliances. When shopping for large kitchen appliances, compare the Energy Guide labels and look for safety and performance seals.

Be sure to read and keep the owner's manual for all appliances. Each manual contains valuable information about using and caring for your appliances.

Fig 26-6
Other Kitchen Utensils

▶ **Cutting boards** serve as a base for your cutting work, keeping knife blades sharp and counters in good shape. Clear plastic boards do not promote bacteria growth.

▶ **Graters** are used to shred and grate vegetables and cheeses. Check out photo-etched graters. They do an amazing job.

▶ **Kitchen shears** are sturdy scissors kept in the kitchen and used for cutting vegetables, pastry, poultry, and meat. Always wash shears with soap and warm water after each use.

▶ **Vegetable peelers** are used to pare vegetables and fruits. Some peelers have a blade that swivels for ease in paring.

Cutting Board

Kitchen shears

Peeler

Grater

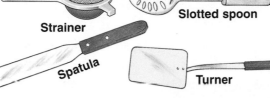
Strainer

Slotted spoon

Spatula

Turner

Colander

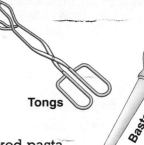
Tongs

Baster

▶ **Colanders** are bowls with holes for draining foods, such as cooked pasta.

▶ **Basters** are used for basting foods and are great for removing liquid.

▶ **Strainers** are wire mesh baskets with handles used to strain liquids from solid foods, such as water from steamed vegetables. Strainers are available in different sizes of mesh.

▶ **Slotted spoons** are helpful for lifting solid food from liquid, like separating vegetables from their cooking juices.

▶ **Metal spatulas** have dull, narrow metal blades. They're useful in leveling dry ingredients, such as flour, in measuring cups.

▶ **Turners,** or wide spatulas, are used to lift and turn foods, such as pancakes or hamburgers.

   ▶ **Tongs** grasp or hold foods, such as a chicken drumstick or a corncob.

   ▶ **Ladles** help spoon out hot soup and stews.

   ▶ **Cooling racks** are made of wire and allow air to circulate around hot baked products so that they cool evenly.

Thermometer

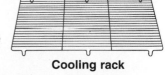
Cooling rack

Ladle

   ▶ **Thermometers** are used to measure the temperature of food. Rapid read thermometers can be placed in food at any time during cooking for an instant read.

Fig 26-7
Small Kitchen Appliances

▶ **Toasters** brown and crisp slices of bread. Some can adjust for thicker breads, such as bagels or English muffins.

▶ **Blenders** have push-button or touch-pad controls and short blades that rotate quickly to blend, chop, mix, and purée. Handheld blenders, known as immersion blenders, blend foods directly in pots and bowls.

▶ **Handheld mixers** can be used for mixing cake batter and whipping cream, potatoes, or anything with a light to medium batter. They are lightweight, easy to manage, and convenient to store.

▶ **Stand mixers** are used for larger amounts or thicker batters and do not require you to hold either the mixer or the bowl.

▶ **Food processors** perform many cutting and mixing tasks using blades and disks.

▶ **Electric skillets** fry, roast, and simmer foods. The skillet's thermostatic controls regulate cooking temperatures. It also works to keep foods warm during an event.

▶ **Toaster ovens** take little time to preheat and are ideal for toasting bread and baking or broiling small amounts of food. Some toaster ovens have a broil feature.

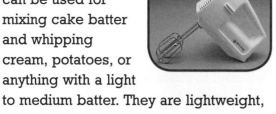

▶ **Slow cookers** allow you to safely cook one-dish meals for several hours.

▶ **Indoor or outdoor grills** are electric grills with temperature controls that allow low-fat cooking, indoors or outside.

Fig 26-8 Manufacturers of large appliances usually provide warranties, which cover repairs when appliances break. Read all warranty information carefully.

Refrigerators

Refrigerators keep perishable foods cold. Refrigerators can come with a freezer on top, at the bottom, or on the side, or they can come without a freezer. Sizes and features of refrigerators vary. People with smaller kitchens usually have a small refrigerator with few extra features. If you have more space, you can have a larger refrigerator, with features such as an ice and water dispenser, although the larger size and greater number of features will cost you more. Large refrigerators also come in handy if you live far from the grocery store. A large refrigerator can store more food, which means you can make fewer trips to the store. See **Fig. 26-8**.

Ranges

Think about the food prepared in your kitchen. How much is cooked on a range? Standard ranges have a cooktop, an oven, and a broiler and are powered by electricity or gas. Gas-range heating units are called burners. The gas flame on a burner is visible and can be raised or lowered quickly to control the heat flow. The heating units on electric ranges are called elements. When you turn on a heating element, it gradually becomes red. As it cools, it returns to gray or black. Be aware, however, that heating elements retain heat long after you turn them off. Some ranges have a warning light that stays on until the cooktop is safe to touch. Older ranges often do not have this safety feature.

When using a range, make sure you do the following:

- Avoid touching electric heating elements or gas burners until they are completely cooled.

- Turn up the flame on gas burners slowly to keep the fire from flaring.

- Never place towels or paper near gas burners or heating elements.

- Always keep pot handles turned inward so that people passing by don't knock them off the range.

- Always keep long hair and loose clothing away from gas burners and heating elements.

- Use potholders when removing anything from the oven or when moving pots with handles.

Standard and Convection Ovens

If you shop for traditional ovens, you will find two types: standard and convection ovens. In standard ovens, the hot air rises naturally from the bottom to the top of the oven. Convection ovens use a fan to move hot air around rapidly. This allows convection ovens to cook faster than standard ovens, often cutting cooking time in half. This is not true of all convection ovens. If you buy one, experimentation is key. You will have to check times and compare them to the recipes you are preparing. The rapid airflow also helps food cook more evenly. Both types of ovens are available with a self-cleaning feature, which reduces food to ash so that it can be easily wiped away.

Microwave Ovens

Microwave ovens use **microwaves**, or energy waves, to heat food. Microwaves pass through glass, plastic, and paper. These microwaves are absorbed by the molecules in food and cause vibrations. This in turn produces friction, and the friction produces heat to cook the food. Rotating food during cooking allows even cooking in the microwave. Nothing metal should be used in a microwave oven! Metal will cause electrical sparks that can destroy the microwave and lead to a fire.

Be careful when handling microwaved food. You sometimes don't expect the containers to be as hot as the food. It's important to use potholders when removing containers from a microwave oven. Use only microwave-safe containers for cooking. Most dishes safe for the microwave will be marked. Special microwave bags are available for microwaving food.

Cookware

Just about anything you prepare in the kitchen requires cookware. **Cookware** includes pots, pans, and other containers for use on top of the range, in the oven, or in the microwave. Cookware items are made of metal, glass, or plastic. When buying cookware, be sure that the bottoms of pots and pans are heavy and flat, the handles are riveted to the pan, and the covers fit securely. If the handles are oven safe (not plastic), the pan can be safely put into and used in the oven. Skillets also are available with a nonstick finish. The nonstick coating keeps food from sticking to the cookware and makes it easier to clean. See **Fig. 26-9**.

Fig 26-9 ▶
Cookware & Bakeware

▶ **Skillets** are shallow pans and generally have long handles. They come in assorted sizes and sometimes have covers.

▶ **Saucepans and stockpots** are deeper than skillets. They come in a variety of sizes, usually measured in quarts or liters. Some have covers. Saucepans have one handle, and stockpots have two, one on each side.

▶ **Cake pans** come in different sizes and shapes. They can be used for baking many foods . Cake pans can be made of glass, metal, or silicone.

▶ **Loaf pans** come in different sizes and are used for breads and meat loaves. Loaf pans can be made of glass, metal, or silicone.

▶ **Casseroles,** or baking dishes, come in a variety of shapes and sizes. They're deep enough to hold a main-dish mixture and often have covers.

▶ **Baking sheets** are rectangular, low-sided pans. They're most often used for baking cookies and making sweets.

▶ **Pie pans** are round and come in different sizes and depths. Pie pans can be made of glass, metal, or silicone.

▶ **Muffin pans** have from 6 to 12 individual cups to hold muffins and cupcakes.

▶ **Custard cups** are made from heatproof glass. You can use them to bake custard or to microwave eggs.

Stock pot

90x130 Cake pan

Loaf pan

Saucepan

Round cake pan

Casserole

Skillet

Pie pan

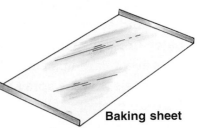

Baking sheet

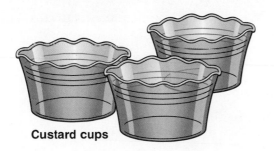

Custard cups

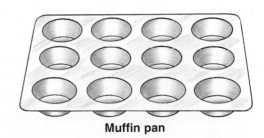

Muffin pan

HOW TO GRILL HEALTHY FOOD

People have enjoyed the taste and aroma of grilling since they first learned to put food over fire. Quickly cooked with little added fat, grilled foods can also be nutritious. Remember these tips for safe and healthful outdoor cooking:

STEP 3 **Choose the food.** Thin cuts of meat and poultry pieces are popular because they cook quickly. You can thread a skewer with chunks of vegetables, fruits, shellfish, or meat. Grill whole ears of corn right in the husk. Place fish in aluminum foil or a grill basket. To speed cooking without burning the food, keep the grill closed as much as possible. Note: If using bamboo skewers, make sure they are soaked in water for 30 minutes before threading them with food. This prevents the skewers from burning.

STEP 1 **Practice fire prevention.** Flames can burn more than food. Always keep a fire extinguisher handy. Set the grill on a level surface, in a well-ventilated area, and away from anything that could catch fire. Trim fat from meat and poultry to prevent flare-ups caused by fat dripping onto coals. Keep a spray bottle of water for flare-up control.

STEP 2 **Assemble the equipment.** Some items make grilling more successful. Fireproof mitts and long-handled brushes and turning utensils are safety "must-haves." Wire baskets and metal rods, or skewers, let you grill small or delicate foods.

STEP 4 **Flavor for health.** Grilled foods have a naturally smoky taste. Some woods also impart a distinct flavor. Chips of hickory, maple, mesquite, alder, apple, or pecan can be used alone or with charcoal. You might experiment with a rub (a blend of seasonings). Add fat only to keep certain foods from drying out. Vegetables may be lightly brushed with melted margarine, and skinless chicken can be thinly coated with barbecue sauce. Try fish with low-fat salad dressing or a marinade, a seasoned blend of oil and vinegar or fruit juice that forms a sauce used to flavor food.

STEP 5 **Handle meat with care.** Use tongs, rather than a fork, to move meat on and off a grill. Forks pierce the flesh, letting out natural fats and juices. Saving these flavorful fluids reduces the need for added fat or salty condiments. Make sure meat is cooked evenly on both sides. A rapid read thermometer is a great tool when grilling.

TAKE **ACTION**

Look through a print or online catalog of grilling equipment. Compare similar items on price, usefulness, and safety. Choose three items that you think are the best buys. Explain your choices.

26

Review & Activities

Chapter Summary

- Selecting kitchen equipment requires careful consideration and decision making.
- Kitchen utensils allow you to cut, measure, and mix, as well as perform other food preparation tasks with accuracy.
- Small kitchen appliances help make your food preparation time more efficient.
- Large kitchen appliances include refrigerators, ranges, and ovens.

Reviewing Key Terms & Ideas

1. What are **utensils** and how are they helpful in the kitchen?
2. List three types of knives.
3. What are the standard sizes of liquid measuring cups?
4. Describe how mixing spoons, plastic or rubber scrapers, and wire whisks are used.
5. Why is it important to use a cutting board when working in the kitchen?
6. What is the advantage of **immersible** appliances?
7. What is a gas burner? What is an element?
8. What is the difference between a convection oven and a standard oven?
9. What are **microwaves** and why do they cook foods faster?
10. What does **cookware** include?

Thinking Critically

1. **Analyzing situations.** What advice would you give a person buying kitchen equipment for the first time?
2. **Justifying decisions.** Explain why people should consider spending more money for better-quality equipment when shopping for kitchen utensils.
3. **Drawing conclusions.** Imagine you have an opportunity to acquire only two small kitchen appliances. What small appliances would help you make good use of your time in the kitchen? Explain your decision.

Review & Activities

Applying Your Learning

1. **Kitchen inventory.** List the kitchen equipment you have at home. Identify the equipment you feel is most or least helpful to your family. If you could replace three items, which would you replace? Why?

2. **Product promotion.** Imagine you work for an advertising company that has been hired to create a print advertisement for a kitchen utensil. Working in a small group, select a utensil and create an advertisement that showcases the utensil's use and features.

3. **Utensil critique.** Select one small utensil to evaluate. Using catalogs, consumer publications, or actual items, critique three brands or designs of the utensil you chose. If possible, try preparing food with each of the utensils. Present your critique to your class.

4. **Design improvement.** Select one small appliance with which you are familiar. Explain how you would improve the design to make it more user-friendly.

5. **Range safety.** Using the range in the food lab, identify common safety hazards and demonstrate proper safety procedures when using a range.

6. **Technology research.** Research new technology available in kitchen appliances, such as a refrigerator–oven combination. Present your findings to the class.

Making Connections

1. **Math** Measure 1 cup of flour into a 2-cup liquid measuring cup. Carefully pour the flour from the liquid measuring cup into a 1-cup dry measuring cup. How do the measurements compare? What conclusions can you draw?

2. **Reading** Locate studies in a consumer magazine that compare the safety, features, and performance of a small kitchen appliance. Based on your reading, which model would you choose and why?

3. **Writing** Learn about the features of a standard range or flattop range and how to use them. Write a short instruction manual for the appliance. Have classmates evaluate your instructions.

CAREER Link

Being on Time.
In the workplace, one way people are judged is by their punctuality—their ability to arrive on time. Right now, being punctual is important for you to meet your responsibilities in school. You'll also need to be punctual on the job. Interview local employers to find out how punctuality affects their business. How much do they value punctuality? What role does punctuality play in employee evaluations? Present your findings to your class.

Safety & Sanitation

Objectives

- Identify the cause of foodborne illness.
- Explain how foodborne illness can be prevented.
- Demonstrate personal cleanliness in the kitchen.
- Describe safe food storage techniques.
- Provide ways to use kitchen appliances safely.

Vocabulary

- **foodborne illness**
- **bacteria**
- **cross-contamination**
- **sanitize**
- **marinades**

Reading with Purpose

1. **As you read** Chapter 27, create an outline in your notebook using the colored headings.

2. **Write** a question under each heading that you can use to guide your reading.

3. **Answer** the question under each heading as you read the chapter. Record your answers.

4. **Ask** your teacher to help with answers you could not find in this chapter.

Working Safely in the Kitchen

Think about the safety guidelines you typically follow in the kitchen. How long do you wash your hands before preparing your food? Do you keep raw meat and poultry separate from other foods? How do you check meat to be sure it's cooked thoroughly? What do you do to prevent cuts and burns? Kitchen safety guidelines seem almost endless, yet routinely taking basic precautions can prevent most accidents and food-related illnesses.

Sanitation in the Kitchen

Health experts estimate that every minute of every day someone is stricken with foodborne illness, or food poisoning. **Foodborne illness** is an illness caused by eating spoiled food or food containing harmful bacteria. **Bacteria** are one-celled living organisms so small that they can be seen only with a microscope. When harmful bacteria are transferred from one food or surface to another, **cross-contamination** occurs. For example, raw meat cut on a cutting board can cross-contaminate a salad if the cutting board is not washed thoroughly before it's used as a cutting surface for salad vegetables. Some people use separate cutting boards to avoid cross-contamination. See **Fig. 27-1**.

The good news is that simple precautions prevent foodborne illness. Experts believe that 85 percent of all foodborne sickness is avoidable. Taking the time to **sanitize**—or clean to get rid of bacteria—is the first step in preventing foodborne illness. See **Fig. 27-2**.

Fig 27-1 ▶ After cleaning countertops, wash towels in hot water in the washing machine to kill any bacteria.

Fig 27-2

Sanitation in the Kitchen

▶ Wipe lids of cans before opening them, and wash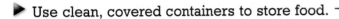
your can opener after each use.

▶ Keep sponges clean. You can boil them in
water for a short time, or you can saturate
them with a diluted bleach solution (2
teaspoons of chlorine bleach in 1 quart of
water). You can even moisten them with water
and heat them in the microwave until they
steam. You can also put them in the dishwasher to
be run at the same time as the dishes.

▶ Use clean, covered containers to store food.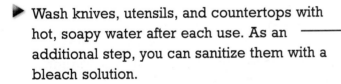

▶ Run the garbage disposal immediately after
placing food in it to keep it free from rotting
food. Make sure your hands and utensils are
completely out of the disposal before turning
it on.

▶ Wash knives, utensils, and countertops with
hot, soapy water after each use. As an
additional step, you can sanitize them with a
bleach solution.

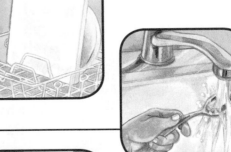

▶ Wash cutting boards in hot, soapy water
after each use, particularly after cutting raw
meat or poultry. Most cutting boards can
be put into the dishwasher to be cleaned.
Replace heavily scratched cutting boards,
which are difficult to clean.

▶ Use a clean spoon every time you taste food
during cooking.

▶ Dishtowels and dishcloths provide a safe
haven for unsafe bacteria. Make sure that you
wash your dishtowels and dishcloths often in
the washing machine's hot cycle.

Personal Cleanliness

Imagine you and your family are eating out at a restaurant. As you pass the kitchen, you notice an employee's hair is dangling into food. You spot another employee handling food with dirty hands. How would you feel about eating food prepared by these employees? Your home isn't a restaurant, but your personal cleanliness in your own kitchen still counts.

Personal cleanliness in the kitchen begins with clean hands. Always wash your hands thoroughly with soap and warm water, rubbing them together for at least 20 seconds. After washing your hands, dry them before handling food. If you take a break from preparing food to use the restroom, make sure your hands are washed! You'll also need to wash your hands after handling anything dirty or potentially hazardous, such as cleaning solutions. If you have cuts or scrapes on your hands, wear plastic gloves while preparing food.

Other personal cleanliness tips include turning your face away from food to sneeze or cough, tying back your hair if it's long, having clean nails, and not touching your hair while working in the kitchen. Also, always wear clean clothes to prevent dirt from transferring from your clothes to the food.

Safe Food Preparation

Cleanliness isn't the only way to combat foodborne illness. The following cooking and reheating tips can help you prevent the spread of harmful bacteria:

- **Wash produce thoroughly.** Wash fresh fruits and vegetables under cold running water. Use a vegetable scrub brush to loosen dirt on hard vegetables, such as potatoes. Do not use soap or detergent. Be sure to wash the rind or skin to prevent bacteria from spreading to the inside of the food when it's cut or peeled. Also, prewash any packaged salad mixes.

- **Wait before tasting.** Do not taste-test meat, poultry, eggs, or fish until they're thoroughly cooked.

- **Thaw food safely.** Never thaw frozen meat, poultry, or seafood on the counter or in a sink of water. Thaw them in the refrigerator.

- **Cook food until done.** Meat, poultry, and seafood should be cooked at a temperature of 325°F or higher. The best way to check for doneness is to use a meat thermometer. Pork should be cooked to 160°F, poultry to 180°F, ground meat to 160°F to 165°F, and fish fillets to at least 145°F. When preparing eggs, cook them until the yolk and white are firm, not runny.

- **Finish cooking once you start.** Don't let interruptions stop you from finishing any food you've begun to cook. Never refrigerate partially cooked food to finish cooking later.

- **Heat leftovers properly.** When reheating leftovers, bring sauces, soups, and gravies to a boil. Heat other leftovers thoroughly to 165°F or until hot throughout.

Serving Food Safely

Serving delicious food is just one reward of preparing food. The following tips will help you serve delicious food safely:

- **Use sauces carefully.** Never brush foods you are ready to serve with a marinade that was used on raw foods. **Marinades** are sauces used to flavor food, such as barbecue sauce. The bacteria in the marinade from the raw food can be transferred easily to the cooked food.

Fig 27-3 Potholders can be used when taking dishes out of the oven or removing pots from the range. What precautions should you take when using potholders?

- **Clean serving plates.** Never put cooked food on a plate that held raw meat, poultry, or seafood without thoroughly washing the plate first.

- **Serve food in time.** Do not serve food that's been at room temperature for more than two hours. If you are eating outside on a hot day, do not serve food left out for more than 15 to 30 minutes. It's best to keep all foods chilled. Use ice packets or insulated containers.

- **Keep temperatures consistent.** Always keep hot food hot and cold food cold.

Preventing Accidents in the Kitchen

More accidents take place in the kitchen than in any other room in the home. Prevent accidents by thinking ahead and working safely in the kitchen. The following sections offer some guidelines to help you make the kitchen a safe place to work. What other safety rules can you add? See **Fig. 27-3.**

Cooking Safely with a Range

Being careless while using the range and oven can lead to fires and burns. Fires can start easily and quickly. If a grease fire starts, smother the fire with a pan cover, salt, or baking soda—not flour or water. Never use water on a grease fire because the water spreads the flames. If the fire is in the oven, turn the controls off and close the door tightly to smother the flames. Always keep a fire extinguisher in the kitchen and know how to use it. Here are some additional tips to keep you injury free at the range or oven:

- **Mind cooking food.** Don't leave food cooking in the kitchen without watching it. Leaving food unattended is the main cause of kitchen fires.

- **Keep appliances clean.** Always make sure the oven and cooktop are clean. Grease and food left on surfaces can catch fire.

- **Keep pot handles inward.** If pot handles point away from the front edge of the range, they may stick out and cause injury. Also, be sure they're not over another gas flame or hot heating element.

- **Use a potholder.** Make sure the potholder is dry. Wet dishtowels used as potholders can cause steam burns.

- **Wear proper clothing.** Avoid wearing dangling jewelry or loose-fitting clothes that can become tangled on cookware handles or catch on fire.

- **Keep flammables away from the range.** This includes towels, dishcloths, paper, cookbooks, and curtains.

- **Use utensils properly.** Flat-bottomed cookware and well-balanced cooking utensils that won't tip or spill work best. Also, use kitchen tongs, long-handled spatulas, or long silicone mitts to remove food from hot water and to turn frying food. See **Fig. 27-4**.

- **Open covers carefully.** Remove a pan cover by tilting the cover away from you so that the steam flows away from you.

- **Fry foods with caution.** Dry foods thoroughly before placing them into hot fat, because water can cause fat to pop and spatter. Cover skillets with frying screens or covers to keep hot fat in the pan.

- **Use cookware properly.** Don't put ovenproof glass dishes, such as casserole dishes, on hot burners or heating elements. The glass can easily shatter, scattering glass shards and destroying your meal.

Cooking Safely with a Microwave

Microwaves are so easy to use you may forget that they can be the cause of injuries. Safe microwave cooking begins with the proper cookware. Choose "microwave-safe" plastic containers or cookware made of glass, microwave cookware, and microwave dishware to heat food in the microwave. Special bags are also available for microwave cooking. Alternatively, you can use paper plates and paper towels as long as they're not made of recycled paper, which can catch fire.

When microwaving plastic containers and pouches, puncture or vent them to keep steam from building. If steam continues to build, it can cause the pouches and containers to burst. A process called superheating can cause another type of explosion. Superheating occurs when a liquid's container does not allow bubbles to form, causing the liquid to explode. To prevent superheating, heat liquids a little at a time, stopping every few seconds to check the temperature.

Food cooked in a microwave continues to cook after the microwave timer goes off, which means it's still hot. Allow it a few minutes to cool slightly.

Stay in the room while food is cooking in the microwave in case an emergency arises. If you see sparks inside the microwave, turn it off or unplug it immediately and seek help. If the microwave makes unusual sounds, tell an adult right away. Remember: No metal in microwaves!

Using Small Appliances Safely

Many small appliances are so simple to use that people become careless with them. The result is electrical shock, a burn, or a fire. Staying safe while using small appliances isn't difficult, but it does require you to think about what you're doing. The following guidelines can help:

Fig 27-5 Whenever using a kitchen appliance, follow the safety guidelines given in the user's manual.

- **Use caution with blades.** Be careful when using or cleaning appliances with blades, such as food processors and blenders. Never put utensils or your hands near blades of running appliances. When cleaning sharp blades, wash them separately and carefully. See **Fig. 27-5**.

- **Keep cords under control.** Avoid letting appliance cords dangle over the edge of countertops or tables.

- **Make sure your hands are dry.** Dry your hands before touching any electrical equipment, and never plug in an appliance while standing on a wet surface.

- **Unplug with care.** Always unplug a cord from the wall outlet before removing it from the appliance. When you unplug it, be sure to pull on the plug, not the cord.

- **Keep utensils out of toasters.** If bread becomes stuck in a toaster, disconnect the toaster and try to shake the bread loose.

Children in the Kitchen

Many families enjoy preparing food together, but cooking with young children can be hazardous. When you're cooking with young children present, supervise them carefully. Keep them at a safe distance from hot items, such as the cooktop, toaster, and indoor grill, and watch for them when you move hot or heavy items. Also, young children should never handle knives, cleaning products, or other hazardous chemicals.

Very young children who are learning new motor skills present special challenges in the kitchen. They might try to pull themselves up to stand on a hot, open oven door. Some might pull a tablecloth out of curiosity, causing plates of hot food to spill on them. In this case, placemats would be a better choice of table covering. Electrical cords are also tempting to young children. Be sure to always use small appliances out of reach of children. Following a few simple guidelines can help everyone remain safe while enjoying special family time in the kitchen.

Safety Check

To prevent falls in the kitchen, do the following:

- Wipe up spills immediately.

- Stand on a step stool to reach high shelves, not on a chair or box.

- Never leave anything on the floor where someone might trip over it.

- Close cabinet drawers and doors when they are not in use. Otherwise, someone could fall over them.

HOW TO STORE FOOD SAFELY

Thanks to the work of people in a lot of government and private agencies, your food supply, from farm to supermarket, is one of the safest in the world. To keep the chain going, take care of foods properly after you bring them home. Start by buying only as much as you can use before it begins to spoil. Then store the food using these guidelines:

mark the purchase date on the package.

- **Place food containers in cabinets or on darkened shelves.** Light can diminish their quality.

- **Store foods in their original package until opened.** Bulk foods may be an exception. If you transfer food to another container, mark the date of storage on the new container.

- **Keep foods well separated from hazardous household materials.** Besides the risk of contamination, there is the chance that someone may accidentally grab the cleansing powder instead of the garlic powder.

- **Clean storage spaces often.** Bacteria thrive in dirt.

- **Store food in cool, dry places.** This rules out spaces near a radiator, over the oven, and under the sink.

- **Follow storage directions on the food package.** Note whether storage needs change after the package has been opened. Also pay attention to expiration and use-by dates. If no date appears,

- **Store more perishable foods in the interior of the refrigerator or freezer, not in the door.** Temperatures in doors can increase when the door is open, causing foods to warm.

- **Keep track of foods in the freezer.** If you use the freezer to stock up on foods on sale or to freeze foods at home, post a chart on the door listing what's inside. Include the foods and their amounts, purchase dates, and use-by dates. This way, you won't need to open the door to check your supplies. Update the chart as you use the foods.

- **Use only packages and wraps intended for food.** Aluminum foil, wax paper, and empty containers from other foods are safe choices. Seal them tightly to keep them from leaking.

- **Keep cold items cold.** In the freezer, cluster previously frozen items together so that they act as ice packs for each other. In the refrigerator, leave space around items so that the cold air can circulate around them, keeping them cold.

- **Set the right temperature.** Be sure your refrigerator is set to 40°F or cooler and the freezer is 0°F or below.

- **Use moisture-proof containers and wraps to freeze foods for longer storage.** Heavy-duty aluminum foil and freezer bags and sturdy plastic containers are made for this purpose.

TAKE **ACTION**

Use the tips given here as a checklist to evaluate storage conditions and practices in the food lab kitchen. Make any needed changes. Post signs to promote safe practices.

Review & Activities

Chapter Summary

- Basic safety precautions can prevent most accidents and food-related illnesses.
- Foodborne illnesses can be avoided by following proper sanitation procedures.
- Personal cleanliness begins with hand washing.
- Food should be stored properly to avoid foodborne illnesses.
- Proper use of kitchen appliances can prevent accidents, such as burns, cuts, and bruises.

Reviewing Key Terms & Ideas

1. What causes **foodborne illness**?
2. What are **bacteria**?
3. Define **cross-contamination**.
4. What does it mean to **sanitize** a surface?
5. List three tips for personal cleanliness.
6. How should frozen meat be thawed?
7. How can **marinades** cross-contaminate food?
8. How should you put out a grease fire?
9. What types of containers are safe for the microwave oven?
10. List three safety precautions to use with young children in the kitchen.

Thinking Critically

1. **Drawing conclusions.** Why is personal cleanliness important when you're working in the kitchen? Why do you think people sometimes overlook this aspect of sanitation?
2. **Making comparisons.** Which kitchen equipment do you think is most dangerous? Justify your answer.
3. **Analyzing situations.** What kitchen safety tips would you give to new parents?

Review & Activities

Applying Your Learning

1. **Sanitation evaluation.** Create a sanitation checklist and use it to evaluate your sanitation procedures either at home or in the food lab. How well do you meet sanitation guidelines?

2. **Restaurant sanitation.** Research the sanitation requirements of restaurants in your local community. Which requirements would benefit you in your home? How do the requirements compare with the guidelines in this chapter?

3. **Safety posters.** Choose a food preparation guideline from this chapter and create a poster to illustrate it. Display the poster in the food lab or your classroom.

4. **Meal planning.** In a small group, plan a picnic or outdoor party. Brainstorm foods you would like to serve. Then explain how to prepare and serve the food safely.

5. **Emergency response.** Research first aid procedures for minor kitchen injuries, such as burns and cuts. Present the procedures to your class, using visual aids or first aid supplies if necessary.

6. **Life simulation.** Enact a scene in which a student responds to a grease fire. Ask the audience to provide feedback.

Making Connections

1. **Reading** Read an owner's manual for a small appliance, such as a blender or food processor, and identify the manufacturer's safety precautions.

2. **Math** Research the number of cases of foodborne illness in the United States each year for the last five years. Draw a graph of the information. What conclusions can you draw from the information?

3. **Writing** Organize a kitchen safety slogan-writing contest. Develop a score sheet and judge the effectiveness of the slogans created.

CAREER Link

Professionalism.
Your attitude and work ethic on the job reflect your level of professionalism. When you work to the best of your ability, respect coworkers, and display a positive attitude, you're showing others that you can act professionally. Professionalism also includes punctuality and good grooming. Teens can also act professionally in school. In what ways do you show professionalism? In what other ways can you display professionalism at school?

Recipes & Measuring

Objectives

- Evaluate a recipe.
- Demonstrate how to measure ingredients accurately.
- Define commonly used recipe terms.
- Calculate the yield of a recipe.
- Explain how to make healthful substitutions.

Vocabulary

- **recipe**
- **abbreviation**
- **equivalents**
- **yield**

Reading with Purpose

1. **Read** the title of this chapter and describe in writing what you expect to learn from it.

2. **Write** each vocabulary term in your notebook, leaving space for definitions.

3. **As you read** Chapter 28, write the definition beside each term in your notebook.

4. **After** reading the chapter, write a paragraph describing what you learned.

Selecting a Recipe

What kinds of foods do you enjoy? Your mother's chicken enchiladas or your dad's meat loaf may be your special favorite. During holidays, you and your family might prepare dishes that your grandparents and their parents cooked in the past. Do you know where your favorite recipes came from?

A **recipe** is a set of directions used in preparing food. Recipes are written by cookbook authors, chefs, food magazine and newspaper editors, Internet sites, family members, friends, and local charity and organizational groups.

Perhaps your favorite cookies are made with a recipe handed down by your great-grandmother. Maybe your next-door neighbor shared a barbecue recipe with your family, or a local restaurant owner gave you a recipe for spaghetti. By trying different recipes, you will expand your food experiences and develop tastes and favorites. See **Fig. 28-1**.

Selecting recipes usually begins with reading them. As you read a recipe, ask yourself these questions:

- Does this recipe sound good? Are there foods I like included? Are there new foods I want to try?

- Does everyone sharing the meal like the ingredients?

- How long will it take to prepare the recipe? Do I have enough time?

- Do I have all of the equipment and ingredients I need to prepare the recipe?

- Do I understand all of the directions? Do I have the skills needed to do the job?

If you are less experienced in the kitchen, try to find recipes with fewer ingredients and fewer steps. They're usually easier to prepare.

Fig 28-1 ▶ Some cookbooks provide recipes for every mealtime dish, and others focus on one type of dish, such as grilled foods or desserts.

Measuring Ingredients

When you cook, you can choose to make something from scratch—that is, put all of the ingredients together yourself—or to use a mix, which contains most or all of the ingredients you need. In either case, you need to know how to measure and combine ingredients. Learning some basic abbreviations, equivalents, and measuring techniques will get you off to a good start.

Measuring Dry Ingredients

Sugar, flour, salt, and baking powder are dry ingredients. Use a dry measuring cup to measure $\frac{1}{4}$ cup (50 mL) or more. Hold the cup over waxed paper, a dry paper towel, or the ingredient's container. Spoon the ingredient into the cup and heap it a little over the top. Then level off the ingredients with the straight edge of a spatula or table knife. When measuring smaller amounts, use a measuring spoon in the same way.

When measuring flour and brown sugar, keep the following points in mind:

- **Flour.** Always spoon flour into your measuring cup. Do not scoop your measuring cup through the flour. The tiny granules of flour tend to pack together in the flour container. If the recipe calls for sifted flour, sift the flour first, and then measure it in the usual way. Sifting flour before mixing helps remove any lumps it may have. Do not tap the cup. Tapping packs the flour down and will give you more flour than you need. **Fig. 28-2**.

- **Brown sugar.** To accurately measure brown sugar, pack the sugar firmly into a measuring cup and then level it off. If a recipe specifies packed sugar, pack it tightly. Some recipes do not require packing.

Fig 28-2 If a recipe calls for sifting, don't skip the step. What might happen if you do?

Measuring Liquid Ingredients

Water, milk, and oil are considered liquid ingredients and are measured in liquid measuring cups, usually clear. For accurate measurements, put the cup on a flat surface and read the measurement at eye level. You can measure small amounts of liquid in measuring spoons. Simply fill the spoon to the brim.

Measuring Fats

Sticks of margarine and butter have measurements marked on the wrapper to make it easier to measure the amounts needed. Each line represents 1 tablespoon. Each stick equals $\frac{1}{2}$ cup (125 mL). If you need just part of the stick, cut through the wrapper on the appropriate line. When using brands of butter that are in 8-oz. packages, this would not be the case. You would have to measure or weigh the amount called for in the recipe.

Solid fats, such as shortening or margarine in a tub, are measured in a dry measuring cup. First, pack the fat into the cup, trying to avoid any air pockets. Then, level it off. Use a plastic scraper to remove the fat from the cup.

Abbreviations and Equivalents

An **abbreviation** is a short form of a word. Abbreviations are used in recipes to save space. Most recipes you will use are written using customary measurements, such as cups and tablespoons. Other recipes use metric measurements, such as milliliters. It's best to use the correct measuring equipment, customary or metric, for the recipe you're following.

Units of Measure

Type of Measurement	Customary Units and Abbreviations	Metric Units and Symbols
Volume	teaspoon (tsp.) tablespoon (Tbsp.) fluid ounce (fl. oz.) cup (c.) pint (pt.) quart (qt.) gallon (gal.)	milliliter (mL) liter (L)
Weight	ounce (oz.) pound (lb.)	gram (g) kilogram (kg)
Temperature	degrees Fahrenheit (°F)	degrees Celsius (°C)

Equivalents

Dash	Less than $\frac{1}{8}$ tsp.	Less than 0.5 mL
$\frac{1}{4}$ tsp.		1 mL
$\frac{1}{2}$ tsp.		2.5 mL
1 tsp.		5 mL
1 Tbsp.	3 tsp.	15 mL
1 fl. oz.	2 Tbsp.	30 mL
$\frac{1}{4}$ c.	4 Tbsp. or 2 fl. oz.	50 mL
$\frac{1}{3}$ c.	5 Tbsp. + 1 tsp.	75 mL
$\frac{1}{2}$ c.	8 Tbsp. or 4 fl. oz.	125 mL
$\frac{2}{3}$ c.	10 Tbsp. + 2 tsp. or 6 fl. oz.	175 mL
1 c.	16 Tbsp. or 8 fl. oz.	250 mL
1 pt.	2 c. or 16 fl. oz.	500 mL
1 qt.	2 pt. or 4 c. or 32 fl. oz.	1 L (1,000 mL)
1 gal.	4 qt. or 16 c. or 128 fl. oz.	4 L
1 lb.	16 oz. (weight)	500 g
2 lb.	32 oz. (weight)	1 kg (1,000 g)

Fig 28-3 Units of measure and equivalents.

Fig 28-4

Estimates of Common Ingredients

The more you cook, the more skilled you'll become at estimating.

- ☑ 1 cup chopped onion = 1 large onion
- ☑ 1 cup chopped bell pepper = 1 large bell pepper
- ☑ 1 cup chopped tomato = 1 large tomato
- ☑ 1 cup chopped carrot = 1 large carrot
- ☑ $\frac{1}{2}$ cup chopped celery = 1 large rib of celery
- ☑ 1 teaspoon chopped garlic = 1 large clove of garlic
- ☑ 3 tablespoons lemon juice = 1 medium lemon
- ☑ 2 tablespoons lime juice = 1 medium lime
- ☑ $\frac{1}{3}$ cup orange juice = 1 medium orange
- ☑ $\frac{1}{2}$ cup mashed banana = 1 medium banana
- ☑ 1 cup soft bread crumbs = 2 slices of fresh bread
- ☑ 1 cup bread cubes = 2 slices of fresh bread
- ☑ 2 cups shredded cheese = 8 ounces of cheese
- ☑ 1 pound dry pasta = 6 to 9 cups of cooked pasta, depending on the shape

You will also find it helpful to know some basic equivalents. **Equivalents** are amounts that are equal to each other. For example, 3 tsp. are equal to 1 Tbsp. Equivalents come in handy when you are preparing a recipe. They are also helpful when you don't have the right measuring tool or if you've already used the one needed. **Fig. 28-3** shows abbreviations, units of measure, and equivalents commonly used in recipes.

Estimating Amounts

To celebrate her father's birthday, Sarah decided to make him dinner. The recipe Sarah wanted to make called for $\frac{1}{4}$ cup of chopped onion. Sarah looked in her refrigerator. "I have one onion. Is that enough?" What do you think?

Deciding whether you have enough of certain ingredients to make a recipe can be tricky. In **Fig. 28-4**, estimates are provided for some common ingredients. According to the chart, one onion is enough for Sarah to make her recipe.

Understanding Recipe Terms

Certain words or terms have special meanings when used in food preparation. To prepare a recipe successfully, you'll need to pay careful attention to the terms in the recipe. See **Fig. 28-5**, **Fig. 28-6**, and **Fig. 28-7**.

Fig 28-5 ▶ Mixing Terms

Several recipe techniques are used to describe methods of combining ingredients. Each method produces slightly different results. Here are some of the most common methods:

▶ **Stir.** Use a spoon to make circular or figure eight motions, as in stirring soup when it warms or making a sauce.

▶ **Blend, mix, or combine.** Use a spoon to stir two or more ingredients together thoroughly.

▶ **Beat.** Use this technique to add air to foods, as in beating eggs. When beating cake batter, you can use a quick, over-and-under motion with a spoon or a wire whisk, rotary beater, or electric mixer.

▶ **Whip.** Use a wire whisk, rotary beater, or electric mixer to whip ingredients. This rapid movement adds air and makes foods fluffy.

▶ **Cream.** Use a spoon, beater, or mixer to combine ingredients until soft and creamy, as in combining fat and sugar for a cake.

▶ **Cut in.** Use a pastry blender or two knives and a cutting motion to mix solid fat with dry ingredients, as in cutting fat into flour for a pie crust.

▶ **Fold.** Use a rubber scraper to gently combine ingredients in a delicate mixture, such as adding a lighter ingredient to a heavier one. Folding keeps air in the mixture.

Fig 28-6 ▶ Cutting Terms

What is the difference between mincing and chopping or between dicing and cubing? At first glance, some of the differences may seem minor, but they make a significant difference in the appearance and texture of a dish.

▶ **Chop.** Cut food into small, irregular pieces, as in chopping carrots or green peppers.

▶ **Mince.** Chop food into pieces that are as small as possible, as in mincing an onion.

▶ **Cube.** Cut into evenly shaped pieces about ½ inch on each side, as in cubing bread.

▶ **Dice.** Cut into evenly shaped pieces about ¼ inch on each side, as in dicing ingredients for a salad.

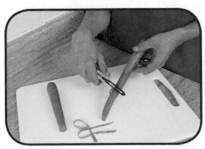

▶ **Pare.** Cut off the outside covering of a fruit or vegetable, as in paring an apple or a potato.

▶ **Grate and Shred.** Rub food over a grater to make fine particles or shredded food, as in grating cheese. New photo-etched graters easily grate and shred food.

Fig 28-7 ▶ Other Cooking Terms

You will probably see some of the following terms as you look through recipes:

▶ **Baste.** Moisten foods, such as meat, while cooking. Basting adds flavor and helps keep food from drying out.

▶ **Brush.** Use a brush to lightly cover the surface of one food with another, as in brushing butter sauce on fish.

▶ **Coat.** Cover the surface of a food with a dry ingredient, such as flour, cornmeal, dry bread crumbs, or sugar. Coatings can also include liquid ingredients.

▶ **Garnish.** Decorate a food dish with a small decorative food item, such as parsley sprigs, vegetable confetti, carrot curls, or an edible flower.

▶ **Grease.** Rub lightly with fat, such as butter, margarine, oil, or shortening, as in greasing a baking sheet or muffin tins.

▶ **Season.** Add seasonings, such as salt, pepper, herbs, or spices, to flavor a food.

▶ **Drain.** Remove excess liquid by placing food in a colander or strainer, as in draining pasta.

Altering Recipes

You don't always have to follow a recipe exactly as it's written. Sometimes you'll alter, or change, a recipe to increase or decrease the number of servings. You can also alter a recipe by substituting one ingredient for another or changing spices and herbs. Knowing how to alter recipes allows you more creativity in your food preparation.

Changing the Yield of a Recipe

The **yield** is the amount of food or the number of servings a recipe makes. If you want more or fewer servings, you need to alter the recipe. Not all recipes can be altered successfully, but many can. To do this, put your math skills and knowledge of equivalent measurements to work. For example, if you're preparing a recipe that yields eight servings but you only want four, follow these steps:

1. **Divide the number of servings you want by the original yield.** The answer is the number you'll use to calculate the new amount of each ingredient. In this example, $4 \div 8 = \frac{1}{2}$.

2. **Multiply the amount of each ingredient by the answer in step 1.** If the recipe calls for 2 pounds of ground beef, you'd use 1 pound ($2 \times \frac{1}{2} = 1$).

3. **Convert measurements as needed.** If a recipe calls for $\frac{1}{4}$ cup grated cheese, the new amount would be $\frac{1}{8}$ cup ($\frac{1}{4} \times \frac{1}{2} = \frac{1}{8}$). If you don't have a $\frac{1}{8}$ cup utensil, use the chart on page 456 to help you figure out an equivalent measure.

4. **Calculate the new amount for each ingredient in the recipe.** Afterward, write the amounts down so that you don't forget them.

To double a recipe, simply multiply the amount of each ingredient by 2. To triple it, multiply by 3, and so on. Remember that increasing the number of servings requires larger pans. The baking or cooking time may also need to be increased for a larger number of servings. See **Fig. 28-8**.

TIPS
Use Herbs and Spices

Herbs and spices can jazz up a dish without adding fat. Herbs are the fragrant leaves of plants. Spices come from the bark, buds, roots, fruit, seeds, or stems of plants and trees. When cooking with herbs and spices, keep these points in mind:

▶ **Don't overdo it.** Too many herbs or spices in one dish can overpower the food. Use only a few herbs and spices to accent the flavor of the food.

▶ **Make accurate substitutions.** If you're using dried herbs instead of fresh ones, you can use half as much dry herbs as fresh.

▶ **Mind the time.** For recipes with long cooking times, such as soup, add herbs, salt, and spices toward the end of cooking.

▶ **Cut finely.** Cut surfaces to release more flavor.

Fig 28-8

If you have additional guests, you may have to adjust the yield of a recipe—the number of servings!

Making Substitutions

Have you ever been in the middle of preparing a recipe and suddenly discovered you were missing an ingredient? To avoid this situation, read through the ingredients list and make sure you have all necessary items on hand before you begin preparing food.

If you don't have an ingredient, you may be able to make a substitution. For example, if you are making oatmeal cookies and you don't have raisins, you can substitute nuts or dried cranberries for the raisins. Experienced cooks know that some ingredients can be used in place of others with good results. Some cookbooks list substitutions. **Fig. 28-9** provides some substitution suggestions.

Creative and Healthy Changes

When you first try a recipe, it's a good idea to follow the instructions closely. After you have used the recipe, you may want to exercise your creativity and try some variations.

Substitutions That Work

Ingredient	Substitutions
2 Tbsp. (30 mL) flour (for thickening)	1 Tbsp. (15 mL) cornstarch
1 c. (250 mL) sifted cake flour	1 c. + 2 Tbsp. (260 mL) sifted all-purpose flour
1 c. (250 mL) whole milk	½ c. (125 mL) evaporated milk + ½ c. (125 mL) water
1 c. (250 mL) sour milk or buttermilk	1 c. (250 mL) fresh milk + 1 Tbsp. (15 mL) vinegar or lemon juice
1 square (1 oz. or 28 g) unsweetened chocolate	3 Tbsp. (45 mL) unsweetened cocoa powder + 1 Tbsp. (15 mL) butter or margarine
1 c. (250 mL) granulated sugar	1 c. (250 mL) packed brown sugar or 2 c. (250 mL) sifted powdered, or confectioner's sugar

Fig 28-9 Ingredient substitutions that work!

You can begin by changing the seasonings and a few ingredients. If you're making pasta, you can add extra onion or garlic to the sauce for more "punch." You can also add diced bell pepper or diced carrots to change the texture and taste and boost the nutrition. If you like meat in your sauce, you can add lean ground beef or ground turkey.

To cut back on the fat for a healthier dish, you can substitute vegetable oil and olive oil for butter or margarine. Olive oil is delicious drizzled over vegetables. Vinegar makes a delicious and low-calorie salad dressing. Low-fat yogurt is a great replacement for sour cream in dips. What other things can you do to decrease the amount of fat in the foods you eat?

Chefs and test-kitchen experts change recipes all the time. They are always developing new recipes and new approaches to eating. You can do the same thing in your own "test kitchen." You can use your understanding of measuring, combining, and cooking terms to create dishes that will bring a new adventure in eating to your family dinner table.

HOW TO MAKE SALSA

Did you know that salsa, a longtime favorite in Mexican cooking, outsells ketchup in the United States? Salsa has become mainstream. Salsas are popular, healthful, and flavorful. They can be a dip for chips or toppings for tacos or scrambled eggs. Even novice cooks can make them, using different amounts or combinations of ingredients cooked or not cooked to suit their creative tastes. No special skills or equipment are required.

Traditional salsas are based on tomatoes, onions, and chili peppers. The variety and amount of peppers determine the recipe's heat. Zucchini, carrots, corn, and beans are other popular additions. You can make a sweet-hot fruit salsa using apples, pears, apricots, bananas, pineapple—whatever intrigues you. Choose fresh ingredients when possible.

With foods this flavorful, seasonings are used sparingly. Traditional choices include seasonings that are popular in Mexican cooking: lime juice, an herb called cilantro, and cumin, a spice. Depending on your tastes and ingredients, you might try flavored vinegar, garlic, chili powder, honey, or sugar.

Once you have settled on your ingredients and seasonings, it's time to assemble the salsa:

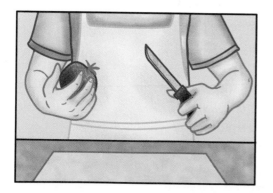

STEP 1 Peel the tomatoes. To loosen the skin, place the tomatoes one at a time into boiling water for about 40 seconds then into a bowl of ice water until cool enough to handle. The skin should slip off.

STEP 2 Halve the tomatoes and scoop out the seeds. Chop the tomatoes into small chunks, about ½ inch. You can use a knife or a food processor. Place the tomatoes in a large bowl.

STEP 4 | **Add the seasonings.** Combine the seasonings with the ingredients gently but thoroughly. Chill, covered, for at least 30 minutes to let the flavors blend.

STEP 3 | **Chop other foods into smaller pieces, about ¼ inch.** Add them to the bowl with the tomatoes. Handle hot chilies with extreme care. The heat-producing substance, called capsaicin (cap-SAY-ih-sin), can burn your eyes and nose. Always wear rubber or latex surgical gloves and keep your hands away from your face. Most of the capsaicin is found in the seeds and membranes of the peppers. Remove these parts before cooking to cool the chilies' "bite."

To vary the texture, purée some of the ingredients (put them through a blender) to create a smooth base. Salsas can be smooth or chunky, spicy hot or mild, thick or thin, or cooked or uncooked. These are personal decisions—make some choices when preparing your salsa.

TAKE **ACTION**

Compare salsa recipes to learn what amounts and ratios of ingredients are commonly used. Use them as a guide to create your own recipe. Prepare your recipe for a class taste test.

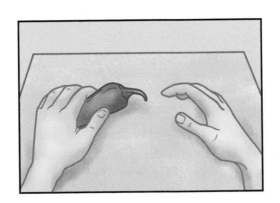

Review & Activities

Chapter Summary

- Recipes can come from many different places.
- Selecting a recipe begins with reading it.
- To follow recipes accurately, you need to carefully measure all ingredients.
- Estimation skill comes with experience.
- Many recipe terms have meanings unique to specific food preparations.
- Recipes can be successfully altered to change the yield and to allow creativity.

Reviewing Key Terms & Ideas

1. List three questions to ask when selecting a **recipe**.
2. Describe the best way to measure dry ingredients.
3. What is the best way to measure liquid ingredients?
4. How much does one stick of butter or margarine measure?
5. Define **abbreviation**.
6. When would you use **equivalents**?
7. What is the difference between stirring and whipping?
8. What does it mean to mince food? How does this differ from dicing food?
9. Define **yield**.
10. List two foods you can substitute to lower the fat content in your diet.

Thinking Critically

1. **Drawing conclusions.** Imagine you're selecting two recipes, one for a weeknight family dinner and one for a holiday meal. What do you need to consider in your selection?
2. **Analyzing situations.** What advice would you give a friend who wants to prepare a difficult recipe?
3. **Making predictions.** If you did not have access to standard measuring utensils, which recipes would you attempt and which recipes would you avoid? How would you measure ingredients for the recipes you would attempt to prepare?

Review & Activities

Applying Your Learning

1. **Recipe file.** Look through cookbooks, magazines, and a cooking Web site to find recipes you would like to prepare. Copy the recipes and organize them in a recipe box, binder, or expandable file.

2. **Recipe evaluation.** Look for five appealing and healthful recipes you think would be good choices for less experienced cooks to prepare. Identify the criteria you used to select these recipes.

3. **Measurement demonstration.** Demonstrate how to measure dry and liquid ingredients. Ask your classmates for feedback.

4. **Recipe analysis.** Select three recipes you would like to make. Identify the mixing terms used in the recipe. Look up any unfamiliar terms. Which recipes do you think are easiest to prepare, based on the mixing techniques?

5. **Test kitchen.** Express your creativity by changing a recipe to create your own version of a dish. Prepare the dish and share it with your class. Have copies of your recipe and the original on hand to share with classmates.

6. **Healthy alterations.** Select a recipe that is a family favorite. Think of ways to alter the recipe to make it healthier to eat. Prepare your recipe for your family and ask for a critique.

Making Connections

1. **Writing** Choose a recipe. Prepare the recipe. Then, write a short evaluation of your experience, noting what was successful and what you could do to improve.

2. **Math** Select a recipe you would like to make. Change the yield of the recipe by doubling it. Then cut the recipe in half. Did they both come out as expected?

3. **Writing** In the food lab or at home, develop a simple, original recipe. Write the recipe instructions and ask people to critique the organization and clarity.

4. **Reading** Read print cookbooks or cooking Web sites to identify cooking terms that are new to you. Research the meaning of the terms.

CAREER Link

Writing Skills.
Effective written communication is necessary in the workplace. To write effectively, you need to organize your thoughts and use correct spelling and grammar. You also need to think about your choice of words and your audience. Try your hand at effective communication by writing a business letter to your family and consumer sciences teacher about a classroom topic. Ask a classmate to critique your letter for organization, spelling, and grammar.

Quick Meals & Snacks

Objectives

- Explain how lack of time affects food choices.
- Identify the elements that create an appealing meal.
- Explain meal patterns and the role they play in family meals.
- Summarize timesaving strategies for meal preparation.
- Rate snacks according to nutrition guidelines.
- Create a food preparation plan.

Vocabulary

- **graze**
- **meal pattern**
- **convenience foods**
- **dovetail**

Reading with Purpose

1. **Write down** the colored headings from Chapter 29 in your notebook

2. **As you read** the text under each heading, visualize what you are reading.

3. **Reflect** on what you read by writing a few sentences under each heading to describe it.

4. **Continue** this process until you have finished the chapter. Reread your notes.

It's Time To Eat!

Personal food choices are just that—personal. For many people, the focus may be on how something tastes. For others, it's about convenience. Time is a great factor in food choices because of hectic schedules. Family members juggle classes at school, job responsibilities, after-school activities, and volunteer work. Often, little time is left over for meals. This means families sometimes eat on the fly, buy take-out foods at the supermarket for dinner, or order a pizza and make

a quick salad at home. Other times, family members pitch in together to prepare a family meal.

The pressure to accomplish daily routines can often cause families to make unhealthy food choices. For example, families might stop at a fast-food restaurant for a quick meal, rather than shop at the supermarket for a salad they need to prepare at home. Consistently choosing less nutritious food can lead to serious health issues, such as diabetes and high blood pressure. Keep in mind that no matter how busy you are, you're still responsible for selecting healthy food items.

Preparing Meals and Snacks

Some families make a meal schedule for family members, assigning each member a certain day or task. If you are called to be the "chef for the day," it will be your responsibility to plan the meal.

Planning for Meal Appeal

Imagine your favorite meal. What does it look like? Does it have different colors, shapes, flavors, and textures? All of these elements work together to make a meal attractive or give it eye appeal. If a meal is attractive, it will be more pleasing to eat. When you're putting a meal together, think about the following elements:

- **Color.** Combine different colors in a meal to make it visually interesting. Red tomatoes pieces, green pepper slices, carrot sticks, and some fruited brown rice would definitely add visual interest to an entrée of chicken.

- **Shape.** Carrot and zucchini strips, bow-tie pasta, and a mound of garlic-mashed potatoes offer contrasting shapes to a round beef patty.

- **Flavor.** Experiment with different flavors in a meal to stimulate people's taste buds. Added flavors can come from herbs, spices, sauces, vinegars, a small drizzle of healthy oil, or a splash of citrus (lemon or lime).

- **Texture.** All meals should contain a variety of textures. If all foods in a meal were soft, you would think you were eating baby food. Include crunchy or crisp, soft, and chunky or chewy foods to incorporate texture in meals.

Fig 29-1
Omelets can be stuffed with leftover meats or vegetables. They make a quick nutritious meal any time of the day.

Meal Patterns

How are meals organized in your family? Every family does it differently. Some sit down and eat three meals a day. Other people **graze**, or eat several small meals throughout the day. Over time, most people establish a **meal pattern**, or a way of grouping daily food choices into meals and snacks.

There is no one way to eat smart. When you select your food or help plan meals, keep MyPyramid in mind. Use foods from all of the food groups. Try incorporating more foods represented by the wide bands of color in MyPyramid. The results will be not only delicious but also healthy.

Think about your current meal patterns. Do you frequently skip meals? What are your reasons for skipping a meal—not hungry, no time, no available food, nothing interesting to eat, or no original meal ideas? Most people skip a meal once in a while, but skipping meals as a habit is potentially unhealthy. Eventually, you may pay the price with fatigue and poor concentration. Skipping meals can also cause people to overeat later in the day, which can lead to unwanted calories.

Mealtime Timesavers

Few people have a day in the kitchen to cook, unless it's a weekend. However, families can still prepare nutritious meals by managing food preparation time effectively. How many of the following ideas does your family use? See **Fig. 29-1**.

- **Keep easy-to-fix foods on hand.** A few possibilities include cut vegetables, prepared pasta sauce, and salad ingredients.

- **Serve leftovers.** Leftovers are a great timesaver, and they can often be used as the basis for another meal. For example, leftover spaghetti noodles or cooked rice can be combined with teriyaki sauce and a bag of frozen stir-fry vegetables for a delicious and healthful meal.

STEPS TO SUCCESS

I Can Help with Family Meals

Sitting down with your family and eating a home-cooked, healthy meal is important, but bringing everyone to the table is never easy. With working parents or guardians, after-school activities, and homework, eating on the go is often a necessity. Fortunately, there are ways you can help bring your family together to share a meal.

- **Create a meal plan.** Sometimes just figuring out what to prepare makes family meals easier to accomplish. First, talk with your family and decide when everyone can meet for dinner. Then, choose a recipe for each family meal. Choose recipes that aren't too complicated. Those that have many ingredients or require a lot of kitchen time can be overwhelming, especially on a busy weeknight.

- **Make a grocery list.** Once you've created your meal plan, make a grocery list. Find out which ingredients you have on hand. Then make a shopping list for the store. If the list isn't too long and you live close to the store, offer to pick up the ingredients yourself. Ride your bike or walk, and you're also getting in some exercise! If this is not possible, offer to go along and help with the shopping.

- **Use convenience foods.** Prepared or partially prepared foods are called **convenience foods**. Examples include salad greens in bags, precut fruit and vegetables, grated cheese, precut and cooked meat and poultry, and frozen dinners. One drawback to prepared foods is their higher cost.

- **Help with meal preparation.** Depending on the meal, you can do part or all of the food preparation. If you're not able to do it all, you can prepare the kitchen for the "cook." Measure all ingredients, clear the kitchen counters of dirty dishes, and set the table. You also can prepare part of the main course or side dish. By pitching in, you help the meal reach the table faster.

- **Take care of the cleanup.** Some families are simply overwhelmed by the cleanup involved in making family meals. You can do your part by clearing the table, loading the dishwasher or washing dishes, and wiping down the counters and table. Be sure to store leftovers properly in the refrigerator or freezer.

- **Create a family-meal recipe box or notebook.** Each time your family enjoys a new recipe, add it to the recipe box or notebook. For example, you can copy the recipe or, if it's from a magazine or newspaper, cut it out and attach it to a note card or piece of paper. Having surefire recipes on hand helps make meal planning a snap!

- **Make meals ahead of time.** Some families prepare larger meals on the weekends, store the meals in the freezer, and cook them during the week. Casseroles and chili are examples of good make-ahead meals.

- **Use fast-cooking methods.** Microwaving, stir-frying, broiling, and indoor grilling are examples of fast cooking methods. Cutting food into small pieces also helps it cook faster.

- **Create one-dish meals.** Try a chef's salad or stuff a pita pocket with tuna fish and chopped vegetables.

Snacks

What's the first thing you do after you arrive home in the afternoon? Chances are you eat a snack. Snacking is part of the lifestyle of most teens. Think about the last time you visited the mall or attended a sports event or movie. Did you have a snack? See **Fig. 29-2**.

Snacks can be a healthy habit or an unhealthful one, depending on your choices. Choosing snack foods high in fat and sugar can negatively affect your health. On the other hand, snacking can be good if you are an active teen who sometimes needs extra energy and chooses healthy foods. To make snacking part of a healthy lifestyle, follow these guidelines:

- **Don't snack when you're bored.** Substitute another activity for snacking when you're bored. Read a book, call a friend, play games, spend some time with your family pet, or develop a new hobby.

- **Munch snack-size portions.** Snacks aren't meant to replace entire meals. Try putting snacks onto a small plate to make sure you're eating appropriate portions. Also, match your snack size to your energy needs. If you're physically active, eat a larger portion.

- **Make snacks a part of your daily meal plan.** Think about snacks as part of good nutrition. Instead of eating candy bars, cupcakes, and cookies, try snacking on fresh fruit with peanut butter or yogurt.

Fig 29-2 Fresh fruit smoothies are healthy alternatives to ice cream.

- **Turn the television off.** When you're watching television, you lose track of how much you're eating.

- **Avoid eating snacks one hour before meals.** Snacks can interfere with your appetite at meals, where a variety of foods are usually available.

- **Plan ahead.** Try to keep nutritious snack foods on hand, such as air-popped popcorn, fresh fruit, low-fat cheese and crackers, and low-fat yogurt.

Meals Away from Home

Think about the meals you ate this week. How many did you eat away from home? Many teens eat lunch at school. They may eat dinner in a restaurant with their families. Some even grab a bagel and eat breakfast on the go.

Eating healthful away from home can be challenging. Food consumed away from home is generally higher in fat, calories, and cholesterol and lower in nutrients than foods eaten at home. Many restaurants serve larger portions than most people need. Some restaurant portions are mega-sized, which can be four to eight times larger than suggested daily portions. See **Fig. 29-3**.

Eating every meal at home is impossible, so how can you eat out and maintain your health?

- **Make healthy choices.** Many fast-food restaurants now offer healthier selections, such as salads, low-fat meat options, yogurt, and low-fat, reduced-calorie sauces and salad dressings. Make a healthy beverage choice as well.

- **Control your portions.** If you eat at a restaurant, eat reasonable portions. Portion sizes served at home are usually smaller than those in restaurants. See **Fig. 29-4**.

- **Get it to go.** If you're going straight home after dining out, take part of your meal home instead of cleaning your plate.

- **Share.** Have your server ask the chef to divide an order and put it on two plates. For example, you could share an entrée and salad with a friend.

Fig 29-3 Meals away from home are often less healthful with portions far too large.

Fig 29-4 Splitting a pizza is a great way to control portions—and save money.

Budgeting for Food

Whether families are buying food for meals or for snacks, they usually have to keep an eye on their spending. Food costs are a major part of a family budget. By making wise food choices, you can make tasty, nutritious meals without overspending.

Preparing larger portions with leftovers in mind can be cost effective. Freeze some leftovers for quick and handy meals, or transform leftovers into new entrées.

Working in the Foods Lab

When you work in the food lab at school, you'll probably work as part of a group or team. This is an excellent opportunity to learn more about teamwork. Each person in the group is important, and you're each responsible for certain jobs. When one member of the team doesn't do a job correctly or on time, everyone else is affected. Working well as a team in the kitchen is important to your success.

Planning Your Work

Everyone needs a plan, and your food lab group is no exception. Your group will need to plan for supplies. For example, your teacher might ask you to list the ingredients and the amounts of food you need. Then your supplies will be added to the total grocery list for the lab. If your list is not accurate, then your group will not have the supplies it needs. See **Fig. 29-5**.

Time is also an important part your food lab plan. Because time in the lab is usually short, you'll need to plan your time wisely. Begin by listing the major jobs in the order they need to be done. Estimate how long it will take to do each job. Don't forget to allow time for getting ready to cook. Before you can begin to prepare food, you will need to take the following steps:

Fig 29-5 Good planning and teamwork help your work in the food lab go smoothly. How can you improve your own work in the food lab?

1. Put on a clean apron, tie back long hair, roll up dangling sleeves, and, most important, wash your hands with soap and water.

2. Review your recipe.

3. Take out all of the equipment and ingredients you will need.

4. Finish any tasks you need to do before combining ingredients. Do you need to preheat the oven, grease baking pans, chop ingredients, or melt fat?

After you have listed all tasks, divide up the cooking responsibilities. Assign work fairly so that everyone has a comparable job. If someone has less responsibility this time, he or she can assume more next time.

Carrying Out Your Plan

Before you go into the lab, know your assigned job. When you enter the lab, post the time plan where it can be seen. Follow the guidelines about dress, behavior, and lab rules for your safety and the safety of others. After you complete your work, volunteer to help someone else. If you see that something needs to be done, do it.

Cleaning Up

No one likes a big cleanup after preparing food. Cleaning as you go will help your group at the end of class. If food spills on the counter or floor, clean it up right away to prevent an accident, such as a slip or fall. Have a sink of warm, sudsy water ready. When you finish using a utensil, soak it in water—but remember not to put sharp knives in the water where they are not easily seen. Wash them separately. While you're waiting for something to cook, take advantage of a few moments to wash and rinse utensils.

At the end of the lab period, wash any remaining dishes, wipe off tables and countertops, and sweep the floor. Always leave the food lab clean for the next group. See **Fig. 29-6**.

Fig 29-6

Don't forget to evaluate your cleanup tasks. Cleanup is an important final step in meal preparation. Why is that true?

Evaluating Your Work

Evaluation is an important part of your lab experience. When you evaluate your work, you judge its quality, how it tastes, and what it looks like. Your evaluation might be in the form of a rating sheet given by your teacher. A rating sheet allows points for work well done. When evaluating teamwork, think about whether the job went as planned. Did team members perform all of their assigned tasks? How many people put forth an extra effort to help someone else? What could you do to improve? Your answers help you build on your success in future labs.

Working in Your Home Kitchen

Preparing food at home is similar to working in the food lab. In both cases, you probably have limited time. To be successful at home, plan to prepare and cook food as you did in the food lab. Organize your work and plan time for each task. Allow some extra time for unexpected delays. Often two or more family members work together. You'll have to decide how to divide tasks.

Even when you work alone in the kitchen, you can still be efficient. Look for ways to dovetail tasks. **Dovetail** means to fit tasks together to make the best use of time. For example, wash salad greens during the time it takes water to boil for cooking pasta.

Planning a schedule is especially important when you're responsible for preparing an entire meal. Your goal is to have all foods ready at the same time. Start with the foods that take the longest to prepare and cook. For example, it may take you 15 minutes to put a casserole together and another 45 minutes to bake it. If you were also microwaving a frozen vegetable to go with the casserole, you would need to begin the casserole first. As you gain experience, you probably won't need to write out a schedule for simple meals. If meals are more complicated, you may want to jot down a rough time schedule.

Family meals don't just happen. Working in the kitchen requires planning and preparation. If you are organized, you'll have more time to eat and enjoy yourself.

TIPS

Organize Your Recipes

An organized recipe collection makes cooking easier. For a more enjoyable kitchen experience, try some of these tips:

▶ Write or paste recipes onto index cards and store them in a card file. You can sort them alphabetically or by food type.

▶ Write or paste recipes onto notebook paper and file them in a three-ring binder.

▶ Type your recipes using your word processing program and store them on your computer. You can also use recipe software to create electronic recipe files.

▶ Store clipped recipes in photo albums or accordion files.

HOW TO Put It All Together

Getting a meal on the table is like conducting an orchestra. The conductor makes sure each musician plays the right notes at the right time. As a cook, you make sure each dish is properly prepared and ready at the right time.

Unlike the conductor, however, you don't just oversee the production. You are involved. You have to keep a hand on the stirring spoon and an eye on the clock. It's almost like leading the band while playing an instrument. This kind of double duty takes a plan like the one outlined here:

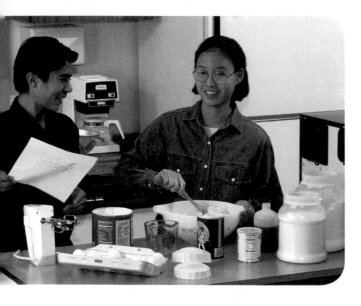

STEP 1 | **List the steps in each recipe and the time needed to complete each one.** Suppose a meal includes refrigerated crescent rolls. The first step, greasing the baking sheet, might take 1 minute. Separating and shaping the rolls might take 5 minutes more. Estimate times generously, especially when trying new skills or recipes.

STEP 2 | **Next to the task times, list any added time needed for cooking.** The rolls mentioned in Step 1 might need 10 to 12 minutes more to cook.

Cooking Times

| Rolls: 10-12 minutes |
| Chicken: 45 minutes |
| Vegetables: 10-12 minutes |

Total Preparation Time

| Rolls: 16-18 minutes |
| Chicken: 50-60 minutes |
| Steamed or stir-fried Vegetables: 20 minutes |

STEP 3 | **Add the task and cooking times.** This total time will help you decide when to start each task. Total preparation time for the rolls would be 16 to 18 minutes.

STEP 4 | **List tasks with flexible starting times.** Some tasks can be done in advance or dovetailed with others—setting the table, for example, or washing a saucepan.

STEP 5 | **Figure out the starting time.** Subtract the total time from the time at which the meal should be ready. Again, add a few minutes. To serve dinner at 6 p.m., roll preparation might start at 5:40 p.m.

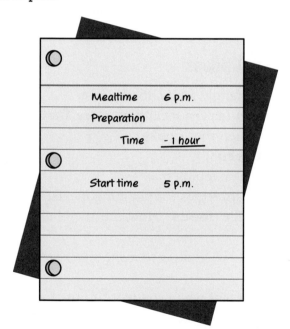

STEP 6 | **Make a schedule.** Put the tasks in order based on starting time, working backward from the time the meal should be ready. Fill gaps with tasks that have flexible starting times and others that can be dovetailed. If leftover soup is on the menu, for instance, you'll need to reheat the soup while the rolls bake. Make adjustments to fit in any tasks that have the same starting time.

STEP 7 | **Carry out the plan.** Check off tasks as you complete them so that nothing is forgotten. Note any problems that arise on your schedule to help improve the results next time.

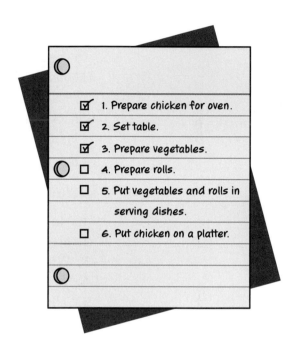

TAKE **ACTION**

Plan and prepare a three-course meal of simple recipes, using the steps listed here. Was preparing the meal easier or harder when you put yourself on a schedule? How can the habit of scheduling prepare you to make larger, more complicated meals?

29

Review & Activities

Chapter Summary

- Many families have hectic schedules that affect their food choices.
- You can use the elements of color, shape, flavor, and texture to create meal appeal.
- Meal patterns may vary, but all meals can all be nutritious.
- A variety of food preparation strategies can help you save time in the kitchen.
- Meals eaten away from home can be as nutritious as those prepared at home.
- Snacks can be a part of a nutritional food plan.
- Planning your work in the kitchen is important to successful meal preparation.

Reviewing Key Terms & Ideas

1. How does time affect family food choices?
2. List four elements that make a meal look more attractive.
3. What do people do when they **graze**?
4. What is a **meal pattern**?
5. What are the effects of skipping meals?
6. List three timesaving strategies for planning meals.
7. What are **convenience foods**? How are they helpful to families?
8. What guidelines should you follow to make snacking part of a healthy lifestyle?
9. Why is planning important when you work in the food lab?
10. Define **dovetail**.

Thinking Critically

1. **Comparing elements.** In your opinion, what is the most important element in creating meal appeal? Why is this element more important than others?
2. **Drawing conclusions.** Why are convenience foods so appealing to people?
3. **Solving problems.** What advice would you give to a friend who has trouble managing time in the food lab?

Review & Activities

Applying Your Learning

1. **Mealtime schedules.** With your family, create a schedule that includes one healthful family meal each day for a week. Follow your plan. How difficult was it to stick to your schedule?

2. **Meal appeal.** Prepare a quick meal or snack that uses the elements of color, shape, texture, and flavor. Share your dish with classmates, and ask them to rate the meal's appeal.

3. **Recipe collection.** Use magazines, newspapers, family cookbooks, and the Internet to collect a variety of quick one-dish meals. Note which meals can be frozen to eat at a later time. Share your recipes with your family.

4. **Snack classification.** Bring several snack food labels to class. In a small group, analyze the snack food labels and use MyPyramid (on page 377 or the MyPyramid.gov Web site) to classify the snacks as healthy or unhealthy choices.

5. **Restaurant choices.** Gather several menus from local restaurants, including fast-food restaurants. With a partner, create a list of healthy dishes offered by each restaurant and explain what makes them wise choices.

6. **Cooking plan.** Think of a meal you would like to prepare for your family. Create a plan for cooking that lists all tasks that need to be done and a schedule for preparation. If possible, prepare the meal. How did your plan work out? Did your meal come out as expected?

Making Connections

1. **Reading** Read a book on time management. What tips offered in the book could be used in the kitchen? Make a list of useful tips from the book. Is there a correlation between time management and meal patterns? Discuss your opinion with the class.

2. **Writing** Write an article titled "Snacking the Healthy Way." Include information from this chapter, as well as from other resources. Share your article with the class.

3. **Math** Identify a convenience food and compare its cost to the cost of making the dish yourself. Which is less expensive?

CAREER Link

Time Management. At first glance, time management seems simple, but for some it can be one of the most challenging things they do. Without time management, even the smallest projects can be disastrous. Employers and employees both manage time to reach their goals. People who can successfully manage time are viewed as responsible employees and effective team members. Track your time for a day. When did you use time effectively? How can you improve your time-management skills?

Basic Cooking Techniques

Objectives

- Demonstrate different dry-heat and moist-heat cooking methods.
- Practice cooking with a convection oven.
- Compare different methods for cooking with fat.
- Explain microwave cooking techniques.
- Give guidelines for conserving nutrients while cooking.

Vocabulary

- **roasting**
- **broiling**
- **boiling**
- **steaming**
- **poaching**
- **simmering**
- **braising**
- **stewing**
- **deep-fat frying**
- **panfrying**
- **stir-frying**

Reading with Purpose

1. **As you read** Chapter 30, create an outline in your notebook using the colored headings.

2. **Write** a question under each heading that you can use to guide your reading.

3. **Answer** the question under each heading as you read the chapter. Record your answers.

4. **Ask** your teacher to help with answers you could not find in this chapter.

Choosing Cooking Techniques

Have you ever looked through cookbooks and recipes and discovered terms you had never heard? Cooking has its own language, and once you have mastered it, food preparation will be much easier.

When you cook food, heat transfers from the heat source, such as a flame, to the food. The heat causes molecules in the food to vibrate and cook the food. This transfer of heat occurs in all cooking methods: dry-heat, moist-heat, cooking with fat, and microwave cooking.

Fig 30-1 ▶

Cooking with Dry Heat

▶ **Broiling.** Popular broiled foods include steak, hamburgers, chicken, and some vegetables (especially if cheese is involved).

▶ **Roasting.** Foods often baked or roasted include meat, poultry, and fish.

▶ **Baking.** Breads, pies, cakes, and cookies are baked.

Dry-Heat Cooking

When you put dinner rolls in the oven to bake, you're using a dry-heat method. Dry-heat methods require that food be cooked uncovered without adding liquid. Dry-heat methods include roasting, baking, broiling, and grilling. Naturally tender foods are best cooked by dry-heat methods. For example, you might bake a meatloaf or roast a whole chicken using dry-heat methods of cooking. See **Fig. 30-1**.

Roasting most often refers to cooking large pieces of meat or poultry in a shallow pan. Sometimes the food is placed on a metal rack inside the pan to keep the fat away from the food. Air in the oven circulates around the food being baked or roasted. Baking can include cookies and cakes, as well as meat and vegetables. Always preheat the oven for 10 to 15 minutes before you bake or roast food, unless the instructions say otherwise.

Broiling means cooking food directly under a heat source (heating element). You can broil food in the oven by placing the food on the broiler pan. Broiling pans have two parts: the grill rack or grid and a lower pan that sometimes can be attached to the grill rack. Grilling is the opposite of broiling. With grilling, the heat source is below, not above.

Convection Oven Cooking

Convection ovens have become very popular. They are now more affordable and often found in home kitchens. Convection ovens have both upper and lower heating elements and a fan on the back wall, which blows hot air from the elements. Some convection ovens have a third heating element in the back of the oven, near the fan. The rapidly circulating air cooks food faster and helps regulate the oven temperature, which prevents hot spots in the oven.

The main advantage of convection oven cooking is reduced cooking time. Besides saving you time, quick cooking helps foods retain their nutrients and stay moist. For example, when cooked in a convection oven, meat, poultry, fish, and seafood develop brown crusts on the outside while remaining juicy on the inside.

Cooking may vary from convection oven to convection oven. You will need to experiment to find the cooking speed of your convection oven. When experimenting with cooking times, you can do the following:

- Bake food at the temperature recommended for the standard oven and reduce the time.

- Bake food for the time recommended for the standard oven and reduce the temperature by 25°F. See **Fig. 30-2**.

The cookware you choose is one factor in determining whether to use a convection or a standard oven. Casserole lids and high-sided cooking pans block the air from circulating and prevent convection ovens from cooking efficiently. For better

Fig 30-2
For dishes that require more than 45 minutes of cooking time, cover the dish for the first half of the cooking time to keep the food from drying out.

air circulation, the cookware should be open and not much higher than its contents. For example, cookie sheets and shallow pans with 1-inch sides are good choices for a convection oven. Covered dishes, roasting bags, and deep roasting pans are better used in a standard oven.

Moist-Heat Cooking

Moist-heat methods of cooking use added liquid or steam to cook and tenderize foods. Moist-heat methods generally require a longer cooking time than dry-heat methods. Water, broth, and even vegetable or fruit juices can be used in moist-heat cooking. The amount of liquid you need to use varies depending on the type of food you're cooking and the recipe. Foods cooked with this method can be prepared in a casserole dish with or without a tight-fitting cover. Which of the following moist-heat cooking methods have you used? See **Fig. 30-3**.

- **Boiling** food involves heating liquid at a high temperature so that bubbles rise and break on the liquid surface. When you boil food, you bring food to a boiling point (212°F). Boiling can rob foods of their nutrients. You can counteract the nutrient loss by adding cooking liquid to sauces and soups and using it to cook rice or beans.

- **Steaming** means cooking food over boiling water, rather than in it. When you steam food, you put it in a metal steam basket and place the basket over the boiling water. You can also use an electric steamer. When you steam foods, make sure there is water left in the pot. Keeping some liquid in the pot prevents the pot from boiling dry and burning.

- **Poaching** refers to cooking whole or large pieces of food in a small amount of liquid. When poaching, the cooking temperature should be just below simmering (185°F). Any liquid can be used for poaching, including water, milk, or broth. The liquid can be seasoned to add flavor to the food.

- **Simmering** is heating liquid to a temperature just below the boiling point until bubbles barely break on the liquid surface. Fewer nutrients are lost when you simmer food than when you boil it.

- **Braising** is simmering and steaming food in a small amount of liquid. Braising can be done on a cooktop, in an oven, or in a slow cooker. Braising works well for less tender cuts of meat. Generally, meat is browned before it is braised.

Fig 30-3

Cooking with Moist Heat

▶ **Boiling.** Foods that you would typically boil include potatoes, pasta, rice, and eggs.

▶ **Simmering.** Vegetables, meat, poultry, dry fruits, and fish can be cooked by simmering liquid.

▶ **Steaming.** Steaming vegetables, such as broccoli, is considered a healthy way to cook because more of the food's nutrients are conserved.

▶ **Poaching.** A gentle cooking process, poaching helps food keep its shape. You can poach poultry, fish, eggs, and dry fruit.

▶ **Braising.** Less tender cuts of meat, such as pork chops, are frequently braised in a covered pan to keep the moisture in the pan.

▶ **Stew**ing. Poultry, less tender cuts of meat, and vegetables are often stewed.

- **Stewing** is long, slow cooking in liquid. This cooking method is similar to braising, but stewed food is generally cut into smaller pieces and more liquid is used.

Cooking with Fat

What do onion rings, omelets, and stir-fried vegetables have in common? They're all fried. Frying food involves cooking with fat. You can use melted fat, such as butter or shortening, or you can use liquid fat, such as vegetable oil or olive oil. When using vegetable oil sprays, so little is used that it's not considered cooking with fat.

Deep-fat frying means food is cooked by completely covering it in fat. French fries, fried chicken, fried okra, and onion rings are deep-fat fried. Foods that are deep-fat fried are high in fat, so you'll want to eat them only occasionally.

In the **panfrying** method, smaller amounts of fat are used to fry tender cuts of meat, fish, and eggs in a skillet. Cooking thinly sliced vegetables in a small amount of fat over low to medium heat is called sautéing.

Teens Speak About Cooking Techniques

Vanessa and Jeremy flipped through the cookbook, looking for recipes for a foods lab project. "How should we cook the potatoes?" Vanessa asked.

"How about oven fried?" Jeremy suggested.

"How do you fry in an oven?"

"They're not fried, really," Jeremy explained. "You cut them into chunks and toss them in vegetable oil, then in cornflake crumbs. They come out crusty like French fries, but without all the fat."

"They sound easy, too," Vanessa said. "Where did you learn that?"

"From my stepdad. He's on a low-fat diet because of his diabetes. He's taught us all kinds of ways to cook food. He says, 'I want you to learn about healthy cooking now, not later from the doctor, like I did.'"

"Well, I like that idea," Vanessa said. "It'll impress Mrs. Ortega. Next time your stepdad cooks, take notes!"

Teen Connection

Locate recipes designed for teens' skills and abilities. What cooking methods are used? Choose one that you are less familiar or experienced with. Try to master this technique as you study this chapter.

Stir-frying involves stirring and cooking small pieces of food quickly at high heat in little fat. Vegetables, meat, fish, and poultry can be stir-fried. Because it uses so little fat, stir-frying is suggested for those trying to reduce fat in their diet. Stir-frying is often done in a wok, a bowl-shaped pan, although a skillet works just as well. A small amount of seasoned liquid can be added to flavor stir-fried food.

Microwave Cooking

You probably have witnessed how quickly food can cook in a microwave. Did you also know that microwaving is a good method of preserving nutrients?

In microwave cooking, electricity is converted into microwaves. Microwaves pass through glass, ceramic, paper, and plastic to cook food. However, they bounce off metal. This is why metal pans made for conventional ovens shouldn't be used in microwave ovens. You should also avoid using brown paper bags and towels made of recycled paper because they can burn when heated. Recent studies have discouraged the use of plastic wrap to cover food while microwaving. Plastic containers should be labeled as microwave-safe. See **Fig. 30-4.**

Microwaving food is easy and fast. To ensure successful microwave cooking, follow a few guidelines:

- Choose a microwave-safe container that fits your microwave.

- When you heat liquids, use a container two or three times larger than the amount of food to help prevent contents from boiling over.

- Cut pieces of food into uniform sizes to help food cook evenly.

- Arrange foods as indicated in your instruction manual to ensure even cooking.

- Cover foods to prevent them from drying out and spattering the inside walls and ceiling of the microwave.

- Follow package instructions on microwavable conve nience foods.

Fig 30-4
Microwaving allows you to cook food nutritiously a ckly this teen without creating a big mess. What safety proced· following for microwave cooking?

Conserving Nutrients

During the cooking process, foods can lose some of their nutrients. You can help preserve as many nutrients as possible by following these guidelines:

- **Choose methods wisely.** When choosing cooking methods, consider nutrition. Cooking in a small amount of water generally conserves more nutrients.
- **Avoid overcooking food.** Carefully follow directions for cooking temperature and time. The longer food cooks, the more nutrients it loses.
- **Leave the skins on.** The skins of fruits and vegetables

HOW TO CHECK FOOD FOR DONENESS

"It looks a little pale. Give it a few more minutes."

"It smells like it's burning."

As those lines show, some people use their senses to decide whether food has cooked long enough. Sight, touch, and smell can be good guides if you know how to use them. At stake is more than eating enjoyment or wasted food. As you know, some foods can be unsafe if not thoroughly cooked.

Recognizing signs of doneness is important throughout a recipe, not only when testing the final product. For example, when you cook garlic to flavor a dish, it should be sautéed until soft. Browned garlic is burned and will spread its bitterness through the food.

Apply these guidelines to help determine doneness in different foods:

- **Appearance.** The recipe and your experience can help you use appearance to judge when a food is ready. A coffee cake may be golden brown. Pancakes are flipped when bubbles appear on the surface. Ground beef is browned when no pink remains. Clear juices indicate a cooked piece of poultry. Check temperature to be sure!

- **Texture.** Touch is a clue for some food. A food might feel springy, like cookies, or fluffy, like rice. Pasta is done when it's tender but firm. Meat will vary depending on the method of preparation

and the cut of the meat. Fish should separate into flakes. Many people prefer their vegetables tender-crisp.

contain vitamins, minerals, and fiber. Leave them on whenever possible.

- **Save the liquid.** If possible, save liquid in which food is cooked. It contains valuable nutrients. If the liquid will not be eaten with the food, save it to make soup.

Now that you are familiar with some basic cooking methods, you'll be able to explore recipes with confidence, and your family and friends will enjoy the results.

- **Consistency.** The moisture left in a food is sometimes a gauge of doneness. Gravy is simmered to one consistency, pudding to another. Inner consistency of baked foods, from cake to custard, can be tested by inserting a knife or toothpick.

- **Aroma.** Properly cooked foods smell pleasant but not potent. Toasted seeds and nuts are fragrant; burned nuts smell sharp. Many people avoid some cooked vegetables, including cauliflower and cabbage, because they have a strong odor. If it is that strong, it is a sign of overcooking. A harsh odor in a spicy food can mean that the seasonings have burned.

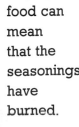

- **Temperature.** Although a food's observable qualities are helpful, remember that internal temperature is the "gold standard" of safety, especially for protein foods. Cooking meat, poultry, fish, and egg dishes to the temperatures specified on page 443 helps ensure that the food is safe and enjoyable to eat.

TAKE **ACTION**

Interview a cooking professional, such as a chef or restaurant owner. What tests for doneness does the professional use? Why?

Review & Activities

Chapter Summary

- Naturally tender foods are best cooked by dry-heat methods.
- Convection ovens speed cooking times and help conserve nutrients.
- Moist-heat cooking methods generally require a longer cooking time than dry-heat methods.
- Cooking with fat includes deep-fat frying, panfrying, and stir-frying.
- Microwaving is an easy and effective method of cooking food.
- Some cooking methods are better than others at conserving nutrients.

Reviewing Key Terms & Ideas

1. List four cooking methods.
2. Compare **roasting** food with **broiling** food.
3. Which cookware is best for a convection oven?
4. List four methods of moist-heat cooking.
5. How is **boiling** different from **steaming**?
6. What does **braising** involve?
7. What foods are good for **stewing**?
8. Which method of cooking with fat is the healthiest?
9. Explain sautéing.
10. Which containers are safe for use in a microwave?
11. List three guidelines for conserving nutrients when cooking.

Thinking Critically

1. **Making predictions.** In the future, do you think ranges will be replaced with convection ovens? Explain your answer.
2. **Making generalizations.** Stir-frying is becoming increasingly popular. Why do you think this is happening?
3. **Analyzing situations.** Imagine a friend prepared a hamburger in the microwave oven. Your friend was displeased with the results because the hamburger was "leathery" and lacked flavor. What advice would you offer?

Review & Activities

Applying Your Learning

1. **Method selection.** With a partner, select three different foods from a supermarket flyer or magazine. Discuss which cooking method would be appropriate for each food.

2. **Vegetable cook-off.** Select a vegetable, such as broccoli, green beans, or carrots. Prepare the vegetable using three different cooking methods. Have your classmates taste the vegetables and decide which method of preparation was best.

3. **Cooking safety.** Create a pamphlet of safety tips for each cooking method. Distribute the pamphlet to your class.

4. **Recipe improvements.** Locate several recipes that require deep-fat frying. Modify the recipes so that they can be cooked with a healthier method. Share your improved recipes with your class.

5. **Stir-fry recipe.** Find a stir-fry recipe and prepare it for your family. How did the recipe turn out? What health benefits does your recipe have?

6. **Nutritious cooking.** Invite a chef or dietician to demonstrate cooking methods that conserve nutrients. (Make sure this is approved by your teacher.)

Making Connections

1. **Reading** Read vegetable recipes in cookbooks and on the Internet. Which techniques have you used before? Which techniques were the most unusual?

2. **Writing** Research the health benefits of olive oil. Write an essay explaining the benefits of olive oil and why people should consider healthier oils for cooking.

3. **Math** Find two recipes for the same food, one that uses the microwave oven and one that uses another method of preparation. Compare estimated cooking times. About how much time would you save by using the microwave?

4. **Reading** Read healthy-cooking magazines. Analyze the recipes and techniques described in the magazines. Which cooking methods do the recipes share?

CAREER Link

Seeking Employment. People often say that finding a job is a job all its own. Finding employment can be time-consuming, but job-search techniques can help you. You can talk to your family, friends, and teachers about job openings, or leads, they may know about. You can also check the classified ads in your local newspaper for available jobs or browse company Web sites to read job postings. Make an action plan for a job search. List the career field that interests you. Then list three specific sources of job leads in this field.

CHAPTER 31

Preparing Grains, Fruits & Vegetables

Objectives
- Describe the nutritional benefits of grains.
- Demonstrate preparation techniques for grains.
- Discuss the nutritional value of fruits and vegetables.
- Explain proper handling of fresh produce.

Vocabulary
- bran
- endosperm
- germ
- enriched
- al dente
- leavening agent

Reading with Purpose

1. **Read** the title of this chapter and describe in writing what you expect to learn from it.

2. **Write** each vocabulary term in your notebook, leaving space for definitions.

3. **As you read** Chapter 31, write the definition beside each term in your notebook.

4. **After** reading the chapter, write a paragraph describing what you learned.

Grains in Your Diet

When you make a sandwich or toast, what kind of bread do you use? If you've only ever eaten white bread and haven't tried whole-grain foods, you are missing out on some adventuresome taste experiences. Barley, buckwheat, bulgur, cornmeal, kamut, millet, oats, and wild rice are just some of the grains you can add to your diet. If you lived a century ago, white bread wasn't available, and whole grains would have been the basis of your diet.

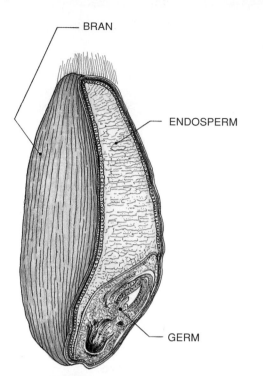

Fig 31-1 Whole grains are loaded with fiber, which has many nutritional benefits. What whole-grain foods have you eaten?

Nutrients in Grains

Grains pack a strong nutritional punch. Grains, especially whole grains, are excellent sources of complex carbohydrates and fiber. Grains also contain B vitamins, iron, and zinc. Most important, because they're plant foods they don't contain saturated fat or cholesterol.

Grains are the small dried fruits of cereal grasses often called kernels. **Fig. 31-1** shows the main three parts of the grain kernel:

- **Bran.** The **bran** is the kernel's edible outer covering.

- **Endosperm.** The **endosperm** is the largest part of the grain kernel, and is made of starch and protein.

- **Germ.** The **germ** is the seed of the kernel that grows into another plant. Some grains also have an inedible covering called the hull.

When grains are processed, or refined, for flour and cereals, the bran and germ are removed, as are some of the fiber, vitamins, and minerals. Because so many nutrients are lost in processing, the government requires that refined grains be **enriched**, or have nutrients added back after processing. Food labels indicate which grains are enriched.

For a healthful diet, make sure at least half of the grains you eat each day are whole grains. When selecting grains, check the food label first. Whole grains are indicated by the word "whole" on the label. The amount of grains you eat each day depends on your age, gender, and activity level.

Preparing Grains

You probably enjoy a lot of ready-to-eat grain products already, such as dry cereal, snacks, and packaged breads. Other grains require at least some preparation. Because you likely enjoy grains, why not find out more about preparing them?

Cooking Pasta and Rice

Pasta and rice are favorite foods for many people in cultures around the world. Pasta and rice not only taste good but also are easy to prepare. When you cook pasta and rice in water, the starch absorbs water, becomes soft, and expands in size. Rice increases up to three times its original volume, and pasta generally doubles in volume.

When you cook pasta, you need a large pot to allow the food to expand. Additional space is also needed for the water to boil. You'll need quite a bit of water, usually 4 quarts of water for 1 pound of pasta. Follow the package directions for cooking. Sample the pasta near the end of the cooking period to determine doneness so that it does not overcook. Experienced pasta makers cook pasta only until it is **al dente**, tender but firm to the tooth. Use a colander to drain the cooking water from the pasta. Avoid rinsing the pasta after you drain it. Rinsing washes away the pasta's nutrients.

When you cook rice, use the amount of water called for in the recipe or the package instructions. To cook rice, boil the water first, then add the rice. The rice absorbs all or almost all of the cooking water. If some cooking water remains in the rice, drain the rice but do not rinse it.

Making Muffins and Biscuits

Muffins and biscuits are called quick breads because they rise, or increase in volume, quickly. They use baking powder or baking soda, which is a **leavening agent**—it causes baked products to rise. Quick breads take less mixing and rising time than yeast breads do.

You can find delicious recipes and box mixes for whole-grain muffins, such as bran muffins, and for popular flavors, such as blueberry and banana nut muffins. When making muffins, you generally do the following:

1. Measure the ingredients accurately.

2. Mix together the dry ingredients—usually flour, sugar, salt, and baking powder.

Store Your Grains

Follow these guidelines when storing grains:

▶ Place grains in a cool, dry location.

▶ Seal containers and packages of grains tightly to retain freshness and keep them free of insects.

▶ Bread can be stored at room temperature. However, in hot and humid weather, refrigerate or freeze it.

Banana Muffins

Yield	Nutrition Analysis
30 medium muffins	**Per Serving:** 190 calories, 6 g total fat, 4.5 g saturated fat, 0 g trans fat, 30 mg cholesterol, 180 mg sodium, 31 g total carbohydrate, 1 g dietary fiber, 18 g sugars, 2 g protein **Percent Daily Value:** vitamin A 4%, vitamin C 2%, calcium 2%, iron 6%

Ingredients

Butter or margarine for greasing pans
1 cup unsalted butter (2 sticks), softened
1½ cups plus 4 tablespoons dark brown sugar

¼ cup light corn syrup
¼ cup dark molasses
2 large eggs, lightly beaten
2 cups ripe bananas (about 4 bananas), mashed

3½ cups all-purpose flour
2 teaspoons baking soda
¼ teaspoon ground ginger
⅛ teaspoon ground cinnamon
1 teaspoon salt

Directions

1. Preheat oven to 375°F. Grease muffin pans.
2. In the bowl of an electric mixer, cream butter and brown sugar. Beat until light and fluffy (about 3 minutes). Add corn syrup and molasses. Mix well. Add lightly beaten eggs and mashed bananas. Mix batter well.
3. In a separate mixing bowl, thoroughly combine flour, baking soda, ginger, cinnamon, and salt.
4. Add dry ingredients to batter a little at a time, beating after each addition.
5. Spoon batter into muffin cups, each about three-quarters full.
6. Bake for 22 to 25 minutes or until tops of muffins are firm to the touch and lightly browned.

Fig 31-2 ▶ Banana Muffins

3. Mix together the wet ingredients—usually milk, eggs, and oil.

4. Make a well in the dry ingredients and add the wet ingredients. Fold or mix the wet and dry ingredients. Do not overmix the batter. It should be somewhat lumpy, not smooth. See **Fig. 31-2**.

To make biscuits, you follow these steps:

1. Measure all ingredients accurately.

2. Sift dry ingredients together.

3. Cut fat into the dry ingredients. "Cutting in" means breaking the solid fat, usually shortening, into pea-size pieces, which makes biscuits flaky.

4. Make a well and mix the wet ingredients with the dry ingredients. Do not overmix the batter.

5. If you roll out the dough and cut the biscuits with a cutter, they are called rolled biscuits. If you spoon them out, they are called drop biscuits. When baking either rolled or dropped biscuits, expect them to enlarge with baking.

Fruits and Vegetables in Your Diet

Have you ever looked carefully at the selection of fruits and vegetables in a supermarket? More fresh produce is available today than ever before. New agricultural developments, increasing international trade, and the influence of different ethnic groups have introduced an array of fruits and vegetables throughout the year.

How many different fruits and vegetables have you tried? Jicama (HEE-kuh-muh), mango, tomatillo (toh-muh-TEE-yoh), bok choy (BAHK choy), taro (TAHR-oh), plantain, papaya (puh-PY-uh), and more are available in many stores. Add carrots, celery, apples, lettuce, broccoli, oranges, green beans, watermelon, potatoes, and corn to this growing list and you might have a difficult time saying, "I don't eat fruits and vegetables."

Nutrients in Fruits and Vegetables

Everyone benefits from eating a variety of fruits and vegetables. When choosing vegetables, remember that variety is as important as quantity. No single fruit or vegetable has all of the nutrients you need to be healthy. Also, eating the same foods is boring, no matter how good the food tastes. Eating a variety of fruits and vegetables makes meals interesting. See **Fig. 31-3.**

Buy Canned Fruits and Vegetables

Canned fruits and vegetables come in many different varieties. Here are some tips for buying canned goods:

▶ Check the style of the fruit or vegetable to see whether the recipe calls for whole or halves, slices, or pieces.

▶ Look for added seasonings, preservatives, and other spices that may be added. Be sure these are the flavors you want.

▶ When buying "juices" purchase only those labeled 100-percent juice.

▶ Do not buy dented or bulging cans, which may carry harmful bacteria.

Fig 31-3 ▶
If you'd like to try different juices, look for carrot, pineapple, and tomato juice at the store or try making your own juice at home.

HOW TO BUY GREAT GRAINS

Food trends come and go, but grains remain the most plentiful and popular foods in the world. Supermarkets, specialty bakeries, and online vendors offer an array of products, from "ancient" grains like amaranth to microwavable bowls of macaroni and cheese.

To get the most nutrition from among all of these options, remember that whole grains are most healthful. They contain all of the grain's nutrients, including phytonutrients, and fiber. Here are some tips to follow when buying the following grains:

- **Breads.** Whole-grain flour, either wheat or some other grain, is key when comparing bread choices. It should be the first ingredient listed. Rye and oats are particularly healthful. Don't be misled: a brown color may suggest "wholeness," but it may simply come from molasses. Multigrain breads, such as seven- or nine-grain bread, contain different types of grain but may not use the entire grain. Again, read labels carefully.

- **Cereals.** If you shop for groceries regularly, you may have noticed more cereals made with whole grains. This is good news for health-conscious consumers. For maximum grain nutrition, however, plain oatmeal is hard to beat. "Old-fashioned" and some quick-cooking varieties use the whole grain. However, flavored instant oatmeal has added sugar and sodium. If plain oats don't excite you, choose unflavored varieties and add fruits, cinnamon, vanilla extract, a sprinkle of sugar, or a drizzle of maple syrup.

- **Rice.** Brown rice includes the whole grain, except the inedible hull. Overall, it is the most nutritious type. Enriched white rice, which contains the endosperm only, also contributes to a healthful diet. Instant rice, which is precooked and then dried, has the least nutrients. Rice is also classified by the length of the grain: long, medium, or short. Each type is specially suited for different uses. Many varieties of white rice have brown alternatives.

- **Pasta.** Whole-grain pasta is available in most grocery stores. Online sellers and health food shops carry pasta made from buckwheat, spelt, brown rice, quinoa (KEEN-wah), and other less common grains.

TAKE **ACTION**

Choose a favorite recipe that uses a refined grain, such as white flour or instant rice. Prepare the recipe using a similar, whole-grain substitute. Compare the two versions on taste, texture, and appearance.

When preparing fruits and vegetables, keep these pointers in mind:

- Place a damp dishcloth or towel under the cutting board to keep it from slipping when you cut produce.

- Keep your fingertips away from the sharp edges of graters, peelers, chopping tools, and can lids.

- When you wipe knives, point the blade away from you.

- If a knife starts to fall, don't try to catch it. After it's on the floor, pick it up.

Fruits and vegetables are low in calories but packed with generous amounts of vitamins, minerals, and phytonutrients. Although nutrient amounts may differ, fruits and vegetables are good sources of carbohydrates, vitamin A, vitamin C, and minerals, such as calcium and potassium. Scientific evidence shows that fruits and vegetables protect against heart disease, stroke, cancer, and other serious health problems.

One characteristic that indicates the amount of nutrients in fruits and vegetables is color. Deeper yellow or dark green vegetables are better sources of vitamin A than those with a paler color. Look for yams, apricots, cantaloupe, carrots, broccoli, spinach, kale, and green peppers for vitamin A. Citrus fruits, such as oranges and grapefruit, are outstanding sources of vitamin C. Other good sources include tomatoes, strawberries, red sweet peppers, and white potatoes.

Everyone needs a different amount of fruits and vegetables each day depending on their age, gender, and physical activity. For adequate fiber and nutrients, eat more dark green and orange vegetables than other varieties. Limit the amount of starchy vegetables you eat. Make sure to eat a variety of vegetables. When choosing fruit, think fresh. Also, limit the amount of fruit juices you drink to less than half of your fruit intake.

How can you increase the amount of fruits and vegetables you eat each day? Be creative. Add lettuce, tomato, green pepper, and onion to sandwiches, or dip fruit into low-fat yogurt. You can also add vegetables to casseroles and experiment with various fruits and vegetables in salads.

Preparing Fruits and Vegetables

Depending on personal preferences and the season, your family may use fresh, frozen, canned, or dried fruits and vegetables. You will need to cook most fresh and frozen vegetables and only warm canned vegetables to the desired temperature. See **Fig. 31-4.**

Handling Fresh Produce

Be sure to wash fresh fruits and vegetables thoroughly under cold running water. Use a brush to clean firmer vegetables, such as potatoes and carrots. Proper washing of produce helps prevent foodborne illness—illness caused by eating contaminated food. However, avoid soaking vegetables in water, which causes the loss of water-soluble nutrients. Some fruits and vegetables, such as apples and cucumbers, have a wax

Fig 31-4 ▶
Use your creativity when cooking vegetables. Added herbs or drizzled olive oil can make a big difference in taste.

coating. This protective coating, which is safe to eat, keeps the produce moist and protects against bruising.

Cut vegetables just before you use them to conserve nutrients destroyed by air. Also cut fresh fruits, such as bananas, apples, peaches, and pears, just before serving. They darken when cut and exposed to the air. To prevent browning, you can squeeze lemon, orange, lime, or grapefruit juice on fruits just after you cut them.

Making Salads

When you think of salad, what do you imagine? Many people think of salad as lettuce with a few tomato slices on top. Fortunately, salads are much more than that. Main dish and side salads can be made from a number of ingredients, including vegetables, fruits, pasta, grains, legumes, eggs, meat, fish, poultry, and cheese.

Salad greens taste best when they're crisp, so keep them in the refrigerator until you're ready to use them. Remove any discolored leaves, and rinse the greens thoroughly in cold

Green Bean Salad

Yield	Nutrition Analysis
8 servings (1 cup each)	**Per Serving:** 300 calories, 28 g total fat, 2.5 g saturated fat, 0 g trans fat, 0 mg cholesterol, 630 mg sodium, 13 g total carbohydrate, 3 g dietary fiber, 4 g sugars, 1 g protein **Percent Daily Value:** vitamin A 6%, vitamin C 10%, calcium 4%, iron 2%

Dressing Ingredients

1 whole garlic bulb, roasted
Vegetable oil spray
½ cup light olive oil, divided
¼ cup balsamic vinegar
2 tablespoons fresh oregano, chopped
1 tablespoon fresh chives, chopped
¼ teaspoon salt
¼ teaspoon black pepper

Dressing Directions

1. Preheat oven to 400°F.
2. Spray garlic bulb with vegetable oil spray. Place bulb on an ovenproof plate or container. Bake for 20 to 30 minutes until cloves feel soft and tender to the touch. Remove. Cool bulb enough to handle.
3. In the bowl of a food processor or blender, squeeze each clove of garlic. Process the garlic and 2 tablespoons olive oil until a smooth paste forms. Add vinegar and process until well blended.
4. With the motor running, add the remaining olive oil in a steady stream.
5. Add chopped oregano and chives. Mix well. Season with salt and pepper.

Salad Ingredients

1 pound fresh, thin green beans, trimmed
1 medium Vidalia onion (or any sweet onion), thinly sliced (equal to 1½ cups)
1 can pitted black olives (15 ounces), halved vertically

Salad Directions

1. In a large pot of boiling water, cook green beans about 2 minutes.
2. Remove beans with a large slotted spoon, and plunge into a large bowl of ice water to stop the cooking process. They should be crisp.
3. When beans are cool, drain in a colander and slice on the diagonal.
4. In a large bowl, gently toss together the cut green beans, thinly sliced onions, and black olives. Toss with dressing.
5. Serve at room temp.

Fig 31-5 Green Bean Salad

water. Be especially careful of the dirt clinging to some greens, such as spinach and escarole. Put them in cold water, move them around, and lift them out of the water. The dirt usually settles to the bottom. You should rinse them more than once.

To keep salad dressing from diluting or clinging to wet leaves, dry greens in a salad spinner or clean towel before adding them to a salad. If you make a tossed salad, tear the greens into small pieces. When you add other vegetables or fruits to a salad, be sure they are clean as well. Pour salad dressing on just before serving to keep the greens from wilting. See **Fig. 31-5**.

Cooking Fruits and Vegetables

Fruits and vegetables change dramatically when they are cooked. They become less crisp because their starch and fiber soften. You can save nutrients by careful cooking. Some water-soluble nutrients dissolve in water, and others are destroyed by heat. To conserve nutrients in cooked fruits and vegetables, follow these guidelines:

- **Save the skin.** Whenever you can, leave the skin on fruits and vegetables. When fruits and vegetables are cooked whole or in large chunks, fewer nutrients are lost. Also, many important nutrients are contained in the skin and next to the skin.

- **Keep them crisp.** Cook fruits and vegetables until just tender. Slightly crisp is even better. Keep in mind that larger pieces take longer to cook than smaller pieces.

- **Limit the water.** Use as little water as possible to cook vegetables. Steaming vegetables or microwaving them in very little water conserves nutrients. Starchy vegetables, such as potatoes, are an exception and need to be cooked in more water. You can also grill vegetables on an indoor or outdoor grill. Grilling adds flavor yet retains the food's crispness and nutrients.

- **Follow the directions.** Follow package directions when you cook frozen vegetables. The flavor and nutrition will be better if you put the food in boiling water when it is still frozen. Separate frozen pieces with a fork after cooking begins so that the pieces cook evenly.

- **Don't overcook canned varieties.** Remember that canned vegetables are already cooked and only need to be warmed.

Keep the Color

Fruits and vegetables can change color during preparation and cooking. To retain the vibrant colors of produce, follow these tips:

- ▶ Toss fruit in a tablespoon of lemon juice to keep them from turning brown before you serve them.

- ▶ Cook vegetables al dente, or tender but firm to the tooth.

- ▶ Soak fruits and vegetables in water with ascorbic acid, a commercially available product.

- ▶ For cut vegetables, rub the cut edge with lemon juice to prevent the vegetable ends of discoloring.

Review & Activities

Chapter Summary

- Grains are excellent sources of complex carbohydrates, fiber, B vitamins, and iron.
- Pasta and rice absorb water when cooked and increase in volume.
- Quick breads include muffins and biscuits and can be easily prepared.
- Fruits and vegetables contribute a variety of essential nutrients to the diet.
- Proper handling and cooking of produce helps conserve nutrients and prevent foodborne illness.

Reviewing Key Terms & Ideas

1. Describe the **bran**, **endosperm**, and **germ** in a grain kernel.
2. Why are bread products **enriched**?
3. How much do pasta and rice increase in size when cooking?
4. What does **al dente** mean?
5. What does a **leavening agent** do?
6. Why should you eat a variety of fruits and vegetables?
7. What nutrients do produce foods contribute to the diet?
8. Why should you choose deeper yellow or darker green fruits and vegetables?
9. How can you prevent a banana or apple from turning brown after it is cut?
10. How can you keep salad greens crisp?

Thinking Critically

1. **Analyzing viewpoints.** Some people consider salads to be "rabbit food." What factors do you think contribute to this viewpoint? Why is this viewpoint a limited one?
2. **Making generalizations.** Why do people think all grains taste the same? Why are they considered the same nutritionally?

Review & Activities

Applying Your Learning

1. **Label analysis.** Gather several labels from grain products. Compare the nutritional information found on the labels. Decide which products provide better nutrition.

2. **Grain evaluation.** List the grain products you generally eat during a week. Rate them from the most to the least nutritious. How did you rate the majority of the products?

3. **Grain research.** Research an unusual grain found in a supermarket. Find out the health benefits and uses of the grain. Then locate a recipe for the grain and prepare it for your family.

4. **Muffin creation.** Put a healthy and creative spin on the muffin recipe in the chapter by adding fruit, nuts, or chopped vegetables to it. Taste-test your creation. What do you like about it? What would you do differently next time?

5. **Produce research.** Locate several unusual fruits or vegetables in the market. Where were they grown and how are they served? Prepare a few and evaluate the results.

Making Connections

1. **Reading** Read books about the history of grains. When were grains first used in people's diets? How were they prepared?

2. **Writing** Imagine you work in the produce department of a large supermarket. Your job is to write brief descriptions of produce to print in the weekly sales flyer. Select six fruits and vegetables and write brief, appealing descriptions of each.

3. **Reading** Read cookbooks and magazines that explain methods of preparing fruits and vegetables. Which method seems most appealing? Try the recipe and evaluate the results.

4. **Math** Fresh green beans are $1.29 per pound. A ½-pound package of frozen green beans costs $0.59. If you needed 1½ pounds of green beans, which would be cheaper—fresh or frozen?

CAREER Link

Accepting a Job.
If you receive a job offer and are uncertain whether it's the job for you, ask yourself the following questions: Can I handle the responsibility? Will the work hours fit my schedule? Do I have reliable transportation to work? Does the pay fit my needs? If you answer "yes" to most of these questions, you might want to accept the job. Talk to parents and other adult family members. Find out which factors affect their decision to accept a job.

32

Preparing Protein & Dairy Foods

Objectives

- Describe the nutritional benefits of protein foods.
- Demonstrate safe handling, preparation, and storage of protein foods.
- Identify different types of dairy foods.
- Give guidelines for preparing and storing dairy foods.

Vocabulary

- **legumes**
- **marbling**
- **perishable**
- **salmonella**
- **scorch**

Reading with Purpose

1. **Write down** the colored headings from Chapter 32 in your notebook.

2. **As you read** the text under each heading, visualize what you are reading.

3. **Reflect** on what you read by writing a few sentences under each heading to describe it.

4. **Continue** this process until you have finished the chapter. Reread your notes.

Nutrients in Protein and Dairy Foods

What do meat, poultry, fish, nuts, dry beans, eggs, and dairy products have in common? They're all good sources of nutrients. Meat contains iron and B vitamins. Along with iron and B vitamins, poultry contains phosphorous. Fish and shellfish are good sources of iron and vitamins A and D. **Legumes**, or dry beans, are rich in carbohydrates, fiber, calcium, phosphorus, B vitamins, and vitamin E. Nuts provide fiber, vitamin E, and minerals, such as magnesium and potassium. Dairy products are good sources of calcium, protein, riboflavin (B_2), phosphorous, vitamins A and D, and fat.

Fig 32-1 Protein helps build and repair body tissues. Choose from a variety of protein foods, especially those lower in fat content.

Buying Protein Foods

Buying protein can be confusing. The following facts should help you make good choices:

- **Meat.** Meat is identified by cut, or where it came from on the animal. The meat is labeled by grades. The highest grade is prime, followed by choice and select grades. **Marbling** (tiny veins of fat throughout the meat muscle) adds tenderness and flavor. Processed meats take numerous forms, including sausage and cold cuts. They vary greatly in fat and sodium. Read the Nutrition Facts panels carefully.

- **Poultry.** Poultry parts can be recognized by their names— wing, thigh, and breast. Whole birds are named to suggest how they should be cooked. For example, a stewing chicken would use a moist-heat method, such as stewing, to tenderize it. Poultry should be plump, cream colored, and free of blemishes. Chicken and ground turkey may be found packaged in a variety of forms.

- **Fish.** Purchasing fish can vary from whole fish—containing meat, skin, and bones—to fillets, which are boneless and sometimes skinless. Quality fish has firm flesh, red gills, and clear eyes. It doesn't smell "fishy." Because fresh fish is highly perishable and tends to be expensive, canned forms are popular.

- **Eggs.** Egg size reflects weight per dozen. Most recipes are made using large eggs. Check cartons for cracked or broken eggs.

- **Legumes.** Legumes come in dried, canned, fresh, or frozen forms. When buying dry versions, look for unbroken and stone-free peas and beans.

Preparing Protein Foods

When cooking protein foods, try to use low to moderate cooking temperatures. Lower temperatures help keep protein tender. In contrast, higher temperatures make it tougher. Broiling and grilling are exceptions because the higher temperatures seal in the juices. See **Fig. 32-1**.

Cooking and Handling Meat, Poultry, and Fish

No backyard barbecue or holiday dinner seems complete without protein foods. However, certain protein foods require extra care for safe handling and preparation. Meat, poultry, and fish are **perishable**, which means they are likely to spoil easily. Spoiled food can cause foodborne illness. To keep meat, poultry, and fish safe to eat, you need to defrost and cook it properly.

Defrosting Safely

The safest way to thaw, or defrost, protein foods is in the refrigerator. Smaller pieces usually defrost within a day. Larger pieces, such as roasts, may take two days. Never thaw meat, poultry, or fish on the countertop at room temperatures or in a sink filled with water. Bacteria begin to multiply at temperatures above 40°F. Considering most homes are about 70°F, room-temperature defrosting is dangerous.

You can also carefully thaw protein foods in the microwave at a reduced power level. Check your microwave owner's manual for defrosting procedures. You must be cautious when defrosting in a microwave, as the food can begin to cook. The result is unevenly cooked food. Never keep thawed food in a microwave while you wait to cook. The inside of the microwave is room temperature—a suitable temperature for bacteria to multiply.

Cooking Safely

Meat, poultry, and fish should be cooked immediately after thawing. You don't need to rinse these foods before cooking them. Doing so only spreads bacteria. Also remember that once you start cooking, don't stop. Partially cooked foods can harbor bacteria. Thoroughly cook all meat, poultry, and fish products. See **Fig. 32-2**.

Cookbooks give guidelines for suggested cooking times based on weight and size. However, these are only guidelines. Brownness on the outside of hamburgers and poultry does not mean they're done and safe to eat. Meat can be cooked to different levels of doneness. Cooking times vary depending on the type of meat, the cut, and the desired doneness. It is important that you cook poultry long enough that there is no pink remaining, the juices run clear, and the temperature is safe. Because fish is naturally tender, it requires a shorter cooking time. The general fish-rule of thumb, is to allow 10 minutes of cooking time for every inch of thickness. You can tell when fish is finished cooking because it separates and flakes easily with a fork.

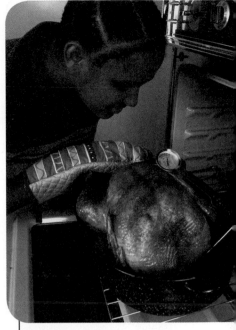

Fig 32-2 Cook meat thoroughly to prevent foodborne illness.

The only accurate method of determining whether meat, poultry, and fish are done is to check for safe temperatures using a meat thermometer. Insert a rapid-read thermometer into the center of the meat or poultry. Ground meat dishes, such as hamburgers and meatloaf, should be cooked to 160°F. Other cuts of meat, such as venison and beef steaks, should be cooked to at least 145°F. Whole poultry, such as a roasted chicken, should be cooked to 180°F, and poultry pieces to 170°F. Pork should be cooked to at least 160°F.

Cooking Methods

Tender cuts of meat are usually cooked by grilling, roasting, broiling, sautéing, or frying. Less tender cuts of meats are generally cooked using a moist-heat method, such as braising or stewing. Cook poultry labeled "broiler-fryer" just as the name states, or microwave it. Broil, bake, or fry fish.

If you purchase fully cooked beef and poultry, make sure it is held at the appropriate temperature. If the meat or poultry cools down, reheat it and check the internal temperature before serving.

Cooking Eggs

How do you like your eggs—poached, fried, or boiled? Do you like eggs in omelets, salads, or sandwiches? They can be used in a variety of ways, for breakfast, lunch, and dinner meals, or as an added ingredient. However, eggs are as perishable as raw meat, poultry, and fish and need to be handled and cooked with care. If not handled properly, you may not destroy the **salmonella**, bacteria that can cause foodborne illness, found in some eggs.

You can enjoy eating eggs if you follow these safe handling guidelines:

• **Do not eat raw eggs.** This includes any products made with uncooked eggs, such as raw-egg drinks.

• **Handle eggs safely.** Wash your hands and utensils with warm soapy water before and after cooking with eggs.

• **Cook eggs thoroughly.** Many cooking methods can be used to cook eggs safely, including poaching, boiling, frying, and baking. However, eggs must be cooked thoroughly until the yolks are firm. Scrambled eggs should not be runny.

Cooking Legumes

How many types of dry beans and peas can you name? You may have heard of black beans, kidney beans, navy beans, pinto beans, black-eyed peas, split green or yellow peas, garbanzo beans, and pink and green lentils. People today are rediscovering legumes and their benefits. Legumes are naturally low in fat and rich in fiber and complex carbohydrates, they're easy to prepare, and they don't harbor dangerous bacteria. They can also be easily substituted for one another and substituted for meat.

To prepare dry beans, sift through them and remove any debris or stones. Then wash them thoroughly and remove the discolored ones. Presoaking beans helps them cook more thoroughly and in less time. It also dissolves gas-causing substances and allows better digestion. Most presoaked beans cook within one to one and a half hours. Lentils and split peas will be tender sooner than whole beans. See **Fig. 32-3**.

Beans on the Menu

There are many delicious ways to include legumes at mealtime or as a snack. Look for these recipes in a cookbook and try a few:

- ▶ Black beans and rice
- ▶ Chili con carne
- ▶ Refried beans
- ▶ Hoppin' John
- ▶ Mixed bean salad
- ▶ Lentils and rice
- ▶ Falafel

Fig 32-3 ▶ Minted beans and potatoes

Minted Beans and Tomatoes

Yield	Nutrition Analysis
8 servings	*Per Serving:* 160 calories, 7 g total fat, 1 g saturated fat, 0 g trans fat, 0 mg cholesterol, 790 mg sodium, 24 g total carbohydrate, 8 g dietary fiber, 5 g sugars, 8 g protein *Percent Daily Value:* vitamin A 2%, vitamin C 15%, calcium 6%, iron 10%

Ingredients

3 cans great Northern beans, (15 oz.), rinsed and drained
¾ cup tomatoes, diced
2 teaspoons dried mint
1 large garlic clove, finely minced

⅓ cup fresh lemon juice (2 medium lemons)
¼ cup light olive oil
½ teaspoon salt
½ teaspoon sugar
Sprig of fresh mint (optional)

Directions

1. In a large bowl, combine drained beans, diced tomatoes, dried mint, and garlic.
2. In a small bowl, whisk together lemon juice, olive oil, salt, and sugar.
3. Pour liquid mixture over beans. Toss gently with a rubber spatula to coat thoroughly.
4. Cover and chill for at least three hours. Garnish with fresh mint if desired.

Tips

- Dried beans may be used. Follow package directions for cooking.
- To get the most juice from fresh lemons, firmly roll them on the countertop. Applying pressure releases juice before cutting.

You can soak dry beans overnight using 3 cups of water to 1 cup of dry beans. Remember to always discard the soaking water. If you forget to soak them overnight, you can cover the beans with water and simmer them until they swell. Avoid boiling the beans, which breaks the skin and makes them mushy. Then, take the pan off the heat, cover it, and let the beans stand for one hour. Drain and rinse the beans and follow your recipe's directions. Many recipes for legumes are available in cookbooks and on the Internet. Various ingredients, along with spices and herbs, can bring out the flavor of beans and peas.

Dairy Foods

If you're like most people, milk was one of the first foods you had as an infant. Today, you probably have milk in your cereal or drink it with lunch. Milk is classified as dairy food. Other dairy foods include cheeses and yogurt.

Dairy Substitutions

Tara has a milk allergy, and Dan eats a vegan diet, which means he eats no animal products. How do they get the nutrients in dairy without eating dairy products? They eat dairy substitutes such as rice milk, a processed drink usually made with brown rice. Other substitutions include soy, a complete protein made from soybeans.

Preparing Dairy Foods

A lot of dairy products you eat are convenience foods that don't require cooking. You can pour milk into a glass, eat yogurt from the container, or snack on a cube of cheese. However, you may decide to make a melted cheese sandwich, a quesadilla (k-suh-DEE-luh), macaroni and cheese, or a cup of cocoa, which all need to be cooked or heated. See **Fig. 32-4**.

To successfully prepare dairy products, keep the following tips in mind:

● **Avoid high heat.** Use low to moderate heat when cooking dairy foods. High heat will **scorch**, or burn, heat-sensitive proteins in dairy foods. Also, add cold milk to hot foods slowly so that the milk does not curdle, or thicken into lumps.

● **Cover or stir.** When heating milk, use a cover to prevent a film from forming on top. If you do not use a cover, stir it often.

Foolproof Cheese Soufflé

Yield	Nutrition Analysis
8 servings	*Per Serving:* 270 calories, 22 g total fat, 12 g saturated fat, .17 g trans fat, 220 mg cholesterol, 480 mg sodium, 4 g total carbohydrate, 0 g dietary fiber, 1 g sugars, 14 g protein *Percent Daily Value:* vitamin A 15%, vitamin C 0%, calcium 20%, iron 8%

Ingredients

Butter or margarine for greasing soufflé dish
6 large eggs
½ cup heavy whipping cream, not whipped
¼ cup Parmesan cheese, freshly grated
½ teaspoon prepared mustard

½ teaspoon salt
¼ teaspoon white pepper
4 ounces sharp cheddar cheese, shredded
11 ounces low-fat cream cheese, softened

Directions

1. Preheat oven to 375°F. Grease an ovenproof soufflé dish well.
2. Place the eggs, whipping cream, Parmesan cheese, mustard, salt, and pepper into a blender or a food processor fitted with the steel "s" blade. Process until well blended.
3. Add the cheddar cheese and process. Add the cream cheese and process.
4. Spoon mixture into the soufflé dish. Bake for 40 to 45 minutes or until top is slightly golden and springs back when gently tapped. Remove from oven and serve immediately.

Fig 32-4 Foolproof Cheese Soufflé

Storing Dairy Foods

Almost all dairy foods are highly perishable, so you will need to store them properly to avoid spoilage. Keep all dairy foods in their original containers. Refrigerate milk and use it by the date indicated on the package, usually two to seven days. To store cheese, be sure it's wrapped tightly before refrigerating. Fresh cheese should be used within two weeks. Throw out any fresh cheese that contains mold. Cheeses usually last several weeks in the refrigerator. You can also freeze cheese for later use.

Picture the contents of your refrigerator. What dairy products do you see? If you're like many people, you saw milk—white, maybe chocolate. Although milk is a mainstay of many Americans' diets, it is not your only dairy option. If you are bored with your usual dairy choices, the following information can help you embark on an exploration of the many varieties of dairy products available today:

- **Cheese.** A concentrated form of milk, cheese is grouped into two categories: fresh and aged, or ripened. Fresh cheese has a mild flavor and is highly perishable. Cottage cheese, a bland cheese made with large or small curds (solid clusters), and cream cheese are two popular fresh cheeses. Another option is farmer's cheese—a mild, slightly tangy cheese usually shaped into a loaf. Aged, or ripened, cheese is available in firm, semisoft, soft, and blue-veined forms. Hundreds of ripened cheeses, each with a distinctive flavor, can be found in stores. Try cheddar, mozzarella, Monterey Jack, feta (FEH-tuh), or blue cheese.

- **Milk.** This creamy beverage comes in whole, low-fat, and nonfat varieties. You can find not only white and chocolate flavors but also strawberry, caramel, and coffee. If you have a sensitivity to lactose (the sugar contained in milk), you might choose lactose-free or reduced-lactose milk. For a calcium boost, try calcium-enriched milk, which contains 500 milligrams of calcium per cup. You can also find canned milk, such as evaporated and sweetened condensed milk, and nonfat dry milk.

- **Dairy desserts.** Whether on a cone, on a stick, or in a cup, frozen dairy desserts are one of the most popular desserts in America. Hundreds of flavors of ice cream are sold each year in regular, low-fat, nonfat, and sugar-free forms. Besides ice cream, you can choose frozen yogurt or sherbet, a dessert containing milk fat, fruit or juice, sugar, water, and flavorings. Try making some healthful choices. When making some dairy desserts, add fresh fruit, nuts, granola, or crushed trail-mix (a combination of nuts and dried fruit).

- **Yogurt.** A thick, dairy-based product, yogurt is packed with calcium and provides bacteria that aids digestion. Try plain yogurt or one of the many flavored varieties—either regular, low-fat, or nonfat. If you're looking for more flavor and texture, try yogurt with added fruit. For a drink on the go, choose a yogurt smoothie. Replace sour cream with yogurt in your favorite recipe. Try straining yogurt in a fine mesh strainer or a bowl lined with cheesecloth. You will create a type of semi-soft cheese by draining the liquid from the yogurt.

TAKE **ACTION**

As a class, host a Dairy Day tasting event. Bring to class a variety of dairy products for classmates to try. Be sure to choose varieties that can be easily eaten and make sure to have some dairy substitutes so that everyone can participate. After the event, vote on class favorites and discuss ways to include a variety of dairy in daily meals.

32

Review & Activities

Chapter Summary

- Protein foods contribute a variety of important nutrients to the diet.
- Protein foods are perishable and should be handled and cooked carefully.
- Dairy products are heat sensitive and need to be carefully prepared.
- Almost all dairy products are perishable and should be stored properly to prevent spoilage.

Reviewing Key Terms & Ideas

1. What is the difference in the type of protein found in meat, poultry, and fish and the type of protein found in legumes?
2. Define **marbling**.
3. What cooking temperatures are recommended for protein foods? Explain.
4. What are **perishable** foods?
5. Why should you avoid thawing frozen protein foods at room temperature?
6. How can you tell when fish is finished cooking?
7. What temperatures indicate doneness in meat, poultry, and pork?
8. What is **salmonella**?
9. Why are legumes soaked before cooking?
10. What does it mean to **scorch** dairy foods?

Thinking Critically

1. **Analyzing trends.** Which protein foods do you think are most popular? How can you explain their popularity?
2. **Making comparisons.** Regarding flavor and nutrition, which protein food do you think provides the most benefits? Explain.
3. **Defending statements.** Imagine a friend made the statement, "Milk is for babies." How would you respond, given what you read in this chapter?

CHAPTER 32

Review & Activities

Applying Your Learning

1. **Protein investigation.** Using the Internet, explore the different varieties of wild game, such deer, bison (buffalo), quail, and pheasant. Choose one variety and research the nutritional benefits of the food and proper cooking methods. Share the information with your class.

2. **Defrosting guidelines.** With a partner, create a poster that shows how to safely defrost protein foods. Display your poster in the food lab.

3. **Food bulletin.** Develop a bulletin explaining the latest breaking news about legumes. Include nutritional benefits and information on healthy preparation of legumes.

4. **Preparation guidelines.** Select and demonstrate one method of cooking eggs. Stress the guidelines you would follow for safe preparation.

5. **Dairy recipe.** Imagine you're employed as a recipe creator at a dairy foods company. Using nuts, fruit, and other healthy ingredients, create a new yogurt recipe. Name your product and create a food label that details the ingredients and nutrients in the food. If possible, prepare your recipe and share it with your class.

Making Connections

1. **Reading** Read recent news articles about illnesses caused by contaminated or spoiled meat. What government restrictions are in place to prevent consumers from purchasing unsafe meat?

2. **Math** Using the Internet or print resources, find out the number of pounds of beef, poultry, fish, and wild game sold in the United States in the last year. Create a graph of the information and calculate the range of values.

3. **Reading** Most eggs available in stores are chicken eggs, but other types of eggs can be used in cooking. Read about ostrich, quail, and duck eggs and find out how they're used. How does their nutritional content compare to that of chicken eggs?

4. **Writing** Obtain samples of three cheeses you have never tried before. Sample the cheeses and write a brief critique of each.

CAREER Link

Resignation Letter
When you leave a job, you'll need to submit a letter of resignation to your employer. In your letter, explain why and when you are leaving. Thank your employer for having given you the opportunity to work. You can also mention what you learned on the job and how it will help you in future jobs. If you were an employer, why would you be pleased to receive a resignation letter including this information?

Clothing That Suits You

CHAPTER 33

Objectives

- Plan an outfit using the elements and principles of design.
- Organize clothes using a clothing inventory.
- Categorize clothing as high- or low-priority needs.
- Summarize clothes-shopping strategies.

Vocabulary

- **fashions**
- **illusion**
- **elements of design**
- **silhouette**
- **principles of design**
- **fads**
- **accessories**

Reading with Purpose

1. **As you read** Chapter 33, create an outline in your notebook using the colored headings.

2. **Write** a question under each heading that you can use to guide your reading.

3. **Answer** the question under each heading as you read the chapter. Record your answers.

4. **Ask** your teacher to help with answers you could not find in this chapter.

The Importance of Clothing

What is the first thing people notice about you—your personality, your sense of humor, your intelligence? Yes, these are important traits, but chances are what people notice first is your clothing. Clothes can convey many messages. People with positive self-esteem display a sense of pride in their appearance. For some teens, wearing designer labels and trendy **fashions**, or styles that are currently popular, is important. This may influence their clothing choices and how they care for their clothing.

To make sure your clothing speaks the truth about who you are, you need to consider several factors, such as your needs, wants, budget, and how you want others to perceive you. Good planning and resource management can help you develop a wardrobe—a collection of clothes—that makes you feel good about the way you look.

Individualizing Your Clothing

Every person is different, with a specific body shape, a different texture and color of hair, and a unique skin complexion. Your clothing can help you enhance and personalize your individual style. Before you shop for or make clothes, consider how you can make garments work for you to improve your appearance.

One way to enhance how you look is to use clothing to create an **illusion**, which can influence or lead the eye to see something that does not exist. A short person who wears vertical stripes creates the illusion of height. On the other hand, a tall person can appear shorter by wearing horizontal stripes. Black and other dark colors can create an illusion of a sleek appearance. You can use illusion to draw attention to your best features. You create these by using the elements and principles of design. See **Fig. 33-1**.

Elements of Design

The **elements of design** are line, shape, space, texture, and color. Understanding how these elements work will help you choose styles that look good on you. Some computer programs can show how various garments will look on you without trying them on.

- **Line.** Line guides your eye movement up, down, and across an area. Lines can be straight or curved and can flow vertically, horizontally, or diagonally.

- **Shape.** Sometimes called a **silhouette**, shape is the form created when lines are combined. Types of shapes include natural (following the body's line), tubular (forming a rectangular shape with no waistline), bell (combining diagonal and horizontal lines to create a bell outline), and full (combining horizontal and curved lines).

- **Space.** The area inside the silhouette is the space. Space can be divided by accessories, decorative trim, and seams.

- **Texture.** Texture is the surface characteristic that you see or feel in a fabric. Textures can be soft or crisp, bulky or smooth, and dull or shiny.

- **Color.** Color is one of the most important design elements. Your best colors are the ones that flatter the color of your hair, skin, and eyes.

Using Color

Of all design elements, color is the one most people notice first. Many people choose their clothes based on their favorite color—whether the color flatters them or not. If you understand color and know how to use it, you can choose clothing in colors that suit you. See **Fig. 33-2**.

The Effects of Color

Sharon wears one-color outfits because they make her look taller. Jake wears darker colors for a slimming effect. You, too, can create illusions with color. If you can control the following qualities, you can enhance your appearance:

- **Value** is the lightness or darkness of a color. For example, the lightest value of red is pink, and its darkest value is maroon. Light values are called tints and make things look larger. Dark values are called shades and make things look smaller.

- **Intensity** describes how bright or dull a color appears. A color at full intensity, such as bright red, tends to stand out. Colors with lower intensity, such as dusty rose, are less obvious. In general, low-intensity colors are used for larger pieces, such as jackets. Bright colors are better for smaller pieces, such as tops.

- **Warm and cool** describes how color can make you feel. Yellow, orange, and red are associated with warmth. Warm colors make areas appear larger and closer to you. Green, violet, and blue may remind you of cool water, trees, and sky. Cool colors tend to make areas look smaller and farther away.

TIPS

Choose Clothing for Special Needs

Clothing needs vary for people with special needs, depending on the specific disability. Here are some features that can make dressing easier for people with disabilities:

▶ Easy-to-manage fasteners, such as big buttons and buttonholes, hook-and-loop tape fasteners, large zipper pulls, and even antique buttonhooks.

▶ Soft fabrics that don't irritate the skin.

▶ Large or colorful buttons that are easy to see.

▶ Designs that won't hang loosely and become caught in wheelchairs or other mobility devices.

▶ Two-piece outfits with front zippers to improve ease in handling and to increase size and fit options.

▶ Pants and skirts with adjustable waistlines.

▶ Large seam allowances that permit necessary alterations.

▶ Lines that draw attention to a person's best features.

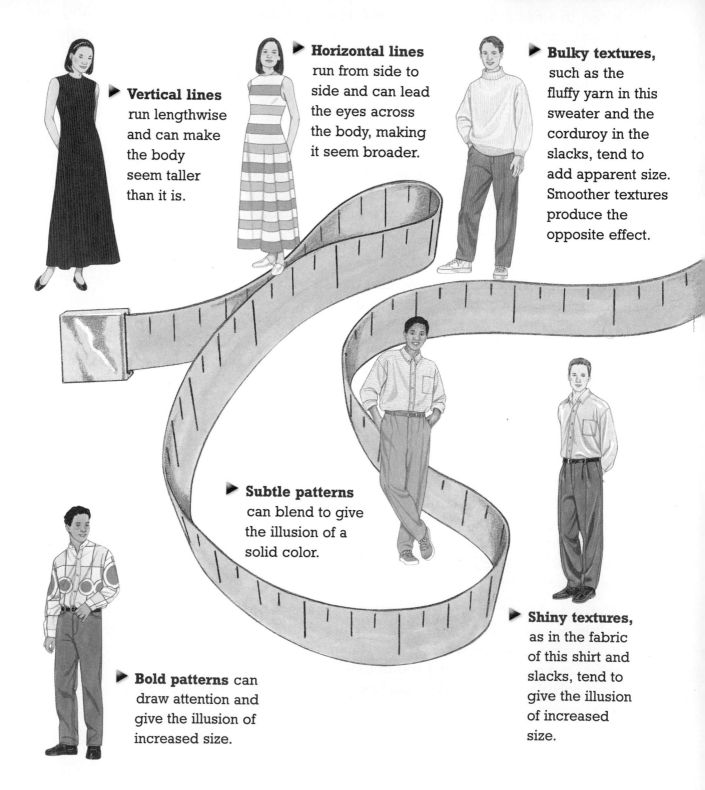

Fig 33-2

Using the Elements of Design

▶ **Vertical lines** run lengthwise and can make the body seem taller than it is.

▶ **Horizontal lines** run from side to side and can lead the eyes across the body, making it seem broader.

▶ **Bulky textures,** such as the fluffy yarn in this sweater and the corduroy in the slacks, tend to add apparent size. Smoother textures produce the opposite effect.

▶ **Subtle patterns** can blend to give the illusion of a solid color.

▶ **Bold patterns** can draw attention and give the illusion of increased size.

▶ **Shiny textures,** as in the fabric of this shirt and slacks, tend to give the illusion of increased size.

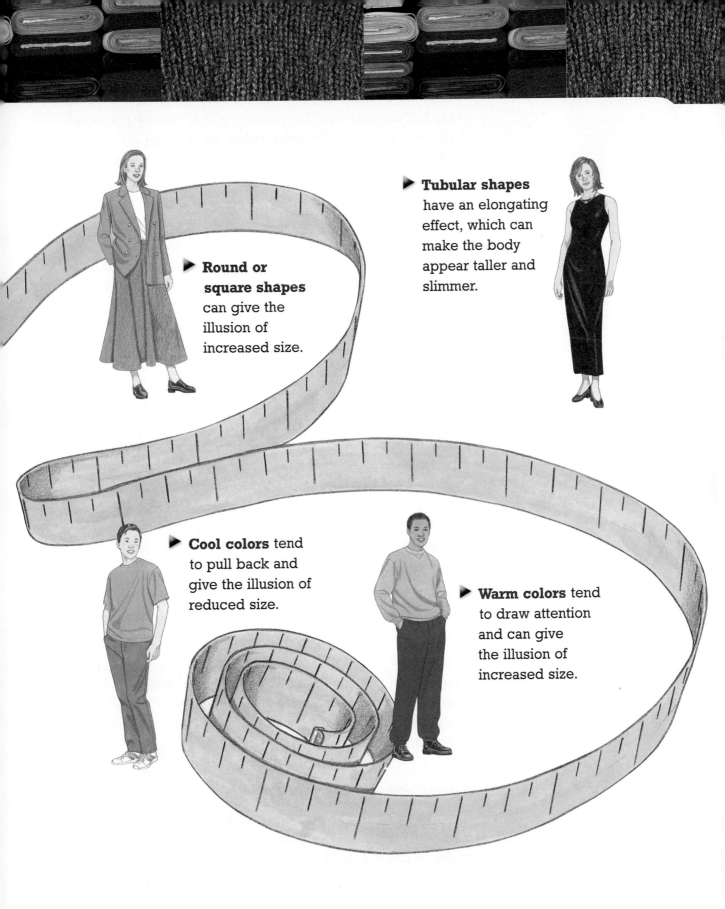

Round or square shapes can give the illusion of increased size.

Tubular shapes have an elongating effect, which can make the body appear taller and slimmer.

Cool colors tend to pull back and give the illusion of reduced size.

Warm colors tend to draw attention and can give the illusion of increased size.

Principles of Design

Sandra examined the garments laid out on her bed. She had tried on all of them and still wasn't sure which combination worked. Does this ever happen to you? If so, the principles of design can help. The **principles of design** are artistic guidelines that help you combine the elements of design:

- **Proportion** involves the relationship of one part to another and to the whole. If you make one section of your body look long, wide, or large, the other section will appear shorter, narrower or smaller. For example, if you tuck a shirt into your slacks, your legs will appear longer. Wearing an untucked, long shirt will make your legs look shorter.

- **Emphasis** is the point of interest that the eyes see first. It can be used to draw attention to your best features. A colorful belt emphasizes the waist. A bright tie or scarf draws attention to the face.

- **Balance** gives a feeling of equal weight among all parts of a design. Balance is either symmetrical or asymmetrical. When one side of a garment or outfit is exactly the same as the other side, it is called symmetrical balance. Asymmetrical balance occurs when the two sides of the garment or outfit are different in size, form, texture, or color. An example is a trendy top with only one sleeve or a skirt that is long in the back and short in the front.

- **Rhythm** is the feeling of movement, leading the eye around a garment or outfit. For example, when you repeat the color of an outfit in a scarf or you choose square patch pockets to repeat a jacket's boxy shape, you create rhythm.

- **Harmony** occurs when the design elements work together. That doesn't mean all items have to match. Variety is interesting if the design details grouped together have something in common, such as shape, style, color, or size. See **Fig. 33-4**.

Wardrobe Assessment

You know the look you want, and you understand the elements and principles of design. So how can you use this information to create a wardrobe that showcases your style? Begin by taking a look at what you already have. A clothing inven-

Fig 33-4

Using the Principles of Design

► **Proportion** refers to how separate parts of an outfit relate to each other and to the whole outfit. Clothing looks best when it's in proportion to your own size. When an outfit does not relate well to your body size, or the parts of the outfit don't relate well to each other, the outfit is said to be out of proportion.

► **Emphasis** is the focal point of a garment. Emphasis can be used to make an outfit more interesting or to draw attention to your best features. You can create emphasis with a bright belt, a colorful scarf, or a bright tie, among other items.

► **Harmony** occurs when the elements of design complement each other. When an outfit is harmonious, each part looks like it belongs. To achieve harmony, plan your accessories along with your outfit so that together they create a unified theme.

Fig 33-4 ▶ cont.

Using the Principles of Design

▶ **Rhythm** leads the eye from one area of an outfit or garment to another. For example, a repeated pattern, such as square pockets on a boxy jacket, produces rhythm. A color that changes gradually from red to yellow also shows rhythm. When rhythm is good, the lines of an outfit work well together. When rhythm is poor, the look of the outfit is upset.

▶ **Balance** occurs when the spaces on both sides of a central line appear equal. A balanced design gives the feeling of stability. Balance can be symmetrical or asymmetrical. When balance is symmetrical, two identical sides are divided by a center line. When balance is asymmetrical, the sides of a garment or outfit are visually different.

tory, or an organized list of your clothes, helps you decide which garments you need to fill the gaps in your wardrobe. When taking a clothing inventory, sort your clothing into the following groups:

- Clothes you like or wear regularly and want to keep.

- Clothes you don't want.

- Clothes you are unsure about. See **Fig. 33-3**.

Jot down all garments in your "keep" group. Then look again at the clothes in your "unsure about" group. Would updating or repairing any of these clothes make them work in your wardrobe? Could you wear any of these clothes during messy activities, such as painting, house cleaning, or working out? If so, add these garments to your list. Now consider the clothes in the "don't want" group. If they are in good conditions, you could donate them to a charitable organization or give them to a sibling, friend, or relative. You could also sell them in a yard sale, in a resale shop, or on the Internet.

Expanding Your Wardrobe

After you complete your clothing inventory, look over the clothes you decided to keep. Make sure you have clothes for daily wear and those you wear for special activities. You should have a few items for special occasions, such as weddings, special celebrations, or funerals. Clothing for different seasons is also needed, such as swimwear and shorts in summer and sweaters and heavy socks in winter.

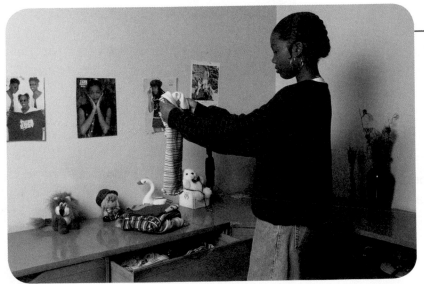

Fig 33-3
Taking a clothing inventory helps you determine your clothing needs. How do you determine your clothing needs?

Finding Gaps in Your Wardrobe

Do you see any gaps in your wardrobe? If so, you will need to expand your clothing options by making, restyling, or purchasing clothes. Before taking any steps to expand your wardrobe, you will need to do the following:

- **Consider your needs and wants.** Which items do you really need? Which do you want but could do without? Needs are usually more important than wants.

- **Consider accessories to fill in gaps.** Are there some accessories to recycle that might just be a perfect touch?

HOW TO SELECT QUALITY CLOTHING

Fashions may change every year, but clothes should last as long as you want to wear them. To improve your chances for a long and happy relationship with a garment, check these features:

- **Wrinkling.** Crush the material in your hand, then release it. Any wrinkles should smooth or shake out easily. Otherwise, the garment will take on that "slept in" look soon after you put it on. Remember, however, that some fabrics, such as linen, wrinkle.

- **Wear.** Hold the garment to the light to check that the weave is tight and even throughout. Loose weaves tend to lose their shape. An uneven weave means uneven wear. Check for a lining. Clothes with linings are typically higher quality.

- **Care.** Read the garment labels. Like plants, some clothes require more care than others. Decide whether the garment is worth the upkeep.

- **Plan for core clothing pieces.** Core clothing pieces—garments that can be used in a variety of situations—are the backbone of your wardrobe. A closet full of trendy clothes, which will not last long before they fall out of fashion, is not ideal. However, a few core pieces, or those considered classic, are timeless and will last much longer. Males might choose a pair of well-fitting jeans, a pair of khaki pants, and a few solid-color knit shirts with collars as core pieces. Females might select a solid-color skirt, a few solid-color shirts or some shirts with a simple design, and a pair of well-fitting jeans.

- **Pattern.** A plaid or print should run in the same direction throughout the garment. It should match at the seams, including pockets and collars.

- **Fastenings.** Fastenings should open easily, close smoothly, and stay closed during wearing. Look for evenly spaced buttons and buttonholes that are well defined with tight, even stitching. Zippers should lie flat. Metal zippers are more durable than plastic ones. All fastenings—for example, hooks, eyes, and snaps—should be securely sewn.

- **Seams.** Garment sections should meet smoothly at the seams, without pulling or puckering. Check for tight stitches on the underside. About 8 to 12 stitches per inch indicate sturdy construction.

- **Hems.** Hems should be straight and flat, not wrinkled or rumpled. Stitches should be invisible from the outside. Turn the hemmed area over to check for secure stitching on the underside.

- **Corners.** Points on collars, lapels, and pocket flaps should be clean and symmetrical. They should lie flat and smooth, with no lumps, bumps, or puckers.

- **Trims.** Decorations such as patches, braids, and ribbons should be neatly but securely attached. The thread should blend into the fabric, unless it is meant as part of the decoration.

TAKE ACTION

Evaluate a favorite piece of clothing using these criteria. How does the garment compare? Can you correct any flaws with simple techniques? Is doing so important? Why or why not?

• **Keep your budget in mind.** How much money do you have to spend on garments or fabric to make them? Be sure to consider the cost per wearing of each garment. To figure this out, take the garment's purchase price, add the cleaning costs over time, and divide the sum by the number of wearings you expect to get out of it. Some garments, such as jeans, are worn often and have a lower cost per wearing. Also, beware of **fads**, or fashions that last only a short time. Because clothing fads come and go quickly, their cost per wearing is usually high. To save money, consider using **accessories**, or small items of clothing that complete an outfit. Accessories add interest to an outfit and in most cases are less expensive than new clothes.

Shopping for Clothes

You have learned about the elements and principles of design and have taken a clothing inventory. Now you need to shop for new clothes. Are you prepared? To be a savvy shopper, use a plan. If you shop with a plan, you are more likely to be pleased with your purchases.

To create your plan, prioritize your clothing needs. You need to buy your highest-priority items first. If you start at the bottom of your list, you may run out of money before you reach the top. Use catalogs, sales flyers, and the Internet to find out prices of clothing and create your priority list.

Shopping Options

Once you have your needs prioritized, you are ready to shop. What shopping options do you have? If you live in a large city, you may have many shopping options, including specialty stores or boutiques, discount stores, resale shops, outlet stores, and department stores. If you live in a rural area, your choices will probably be limited. However, online shopping allows people in rural areas to shop almost anywhere without making a trip to a city or store. If you shop online, you will probably need a credit card. Also, remember to add the shipping costs to the price of the item. Some companies offer free shipping if you spend a certain amount. See **Fig. 33-5**.

Fig 33-5
You can't inspect clothing firsthand when you shop online. Read product descriptions carefully before making an online purchase.

Consignment shops and thrift stores often have many items that are like new without the new-clothing price tag. For special-occasion clothes, such as a tuxedo or formal gown, you can rent an outfit from a rental shop.

Shopping Strategies

When you shop, remember your priority list. If you are not able to locate the exact item you want, look for a good substitute at a comparable cost. Here are some other tips to keep in mind as you shop:

- **Check the care label.** Be sure you can give the garment proper care. A dry-clean-only garment means continuing costs not only for the garment but also for the trip to and from the dry cleaners.

- **Check the fit.** Buy only what fits comfortably. Try the garment on to be sure it doesn't pull, wrinkle, or feel uncomfortable when you sit or bend. Buy clothes that fit you right now. Your body size, clothing styles, and even your taste in clothes may change.

- **Check the quality.** Choose the best quality you can afford to buy. The garment will have to stand up to repeated laundering and wear.

- **Check the price tag.** Does the price fit into your clothing budget? If items in a store seem expensive, shop around. Try a resale shop, a discount store, or a sale for better value. On the other hand, do not buy items simply because they are on sale. You might end up with good deals that you never wear.

Deciding to Buy

After checking the care instructions, fit, quality, and price, you should have a good idea of whether a garment is the right one for you. If you have doubts about a garment, do not buy it. If you decide to buy an item, check the exchange or return policies of the store before you pay. If the store's policy is "exchanges only, no returns," you know you will not get your money back. You will only be able to exchange an item for one of equal value. Keep the sales receipt—and keep the tags on the clothing—until you are sure you're keeping the item. See **Fig. 33-6**.

Fig 33-6 When shopping online or by catalog, you'll need to ship any returns back to the manufacturer. Check the return policies stated in the catalog or on the Web site before you make a purchase.

33

Review & Activities

Chapter Summary

- You can use the elements and principles of design to create outfits that work for you.
- A clothing inventory is a good first step in putting together a wardrobe.
- Prioritizing your needs and wants will help you be more satisfied with your purchases.
- Shopping strategies can help you obtain good-quality garments within your budget.
- Before buying an item, check the store's exchange or return policy.

Reviewing Key Terms & Ideas

1. Define **fashions**.
2. What is an **illusion**?
3. List the **elements of design**.
4. What is a **silhouette**?
5. Name the **principles of design**.
6. How can a clothing inventory help you?
7. What are **fads**?
8. What are the benefits of **accessories**?
9. What four things should you check when shopping for clothes?
10. Why should you keep your sales receipt and tags on the clothing until you're sure of your purchase?

Thinking Critically

1. **Recognizing viewpoints.** How do you think adults view teens who wear torn, mismatched, or wrinkled clothing? Do you think this view accurately represents the teen? Why?
2. **Making comparisons.** How do teens' clothing needs differ from those of adults?
3. **Analyzing situations.** Imagine a friend of yours is feeling pressured by classmates to wear expensive designer clothing that does not fit in your friend's budget. What advice would you give your friend?

Review & Activities

Applying Your Learning

1. **Advice column.** Imagine that you write a fashion advice column for a local paper. Respond to a teen who has written asking how to develop a personal style.

2. **Clothing makeover.** Imagine you are a fashion consultant. Create clothing makeovers for two clients: one is short and heavy, and the other is tall and thin. How would you advise each to dress?

3. **Color assessment.** Gather fabric pieces in various colors. Hold the pieces up to your face and identify the colors that seem best for your complexion, hair, and eye colors.

4. **Emphasis techniques.** Examine photographs of fashions from magazines and catalogs. Determine the point of emphasis in each outfit. How does the emphasis improve the look of the outfit?

5. **Core clothing.** Develop a list of core clothing pieces for your wardrobe. Be sure to consider your routine activities.

6. **Shopping strategies.** Create a list of clothing items you need to fill gaps in your wardrobe. Use catalogs and the Internet to determine the cost of the items and prioritize your list. Talk with your family to create a budget and plan for purchasing the items.

Making Connections

1. **Writing** Some people think that school uniforms prevent teens from expressing their individual styles. Write a position paper either for or against school uniforms.

2. **Math** Assume you have purchased a washable jacket for $50. All washings cost $1. You plan to wear the jacket 40 times. What is the total cost per wearing (garment cost + cleaning costs ÷ number of wearings = cost per wearing)?

3. **Reading** Read a book on seasonal colors—winter, summer, spring, and autumn. Which color best suits you?

4. **Writing** Write a smart-shopping guide for teens. Include information on inspecting clothes for quality and sticking to a budget.

CAREER Link

Interviews.
An interview is your chance to make a positive first impression on an employer. The clothes you wear to an interview might determine whether or not you obtain the job. When choosing clothes for an interview, wear clothing that is slightly dressier than what you would wear on the job. Think of a job you would like to have. What clothes would you wear to an interview for that job?

Fibers and Fabrics

Objectives

- Identify natural and manufactured fibers.
- Summarize the benefits of microfibers.
- Compare the types of fabric construction.
- Explain various dye methods.
- Describe different fabric performance finishes.

Vocabulary

- **fibers**
- **natural fibers**
- **manufactured fibers**
- **generic name**
- **trade name**
- **microfiber**
- **finishes**

Reading with Purpose

1. **Read** the title of this chapter and describe in writing what you expect to learn from it.

2. **Write** each vocabulary term in your notebook, leaving space for definitions.

3. **As you read** Chapter 34, write the definition beside each term in your notebook.

4. **After** reading the chapter, write a paragraph describing what you learned.

Selecting Fabric

The story of fabrics is both ancient history and today's news. People have been making fabric for thousands of years. Through technology and people's creativity, more fabric choices are available today than ever before.

Fabric is an important factor to consider when you buy or sew clothes. You may want your clothes to be wrinkle free, soft to the touch, or able to wick (take away) perspiration

Fig 34-1 Clothing often has to serve a purpose, and fabric helps clothing accomplish its purpose. What is the purpose of this teen's clothing?

from your body. Some qualities you are looking for are a natural part of the fabric. Other qualities are created during the manufacturing process. See **Fig. 34-1**.

Fibers

All yarns and fabric are made of fibers. **Fibers** are hairlike substances twisted together to make yarns and fabric. Just as people have individual personality traits, fibers have unique characteristics. Some fibers have greater strength, others are stretchable, and still others are sensitive to heat. Fibers are grouped into two categories: natural and manufactured.

Natural Fibers

Natural fibers are produced by nature and come from plant and animal sources. Natural fibers have been used for thousands of years. The jeans you wear today are manufactured from the same type of cotton fiber people made their clothes from centuries ago. Of course, today's jeans may have more stretch or be softer than the cotton garments of yesteryear. The following fibers are some of the more common natural fibers:

- **Cotton,** which comes from the seed pod of the cotton plant, is the most widely used natural fiber. It absorbs moisture, is cool in hot weather, and is easy to launder. Its negative features, such as wrinkling and shrinking, can be corrected with special finishes.

- **Flax** comes from the stalk of the flax plant. Linen is made from flax. Linen wrinkles easily.

- **Ramie,** a strong, durable fiber, comes from the stalk of China grass, which is grown mainly in Southeast Asia. It is often blended with other fibers, such as cotton or flax.

- **Wool** is made from the fleece of sheep and is valued for its warmth. It shrinks when washed in hot water, so it is best to dry-clean wool clothing or wash it in cold water. Wool can be damaged by insects, such as moths.

- **Silk** is spun by silkworms. It resists wrinkles and has a luxurious feeling. It is often cleaned professionally, but some silks can be hand washed. Always check your labels for safe cleaning.

Manufactured Fibers

Manufactured fibers are produced in laboratories through chemical processes and are made from substances such as wood pulp, petroleum, and other chemicals. Chemical engineers have designed these fibers to have special, desirable characteristics. They are generally strong and can spring back to their original shape, so they don't wrinkle and are easy to maintain. They are less likely to absorb water. As a result, they dry quickly and have little shrinkage.

- **Rayon** was the first manufactured fiber. Rayon is comfortable to wear and is often combined with other fibers. Some rayon fabrics can be washed, but most need to be dry cleaned. Rayon fabrics can easily shrink and should not be put in a clothes dryer.

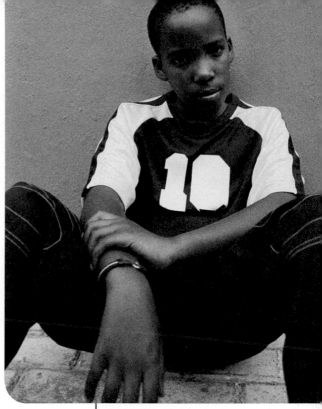

Fig 34-2 Many garments contain manufactured fibers, such as spandex. Why might this be so?

- **Polyester** is a popular manufactured fiber both in combination with other fibers or alone. Most often it is mixed with cotton to make easy-care shirts, pants, and table and bed linens. When enough polyester is blended with other fibers that require dry cleaning, such as wool and acetate, the fabric is made washable.

- **Spandex,** an elastic fiber, has replaced rubber in most clothing uses. It is often combined with other fibers to make undergarments, sportswear, and swimwear. See **Fig. 34-2**.

- **Elastoester** is a stretchable fiber that replaces spandex. You can find it in sportswear, swimwear, sweaters, hosiery, and socks.

- **Acetate,** which is similar to rayon, has a silky appearance and can drape well. Most acetate fabrics must be dry cleaned, but some can be washed. Acetate is used in special occasion dresses, blouses, and home fashions, such as draperies.

- **Triacetate** is similar to acetate, but triacetate is stronger, resists shrinking, and can be easily laundered. Triacetate is used in skirts, dresses, and sportswear.

- **Acrylic** is a soft fiber that provides warmth without being heavy. It resembles wool, yet it is easy to care for and is machine washable. It is also resistant to moths.

- **Lyocell** is similar to rayon in appearance, but it can be machine washed and dried. It is a strong fiber, absorbent, and generally comfortable to wear. Any wrinkles can be easily removed with light ironing.

- **Nylon** is a strong, lightweight, resilient fabric used in pantyhose, swimwear, and jackets. It is easy to wash, quick drying, and needs no pressing. However, it does not absorb moisture well and can be uncomfortable to wear in hot weather.

- **PLA fiber,** a new fiber whose letters stand for poly-lactic acid, is similar to cotton in appearance. It can be used alone or blended with cotton or polyester. Swimwear, sportswear, and undergarments are being made from this new fiber.

- **Polyolefin** is strong, fast drying, and able to float. Traditionally used in clothing for backpacking and canoeing, it is now being used in swimwear. It is also blended with cotton to make jeans.

Generic and Trade Names

Every manufactured fiber carries two names—a generic name and a trade name. A **generic name** is the common name for a group of similar fibers. Cotton, wool, acrylic, and spandex are examples of generic names. All members of a generic group have similar characteristics and need the same type of care. Labels on garments must list the generic name. See **Fig. 34-3.**

A **trade name** is a company's name for a specific fiber it manufactures. For example, Cresloft® and Duraspun® are both trade names for acrylic. Trade names are protected by law, which means no other company can use the name. Labels on garments may or may not list the company's trade name.

Blends

Every fiber has good qualities, but no fiber is perfect. As a result, manufacturers produce fabric blends—fabrics containing two or more fibers. Blends combine the best qualities of each fiber. For example, fabric made of a cotton-polyester blend contains the moisture absorbency of cotton and the strength and wrinkle resistance of polyester.

Microfibers

Imagine a fiber twice as fine as the finest silk and 100 times finer than human hair! This superfine manufactured fiber is known as **microfiber**. Microfibers are made from polyester, nylon, rayon, and acrylic. They also can be blended with natural fibers.

Microfibers repel water, yet they are comfortable to wear. Air passes through the fabric, and body moisture is taken from the skin's surface to the outside of the fabric. This makes microfiber perfect for undergarments and outerwear. Nylon microfiber fabrics are used mostly in active wear. Polyester microfibers are popular for luxurious blouses, skiwear, and rainwear. Polyester microfibers have the look and feel of fine silk, but they wear better, are less expensive, and can be washed like other polyesters.

Teens Speak About Fabric and Function

Trent unzipped the garment bag to reveal the navy blue blazer inside. "What do you think?"

Aaron fingered one soft, smooth sleeve. "It looks great. You'll fit right in."

"Good. I want to look right. My brother doesn't graduate from college every day, you know. But I don't want to upstage you. You'll be the man of the hour."

Aaron swallowed nervously. "Don't remind me. I hope you didn't spend too much, though. That feels like wool."

"A wool blend," Trent said, reading the label. "Dacron polyester and worsted wool. 'Looks like wool, wears like leather'—that's what the salesman said. It was a lot cheaper than pure wool. Besides, it doesn't hurt a guy to have nice clothes."

Aaron grinned. "I hear you, bro!"

Teen Connection

Imagine you need to buy clothing for a special event, such as a sibling's graduation or wedding. Which fibers would you look for on the clothing labels? How would these fibers fill your needs?

Fig 34-4

The construction of the fabric affects its appearance. What characteristics does this teen's dress have?

Fabric Construction

Fibers are twisted together to make yarns. These yarns are usually about the thickness of sewing thread. Yarns are then put together to form fabric. The way the yarns are finally arranged affects the appearance of the fabric and the wear you can expect. It also affects the care a fabric requires. See **Fig. 34-4**.

Weaving

To weave fabric, lengthwise and crosswise yarns are laced together at right angles. The tightness of the weave determines the firmness of the fabric and affects how it will wear. In general, tightly woven fabrics wear better than loosely woven fabrics. See **Fig. 34-5**.

Four types of weaves are used to make fabric:

- **Plain weave.** Each crosswise yarn passes over and under each lengthwise yarn in a plain weave. The plain weave is the simplest of all weaves. Broadcloth, chambray, and canvas are examples of plain weave.

- **Twill weave.** In a twill weave, the lengthwise yarns pass over two and then under two crosswise yarns. You see the diagonal ridges made by yarns on the surface of the fabric. The twill weave produces a stronger fabric than other weaves do. Denim is an example of a twill weave.

- **Satin weave.** The lengthwise yarns in a satin weave pass over four or more crosswise yarns and generally under one crosswise yarn. This produces a shiny surface, but the weave is not as strong as the twill and plain weaves. Satin fabrics are used for blouses and eveningwear.

- **Pile weave.** Three sets of yarn are used to make the pile weave. Pile fabrics are first woven in a plain, twill, or satin weave. Then an extra set of yarns is woven in so that loops or cut ends are produced on the fabric surface. The loops are cut to make corduroy and velvet. If left uncut, the fabric is terrycloth.

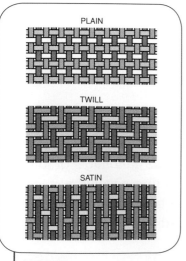

Fig 34-5 Almost all woven fabrics are based on plain, twill, and satin weaves.

Knitting

Fabrics can also be made by knitting, either by hand or machine. Knitting consists of interlocking loops of yarn row after row. Different fibers, weights, and textures are used to create distinctive designs. Knitted fabrics are stretchy and comfortable, and they generally hold their shape well. However, knits can snag more easily than woven fabric. When making knitted clothes, measurement is important. See **Fig. 34-6**.

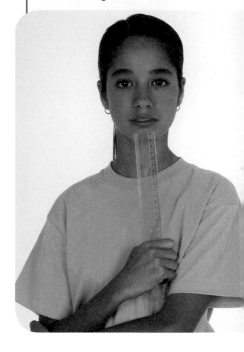

- **Single knits.** T-shirts and simple dresses are most often made with single knits. Single knits, sometimes called jersey knits, have a flat, smooth appearance on the front side and horizontal loops on the back side. Single knits have a tendency to curl at the edges.

- **Rib knits.** Rib knits have a lot of stretch, making them ideal for close-fitting tops and neck, wrist, and bottom bands on sweaters and jackets.

- **Interlock knits.** This variation of the rib knit has an identical smooth surface on both sides. Interlock knits have less stretch than rib knits, so they are used for soft, casual garments.

- **Double knits.** These knits are made with two interlocking layers on the front and back that cannot be separated. Double knits are durable and wrinkle resistant.

- **Tricot knits.** Tricot (TREE-koh) knits have narrow vertical ribs on the front and crosswise ribs on the back. They have plenty of stretch and are run proof, snag resistant, and do not ravel. Tricot knits are used for undergarments, nightgowns, and uniforms.

Other Construction Methods

Other fabrics can be made using methods other than knitting or weaving. Nonwovens are created by bonding fibers with heat, moisture, pressure, or adhesives. Felt, sew-in and fusible interfacings, and disposable surgical gowns are made from nonwoven fabric. Quilted fabrics consist of two fabric layers with a batting, or stuffing, between them.

TIPS

Learn about Fabrics

Find out what these fabrics are and how they are used:

▶ **Broadcloth.** Closely woven plain-weave fabric that is mostly cotton; used for shirts and sportswear.

▶ **Flannel.** Soft, napped fabric that is made of cotton, wool, or rayon; used for shirts, nightwear, and sheets.

▶ **Fleece.** Thick, lightweight nap; used for warm jackets and sweat suits.

Fabric Finishes

Finishes are special treatments that make a fiber or fabric more useful and appealing. They are one of the final touches put on yarns and fabrics. Clothing can have different types of finishes, including performance finishes and color.

Performance Finishes

Some finishes help the fabric perform better. For example, a shirt might have a finish that prevents wrinkling or creasing. Which of the following finishes would you like your clothing to have?

- **Crease-resistant,** sometimes called durable press, finishes are most often applied to fabrics that wrinkle easily.

- **Shrinkage control** finishes limit shrinking, though some shrinking might occur. If a fabric is labeled "preshrunk," a shrinkage finish has been applied.

- **Soil-release** finishes allow dirt and stains to be removed more easily.

- **Water- and stain-repellent** finishes help fabric repel water and oil-based stains. The water or staining liquid stays on the surface of the fabric in small beads.

- **Waterproof** finishes prevent fabric from absorbing water, which keeps the wearer dry.

- **Flame-retardant and flame-resistant** finishes reduce flaming and burning in fabrics that have been exposed to flame or high heat. See **Fig. 34-7**.

Color

Some fabric dyes come from nature, and others are developed in the lab. Dyes can be applied in various ways. Sometimes dye is applied to the yarn before it is woven into fabric. In the most common method of dyeing, called piece dyeing, dye is applied after the yarn is made into fabric. A printing process can also be used to apply color.

HOW TO ⟩ CHOOSE THE RIGHT FABRIC

Not every fabric is equally suited for every need. Knowing about the following fabric traits can help you decide whether a fabric suits your needs:

- **Strength.** A fabric should meet the wear needs of its intended use. For example, work shirts should be made of a rugged fabric.

- **Texture.** A fabric's feel and appearance affect the "mood" of the finished garment. For example, a silk scarf adds elegance to an outfit.

- **Breathing.** Air circulation helps moisture evaporate, so breathable fabrics (those that let air flow freely) are more comfortable in warm weather than in cold.

- **Weight.** A fabric's lightness or heaviness affects how it feels on your body.

- **Hand.** Hand is the term for how a fabric behaves when handled. For example, silk falls in soft folds. Hand affects a garment's wear and appearance.

- **Care needs.** Weigh the care needs of a fabric against the use you expect from the garment. Is a dry-clean-only garment worth the cost? Also, compare its needs with those of other fabrics. Does it require extra energy for a separate wash?

TAKE **ACTION**

With a partner, describe a garment that meets a specific purpose, such as a dress shirt for office work. Using the characteristics given here, suggest good fabrics for that garment.

Review & Activities

Chapter Summary

- Natural and manufactured fibers have characteristics that affect how they wear.
- Microfibers have many benefits and are often blended with natural fibers.
- The way yarns are woven affects the appearance of the fabric and the wear you can expect.
- Various methods can be used to dye fabric.
- Performance finishes are applied to improve a fabric's appearance, wear, and care requirements.

Reviewing Key Terms & Ideas

1. What are **fibers**?
2. Where do **natural fibers** come from?
3. Identify four natural fibers.
4. What are the advantages of **manufactured fibers**?
5. List four manufactured fibers.
6. What is the difference between a **generic name** and a **trade name**?
7. Why are fabric blends popular?
8. What is a **microfiber**?
9. Name four types of weaves.
10. What are the advantages of tricot knits?
11. What are **finishes**?

Thinking Critically

1. **Making comparisons.** Compare the different types of natural fiber. Which would you prefer for your lifestyle? Why?
2. **Predicting outcomes.** If manufactured fibers had not been developed, how would clothing design and care be different today?
3. **Analyzing situations.** What fibers and fiber finishes would you suggest to a friend looking for clothes to wear on a camping trip? Why would you suggest these finishes?

Review & Activities

Applying Your Learning

1. **Wardrobe assessment.** Review the clothes in your wardrobe. What fibers are most frequently represented? Why do you think these fibers were selected by the manufacturer? How have these clothes met your expectations?

2. **Fabric comparison.** Select a fabric that contains only natural fiber, such as 100 percent cotton. Select another fabric made only of manufactured fibers. Compare the care labels. How are the care requirements similar and different? Which fabric requires the least amount of care?

3. **Fiber design.** Assume you are developing a new manufactured fiber to be used in sportswear. Describe the characteristics of the fiber and the care requirements.

4. **Fabric research.** Use print and online sources to find out about fibers used in specialty clothing, such as the uniforms of professional athletes, firefighters, or astronauts. How have fibers affected people's performance on the job?

5. **Fabric analysis.** Gather a variety of fabric samples. Identify each type of fabric and write its name on an index card, along with its care requirements.

6. **Dye process.** Decorate a T-shirt using a tie-dye process. Observe how the dye interacts with the fiber. Research any special care requirements needed for your T-shirt.

Making Connections

1. (**Reading**) Read reference books and Internet sources to research the early history of a natural fiber. Where was it discovered? How was the fiber identified? How has its use changed since its early history?

2. (**Writing**) Select one manufactured fiber and write a promotional article telling consumers about the advantages of buying garments made with this fiber. Emphasize wear and care features.

3. (**Reading**) Read online sources to find out how microfibers were developed and how they are currently manufactured.

CAREER Link

Thank-You Letter.
After an interview, always send a handwritten thank-you letter to the person who interviewed you. Thank the interviewer for his or her time. Express your enthusiasm for the job and stress your experience and skills. Be sure to include your contact information, such as your phone number or e-mail address. How do you think a thank-you letter affects an employer's impression of you?

Caring for Clothing

Objectives

- Give guidelines for routine clothing care.
- Identify clothes-storage strategies.
- Demonstrate laundering procedures.
- Compare pressing and ironing techniques.
- Practice simple clothing repairs.

Vocabulary

- **pretreatment**
- **pressing**
- **ironing**
- **dry cleaning**

Reading with Purpose

1. **Write down** the colored headings from Chapter 35 in your notebook.

2. **As you read** the text under each heading, visualize what you are reading.

3. **Reflect** on what you read by writing a few sentences under each heading to describe it.

4. **Continue** this process until you have finished the chapter. Reread your notes.

Routine Clothing Care

Michael picked up his pants from the heap of clothes on the floor. "Great," he thought. "My only dress pants are a wrinkled mess." He pulled a white button-down shirt from a hanger and noticed a tear in the sleeve. "I can't believe I have to accept my sports award in clothes like this. The varsity coach isn't going to be very impressed."

Have you ever been in a situation like Michael's? If so, you probably need to take routine care of your clothing. A routine

When caring for clothing, be sure to:

- Always keep detergents and chemicals out of reach of children and pets.

- Use sharp sewing equipment, such as needles and scissors, properly and store equipment in closed containers.

- Never use a razor blade to cut pills off clothing.

is something you do regularly. Taking a little extra time each day to wash, mend, and properly store clothes can prevent you from having big clothing problems later. Make the following suggestions part of your daily clothing care routine:

- **Dress and undress carefully.** Open clothing fasteners, such as buttons, zippers, and snaps, to prevent clothing tears. Remove your shoes before getting in and out of shorts and pants.

- **Treat stains.** Look for any stains on your clothes and try to remove them right away. The longer a stain remains, the harder it is to take out.

- **Remove lint and pills.** Use a lint roller, a lint brush, or a battery-operated or electric lint and pill remover. Rubbing fabric softener sheets across clothes also removes lint.

- **Repair clothes regularly.** Check for repairs you need to make, such as replacing buttons or fixing a seam, and make the repairs as soon as possible.

- **Store clothes properly.** Put dirty clothes in a laundry basket or hamper. Fold or hang up clean clothes. See **Fig. 35-1**.

Clothing Storage

Do you have a small closet or dresser? Organizing your clothing can increase your storage space. Proper storage can also keep your clothes from wrinkling or stretching out of shape. Here are some tips to help you properly store your clothes:

- **Fold clothing for drawer storage.** Folded storage is good for garments such as sweaters and knitwear. Avoid stacking too many folded items into a drawer. Stuffing drawers will cause clothing to crease. Also, fold garments a different way each time to prevent permanent creasing. You can also put tissue paper between garment folds to keep items from wrinkling. Roll items that won't wrinkle, such as undergarments and socks, to save space. Always place the heaviest folded garments on the bottom of a drawer. Smaller items can be placed in boxes or in drawer dividers to keep them in place.

Fig 35-1
There are numerous ways to organize a closet. Which organizational strategies in this photo can you try in your own closet?

- **Hang clothing properly.** Avoid all-wire hangers, unless they are covered. Wire hangers can become rusty and stain clothing, and the metal edges can snag the fabric. Plastic hangers provide good support for tightly woven, light-weight shirts and blouses. Padded fabric hangers are good for sheer-fabric blouses, jackets, and dresses. Use garment fasteners at the neckline of shirts and blouses and at the waistline of slacks and skirts to keep them positioned on the hanger. Whenever possible, provide enough space between hanging garments to allow the air to circulate around the clothes. This helps prevent wrinkling and musty odors.

- **Store clothing that is out of season.** Be sure the clothes and the storage area are clean. Attic and basement areas are often too damp, too hot, or too cold for good storage. Use garment bags or storage boxes to protect clothes from dust, dirt, and insects. Cedar chips, cedar blocks, herbal bags, or just loose bay leaves work well in closets.

When removing stains, place a clean cloth behind the stained fabric layer to keep the stain and the remover from bleeding through to another layer of fabric. The following tips can help you with problem stains:

▶ **Blood.** Soak the fabric first in cold water for 30 minutes and then in a presoak product. Wash in cool water only.

▶ **Oil and grease.** Use a stain remover according to label directions. Wash as directed on garment care label.

▶ **Soft drinks, tea, and coffee.** Sponge the stain with cool water. Use stain remover. Wash as directed.

▶ **Food stains.** Soak a clean cloth with club soda. Press the wet cloth on the stain, blotting until the stain is removed. Do not rub.

Washing Clothes

Leigh's mother had been out of town for a week, and Leigh's dirty clothes were spilling out of her hamper and onto the floor. "I'll just toss all of these clothes into the washer and surprise Mom when she gets home. I've seen her do laundry a ton of times. How hard can it be?"

Doing laundry isn't difficult, but carelessness can create some clothing disasters, such as shrunken or stained garments. However, laundry must be done. Keeping your clothes clean keeps them free of dirt, stains, and odors. When done correctly, laundering, or washing, clothes keeps their colors brighter and helps them last longer.

Care Labels

Clothing labels are your guide to keeping your clothes looking fresh and clean. Clothing manufacturers are required to attach or stamp care labels onto garments. The labels explain, using either words or symbols, how to properly wash the clothes. Common fabric symbols are shown in **Fig. 35-2**. You can also use labels to sort your clothes (see page 552). Always read the care instructions on a garment before you begin a wash!

Pretreating Clothes

Pretreatment refers to any special attention you give a garment before laundering. Pretreatment helps remove heavy soil and stains that washing alone may not remove. Necklines and the cuffs of long-sleeve shirts often need pretreatment. You can use a soil-and-stain remover or an enzyme presoak. Always read the package directions.

If the stain is not entirely removed after washing, pretreat and wash the item again before drying. The heat from a clothes dryer can set a stain, making it impossible to remove. Wash again before drying!

Fabric Care Symbols

WASH	Cool/Cold Temperature / Normal Cycle	Warm Temperature / Permanent Press Cycle	Hot Temperature / Delicate/ Gentle Cycle	Hand Wash	Do Not Wring / Do Not Wash
BLEACH	Bleach As Needed	Nonchlorine Bleach As Needed			Do Not Bleach
TUMBLE	No Heat/ Air / Any Heat/ Normal Cycle	Low Heat / Permanent Press Cycle	Medium Heat / Delicate/ Gentle Cycle	High Heat	Do Not Tumble Dry
DRY	Line Dry	Drip Dry	Dry Flat	Dry in the Shade	Do Not Dry (Used With Do Not Wash)
IRON	Low Heat	Medium Heat	High Heat	Do Not Iron with Steam	Do Not Iron
DRY-CLEAN	Dry-Clean				Do Not Dry-Clean

Fig 35-2 Checking fabric care symbols before doing laundry will help you prevent laundry mishaps.

Machine Washing

You have probably seen the commercials for laundry products on television—detergents, bleaches, and fabric softeners, each with a different job. Do you know what those jobs are? The primary job of detergents is to remove dirt from clothes. Bleaches are used to remove stains and to whiten and brighten 100 percent cotton fabrics. Fabric softeners reduce static cling, make fabrics softer, and reduce wrinkling.

I Can Sort My Laundry

As a young child, you were not expected to do the laundry. You couldn't read the care labels, reach the controls on the washing machine, or use the detergent. Now, you can do all of those things—you can do the laundry. Before you can start the washing machine, however, you need to prepare your clothing. One important laundry task is sorting clothes.

Get Organized

Gather four different-colored duffle bags. If you don't have duffle bags, you can use pillowcases or laundry baskets. You'll use one bag for light and another for dark clothing. The third bag will be used for heavily soiled clothes, and the fourth for clothing requiring special care.

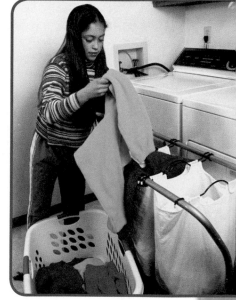

the care labels on each garment. The labels will tell you the washing method, safe washing temperature, and the method and safe temperature for drying. Be sure to pretreat any stains, following package instructions. Your clothes can remain in the bags until laundry day.

Laundry Day

When laundry day arrives, empty a bag of clothes into the washing machine. If the bag is dirty, toss it in, too! Each bag is its own wash load, so you might do two, three, or four loads of wash. Be sure you do a wash only if you have a full load. If a bag doesn't contain a full load, wait until the next laundry day or ask family members if they would like to combine their clothes with yours to make a full load.

Daily Tasks

Place the clothing in the appropriate bag or pillowcase as you undress each day. Check

In addition to detergent, you need to consider the water temperature and the wash cycle when machine washing. Different fabrics and types of clothing require different water temperatures and wash cycles. Place clothes loosely in the washer tub, and be careful not to overload the washer.

Hand Washing

Some clothing requires hand washing. To hand wash a garment, follow these steps:

1. Select a detergent suitable for delicate garments and follow the package directions.
2. Put water into a sink or container large enough for the clothes to move freely.
3. Add the detergent and mix.
4. Add the clothes and soak for 5 to 30 minutes to release the dirt.
5. Gently squeeze the sudsy water through the garment. Do not twist the clothing.
6. Drain the sink and add fresh water. Rinse at least twice in fresh water to remove both suds and soil.
7. Gently squeeze water from the garment and either lay it flat or hang it to dry, according to care label directions. See **Fig. 35-3**.

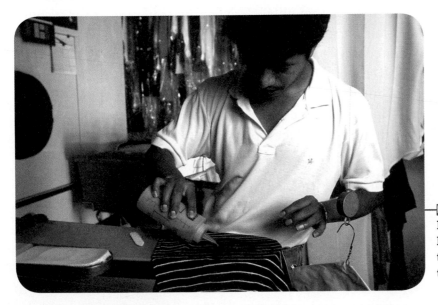

Fig 35-3
Many hand-wash-only clothes can be pretreated for stains. Read the garment's care label before treating for stains.

TIPS
Take Environmental Action

Here are some actions you can take to minimize the effects of laundry products on the environment:

▶ Always follow the manufacturer's directions.

▶ Use concentrated liquids or powders.

▶ Use combination products that blend two or more functions.

▶ Buy refills whenever possible because they use less packaging and storage space.

▶ Dispose of unused laundry products properly. Flush most laundry products down the drain with plenty of water. Dispose of solid products, such as dryer sheets, in the trash or recycle them as dust cloths.

Drying Clothes

Generally, articles that can be washed together can be dried together. However, some need to be dried in a particular way. Always follow instructions on the care label.

Pressing and Ironing

After washing and drying, some clothes wrinkle and need to be pressed or ironed. **Pressing** is the process of lifting and lowering an iron onto areas of the fabric. **Ironing** involves moving the iron back and forth over the fabric to remove wrinkles. Use the iron temperature setting shown on the care label.

Leaving the iron on too long in one spot can cause damage to the fabric. It can quickly burn the garment. Also, never leave an iron unattended!

Steamers can also be used to remove wrinkles. Fabric steamers use heat to turn water into steam. The combination of heat and steam releases the wrinkles. Steamers work faster than irons and do not scorch or burn fabrics. They come in large sizes for home use and smaller travel sizes.

Dry Cleaning

Some clothing care labels say to dry-clean garments. **Dry cleaning** means to clean with chemicals rather than with water and detergent. The cleaned garment is then steamed to remove wrinkles.

You will find two types of dry-cleaning services. Professional dry cleaners, although more expensive, can remove most spots and stains. Professional pressing is part of that service. Coin-operated dry-cleaning machines cost less. However, they do not always provide special spot and stain treatment, and you must do your own pressing. You can buy products to do your own dry cleaning at home, but you need a dryer to do so. Be sure to follow product directions.

Repairing Clothing

Your clothes look better when they are kept in good repair. Simple repairs are not difficult to make, but you must do some planning. Before you plunge into repair work, ask yourself a few questions. Do you have the skills to make the repair? If the garment is too severely damaged and not wearable, you may want to pass up the repair. If you can make the repair, do you have the right supplies and equipment? If not, you will need to ask someone to help you. Make sure you have all of the supplies and equipment you need before you start. See **Fig. 35-4**.

Fig 35-4 Gathering your supplies before making a clothing repair will save you time and frustration.

Rips and Tears

Ripped seams are generally easy to repair. By hand or with a sewing machine, make a new line of stitching. Begin and end the stitching just beyond the ripped section and secure each end of stitching. If handstitching, backstitch to strengthen the seam.

Iron-on mending tape can help you repair a tear. Iron the tape to the inside of the garment. Be sure to follow the package directions. Tears can also be repaired with patches on the right side of the garment. Use hand or machine stitching to attach the patch. You can also use fusible patches or iron-on patches to repair tears. Each of these is pressed onto the garment with an iron.

Buttons

There are two types of buttons: sew-through and shank. With sew-through buttons, the thread comes up through the button and shows on the top side. Shank buttons have a shank, or stem, underneath to hold the thread. The shank gives you room to work the button through the buttonhole. Because sew-through buttons do not have shanks, you should make a thread shank as you sew them on.

Follow these steps when replacing a sew-through button; see **Fig. 35-5**:

1. Place a pin where the missing button was located. Select a matching thread color.
2. Double the thread in the needle and knot both ends together. Bring the needle up from the wrong side to the right side of the garment.
3. Take a small stitch to secure the thread knot. Remove the pin you used to mark the button replacement.
4. Bring the needle through the button. Place a toothpick or needle across the top of the button to allow a thread shank.
5. Make several stitches through the fabric, the button, and over the toothpick or needle.
6. Remove the toothpick or needle. Bring the sewing needle and thread between the button and the fabric. Wrap the thread around the threads under the button several times to make a thread shank.
7. Bring the needle back to the wrong side of the fabric and fasten the thread securely to the fabric. Clip the thread. Your button is now securely attached.

Fig 35-5 You can sew a button in a few easy steps.

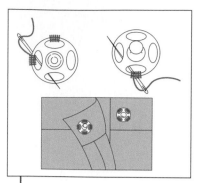

Fig 35-6 To sew a snap, first sew the ball section, then sew the socket section.

Snaps

An opening that does not have much strain is often fastened with a snap. Hooks and eyes are often used to fasten openings on which there is a strain. To sew snaps, follow these steps:

1. Place the ball section of the snap about ⅛ inch (3 mm) from the underside of the overlap. Make several small stitches through each hole of the snap using a single thread. Sew through only one layer of fabric so that the stitches do not show on the right side.

2. Pin the closing together and mark the socket location, for the flat part of the snap. Mark the position of the socket by placing a pin through the center hole of the ball section. Sew the socket in place as you did the ball section. Carry the thread under the snap and secure. See **Fig. 35-6**.

HOW TO PACK A BAG

Packing a bag, or suitcase, is an exercise in engineering, as well as in clothing care. The goal is to fit as many items as you can into a space about the size of a school locker and find them still looking good when you take them out. To achieve this feat, remember these packing pointers:

STEP 1 | **Make a list of needed items.** Refer to it when packing. If traveling by plane, make sure you know what items are forbidden in carry-on luggage.

STEP 2 | **Find out what you can leave behind.** If you will be staying at a hotel, call ahead or check the Web site to learn whether items such as irons and hair dryers are available to guests.

STEP 3 | **Plan your wardrobe.** To get the most use from the fewest garments, choose mix-and-match clothing and accessories to suit whatever occasions you expect.

STEP 4 | **Prepare your clothing.** Iron clothes just before packing. Close buttons and zippers.

STEP 5 | **Pack heavy and large items.** To make the most of space, fill the suitcase in layers. Fill the bottom first, then lay clothes on top. Place shoes, guidebooks, and other heavy objects on the bottom. Place shoes sole-to-sole and heel-to-toe in plastic bags to keep clothes clean. Stuff them with socks or pantyhose.

Hooks and Eyes

To properly sew hooks and eyes, follow these steps:

1. Place the hook on the underside of the overlap at least ⅛ inch (3 mm) from the edge. Stitch through each loop, around the curve. Sew through only one layer of fabric so that the stitches will not show on the right side.
2. Take three to four stitches around the shank of the hook so that it is held down firmly.
3. Overlap the edge and mark the position of the straight eye on the left-hand side with a pin. Stitch the eye in place through both loops. Fasten the thread. See **Fig. 35-7**.

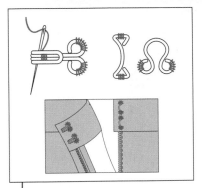

Fig 35-7 To sew a hook and eye, first sew the hook, then sew the eye.

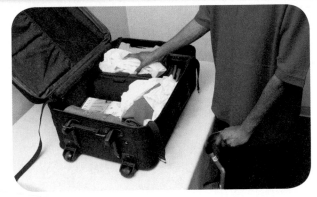

STEP 6 | **Minimize wrinkling.** If your clothes are in dry-cleaner bags, pack them in the bags. Roll jeans, T-shirts, and other wrinkle-resistant clothes tightly. Rolling two or more items together "fattens" the rolls, making fewer wrinkles. To reduce wrinkles, layer clothes with white tissue paper. If you are staying at a hotel or motel, use the tissue paper to line the dresser or cabinet drawers.

STEP 7 | **Pack the small stuff.** Fill corners and small spaces, such as the inside of shoes, with nonbreakable belongings, such as a travel clock and boxed jewelry. Place travel-sized liquid toiletries in a zippered plastic bag. Add a plastic bag for dirty laundry.

TAKE **ACTION**

Use these suggestions to pack a suitcase with items you would need for a trip you plan to or would like to take. Leave the bag packed for at least six hours, if possible. Remove the clothes and assess the results.

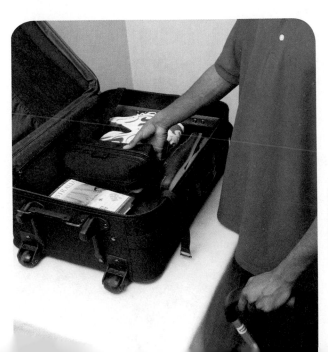

Review & Activities

Chapter Summary

- Routine care helps keep clothes in good condition.
- Organizing your clothing can increase your storage space and keep clothes from wrinkling and stretching.
- Always follow care labels when laundering clothes.
- You can remove wrinkles from clothing by pressing or ironing them.
- Simple clothing repairs maintain the appearance and extend the use of garments.

Reviewing Key Terms & Ideas

1. What are five things you can do to take routine care of your clothes?
2. Why should space be left between hanging garments?
3. Why is it important to sort clothes?
4. What does **pretreatment** mean?
5. List three types of laundry products.
6. What is the difference between **pressing** and **ironing**?
7. Define **dry cleaning**.
8. What questions should you ask yourself before repairing a garment?
9. What tools can you use to repair tears?
10. Explain the difference between sew-through and shank buttons.

Thinking Critically

1. **Analyzing problems.** Imagine that you just finished a load of wash and your white garments are now pale pink. What could have happened? How can you prevent the problem next time?
2. **Making generalizations.** What do you think is the most important step in the laundry process? Why?
3. **Defending positions.** Some adults think teens are not capable of washing their own clothes. How would you respond to that viewpoint?

Review & Activities

Applying Your Learning

1. **Routine care.** Follow the routine care steps in the chapter for one week. Evaluate your results. How did routine care of your clothes affect your appearance?

2. **Storage plan.** Create a storage plan for your clothes. Consider closet and drawer space. List the steps you need to take to organize your clothing. Then put your plan into place. Afterward, evaluate your results. How do you think your organizational plan will help you?

3. **Care labels.** Bring several garments with care labels to class. In a small group, read and discuss the care labels. What do the symbols mean?

4. **Stain removal.** Stain two or three light-colored fabric swatches with different stains, such as chocolate, grass, or ketchup. Use a pretreatment product on the stains, following package instructions. Leave the product in for a day, if possible, before rinsing. Which stains came clean? How do you think the type of fabric affected the results?

5. **Tear repair.** Choose a torn garment and organize the supplies and equipment you need to repair it. If necessary, have your teacher show you how to make the repair. Make the repair and share the results with the class.

6. **Button workshop.** On a garment or on a swatch of fabric, follow the directions in this chapter to attach a sew-through button. Evaluate the quality of your work. Is the button secure?

Making Connections

1. **Reading** Read magazines and catalogs that contain storage products and strategies. How can you recreate these organizational strategies in your own home for little or no cost?

2. **Writing** Write a laundry handbook for teens who have no experience laundering clothes. Include art or photographs to illustrate your instructions. Share your handbook with the class.

3. **Math** A bottle of liquid detergent costs contains 100 oz. of detergent. You use 4 oz. of detergent for each load of wash. How many loads of wash can you do with one bottle of detergent?

CAREER Link

Applying for a Job. When applying for a job, your appearance counts. In addition to selecting the right type of clothes, you need to make sure your clothing is clean and in good repair—that means free of tears and wrinkles. Imagine two people dressed for a job interview, one in a clean, neat outfit and the other in a wrinkled, dirty one. In a small group, discuss the impression you have of each person. How do clothes make a difference?

Preparing to Sew

Objectives

- Demonstrate the use of sewing tools and equipment.
- Practice measuring to determine correct pattern size.
- Interpret information on a pattern envelope.
- Summarize guidelines for selecting fabric and notions.
- Explain how to use a pattern to construct a garment.

Vocabulary

- tension
- interfacing
- notions
- ease
- selvage
- bias

Reading with Purpose

1. **As you read** Chapter 36, create an outline in your notebook using the colored headings.

2. **Write** a question under each heading that you can use to guide your reading.

3. **Answer** the question under each heading as you read the chapter. Record your answers.

4. **Ask** your teacher to help with answers you could not find in this chapter.

Learning About Sewing Equipment

Welcome to the world of sewing! Sewing gives you the opportunity to use patterns and your own creativity to create your own clothing and home fashions. If you have not sewn before, you may be a bit anxious. The information in this chapter will help make your sewing tasks successful, in addition to keeping you safe and your sewing equipment in good working order.

Small Sewing Equipment

If you have the right tools, sewing projects will be more fun and your work will be faster and easier. Small sewing equipment consists of cutting and measuring equipment, marking equipment, and pressing equipment, as well as a few other assorted items.

Measuring and Cutting Equipment

You will use cutting equipment to cut fabric and thread. Keep your cutting equipment sharp by using it only for sewing. You will use measuring equipment to measure patterns, fabric, and garment pieces accurately as you sew. See **Fig. 36-1**. Here are the basics:

- **Small scissors.** Use small scissors to clip threads and trim (cut off) fabric.

- **Shears.** Cut fabric with shears. Shears have long blades with one handle for the thumb and one handle for two or more fingers. Bent-handled shears improve your accuracy because the fabric lies flat and is hardly lifted from the table as you cut.

- **Seam ripper.** The seam ripper has a hooklike point. It is used to cut and remove stitches, mostly in seams.

- **Tape measure.** This is a flexible, narrow strip of durable plastic or cloth used to take body measurements and measure fabric.

- **Yardstick.** This ruler, which is 36 inches (91.5 cm) or one yard long, is useful for measuring patterns and fabrics on a flat surface and for checking hemlines.

- **Sewing or seam gauge.** This small, metal ruler has a slide marker that can be set to gauge specific measurements, such as the width of a seam or hem.

Marking Equipment

Marking equipment helps you transfer construction markings, such as buttonhole and pocket positions, from your pattern pieces to the fabric. See **Fig. 36-2**. The following items are most commonly used:

- **Tracing wheel.** Use a tracing wheel and a special, colored waxed paper to transfer pattern markings to the wrong side of fabric.

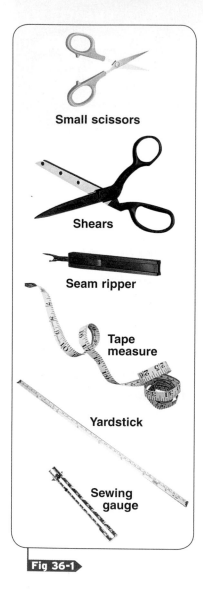

Small scissors

Shears

Seam ripper

Tape measure

Yardstick

Sewing gauge

Fig 36-1 ▶

Tracing wheel

Tailor's chalk

Fabric marker

Fig 36-2 ▶

- **Fabric marker.** This special pen marks fabrics temporarily. Some fabric pen marks can be removed with water. Others fade after a short period. Test fabric markers on a fabric scrap before using them.

- **Tailor's chalk.** Pencils, small squares, or small wheels of chalk or wax are also used to mark fabric.

Pressing Equipment

Pressing your project as you sew helps keep your work neat and gives it a finished and professional look. Basic pressing equipment includes an iron and ironing board. Choose a steam iron and a well-padded ironing board with a tight-fitting cover. You also need a press cloth when pressing certain fabrics to keep them from scorching or developing a shine or glossy marking. You can buy ready-made press cloths or use a clean handkerchief or large, lightweight cloth.

Other Small Equipment

Some other small sewing aids can help you as you work on your sewing project. **Fig. 36-3** shows some common sewing aids.

Safety Check

To help prevent injuries while sewing, take these precautions:

- Store pins and needles in a pincushion rather than in a box to avoid spills. Do not put pins in your mouth.

- Keep shears, scissors, and seam rippers closed when not in use. Pass sharp objects handle first.

- Use small boxes or plastic bags to store small items such as thimbles, fabric markers, buttons, and other fasteners.

- Store all sewing equipment away from small children.

- After use, allow an iron to cool. Wrap the cord properly before putting it away.

Straight pins. These are used to anchor the pattern to the fabric and to hold layers of fabric together for sewing.

Pincushion. Use a pincushion to keep needles and pins handy while you work. Many pincushions come with an attached emery bag. Push rusty or sticky needles and pins into the bag a few times and it will clean them.

Thimble. A thimble can be used to push the needle through fabric while hand sewing. A thimble should fit snugly on the third finger of the hand that holds the needle.

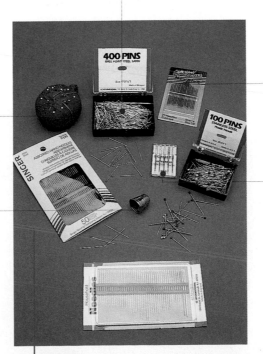

Hand sewing needles. Needles are numbered from 1 (very thick) to 12 (very fine). A sharp point and medium length make "sharps" best for general hand sewing, try a size 7 or 8.

Machine needles. Machine needles range from 60 (very fine for delicate fabrics) to 110 (very thick for coarse, heavy fabrics). Select the size best suited for your fabric. Use ballpoint needles for knit fabric. A needle that's dull, bent, or rough needs to be replaced.

Fig 36-3 Sewing aids help make sewing jobs easier. You can find these and other sewing aids at local or online stores.

Sewing Machines

A sewing machine is one of the most important and most expensive pieces of sewing equipment you will use. Machines range from basic models to computerized machines that allow you to embroider and monogram with the touch of a button. However, you don't need a fancy machine. Basic models can handle most general sewing. Take some time to learn about the parts of the sewing machine and how to use it safely. Read the machine's operating manual or ask someone to show you how to operate and care for the machine.

Parts of the Machine

All sewing machines operate in a similar manner. Knowing the major parts helps you operate it successfully and safely. The parts shown in **Fig. 36-4** are found on most machines. Check your manual to see where they're located on your machine. Machines that embroider and monogram have additional parts or components.

1. **Hand wheel.** This large wheel on the right side of the machine controls the up-and-down movement of the needle and thread take-up leaver.

2. **Thread take-up lever.** This lever feeds thread from the spool to the needle.

3. **Throat plate.** This is the metal plate under the machine needle. On most machines, the throat plate is also etched with seam allowance markings for accurate sewing.

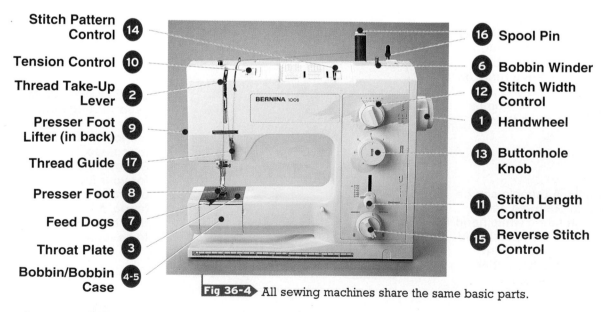

Stitch Pattern Control 14
Tension Control 10
Thread Take-Up Lever 2
Presser Foot Lifter (in back) 9
Thread Guide 17
Presser Foot 8
Feed Dogs 7
Throat Plate 3
Bobbin/Bobbin Case 4-5

16 Spool Pin
6 Bobbin Winder
12 Stitch Width Control
1 Handwheel
13 Buttonhole Knob
11 Stitch Length Control
15 Reverse Stitch Control

Fig 36-4 All sewing machines share the same basic parts.

4. **Bobbin.** This small, flat spool holds the bottom thread.

5. **Bobbin case.** This holds the bobbin and is found beneath the throat plate.

6. **Bobbin winder.** This spindle holds the bobbin while thread is wound from the thread spool to the bobbin. The location of this spindle varies with each machine.

7. **Feed dogs.** The feed dogs are a set of metal "teeth" that move the fabric during stitching.

8. **Presser foot.** This holds the fabric firmly in place against the feed dogs for sewing.

9. **Presser foot lifter.** This lever raises and lowers the presser foot.

10. **Tension control.** This dial adjusts the tightness or looseness of the needle thread.

11. **Stitch length control.** This is used to adjust the length of stitches from short to long.

12. **Stitch width control.** This control is used to adjust the width of other stitches, such as the zigzag stitch.

13. **Buttonhole control.** The built-in buttonhole maker creates perfect buttonholes.

14. **Stitch pattern control.** The stitch pattern control can be adjusted to make different stitching patterns.

15. **Reverse stitch control.** This button or lever allows backward stitching.

16. **Spool pin.** This pin holds the spool of thread.

17. **Thread guides.** These guide the thread as it travels from the spool to the needle.

18. **Foot or knee control.** This control regulates the starting, running, and stopping of the machine (not shown).

Threading the Machine

Before threading the machine, raise the presser foot and turn the hand wheel toward you to raise the needle and take-up leaver to the highest position. Thread must also be wound onto a bobbin. Follow directions in the owner's manual for threading the machine.

Buy a Sewing Machine

Here are some things to check when buying a sewing machine:

▶ The machine starts and stops smoothly.

▶ The bobbin is easy to wind and insert.

▶ The foot pedal is comfortable and easy to use.

▶ The needle area is well lit.

▶ Machine stitching is even and attractive.

▶ You understand the owner's manual and know whom to contact if you have a problem with the machine.

Fig 36-5

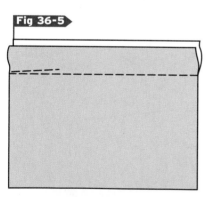

Reverse stitching or backstitching

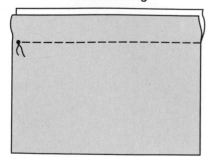

Tied threads

After threading the machine and putting the filled bobbin into the bobbin case, bring the bobbin thread up through the hole in the throat plate. To do this, hold the end of the needle thread while turning the hand wheel toward you one full turn. The needle thread will pull up a loop of bobbin thread. Pull up on this loop until the thread end is out of the throat plate.

Machine Stitching

All machines do straight stitching the same way. If you haven't sewn before or will be using a different machine, practice stitching. Here are the general directions:

1. **Raise the take-up lever and needle to the highest point.** Do the same when you finish stitching. This keeps the thread from pulling out of the needle or tangling in the bobbin.

2. **Pull the needle thread and bobbin thread to the right side of the presser foot.** The threads should also be underneath the presser foot.

3. **Place the fabric under the presser foot.** First lower the needle into the fabric at the beginning of the stitching line and then lower the presser foot. The bulk of the fabric should be to the left of the machine.

4. **Start the machine slowly.** A smooth, steady speed allows better control.

5. **Use the throat plate markings to guide your fabric through the machine.** This helps you keep an even seam width.

6. **Slow the machine speed for the last few stitches.** This helps prevent stitching beyond the edge of the fabric.

7. **Secure stitching at both ends of a seam.** There are several ways to do this. Backstitching, or retracing your stitches about ½ inch (1.3 cm), is done by using the reverse stitch control on the machine. Another way to secure stitching is to tie the threads at the end of the seam. See **Fig. 36-5**.

Adjusting Stitch Length and Tension

The correct stitch length and tension make a seam attractive and strong. A medium-length stitch (2 to 2.5 mm or 10 to 12 stitches or per inch) is used for most fabrics. Some fabrics and sewing steps require different stitch lengths. Check the machine stitching on a two-layer scrap of your fabric before beginning to sew. You can make changes in the stitch length by adjusting the stitch length control.

Tension refers to the tightness or looseness of the thread. The tension is balanced when the stitching looks the same on both sides. It is not in balance if thread loops form on either side of the fabric. Newer machines seldom require tension adjustments when regular sewing thread is used in the needle and the bobbin. If tension problems occur, check the machine and bobbin threading before adjusting the tension dial. Incorrect threading is often the cause. If the tension needs adjusting, your machine manual will tell you how to correct it. If the machine jams because thread has become tangled in the bobbin area, the thread must be carefully removed. Turn off the machine and check the manual or ask your teacher for further directions. See **Fig. 36-6**.

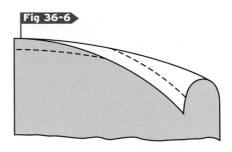

Fig 36-6

Balanced tension

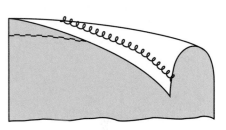
Upper tension too tight

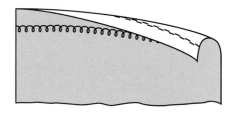
Lower tension too tight

Serger Sewing

Why do the seams in ready-to-wear clothes appear so smooth and neat? You can make garments that look as good as ready-to-wear clothing by using a serger. A serger, or overlock machine, stitches, trims, and finishes a seam in one step, and it's twice as fast as a sewing machine. Some garments, such as sweatshirts, can be sewn entirely on the serger. However, many projects require a sewing machine and a serger.

Comparing Sergers and Sewing Machines

Unlike sewing machines, sergers have cutters that trim the seam before it is stitched, and they can also use two needles, depending on the model. Sergers use more thread than sewing machines. Most serger thread comes on cones that hold 1,000 or more yards. Some sergers use two or more cones of thread for stitching. Sergers also have no bobbin. Two loopers take the place of bobbins.

When sewing with a serger, it is not necessary to lift the presser foot when starting to sew, unless the fabric is thick. The serger feed dogs grip the fabric as you begin to sew. Also, you should never sew over pins with a serger because the pins will damage the serger's cutting knives and the pins could fly out and hurt you.

Using a Serger

All brands of sergers sew basically the same way. When you feed the fabric into the machine, the feed dogs grip the fabric and pull it toward the cutters. The cutters trim the fabric edges before the fabric reaches the loopers and needles for stitching. Rather than backstitching, you simply run the fabric off the serger behind the needles. Securing the ends of stitching is not necessary for most projects. See **Fig. 36-7**.

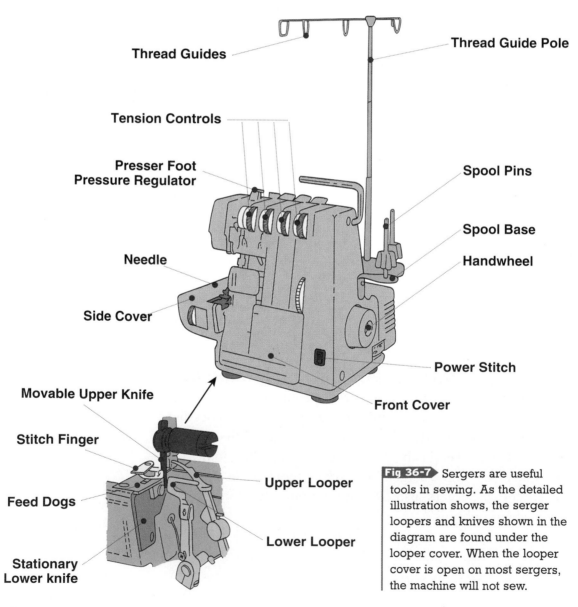

Fig 36-7 Sergers are useful tools in sewing. As the detailed illustration shows, the serger loopers and knives shown in the diagram are found under the looper cover. When the looper cover is open on most sergers, the machine will not sew.

Selecting a Pattern

You can find hundreds of sewing projects by looking through a pattern catalog, either in the fabric store or online. Catalogs are organized into different sections, such as easy-to-sew styles, sportswear, and dresses, and show different views of a garment. Patterns in catalogs have assigned numbers. When you find the pattern you want, write the number down. You can find the pattern in the numbered cabinet drawers at the fabric store.

Pattern Envelopes

The front and back of the pattern envelope contain important information that you can use to select a project. It also provides a list of the supplies you need for a project. **Fig. 36-8** shows the parts of a pattern envelope.

Taking Measurements

When you construct garments, you must take body measurements. Take the measurements over close-fitting clothes. Remove bulky sweaters, jackets, and belts. **Fig. 36-9** gives guidelines for measuring specific body parts. When you take measurements, hold the tape measure, with two fingers beneath the tape, so that it fits snugly. Be sure it is not too tight or too loose. It is easier to work with a partner so that you can measure each other. Write each measurement down as you take it. You will use your body measurements to determine your figure type and the pattern size.

- **Figure types** are size categories, such as juniors and misses, based on height and body proportions. Girls also need to know back waist length to identify figure type. Compare this information with the body measurement charts in the back of the pattern catalog to determine your figure type.

- **Pattern size** is determined by comparing your chest or bust, waist, and hip measurements with those listed on the pattern envelope. You will choose your pattern size for most garments according to your chest or bust measurement. When making pants or a skirt, use your waist measurement. However, if your hips are large compared with your waist, use the hip measurement for the best fit. When your measurements fall between two sizes, pick the smaller size unless the design is close fitting.

Care for Your Machine

Routine care will keep your sewing machine in good working order. To care for your machine, follow these steps:

1. Unplug the machine before cleaning or doing other machine maintenance.

2. Use a soft cloth to remove lint from the needle bar and the base of the machine.

3. Use a soft brush to clean the bobbin case and bobbin. Follow the manufacturer's directions to remove the entire bobbin case for further cleaning.

4. Oil your machine, following the manufacturer's directions. Use only high-grade sewing machine oil. After oiling the machine, wipe away any drips. Plug in the machine and stitch on a scrap of fabric to remove excess oil. (Note: Newer machines are sealed and do not need to be oiled.)

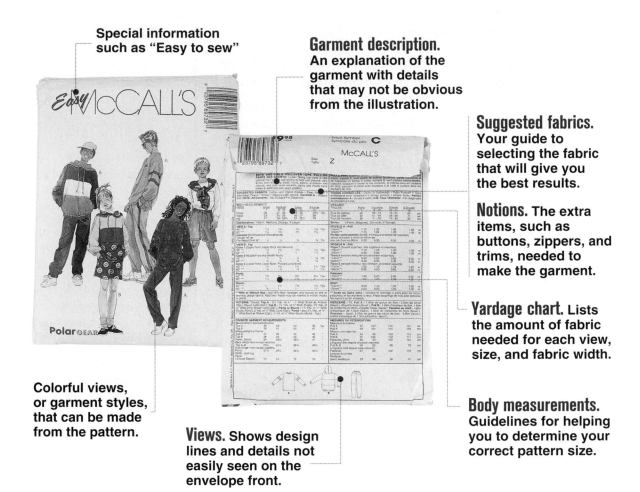

Special information such as "Easy to sew"

Garment description. An explanation of the garment with details that may not be obvious from the illustration.

Suggested fabrics. Your guide to selecting the fabric that will give you the best results.

Notions. The extra items, such as buttons, zippers, and trims, needed to make the garment.

Yardage chart. Lists the amount of fabric needed for each view, size, and fabric width.

Body measurements. Guidelines for helping you to determine your correct pattern size.

Colorful views, or garment styles, that can be made from the pattern.

Views. Shows design lines and details not easily seen on the envelope front.

Fig 36-8 The front of a pattern envelope shows the item. The back of the envelope is your guide for selecting the proper fabric and notions.

Selecting Fabric and Notions

Before purchasing garment fabric, ask yourself several questions: How appropriate is the fabric for your pattern and your sewing skills? How will the fabric look on you? What kind of care will the fabric need?

Buy fabric you like and will enjoy working with. If you are making an active sportswear garment, concentrate on fabrics that are durable. On the other hand, if you are making something for a special occasion, you may want a dressier fabric. When you purchase your fabric, remember to ask for the fabric care label and attach this to your garment.

Interfacing is a special fabric that gives support and body to a garment or project. It is placed between the facing and the outer fabric and is not visible. It can be found in hats, belts, bags, and around necklines to keep them from stretching.

Taking Measurements

For Males	For Females
Neck. Measure around the base of the neck and add ½ inch (1.3 cm) or buy a pattern based on the shirt size you regularly purchase.	**Back waist length.** Measure from the base of the neck to the waistline.
Chest. Measure around the fullest part of the chest.	**Bust.** Measure around the fullest part of the bust and under the arms.
Waist. Tie a string around the waist to identify where the measurement should be taken.	**Waist.** Tie a string around the waist to identify the narrowest point. Measure around the body exactly where the string settles.
Hip/Seat. Measure around the fullest part of the hip or seat, usually about 8 inches (20.5 cm) below the waist.	**Hip.** Measure around the fullest part of the hips, 7 to 9 inches (18 to 23 cm) below the waist.
Outseam. Measure along the outside of the leg from the waist to the desired length of the pants, usually where the pants bottom breaks slightly on the shoe.	**Outseam.** Measure along the outside of the leg from the waist, over the hips, to the desired length of the skirt or pants.
Inseam. Place pants that are the correct length on a flat surface. Measure along inner seam from the bottom of one leg to where the two legs meet.	**Inseam.** Place pants that are the correct length on a flat surface. Measure along inner seam from the bottom of one leg to where the two legs meet.

Fig 36-9 Use these measuring methods to determine your pattern size.

You can buy sew-in or fusible interfacing. Sew-in interfacing is stitched to the garment. Fusible interfacing is pressed on with a hot iron. Choose an interfacing that has similar weight, body, and care requirements as your fabric. If you are unsure about a fabric, talk to a salesperson or your teacher.

Notions

Notions are the small items, such as thread, zippers, buttons, trim, seam binding, hooks and eyes, and snaps, needed to complete a garment. The back of the pattern envelope lists the notions you will need.

Select thread just slightly darker than the fabric. If you have a print, match the thread with the main color in the print. Zippers come in a variety of colors, lengths, and styles. Check the pattern envelope for the zipper length and type suggested. Match the color of the zipper to the fabric as closely as possible. If the fabric has several colors, match the zipper to the background color.

HOW TO SELECT NOTIONS

The name sounds fanciful, but notions are a practical part of a garment. Choose notions with as much care as you choose fabric. In fact, choose them when you choose the fabric because notions and fabric should complement each other. In particular, make sure they have the same care needs. With your pattern as a guide, look at these basic notions:

- **Thread.** Polyester or polyester–cotton thread works nicely for most garment-sewing tasks. It combines strength, flexibility, stretch, and shrink resistance. Heavier threads are available for crafts or decorative stitching. Whatever your needs, use a quality brand. Inferior thread may break or tangle in machines.

- **Buttons.** Besides usefulness, buttons offer a chance to enhance the look of a garment. Designs run from plain discs to bow ties. Materials range from mother-of-pearl to plastic. You can even find wooden buttons "designed" by termites. They were shaped by the patterns created as the termites ate through the wood.

- **Zippers.** A look through your closet will likely show a variety of zippers that meet a number of applications. Conventional zippers are used in pants and dresses. A jacket shell needs a separating zipper. Invisible zippers blend into the seam. Decorative zippers are meant to stand out.

- **Other fasteners.** Depending on the garment, you may need buckles or two-piece fasteners such as snaps or hooks and eyes. Check the pattern for the recommended size and style.

Using the Pattern

You will find the guide sheet and pattern pieces inside the pattern envelope. The guide sheet contains the following:

- Sketches of different styles or views that can be made from the pattern.

- A list and diagram of pattern pieces.

- **Elastic.** Width is the main difference in elastics used in garments. Both woven and knitted elastic maintain their width when stretched and can be sewn directly onto fabric. Read labels to learn other qualities, such as shrink or roll resistance.

- **Trim.** Trim can be used to achieve far-ranging effects. Ribbons and lace add softness and elegance. Peacock feathers are showy and bold.

TAKE **ACTION**

Choose a garment that you own. Think of three ways you could change or improve the look or fit by changing or adding notions. Sketch your ideas or implement the changes.

- Cutting layouts, or diagrams, that show how to lay pattern pieces on the fabric for different sizes, fabric widths, and types of fabric.

- Step-by-step instructions for sewing the garment or project.

Each pattern piece has pattern symbols or markings that serve as guides for laying out and sewing your project. See **Fig. 36-10**. These are common symbols you will see:

1. **Cutting line.** The heavy line you follow on the outside of the pattern to cut out the fabric.

2. **Grainline.** A straight line with arrows on each end to be placed in the direction of the lengthwise grain, crosswise grain, or bias.

3. **Place on fold.** A bracketed grainline that indicates the pattern edge to be placed exactly on the fold of the fabric.

4. **Darts.** Triangular or diamond shapes indicated by dots and broken lines. They are folded and stitched.

5. **Placement line.** A solid line to show where to locate pockets, trims, and other features.

6. **Seamline or stitching line.** A broken line, usually ⅝ inch (1.5 cm) inside the cutting line that shows where to stitch the seams.

7. **Adjustment line.** Two parallel lines that indicate where to cut or fold a pattern for lengthening or shortening.

8. **Notches.** Diamond-shaped symbols along the cutting line that show where to join the pattern pieces together.

9. **Dots, squares, and triangles.** Symbols that help you match and join project sections together.

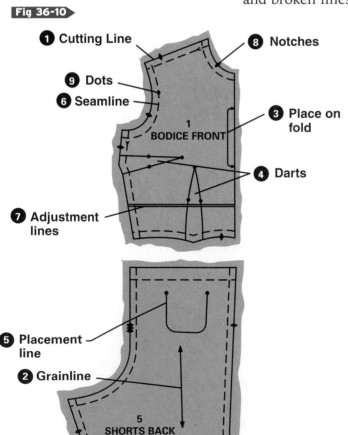

Fig 36-10

❶ Cutting Line
❽ Notches
❾ Dots
❻ Seamline
❸ Place on fold
1 BODICE FRONT
❹ Darts
❼ Adjustment lines
❺ Placement line
❷ Grainline
5 SHORTS BACK

Fitting the Pattern

When you make a garment, you need to check to see how well the pattern fits you. You can do this by comparing your measurements with those of the pattern. Follow these steps:

1. Smooth out the pattern with your hands or press the pattern pieces with a warm, dry iron.

2. Measure the pattern between stitching lines at the same places where the body measurements were taken and write them down.

3. Do not include seam allowances (the fabric between the cutting line and the stitching line) or darts when measuring the pattern pieces.

In most cases, you can expect the pattern pieces to be larger than your exact body measurements. Don't worry! Your pattern should be larger to account for wearing and design **ease**—the extra room needed for movement and comfort. Some garments have plenty of ease. However, if the garment is close fitting and the pattern measurements are much larger (or smaller) than your body measurements, you need to make some adjustment in the pattern. See **Fig. 36-11**.

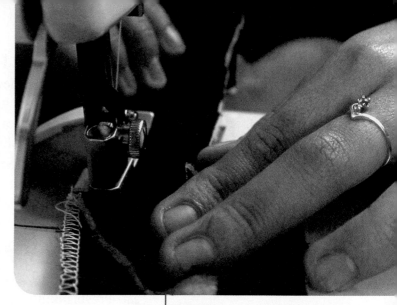

Fig 36-11 ▶ When guiding fabric through the machine, keep one hand in front and one hand in back of the presser foot.

Preparing Fabric

All woven fabric is made up of two sets of yarn, or grain—lengthwise and crosswise. The lengthwise grain, running the length of the fabric, has little or no stretch. The **selvage** is the finished lengthwise edge of the fabric. It will not ravel. The crosswise grain, running from selvage to selvage, has more stretch than the lengthwise grain. The true bias has the most stretch. **Bias** is the diagonal line formed when the fabric is folded with the crosswise grain parallel to the selvage. See **Fig. 36-12**.

A fabric's crosswise and lengthwise grains must be square (at right angles to each other) when you cut out your pattern; otherwise, the finished garment may not hang properly.

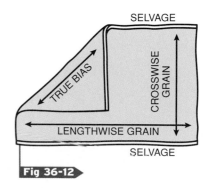

SELVAGE
TRUE BIAS
CROSSWISE GRAIN
LENGTHWISE GRAIN
SELVAGE

Fig 36-12 ▶

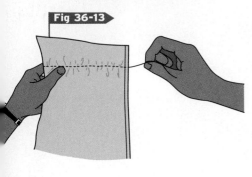
Fig 36-13

Straightening Fabric Ends

It's difficult to check whether the fabric grain is straight if the crosswise edges are uneven. To straighten the fabric ends, clip into the selvage and pull one crosswise thread (yarn) with one hand while pushing the fabric back with the other hand. Cut along this pulled-thread line. If the thread breaks before you reach the other selvage, pick up the end of the broken thread and continue pulling and cutting as necessary. See **Fig. 36-13**.

Preshrinking Fabric

Fabrics need to be preshrunk before you make your project. Preshrinking keeps your project from shrinking after you make it. It also removes fabric finishes that could cause stitching problems. Preshrink washable fabrics in the same manner you plan to launder the finished garment. Follow the care label you received when you purchased your fabric. For fabrics that ravel easily, zigzag stitch or serge the cut edges before washing the fabric. All woven interfacings, zippers, and trims should also be preshrunk.

Pattern Layout

The pattern guide sheet lists the pattern pieces needed for each view. Before you lay out the pattern, cut apart the pattern pieces you need. Leave some extra paper outside of the cutting lines on all pieces. On the guide sheet, check off the pattern pieces needed as you find them, and put the extra ones back into the envelope. Press the pattern pieces with a warm, dry iron if they're wrinkled. If you're working in the clothing lab, write your name on the pattern pieces so that you don't lose them.

Positioning Pattern Pieces

It is important to place pattern pieces on the fabric correctly. Once fabric has been cut, it is difficult to correct layout mistakes. Follow these steps:

1. **Circle the layout you are using on the pattern guide sheet.** The layout shows how to place the pattern pieces for the view, fabric width, and size you are making.
2. **Check the layout instructions carefully.** Note the following markings: the right and wrong sides of the fabric, the right and wrong sides of the pattern, the pattern pieces to be cut a second time, and any pattern pieces to be cut from a single layer of fabric.

3. **Fold the fabric as shown in the layout diagram.** Generally, fabric is folded in half on the lengthwise grain with right sides together.

4. **Position any large pattern pieces that go on the fold first.** Then position the remaining pattern pieces so that their grainline symbols are straight on the fabric grain. See **Fig. 36-14**. Pin the pieces securely, inserting the pins perpendicular to but not on the cutting line.

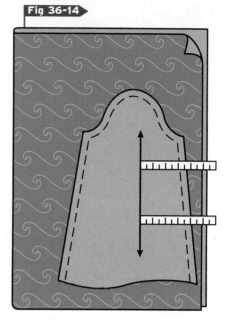

Fig 36-14

Cutting Out the Pattern

Use sharp shears to cut out the fabric. Follow the outside cutting lines carefully. Do not cut on the fold line. Try to hold the pattern and fabric flat with one hand as you cut with the other to prevent the fabric from moving under the pattern. Do not pick up the fabric to cut it. Move around the table as you work instead of moving the fabric. See **Fig. 36-15**.

Cut the notches outward, not inward. When you cut inward, you can weaken the seam. You could also accidentally cut into the garment. If two or three notches are together, cut them across the top as one long notch.

Keep pattern pieces pinned to the fabric for marking and identification. If you are using interfacing, cut out the interfacing when you finish cutting the fabric.

Marking the Fabric

The lines and symbols on your pattern are your guides for sewing accurately. Transfer these markings to the wrong side of your fabric before the pattern is unpinned. They must be visible as you sew but should not show on the outside of the finished project.

You can transfer markings to the fabric in one of several ways. You can make temporary markings on fabric using fabric markers. Test the markers on a fabric scrap first to be sure the markings can be removed. You can also use chalk and pins. Put a pin through the pattern and fabric at the place to be marked. Make a chalk mark on the wrong side of both fabric layers at the pin marking. Another option is to use tracing paper and a tracing wheel. Select a color of tracing paper that will be easily seen yet is close enough to the color of your fabric. Slide the tracing paper under the pattern with the waxy, colored side against the wrong side of the fabric. If you need to mark two layers of fabric, use two sheets of tracing paper, each facing the wrong side of the fabric. Roll the tracing wheel along the marking lines. Using a ruler will help keep the lines straight. Mark dots with an X.

Fig 36-15 Pattern pieces are generally larger than your exact body measurements. Always remeasure before cutting to avoid costly mistakes.

Review & Activities

Chapter Summary

- Knowing how to safely use sewing tools and equipment is important in the success of any sewing project.
- Work with a partner and wear close-fitting clothes to take accurate body measurements.
- Refer to the back of the pattern envelope when selecting fabric and notions.
- It is important to prepare fabric correctly when working on a sewing project.
- Follow the pattern guide sheet carefully when working on a sewing project.

Reviewing Key Terms & Ideas

1. Identify two pieces of cutting equipment and explain their use.
2. What is the purpose of marking equipment?
3. List three basic pieces of pressing equipment.
4. Why is it important to raise the take-up lever and needle to the highest point before machine stitching?
5. What does **tension** refer to?
6. What does a serger do?
7. What are figure types?
8. Define **interfacing**. Where is it used?
9. How do you know which **notions** you need?
10. Why does a pattern need **ease**?
11. What is a **selvage**?
12. Define **bias**.

Thinking Critically

1. **Making generalizations.** What is the most important step in preparing to sew? Explain your answer.
2. **Analyzing situations.** Imagine a friend of yours says, "Sewing is a big waste of time." How would you respond to this statement?
3. **Defending positions.** It has been said that sewing can be a creative experience. Do you agree or disagree? Explain your response.

Review & Activities

Applying Your Learning

1. **Sewing kit.** Using the information from this chapter and online or print resources, assemble a sewing kit for home use.

2. **Special tools.** Research special tools that make sewing easier, such as disappearing basting thread, liquid seam sealant, and fabric stabilizer. If possible, try out the tools and evaluate their effectiveness.

3. **Machine parts.** Use the diagram on page 574 to identify the parts of a sewing machine in the clothing lab or at home.

4. **Safety practices.** Demonstrate safe practices for using a sewing machine or serger, including proper machine care. Ask the class for feedback.

5. **Measurement demonstration.** Demonstrate to the class how to take measurements and find the figure type and pattern size using a sample pattern.

6. **Layout comparison.** Lay out a pattern on fabric. Have a partner lay out the same pattern on another piece of fabric. Compare your layout with your partner's. Discuss any differences in the layout and make corrections.

7. **Pattern cutting.** Demonstrate the correct way to cut out a pattern. Explain what you are doing and why you are doing it.

Making Connections

1. **Reading** Read books or magazine articles about famous fashion designers, such as Calvin Klein, Coco Chanel, Oleg Cassini, or Edith Head. Share your information with the class.

2. **Math** Select a pattern and estimate the total cost of constructing the view you selected. Include the pattern, fabric, and notions in your estimate.

3. **Writing** Research the sewing tools and equipment and the garment construction techniques of settlers in colonial America. Write an essay comparing their tools and techniques with those used today.

CAREER Link

Cover Letter.
Most jobs require a cover letter with a résumé. In your cover letter, introduce yourself. State the job you are applying for and how you found out about it. Let the employer know how your skills and experience would benefit the company. Finally, ask for an interview and thank the employer for reviewing your résumé. Before mailing, check your letter for correct grammar and spelling. Read a job-search book that includes samples of cover letters. Then try writing one for a job you would like to have.

Basic Sewing Techniques

Objectives

- Demonstrate basting techniques.
- Compare directional and staystitching.
- Create finished seams, facings, gathers, and casings.
- Demonstrate hemming a garment.
- Produce simple alterations.

Vocabulary

- **basting**
- **directional stitching**
- **staystitching**
- **grading**
- **notching**
- **clipping**
- **understitching**
- **gathers**
- **casing**

Reading with Purpose

1. **Read** the title of this chapter and describe in writing what you expect to learn from it.

2. **Write** each vocabulary term in your notebook, leaving space for definitions.

3. **As you read** Chapter 37, write the definition beside each term in your notebook.

4. **After** reading the chapter, write a paragraph describing what you learned.

Developing Your Sewing Skills

Everyone in Jamie's family sews. Jamie sews to repair her clothes, which helps her stick to her clothing budget. Her little brother can sew buttons onto clothes. Her older sister makes her own clothes and recently made a dress for a friend. Her mom owns a tailoring shop and makes custom clothing for clients. Although Jamie may never be a professional tailor, she knows she will use her sewing skills throughout her life.

Sewing skills allow you to personalize your clothing and items in your home. With a few skills, you can also repair and alter garments. The techniques in this chapter will help you develop your sewing skills.

Basting

To be certain about the fit of a garment or the way a project is going to look, you may need to baste parts of a garment together. **Basting** means holding two or more pieces of fabric together temporarily until they are permanently stitched. See **Fig. 37-1**. There are several types of basting:

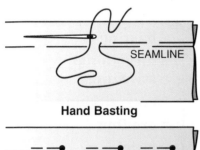

Hand Basting

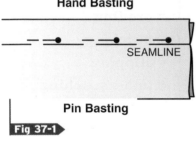

Pin Basting

Fig 37-1

- **Hand basting.** Thread basting by hand uses long stitches, about ¼-inch (6 mm) long.
- **Machine basting.** Thread basting by machine uses a stitch length set at 4 or longer.
- **Pin basting.** For pin basting, the pins substitute for stitching. You may want to experiment with basting tape or disappearing basting thread, which dissolves when you wash or iron it.

When basting, make sure the stitches or pins are next to, but not directly on, the seamline. Remember, basting is temporary. This makes the basting easy to remove after the permanent seam is sewn.

Machine Stitching

Machine stitching is used for the major seams of your sewing project and for directional stitching and staystitching. You will use a stitch length setting of 2.5 for most fabrics.

Directional Stitching

All stitching on a garment should be sewn with the grain of the fabric. When you sew with the grain, you are less likely to stretch the fabric. Stitching in the direction of the grain is called **directional stitching**. How do you identify the direction for stitching? Move your finger along the raw edge of the fabric. The direction that smooths the yarns against the fabric is going with the grain. You can also look at the pattern. Pattern tissues have arrows pointing to the grain direction. As a rule, stitch from the wide to the narrow part of the garment. For example, sew from the hem to the waist of a skirt. See **Fig. 37-2**.

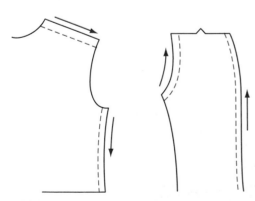

Fig 37-2 Directional stitching prevents the fabric from stretching as you sew.

Staystitching

Before you begin to put a garment or project together, it should be staystitched. **Staystitching** is a row of stitching on one layer of fabric that prevents the edges from stretching as you handle the fabric. Follow these guidelines for staystitching:

- Staystitch after you mark the fabric but before pinning or basting.

- Staystitch in the direction of the grain.

- Use the same thread tension and stitch length you will use for the project seams.

- Staystitch ½ inch (1.3 cm) from the raw edge. This is ⅛ inch (3 mm) inside the seamline. Staystitching should not show on the outside of a project.

- Staystitch edges that are curved, on the bias, or cut off-grain, such as shoulder seams, necklines, and armholes. See **Fig. 37-3**.

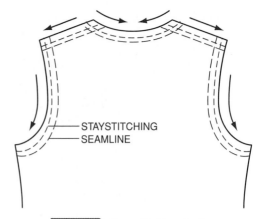

Fig 37-3 Staystitching is done on curved areas to prevent the fabric from stretching.

Sewing Techniques

Pattern instructions dictate the sewing techniques you need to use to complete a garment. Some basic techniques you will probably see in pattern instructions are explained here.

Seams

Seams hold a garment together. A seam is made by sewing two pieces of fabric together. In general, seams are ⅝ inch (1.5 cm) wide. The fabric between the seamline and the cut edge is the seam allowance.

Before you begin to sew, make a sample seam on a scrap of your fabric. Examine the seam to check the tension, stitch length, and general appearance. Then follow these steps to make a plain seam:

1. Place the right sides of the fabric together. Match notches, cut edges, and both ends of the fabric. Place pins at right angles to the seamline at the ends and notches. Pin the rest of the seam. Placing pins 2 to 3 inches (5 to 7.5 cm) apart with the pin heads outward.

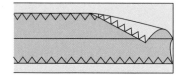

Zigzag seam finish

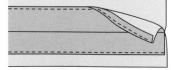

Clean finish

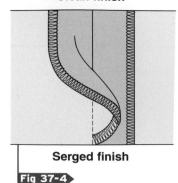

Serged finish

Fig 37-4 ▶

2. Place the fabric under the presser foot with the cut edges of the seam allowance lined up with the proper seam guide numbers on the throat plate. Turn the hand wheel to lower the needle into the fabric ½ inch (1.3 cm) from the top of the seam. Lower the presser foot.

3. Backstitch to secure the top end of the seam. Backstitch by retracing your stitches about ½ inch (1.3 cm). Use the reverse button or lever on your sewing machine.

4. Using a medium speed and an even pace, stitch to the other end of the seam.

5. Backstitch to secure the bottom end of the seam.

6. Seams are usually pressed open flat.

Seam Finishes

Seam finishes are used to prevent raveling on the cut edges of seams and facings. The seam finish to use depends on the type of fabric and the amount of raveling. If you are unsure which finish to use, try different finishes on your fabric scraps. See **Fig. 37-4**.

• **Zigzag finish.** For fabrics that ravel, zigzagging is a practical seam finish. Use a medium-width machine zigzag stitch and sew along the edge of each seam allowance.

• **Clean finish.** Also called a turned-and-stitched finish, a clean finish is a turned and stitched finish used on lightweight and medium-weight fabrics. Turn the edges under ¼ inch (6 mm) and press. Machine stitch close to the folded edge.

• **Serged finish.** This may be used on any fabric. Serge along the cut edge of the seam, just skimming the edge as you sew. A serged finish is especially helpful on heavy or bulky fabric and fabric that ravels easily.

Interfacing

Interfacing is applied before the facing is attached to the garment. **Fig. 37-5** shows two ways to apply interfacing.

Facings

Facings are often used to finish raw edges, such as necklines, front openings, armholes, or collars. There are several different types of facings. A shaped facing is used most often. It is cut the same shape as the edge onto which it is sewn. Before sewing a facing to a garment, you need to understand several techniques:

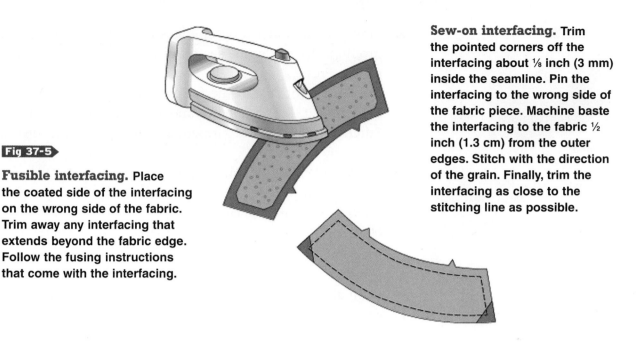

Fig 37-5

Fusible interfacing. Place the coated side of the interfacing on the wrong side of the fabric. Trim away any interfacing that extends beyond the fabric edge. Follow the fusing instructions that come with the interfacing.

Sew-on interfacing. Trim the pointed corners off the interfacing about ⅛ inch (3 mm) inside the seamline. Pin the interfacing to the wrong side of the fabric piece. Machine baste the interfacing to the fabric ½ inch (1.3 cm) from the outer edges. Stitch with the direction of the grain. Finally, trim the interfacing as close to the stitching line as possible.

- **Grading.** After facings are joined to a garment, the seams may be thick and bulky. **Grading**, or trimming the seam allowances in layers, is done to reduce the bulk.

- **Notching or clipping.** Outward-curved edges, as on collars, and inward-curved edges, as on necklines, need special treatment to lie flat. Outward curves need **notching**, which means clipping V-shaped notches from the seam allowance. Inward curves need **clipping**, or making small, straight cuts in the seam allowance.

- **Understitching.** This row of stitching gives facings a smooth, flat edge. **Understitching**, or stitching the facing to the seam allowances, also keeps seams and facings from rolling to the outside of the garment.

Sewing a Facing

After learning about grading, notching, and understitching, it is easier to sew on a facing. See **Fig. 37-6**. Follow these steps to attach a facing:

1. Staystitch curved facing edges that are to be attached to the garment. Sew facing pieces together as directed in the pattern. Trim the seams to ¼ inch (6 mm) and press open.

Fig 37-6

Step 1

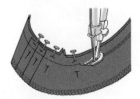

Step 2

Fig 37-6 cont.

Step 3

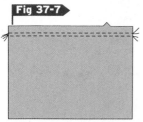

Understitching

Step 4

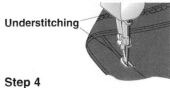

Fig 37-7

Step 1

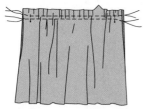

Step 2

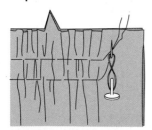

Step 3

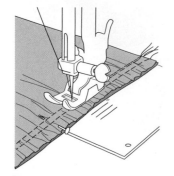

Step 4

2. Finish the unnotched outer edges of the facing to prevent raveling. Use one of the seam finishing methods described earlier. Press.

3. Place the right side of the facing against the right side of the garment. Match notches and seams and pin together.

4. Stitch the facing to the garment at ⅝ inch (1.5 cm), sewing as evenly as possible.

5. Grade and clip the seams to reduce bulk.

6. Press the facing and seam allowance away from the garment and toward the facing.

7. Understitch the seam allowance to the facing. Turn the facing to the inside and press.

8. Hand sew the facing to the inside of the garment at the seam allowances only. Do not hand sew the facing to the garment.

Gathers

Gathers are soft folds of fabric. They are formed by pulling up basting stitches to make a larger piece of fabric fit onto a smaller space. Fullness on shirts, skirts, and sometimes window curtains is often created by gathers. See **Fig. 37-7**. Follow these steps to make gathers:

1. Sew two parallel rows of machine basting on the right side of the fabric, with a stitch length of at least 4. Leave a 2-inch (5-cm) tail of thread at the beginning and the end of each row. Do not backstitch because you will be pulling the thread tails. Stitch the first row on the seamline. Stitch the second row about ¼ inch (6 mm) from the seamline inside the seam allowance.

2. Place the edge of the piece to be gathered against the fabric piece it is to be sewn to (such as skirt to waistband or ruffle to curtain edge). Put right sides together and make edges even. Match all markings, notches, and seams, and pin only at these locations.

3. Tie a knot in each pair of bobbin-thread tails (now facing you). Gently pull these bobbin-thread tails at each end to gather the fabric. Slide the fabric along with your fingers until the gathered fabric fits the shorter fabric piece. At both ends, wrap the excess bobbin thread around the pins in figure eights.

4. Adjust the gathers evenly. Pin about every ½ inch (1.3 cm).

5. Stitch the seam with standard stitching. Sew with the gathered edge on top. This way, stitching is more accurate and the gathers will not be caught in the stitching. For safe sewing, remove the pins as you sew.

Casings

A **casing** is a closed tunnel or space of fabric that can hold a piece of elastic or a drawstring in a waistband. Casings are also used as curtain rod pockets for simple curtains or valances. A casing is made like a hem. You generally fold over the edge of the waistband or the top of the curtain and sew it in place. The width of the casing will vary depending on the size opening needed. For example, waistband casings are usually 1 inch (2.5 cm) wide. See **Fig. 37-8**. To sew a self-casing, follow these directions:

1. Finish the raw edge of fabric by turning it under ¼ inch (6 mm) and press. Otherwise, zigzag or serge the raw edge.

2. Turn the casing to the inside on the fold line with wrong sides together. Pin in place. Press the outer edge of the casing.

3. Stitch close to the inner pinned edge of the casing. If you are inserting elastic or a drawstring, you need to leave a small opening.

Elastic Waistband

The width of the elastic needs to be about ¼ inch (6 mm) narrower than the finished casing so that you can pull it through the casing. If the casing is too wide, the elastic will twist inside the casing when the garment is worn. See **Fig. 37-9**. Follow these steps to sew an elastic waistband:

1. Leave a 1½-inch (3.8-cm) opening when stitching the inner edge of the casing to insert elastic. Backstitch at each end of the seam.

2. Cut a piece of elastic to fit snugly around your waist. Remember, it must be able to slide over your hips. Add 2 inches (5 cm) to overlap.

3. Put a safety pin in one end of the elastic. Insert the pin and elastic into the casing opening. Pull the pin and elastic through the casing, using the pin to guide the elastic. Hold onto the loose end of the elastic.

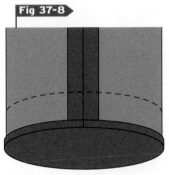

Fig 37-8

Finish casing edge.

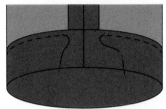

Opening for elastic or drawstring.

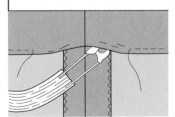

Fig 37-9 Follow these steps to sew an elastic waistband.

Steps 1–3

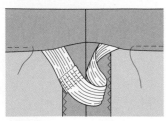

Step 4

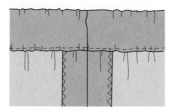

Step 5

Fig 37-9 cont.

Fig 37-10

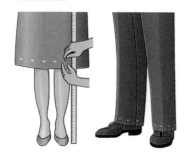

Marking with chalk   **Marking with pins**

4. Overlap the elastic ends 1 inch (2.5 cm). Machine stitch the overlap securely in a square pattern.

5. Stitch the opening of the casing closed. Backstitch at each end of the opening. See **Fig. 37-9**.

Hems

The bottom edges of pants, skirts, sleeves, and window treatments are finished with hems. The type of hem you will use depends on the type of fabric and the design of the project.

Marking the Hem

To mark the length of the hemline, put on shoes of the heel height you expect to wear with the finished garment. Have another person measure the correct length up from the floor using a yardstick. Place pins or chalk marks at the same distance all the way around the garment. Check to be sure that the markings form an even line. See **Fig. 37-10**.

Using the marked line as a guide, turn the hem to the wrong side of the garment. Insert pins at right angles along the fold line. The depth of the hem varies depending on the fullness of the garment. Pants usually have a hem of 1½ to 2 inches (3.8 to 5 cm). Skirt hems vary from 1 to 3 inches (2.5 to 7.5 cm), depending on the fullness. Use a narrower hem depth for a fuller skirt.

Measure the hem depth needed plus ¼ inch (6 mm) for finishing. Cut off the extra fabric from the edge of the hem. Machine stitch or hand sew ½ inch (1.3 cm) from the cut edge. Stitch only through the hem, not the outside of the garment.

Finishing the Hem

When a garment has extra fullness, it has to be eased in so that it fits flat against the garment. Otherwise, it will be bulky and lumpy. There are several ways to finish raw edges of hems, such as zigzagging, clean finishing, and serging. Choose a method that best suits your fabric. Next, attach the hem to the garment. Two methods include slipstitching (a method of hand stitching) and machine stitching. See **Fig. 37-11**.

Fig 37-11
Finishing the Hem

1. Pin and baste the hem along the fold.

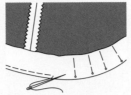

2. Mark and trim the hem depth to make it even.

3. In fabrics that shrink, use steam to shrink hem fullness.

4. For fabrics that do not shrink with steam, machine baste close to the cut edge. Pull up the bobbin thread to ease in fullness.

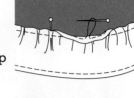

5. For serged edges, slipstitch the hem edge to the garment.

6. Slipstitch the hem edge to the garment.

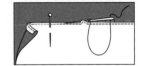

- **Slipstitching.** To slipstitch a hem, use a single strand of thread in the needle. Make sure the stitches do not show on the outside of the garment. Keep the stitches somewhat loose so that the fabric does not pull. Start by attaching the thread to a seam. Pick up only one or two threads on the outer layer of the garment or fabric. Then insert the needle into the fold of the hem edge. Space the stitches about ¼ inch (6 mm) to ½ inch (1.3 cm) apart.

- **Machine stitching.** Blindstitching or topstitching can also be used to attach a hem to a garment. If your machine has a built-in blindstitch, follow the machine manual. For topstitching, fold the hem to the width you want and press. Stitch close to the inside edge of the hem.

Simple Alterations

Garments do not always fit perfectly. Simple alterations can extend the usefulness of a garment. All it takes is a little planning, organizing, skill, and time management. See **Fig. 37-12** for instruction on altering garments.

Fig 37-12
Follow these steps to make simple alterations.

Lengthening or Shortening a Garment

1. Remove the old hem stitching.
2. Put on the garment and have someone mark the bottom of the hem.
3. Turn the hem under along the new hemline and pin in place.
4. Baste the hem close to the folded edge. Try on the garment to make sure the hem length is correct.
5. Measure and mark the desired hem depth. Trim off the extra fabric when shortening a garment. When lengthening a garment, if the hem allowance is too narrow, sew hem tape to the hem edge to create a new hem allowance.
6. Finish the raw edge of the hem using one of the edge finishes described on page **584.**
7. Pin the top of the hem edge to the garment. Ease the hem fullness to the garment as needed.
8. Machine stitch or slipstitch the hem to the garment. Remove the basting. Press.

Adjusting the Width of a Garment

To make a garment larger, follow these steps:

1. Check the seam allowances to be sure there is enough fabric for new seams.
2. Remove the old stitching from the section of the seam to which the width will be added.
3. Try on the garment inside out and have someone pin the new seams.
4. Machine baste the new seams, removing the pins as you sew.
5. Try the garment on to check the fit.
6. Machine stitch the new seams with a regular stitch length, carefully tapering the stitching into the old seam.
7. Backstitch at each seam end. Remove the basting.
8. Press the seams open.

To make a garment smaller, follow these steps:

1. Put the garment on inside out. Have someone pin the new seams on each side. Machine baste on the pin line, removing the pins as you sew.
2. Try the garment on to check the fit.
3. Stitch the new seams using a regular machine stitch, carefully tapering the new stitching into the old.
4. Remove the basting and old seam.
5. Press the seams open.

HOW TO SERGE SEAMS

In a world where everyone from a doctor to a chef may be a specialist, the serger is right at home. A serger does one thing—makes seams—and does it well. Using a serger requires basic sewing skills. You will need to distinguish the seamline, where the needle enters the fabric, from the serger cutting line, generally 1/4 inch (6 mm) beyond the seamline.

Once you've gained some serging savvy, these steps can help you take advantage of this multitalented machine:

STEP 1 | **Baste or pin the seam.** If you use pins, make sure they run parallel to the seamline, about 1 inch (2.5 cm) to the inside. Remove pins as you sew.

STEP 2 | **Stitch a 4- to 5-inch (10-cm to 12.5-cm) lead-in thread chain.** Then ease the fabric under the presser foot.

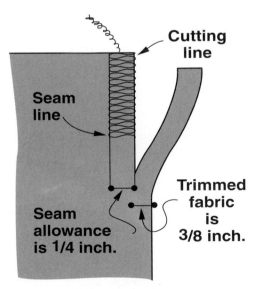

Cutting line

Seam line

Seam allowance is 1/4 inch.

Trimmed fabric is 3/8 inch.

STEP 3 | **Serge off the fabric.** Run another 5-inch (12.5-cm) thread chain after finishing the seam. Turn the chain to the front and let the knife cut it, being careful not to cut into your fabric.

STEP 4 | **Secure the thread ends.** Serged ends are fairly ravel proof, especially if stitched over by another seam—at the cuffs and sleeves of a sweatshirt, for example. As a safeguard, you can pull the thread chain back through the seam stitches using a small crochet hook or a large-eyed needle. Alternately, knot the threads using this technique: make a slip knot in the thread close to the fabric; slip the knot around a pin; holding the pin tip next to the fabric edge, pull the thread to tighten it around the pin tip; and remove the pin.

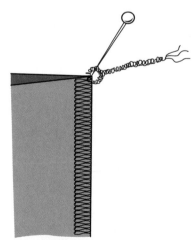

TAKE ACTION

Practice making two seams—one on a serger and one on a traditional sewing machine. Finish the traditional seam according to the steps on page 583-584. Which seam appeared to require more skill? For what types of garments or home fashions projects would each be appropriate? Why?

Review & Activities

Chapter Summary

- You may need to baste parts of a garment together to check the garment's fit.
- Machine stitching is used for directional and staystitching.
- Pattern guide sheets explain where seams, facings, gathers, and casings are needed.
- The type of hem you will use depends on the type of fabric and the design of the project.
- Simple alterations can extend the usefulness of a garment.

Reviewing Key Terms & Ideas

1. What is **basting**?
2. Explain **directional stitching**.
3. What is the purpose of **staystitching**?
4. Identify three types of seam finishes.
5. List two types of interfacing.
6. Where are facings often used on a garment?
7. What is **grading**?
8. Compare **notching** and **clipping**.
9. What is **understitching**?
10. How are **gathers** made?
11. What is the function of a **casing**?
12. Which methods can you use to attach a hem to a garment?

Thinking Critically

1. **Drawing conclusions.** What factors influence sewing success and confidence? How could you encourage others in pursuing sewing success?
2. **Making predictions.** What might happen if you hung a skirt at the waistline for a day before hemming it?
3. **Analyzing situations.** If you were making a decision about altering a garment, what factors would you take into consideration?

Review & Activities

Applying Your Learning

1. **Sewing video.** Create a video for teens that demonstrates the sewing techniques in this chapter. Prepare a script for your video and practice the techniques before taping.

2. **Basting samples.** Experiment with different methods of basting on 4-inch-square scraps of fabric. When would you use each of these basting methods? Mount your samples on paper and start a sewing portfolio.

3. **Stitching identification.** On a fabric scrap, identify the grain for directional stitching. Try sewing with the grain and evaluate your results. Did you sew with the grain?

4. **Seam sample.** Using scrap fabric, make a finished seam. How can you improve the seam next time?

5. **Facing instructions.** Choose a pattern for a garment you would like to make that includes facings. Study the pattern guide sheet. Then explain to the class how to make the facings for the garment.

6. **Hemming practice.** Hem a garment of your own, or hem one for someone you know. Evaluate your results. Is your hem straight?

Making Connections

1. **Math** Compare the cost of making a garment (including the pattern, fabric, thread, and notions) with buying a similar ready-made one. What is the difference in cost? What do you think contributed to this difference?

2. **Writing** Write an essay to persuade young children to learn sewing techniques. Emphasize the use of sewing skills throughout life.

3. **Reading** Read online information about careers in the garment-making industry. What education is required for one of the careers? Report your findings to the class.

4. **Writing** Collect photographs that show the use of gathers in a variety of places on clothing or home fashions. For each photo, write a brief description that explains how the gathering creates interest. Arrange the photos and descriptions in an attractive display.

CAREER Link

Pride in Your Work. Hard work and pride go hand in hand. Think about how you feel after finishing a sewing project that went well. You probably feel a sense of pride and accomplishment. Feeling good about the work you do drives you to work harder. The result of your hard work is a job well done. In the workplace, pride in your work matters, too. Observe employees in a workplace. Which employees seem to take pride in their work? How can you tell?

Where You Live

Objectives

- Explain how housing fulfills human needs.
- Describe factors that influence housing decisions.
- Classify different types of housing.
- Discuss housing trends.
- Compare the advantages of renting and buying a home.

Vocabulary

- **utilities**
- **duplex**
- **multiplex**
- **townhouse**
- **apartment**
- **landlords**
- **lease**
- **mortgage**
- **condominiums**
- **cooperative**

Reading with Purpose

1. **Write down** the colored headings from Chapter 38 in your notebook.

2. **As you read** the text under each heading, visualize what you are reading.

3. **Reflect** on what you read by writing a few sentences under each heading to describe it.

4. **Continue** this process until you have finished the chapter. Reread your notes.

Housing to Fulfill Human Needs

What does an apartment in the city have in common with a house in the suburbs? Or a houseboat with a cabin in the woods? Each living unit is someone's home. Whether large or small, each structure fulfills its residents' basic needs:

- **Physical needs.** Housing provides people with shelter. It enables them to create an environment that suits their particular needs.

- **Emotional needs.** Housing meets people's emotional needs by allowing them to relax and pursue their own interests in privacy and comfort. Decorating a home to reflect personal tastes also fulfills emotional needs.

- **Social needs.** A home promotes family strength by giving family members a place to live, share their lives, work, play, entertain guests, and relax. See **Fig. 38-1**.

Influences on Housing Decisions

Although people share basic human needs, they also have individual needs and wants. When people choose a place to live, they first need to consider their specific needs and wants. Then they have to find a way to balance those with their available resources.

Considering Needs, Wants, and Priorities

People's needs, wants, and priorities differ. What one family sees as a necessity might be a drawback or unimportant to another family. When considering housing, people need to think about the following:

- **Family size.** How much room does the family need? Suppose your friend lives with foster parents and five other children. His family's need for space is quite different from that of another friend's family, which includes herself, her brother, and her father.

- **Family changes.** Changes that families experience can affect housing needs. A young couple expecting a baby may need a larger house with an outdoor play area. In contrast, an older adult who lives alone might prefer a smaller space that requires little upkeep.

- **Special needs of family members.** Do any family members require special considerations? Someone with limited vision or mobility may require a single-level home. A person who uses a wheelchair or walker requires an accessible home and environment. Accessible homes have wide doorways and hallways, which allow wheelchairs and walkers to easily move from room to room.

- **Location.** It may be important for a family member to be close to a job or transportation. The family may prefer a quiet location, a busy neighborhood, or an area with access to stores and public transportation.

- **Environmental concerns.** Many people are concerned about the environment. They want housing with features that conserve resources.

- **Technology.** Is the home wired for high-speed Internet access? Is there a security system? What other technology might be available?

- **Lifestyle.** What interests and activities are part of the family's lifestyle? Does the family want a large living area for watching movies? Would a large yard for outdoor activities be required?

TIPS

Keep Your Family Strong

Housing affects the strength of a family. Here are some housing tips for keeping your family strong:

▶ If space is limited, make sure everyone can enjoy privacy.

▶ If your home is large, make time to enjoy being together.

▶ If housing costs are causing parents to work too many hours, find ways to cut expenses.

▶ Patience, courtesy, and compromise all strengthen family relationships.

People come in all shapes and sizes, with widely ranging abilities, and all of them need or want to live as independently as possible. Think of how satisfying it feels when you are self-reliant. Would that feeling disappear if a condition limited your ability to get around your home? Increasingly, architects and home planners are incorporating elements of universal design, creating living and working spaces that are accessible to as many people as possible. Using this idea, families can make simple changes to make a home "user friendly" to members and guests who have physical limitations:

- **Limited mobility.** People who use wheelchairs or walkers need safe, clear, wide pathways. Outside the home, sidewalks can be widened and ramps can be built over steps. Inside, furniture can be rearranged or put on casters or carts. Deep carpeting, throw rugs, and thresholds between rooms should be removed. Installing a lazy Susan or storing frequently used items at lower levels can accommodate a limited reach.

"Grabbers" or tongs are handy devices for extending a reach. Comfortably rounded handrails and grab bars help people maneuver on their own.

- **Visual impairment.** Good lighting is a good idea for everyone. Large digital clocks are easy to read. Bright colors or colored tape highlight edges of counters and changes in surface levels. Use textural cues to help people identify

- **Limited strength.** Weakness in arms and hands can be overcome by exchanging doorknobs for easy-to-grip, D-shaped handles. Spray attachments on sinks eliminate the need to turn faucets. In the kitchen, clear counters of small appliances to allow sliding, rather than carrying, of heavy objects.

items by feel. Put salt in a round shaker, for instance, and pepper in a square one. Label items when proper use is essential to health and safety, as with medicines and household chemicals. Rearrange objects as little as possible.

- **Hearing impairment.** Furniture and lighting should be arranged to help hearing-impaired family members see and focus on speakers. Families can buy plug-in signalers that trigger lamps to flash when a baby cries, an oven timer goes off, or a doorbell rings. Amplified phones make incoming calls louder and clearer. A TTY (teletypewriter) lets users carry on phone conversations by typing their words on a keyboard.

TAKE **ACTION**

Identify and carry out two changes to your home that make it more accessible to people with disabilities. After one week, describe the difference the changes made in your routines.

Considering Family Resources

After considering needs, wants, and priorities, a family will have a good idea of the location and type of housing that would suit everyone in the family. If the family members cannot find what they're looking for, they may have to rethink their housing needs and wants or design exactly what they want, assuming they have adequate resources.

Families need to choose affordable housing. When calculating the cost of housing, take all expenses into account. In addition to monthly payments for the housing unit, consider other possible costs, such as insurance, taxes, repairs, outdoor maintenance, and utilities. **Utilities** are basic services, such as electricity, cable, gas or oil, phone, water, and sewer service. Some homes have wells that provide water and septic tanks that take care of waste. See **Fig. 38-2**.

Most people must make some compromises to find housing that fits their budget. One family hoped to find a home where two sisters could have their own bedrooms. The family also had a need for an office space. The best value the family could find met all of family members' needs, except for separate bedrooms for the girls. Here the family members had to compromise.

Human resources, such as construction and decorating skills, time, energy, and creativity can save families a considerable amount of money. For instance, a family bought a large older house that needed a lot of repairs. Without skills and willingness to make improvements, the family would have had to settle for a much smaller house. See **Fig. 38-3**.

Fig 38-2 Larger homes tend to have larger utility bills.

Types of Housing

Two basic categories of housing are single-family housing and multiple-family housing. Single-family housing is built to house one family. Multiple-family housing contains several single-family housing units in one structure. Learning about the types of single-family and multiple-family housing, and understanding the advantages and disadvantages of each, can help you make good housing decisions in the future.

Single-Family Housing

Single-family homes are freestanding homes for one family. They don't share any walls with another housing unit. They may be small or large, one story or several stories.

Single-family homes offer more privacy than other types of housing. They are also usually more expensive because they require more land and building materials. There are many types of single-family homes. Some single-family homes are tract homes, or mass-produced homes with similar floor plans. Some are custom-built homes. Others are "spec homes," which are built on speculation; subdivisions developed by builders; or historic structures. Single-family homes can also be prefabricated homes, which are system-built homes with parts made in a factory and assembled on-site.

Manufactured, or mobile, homes are also considered single-family homes. Manufactured homes are built in a factory and are moved to a specific site. Some communities restrict where manufactured homes can be placed. Most manufactured homes are less expensive than a traditional single-family home. They also may come completely furnished.

Stan gazed up at the soaring apartment building. "When you said you live in a high-rise, you weren't kidding."

Javier laughed. "And we're only on the sixth floor!"

They rode the elevator to Javier's apartment. Javier gave his new friend a tour of the family home.

Stan took in the view from the balcony. "What—no backyard?"

Javier grinned and pointed to the park a few blocks away. "That's my backyard. It has biking trails, a soccer field, a lake. How about yours?"

"I don't have to share mine with a hundred other people," Stan replied.

"I've made some good friends there," Javier said. "That's where I found my soccer team."

Stan nodded. "I guess I could get used to city life. But my mom would go nuts without her vegetable garden."

"We're city folks," Javier said. "See that yellow awning on the corner? That's the green grocer. That's our vegetable garden."

Teen Connection

With one or two classmates, write a description of a "teen dream home." Stress those features that would make a home most appealing for the typical teen. Compare your ideal home with most family homes. How do differences and similarities reflect different and similar needs and concerns of teens compared with families?

Multiple-Family Housing

Multiple-family dwellings are connected to one another and may be more affordable. Cost, however, varies with location, size, and features. Individual units may be small or large. Residents may or may not share the use of a laundry room, swimming pool, and other special features. See **Fig. 38-4**.

Multiple-family dwellings require much less land per person than single-family houses, which means less or no yard maintenance. However, these dwellings tend to be noisier and less private than single-family homes, depending on the structure and the insulation. Storage space may be limited, and pets may not be allowed. The following dwellings are considered multiple-family houses:

- A **duplex** is one structure that contains two separate units. The units may be side by side and share one wall, or they may be on separate floors.

- A **multiplex** is similar to a duplex, but three or more units share one building.

- A **townhouse** is a house built in a row of other townhouses. It is attached to another townhouse at a side wall.

- An **apartment** is a rental unit in a building, or a structure that houses units for more than two families. Some apartments are not just one building. Some are an actual complex, or a community of apartments.

Ways to Obtain Housing

Some people own the housing unit in which they live. Others rent their home from the person who owns the house. Renting and buying both have advantages and disadvantages.

Renting a Home

Renting means paying money to live in a housing unit owned by someone else. Owners of rental housing are sometimes called **landlords**. Many different types of housing

units are available for rent. People can rent apartments, duplexes, houses, and even individual rooms in houses. Some rental units come furnished, usually for an extra fee. Typically, the larger the housing unit, the higher the cost of rent.

When you rent a housing unit, you may have to fill out an application and sign a **lease**, a written rental agreement. The lease states that you agree to pay rent for a certain period of time. It specifies the monthly fee, what is included, and what is not included—for example, utilities and maintenance. It also includes any rules you must follow. Always read a lease carefully before you sign it. If you don't understand the lease, ask a qualified person to explain it. Even if you understand it, having a lawyer look over lease is a wise decision. It is a legal document. Many landlords require a security deposit, often equal to one month's rent or the first and last months' rent. This is returned when you move out if the unit is clean and hasn't been damaged. If damage has occurred, you will receive a partial refund of your security deposit. Make sure there is an agreement to the condition of the rental when you move in and when you move out. See **Fig. 38-5**.

Fig 38-5 Landlords can answer questions you have about a house before you sign a lease agreement.

Many people enjoy the following advantages of renting:

- **Convenience.** The landlord rather than the tenant usually handles painting, maintenance, and any household repairs.

- **Flexibility.** Renters don't have to sell their home when it's time to move. Selling a home can be a long and costly process.

- **Financial advantages.** People who rent homes do not have to pay for general repairs. If something breaks, the owner is obligated to fix it. This also usually applies to property taxes and any upkeep of the facility. Homeowner's insurance is the responsibility of the homeowner. Renters should have renter's insurance for their personal items.

Owning a Home

Many people choose to buy a home because they value a feeling of permanence. Owning a home also offers freedom. Homeowners can redecorate or remodel their home to meet their personal needs and tastes. The major reason for owning a home is to develop an investment that can provide a sense of financial security.

Purchasing a place to live isn't a decision to be made lightly. A home is usually the most expensive purchase families will ever make. To buy a home, most people take out a long-term loan called a **mortgage**. The mortgage is typically for 15 to 30 years. The interest paid on the mortgage can be deducted on the homeowner's income tax return. This is an incentive for many people to buy instead of rent a home.

The part of the purchase price paid up front is called a down payment. The down payment can be quite large, often at least 10% of the total house cost. Other costs must also be considered. A homeowner usually must pay property taxes and insurance, along with utilities and repair fees. See **Fig. 38-6**.

Fig 38-6 Some single-family homes are older, preowned homes. These homes might need repairs that new homes do not. Why might people choose a preowned home over a new home?

Many people want to invest in a home but don't want the responsibilities of yard work and maintenance outside of the main living space. Two special kinds of housing, which combine some advantages of home ownership and apartment living, offer a solution. **Condominiums** are individually owned units in a multiple-family dwelling. Some are physically connected, and some are freestanding. The owner of each unit pays a fee to help cover the cost of maintaining hallways, landscaping, parking lots, and other common areas. A less common form of ownership is a **cooperative**, or co-op. In a co-op, residents of a multiple-family dwelling form a corporation that owns the building. Instead of buying or renting a housing unit, owners buy shares in the co-op and contribute to its monthly costs. In return, each member receives use of one of the units.

Fig 38-7

When two people share a home, they usually share the expenses and the household chores.

Condominium and co-op owners often have less freedom to make decisions about their homes compared with single-family housing owners. For example, the exterior color of the home and the landscaping, such as flowers, trees, and lawn ornaments, may be restricted.

Sharing a Home

Many people choose to share a home. When they share a home, individuals combine their finances to meet their housing needs yet stay within their spending plans. Classmates may share an apartment to save money. Adult children sometimes return to live with a parent for a time. Older adults may move in with their adult child for care and companionship. Siblings will sometimes live together right out of the family nest, when they are older adults, or at any time during their life span.

Sharing a home only works if people are thoughtful of one another. Every member of the household should have a degree of privacy. See **Fig. 38-7**.

Choosing a Place to Live

Most people live in several types of housing and several locations during their lifetime. People often change housing as their needs and resources change. For example, people may move from an apartment in the city to a home in a suburban area.

The decision to move should be made carefully. Moving can be expensive. You may need to hire movers or rent a truck to move on your own. Having the phone or electric and gas service hooked up, for instance, involves additional fees. When it makes sense to move, the more information you have with which to make a housing decision, the happier you're likely to be with your choice.

Prepare to Move

Moving can be a major project. What can you ask yourself ahead of time to make it easier?

▶ Are you going to move yourself or have someone do it for you? Have you obtained more than one estimate from a professional mover?

▶ Who is going to do the packing, you or the mover? Have you made provisions for fragile items?

▶ Who will inventory your household items and decide what you are taking with you? Will you donate items left behind to a charitable organization or give them to friends?

▶ Will you put things in storage? What will this cost?

▶ How are you organizing moving day? What needs to be done? Who will do it?

Review & Activities

Chapter Summary

- Housing fulfills people's basic needs.
- People's needs, wants, priorities, and resources influence their housing decisions.
- Single-family and multiple-family housing options have advantages and disadvantages.
- Buying a home is a major decision that should be considered carefully.
- Most people live in several types of housing and several locations during their lifetime.

Reviewing Key Terms & Ideas

1. What basic human needs does housing fulfill?
2. List five needs, wants, and priorities that influence housing decisions.
3. What should be considered when calculating the cost of housing?
4. What do **utilities** include?
5. Explain the difference between single-family and multiple-family housing.
6. Describe a **duplex**, a **multiplex**, a **townhouse**, and an **apartment**.
7. Define **landlords**. Why would a landlord want a renter to sign a **lease**?
8. What is a **mortgage**?
9. What is the difference between a **condominium** and a **cooperative**?
10. What expenses are involved in moving?

Thinking Critically

1. **Making comparisons.** How do your family's housing needs differ from those of single young adults and older adults?
2. **Analyzing situations.** What advice would you offer a friend whose family is considering buying a home in your community?
3. **Predicting consequences.** Describe possible consequences that might occur when two people with different housekeeping or privacy standards share housing.

Review & Activities

Applying Your Learning

1. **Housing needs.** Talk with your parents or guardians about housing features they consider important. How did these features affect their choice to move into your current home?

2. **Housing evaluation.** Many people with special needs require modifications to their home so that they can be independent. Research the types of modifications builders use to make homes accessible for people with special needs. Use this information to rate the accessibility of your home.

3. **Local housing.** Look around your community or use the real estate section of your newspaper to find out which types of housing are available in your neighborhood. What type of housing seems to be most available? Why do you think this is so?

4. **Rental agreements.** Interview a landlord or property management company to find out what a standard lease agreement involves. Is there a minimum age for renters? What documents are required for a person to rent the housing? Share your findings with the class.

5. **Service project.** Habitat for Humanity International is an organization that helps renovate and build homes for people who would otherwise not be able to afford a home. Find out more about this organization and how you can help.

Making Connections

1. **Writing** Write a classified ad describing a home for sale or rent. Emphasize the features you believe would best fulfill people's needs. What might be the "hook" (something to grab the buyer)?

2. **Reading** Read online or print sources on universal design. Choose one adaptation to present to the class.

3. **Math** Use the classified ads in your local newspaper to find an apartment rental. What is the total rent for six months? Make sure to add the approximate cost of utilities if they are not included.

JAMES SMITH
123 Main Street, Springfield, IN 77007
(555) 555-555 (Telephone)
(555) 223-4568 (Fax)

OBJECTIVE A paid position as a preschool teacher assistant.

SUMMARY
- Three years of experience baby sitting for five families.
- Two years as an assistant coach for Little League baseball my two younger brothers.
- Class president of Family, Career, and Community Lead
- Completed Red Cross CPR training course and D. A. R.
- Sophomore student at Hayes High School, currently on first semester.

WORK EXPERIENCE AND ACCOMPLISHMENTS ●
2003 - Present   Child Care Worker   Mr. & Mrs. Greg

CAREER Link

Résumés.
When you apply for a job, you may be asked to submit a résumé. A résumé is a summary of your education, work experience, and skills. Information on your résumé should be organized, accurate, and free of errors. Use the Internet to find different types of résumés, such as functional or reverse chronological. Which do you think would best present your qualifications?

Decorating Living Space

Objectives

- Give guidelines to consider when planning a decorating project.
- Describe the elements of design and the effects they create.
- Explain how to apply the principles of design to a decorating project.
- Demonstrate the selecting and arranging of furniture and accessories.
- Propose strategies for sharing space.

Vocabulary

- **unity**
- **backgrounds**
- **functional furniture**
- **traffic patterns**

Reading with Purpose

1. **As you read** Chapter 39, create an outline in your notebook using the colored headings.
2. **Write** a question under each heading that you can use to guide your reading.
3. **Answer** the question under each heading as you read the chapter. Record your answers.
4. **Ask** your teacher to help with answers you could not find in this chapter.

Using Design

Some people seem to have a natural talent for decorating a room. However, in most cases, good design doesn't just happen. Effective interior design requires careful planning. Whether your project is simple, such as painting your bedroom walls a new color, or complicated, such as a complete remodel, think about the project before you begin. If you do a little

planning, you are more likely to be pleased with the results See **Fig. 39-1**. When planning a decorating project, do the following:

- **Identify what you need.** What is your major goal? How will the space be used? What type of storage is needed?

- **Evaluate your current space.** What parts of the present design work well? What needs improvement? What specifically would you like to keep or change?

- **Keep your resources in mind.** How much can you afford to spend? There's no point in planning expensive changes if they are beyond your budget. Remember that skills are resources, too. Changing a room's look can mean adding a few new touches to what you already have.

- **Identify your preferences.** What look do you want? What styles do you like?

Elements of Design

Many people attempt to design living space with little success. No matter how they arrange furniture or what colors and accessories they add, they are never pleased with the results. To achieve a satisfying look, people should use the elements of design. These elements include space, line, form, texture, and color. See **Fig. 39-2**.

- **Space** refers to the three-dimensional area to be designed, such as a room, as well as to the area around or between objects within that expanse. Whatever the size of the space, you have two basic choices: fill the space or leave much of it empty. Your choice can make a room seem quite different. For example, a room with a lot of furniture may give some people a cozy feeling, but others may feel cramped. On the other hand, too much empty space creates the feeling that something is missing.

- **Line,** often considered the most basic design element, refers to the outline of an object or to the obvious lines within it. All lines are either straight or curved and are placed in a direction—vertical, horizontal, or diagonal. Lines can be combined to make zigzags or other variations and can cause your eyes to move up and down or across an object. Lines delineate space when they intersect, such as at the edges of a wall, floor, or ceiling. You can combine and place lines to create certain effects and feelings. For example, tall bookcases give the illusion of height, and the long, horizontal lines of a sofa direct your eyes across a room.

- **Form,** or the shape and structure of solid objects, is created when lines are combined. Form may be two-dimensional or three-dimensional. Examples of two-dimensional forms are walls and rugs. They have length and width but little or no depth. A piece of furniture is a three-dimensional form. It has depth in addition to length and width. An object's form can make it seem heavy or light. A large, heavy sofa gives a feeling of stability to a room, and spindly chairs in the same space produce the opposite effect.

- **Texture** describes the way an object's surfaces look and feel. People respond to texture in different ways. For example, plush rugs and furniture covered with soft fabric provide a sense of warmth and luxury. Glass, metal, and stone tend to give a feeling of coolness. Texture can also affect color. Smooth textures appear lighter in color than rough textures.

- **Color,** often called the most important of all decorating elements, influences how people feel and can be used to create a certain mood. For these reasons, color should be chosen carefully. For example, red often conveys strength and excitement. Many greens and blues have a calming effect. Yellow can give a feeling of cheerfulness, but large expanses of gray may do the opposite. Colors associated with the sun—red, orange, and yellow—are called warm colors. Blues and greens, like the colors of the sea, are considered cool colors. For more information about using color, see **Fig. 39-3**.

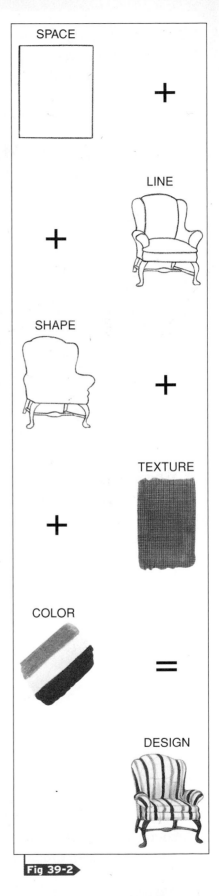

SPACE

LINE

SHAPE

TEXTURE

COLOR

DESIGN

Fig 39-2

Fig 39-3 ▶ Using Color

The color wheel, which is shown in Fig. 39-2, is a helpful tool for understanding and using color. The wheel is divided into 12 pie-shaped sections that display three types of colors: primary, secondary, and intermediate.

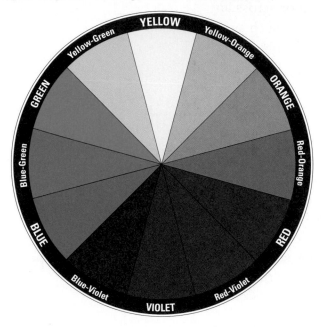

To make violet, red and blue are mixed together. Green is a mixture of yellow and blue, and orange is made from red and yellow. On the color wheel, the secondary colors are halfway between the primary colors from which they're made.

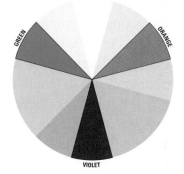

▶ **Primary colors.** Red, yellow, and blue are primary colors and are placed an equal distance apart on the wheel. The other colors on the wheel can be made from them.

▶ **Intermediate colors.** When a primary and a neighboring secondary color are mixed, an intermediate color is made. The six intermediate colors are yellow-green, blue-green, blue-violet, red-violet, yellow-orange, and red-orange. (Note that the primary color comes first in the name of the intermediate color.) The intermediate colors fill the remaining spaces on the wheel.

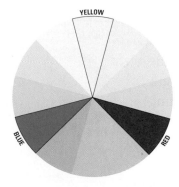

▶ **Secondary colors.** When two primary colors are mixed, the result is a secondary color. The three secondary colors are violet, green, and orange.

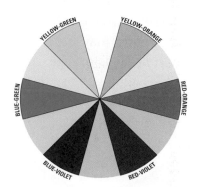

You may have noticed that neutral colors—black, white, and gray—are not on the color wheel. However, neutral colors can be used to change the lightness or darkness of a color.

Color schemes, or combinations of color, are also important in the study of color. Color schemes are pleasing to the eye and are based on the color wheel:

▶ **Monochromatic** schemes use variations of only one color. For example, you could combine light and dark or dull and bright greens.

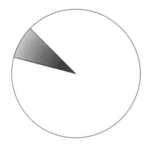

▶ **Analogous** schemes are made up of two or more colors next to one another on the color wheel. Blue-green, green, and blue, for example, form an analogous color scheme.

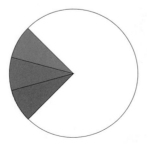

▶ **Complementary** schemes are made up of two colors directly opposite each other on the color wheel, such as red and green.

▶ **Split-complementary** schemes result when a color is combined with colors on each side of its complement. Blue, red-orange, and yellow-orange are examples.

▶ **Triadic** schemes use three colors the same distance from one another on the color wheel. For example, green, orange, and violet form a triadic scheme.

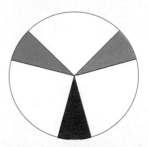

Principles of Design

All good designs follow certain principles that have evolved over time. By applying the following principles to the elements of design, you can achieve appealing decorating results that fit your personality:

- **Proportion** is the way one part of a design relates in size to another part and to the whole design. For example, wooden chairs with thick legs and backs would be in proportion to a bulky oak table. Small, spindly chairs would not. When considering proportion, think of shape, as well as size. Designers know that certain shapes are more pleasing than others because of their proportions. For example, rectangles are often more desirable than squares. Consider how often you see rectangular rugs, windows, and picture frames compared with square ones. However, a rectangle that is too long and narrow may not work visually.

- **Scale** refers to the overall size of an object compared with other objects, especially humans. Scale is not the same as proportion. A lamp may be well proportioned, with a pleasing ratio of shade to base. To be in scale with a room, however, it must also be an appropriate size in relation to the other furnishings. A small lamp might be the right scale for a medium-sized nightstand but out of scale if placed on a large table.

Fig 39-4

The principles of design can help you design attractive living spaces.

- **Balance** gives a feeling of equal weight to objects on both sides of a design's center point. Symmetrical balance is achieved when objects on one side of an imaginary center line are the mirror image of those on the other side. Symmetrical balance is also known as formal balance. In asymmetrical balance, objects on each side are unmatched but appear balanced. Asymmetrical balance is also referred to as informal balance.

- **Emphasis,** or focal point, is the point of greatest interest in a room or a living area. Examples of emphasis include a brightly painted headboard, a large poster or painting, a large couch, or a bookshelf. The focal point doesn't have to be expensive, and it can be more than one item. Instead of one large framed painting, you can create a center of interest on a wall with a collection of smaller items, such as photographs or drawings. See **Fig. 39-5**.

Fig 39-5 When people enter a room, they are drawn first to its focal point. What is the focal point of this room?

- **Unity** is the feeling that all parts of a design belong together. However, everything doesn't have to match for unity to be achieved. A design should also have variety, or the combination of different but compatible styles. Without some variety, rooms can be dull and monotonous. Too much variety, on the other hand, can be visually distracting. To be effective, unity and variety need to be combined to create a harmonious effect.

- **Rhythm** is a feeling of movement, leading the eye from one point to another. A specific color repeated at various points in a room creates a sense of rhythm. So do different sizes of candles, candlesticks, or flower vases, arranged from tall to short, or chairs arranged around a circular table. Arched doorways, draperies with flowing swags, and a sofa with a back curving into the arms are other examples of rhythm.

Backgrounds

The background of your room is the artist's canvas for the elements of design. **Backgrounds** are the walls, floors, windows, and ceilings of a living area. Sometimes, a room's background may be the center of interest. At other times, a background may go almost unnoticed, only helping display furniture and other possessions to their best advantage.

Walls

Walls define areas, provide privacy, and help absorb noise. Although walls serve as boundaries, the number of ways you can decorate walls is limited only by your imagination. The two most popular ways to decorate walls are painting and wallpapering. If you paint, you can choose from many colors and techniques. You can paint a mural or stencil on all or part of a wall. Wallpaper adds interesting patterns and textures to all or a portion of a wall.

Windows

Sometimes windows are left bare to expose a beautiful view. Usually, however, they are covered in some way for privacy. Window treatments, or window coverings, can provide both privacy and decoration. Window treatment choices include curtains, drapes, shutters, blinds, and shades in a variety of

Fig 39-7
This contemporary table helps this couple combine work and recreation in one room. What other options can you visualize for this setting?

colors and materials. Some people like to combine treatments. For example, you might use shutters and curtains on the same window. See **Fig. 39-6**.

Floors

Flooring materials—such as concrete, wood, ceramic, and stone, including granite, marble, slate, and brick—are a permanent part of the floor. Floor coverings, which aren't considered permanent, may be installed over permanent flooring. They can add comfort, warmth, and beauty to a room. Vinyl, for example, is easy to clean. It's warmer and quieter to walk on than ceramic tile and other hard materials, but vinyl is more easily damaged. Carpets and rugs provide extra warmth and comfort, muffle noise, and add color. Wood laminate is durable, attractive, and usually more affordable than solid hardwood floors.

Ceilings

Ceilings are an often-forgotten but important feature of a room. Higher ceilings, common in older homes, give a feeling of dignity and elegance. Lower ceilings create a warm, informal feeling, although ceilings that are too low can convey a cramped feeling. Wallpaper, paint, and window treatments can be used to create the illusion of ceiling height.

Furniture

Furniture provides a place for various activities. Most furniture is **functional furniture**—it meets specific needs. Chests, for example, are used to store things. Tables provide space for eating, doing homework, or playing cards. Functional furniture is usually decorative as well. See **Fig. 39-7**.

Fig 39-8 Furniture comes in a variety of formal and informal styles. Can you identify these furniture styles?

Furniture Styles

Because people's tastes differ, manufacturers make many styles of furniture. These styles can be divided into two basic types: traditional and contemporary. Traditional styles are based on designs used for hundreds of years. Traditional furniture can be formal or informal, fancy or plain. Contemporary furniture is simple and reflects today's lifestyles. It has straight or gently curved lines with little or no decoration. Plastic, glass, and metal are often used for contemporary furniture, but wood and fabric can also be used. See **Fig. 39-8**.

Choosing and Arranging Furniture

Before selecting furniture, think about what you need and what you have. If your budget is limited, put your creativity to work. Garage sales, flea markets, and consignment stores often have used furniture bargains. With a fresh coat of paint or a new cushion, these pieces might become just what you have in mind.

When choosing furniture for a room, look for styles that have a similar feeling, such as different wood furniture pieces with similar simple lines. Every piece of furniture in a room doesn't have to match exactly. Even if the pieces are from different time periods, they still can be interesting.

The smart way to arrange furniture is to use graph paper or a computer program before using your muscles. Take time to think about your arrangement. Ask others for their ideas. Check to see whether the **traffic patterns**, or the paths people use to get from one area or room to another, are uncluttered and fairly direct. Avoid blocking traffic patterns with furniture or other obstacles.

Accessories

What's the easiest and least expensive way to change a room? Accessories, such as lamps, plants, posters, books, baskets, pictures, and mirrors, can change a room dramatically. When selecting accessories, keep in mind the elements and principles of design and use them to create the effect you want.

When you consider accessories, let your imagination soar. You might choose to accessorize a room by displaying your collection of sports memorabilia, CDs, old record album covers, baseball caps, hats, jewelry, or other items that express your personality and interests.

Lighting

Lighting is part of interior design and should be considered when you're planning a project. Each of the three main types of lighting has a unique purpose:

- **General lighting,** such as an overhead ceiling light, provides enough light that you can move around a room safely and comfortably. In most cases, general lighting isn't good light for reading or studying.

- **Task lighting** focuses light where it's needed. You use task lighting to prevent eyestrain when reading, working on hobbies, and playing games. Task lighting should be free of distracting glare and shadows. If you use a table or floor lamp for reading, the bottom of the shade should be slightly below eye level when you are seated. If the lighting is above your eye level, the lamp should be about 10 inches (4 cm) behind your shoulder. See **Fig. 39-9**.

Accessorize Your Walls

You can hang pictures and other items on the walls to give a room a warm, personal look. When planning wall decorations, keep these tips in mind:

▶ Hang decorations at eye level.

▶ Choose items that are in proportion to the area in which they will be hung or to the pieces of furniture that will be under them.

▶ Use an uneven number of items if you are creating a wall arrangement. Uneven numbers are more interesting and pleasing to the eye.

▶ When arranging a wall grouping, trace each item on paper and cut out the shapes. Practice arranging these paper "wall decorations" (using masking tape on the back) before fastening the hangers or nails to the wall.

Fig 39-9 Lighting is an important but often-overlooked feature. Which types of lighting are in this photo?

- **Accent lighting** is an intense beam of light aimed at a painting, sculpture, or other object to create a dramatic or directed effect. Accent lighting can be installed in the ceiling or can be freestanding.

Sharing Space

Everybody has to share space. Sharing space is part of life whether you're at school, at home, or at work. In a family, everyone shares common areas, such as the kitchen and living room. Bathrooms are usually shared, too. Many teens share a bedroom with one or more siblings. If you share a room, you have probably discovered that differences in age, interests, friends, and study habits can create occasional conflicts.

That's where furniture arrangement might offer a solution. Is there a way you can arrange your furniture to help make sharing easier? In a shared bedroom, you might try separating the sleeping and activity areas of the room. Another possibility is to divide the room so that you each have a private area.

Whenever people share the same space, it also helps to agree on a few ground rules. Rules will keep conflicts to a minimum and help you enjoy your time together. Respect and consideration for everyone sharing the space are the keys to effective rules. You might, for example, agree not to use one another's books or clothes without permission. Once you agree on a list of rules, make a commitment to stick to them.

Think of sharing space as a plus, not a minus. Learning how to share space can teach you a lot about yourself and others. The cooperation and communication skills you develop will help you now and in the future. See **Fig. 39-10**.

HOW TO HANG BORDERS

How can you dress up plain walls without tackling full-scale wallpapering? You can add a border, a decorative strip of wallpaper, as an accent. You can hang a border near the ceiling or in the middle of the wall as a chair rail. You can also hang borders around doors or windows. Hanging borders doesn't take special skills, but patience and attention to detail are vital. To hang borders successfully, follow these steps:

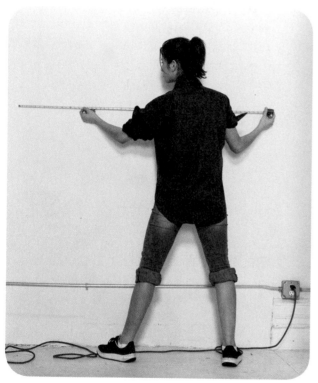

STEP 1 | **Measure the area to be covered.** By measuring the area, you will know how much border to buy. Measure walls from corner to corner with a tape measure, instead of taking one continuous measurement. Add the wall measurements. For a chair rail, measure the height from the floor. Double-check all measurements. Draw a line on the wall with a pencil showing where the border will go. Use a level while drawing to make sure the line is straight.

STEP 2 | **Prepare the walls.** Wash and dry the border area thoroughly. If the area is painted with a gloss or semigloss paint, sand it or brush on an undercoat of wallpaper primer, which helps the border stick.

STEP 3 | **Measure and cut the roll of border to the right length.** Add a few inches to allow for overlap in corners and at the ends of rolls, especially if you need to match the pattern. Cut the border with a razor knife.

STEP 5 **Hang the border.** Place the border as desired, unfolding as you go. The glue takes a few minutes to set, leaving time for adjustments. Wipe with a damp sponge to remove any seeping glue, pressing out air bubbles and creases.

STEP 6 **Trim the overlap.** Continue hanging border pieces, lining up the designs of each piece. Carefully cut through both pieces of overlapping border using a razor knife and a straight edge. Use a pin to pop any bubbles that remain after drying and flatten the bubbles with your fingers.

STEP 4 **Activate the adhesive.** The easiest borders to use are self-adhesive. Simply pull off the backing to reveal the sticky side. To use prepasted borders, loosely fold the paper pattern side in and place it in a tray of water. Leave the paper in the tray as long as indicated on the package instructions. Pull it out and let it drip a few seconds, holding it in loose, accordion folds with the paste side together.

TAKE ACTION

With a classmate, practice hanging border using scraps of border and sheetrock, sometimes available at discounted prices from home improvement stores. Give a demonstration for the class.

Review & Activities

Chapter Summary

- You will be more pleased with a decorating project if you do a little planning.
- Use the elements and principles of design to create living space that you and your family enjoy.
- Backgrounds are the walls, floors, windows, and ceiling of a living area.
- Before moving furniture, take time to plan your arrangement.
- Respect and consideration can help make sharing space easier.

Reviewing Key Terms & Ideas

1. Why is it important to consider your resources when making plans to decorate a room?
2. Explain the relationship between line and form.
3. Which element of design is often considered the most important? Why?
4. What is the difference between symmetrical and asymmetrical balance?
5. What is **unity**?
6. Name two ways **backgrounds** in a home may be used.
7. What are three purposes of walls?
8. List five types of window treatments.
9. Give an example of **functional furniture**.
10. What are **traffic patterns**?
11. What can help people share space successfully?

Thinking Critically

1. **Making comparisons.** Visualize some of the colors in nature. Compare colors you see in spring with colors you see during winter. How do seasonal colors make you feel?
2. **Analyzing situations.** Some people rent furniture and pay a monthly fee to use it. In what situations might renting furniture be beneficial?
3. **Drawing conclusions.** Think about siblings who share a room. What do you think they may learn from sharing space? How can they use these lessons in the future?

Review & Activities

Applying Your Learning

1. **Design display.** Create a display of photos from decorating magazines that show the elements and principles of design. Label and discuss each example.

2. **Class project.** Plan a decorating project for a room in your school, such as your classroom, a conference room, or a hallway. Incorporate the elements and principles of design in your plan. Present your plan to the school principle.

3. **Family discussion.** With your family, discuss ideas for using color in your home. Discuss the use of color on walls, window treatments, and furniture. If possible, carry out an idea and evaluate the results. Did you achieve the desired effect?

4. **Furniture arrangement.** Use graph paper and paper furniture to rearrange furniture in your bedroom or another room of your home. Make sure traffic patterns are clear. Show your arrangement to classmates to see what suggestions they can offer.

5. **Life simulation.** With a partner, enact a scene in which two family members are in conflict over a shared space. With the audience, brainstorm ground rules that will help the family members share space successfully.

Making Connections

1. **Reading** Read career information to learn about jobs in the interior design field. What are some job opportunities in the field? What education and skills are required?

2. **Writing** Use the Internet or interior design magazines to research the work of a particular designer. How does the designer use the elements and principles of design? Write an essay evaluating the designer's work.

3. **Math** Make a list of new furniture you would like for your bedroom. Estimate the total cost of the furniture. Check a furniture store or newspaper ads for pricing and calculate the actual cost. How close was your estimate?

4. **Reading** Read books or Internet sources about folk art, wicker, or twig furniture or any furniture other than traditional or contemporary. Present the information to your class.

CAREER Link

Social Skills.
You first learn social skills at home as you interact with your family. As you grow, you also learn from your friends, classmates, and people on the job. Friendliness, enthusiasm, courtesy, and respect for others' opinions are important not only at home but also at work. Write a brief evaluation of your social skills. How do you think they can help you in the workplace?

Clean & Safe Environments

Objectives

- Describe renewable and nonrenewable resources.
- Demonstrate strategies for conserving resources.
- Give guidelines for making wise consumer decisions.
- Create a home maintenance plan.
- Explain home safety procedures.

Vocabulary

- **global environment**
- **natural resources**
- **renewable resources**
- **nonrenewable resources**
- **conservation**
- **home maintenance**
- **hazard**

Reading with Purpose

1. **Read** the title of this chapter and describe in writing what you expect to learn from it.

2. **Write** each vocabulary term in your notebook, leaving space for definitions.

3. **As you read** Chapter 40, write the definition beside each term in your notebook.

4. **After** reading the chapter, write a paragraph describing what you learned.

The Earth–Your Home

Imagine a giant billboard with a picture of the earth on it. The sign's slogan reads, "What have you done for me lately?" How would you answer the question? Would you be proud of your answer?

Today, the earth faces many challenges. Pollution, the presence of harmful substances on land, in water, and in the air, is just a problem that communities everywhere need to solve. The **global environment**—all living and nonliving elements on earth—needs your care. Fortunately, there is some

Fig 40-1▸ Many teens are taking responsible action against pollution. What can you do to help fight pollution?

good news. Many people are becoming aware of environmental problems and are making positive changes. Are you among those making a difference? See **Fig. 40-1**.

The Earth's Natural Resources

Air, water, and trees are some of the earth's **natural resources**, or resources that occur in nature. Think about what life would be like without forests, rivers, lakes, and blue skies. The air you breathe and the water you drink help keep you alive and healthy. Other natural resources include coal and natural gas. These fuels are used to provide heat, light, and energy to run machines.

The Supply of Natural Resources

Some resources, called **renewable resources**, replace or renew themselves over time. Plants renew themselves by producing seeds, which in turn produce new plants. Air, water, and soil are also renewed through natural cycles, unless something interferes with them.

Nonrenewable resources do not replace themselves, and their supply is limited. For example, once current world supplies of oil, copper, iron, and other minerals are used up, no more will be available. Supplies of nonrenewable resources could last indefinitely, but only if people use them wisely.

Conserving Earth's Resources

Everyone has the responsibility to help manage the earth's natural resources. You can do your part by practicing **conservation**, or the protection of resources against waste and harm.

Water Resources

What if you turned on the faucet one morning and no water came out of the tap? Severe water shortages exist in many parts of the world. In other areas, water supplies are polluted and unusable. No matter where you live, clean, fresh water is a precious resource that should not be wasted. Here are some simple ways you and your family can conserve water:

• **Make a compost pile.** Instead of putting fruit and vegetable scraps in the garbage disposal, which requires water, put them in a compost pile, which in time turns the material into fertile organic matter for plants. You might even see unusual new plants come out of your compost pile. See **Fig. 40-2**.

- **Avoid wasting water.** Take quick showers instead of long baths. Turn faucets completely off while brushing your teeth or washing dishes. Wait until you have a full load before running the dishwasher or washing machine. Also, do not overwater your lawn or garden. Talk to your parents about low-flow showerheads and toilets and aerators on your faucets. These devices use less water yet supply the same water pressure.

- **Make needed repairs.** Leaky faucets can waste gallons of water each day. Help repair plumbing leaks promptly.

- **Keep water supplies clean.** Improperly disposing of household chemicals, such as detergents and pesticides, can pollute local streams, rivers, and lakes. Always follow package instructions when disposing of household chemicals.

Heating and Cooling Energy

It takes natural resources to heat and cool a home. Some heating requires nonrenewable fuels, such as oil. Other kinds of heating and air conditioning depend on electricity—often produced by burning a nonrenewable fuel. For fuel supplies to last, it's important to use less. Home improvements, such as installing weather stripping around doors and windows, plastic film for windows, clear removable weather stripping, and insulation in the attic, can help conserve fuel. Here are some other ideas to help conserve heating and cooling resources:

- **Heating resources** can be conserved by setting the heater no higher than 68°F (20°C) during the day and turning the thermostat down at bedtime. Close shades and draperies at night in cold weather to keep in the heat and keep out the cold. On sunny days, open shades and draperies to let the sun's energy heat your home. Also, layer clothing by wearing sweaters and turtleneck shirts under clothes and wearing additional heavy socks in cooler months.

Fig 40-2 Natural compost provides much-needed nutrients to gardens while saving consumers money.

- **Cooling resources** can be conserved by setting the air conditioner thermostat no lower than 78°F (26°C) during summer months. Be sure to clean or replace the air conditioning filter when it is dirty. Choose fans over air conditioners whenever possible. Fans use less electricity. Install solar screens to keep the sun's heat from entering through windows, and close draperies during the day to keep heat out. Also, dress in lightweight clothing to keep cool in warm weather.

Energy for Lighting and Appliances

Lighting and appliances use the earth's fuel. The following tips can help you and your family stretch those resources:

- **Lighting.** Replace lightbulbs with compact fluorescent lights, which use less electricity. Use only the number of lights you need in a room. For example, if you can get a job done with one lamp, turn off all others. Also, always turn off lights when you leave a room.

- **Appliances.** Keep oven doors closed when cooking, and avoid opening the refrigerator door unnecessarily. Try air drying dishes and clothes. If using a dryer, remove clothes as soon as they are dry and clean the dryer's lint filter at each use. Also, use an appliance that requires the smallest amount of energy for the specific task. For example, hand chop a small onion instead of using a food processor. Save appliances for bigger jobs.

Efficient Transportation

Some of today's vehicles, known as hybrid vehicles, are powered by a combination of gasoline and electric power. However, most vehicles are powered either by gasoline or by diesel fuel. These fuels are made from crude oil, or petroleum, which is a nonrenewable resource. To cut fuel use and still meet transportation needs, your family can use transportation that doesn't require fuel, such as biking and walking, or public transportation, such as buses and subways. Family members can also form carpools to share rides.

Combining errands into one fuel-saving trip also conserves fuel. When in line at a bank or fast-food restaurant, avoid wasting fuel by idling the car. Instead, go inside. Vehicle maintenance also affects a vehicle's energy efficiency. Change the family vehicle's oil at recommended intervals (about 3,000 miles), check tire pressure monthly, have tires rotated regularly, and schedule tune-ups to keep the vehicle running properly.

Consumer Choices

Many products are manufactured using natural resources as raw materials. Paper, for example, is made from wood pulp, a substance from the wood of trees. Some of these raw materials, such as trees, are renewable. Others can only be used once. See **Fig. 40-3.**

Although government regulations restrict pollution, you, the consumer, also play an important role. Think before you buy. You can help conserve natural resources and reduce pollution by taking the following steps:

Fig 40-3 Simple habits, such as saving and reusing bags or using cloth bags, can make a big difference in the environment.

- **Recycle as many products as possible.** Plastic containers with specified numbers and bottles and cans are recycled in many communities. Some stores give customers incentives to recycle printer cartridges and film containers.

- **Buy products that feature the recycling symbol.** This symbol is on packages that can be recycled and packages made from recycled materials.

- **Choose items that are long lasting.** Examples include rechargeable batteries and long-lasting lightbulbs.

- **Select items with little or no packaging.** It takes resources to make wrappers and boxes that are quickly discarded. If you buy something with packaging material, see if you can recycle it. Use embellishments, such as stamping and embossing, to create new wrapping.

- **Reuse plastic, sturdy paper, and cloth shopping bags.** Keep them handy so that you'll remember to use them each time. Some stores will actually pay you or deduct an amount on your grocery bill if you bring in your own bags.

- **Buy energy-efficient appliances.** EnergyGuide and EnergyStar labels will help you choose appliances that make good use of fuels.

- **Buy vehicles that get good gas mileage.** When purchasing a vehicle, compare the miles per gallon of various models. Select a model that gets the most mileage for the least amount of fuel.

I Can Take Action Against Trash

Unfortunately, you see it everywhere—in parks, on the streets, around your school, and even in lakes and rivers. What is it? It's trash. Not only is trash unpleasant to look at, but it also can be harmful to people, animals, and the planet. The good news is you can take action against trash by precycling, reusing, and recycling.

Precycling

When you precycle, you reduce the amount of trash you produce. There are many ways to become a precycler:

- **Buy fewer fast foods.** Each part of a fast-food meal is individually wrapped. Skip the fast-food lines and bring your meal in a reusable lunch bag.

- **Buy in bulk.** Buy bulk snacks and store them in reusable containers.

- **Avoid disposable items.** Razors, cameras, and cups are a few disposable goods that increase the load on landfills.

- **Use environmentally friendly cleaning products.** Manual pump spray products are better for the environment then aerosols, and the bottles can be refilled and reused.

- **Choose products with little or no packaging.** You can also buy products that come in recyclable packaging—be sure to recycle it.

- **Bring your own shopping bag.** Either use a cloth bag or reuse a sturdy paper or plastic bag from the store. If you're buying just one item, skip the bag.

Reusing

Many things you throw away can be reused. If you use your imagination, you will find there are ways to use almost everything at least twice. Here are some ideas to get you started:

- **Plastic containers.** Use these items to organize your belongings. They can also be donated to a child or adult care facility. They use these items for many things, including art projects.
- **Old, ripped towels and sheets.** Cut these items into small pieces for housecleaning chores, such as cleaning and dusting.
- **Books and magazines.** School and local libraries, community centers, and homeless shelters will usually gladly accept these donated items.

- **Old clothing and toys.** You can donate these to charity or sell them in a yard sale or on the Internet.
- **Wrapping paper, plastic bags, and boxes.** All of these items can be reused if they're in good condition.

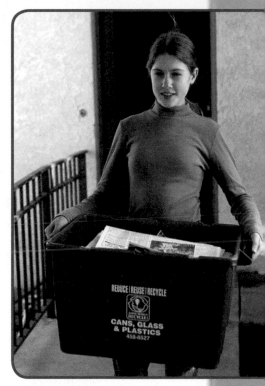

Recycling

Recycling is the treating of trash so that it can be reused rather than buried in landfills. Many communities have recycling programs. Check for your local recycling facilities. You and your family can likely recycle the following items:

- Paper and cardboard
- Glass bottles and jars
- Aluminum cans and containers
- Certain recyclable plastics
- Motor oil
- Tires

Creating a Clean and Safe Home Environment

A place where you feel comfortable and safe doesn't just happen. Maintaining a home so that it benefits everyone who lives there takes careful planning. **Home maintenance** includes eliminating clutter, organizing household and personal items, cleaning, making minor repairs or changes, and keeping household equipment in good working order. A home maintenance plan can catch small problems before they develop into large and costly ones. See **Fig. 40-4**.

The most successful home maintenance plans are those that family members develop together. To develop a plan, list maintenance tasks for each room of your home. Then, decide how often each task should be done—daily, weekly, monthly, or annually. Consider how much time each job will take and whether it needs to be done in a certain order. Then decide who will be responsible for each job and whether jobs can be rotated. Even young children can be given simple tasks.

Fig 40-4
Washing dishes is a small task that should be done daily. What might result if dishes are left unwashed?

Daily and Weekly Tasks

Everybody needs to agree on daily and weekly household tasks that are important for health and safety. These tasks don't take long to accomplish and can quickly turn into habits.

Daily tasks include putting away clothes and other belongings, making beds, disposing of trash, caring for pets, and washing dishes with hot, soapy water. Also, wiping up spills as they occur and keeping traffic patterns, stairs, and doorways free of clutter are important for safety.

Many families do overall cleaning once a week. Individual families can determine how often to vacuum, dust, change bed linens, clean bathrooms, wash floors, do laundry, and perform other cleaning tasks that must be done. If you do have pets, you may have some extra cleaning to do. Pets need a clean environment as well.

Occasional Tasks

Some maintenance tasks only need to be taken care of occasionally—once a month, every few months, or once a year. These tasks include cleaning the oven and refrigerator, shampooing carpets, washing walls and windows, cleaning blinds and curtains, and cleaning closets and drawers.

Keep and file instruction booklets that come with furnishings and equipment, and check to find out what special care is required. Add these jobs to the list. Also, you may need to add outdoor jobs, such as raking leaves and cutting grass, to your home maintenance task list. Even if you live where outdoor maintenance is done by others, do your part to keep the area clean.

Storage

The best way to control clutter is to pick up and put away your belongings immediately after you use them. How you organize your storage depends on what you have to store and the kind and size of storage space you have available. If possible, it is best to store items near the area where they are used and to store frequently used items where they can be reached easily.

Cleaning Products and Equipment

Part of becoming organized includes selecting products and equipment for cleaning jobs. Products that clean more than one type of surface often are a good buy. Some jobs, however,

Safety Check

The following steps will help keep you safe as you use cleaning products:

- Keep cleaning products in their original containers so that you will know what they are and how they should be used.

- Never store cleaning products near food.

- Store cleaning products out of the reach of small children. Keep chemicals in a locked cabinet.

- When using products with powerful fumes, make sure there is adequate ventilation. Use a fan and open windows to bring in fresh air.

- Never mix products. The results could be poisonous, explosive, or fatal.

may require a specific product. As you shop, compare labels on various brands to get the best quality for your money. Reading the labels is key.

Using the proper equipment also makes cleaning easier. A broom, mop, bucket, and vacuum cleaner, as well as scrub brushes, discarded toothbrushes, sponges, and dusting cloths, are basic cleaning tools.

HOW TO KEEP UP WITH CLEANUP

"Clean as you go" is a good way to avoid being overwhelmed by dust, dirty dishes, and piles of clothes. Taking a few minutes or less for small cleanups makes the tasks less burdensome. That not only saves your personal energy supply but also reduces the need for harsh cleaners that can be toxic. You're also rewarded with the satisfaction of knowing that you are caring for your home.

Quick cleaning takes a little planning. Keep needed supplies handy and add the needed time to your schedule. Then, with practice, the following tasks can more easily become part of your routine:

- Wipe down sinks, the bathtub, and the shower after using them. Keep spray cleaner on the side of the tub for ease in cleanup.

- Put clothes away, either in a clothes hamper or in a closet or drawer, immediately after wearing them.

- Pick up crumbs or small bits of dirt as you notice them. Keep a dust pan and brush handy for small jobs.

- Straighten magazines, CDs, and videotapes while passing through a room.

- Have a box or container specifically for daily mail.

Maintaining a Healthy Home Environment

Keeping your home free of dirt and bacteria that can lead to illness is important. By removing dust and dirt, disposing of garbage, and controlling pests, you help make your home a healthy place to live.

- Unless you plan to reuse them, dispose of containers as soon as they are empty, either in a recycling bin or trash can.

- Recycle plastic bags. Plastic bags from the grocery store recycle into great liners for small waste baskets.

- When you take an item from a counter, shelf, or cabinet, check the space for dust or dirt. Wipe clean as needed.

- Pick up litter in your yard on your way to school and place it in the trash. Never throw trash out of a car window.

- Throw out or recycle unwanted mail as it comes in. A paper shredder works wonders on unwanted mail and fliers. Mail shreds make great packing material for outgoing packages.

TAKE ACTION

Choose one of the tips here and ask family members to help you carry it out. If necessary, assemble a kit of needed cleaning supplies (look for environmentally friendly choices) and store it in a safe and convenient location. Assess the results. Does the area stay cleaner? Are larger cleaning tasks easier? If not, what added steps could you take?

Dust and Dirt

Dust and dirt can be removed by sweeping, dusting, vacuuming, washing, and mopping. Sweeping with a broom removes dirt from hard floors. You can also use brooms for seasonal jobs, such as cleaning window screens and dusting cobwebs from walls and ceilings.

Vacuum or wipe windowsills and baseboards. Then dust all furnishings except upholstered pieces. Don't forget areas such as chair legs and lampshades. Wood furniture needs occasional polishing to keep it in good condition. Make sure that what you put on wood furniture is compatible with the furniture you have.

A vacuum cleaner can remove dust and dirt from carpeting, hard floors, upholstered furniture, and draperies. Its suction draws soil particles into the machine, where it's trapped inside a bag or container. For proper operation, change vacuum bags, filters, and containers frequently. See **Fig. 40-5**.

Washable hard floors need regular washing to remove stubborn dirt. Use a mop—there are all kinds available to choose from—water, and a cleaner that is safe for the type of floors you have.

Cleaning is usually most efficient if certain tasks are performed in a particular order. For example, as you dust, work from the top to the bottom to keep dust from ending up on already dusted areas. Some people prefer cleaning the outside edges of a room first. Then they clean the center and finish with the floor. This sequence helps make sure no areas are skipped.

Fig 40-5
Picking up clothing before you vacuum will allow you to vacuum more thoroughly.

Garbage

An overflowing garbage can and dirty dishes in the sink can make an otherwise clean house look dirty. Because standing garbage may contain thousands of germs, it is also a safety hazard. Garbage gives off a bad odor. Make sure to secure garbage can covers. To keep garbage under control, dispose of garbage daily.

Pests

Roaches, ants, flies, and mice are household pests that carry germs that can cause illness. With regular home maintenance, you can usually keep pests under control. If you use pest control products, read and follow directions carefully. Always store the products out of the reach of children, and wear rubber gloves when using them. If a pest problem becomes severe, call a professional to get rid of the pests.

Keeping Your Home Safe

Proper home maintenance can't guarantee your family's safety. However, it can prevent **hazards**, or sources of danger. Avoid falls, electric shocks, fires, and poisoning by eliminating hazards.

Falls

Falls are one of the most common accidents to occur in homes. Fortunately, most falls are preventable. You can avoid such falls by using a nonskid backing on throw rugs and keeping traffic patterns, stairs, and doorways free of clutter and furniture. Use a sturdy ladder or stepstool to reach high items. When climbing stairs, always use the handrail and keep the stairs illuminated.

Electrical Hazards

It's easy to forget that electricity can be dangerous or even fatal. To avoid electrical hazards, keep electrical appliances away from water. Never touch them with wet hands or use them while standing on a wet floor. Don't overload an outlet with too many cords, and never run cords under rugs or carpeting. Keep all appliances and cords in good repair, and cover outlets that small children can reach. See **Fig. 40-6**.

Focus on the Positive

Home maintenance tasks don't have to be a grind. If you approach them with a positive attitude, most of them can be easier and even enjoyable. Consider these suggestions:

▶ Play your favorite music as you work.

▶ Think of vigorous chores as part of your exercise program.

▶ Work with a friend or family member and socialize as you work.

▶ Use household tasks as a way to reduce stress.

▶ Enjoy the benefits of a clean home.

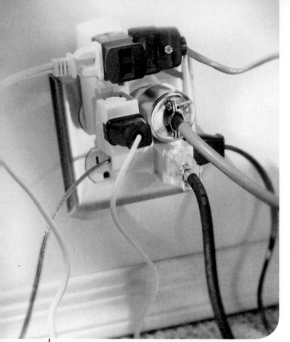

Fires

Most fires in the home are caused by matches, candles, cigarettes, grease, incense, and electrical appliances. Garbage cans, kitchen ranges, mattresses, and upholstered furniture are common places for a fire to start.

Every home should have fire extinguishers and an exit plan. All two-story homes should have a rope ladder for escape. Make sure family members know where the rope ladder is kept and how to use it properly. Keep a chemical extinguisher near, but not above, the kitchen range for grease and electrical fires. Be sure you know how to use it. Keep matches out of children's reach and always monitor candles after you light them. Store flammable products away from all heat sources. If you smell gas in your home, leave the home immediately and call the gas company from a cell phone or a neighbor's home.

Smoke detectors can provide early warning in case of fire and smoke. Make sure your home has smoke detectors near bedroom areas and on each floor. Check all detectors once a month to see that they function properly, and replace batteries twice a year.

Saving your home isn't as important as saving your life. Schedule fire drills so that everyone in the family knows the emergency plan and the quickest way to exit your home in case of fire or another emergency.

Poisons

Poisons can be found in nearly every room of your home. Prescription drugs, pest control products, and some cleaning products are just a few poisonous items you may have in your home. Make sure that poisonous products are stored out of children's reach, preferably in a locked cabinet. Never store poisons in another container, such as a soda bottle, because they can be mistaken for something else. Also, never encourage children to take medicine by telling them medicine is candy. They may go back for more.

Carbon monoxide, an odorless and poisonous gas, is produced by defective gas appliances. If you have gas appliances, install a carbon monoxide detector that alerts you to the presence of carbon monoxide.

Making Repairs

Would you know what to do if you were the only person at home and a toilet overflowed? Do you know where to find the water shut-off valve? What about a blown fuse? Learning to handle minor repairs can save your family money now and prepare you to handle these tasks later in your home. When repairs have to be made in your home, take advantage of the opportunity to watch the person who handles the problem and ask questions. Also, check to see whether your community offers classes that teach home repair skills. See **Fig. 40-7**.

Fig 40-7 Have an adult show you how to make simple home repairs. What you learn now can come in handy later in your own home.

Review & Activities

Chapter Summary

- Unless something interferes with natural cycles, renewable resources replace themselves over time. Nonrenewable resources do not replace themselves.
- You can protect natural resources by doing your part to conserve water and fuel.
- Tomorrow's trash often comes from what you buy today, so make wise consumer decisions.
- A home maintenance plan can help stop small problems from developing into large and costly ones.
- Household tasks that protect health and safety should be carried out regularly.

Reviewing Key Terms & Ideas

1. What is the **global environment**?
2. What is the difference between **renewable** and **nonrenewable resources**?
3. Define **conservation**.
4. Why should plumbing leaks be repaired promptly?
5. What are hybrid vehicles?
6. Name two consumer items that are long lasting and help conserve resources.
7. What does **home maintenance** involve?
8. List four daily tasks.
9. What guidelines should you follow when storing items?
10. What is a **hazard**?
11. What causes most fires?

Thinking Critically

1. **Drawing conclusions.** How is composting an example of reusing and recycling?
2. **Making comparisons.** Think about people you know who have little clutter in their home. How do their clutter control tasks differ from those of people whose homes are filled with clutter?
3. **Evaluating safety.** What are some ways you and your family can make your home safer? Which of these examples would you choose to carry out in your home someday?

Review & Activities

Applying Your Learning

1. **Composting education.** Create a leaflet that shows the steps required to make a compost pile. Share your leaflet with the class. If possible, use the leaflet to create a compost pile in your yard.

2. **Conservation checklist.** Create a conservation checklist for your family members to follow. Include conservation steps for water, heating and cooling resources, and electrical appliances. Share your checklist with your family.

3. **Safety evaluation.** Rate the home safety procedures your family uses on a scale of 1 to 5. A 1 means "poor," and a 5 means "excellent." Afterward, reflect on the hazard prevention strategies in place in your home. What can you do to improve them?

4. **Animal safety.** Home hazards can also harm family pets. Use print and Internet resources to make a list of tips to keep family pets safe in the home. Post your tips list in the classroom.

5. **Fire drill.** Discuss fire drills with your family and create an escape plan for each member. Be sure to include escape routes from each room in the home. Practice your drill until everyone can evacuate quickly.

Making Connections

1. **Writing** Write a letter of appreciation to an individual in your community whose actions show concern for the environment. Identify the actions and how they have affected you, your family, and your community.

2. **Math** Many people are concerned about the amount of trash being put into landfills. Imagine that you throw away 15 pounds of trash each week. How much trash would you throw away in a month? If everyone in your family threw away 15 pounds a week, how much trash would your entire family throw away in a month?

3. **Reading** Using product brochures or Internet sources, read and compare information about various types of home fire extinguishers. Give a short presentation, sharing what you learned.

CAREER Link

Environmental Practices.
Many companies, as well as various state and local agencies, have chosen to incorporate wise environmental practices in the workplace. Employees are encouraged to precycle, recycle, and reuse items. Interview family members or friends about the recycling practices they follow in the workplace. Summarize your interviews in a short report.

Family, Career and Community Leaders of America, Inc. (FCCLA) is a national student organization for students enrolled in family and consumer sciences courses. Involvement in FCCLA offers members the opportunity to develop life skills, expand their leadership potential, and explore careers.

FCCLA promotes personal growth and offers members opportunities to participate in a number of individual and chapter programs that strengthen life skills. Some examples of specific FCCLA programs follow.

Power of One

Power of One helps students find and use their personal power by setting and achieving goals. Members complete projects that focus on improving personal traits, getting along with family members, exploring career options, and developing leadership qualities.

Career Connection

This FCCLA program helps members target career goals. Students focus on six aspects of career development: Plug In to Careers; Sign On to the Career Connection; Program Career Steps; Link Up to Jobs; Access Skills for Career Success; Integrate Work and Life.

Community Service

FCCLA helps members strengthen their contributions to their community through this program. Students develop, plan, carry out, and evaluate projects that improve the quality of life in their communities.

Leadership Programs

FCCLA offers two leadership programs.
- *Dynamic Leadership* offers activities and project ideas that help students learn to model good character, solve problems, foster relationships, manage conflict, and build teams.
- *Leaders at Work* recognizes FCCLA members who create projects to strengthen leadership skills on the job in one of six career areas related to Family and Consumer Sciences.

STAR Events

Students Taking Action with Recognition (STAR) Events are competitive events in which FCCLA members are recognized for proficiency in individual and chapter projects, leadership skills, and career preparation. Here are a few of the *STAR Event* categories:
- Illustrated Talk
- Interpersonal Communications
- Career Investigation
- Job Interview
- Entrepreneurship
- Applied Technology

For more information, contact FCCLA at www.fcclainc.org

Glossary

A

á la carte: Each item has an individual, or separate, price. (Ch. 25)

abbreviation: A short form of a word. (Ch. 28)

abstinence: Not engaging in a sexual activity. (Ch. 20)

academic skills: Competencies in reading, writing, mathematics, and science. (Ch. 5)

accessories: Small items of clothing that complete an outfit. (Ch. 33)

acne: A skin problem that develops when glands below the pores (tiny openings) in the skin become blocked. (Chs. 13, 19)

acquaintances: People an individual may know but who are not personal friends. (Ch. 10)

acquired immunodeficiency syndrome (AIDS): A life-threatening disease that interferes with the body's natural ability to fight infection. (Ch. 20)

addiction: A physical or psychological dependence on something, such as stimulants, depressants, marijuana, or hallucinogens. (Ch. 20)

additives: Substances added to food for a specific purpose. (Ch. 23)

adolescence: The stage of growth between childhood and adulthood. (Ch. 1)

age span: The number of years between siblings. (Ch. 11)

al dente: Tender but firm to the tooth. (Ch. 31)

alcoholics: People addicted to alcohol in the form of beer, wine, or other liquor. (Ch. 13)

alcoholism: Physical and mental dependence on alcohol. (Ch. 12)

allergies: Reactions of the body's immune system, for example, to ingested food. (Ch. 23)

amino acids: Chemical compounds, known as the body's building blocks, that make up protein foods. (Ch. 22)

anabolic steroids: Manufactured substances that alter body characteristics. (Ch. 20)

anorexia: An eating disorder characterized by self-starvation. (Ch. 19)

apartment: A rental unit in a building, or a structure that houses units for more than two families. (Ch. 38)

appetizer: An optional first course, and generally a small portion. (Ch. 25)

aptitudes: Natural tendencies that make it easy for someone to learn a certain skill. (Ch. 4)

assertive: People who stand up for themselves and for their beliefs in firm, but positive, ways. (Ch. 7)

B

backgrounds: The walls, floors, windows, and ceilings of a living area. (Ch. 39)

bacteria: One-celled living organisms so small that they can be seen only with a microscope. (Ch. 27)

basal metabolic rate (BMR): The rate at which the body uses energy when someone is inactive. (Ch. 19)

basting: Holding two or more pieces of fabric together temporarily until they are permanently stitched. (Ch. 37)

benefits: Rewards for employment, besides salary, that may include health insurance, personal financial savings plans or retirement plans, and paid vacations. (Ch. 6)

bias: The diagonal edge formed when the fabric is folded with the crosswise grain parallel to the selvage, or lengthwise grain. (Ch. 36)

binge eating disorder: A disorder characterized by compulsive overeating. (Ch. 19)

body language: The use of gestures and body movements to communicate. (Ch. 7)

boiling: Heating liquid at a high temperature so that bubbles rise and break on the liquid surface. (Ch. 30)

braising: Simmering and steaming food in a small amount of liquid. (Ch. 30)

bran: A grain kernel's edible outer covering. (Ch. 31)

broiling: Cooking food directly under a heat source (heating element). (Ch. 30)

budget: A plan for spending and saving the money available. (Ch. 17)

bulimia: A condition in which people eat large quantities of food in a short period of time and then purge. (Ch. 19)

C

calories: Units for measuring energy that measure the energy contained in food and the energy used when someone is active. (Ch. 22)

carbohydrates: The nutrients that provide the body with most of its energy. (Ch. 22)

cardiopulmonary resuscitation (CPR): A technique used to keep a person's heart and lungs functioning until medical care arrives. (Ch. 14)

career: A series of related jobs in a particular field over a lifetime. (Ch. 4)

career cluster: A large grouping of occupations that have certain characteristics in common. (Ch. 4)

casing: A closed tunnel or space of fabric that can hold a piece of elastic or a drawstring in a waistband. (Ch. 37)

character: A combination of traits that show strong ethical principles and maturity. (Ch. 2)

childproofing: Taking steps to identify possible hazards and removing them. (Ch. 14)

cholesterol: A soft, fatlike, waxy substance found in the bloodstream and in all of the body's cells. (Ch. 22)

citizen: A member of a community, such as a city, town, or country. (Ch. 2)

citizenship: The way in which people handle their responsibilities as citizens. (Ch. 2)

clipping: Making small, straight cuts in the seam allowance. (Ch. 37)

cliques: Groups that exclude others from their circle of friendship. (Ch. 10)

closure: Finality that helps people deal with the reality of a loss. (Ch. 12)

communication: The process of sending messages to—and receiving messages from—others. (Ch. 7)

comparison shopping: Comparing products, prices, and services to get the most value for the money. (Ch. 17)

complete proteins: Meat, fish, poultry, milk products, eggs, and other foods from animal sources, which have all of the nine essential amino acids the body needs. (Ch. 22)

compromise: The process of settling a conflict by each person involved agreeing to give up something that he or she wanted. (Ch. 8)

concussion: A type of head injury characterized by eye pupils that are different sizes, vomiting, or sleepiness after an injury. (Ch. 14)

condominiums: Individually owned units in a multiple-family dwelling for which the owner of each unit pays a fee to help cover the cost of maintaining common areas. (Ch. 38)

conflict: A disagreement, dispute, or fight between people with opposing points of view. (Ch. 8)

conflict resolution: The process of settling a conflict by cooperating and problem solving. (Ch. 8)

conscience: An inner sense of right or wrong. (Ch. 13)

conservation: The protection of resources against waste and harm. (Ch. 40)

consumer: Someone who buys and uses goods and services produced by others. (Ch. 17)

convenience foods: Prepared or partially prepared foods. (Ch. 29)

cookware: Items including pots, pans, and other containers for use on top of the range, in the oven, or in the microwave. (Ch. 26)

cooperative: A unit in a multiple-family dwelling that is owned by a corporation. (Ch. 38)

cooperative play: Playing with other children and learning to share, take turns, solve problems, and control emotions. (Ch. 13)

cost effective: Fewer expenses for greater benefits. (Ch. 18)

courses: Parts of a meal. (Ch. 25)

cover letter: A letter that tells the employer someone is applying for a position in the company. (Ch. 6)

credit rating: A record that shows people's ability and willingness to pay their debts. (Ch. 12)

creditors: People or companies someone owes money to. (Ch. 12)

crime: An illegal act committed against someone or something. (Ch. 21)

crisis: An immediate difficulty that can be life altering. (Ch. 12)

cross-contamination: When harmful bacteria are transferred from one food or surface to another. (Ch. 27)

D

dandruff: Scales and flakes on the scalp. (Ch. 19)

decision making: The act of making a choice. (Ch. 3)

deep-fat frying: Cooking by completely covering the food in fat. (Ch. 30)

deficiency: A shortage, such as when the body does not get enough nutrients. (Ch. 22)

dependable: People who can be counted on and who keep their word. (Ch. 10)

depressants: Drugs that reduce blood pressure and slow heart and breathing rates. (Ch. 20)

dermatologist: A doctor specializing in skin problems. (Ch. 19)

developmental milestones: Skills achieved at a particular stage of life. (Ch. 13)

Dietary Guidelines for Americans: Scientifically based advice for making smart food choices, balancing food choices and physical activity, and getting the most nutrition out of calories. (Ch. 23)

dietary supplements: Pills, capsules, powders, and so on, taken in addition to a person's diet. (Ch. 23)

directional stitching: Stitching in the direction of the grain. (Ch. 37)

discipline: A process that helps children learn to get along with others and control their own feelings. (Ch. 15)

discrimination: Unequal treatment based on factors such as race, religion, nationality, gender (male or female), age, or physical appearance. (Ch. 5)

dovetail: Fitting tasks together to make the best use of time. (Ch. 29)

downsizing: A process that occurs when a company eliminates jobs to save money. (Ch. 5)

dry cleaning: Cleaning with chemicals rather than with water and detergent. (Ch. 35)

duplex: One structure that contains two separate units. (Ch. 38)

E

ease: The extra room in clothes needed for movement and comfort. (Ch. 36)

elements of design: Line, shape, space, texture, and color. (Ch. 33)

empathy: The ability to understand what someone else is experiencing. (Ch. 7)

empty nest: A home the children have left to be on their own. (Ch. 11)

endorse: To sign your name on the back of a check. (Ch. 17)

endosperm: The largest part of the grain kernel, made of starch and protein. (Ch. 31)

enriched: Items that have nutrients added back after processing. (Ch. 31)

entrée: The main course, and a larger portion than the appetizer. (Ch. 25)

entrepreneur: Someone who sets up and operates a business. (Ch. 4)

environment: Everything around you, including people, places, things, and events. (Ch. 1)

equivalents: Amounts that are equal to each other. (Ch. 28)

escalate: To grow into disagreements that are destructive or unsafe to everyone concerned. (Ch. 8)

ethical principles: Standards for right and wrong behavior. (Ch. 2)

etiquette: The accepted rules of behavior at mealtime. (Ch. 25)

expenses: Goods and services purchased. (Ch. 17)

exploitation: A process that occurs when someone uses someone or something for his or her own advantage. (Ch. 21)

eye–hand coordination: The ability of the eyes and the hand and arm muscles to work together to make complex movements. (Ch. 13)

F

fads: Fashions that last only a short time. (Ch. 33)

familial: Relating to the family. (Ch. 2)

family life cycle: The process families go through as they grow and change. (Ch. 11)

fashions: Styles that are currently popular. (Ch. 33)

fiber: Plant material that does not break down during digestion. (Ch. 22)

fibers: Hairlike substances twisted together to make yarns and fabric. (Ch. 34)

financial: Relating to money. (Ch. 12)

finishes: Special treatments that make a fiber or fabric more useful and appealing. (Ch. 34)

flatware: Eating utensils. (Ch. 25)

flextime: A program that lets workers adjust their work schedules to meet family needs as long as the workers put in the required number of hours on the job. (Ch. 6)

food product dating: The process of dating food to indicate product freshness. (Ch. 24)

foodborne illness: An illness caused by eating spoiled food or food containing harmful bacteria. (Ch. 27)

fraud: Telling lies to steal money or valuables. (Ch. 21)

fringe benefits: Services and products received for little or no cost, such as vacation time, sick leave, child care, health insurance, and retirement programs. (Ch. 4)

functional foods: Foods that provide benefits beyond basic nutrition. (Ch. 23)

functional furniture: Furniture that meets specific needs. (Ch. 39)

G

gathers: Soft folds of fabric. (Ch. 37)

generic name: The common name for a group of similar items. (Ch. 34)

genes: The basic units of heredity, which determine body type and the color of hair, skin, and eyes. (Ch. 13)

germ: The seed that grows into another plant. (Ch. 31)

global environment: All living and nonliving elements on earth. (Ch. 40)

goal: Something a person plans to do, be, or obtain. (Chs. 1, 16)

grading: Trimming the seam allowances in layers. (Ch. 37)

graze: To eat several minimeals throughout the day. (Ch. 29)

grooming: The personal care routine people follow to keep themselves clean, washing away bacteria and helping prevent problems with skin, hair, and teeth. (Ch. 19)

H

hallucinogens: Street drugs that distort the user's thoughts, moods, and senses. (Ch. 20)

harassment: Behavior that is unwelcome and disturbing to others. (Ch. 5)

hazards: Sources of danger. (Ch. 40)

heredity: Characteristics passed from parents to children. (Ch. 1)

home maintenance: Eliminating clutter, organizing household and personal items, cleaning, making minor repairs or changes, keeping household equipment in good working order, and so on. (Ch. 40)

homogenized: The fat particles in the milk have been broken up and distributed throughout the milk. (Ch. 24)

hormones: Chemical substances in the body that help stimulate body changes and the development of the male and female reproductive systems. (Ch. 1)

hybrids: Vehicles that use a combination of electricity and fuel. (Ch. 18)

I

identify theft: Stealing and illegally using personal information. (Ch. 18)

illusion: An occurrence that influences or leads the eye to see something that does not exist. (Ch. 33)

immersible: Describes an entire appliance that can be put safely into water to be washed. (Ch. 26)

impulse purchases: Items someone buys without careful thought. (Ch. 17)

income: The amount of money that a person receives. (Ch. 17)

incomplete proteins: Plant foods such as grains, dry beans and peas, nuts, seeds, and vegetables, which lack one or more of the nine essential amino acids. (Ch. 22)

infatuation: Feelings of love that are experienced based on an intense attraction to another person and may be one-sided. Also called a crush. (Ch. 10)

inhalants: Substances with dangerous fumes that are sniffed to produce a mind-altering high. (Ch. 20)

interest: Money a financial institution pays customers at regular intervals. (Ch. 17)

interfacing: A special fabric that gives support and body to a garment or project. (Ch. 36)

interview: A meeting between a job applicant and an employer. (Ch. 6)

ironing: Moving the iron back and forth over the fabric to remove wrinkles. (Ch. 35)

irradiated foods: Foods that have gone through a process that destroys bacteria, mold, and insects by passing them through a field of radiant energy similar to X rays. (Ch. 23)

J-K

job shadowing: Staying in the background while following a worker for a few days on the job. (Ch. 4)

job sharing: An agreement in which two part-time workers share one full-time job, splitting the hours and the pay. (Ch. 6)

L

landlords: Owners of rental housing. (Ch. 38)

large motor skills: The movement and control of the back, legs, shoulders, and arms. (Ch. 13)

leader: A person who has influence over and guides a group. (Ch. 3)

leadership: The ability to lead. (Ch. 3)

lease: A written rental agreement. (Ch. 38)

leavening agent: An ingredient, such as baking powder or baking soda, that causes baked products to rise. (Ch. 31)

legumes: Plants in which seeds grow in pods, such as beans, peas, and lentils. (Ch. 32)

lifelong learning: Keeping skills and knowledge up-to-date throughout life. (Ch. 4)

M

manipulation: A dishonest way to control or influence someone. (Ch. 9)

manufactured fibers: Fibers produced in laboratories through chemical processes and made from substances such as wood pulp, petroleum, and other chemicals. (Ch. 34)

marbling: Tiny veins of fat throughout the meat muscle. (Ch. 32)

marijuana: A drug made from the hemp plant. (Ch. 20)

marinades: Seasoned blends of oil and vinegar or fruit juice that form sauces used to flavor food, such as barbecue sauce. (Ch. 27)

meal pattern: A way of grouping daily food choices into meals and snacks. (Ch. 29)

mediation: A neutral third party helps everyone reach a solution that's agreeable. (Ch. 8)

mentors: Informal teachers or guides. (Ch. 4)

microfiber: Superfine manufactured fiber. (Ch. 34)

microwaves: Energy waves that can be used to heat food. (Ch. 26)

mortgage: A long-term loan used to buy a home. (Ch. 38)

multiplex: Similar to a duplex, but three or more units share one building. (Ch. 38)

MyPyramid: A personalized way to approach healthful eating and physical activity every day. (Ch. 23)

N

natural fibers: Fibers that are produced by nature and come from plant and animal sources. (Ch. 34)

needs: Those things essential to survival and well-being. (Ch. 3)

neglect: Abuse that occurs when people fail to meet the needs of their children or older adults in their care. (Ch. 12)

negotiation: A process of discussing problems face-to-face to reach a solution. (Ch. 8)

networking: Making use of personal connections to achieve goals. (Ch. 4)

night terror: A type of sleep disorder that is more intense than a nightmare and often occurs when a child has a high fever or illness, causing the child to scream, cry, and act confused while still asleep. (Ch. 14)

nightmares: Bad dreams that can produce a feeling of anxiety and awaken the sleeper. (Ch. 14)

nonrenewable resources: Resources that do not replace themselves and are in limited supply. (Ch. 40)

nonverbal communication: A message sent without speaking. (Ch. 7)

notching: Clipping V-shaped notches from the seam allowance. (Ch. 37)

notions: The small items, such as thread, zippers, buttons, trim, seam binding, hooks and eyes, and snaps, needed to complete a garment. (Ch. 36)

nurturing: Giving love, affection, attention, and encouragement. (Ch. 15)

nutrient density: The amount of nutrients in a food item in relation to the number of calories. (Ch. 22)

nutrients: Substances that are found in food and keep the body in good working order. (Ch. 22)

O

obesity: Being seriously overweight because of an excess of body fat. (Ch. 23)

obligations: Things a person must do. (Ch. 16)

obsolete: Out of date and no longer useful. (Ch. 18)

P-Q

panfrying: Using smaller amounts of fat to fry tender cuts of meat, fish, and eggs in a skillet. (Ch. 30)

parallel play: Play alongside other children but not with them. (Ch. 13)

parenting: The process of caring for children and guiding their growth and development. (Ch. 15)

pasteurized: The milk has been heated to destroy harmful bacteria. (Ch. 24)

peer mediator: A young person who listens to both parties in conflict and helps them to find a solution. (Ch. 8)

peer pressure: The pressure people feel to do what others their age are doing. (Ch. 9)

peers: People the same age. (Ch. 9)

perishable: Foods likely to spoil easily. (Ch. 32)

personality: The combination of feelings, traits, attitudes, and habits that an individual shows others. (Ch. 1)

phytonutrients: Substances that plants produce naturally to protect themselves from harm and that improve the body's immunity, which helps fight diseases. Also known as phytochemicals. (Ch. 22)

place setting: The arrangement of tableware and flatware for each person. (Ch. 25)

plaque: A sticky film formed by food, bacteria, and air in the mouth and that clings to teeth and helps form an acid that eats tooth enamel. (Ch. 19)

poaching: Cooking whole or large pieces of food in a small amount of liquid. (Ch. 30)

poison control centers: Organizations that give advice on treatment for poisoning. (Ch. 14)

portfolio: A collection of work samples demonstrating skills. (Ch. 6)

potential: The possibility of becoming more than you are right now. (Ch. 1)

prejudice: An unfair or biased opinion made without knowledge of the correct facts. (Ch. 7)

pressing: The process of lifting and lowering an iron onto areas of the fabric. (Ch. 35)

pretreatment: Any special attention given to a garment before laundering. (Ch. 35)

principles of design: Artistic guidelines that help someone combine the elements of design. (Ch. 33)

priorities: Things that are ranked in order of importance. (Chs. 1, 16)

proteins: Nutrients used to build, maintain, and repair body tissues. (Ch. 22)

puberty: The time when teens start to develop the physical characteristics of men and women. (Chs. 1, 13)

R

rapport: Harmony or understanding among people. (Ch. 7)

recipe: A set of directions used in cooking. (Ch. 28)

redress: The right to have a wrong corrected quickly and fairly. (Ch. 17)

refusal skills: Basic communication skills someone can use to say no effectively. (Ch. 9)

renewable resources: Resources that replace or renew themselves over time. (Ch. 40)

repetitive stress injuries: Joint injuries caused by repeated motions. (Ch. 18)

resource: Anything a person uses to help accomplish something. (Ch. 1)

responsibility: Accepting the consequences of your own decisions and behavior. (Ch. 2)

résumé: A document that provides a brief history of work experience and education, highlights interests and skills, and includes some personal information. (Ch. 6)

roasting: Most often refers to cooking large pieces of meat or poultry in a shallow pan. (Ch. 30)

role models: People who set a positive example for others. (Ch. 2)

S

salmonella: Bacteria that can cause foodborne illness and that are found in some eggs. (Ch. 32)

sanitize: To clean to get rid of bacteria. (Ch. 27)

scorch: To burn, such as heat-sensitive proteins in dairy foods. (Ch. 32)

sedentary: Inactive. (Ch. 23)

selvage: The finished lengthwise edge of the fabric. (Ch. 36)

sexually transmitted diseases (STDs): Diseases passed from one person to another through sexual contact. (Ch. 20)

shock: A physical condition that is characterized by inadequate blood flow and can be very serious. (Ch. 14)

sibling rivalry: Competition for the love and attention of parents. (Ch. 11)

siblings: Brothers and sisters. (Ch. 11)

silhouette: The shape or the form created when lines are combined. (Ch. 33)

simmering: Heating liquid to a temperature just below the boiling point, until bubbles barely break on the liquid surface. (Ch. 30)

sleepwalking: Walking while still asleep. (Ch. 14)

small motor skills: The movement and control of small body parts, such as the hands and fingers. (Ch. 13)

spouse: A person's husband or wife. (Ch. 12)

staples: Foods someone is likely to use often, such as milk, eggs, pasta, rice, and bread. (Ch. 24)

staystitching: A row of stitching sewn on one layer of fabric to prevent the edges from stretching when handling the fabric. (Ch. 37)

steaming: Cooking food over boiling water, rather than in it. (Ch. 30)

stereotype: The belief that an entire group of people fit a fixed, common pattern—that they're all alike in certain ways. (Ch. 7)

stewing: Long, slow cooking in liquid. (Ch. 30)

stimulants: Drugs that increase a person's heart rate, speed up the central nervous system, increase breathing rates, and raise blood pressure. (Ch. 20)

stir-frying: Stirring and cooking small pieces of food quickly at high heat in little fat. (Ch. 30)

stress: The pressure people feel as the result of their ability or inability to meet the expectations of others and themselves. (Chs. 6, 16)

suicide: The taking of one's own life. (Ch. 12)

T

tableware: Includes dishes, glasses, and flatware. (Ch. 25)

tact: Communicating something difficult without hurting another person's feelings. (Ch. 7)

teamwork: Team members work together to reach a common goal. (Ch. 5)

technology: The application of science to help people meet needs and wants. (Ch. 18)

telecommute: Work at home and communicate with customers and coworkers by phone, fax, and computer. (Ch. 6)

telemarketing: Selling over the telephone. (Ch. 21)

tension: The tightness or looseness of a thread. (Ch. 36)

thinking skills: Mental skills used to learn, make decisions, analyze, and solve problems. (Ch. 5)

tolerance: Accepting and respecting other people's customs and beliefs. (Ch. 8)

townhouse: A house built in a row of other townhouses and attached to another townhouse at a side wall. (Ch. 38)

trade name: The company's name for a specific item it manufactures. (Ch. 34)

traditions: Customs passed from one generation to another. (Ch. 11)

traffic patterns: The paths people use to get from one area or room to another. (Ch. 39)

U

understitching: Stitching the facing to the seam allowances. (Ch. 37)

unit price: The price per ounce, pound, or other unit of measure. (Ch. 24)

unity: The feeling that all parts of a design belong together. (Ch. 39)

universal values: Values that are generally accepted and shared worldwide. (Ch. 2)

utensils: Small kitchen tools. (Ch. 26)

utilities: Basic services, such as electricity, cable, gas or oil, phone, water, and sewer service. (Ch. 38)

V

vaccines: Small amounts of disease-carrying germs introduced to the body so that the body can build resistance to a disease. (Ch. 15)

values: Beliefs and ideas about what is important. (Ch. 2)

vegetarian: Someone who does not eat meat, poultry, or fish. (Ch. 23)

verbal communication: A process that includes spoken messages. (Ch. 7)

video teleconferencing: A service that enables people in different locations to see and hear each other at the same time. (Ch. 18)

W-X-Y-Z

wants: Those things a person desires even though they aren't essential. (Ch. 3)

warranty: A guarantee that a product will work properly for a specific length of time unless misused or mishandled by the consumer. (Ch. 17)

wellness: An approach to life based on healthy attitudes and actions. (Ch. 19)

work ethic: Working hard, being honest, and staying committed to work. (Ch. 5)

work simplification: The easiest and quickest way to do a job well. (Ch. 16)

yield: The amount of food or the number of servings a recipe makes. (Ch. 28)

Credits

Design
Bill Smith Studio

Cover Photography
African American woman laughing: Vincent Benault/Getty
    Images
Laptop: Stockdisc/Getty Images
Musician on laptop screen: Elizabeth Knox/Masterfile
Soccer Ball: Photodisc
Denim Pocket: Ron Leighton
Wrap: Schnare & Stief/Stockfood
Teenage Boy & Girl: Masterfile Royalty Free

Photo Editing
Graphic World Inc.

Alamy, Emilio Ereza, 357
Arnold & Brown Photography, 30, 31L, 31R
Brand X CD/Beautiful Homes, 617
Butterick/Vogue, 621
Comstock, 600
Corbis
    Atlanta Constitution/Corbis Sygma, 212
    Ondrea Barbe, 430L
    Michael Barley, 116
    Paul Barton, 171R, 192, 344
    Peter Beck, 79
    Benelux/zefa, 200
    Ed Bock, 27T, 115
    L. Clarke, 301R
    Darama, 312
    Dex Images, Inc., 229
    Emely/zefa, 497
    Owen Franken, 467
    Guntmar Fritz/zefa, 223
    Rick Gayle, 179
    Raymond Gehman, 204
    Patrik Giardino, 319
    Gulliver/zefa, 168
    Charles Gupton, 59, 528
    K. Hackenberg/zefa, 498L
    Brownie Harris, 622
    John Henley, 114
    Jacqui Hurst, 572
    Richard Hutchings, 144
    Alan Jakubek, 331R
    Japack Company, 408
    Wolfgang Kaehler, 602
    Reed Kaestner, 46R
    U. Kaiser/Kate Mitchell/zefa, 542
    Ed Kashi, 302
    Ronnie Kaufman, 156
    Michael A. Keller/zefa, 298, 354

Michael Keller, 452
Kelly-Mooney Photography, 379
Kim Kulish, 296
Thom Lang, 333
Left Lane Productions, 39
Rob Lewine, 594
Robert Llewellyn, 273
LWA-Dann Tardif, 127
Robert Maass, 351
Simon Marcus, 248
Don Mason, 412
Tom & Dee Ann McCarthy, 256
Will & Deni McIntyre, 322BL
Darren Modricker, 610
Ray Morsch, 173
Gabe Palmer, 32, 158, 159
Jose Luis Pelaez, Inc., 28, 337
David Pollack, 250
Rick Gayle Studio, 642
H. G. Rossi/zefa, 339
Royalty-Free, 40, 42, 44, 46L, 57, 64, 73BL, 81, 82, 100, 104,
    117, 119, 120, 125, 142, 203, 207, 222, 241L, 257, 265,
    271, 300, 301R, 349L, 359, 421, 422TL, 422TR, 423TL,
    423TR, 425TL, 425TR, 427, 429TL, 429TR, 430L, 431L,
    431R, 437TL, 437TR, 441, 448, 471, 474, 482TL, 482TR,
    501, 514L, 514R, 515, 541, 591, 606, 619, 620
Chuck Savage, 84, 94, 132BL, 175, 580
Ariel Skelley, 447, 596
Walter Smith, 205
Joseph Sohm; ChomoSohm Inc., 631
Tom Stewart, 18, 26, 27B, 50, 67, 197, 234, 321, 323TL,
    347, 418, 601
David Stoecklein, 313R
Turbo/zefa, 619L
Bill Varie, 372
Cheryl Fenton, 482BL, 482BR, 485TL, 485TR, 485ML, 485BL,
    485BR
Getty
    Alex & Laila/Stone+, 231
    Ty Allison/Taxi, 415R
    altrendo images, 335
    Tony Anderson/Taxi, 536
    David Arsenault, 322BR
    Vincent Besnault/Taxi, 458
    Nathan Billow/Allsport Concepts, 191
    Leland Bobbe/Photonica, 177
    Phil Boorman/Taxi, 436
    Matt Bowman/FoodPix, 374L
    Brooklyn Productions/The Image Bank, 415L
    Peter Cade/Iconica, 556
    CGSL Photography, 282R
    Chabruken, 21
    Ron Chapple, 314
    Nancy R. Cohen, 68

Robert E. Daemmrich, 533
Digital Vision, 92, 150, 389
Neil Emmerson, Robert Harding World Imagery, 528, 529
Britt Erlanson/The Image Bank, 593
Bruce Forster/Stone, 483
Brett Froomer, 25
Getty Images, 97
Larry Dale Gordon/The Image Bank, 406
Dennis Gottlieb/FoodPix, 375L
Michael Greenburg/Taxi, 185
Howard Grey/Stone, 55
Brian Hagiwara/FoodPix, 356
David W. Hamilton/The Image Bank, 221
Paula Hibble/FoodPix, 244
Holos, 24
Russel Illig, 241R
image100, 269R
Image Source, 169, 472
Janeart Inc./The Image Bank, 247
Chase Jarvis, 182
Sean Justice/The Image Bank, 130
Sean Justice/Photonica, 269L
John E. Kelley/FoodPix, 404
Michael Krasowitz/Taxi, 397
Brian Leatart/FoodPix, 375R
Jeff Maloney, 89
Alex Mares-Manton/Asia Images, 450
Barbara Maurer/Taxi, 492
Medioimages, 643
Rob Melnychuk, 154, 546
Eri Morita/Stone+, 187
Muntz/Taxi, 612
Nancy Ney, 240L
Eric O'Connell/Taxi, 489R
Ian O'Leary/Stone, 190L
David Oliver/Taxi, 166
Lisa Peardon, 329
Photodisc, 47L, 69L, 289, 499R
Plush Studios, 178
Andreas Pollok, 22T
Loretta Ray/Photonica, 131L
Ken Reid/The Image Bank, 294
John Riley, 91TR
Jon Riley/Stone, 276
John A. Rizzo, 498R
Anderson Ross, 43, 434, 445
Royalty Free, 522R, 531, 534, 549, 624, 625, 634L
Rubberball, 540
Lawrence M. Sawyer, 36
Jeanene Scott/Photonica, 268
Mark Scott/Taxi, 137
Ian Shaw/Stone, 261
Zubin Shroff, 543L
Emily Shur/Taxi, 618
Paul Simcock/Iconica, 218
Solstice Photography, 349R
Henrik Sorensen, Image Bank, 528, 529
Square Peg Productions, 278
Lee Strickland, 91L
Stockbyte, 190R, 384, 390, 537, 628
Stockdisc, 410, 464
SW Productions, 133, 238, 258R, 310, 320, 322TL, 328, 336, 342, 353
Jerome Tisne, 326

Mark Thornton, 308
Penny Tweedie/Stone, 215, 272
Rob Van Petten, 198
Simon Watson/ Botanica, 194
Paul Webster/Stone, 499L
Mel Yates, 348
Yellow Dog Productions/The Image Bank, 171L, 552BL
Kevin May, 516L, 516R, 557L, 557R, 599L
PhotoEdit
Bill Aron, 267, 325, 385L, 444R, 517, 538
Davis Barber, 106, 473
Sky Bonillo, 77
Michelle D. Bridwell, 71, 145, 209, 323M, 442, 518, 552TR
Myrleen Ferguson Cate, 33, 78, 122, 225L, 225R, 226BR, 232, 235, 279, 343, 417
Paul Conklin, 332
Gary Conner, 266L
David Kelly Crow, 20, 151, 313L, 577
Bob Daemmrich, 69T, 131R, 237, 317, 340, 476, 633
Mary Kate Denny, 45, 52, 153, 160, 161L, 161R, 213L, 240R, 387, 398, 566TL
Lon C. Diehl, 146
Kayte M. Deioma, 73BR
Laura Dwight, 242
Amy Etra, 525
Eric Fowke, 605
Tony Freeman, 86B, 112, 135, 139, 140, 220, 259L, 259R, 287, 291, 369, 385R, 598
Robert W. Ginn, 363
Spencer Grant, 148, 285, 374R, 545, 559
Jeff Greenberg, 143, 203T, 226TR, 413, 488, 491, 635L
Richard Hutchings, 22B, 38, 126, 213R, 345, 403
Bonnie Kamin, 132R, 217, 281, 634R
Christina Kennedy, 392
Richard Lord, 382
Dennis MacDonald, 149R, 224R, 346, 370
Felicia Martinez, 358
Michael Newman, 47R, 66, 107, 162, 170, 181, 210L, 252, 255, 266R, 293, 297, 305, 309, 414, 444L, 487, 489L, 505, 508, 509, 543R, 553, 554, 573L, 599R, 604, 627
Dwayne Newton, 645
Jonathan Nourok, 323BR
James Shaffer, 306
Clayton Sharrard, 70
Nancy Sheehan, 226L
Skjold Photographs, 113, 258L
Don Smetzer, 330
Susan Van Etten, 210R
Dana White, 93, 111, 165, 284, 393, 445L
Colin Young-Wolff, 23, 401R
David Young-Wolff, 35, 49, 61, 63, 73T, 74, 75, 86T, 88, 91BL, 95, 96, 99, 102, 132TL, 149L, 174, 184, 189, 195, 201, 211, 224L, 251, 253, 262, 275, 282L, 286, 316, 322BM, 331L, 334, 380, 381, 395, 396, 399, 401L, 420, 433, 439, 463, 468, 469, 470, 479, 480, 506, 530, 552BR, 573L, 579, 630, 635R, 636, 640
Punchstock/Photo Disk (RF), 616
SuperStock
BananaStock, 108L
Michael Pole, 124
Stockbyte, 283
Stockdisc, 409

Index

A

À la carte, 413, 647
Abbreviations, in cooking, 451–452, 647
Abstinence, 335, 647
Abuse
    cycles of, 211–213
    sibling, 210–211
    spousal, 209
    stopping, 212–213
    substance, 208–209, 332–333
    verbal, 148
Academic skills, 86, 647
Accessories, 530, 647
Accidents, 237–239, 439–442. See also Safety
Acetate, 537
Achievements, 25
Acne, 228, 311, 647
Acquaintances, 168, 647
Acquired immunodeficiency syndrome (AIDS), 335–336, 647
Acrylic, 538
Activities
    choosing, 330
    with friends, 170, 174
    interests and, 26
    prioritizing, 115, 323
Addiction, 208–209, 647
Additives, 382, 647
Adolescence, 647
    changes during, 20–21
    confidence building during, 21–24
    defined, 19

developmental tasks of. See Careers; Independence; Personal Development
    gaining independence during, 26–27
    moral development during, 21
    parenthood during, 201, 252–253
    period of, 228
    self-concept during, 21–24
Adoption, 185
Advertising
    decision-making and, 55
    product, 280
    purchasing decisions and, 278, 379
    on site, 108
Aerobic exercise, 316, 317
Age span, 194, 647
AIDS, 335–336
Al dente, defined, 495, 647
Alcohol, 330
Alcoholics, 208, 647
Alcoholism, 208, 647
Allergies, 386, 508, 647
Americans with Disabilities Act (ADA), 96
Amino acids, 357, 647
Anabolic steroids, 333, 647
Analogous color schemes, 615
Anger management, 146–147
Anorexia, 320, 647
Anxiety, 273
Apartment, 603, 647
Apparel. See Clothing
Appearance. See Personal appearance

Appetizer, 412, 647
Appliances
    energy conservation and, 632
    large, 424, 426–427
    small, 424, 428, 442–443
Appreciation, showing, 189, 194
Aptitudes, 69–70, 647
Assertive, 129, 647
Assertive communication, 128–129
ATM (automatic teller machine), 289–290
Attitudes, positive, 92
Authority, 217
Automatic teller machine (ATM), 289–290

B

Babysitting. See Child care
Background as design element, 620–621, 647
Bacteria, 436, 509, 510, 647
Baking, 483–484
Balance
    achieving in life, 263–265, 273
    in design, 524, 527, 617
    time factors and, 265–268
    work and family, 113–117
Banking, 288–291
Basal metabolic rate (BMR), 318, 647
Beans. See Legumes
Bedtime, 245
Behavior. See also Etiquette; Guidance
    guiding, 239, 242, 255–256

while driving, 147

Benefits, employment, 116–117, 647

Better Business Bureau (BBB), 280

Bias, of fabric, 575, 648

Binge eating disorders, 320, 648

Blended family, 185

Body image, 569

Body language, 125–126, 648

Body mass index (BMI), 364

Boiling, 484–485, 648

Botulism, 400. *See also* Food-borne illness

Bowls, mixing, 423

Braising, 484–485, 648

Bran, 494, 648

Brand names, 279

Breads, 498

Breakfast, 466

Breast self-examinations, 309

Broiling, 482, 648

Budgets, 286–287, 648
  clothing, 530
  creating, 286
  food, 393

Bulimia, 320, 648

Bullying, 148–149, 158

Businesses, 77, 108–109

Buttons, 572

C

Caffeine, 323

Calcium, 361

Calories, 365–367, 648
  individual needs, 372–373
  per-gram conversion, 394

Carbohydrates, 356, 380, 648

Cardiopulmonary resuscitation (CPR), 239, 351, 648

Career, 66, 648

Career clusters, 71–72, 648

Career paths
  considering, 65–66
  investigating, 68–70

resources, 74

Career profiles
  Chef, 100
  Child Care Provider, 121
  Child Psychologist, 121
  Child Welfare Worker, 120
  Clinical Dietitian, 101
  Consumer Journalist, 83
  Director of Youth Programs, 101
  Employment Counselor, 121
  Extension Agent, 120
  FACS Teacher, 120
  Fashion Buyer, 82
  Fashion Designer, 83
  Food Editor, 101
  Food Marketer, 101
  Food Technologist, 100
  Home Health Aide, 100
  Interior Designer, 83
  Kitchen Planner, 82
  Landscape Architect, 82
  Librarian, 83
  Loan Officer, 82
  Personal Trainer, 101
  Preschool Teacher, 121
  Rehabilitation Specialist, 100
  Social Worker, 121
  Speech Pathologist, 120
  Urban Planner, 83

Careers. *See also* Work
  changing, 73
  in child and family services, 120–121
  in consumer and design services, 82–83
  defined, 66
  educational requirements for, 75
  expert advice on, 69
  fields, jargon, 369
  hobbies and, 67
  in nutrition and wellness services, 100–101
  parenthood and, 252
  planning, 68–69

resources, 74, 76
  technology skills, 296, 305

Careers, entry-level
  Bank Teller, 83
  Caterer, 101
  Food Stylist, 101
  Mortgage Loan Processor, 83
  Nanny, 121
  Teacher Aide, 121

Careers, technical-level
  Assistant Apparel Designer, 83
  CAD Technician, 83
  Dental Hygienist, 121
  Food Services Manager, 101
  Physical Therapy Assistant, 101
  Preschool Director, 121

Careers, professional-level
  Actuary, 83
  Exercise Physiologist, 101
  Family Therapist, 121
  Guidance Counselor, 121
  Hospitality Interior Designer, 83
  Weight Reduction Specialist, 101

Care labels, 528, 550

Caregivers. *See* Child care; Parents

Cell phones, 130–131

Cereals, 498. *See also* Carbohydrates

Character, 648
  building, 37–38
  defined, 37
  guidance, 41
  positive qualities of, 45
  values and, 38

Checking accounts, 288–289

Cheese, 514

Child care
  checklist for, 245
  emergencies, 237–239
  providing, 233–234
  safety, 235–237

Childproofing, 235, 648
Children. *See also* Infants; Toddlers; Preschoolers; School-Age; Adolescents
　accidents and, 237–239
　activities for, 226–227, 240–241
　basic needs of, 243, 354
　bedtime, 245
　being role model for, 258–259
　clothing for, 242
　developmental influences on, 221–222
　developmental milestones of, 222
　developmental stages, 222–228
　discipline and guidance, 225, 239, 242
　entertaining, 240–241
　in healthy environment, 24
　in kitchen, 443
　meals and snacks for, 243–245
　preschool, 227
　reading to, 254
　safety of, 223, 235, 237
　school-age, 227–228
　and self-dressing, 242
　and sleep, 245
　with special needs, 228–230
　teaching, 173
　toddlers, 223–227, 240–242
Cholesterol, 359, 648
Citizen, 42, 648
Citizenship, 42–44, 60, 648
Cleanliness
　germs and, 494
　health and, 310
　kitchen, 436–439
　personal, 436
Cleaning
　as you go, 638–639
　equipment, 637–638
　organizing, 636

products, 426, 637–638
tasks, 634, 637, 641
Cliques, 172, 648
Closure, 205, 648
Clothing. *See also* Fabrics; Sewing
　appropriate, 119
　care labels, 531
　for children, 242
　careers in, 82–83
　design elements and, 520
　design principles and, 524–527
　evaluating, 524, 527–529
　importance of, 520
　individualizing, 520–531
　for job interviews, 108, 110
　quality, 528–529
　shopping for, 530–531
　for special needs, 521
　strategies, 531
　wardrobe, 524–525, 528–529
Clothing care
　dry cleaning, 554
　repair, 554–556
　routine, 547–548
　stain removal, 550
　storage, 548–549
　washing, 550–554
Collaborating, 115
Color
　cool, 521
　design element, 613
　as design element, 521–523, 613
　effects of, 521, 523
　fabrics, 542
　food and, 378, 464
　types, 614
　using, 521, 614–615
Color schemes, 615
Color wheel, 614
Commitments, 32, 49, 190
Common interests, 169
Communication, 124–129, 648. *See also* Listening Skills

with friends, 175
leadership and, 60
mealtime, 406
nonverbal, 125–127
positive, 21
and presentation skills, 403
respect and, 133, 135
role in conflict avoidance, 146
speaking skills, 87, 139
technology, 296–297
verbal, 87, 124–125, 139
written, 87, 463
Community
　emergency resources, 351
　involvement, 42–44, 353
　leadership, 44–45, 58–61
　pride, 163
　resources, 27, 54
　respecting, 134
　safety issues, 297
Community bulletin boards, 108
Community service careers, 82–83, 101, 120–121
Comparison shopping, 279, 648
Compensation, 75
Competition, 147
Complementary color schemes, 615
Complete proteins, 357, 648
Compost pile, 630
Compromise, 145, 648
Concussion, 237, 648
Condominium, 606–607, 648
Confidence. *See also* Self-confidence
　building, 22
　developing, 163
　showing, 148
　speaking with, 129
Conflict resolution, 145, 649
Conflicts, 141–151, 649
　anger management and, 146–147
　causes, 142–144

defined, 142
with family, 186, 192–195
with friends, 177
mediating, 145, 150–151
preventing, 144–149
resolving, 145–147, 151
with peers, 158–159
workplace, 95
Conscience, 227, 649
Consensus building, 197
Conservation, 630, 649
Consequences, 56
Constructive feedback, 389
Consumer Product Safety Commission, 280
Consumers, 277, 284–285, 649
Convection ovens, 427, 483–484
Convenience foods, 469, 649
Conversations, 129. *See also* Communication
Cooking. *See also* Recipes
    dairy foods, 512–513
    determining doneness, 488–489
    with dry-heat, 482–484
    eggs, 510
    with fat, 486–487
    fruits, 503
    grain products, 494–497
    legumes, 511–512
    microwave, 487
    with moist-heat, 484–486
    nutrients and, 488
    pasta, 495
    process, 481
    protein food, 508–512
    safety, 427, 440–441, 486, 509–510
    time, 476–477
    vegetables, 503
Cookware, 428–429, 649
Cooperation, 90, 270
Cooperative play, 226–227, 649
Cooperatives, 606–607, 649

Coping strategies
    for family challenges, 192
    for family changes, 186
    for handling bullies, 148–149
    for peer pressure, 159–161, 330–331
    for stress, 272–273, 322–323
Corporations, 77
Cost effective, defined, 297, 649
Cotton, 536
Counselors, 54
Courage, 351
Courses, meal, 412, 649
Cover letters, 106, 579, 649
CPR (cardiopulmonary resuscitation), 239, 351
Credit, 290–291
Credit cards, 290, 299
Creditors, 203, 649
Credit ratings, 203, 649
Crime, 649. *See also* Violence
    causes of, 342
    defined, 342
    fraud, 345
    prevention of, 342
    theft, 302
    victims, 214
Crises, personal and family, 204–205, 649
Criticism, 94–95
Cross-contamination, 436, 649
Crushes. *See* Infatuation
Culture
    Appreciation of, 22–23
    buying habits and, 278
    decision-making and, 53
    diversity, 58
    food choice and, 379
Cutting
    boards, 425, 438
    terms, 455
    utensils, 421, 562
Cutting in, 454
Cystic fibrosis, 228

D

Daily values, 394
Dairy foods
    buying, 399
    daily requirements, 377
    desserts, 515
    selecting, 373
    substitutes for, 512
    types, 514–515
Dandruff, 311, 649
Dating, 176–177
Death, 205–206
Debit cards, 289–290, 299
Decision making, 649
    consequences, 55–57
    as a coping skill, 51–52
    defined, 52
    process, 56–57
    workplace, 113
Decisions
    blaming others for, 330
    consequences of, 56
    influences, 52–54
    learning from, 55
    options and, 57
    responsible, 51–52
Decorating. *See* Home design
Deep-fat frying, 486, 649
Deficiency, 364, 649
Dependable, 168–169, 188, 649
Depressants, 333, 649
Dermatologists, 311, 649
Design elements, 520–524
Design principles, 524
Development. *See also* Children; Personal development
    milestones, 222, 649
    emotional, 20
    intellectual, 21, 220
    moral, 21
    physical, 20, 220
    stages, 222–228
Dicing, 455

Dietary Guidelines for Americans, 372–373, 376, 649
Dietary supplements, 382, 649
Diets. *See* Nutrition
Digestion, 366
Directional stitching, 582, 649
Disabilities, 96. *See also* Special needs
Disasters, 204
Discipline, 225, 239, 242, 254–256, 649
Discount stores, 281
Discrimination, 96, 649
Diversity, 58, 90–91, 169
Divorce, 206–207
Dovetail, 475, 649
Downsizing, 97, 649
Drugs
    abusing, 208–209, 328–333
    illegal, 332–333
    OTC, 334
    prescription, 334
    risks, 328
    saying no to, 330–331
Dry cleaning, 554, 649
Dry-heat cooking, 482–484
Duplex, 602, 649

E

Early childhood education
    careers, 101, 121
Ease, in clothing, 575, 649
Eating. *See also* Food; Meals
    away from home, 412–413, 471
    disorders, 320
    ctiquette, 405, 409–411
    exercise and, 371–372, 381
    fad diets, 376
    habits, 315, 319, 323, 371–372
    healthy, 373–376, 384
    portion control, 373, 377–378
Education. *See also* Schools

academic skills, 86–88
and career, 75
for parenting, 253
and technology, 299
Eggs, 399, 510
Elastoester, 537
Electrical hazards, 641
Electronic shopping, 282
Elements of design, 520–523, 649
E-mail etiquette, 303
Emergencies
    community resources for, 351
    taking action in, 237–239, 347–351
Emotional development, 20
Emotions
    changes in, 20
    controlling, 33, 41, 146–147
    development of, 221
    family's impact on, 184
    health and, 321
Empathy, 135, 649
    friends and, 168
    showing, 206
Emphasis. *See* Focal points
Employee assistance program, 117
Employment. *See* Careers; Jobs; Workplace
Empty nest, 187, 650
Endorse, defined, 288, 650
Endosperm, 494, 650
Endurance, 316
Energy
    calories and, 366
    conservation, 631–632
    management, 270
Enriched, 494, 650
Entertainment, 298
Entrée, 412, 650
Entrepreneur, 77, 650
Entrepreneurship, 77–78
Environment, 629–643, 650
    defined, 24
    housing and, 597

as influence on development, 24, 221
    outdoors, 636
    protecting, 221, 633–635
    role in buying habits, 278
    workplace, 645
Environmental Protection Agency (EPA), 112
Equal Employment Opportunity Act, 96
Equivalents, in cooking, 452–453, 650
Escalate, 144, 650
Ethical principles, 38, 650
Ethnicity, 23. *See also* Culture
Etiquette, 650
    cell phone, 130–131
    e-mail, 303
    importance of, 228
    mealtime, 405, 409–411
    restaurant, 413
    workplace, 94
Exercise. *See* Fitness
Expenses, 286, 650
Exploitation, 343, 650
Extended family, 185, 214
Eye-hand coordination, 220, 650

F

Fabrics
    bias, 575
    care symbols, 551
    choosing, 543
    construction methods, 540–541
    finishes, 542
    marking, 577
    preshrinking, 576
    selecting, 535–536, 570–571
    selvage of, 575
Factory outlets, 281
Fad diets, 376
Fads, 230, 650
Fairness, 253

Fall prevention, 348–349, 641
Familial, defined, 42, 650
Families, 183–195. *See also* Children; Parents; Relationships
buying habits and, 278
challenges, 192, 199–215
common rules, 176
and culture, 22–23
decision-making and, 52
eating with, 406
factors affecting, 186, 199–215
food budgets, 393
food choice and, 379
health, 309
heritage, 22–23
housing needs, 596–601
making time for, 190–192, 268
meetings, 193
need for, 195
positive self-concept from, 21
relationships within, 176, 186, 193–195
respecting, 134
responsibility to, 42, 176
self-esteem and, 24
social skills and, 627
space sharing, 624–625
strengthening, 189–190
and work balance, 113–117
Family, Career and Community Leaders of America (FCCLA), 60–61
Family challenges
addiction, 208–209
crime, 214
death, 205–206
divorce, 206–207
financial, 202–203
health, 205
homelessness, 204–205
meeting, 199–200
moving, 202
natural disasters, 204
new members, 200–202

seeking help, 214–215
separation, 206–207
substance abuse, 208–209
teen pregnancy, 201–202
unemployment, 202
violence, 209–210
Family life cycle, 186–187, 650
Fashions, 519, 650
Fat
burning, 380
cooking with, 486–487
in food, 374–375, 398–399, 510
limiting, 373
measuring, 451
types, 358–359
Family services careers, 100, 120–121
Fat-soluble vitamins, 359–360
FCCLA (Family, Career and Community Leaders of America), 60–61, 646
Fear, 351
Feedback, constructive, 389
Feedback, nonverbal, 46
Fiber, food, 356, 650
Fibers, clothing, 526–538, 650
Finances. *See* Money
Financial, defined, 202, 650
Financial services. *See also* Money
ATM cards, 289–290
checking accounts, 288–289
credit, 290–291
debit cards, 289–290
savings accounts, 288
statements, 290, 291
technology, 299
Fine motor skills, 227
Finishes, 542, 650
Fire
extinguishers, 440
safety, 239, 642
First aid
giving, 350–351
kits, 343

treatment, 239
Fish, 398–399, 509–510
Fitness
diet and, 315
factors affecting, 309–310, 315–319, 321
nutrients for, 381
programs, 316–317
safety, 317–318
stress control and, 323
weight management and, 319, 373
Flannel, 541
Flare-ups, 143
Flatware, 407–410, 650
Flax, 536
Fleece, 541
Flexibility, 93, 316–317
Flextime, 115, 650
Floors, 619
Focal points
defined, 524
garments, 526
rooms, 617
Food. *See also* Fruits; Meats; Vegetables
allergies, 508
buying, 391–400
doneness of, 488–489
and family meals, 405–407
flavor, 466
frozen, 380, 445
functional, 383
fun with, 240
grilling, 430–431
for infants and children, 240, 243–244
labels, 394
and manners, 409–411
and nutrition, 355–367, 371–387
preparation skills, 466, 475–477, 481–489, 493–503, 507–515
quick meals and snacks, 465–477

safety and sanitation, 399–400
seasoning, 458
storage, 401, 444–445
stores, 393–394
Foodborne illness, 436, 650
Food and nutrition careers, 100–101
Food guide pyramid (MyPyramid), 376–378
Food labs, 472–475
Food product dating, 396–397, 650
Forgiveness, 145, 168
Form, as design element, 613
Foster families, 185
Fraud, 345, 650
Friends, 166–179
  choosing, 26, 168–169, 172–173, 330
  communicating with, 175
  conflicts with, 142
  enjoying, 173–176
  influence on decision-making, 53
  making, 170–171, 202
  qualities of, 168–169
  respecting, 79
  responsibilities to, 174–176
  self-esteem from, 24
  sharing with, 169
  supporting, 206
  time for, 268
Friendships
  diverse, 169
  ending, 177–179
  focus on, 167–168
  long-distance, 177
  peer, 169, 172
  positive, 20
  qualities, 168–169
  strengthening, 169
Fringe benefits, 75, 247, 650
Fruits
  buying, 397–398
  canned, 497

daily requirements, 377
eating, 497
nutrients, 497, 500
preparing, 500–503
selecting, 373
washing, 437
Fuels, 633
Functional foods, 383, 650
Functional furniture, 619, 650
Furniture
  arranging, 623
  choosing, 621–622
  styles, 620

G

Gangs, 159
Garbage. *See* Trash
Genealogy, 23
Generic name, 538, 650
Genes, 221, 650
Germ, 494, 650
Gestures, 126
Global environment, 629–630, 650
Goals
  career, 68–69
  defined, 29, 264, 650
  fixed *vs.* flexible, 31
  group, 30–31
  influences on, 190
  long-term, 29–30
  organizational, 31
  personal, 29–30
  reaching, 32
  and resources, 131
  rewards and, 29
  setting, 29–31
  short-term, 29–30
Gossip, 179
Grading, 585, 650
Grains
  baking, 495
  buying, 498–499
  characterization, 494
  daily requirements, 377

eating, 493
enriched, 494
nutrients in, 494
preparing, 494–497
products from, 400
selecting, 373
storage, 495
whole, 498–499
Gratitude, 228
Graze, 467, 650
Grilling, 428, 430–431
Grooming, 310–314, 411, 650
Group goals, 30–31, 59
Group interaction, 58, 90–91, 270
Guidance, 239, 242, 254–256

H

Hair, 311, 314
Hallucinogens, 333, 651
Harassment, 97, 153, 651
Harmony, 524, 526
Hazards, 641–643, 651. *See also* Safety
Health. *See also* Wellness
  components of, 307–308
  emotional, 321
  and exercise, 315–318
  family, 205, 309
  government standards, 339
  grooming and, 310–311, 314
  and nutrition, 315, 363
  problems, 205
  protecting, 27
  regular checkups, 308–309
  resources, 323
  sleep and, 309–310
  technology, 297–298, 302
  weight and, 364–365
Health risks
  avoiding, 337
  drug abuse, 328–334
  HIV/AIDS, 335–336
  pregnancy, 336
  STDs, 335

Hearing impairment, 599
Heimlich maneuver, 350
Help, sources of, 214–215, 257, 273
Help lines, 213
Heredity, 24, 221, 651
HIV, 335–336
Home. *See also* Housing
  cleaning tasks, 636–641
  healthy, 639
  maintenance, 636, 651
  management, 298
  pests, 641
  repairs, 631, 643
  respect at, 134
  safety, 342–345, 641–643
Home design
  accessories, 621–622
  background elements, 618–619
  color in, 613–615
  furniture in, 619–621
  lighting in, 621–622
  line in, 613
  planning, 611–612
  principles, 616, 618
  space in, 622–623
  texture in, 613
  and traffic patterns, 621
  walls, 618, 625
Homelessness, 204–205
Homogenized, 399, 651
Honesty, 21, 93, 285
Hormones, 20, 651
Housing. *See also* Home
  condominiums, 606–607
  cooperatives, 606–607
  costs, 600, 604–607
  environmental concerns, 596–597
  hearing impairment and, 599
  human needs and, 595–600
  limited mobility and, 598
  location, 597
  moving tips, 607

multiple-family, 602–603
owning, 605–606
renting, 603–604
selection, 607
sharing, 607
single-family, 601
technology, 597
visual impairment and, 598–599
Human immunodeficiency virus (HIV), 335–336
Human nature, 91
Human needs, 54, 243, 254, 354, 595
Human resources, 27
Hybrid cars, 298, 651

I

Identity theft, 282–283, 299, 651
Illusion, 520, 651
Immersible, 424, 651
Impulse purchases, 279, 651
Income, 278, 651
Incomplete proteins, 357, 651
Independence, 26–27, 33
Infants, 222–223. *See also* Children
  bathing, 236
  entertaining, 240
  feeding, 243–244
  older, 223
  young, 222
Infatuation, 177, 651
Influences, 53–54, 221–222
Information skills, 89
Inhalants, 332, 651
Initiative, 93
Intellectual development, 21, 220
Interest, on money, 288
Interests, 651
  activities and, 26
  common, 169
  skills and, 69–70

Interfacing, 570–571, 584–585, 651
Interior design. *See* Home design
Interior design careers, 82–83
Intermediate colors, 614
Internet
  career research, 76
  genealogy search, 23
  safety, 300–301, 343–344
  security, 283
Interpersonal skills, 89, 123–137, 167–179, 189–195
Interview, 651
  follow-up, 110
  job, 107–110, 533
  media, 109
  thank-you letters after, 545
Ironing, 554, 651
Irradiated foods, 383, 651

J

Job application process
  cover letters, 106
  forms, 104
  interviews, 107–108, 539
  portfolios, 106–107
  post-interview follow-up, 110
  résumés, 104–106
  tests, 104
Job market, 79
Jobs. *See also* Careers; Workplace
  accepting, 505
  advancement, 73
  applying for, 103–106
  aptitudes for, 69–70
  benefits of, 75, 116–117, 247
  diversity at, 90
  downsizing, 97
  etiquette, 94
  finding, 28, 491
  full-time, 78
  impact on family, 113–117

interviewing for, 107–110, 533

leaving, 73, 325

losing, 202

networking and, 74

part-time, 71

paychecks from, 287

pride in, 593

punctuality, 433

rewards of, 66–67

safety, 112

school connection, 67

search for, 68–76

simplification, 270

skills for, 69–70, 86–92

starting, 111

stress, 114

success on, 63, 85, 117

teamwork in, 90–92

technology in, 79

telecommuting and, 116

training in, 68

work ethic, 90

Job shadowing, 71, 651

Job sharing, 116, 651

K

Kitchen equipment

cookware, 427, 429

large appliances, 424, 426–427

safety, 424

sanitation, 426

selecting, 419–420

small appliances, 424, 429, 442–443

utensils, 420–425, 440

Kitchens

accident prevention, 439–443

children in, 443

food preparation, 475

safety, 435

sanitation, 436–439

Knitting, 541

L

Labels

care, 550

clothes, 528

food, 394

product, 279

Landlords, 603–604, 651

Large motor skills, 220, 651

Law enforcement, 208, 215

Leader, defined, 58, 651

Leadership

defined, 58, 651

effective, 58

opportunities, 60–61

skills, 59–60, 89

Learned values, 39

Learning

experiences, 68

lifelong, 68

skills, 87

technology for, 303

time for, 266–267

Lease, 604, 651

Leavening agent, 495–496, 651

Legumes

cooking, 511–512

defined, 400, 651

eating, 377

nutrients in, 507

selecting, 373

Life

changes, 19–21, 73, 186, 198–215

effects of decisions on, 57

health and wellness in, 27

personal growth, 21–33

understanding changes in, 19–20

Lifelong learning, 68, 651

Lifestyles, 597

Lighting as design element, 623–624, 632

Line as design element, 613

Listening skills

benefits of, 88

developing, 46–47, 128–130

tips, 132

at work, 181

Living spaces. See Home; Housing

Love, 177

Loyalty, 168

LSD. See Hallucinogens

Lyocell, 538

M

Mail-order companies, 281

Mail security, 282–283

Maintenance, clothing. See Clothing care

Management skills, 59, 265–271

Manipulation, 157, 158, 651

Manners. See Etiquette

Manufactured fibers, 537–538, 651

Marbling, 508, 651

Marijuana, 333, 652

Marinades, 439, 652

Maturity, signs of, 32–33

Meals. See also Eating

appealing, 466

cleanup after, 468–469

family's approach to, 406

helping with, 468–469

patterns, 467, 652

planning, 468–469

preparation, 466–470, 475–477

snacking between, 470–471

table settings, 407–409

Measurements

equipment for, 422, 562

equivalents, 452

ingredients for cooking, 450–451

taking body, 568–569, 571

units of, 452

Meats. See also Fish; Poultry

buying, 398

cooking, 439, 509–510

daily requirements, 377
  sanitation, 436
  selecting, 373
Mediation, 145, 150–151, 652
Mentors, 71, 652
Menus, 412–413, 414
Messages. *See* Communication
Microfiber, 539, 652
Microwave ovens, 428
  cooking in, 487
  safety, 441–442, 487
Microwaves, 428, 652
Milk, 514
Misbehavior, 255–256
Mistakes, learning from, 29
Mixing utensils, 423
Moist-heat cooking, 484–485
Mold, 513
Money. *See also* Budgets; Financial services
  budgeting, 286
  for clothing, 530
  for housing, 600
  importance of, 293
  managing, 286–291
  problems, 202–203
  saving, 28–29
  working for, 67
Monochromatic color schemes, 615
Moral development, 21, 221
Morality, 21
Mortgage, 605, 652
Motivational skills, 59
Motor skills, 220, 227
Multiple-family housing, 600, 602–603
Multiplex, 603, 652
Muscles, 316–317
MyPyramid, 376–378, 652

N

Natural disasters, 204
Natural fibers, 536, 652
Natural resources, 27, 630–634

Needs
  defined, 54, 652
  family, 195
  goals and, 31
  housing, 596–601
  nutritional, 383
  resources and, 31
  work and, 66–67
Neglect, 209–210, 652
Negotiation, 147, 150, 652
Networking, 74, 652
Night terror, 245, 652
Nightmares, 245, 652
Nonrenewable resources, 630, 652
Nonverbal communication, 46, 125–127, 652
Notching seams, 585, 652
Note taking, 266–267
Notions, sewing, 571, 652
Nuclear family, 185
Nurturing, 254, 652, 652
Nutrients
  carbohydrates, 356
  conserving, 488
  consuming, 366
  defined, 356, 652
  density, 367, 652
  effect, 356
  in fat, 358–359
  in fruits, 497, 500
  in grains, 494
  minerals, 361–362
  phytochemicals, 360
  in protein foods, 356–357, 507
  in vegetables, 497, 500
  vitamins, 359–360
  in water, 363
Nutrition
  for athletes, 387
  deficiencies, 364–365
  dental health and, 314
  exercise and, 315
  fad diets and, 376
  individual needs, 383

  skin and, 313
  special needs and, 386–387
  stress and, 323
  for vegetarians, 386
Nutrition facts panel, 394
Nylon fibers, 538

O

Obesity, 373, 652
Objectivity, 46
Obligations, 265, 652
Obsolete, defined, 295, 652
Occupational Information Network (O*NET), 76
Occupational Outlook Handbook (OOH), 76
Occupational Outlook Quarterly (OOQ), 76
Occupational Safety and Health Administration (OSHA), 112, 339
Options
  choosing best, 57
  in conflict resolution, 144
  employment, 78
Organic foods, 381
Organization
  home, 270–271, 612, 622–623
  personal, 266, 268–269, 272–273
Organizational goals, 31
Organizations
  professional, 117, 323
  service, 44–45
  youth, 60–61, 646
Osteoporosis, 361
Overload avoidance, 115
Over-the-counter drugs, 334

P-Q

Panfrying, 486, 652
Parallel play, 227, 652
Parenthood

considering, 249–250
education for, 253
lifestyle changes and, 251–253
positive, 254–255
Parenting, defined, 253, 652
Parents
blaming, 330
careers and, 252
defined, 253
divorced, 206–207
encouragement from, 29
relationship with, 193–194
rule making by, 176
separated, 206–207
step, 186
support systems for, 257
teen, 201, 252–253
traits from, 24
Parent test, 250–251
Partnerships, 77
Pasteurized, 399, 652
Patterns, design, 522, 529
Patterns, sewing
envelopes, 568, 570
fitting, 574–575
guide sheets, 574–575
measurements for, 568–569
selecting, 568
size determination, 569
using, 574–577
Patterns, traffic, 623
Paychecks, understanding, 287
PCP. See Hallucinogens
Peer friendships, 169
Peer mediators, 150, 652
Peer pressure
long-term effects, 165
negative, 157–161
online, 301
positive, 156–157
recognizing, 155
refusal skills, 162–163
responding to, 159–161
role in buying habits, 278
Peers, 156, 652

Perishable foods, 509, 652
Personal appearance
clothing and, 519–530
color and, 521
grooming and, 310–311, 314
impact of, 125–126
at job interview, 108
nutrition and, 313–314, 383
at work, 119
Personal development
areas of, 220–221
emotional, 20
influences, 221–222
intellectual, 220
moral, 20–21
resources for, 27–29
self-concept, 21–22
self-esteem, 21–24
self-evaluation and, 19–24, 26–29, 33
and skill development, 44–45
social, 20
Personal identity protection, 282–283
Personal resources, 27–29, 41
Personality
defined, 24, 652
differences, 143
friendship and, 169
strengths and weaknesses, 21–24
Personal resources, 27–29
available, 31
career, 74, 76
decision-making and, 54
interview, 109
listing, 56
potential and, 27–29
wellness and, 323
Personal responsibility, 42
Physical activity. See Fitness
Physical development, 20, 220.
See also Children
Phytochemicals, 360, 653
Pilling, 538
Place setting, 407–409, 653

PLA fiber, 538
Plaque, 314, 653
Play, 226–227
Poaching, 484–485, 653
Poison control centers, 236, 653
Poisons, 437, 642–643
Polyester, 537
Polyolefin, 538
Popularity, 169, 170
Portfolio, 106, 653
Portion control, 373, 377–378
Possessions, 270–271
Posture, 125
Potassium, 376
Potential, 26–27, 653
Poultry, 398
Power issues, 143
Pregnancy, 201–202, 334–336
Prejudice, 136–137, 653
Preschoolers, 227, 241, 245
Prescription drugs, 334
Presentation skills, 403
Pressing and ironing, 554, 653
Press releases, 109
Pretend play, 226
Pretreatment, 550, 653
Primary colors, 614
Principles of design, 524, 653
Priorities
defined, 26, 265, 653
determining, 265, 268
setting, 261
Problem-solving, 58, 60
sources of help with, 214–215, 257
stress avoidance and, 323
Produce. See Fruits; Vegetables
Products
brands, 279, 395
costs, 279
generic, 395
high-tech, 302, 303
information on, 279–280
labels, 279
quality of, 279

researching, 279–280
safety, 281
satisfaction tips, 279
Professionalism, 94, 447
Proportion as design element, 617
Protein foods. *See also* Legumes; Meats
buying, 398–399, 508
nutrients in, 507
preparing, 508–512
storing, 512
Proteins, 356–357, 653
Puberty, 20, 228, 653
Punctuality, 433

R

Ramie, 536
Rapport, 128, 653
Rayon, 537
Reading
to children, 254
skills, 86, 231
Recipes. *See also* Cooking
abbreviations in, 451–452
altering, 457–459
Cheese Soufflé, 513
common ingredients, 453
cooking terms, 456
cutting terms, 455
defined, 449, 653
equivalents, 451
estimates, 453
herbs used in, 458
measurements, 450–451
Minted Beans and Tomatoes, 511
mixing terms, 454
salsa, 460–461
selecting, 450
spices used in, 458
substitutions, 458
yield changes, 459
Recycling, 633, 635
Redress, 284, 653

Refusal skills, 162–163, 653
Rejection, 179
Relationships. *See also* Families; Friends; Parents
changes in, 179
dating, 176–177
effects of drugs on, 328
effects of stress on, 114, 272
establishing, 170–171, 202
with family, 192–195
long-distance, 23
with parents, 193–194
responsibilities, 174
and self-concept, 33, 206
supportive, 26, 206
Religion, 379
Renewable resources, 630, 653
Renting housing, 603–604
Repairs, clothing, 554–556
Repairs, home, 631
Repetitive stress injuries, 302, 653
Resources. *See also* Personal resources
career, 74
community, 27, 54
defined, 27, 653
emergency, 351
and goals, 27–39
in home design, 612
influence on decisions, 54
listing, 56
managing, 28–29, 265
natural, 630–634
Respect
absence of, 136–137
for authority, 217
communicating, 133, 135
for community, 134, 136
for family members, 19
for friends, 168
giving and receiving, 79
at home, 134
for parents, 193
at school, 134–135
self, 133

tolerance and, 146
Responsibility, 653
consumers', 284–285
demonstrating, 42, 51–61, 162
to family, 176, 193–194
to friends, 174–176
personal, 42, 175
taking, 43
at work, 94
Restaurants, 413
Résumé, 104–106, 579, 609, 653
Road rage, 147
Roasting, 482, 653
Role models, 653
becoming, 38
for children, 258–259
peers as, 156
Rules, family, 176

S

Safety
ATM, 289
away from home, 345–346
child, 223, 235–236, 239
cleaning products, 637
community, 297
cooking, 424, 427, 435, 440–441, 455, 486, 509–510
fire, 239, 642
food, 376, 399–400, 444–445, 484, 509
government standards, 339
home, 342–345, 637, 641–643
Internet, 300–301, 343–344
kitchen, 424, 435, 441–442, 487
outdoor, 236–237
poison control, 437, 642–643
product, 281
sewing equipment, 563

shopping, 281
sports, 346–347
and technology, 289, 297
toy, 223, 236
weight loss, 319
workout, 317–318
workplace, 112–113
Salmonella, 510, 653
Sanitation. See Cleanliness
Sanitize, 436–438, 653
Sarcasm, 128
Saturated fats, 358
Savings accounts, 288
Scale as design element, 617
Schedules, 268
School-age children, 226–228
Schools. See also Education
    age children, 227–228
    respect at, 134–135
    work connection, 67
Scorch food, 512, 653
Seams, 529, 562, 583–587
Secondary colors, 614
Security, 282–283
Sedentary, defined, 373, 653
Self-concept, 21–24
    and achievement, 25
    and relationships, 33, 246
Self-confidence. See also Confi-
        dence
    building, 22–23, 29
    defined, 25
    role in building indepen-
        dence, 26–27
    role in realizing dreams, 25
Self-control tactics, 234
Self-esteem
    and behavior, 22
    bullies and, 148
    decisions and, 55
    defined, 22
    and self-image, 23–24
    positive self-concept and, 22
    strengthening, 23–24
    success and, 25
Self-evaluation, 19–21, 41

Self-improvement, 25–27, 29–32
Selvage, 575, 653
Sensorimotor play, 226
Serger machines, 567–569
    serger seams with, 586–587
Sewing. See also Clothing
    alterations, 590–591
    basting, 582, 647
    casings, 587–588, 648
    clipping, 585, 648
    directional stitching, 582, 649
    fabric selection and prepara-
        tion, 570–571, 575–576
    facings, 584–585
    gathers, 586–587, 650
    hems, 589
    notion selection, 571–573
    patterns, 568–569
    safety, 563
    seams, 583–585
    serging seams, 586–587
    skills development, 581–582
    small equipment, 562–563
    staystitching, 583
Sewing machines, 564–568. See
        also Serger machines
    parts of, 564–565
    stitch adjustments, 567
    stitching, 566–567, 582–583
    threading, 565–566
    understitching, 585
Sexual harassment, 97
Sexually transmitted diseases,
        334–336, 653
Sharing
    benefits of, 169
    resources, 29
    space, 624–625
    values, 40
Shock, 238, 653
Shopping
    alternatives, 281–283
    for clothes, 530–531
    comparison, 279, 395
    for food, 391–400, 498–499,
        508

high-tech products, 303
    and impulse buying, 279
    lists, 468
    planning, 278–280
    smart, 278–283
    technology, 299
Siblings
    abuse, 210–211
    defined, 188, 653
    rivalry, 194–195, 653
Silhouette, 520, 653
Simmering, 484–485, 653
Single-family housing, 601
Single-parent family, 185
Skills. See also Communication
    community, 44–45
    core academic, 86–88
    employability, 89–90
    interests and, 69–70, 70
    leadership, 59–60
    presentation, 403
    problem-solving, 58, 60
    social. See Social skills
    transferable, 69
Skin care, 310–313
Sleep, 309–310, 323
Sleepwalking, 245, 654
Small motor skills, 228, 654
Snacking, 374, 384–385,
        470–471
Social changes, 20
Social development, 221
Social pressures, 52–54. See also
        Culture; Peer pressure
Social skills, 627. See also Com-
        munication; Friends;
        Friendships
Society, 54
Sodium, 376
Sole proprietorships, 77
Soy milk, 399
Space, as design element, 612
Spandex, 537
Special needs
    children, 227–230
    clothing, 521

housing, 599
nutrition, 386
Specialty stories, 281
Spending. *See* Budgets; Money
    management; Shopping
Spices, 374–375, 458
Split-complementary color
    schemes, 615
Spouse, defined, 209, 654
Spouse neglect, 209
Square shapes, 523
Stain removal, 550
Staples, 392, 654
Staystitching, 583, 654
STDs (sexually transmitted dis-
    eases), 334–336
Steaming, 484–485, 654
Stepparents, 186
Stereotype, 136, 654
Steroids, anabolic, 333
Stewing, 485–486, 654
Stimulants, 332, 654
Stir-frying, 487, 654
Stitching
    under, 585
    directional, 582–583
    machine, 566, 582–583
    slip, 590
    stay, 583
Storage
    clothing, 548–549
    clutter control and, 637
    dairy foods, 513
    grains, 495
    groceries, 401
    safe food, 444–445
Strengths, physical, 316–317
Strengths, personal, 24
Stress
    balancing work and family,
        113–114
    causes of, 114, 199–215, 272
    characterization, 321
    defined, 113, 271, 654
    description, 113–114
    managing, 272–273, 322–323

and relationships, 199–215
types, 114
Stretching, 317
Study skills, 266–267
Substance abuse. *See* Drugs
Success, 25–26, 33, 49
Sugar, 376
Suicide, 206, 336–337, 654
Sun exposure, 312–313
Supermarkets, 393–394
Support. *See* Help, sources of;
    Relationships, supportive
Support groups, 214
Symbolic play, 226

T

Tables
    clearing, 411
    coverings, 408
    settings, 407–409
Tableware, 407–410, 654
Tact, 135, 654
Tailor's chalk, 563
Tantrums, 224–225
Team members, 91–92
Teamwork
    defined, 90, 654
    effective, 91
    goals, 31
    skills, 90
    at work, 417
Technology
    benefits of, 296–299
    communication, 295–297
    cost of, 299
    defined, 295, 654
    drawbacks, 299
    food choice and, 379
    health risks and, 302
    housing, 597
    identity theft, 282–283, 299
    and job opportunities, 296
    managing, 302–303
    skills, 89

Teen parenthood, 201, 252–253
Teeth, 314
Telecommute, 116, 654
Telemarketing, 345, 654
Television, 109, 227
Temper tantrums, 224–225
Temperatures
    bacteria growth and, 509
    for bathing infants, 236
    cooking, 439
    food doneness and, 489
Tension, sewing machine, 567,
    654
Test anxiety, 273
Texture as design element, 613
Thank-you letters, 545
Theft, 302
Thinking skills, 89, 654
Time
    budgeting, 115
    cooking, 476–477
    family, 190–191, 268
    management, 265–268, 479
Tobacco, 328–329
Toddlers, 223–227
    clothing for, 242
    entertaining, 240–241
    food for, 244
To-do lists, 268
Tolerance, 146, 654
Tongs, 425
Townhouse, 603, 654
Toy safety, 223, 236
Trade name, 538, 654
Traditions, 185, 190, 192, 654
Traffic patterns, 621, 654
Trans fats, 359, 394
Transportation, 298, 632–633
Trash, 434, 634–635
Triacetate, 537
Triadic color schemes, 615
Trim, 529, 573
Trustworthiness, 97
Truthfulness, 21
Tubular shapes, 523

U

Understanding, 53
Understitching, 585, 654
Unit price, 395, 654
Unity, 618, 654
Universal values, 40, 654
Unsaturated fats, 358
Utensils, 654
    cleaning, 438
    eating, 407
    food preparation, 422–425
    proper use of, 440
Utilities, 600, 654
UV index, 312

V

Vaccines, 254, 654
Values
    character and, 38
    defined, 38, 654
    family's role, 184
    friends' respect for, 168
    function of, 38–39
    influence on decisions, 54
    learned, 39
    shared, 40
    technology and, 303
    types of, 39–40
    universal, 40
Vegetables
    buying, 373, 397–398
    canned, 497
    daily requirements, 377
    eating, 497
    nutrients, 497, 500
    preparing, 437, 500–503

selecting, 373
    utensils for, 425–426
Vegetarian, 388, 654
Verbal abuse, 148
Verbal communication, 87,
    124–125, 139, 654
Verbal messages, 124–125
Video teleconferencing, 297,
    654
Violence, 209–214
Visual impairment, 598–599
Vitamins, 359–360
Volunteer opportunities, 44–45

W

Waistbands, elastic, 588–589
Wallpaper, 618–619
Walls, decorating, 618–619
Wants, 54, 655
Wardrobe. *See* Clothing
Warehouse clubs, 282
Warranty, 285, 655
Water
    nutritional role, 363
    resources, 630–631
    safety, 237
    soluble vitamins, 361
Weaving, 540
Weight
    factors affecting, 318–319
    gain, myths, 380–381
    healthy, 364–365
    management plan, 319
    obsessing over, 320
Wellness. *See also* Health
    components of, 308
    defined, 308, 655

exercise and, 315–318
    health and, 307–308
    medical checkups and,
        308–309
    nutrition and, 319, 356
    resources, 322–323
    skin protection and, 312–313
    sleep habits and, 309–310
    stress reduction and,
        321–323
    weight management and,
        318–319
Windows, 620–621
Wool, 536
Work. *See* Jobs
Work and family balance,
    113–117
Work ethic, 90, 655
Work simplification, 270, 655
Workplace. *See also* Careers;
    Jobs
    conflicts, 95–96
    criticism, 94–95
    discrimination, 96
    environment, 645
    harassment, 97
    harmony, 117
    safety, 112–113
Writing skills, 87, 463
Written messages, 127

X-Y-Z

Yield, 257, 655
Yogurt, 515
Youth organizations, 60–61, 646
Youth violence, 214